D0176093

"*11 Days at the Edge* is an unusual narrative about evolution and enlightenment, as presented by spiritual teacher Andrew Cohen and as received by his student, Michael Wombacher. The teacher, the teaching and the taught come together in a highly engaging manner via Wombacher's clear prose, honest journaling and insightful commentary.

Andrew Cohen places his teaching of enlightenment in a context of evolutionary development for the entire human race, as well as a context of cosmic laws, which operate impersonally and influence us as individuals and as a species.

The clarity, simplicity and integrity of Andrew Cohen's teaching offer important guidance for modern spiritual seekers. Michael Wombacher captures it in a lively, honest account of his experience during an eleven-day retreat with his teacher and fellow students."

—John White,
author of *The Meeting of Science & Spirit* and *What is Enlightenment?*

"Do you want to know what religion (the search for ultimate meaning) might look like in the year 2100? Then read this book. Are you spiritual but not religious, interested in spirituality but estranged from the mythologies, metaphysical doctrines and the cultural baggage of the spiritual traditions? Then read this book. Do you want to directly experience God? Then read this book. *11 Days* is spirituality at the cutting edge of human evolution."

—Jim Marion,
author of *Death of the Mythic God: The Rise of Evolutionary Spirituality*;
Founder/Director – Institute for Spiritual Awareness in Washington, D.C.;
Founding member of Ken Wilber's Institute for Integral Spirituality.

"Michael Wombacher's engaging account of his spiritual journey with Andrew Cohen is a beautiful and compelling read. His book conveys a palpable sense of the "transmission" that an authentic spiritual teacher can give to his or her students. I highly recommend *11 Days at the Edge* to anyone interested in the work of Andrew Cohen in particular, and evolutionary enlightenment in general."

—Steve McIntosh,
author of *Integral Consciousness and the Future of Evolution*

"Michael Wombacher has given us a clear and beautiful story of eleven days spent with Andrew Cohen, an authentic American spiritual master. A delightful introduction to Evolutionary Enlightenment."

—Allan Combs;
consciousness researcher, neuropsychologist, and systems theorist;
Author of *The Radiance of Being: Understanding the Grand Integral Vision & Living the Integral Life.*

"If we're serious about spiritual evolution, we must be willing to go to the edge— of our comfort zone, our understanding, and our aspiration. In this riveting account of his encounter with one of the great spiritual masters of our time, Mike Wombacher shares his own journey to that edge. In the process, he offers us an inside look at one of the most significant spiritual events in history—the emergence of evolutionary spirituality."

—Craig Hamilton,
New Dimensions Radio and evolutionaryspirituality.com

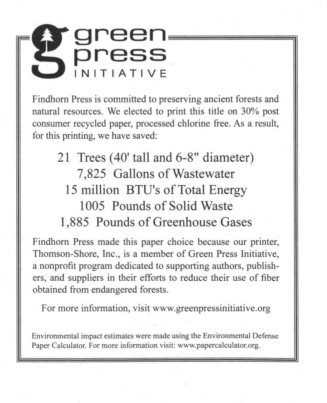

green press INITIATIVE

Findhorn Press is committed to preserving ancient forests and natural resources. We elected to print this title on 30% post consumer recycled paper, processed chlorine free. As a result, for this printing, we have saved:

21 Trees (40' tall and 6-8" diameter)
7,825 Gallons of Wastewater
15 million BTU's of Total Energy
1005 Pounds of Solid Waste
1,885 Pounds of Greenhouse Gases

Findhorn Press made this paper choice because our printer, Thomson-Shore, Inc., is a member of Green Press Initiative, a nonprofit program dedicated to supporting authors, publishers, and suppliers in their efforts to reduce their use of fiber obtained from endangered forests.

For more information, visit www.greenpressinitiative.org

Environmental impact estimates were made using the Environmental Defense Paper Calculator. For more information visit: www.papercalculator.org.

11 Days at the Edge

One man's spiritual journey
into evolutionary enlightenment

Michael Wombacher

FINDHORN PRESS

First published by Findhorn Press 2008

ISBN: 978-1-84409-136-2

British Library Cataloguing-in-Publication Data.
A catalogue record for this book is available from the British Library.

Edited by Jane Engel
Cover design by Will Rogers
Layout by e-BookServices.com
Printed and bound in America

1 2 3 4 5 6 7 8 9 10 11 12 13 14 13 12 11 09 08

Published by
Findhorn Press
305A The Park,
Findhorn, Forres
Scotland IV36 3TE

Tel +44(0)1309 690582
Fax +44(0)1309 690036
eMail info@findhornpress.com
www.findhornpress.com

Table of Contents

Acknowledgements

Of all the people who deserve thanks for their help in contributing to the creation of this book, none stands higher than Andrew Cohen. Not only did he give me permission to use all of the dialogues from the retreat; it is only through my association with him over all these years that I have gained sufficient understanding of both his teaching and myself to be able to write it.

Next in line is my wife Rose who consistently encouraged me and was patient with my long hours gone in the solitude of writing. My sister Birgit deserves a special thanks for reading and re-reading the manuscript in its developmental stages and urging me ever onward when my own enthusiasm would flag and wane. I also want to thank my friends Craig Hamilton, Elizabeth Debold, Gerard Senehi and John White for their ongoing friendship and moral support.

Additionally I am grateful to Thierry Bogliolo of Findhorn Press for taking a chance on this ambitious project with an untested author, to Jo Kaufman for her fantastic work in editing the manuscript and to Will Rogers for his generous contribution of the cover design. I am also indebted to Barbara Marx Hubbard for sending me her truly inspiring words about my work – the first from such a highly respected authority and "evolutionary elder."

I also wish to thank my nine-year old nephew, Lucas Miles Chasin, for serving as an ever-present reminder of the imminent approach of the future and our need to take responsibility for it right now in order to leave a spiritual legacy for the next generation that may nourish and support them. In this way perhaps they, in turn, can evolve and pass it forward.

And lastly, a special thanks to Joel Pitney and Christiana Briddell for being friends and partners in evolution.

To

Lucas Miles Chasin

Author's Note

This book contains seven appendices. Originally their text was contained in the main body of the work. During the editorial process it was decided that their content took the reader slightly too far away from the greater flow of events and therefore they were moved to the back of the book. However, I would encourage the reader not to think of them as literary afterthoughts, thus choosing to skip over them or read them at leisure. The material in these appendices is crucial to understanding the context for and thrust of this entire book. Therefore I strongly suggest that the reader not gloss over them but read them as near to their mention in the main body of the text as possible. Doing so will greatly enhance the understanding and appreciation of the rest of the material in this book.

Michael Wombacher

Foreword

Shortly before boarding an aircraft for an eleven-day retreat with Andrew Cohen in Montserrat, Spain, I was sitting on a grassy patch in my front yard after a Fourth of July barbecue with a longtime friend, gazing up at the majesty of a starlit California sky.

It had been long since the two of us had spent time like this together. After some quiet moments, my friend began relaying a story of a spiritual experience he had had a year or two earlier which had haunted him with whispers of the possible ever since. He spoke with a poignant combination of awe, wonder and melancholy. It was evident that, while he was deeply moved by what had revealed itself to him, he was equally convinced that his life could never be profoundly informed by its unspeakable glory.

We talked into the night and I shared with him my passion for the transformative teaching that would send me off on a jet bound for Spain in a few days. I asked him if he longed for a life in which he could realize the deepest qualities of manhood, courage, vision and a noble willingness to live a life that stands for the highest truth. Yes, he answered, and he meant it. I'd known him for many years and have always been impressed by the depth of his spirit, his sense of true friendship and his quiet appreciation of life's deepest values. In many ways I viewed him as embodying the noble virtues of knighthood. If I had to be in a foxhole, I often thought, this would be the man I'd want next to me.

So it was deeply distressing to see him there, seemingly raped by life, his spirit all but broken. It occurred to me then that in many significant ways he represented millions of spiritually disenfranchised men and women living in the richest country in the world, the beneficiaries of opportunity the likes of which no generation on earth has ever seen. In his early fifties, beset by practical concerns on every side, he reminded me of the saying that "the masses lead lives of quiet desperation."

Like myself, he had been an eclectic spiritual seeker for quite some years. Not only had he been to see various teachers, but he had also ingested a multitude of drugs, walked on coals, sat in drum circles, shared in men's groups and chanted at solstices – yet it had all come to this: utter cynicism about the possibility of leading an entirely different kind of life and a hazy deadness in his eyes.

So a few days later, sitting aboard a plane bound for Europe, I decided that I would attempt to keep a journal while on retreat and share it with him upon my return. I sensed that if he gave himself even in the smallest way to the consideration of the teachings it would contain, he might find renewed hope for living a life of purpose and meaning. This book is the result of that journal – at least in part.

It is also the result of a long-standing desire not only to share my experience of and investigation into the pursuit of what has traditionally been an Eastern concept – Enlightenment – but in a Western context, and also to help redefine the timeless in a very new time, our own. In other words, I have long been interested in exploring the significance of enlightened consciousness, free from its accrued millennia of cultural baggage, in the post-post-modern Western world.

This interest goes back to my early twenties when episodes of enlightened consciousness found their way unsought into my life and transformed me – overnight and altogether unexpectedly – into a spiritual seeker. Even then I sensed that what was essential about this radical upending of the ordinary worldview and its revelation of the Eternal, had little or nothing to do with the cultural trappings and esoteric practices in which it was often couched – though I explored them all – but needed, from time to time, to be reinterpreted in accordance with the rhythms of time, the ever forward-moving thrust of cultural evolution and the increasing span of human knowledge. Therefore, I sought a teacher who embodied the timeless wisdom of the East in a thoroughly Western fashion and, at length, found one. I spent thirteen years with him and through him began to learn to harmonize all aspects of my being, spiritual and material, cosmic and carnal, under the banner of liberation and enlightenment. The experience of this relationship was so extraordinary that I set out to write a book about it (which I never finished), seeking to chronicle the student-teacher relationship as it played itself out on the streets of San Francisco, Manhattan, Miami, Los Angeles, Delhi, Calcutta and the many other places that served as a backdrop for the teachings I received.

However, it was not until I met Andrew Cohen that I found the full fruition of what I had suspected was possible – the perfect integration of the deepest insights revealed in the bottomless depths of the awakened self and the hard-won knowledge of the material universe of a technologically advanced culture freed from the superstitions of the past. In Andrew I saw an explosion of creativity, intellectual acuity and spiritual genius that was and still is, at least to my eyes, peerless. Ever since I became involved with him I have wanted to share what the experience of being on retreat with him was like. This, I discovered early on, was no easy task. Often, upon returning from retreat, friends would ask what it was like, whether I had fun, did I feel relaxed and so on. Unfortunately, other than employing useless adjectives such as awesome, amazing, life changing and indescribable, I was utterly at a loss for words – an unusual state for someone usually blooming with them. The truth was that what Andrew was teaching was so deep, comprehensive and utterly penetrating that nothing short of a three-hour conversation could even begin to do it justice. There was simply too much depth to flatten out into convenient soundbites.

Speaking to my friend that starlit night, I keenly felt this inability to convey in very simple terms what it was that Andrew was teaching. And as I thought about it more, it occurred to me that while Andrew has written a respectable number of books, none gave an overview of the entirety of his teaching and, at least equally significant, none gave a sense of what it was like to be with him. That is when the idea for this book began to percolate. Wouldn't it be great, I thought, to be able to take the reader day by day along on this retreat, not only to discover the radically profound teaching that continues to emerge from Andrew, but to see how that teaching strikes the soul of an average seeker as he daily sinks deeper into it? Wouldn't it also be great to use my own experience as a seeker as a starting point for an examination of the state of the post-modern spiritual world and all its complexities? With that began the writing of this book.

Before diving in, I must mention that Andrew's teaching emphasizes evolution and development, a leaning that is directly reflected in Andrew himself. In the twelve years that I've known him, neither he nor his teachings have ceased, even briefly, to change and evolve, revealing ever deeper layers and potentials of psyche and soul, culture and cosmos. That means that this book, rather than pretending to be some grand and final statement of the entirety of his teaching, is merely a snapshot in time, a short clip depicting the teaching as it was for eleven days in July, 2005, in Montserrat, Spain.

Michael Wombacher

"This is the true joy in life, the being used for a purpose recognized by yourself as a mighty one; the being a force of nature instead of a feverish, selfish little clod of ailments and grievances, complaining that the world will not devote itself to making you happy.

"I am of the opinion that my life belongs to the whole community, and as long as I live it is my privilege to do for it whatever I can.

"I want to be thoroughly used up when I die, for the harder I work, the more I live. I rejoice in life for its own sake. Life is no brief candle to me; it is a sort of splendid torch which I have got hold of for the moment, and I want to make it burn as brightly as possible before handing it on to the future generations."

—George Bernard Shaw,
Man and Superman,
Epistle Dedicatory

Prologue

Into the Looking Glass

It seemed an inauspicious way to begin a journey halfway around the world. I woke at four in the morning, violently ill from an unfortunate encounter with a tainted sandwich during lunch on the previous day and now, in a most miserable state, I had to catch an early flight for Barcelona, Spain.

Moved solely by the force of necessity, I dragged myself from bed, staggered about wearily and managed to get myself together. Before leaving I went downstairs to my office to make sure everything was in order. After all, I would be gone for two weeks and entirely out of touch with my exceedingly active dog training business. Having determined that all was as it should be, I logged on to my Yahoo page where I first saw the morning's headlines: *Bombs Explode in London – Kill Dozens*. It was July 7th, 2005, and terrorists had shocked the world once more with another cowardly attack on innocent civilians as an expression of their faith and hope for the world. It was a sobering reminder of at least part of the reason I was heading on this trip.

I had known Andrew Cohen informally for just over ten years and one of the things that had so attracted me to his teaching was that it embraced both my longing for liberation and my care for the world. In fact, it had awoken me to a care for the world that I had not previously known. His basic message, as I understood it, was this: the pursuit of Enlightened consciousness in today's times only makes sense when it is directly linked to a committed engagement with the world process for the sake of the upliftment of that process. To put it differently, the pursuit of Enlightenment merely for relief from one's own existential tension and neurotic pain, or as a way to transcend the world and its suffering, no longer made any sense and could even be considered selfish. Considering the state of the world and difficult to avoid fact that we, as a species, cannot continue along our present track much longer, gave my pursuit of spiritual liberation a moral context that it had lacked for many years. So, in a strange way, the unconscionable acts of the most recent slew of Islamic terrorists not only helped me to overcome my intense headache and nausea enough to make it out the door, it further fueled my aspiration for radical transformation and sanity.

A few hours later, having passed through a long series of queues and security checkpoints, I found myself seated almost comfortably in a coach seat aboard one of Delta Airlines' aging airliners. As my stomach was still heaving in violent convulsions and threatening to void its contents into a nearby airsick bag, I considered that I should be grateful for not being tempted by the scrumptious fare that I would soon be offered. Relieved of that possibility, I settled back into my window seat and, after watching San Francisco and the Bay Area shrink from a well-detailed skyline glinting in the morning sun to a haze of hills and valleys, I lay back, closed my eyes and considered the path that had brought me here.

Like many others, my first spiritual experiences were directly related to the powerful impact of certain chemicals upon the gray matter between my ears. In these, through some mysterious process, a portal was opened to a radically different perspective on life and my role in it. In this manner, I underwent a series of profound spiritual experiences that utterly unseated me and filled my consciousness with a dimension of knowledge I never knew existed. Not only did I discover, in the most dramatic fashion, the inherently immortal nature of all of life and the ecstatic unity from which it arose, I also discovered an intensely compelling moral context for my own existence. Despite my own testosterone-fueled, narcissistic immaturity at the time, I recognized in the passionate ecstasy of my own Source a demand that my life become an expression of the inherent perfection and wholeness of that timeless Ground. Inwardly I came to my knees in awe, determined to find a way to bridge the gap between what I had seen and the reality of my own condition. No small task, for that gap was more like a yawning gulf.

Further research into the matter suggested that there might indeed exist individuals in whom that extraordinary consciousness, which I had tasted, had become a permanent condition and that such individuals might take on others and endeavor to bring them into that same exalted state. With that supposition I set out in search of a teacher. Thus began a nine-year odyssey of sampling the spiritual marketplace that was as strange as it was thrilling. Over time two things became quite clear to me. First, it became painfully apparent after much dabbling, that the New Age, despite colorful claims to the contrary, was entirely bereft of depth, meaning and profundity. It felt as if a diet of this fare was akin to feeding a starving man junk food, which may have had an interesting taste going down but strangely failed to provide the least bit of nourishment. Second, while I was very attracted to Eastern Enlightenment teachings, having been swept off my feet not only by the Bhagavad-Gita, Upanishads, and Dhammapada, but also by the teachings of the extraordinary Advaita[1] master Ramana Maharshi and others of his kind, I could not see studying a spiritual tradition which expected me to take on a great deal of cultural baggage that I found distracting and unnecessary. Not that I didn't try. I spent a good bit of time with Eastern swamis and their Western devotees but I simply did not wish to play at being Indian. It felt profoundly inauthentic and had little to do with the powerful experiences that had shaken my world and which pointed to a reality radically free from culture or a relative face of any kind. What I sought was an individual who could show me how to embody the timeless revelation of Enlightenment in the busy, Western world of which I was a product and in which I lived.

Nine years after my search began it ended in a series of unlikely events that proved the truth of the old adage that when the student is ready the teacher appears. That teacher, Peter Steward, a bona fide master of the ancient art of kundalini yoga,[2] was a former student of the legendary American spiritual teacher known simply as Rudi (whose extraordinary life colored the streets of Manhattan from the fifties into the early seventies). Peter Steward was just what I'd been looking for - a successful businessman who lived in Manhattan supporting himself in high style with a thriving business and using the money that came to him to support not only his own spiritual pursuit but that of dozens of his students as well. My first encounter with Peter was like being dropped into a vat of LSD. In his presence my mind and heart exploded with the same force and velocity that they had years earlier with considerable pharmaceutical assistance. It was my first experience of "transmission"[3] and it would initiate a thirteen-year relationship during which I was the beneficiary of a great deal of spiritual training and which unfortunately ended with great acrimony. How this came to be, and the important lessons inherent in this tale, will be revealed in more detail in the pages that follow.

I had been studying with Peter for some years when a friend of mine invited me to hear Andrew Cohen speak at the Corte Madera Yoga Center, just outside San Francisco. Initially I declined the invitation, having seen entirely enough of the assortment of spiritual teachers that tended to make their way through the Bay Area. I was also content, after such a long search, to keep my attention focused on what was turning out to be an extraordinary relationship with Peter. However, when my friend handed me a thin newsletter boldly entitled, *What is Enlightenment?* the direction of my life was inexorably altered. The lead article was simply entitled, "The Student-Teacher Relationship." As I read, it became immediately apparent that the person who had written it knew what he was talking about. Word after word, line after line, in language pregnant with spiritual power, he described the deepest essence of what I had been experiencing with Peter over the past five or so years. Whoever this man was, he seemed to possess uncommon depth and authenticity. So, I decided to take my friend up on her invitation and attend the upcoming talk.

When I first saw Andrew walk up to the podium through the gathered crowd of about 150 people, it was not his short, dark hair, neatly cropped mustache or the piercing intensity of his eyes that got my attention. It was his small stature that surprised me. I didn't know why that should be other than that the magnitude of his presence stood in stark contrast to the size of his physique. Similarly, when he spoke his voice was pitched slightly high belying the deep resonance of truth that imbued the words he spoke. Once he began teaching, however, fielding a variety of questions from the gathered crowd, all such concerns quickly faded away. Within a few moments I was shocked to find myself in the presence of that mysterious and powerful transmission to which I had grown so accustomed in Peter's company. Having seen so many teachers who utterly lacked this capacity, I had arrogantly assumed that Peter was the only one, or at least nearly the only one, who stood in possession of such power. As it turned out, I was wrong.

And there was more. Andrew spoke for over two hours, in a way that I had never heard anyone speak of spiritual matters. Whereas most, including Peter, often spoke in a very vague and indefinite way about the mysteries of consciousness, which are, in fact, often defined as ineffable, Andrew did not. He spoke with a level of articulate precision regarding the subtlest aspects of Enlightenment and the spiritual life that to this very day I have found in no one else. The result was that I was not only deeply nourished by the transmission that poured from him ceaselessly but also intellectually satisfied by the clarity of his answers to questions that I had never heard anyone else answer satisfactorily. Andrew's capacity to articulate the smallest points with razor-sharp clarity has often caused him to be accused of intellectualizing, but I have come to realize that this is more a reflection of the rampant sloppy thinking which one tends to find in spiritual circles and which often hides the fact that perhaps people simply don't know the answers to such questions. "Just surrender," "be as you are," "it's only the mind that's a problem," and other overly simple responses to complex inquiries are most commonly heard in the modern spiritual marketplace. Indeed, it was on the same night that I first heard Andrew say, "*I try to teach my students how to think, not to stop thinking.*" This was a revelation to me. I felt as if my intellect had been at least temporarily freed to inquire in a way I never had before. But there was more. I found Andrew's manner of engagement with people, which continues to be controversial to this day, utterly refreshing. Rather than pandering to people's egoic sensitivities he was quite direct, occasionally painfully so. While this quality failed to be appreciated by all, I enjoyed its authenticity and recognized its liberating potential. Finally, and most significantly, it was clear that Andrew was deeply enlightened and that was the most extraordinary recognition of all.

After the teaching my wife Rose and I were able to see Andrew privately and I was impressed by his natural simplicity, openness and kindness. As we drove home we were both in a state of spiritual shock. Neither of us had been prepared for an encounter of such magnitude. "You know, Mike," Rose said to me as we drove beneath the fog-draped towers of the Golden Gate Bridge, "this is what's missing from our teaching." She was referring, of course, to the teaching both she and I were receiving from Peter at that time. I acknowledged her sentiment with a slight shudder, hardly suspecting its profound implications for the future direction of our lives.

Accompanied by Rose, I went to see Andrew teach at the Corte Madera Yoga Center a number of times during the next year or so and in late 1995, during an exchange where he confronted my superficiality by asking me if I was coming to see him merely as a form of spiritual entertainment, he challenged me to attend a long retreat with him. The next one was set for January 1996, in Bodhgaya, India, the birthplace of Buddhism. The gauntlet had been thrown down. Had I not accepted his challenge I would have found it difficult to live with myself and continue to take seriously my own spiritual aspirations. Yet accepting it threw me into quite a quandary, as well. After all, I was deeply involved with another teacher whom I loved dearly and did not wish to betray. I struggled with this issue at some length but at last concluded that Truth itself is the final yardstick of any spiritual endeavor and as such had to come first. With that I decided to go to India.

Bodhgaya marked a turning point in my life. The town itself was less than unassuming despite bearing the considerable distinction of being the site of the Buddha's awakening under the legendary Bodhi tree, the descendant of which still stands today in the shade of an extraordinary stupa[4] that is at least 2,000 years old. However, aside from the spectacular Buddhist temples erected there by each of the world's Buddhist countries, the visitor to Bodhgaya can expect to be greeted by the worst aspects of dehumanizing poverty. The town, strewn with rubble and adorned with grotesqueries of concrete and twisted rebar, seemed inspired by the dreams of Bosch and Breugel and left the distinct impression that war had ravaged this community and no one had bothered to clean up in its wake. The surrounding countryside was an entirely different matter and consisted largely of farmland and neatly arranged rice paddies that stretched to the feet of the mountains in the distance. The land possessed a timeless quality that made it easy, in moments of reverie, to see the Buddha himself traversing those fields on his fateful trip from those very mountains to the sacred tree under which he awoke and realized the Truth. Little had changed here in a very long time and this fact filled the air with a palpable stillness that remained unmoved in the midst of the tumult of Indian village life.

Andrew set the tone for the retreat by asking the 300 or so seekers from around the world to consider what it means to "let everything be as it is." The contemplation of and meditation on this quickly led to one of the most profound recognitions of Truth that I have ever experienced. I discovered that resistance of any kind to the experience of life, inner and outer, as it is, creates the painful illusion of a separate self that then has to struggle for its own existence against the onslaught of forces beyond its control. Simply relinquishing this position results in the overwhelming discovery that one never actually existed as the person one thought one was, a discovery that is simultaneously unsettling and liberating. In that recognition all boundaries disappear, as one's self-sense expands infinitely in all directions and one finds that "the world exists within me, not I in the world."

(This is not, by the way, metaphoric wordplay but simply the actual view from the perspective of the Self Absolute). Equally remarkable was that I was not alone in being immersed in such staggering realizations. In fact, the majority of retreatants shared similar experiences of depth and expansion, which was a reminder of why Andrew had gained a reputation as such a powerful teacher. After all, where else can one go and, within a few days, share enlightened consciousness with a significant number of others simply because of the skilled guidance and transmission of one individual? Nowhere that I knew of.

As the days rolled on and our immersion in the teachings deepened, I noticed that the state and the understanding that had been mine for some days began to fade. I saw myself hold onto a memory and, in my discussion with others, relate from that rather than from the moment-to-moment unfolding of my own experience. I began to pay close attention to what was happening and why, and after some days it became apparent that what lay behind this dissipation was pride. At first I refused to acknowledge it. But, for better or for worse, I have always been slightly more interested in the simple truth of things than in how I would like them to be. With grim determination, I stayed with this stinging realization. I was unprepared for the humiliating truth of my own condition. What I began to see was the degree to which pride had infested nearly every area of my mind and life. Behind almost every motivation I saw its dark face lurk. Like a skulking thief, or a shadow at the edges of my mind, pride had wound its dark way through the very fabric of my being. I was horrified. I'd always thought of myself as a good guy with sincere motivations, but now I could see that even that was simply another manifestation of the selfsame pride. I was emotionally overcome.

It was evening and time for meditation. I tried to rise but my knees buckled, and I fell back in my chair. I wanted to escape from myself. A few friends came over and physically assisted me into the meditation tent. "Let everything be as it is" had been the refrain of the retreat so, drawing on some hidden storehouse of emotional reserve, I determined to do just that. Slowly the crushing emotional pain thinned until ultimately I was left with just my simple insight: pride is the enemy and the enemy is everywhere.

Andrew did not seem the least surprised when I spoke to him the next day. In fact, he pointed out that pride is the only obstacle to Enlightenment and that what I experienced was essentially the simple truth for us all. Putting a positive spin on things, he pointed out that I should be grateful for this realization. Most people, he added, go through an entire lifetime without knowing this and, therefore, no real progress is possible. In short, I had experienced with shocking depth both the goal and the obstacle - not bad for a two-week investment of time.

I recovered my balance and some newfound sobriety about the whole undertaking as the retreat drew to its conclusion, one that ended with Andrew's passionate call for all of us to become "living expressions of the opposite of everything that's wrong with the world." Having climbed to the heights and fallen to the depths, I determined to let what I'd understood inform my life once I was home again.

On the way there I had an extraordinary opportunity to meet someone whose life indeed expressed the spirit behind Andrew's call. While in Calcutta, at the immaculate Oberoi Hotel where we had six or so hours to kill, I discovered that Mother Theresa's mission was only ten minutes away. Upon my arrival there I was shocked to find that the world-renowned mother of the dying and a saint by anyone's standard, was standing right in front of me asking me where I was from. I told her and she smiled, that spider web of wrinkles creasing her face as she pressed a small amulet of the Holy Mother into my hands, gave me a blessing and encouraged me to help the victims of AIDS at her mission in San Francisco. What struck me most about her was not her face but her feet, gnarled and broken from years of work, gripping the earth like the twisted roots of a mighty tree while supporting a life inspired by Heaven. I could not bring myself to have a picture of the two of us taken as I felt it would be an expression of the very pride I wished to destroy while in the presence of the very humility that was the goal. I thanked her and, after a short meditation in her chapel, headed back to the hotel and from there back home.

On the endless flight across that strange time warp known as the international dateline, I had ample opportunity to reflect on the things that, in addition to my unexpected encounter with the enemy within, had most struck me during the retreat. Several things in particular had caught my attention and I wished to speak with Peter about them. That chance would arrive shortly, as I planned to attend a retreat with him in New York just two weeks after my return from India. I wondered, with no small amount of trepidation, whether worlds would collide or a deeper understanding of his teaching would emerge.

In the short time between retreats I was shocked to receive a phone call from Andrew to see how I was doing following my time in India. It seemed to me an expression of unusual care. After all, who was I? Andrew was involved with hundreds of people who'd given themselves to his teaching fully and here he was calling me to see how I was faring after the retreat. After a few brief pleasantries I asked him the question that had been nagging at me since my return: "What do you think of me being involved with two teachers?"

Without missing a beat he responded, *"I think what you need to face into is that your teacher is not meeting you in your interest."*

I felt like I'd taken a body blow. "But," I stammered, "he is a genuine teacher. He's not corrupt (Andrew had, during the foregoing year, been railing relentlessly against corruption in spiritual teachers) and..." ("I love him," I wanted to say).

"That's not what I said," he cut me off. *"I said you need to face into whether your teacher is meeting you in your interest."*

Secretly I had wondered whether my engagement with Peter and his with me could be more intense and focused, but I had not wanted to look too deeply for fear of what I might find.

"I will look into that," I said sheepishly.

We talked for a few more minutes during which I made it clear to him that I was very interested in his teaching. Now, in those days, committing to a deeper engagement with Andrew's teaching could only be accomplished in one way: by moving into his community. We talked about this briefly and our conversation closed first with a warning and then a welcome.

"*Mike,*" Andrew said in a serious tone, "*just know that if you join this teaching you should prepare to have your whole life taken away from you.*"

"Okay," I said rather stupidly, as if there were nothing particularly out of the ordinary in this.

And then, after inviting me to a picnic on the following day, he said, "*Great, Mike. Welcome to the revolution!*"

With that our conversation ended. I sat on my bed terrified. I considered what it would be like to leave my wife Rose, my budding dog training business and my beloved teacher. I cringed. I didn't have the mettle for it and I knew it. I never went to the picnic and I didn't see Andrew for some years thereafter.

However, it was clear to me that I needed to speak with Peter, primarily to address our relationship but also to inquire into two aspects of Andrew's teaching that I had found compelling and had not heard Peter speak about. Two weeks later I found myself sitting in front of him in his vast Manhattan loft; a large, antique desk decorated with a bouquet of flowers and a small collection of Indian and Tibetan bronze sculptures separated the two of us.

"Well, what is it?" he asked in his typically edgy yet not unkind tone.

The first question I asked him concerned a statement I'd heard Andrew make during the retreat. He'd said that it's not our experience that's so important but the conclusions we draw that determine whether we are free or not. This had come as a surprise to me because until that point all of my spiritual understanding told me that it's about having experience until the point that that experience becomes a permanent state of consciousness. I had thought about this after Andrew had said it and it made perfect sense. I realized that two people could enter into the same vastly expanded state of consciousness and draw dramatically different conclusions about what it meant. For example, one individual might conclude from their experience, "I am Jesus," and promptly become a megalomaniac. Another might conclude from the very same experience, "I am nobody," and express an uncommon and powerful degree of humility – a vastly different result. And the "neither here nor there" conclusion which I, and I believe most other spiritual seekers, draw was that while definitely realizing in some fundamental way that "I am That," the felt sense of it was more along the lines of "something amazing happened to me." The powerful experience of the Absolute did not eradicate the separate sense of self; rather, it seemed to become an object in relation to it (which, of course, it is not) and thus its potentially transformative implications were reduced to the level of mere experience and relegated to the halls of memory. The truth is, all of these outcomes have played themselves out countless times since the dawn of human explorations into the depths of our own nature, and in every case the conclusions that were drawn about the experience were more significant than the experience itself. *"This,"* Andrew had said, *"is why I put so much emphasis on understanding."*

When I brought this question of understanding to Peter, however, he was dismissive. "All understanding is in the mind," he said, "and the mind is bullshit. It has all of the answers and none of them at the same time. It's an insane asylum. The only thing that's important is to open and surrender and everything else will take care of itself." It was difficult to take issue with that logic and I wasn't going to argue with my teacher. Still, I felt a bit deflated by his response and he had definitely not met me in my interest.

I moved on to a related question. During his teaching Andrew had made the statement that Enlightenment is as much a perspective on one's experience as a state of consciousness and that in many important ways the perspective was more significant than the experience. After all, he'd said, at the end of the day one wants to be free from all experience. To be honest, I barely understood his point. To me it had been all about experience and I wasn't sure what he meant by perspective. When I put this issue to Peter, he responded, "You know, Mike, I've heard that before and I don't believe it. Perspectives and understanding all have to do with the mind, but an enlightened person knows nothing at all and is simply open to the Higher Creative Energy in the Universe. Their life is one of surrender, mystery and wonderment, not certainty, knowing and perspectives." Once again, it was difficult to argue these points, as even now I know that they are true. But I suspected that this response overlooked layers of depth and subtlety that were significant. Andrew, on the other hand, had grappled with these layers and thus was able to articulate them impressively. This bothered me.

Finally, I addressed Peter regarding the issue of not being met in my interest. Of course, I could not simply raise my concerns in this manner, so I said, "I really want to be taken on; I want for you to do whatever you need to do to break down my ego the way Rudi did with you. I can take it. I want to grow." I was unnerved by the words that came out of my mouth, not knowing what they might bring on. But I meant them and felt ready.

Peter fell silent and leaned back in his chair for a few moments. Then, in a soft tone, he said, "You know, Mike, I don't want to have relationships like that with people anymore. I did that for years and it never worked. People just get angry and leave. They are driven away from God and I don't want to drive people away.

I want them to grow at their own pace and I want to have warm, nourishing relationships with them. My role is to give people energy and a teaching that will help them to build a connection with the Higher Energy in the Universe. What they do with it is up to them. This energy, this shakti[5] that comes through in our classes, marinates and develops people and takes them to the place where they are ready to take the next step in their lives and then on from there. It's like a spiral staircase leading into infinity. My role is to provide the energy. I have a lot and I'm willing to give it, but the work people have to do is their own."

Once again, I felt deflated, unable to argue with either his logic or his sentiment. That more or less finished our conversation. There was a great deal more on my mind but it was clear to me that the dialogue was concluded. It had given me a great deal to think about. However, while questions about Peter's teaching persisted, at this point they were not enough to persuade me to leave. After all, he was a very powerful teacher who surpassed in many important ways most others that I'd met. Not only that, but over the previous six years he had literally taken me by the hand, given me invaluable spiritual training, helped me to start my own business, and mentored me in the business of living in a way that is almost unknown in today's time and culture. In short, it was clear to me that everything that was good in my life at this point had largely to do with his influence. That was not the kind of relationship I was about to turn my back on simply because there were aspects of his teaching that I questioned. Besides, where was I going to go? Andrew's demand had proven too much for me, and this was a teaching that I could objectively see had transformed my life dramatically during the last six years. So I went on for seven more, eventually even teaching under him and allowing the questions to persist.

As time passed, my list of questions grew. A fundamental and increasingly disconcerting one revolved around what I viewed as the dualistic nature of his teaching. That is, in profound episodes of spiritual revelation one discovers "I Am That," which is another way of saying that there is only One. This may seem a subtle point to the uninitiated but it's actually rather important insofar as one's approach to spiritual matters is concerned. *One* means no relationship between this and that. It means **One**, period. This is a truth that the most profound teachings from every time and culture consistently point to. That being the case, the idea that an individual has to develop a chakra system and cultivate a powerful flow of kundalini energy in order to *connect* with the Higher Energy in the Universe, as was taught by Peter, was suspect, especially when the non-dual nature of things was never deeply discussed in the teaching. It was also confusing because the fact is that when the kundalini force is activated, the non-dual nature of things is usually quite obvious. So why was everything always spoken about in dualistic terms? Unfortunately, Peter was never easy to approach on matters like this. In fact, it was clear that penetrating questions into matters of spiritual subtlety annoyed him. His responses to such inquires were usually brief and pointed. "Stop trying to figure it all out in your head. Just bring your attention into the chakra below the navel and open to the Energy. Then all your questions will disappear. Fools think they know something. Wise people know nothing." That was all well and good (and also, in large measure, true) but the problem for me was that, despite following his advice, the questions did not disappear. Apparently I was not sufficiently wise. Once again, Andrew's words resounded quietly in my heart – "*your teacher is not meeting you in your interest.*" Nonetheless, I stayed in the relationship and grew ever closer to Peter. We took trips to India; he often taught retreats at my house; I transcribed his teachings into a book, then got it published and supported him in a myriad of ways as an expression of the gratitude in my heart.

Throughout this time I maintained tenuous contact with Andrew, who kindly exchanged emails with me several times a year and who was always gracious on the few occasions that I attended his public teachings. A thread of connection lay dormant under the surface.

A big moment came when Andrew sent a manuscript of his soon-to-be published book, *Embracing Heaven and Earth*, to Peter for review (he and Andrew had met briefly some years earlier and while the results of that meeting were, shall we say, less than cosmic, I sensed that Andrew had respect for Peter nonetheless) and after he'd read it I asked him what he'd thought of the manuscript.

"You know, Mike," he said, "when I read it the first time I hated it. But when I read it the second time I hated it even more."

"Why?" I asked, taken aback.

"Because it's so absolute," he responded without hesitation. "The thing is, everything he's saying is true, but it doesn't leave any room for one's humanity."

That set off alarm bells in some interior room located in the vicinity of my conscience and its implications would explode into my life within the next two years.

What did he mean by Andrew's teaching not leaving any room for one's humanity? I knew exactly what he meant. When Peter spoke of one's humanity, he was referring to our human foibles, the collection of our assorted shortcomings and neurotic inclinations. The expectation that those would disappear in their entirety over the course of one's spiritual evolution, he viewed as naïve. Even spiritual teachers, no matter how evolved, he held, would always be subject in some degree to their human weaknesses. In this regard he often quoted Rudi: "If you look up a cow's ass you see shit," adding that, "When you go to a cow you don't go to its ass, you go to the udders where the nourishment is." At other times he'd say, "Only God is perfect. All the rest of us are just trying to grow as best as we can every day." In other words, don't expect moral and ethical perfection even from a powerful spiritual teacher, because such a thing is not possible. You take what's good and is helping you and overlook the rest. If you dislike something about the teacher's behavior you can always leave but you are in no way qualified to pass moral judgment on him or her. The basic sentiment is best encapsulated by the statement, "I'm only human."

Andrew, however, had an entirely different take on this statement, one that stood in stark contrast to Peter's proposition. *"What if being human,"* he often asked, *"rather than being a pseudonym for all our weaknesses and shortcomings instead became synonymous with all the highest aspects of what it means to be human. Human beings are capable of the greatest virtues: courage, integrity, generosity, kindness, honor and dignity. What if they became the standard for what it means to be human rather than all our weakness and frailty?"* Ever since I first heard Andrew ask this question it utterly captured my attention because it deeply resonated with my own earliest episodes of spiritual revelation during which I'd intuited this call for a total transformation of our human character. When I first heard Andrew say that one of his definitions of Enlightenment was *"coming to that point in our own evolution where we no longer cause suffering to others due to acting out of ignorance and selfishness,"* my spiritual heart burst open and I felt some inner permission to at least aspire to such a possibility. This aspiration to the perfection of human character, even if never perfectly attainable, struck me as infinitely more compelling than a foregone resignation to ethical mediocrity.

From one perspective, however, Peter's view seemed entirely reasonable and defensible. After all, nearly every spiritual authority figure since the sixties has fallen on their face in a series of twisted ethical scandals that would make an ordinary, spiritually disinterested person red with righteous wrath. That in itself should be proof enough that our human shortcomings are here to stay, no matter what depth of spiritual revelation may have first ignited the passion of these teachers. However, it also throws into question the ultimate value of Enlightenment itself. If individuals who had authentically attained such a level of development were able to behave ethically in a way that a completely ordinary person would never consider, what is the ultimate point of spiritual experience? To feel better about oneself?

It was precisely this point that lay behind Andrew's public assault on corruption in spiritual teachers, which was in full swing when I first met him in the mid-nineties. His main point was that these individuals, through their selfish actions, had so tainted the entire concept of Enlightenment – traditionally understood to be the pinnacle of human attainment – that it had created in the public mind an almost impenetrable wall of cynicism. It was this wall of cynicism – which was perfectly exemplified by the friend I mentioned in the Foreword – which Andrew was constantly up against. When he dared challenge it by naming names and pointing his finger directly at the worst offenders, nearly the entirety of the prevailing spiritual culture turned on him with a vengeance. It was, however, his position that served both to impress me with his character and inspire my own passion for at least attempting to become a different kind of human being. After all, it took an enormous amount of guts to come out the way he did because implied in his position was the claim that "I am going to be different and prove with my very own life that something extraordinary actually is possible." It was an absolute stance that did not seek qualifications with claims of being "only human." It was a dangerous tactic unless one was fully committed to backing it up. It also gave me tremendous confidence in Andrew as a teacher.

All this raised another issue, one that would take me some years to even begin to understand. How is it that a person could be "enlightened" on the one hand and ethically corrupt on the other? It seemed to me that either the Enlightenment, by definition, would have undermined any corruption in the personality or, if the corruption was still present, actual Enlightenment had not, in fact, occurred. How could both exist in the same human being? At this point I had not heard Andrew's teaching on "the enlightened ego," but it would not be long before I would have a full frontal encounter with it myself.

During the year and a half following this incident, my relationship with Peter was more exciting and fulfilling than in all the years that had passed before. We took trips to India, met across the country for retreats and lectures, encountered an endless parade of interesting people and delved ever deeper into consciousness, carried on a surge of shakti that flowed through him like a mighty river coursing through a deep canyon. But quietly and in the depths, change was stirring in the chemistry between us. While Peter's response to Andrew's book lingered at the back of my mind like a faintly bad odor of indeterminate origin, I began noticing other increasingly distressing signals that something was amiss. For instance, I had recently managed to edit and get published a book by Peter and from that moment he developed a growing obsession with fame. "I have karma with fame," he even told me once, a sense of inexorable destiny in his tone. Suddenly more and more of the talk around Peter was about promoting the book, getting on "Oprah," and rubbing shoulders with minor celebrities in L.A. In fact, suddenly more and more of the talk around Peter was about Peter himself.

Alongside this disturbing narcissistic self-obsession, signs of petty selfishness grew like thorny creepers through a garden. A most striking incident occurred one hot August weekend at Peter's beautiful new home nestled in a green embrace of wooded hills in New York State. The occasion was his birthday, which we marked annually with a festive retreat that included many hours of deep meditation, sumptuous feasts and all the work entailed in their preparation, entertainment of various forms and the simple camaraderie of being together. As was always the case, around 40 people had arrived from every corner of the globe and many had arranged to stay at his home. It was the height of summer and the heavy air hung densely around us, the heat slowing time to a crawl. I felt like a stick of melting butter. In that dense oppression we had three classes a day, the shakti shimmering like heat waves between us, all without the least benefit of the readily available air conditioning. The temperature hovered around 100 unrelenting degrees. The nights were not much better, the clammy warmth seeping into sleep and allowing only for fitful turning, tortured dreams and sweaty sheets.

When I raised the issue of using his quite functional and impressively efficient air conditioning system, Peter replied in a somewhat hushed and conspiratorial tone, "Oh, I'd run it if it weren't so expensive." I feigned understanding but was aghast. Gathered at his home were 40 of his closest students, most of whom had supported him in innumerable ways over the years. Each had paid about $300 for the weekend, bringing the total take for three days of teaching to around $12,000. In and of itself, I had no problem with that, as he incurred a good deal of opportunity cost in teaching these retreats and $300 for a weekend retreat, inclusive of food and lodging, was more than reasonable by market standards. However, I simply could not fathom how he could watch these people, some with small children, wither in the heat when a few hundred dollars of air conditioning would have made everyone quite comfortable. It struck me as simply reprehensible and did not line up with the man I'd known even a few years earlier, a man who had at one point paid $7,000 a month simply in order to rent a space large enough to accommodate the 50 to 60 people who attended his nightly meditation classes for free. Something was changing, and while the imperative to change was key to his teaching, I did not think this kind of change was moving in the right direction.

Some months later, Peter sat in my living room in San Francisco, having just finished teaching a retreat at my home. We had eaten dinner and he was engaged in an easy phone conversation with a student and friend of mine in Eugene, Oregon. It was clear from listening to him that the conversation had turned to the issue of healing. Over the years I'd repeatedly witnessed the miraculous healing gift with which Peter seemed to have been endowed. During my early years with him I watched in amazement as he helped a parade of people afflicted with everything from cancer to AIDS, either freeing them from their illness altogether or significantly decreasing its intensity. As with everything else, he never charged a dime. At one point he chose to discontinue his healing work because, he said, "I don't want to run a hospital; I want to help people grow." He felt that in many cases people were sick because they wanted to be, drawing to themselves a kind of attention and care that they did not receive in their ordinary life. Once relieved of their physical burdens, however, most went back to being exactly who they had been prior to the onset of their illness. That was not where Peter's interest lay. He wanted to help people grow and change, not to empower them in "energy vampirism," that is, draining life force and goodwill from others to satisfy their own emotional self-indulgence. Fair enough. On this night, however, I heard him tell my friend in Eugene in a most businesslike tone that he had decided to resume his healing work, but with the proviso that it would cost $100 per session. "I don't care how sick they are or what their financial position is," he added. I cast a sidelong glance at Rose who stood nearby. Obviously she had also noticed. The bell that had begun tolling some time earlier rang another knell that reverberated deeply in my increasingly troubled conscience.

Then came our final trip to India, which in many ways it was one of the most extraordinary experiences of my life. The fact was that despite everything I still deeply loved Peter and held out hope that this was a passing phase that would be swept up and transcended in the dynamics of change that had defined his life every day that I had known him. Together Peter, Rose, Deanna (another student and friend) and I spent three weeks bouncing across that ancient terrain. The trip combined business, tourism and spiritual practice in an adventure as mixed and spiced as the dishes we ate along the way. This whirlwind spiritual odyssey included, among other things, a visit to an orphanage in Calcutta near the Ramakrishna temple at Dakshineswar; an afternoon with Ramesh Balsekar, close disciple of the famed sage Nisargadatta Maharaj[6] (more on that later); and a three-day stay at Tiruvannamalai, formerly home to perhaps the greatest sage of the twentieth century, Ramana Maharshi.[7] This sudden interest on Peter's part in teachers other than those with whom he was already familiar was uncharacteristic and added significantly to the thrill of this trip. Rose and I had long sought to expand his vistas in this regard and something had shifted in him one morning at our home some six months earlier when he saw a picture of Ramana Maharshi propped up in a corner of our bedroom. The timeless gaze from that famous photo had struck Peter in the heart. We explained who he had been and almost immediately, fired by some surge of spiritual illumination, he invited us to accompany him to India, adding, "and I want to see as many teachers as possible while we're there." Rose and I were thrilled at the prospect of the non-dual teachings of Advaita finding their way into his teaching. It was the first time he'd expressed an interest in such teachings, and not a moment too soon, for the dualistic nature of his teaching style had begun to concern us both. Unfortunately, after three days at the sacred mountain of Arunachala, home to Ramana for most of his life, Peter concluded that the calling for his remaining days was to go back and teach Rudi's work as it was. Rose and I were crestfallen and, sitting in the lingering vibrations of the great Maharshi, we suspected that this was the beginning of the end. A few days later, after meditating together near the Kali Temple in Dakshineswar in the room once inhabited by the great Sri Ramakrishna,[8] Peter shared with me that he had been told in a vision, "Want nothing." In itself it was a poignant moment but its significance grew considerably in relationship to what would soon unfold. I never again heard him mention this divine exhortation, unusual for a man who often freely and repeatedly shared the most intimate aspects of his own spiritual evolution.

Back home, Peter's obsession with "name and fame" grew to disturbing proportions and stood in glaring contrast to "wanting nothing." Then, in a series of startling revelations, a whole aspect of his life of which I had been naïvely unaware, was unveiled in painfully short order. As it turned out, Peter, a married man with a child, had been carrying on affairs with a number of his female students. He had always maintained that there was nothing wrong with the practice of Tantric sex between a teacher and his students and had gone even further to assert that, in effect, a man had the right to sleep with any woman at any time and that such escapades were not even the business of his wife. Therefore, he was technically not in violation of his own stated code of ethics, such as it was. However, he had lied not only to his wife about these relationships but to myself and many others as well, including the other women with whom he was involved. In other words, each labored under the misguided impression that she was the only one, though none seemed to have the slightest issue with the fact that he was married.[9] Throughout this whole sordid process he had managed to turn his entire student body against his wife, at one point telling me straight to my face, "My wife is crazy. She thinks I'm having affairs with all my students." This was particularly painful for me for I was, during those years, not only his closest student, but his most staunch defender against any and all accusations. I felt like a total fool, like a knight who had gone into battle for his king only to discover his king in bed with the enemy.

Looking back, it now made perfect sense why Peter should have so despised Andrew's book, *Embracing Heaven and Earth*. After all, that slim volume contained a call to an uncommon level of integrity, a challenge to rise to a relationship to life that would allow each of us to "become a living expression of the opposite of everything that's wrong with the world." Embracing such a view would, of course, utterly destroy the kind of self-serving worldview out of which such grossly selfish actions could arise. "Everything he says in that book is true," Peter had said, in a strange acknowledgement of its ultimate validity, "but it doesn't leave any room for one's humanity." In other words, it didn't leave room for people to do what they want, when they want, how they want, for any reason that they want. It destroyed what Andrew called "negative freedom" and called one to its opposite, "the bondage of liberation." In that state one was shackled by spiritual conscience to doing the right thing for the right reasons even when it didn't *feel* like the right thing to do. Of course, that, as I understood it, was the entire point.

It was then that I knew my time with Peter had run its course. It had been an extraordinary 13 years and it would be quite impossible to overstate the radically positive impact this relationship had on me. In fact, nothing I can say can encompass its magnitude and significance. He had been a combination of father, business mentor and spiritual guide and had expressed a level of care for my well being that leaves in its wake a debt that can never be repaid. However, between the philosophical problems I saw in the teaching itself and the shocking display of ethical misconduct that I saw play itself out, I simply could not go on. It was a momentous and profoundly unsettling realization.

When I told Peter of my decision to leave he exploded in a fit of "narcissistic rage,"[10] accusing me of being a traitor, a hypocrite and "no better than a snake in the grass." "Good riddance," he added after a vitriolic barrage that landed like the psychic equivalent of the bombing of Dresden. My soul was ravaged and I felt the very ground falling from under me, not because I was leaving him but because something that had been so positive and even sacred should end so horrifically. Yet as the emotional firestorm burned, I began to see, dimly at first and with more clarity in time, that what remained in its wake was not a barren desolation but a fertile forest floor ready to sprout new life. In short, I knew that I could now give myself more fully to Andrew's teaching, whose call had haunted me for years and had begun again to grow in its insistence during the foregoing eight months.

This renewed pull to Andrew's teaching had been triggered when, shortly after the horror of September 11th, Andrew appeared in Santa Rosa, about an hour and a half north of San Francisco, to give an evening teaching. It had been years since I had seen him, though throughout that period we had had sporadic communication, so Rose and I decided to go. On that evening I was first exposed to the then newly-emerging evolutionary dimension of his teaching, a dimension that has continued to fuel my inspiration to this very moment. His message, which will become clear further on in the book, was so profoundly awe-inspiring and life positive that my whole body shook when I first heard it. Once again, the power of his transmission swept me into cosmic consciousness and, from that infinite vantage point, I saw the thrill, the glory and the obligation of being human in an evolving universe. It was a dimension of insight and understanding entirely absent not only from Peter's teaching but also from every other teaching I'd ever encountered. The reason for this was simple: it was something utterly new. This was virgin territory on the expanding frontier of human consciousness.[11] It was after Andrew's explosive exposition that, seven years after my first retreat with him, I finally felt ready to throw in my lot with his cause.

Andrew welcomed me heartily after all these years and generously waived the fee for Rose and I for a ten-day summer retreat in Les Courmettes, France, which we could otherwise not have afforded. That retreat was a revelation to me. Not only was it evidence of the fact that Andrew and his teaching were ever evolving – for little of this seemed familiar to me from the days I'd known him in the past – but it was a thrilling new vision that I recognized as being able to bridge the gap between my spiritual longing and my care for the world, enabling me to address both in a way I'd never done with either alone. It set me in earnest upon the road that was now leading me to Montserrat, Spain.

Dwelling on these memories, time seemed to have been lost and emerging from my reverie I found that the end of the first leg of my journey to Spain via New York was surprisingly near. JFK airport, it was announced by the canned yet confident voice from the cockpit, was fifteen minutes away. Pulled back into something close to full consciousness I discovered that the unpleasantness from the previous day's sandwich was still very much with me. A few more minutes, a few deep breaths and the routine ceremony of deplaning followed with predictable certainty: fold up the tray tables, raise your seat backs, wait, land, wait, stand, wait, walk and 20 minutes later I found myself sitting and yes, waiting, this time in the international terminal, for my flight to Barcelona. There I slowly sank back into a trance-like stupor until, unexpectedly, I was pulled from its grasp by the appearance of familiar faces.

"Mike!" I heard a woman's voice shout above the jumble of flight announcements and CNN news feeds droning from nearby televisions.

"Ronnit!" I waved at the thin brunette who had also been a student of Peter and had left along with a number of us during the aforementioned spiritual divorce.

"You're on our flight," she said as she approached and sat down next to me. "Jason and Gerard are here, too."

And there they were. First I spotted Jason, the classically handsome Italian chiropractor who, along with Ronnit, was a "novice" in Andrew's teaching and who lived, with two others, in the "Manhattan Center," a three-story brownstone, which was the focal point for Andrew's teaching in New York. Then, moments later, Gerard appeared. He was a tall, olive-skinned man with dark hair, big puppy eyes, a neatly-trimmed goatee and an accent that blended elements from a variety of languages which created a more pleasing English than that commonly spoken by the rest of us. Gerard, a "formal student" of Andrew's, was not only a world-famous mentalist[12] but also a strong player in the push to bring greater public awareness to Andrew's teaching and what was arising out of it, in order to help create the leading edge of an emerging cultural revolution. Within moments we found ourselves huddled together, excitedly catching each other up on the most recent developments in our lives and sharing our anticipation of the upcoming retreat.

As I talked in animated fashion with Gerard, Jason and Ronnit I also quietly considered how much had changed in the way Andrew approached his relationship with students since the time he had welcomed me to the "revolution" in early 1996. In those days the only real option for a profound engagement with the teaching had been leaving one's entire life behind and moving to the community where, as he'd warned me, one had to prepare to have one's whole life taken away. The lifestyle around Andrew in those days had been essentially monastic in nature and had demanded the surrender of the entirety of one's personal life in favor of the possibility of radical transformation. That's where I'd balked. Had I dared take that outrageous leap at that time I could not have stood behind it. I simply had not been mature enough and would have ended up falling away as abruptly as I'd entered in. Recognizing the reality of different levels of development, Andrew had since created corresponding levels of participation, allowing people to step in and stand behind what they'd stepped in to. He had spoken to a small group of us regarding this topic about a year earlier and emphasized that he was more interested in individuals taking small steps that they could back up without backing off, rather than taking big steps and then, under pressure, retreating. The former built confidence, the latter destroyed it, and in Andrew's view nothing was more injurious to one's progress on the spiritual path than the loss of the delicate and precious confidence in the living possibility of radical transformation.

These new levels of participation were also, as I understood it, a direct reflection of how Andrew had approached his entire teaching career. He did not set out with a grandiose vision of how it was all going to be and then go about systematically implementing it. Rather, he responded to the needs and demands of situations as they evolved around him. For example, in his first years as a teacher, the vision he'd held for his own life involved simply traveling from place to place and sharing his own experience with those who came to him. Such sharing, he had seen from the very outset, seemed to spontaneously immerse those around him in the same illumined state that had become his home. Naïvely, he had assumed that others would respond to that state of revelation with the same depth of surrender that had irrevocably altered his own life. He felt that he would then be free to move on, traversing the globe like a minstrel of consciousness, bringing not only the good news of Liberation, but Liberation itself, to as many seeking souls as possible. I suspect that at that time he had shared Rudi's sentiment that, "if an organization ever formed around me I'd be the first to leave." However, it turned out not to be quite so simple. To his own surprise, he found that people, swept away by what they experienced in his company, were spontaneously leaving their lives behind to follow him from teaching to teaching, from city to city, from country to country, and in such numbers that he had no choice but to respond by creating a structure that could accommodate them.

Similarly, he had assumed that the response of those around him to the explosive revelation of Enlightenment would be surrender and final liberation, as it had been in his own case. What he discovered, to his surprise, was that while people could and did have the most extraordinary spiritual experiences, this in no way guaranteed that they would change on the level of their basic humanity, a connection upon which Andrew insisted. It was this that prompted him to begin examining more closely the nature of ego; thus the bulk of his early teaching emerged as a direct response to presence of the ego and its profoundly negative relationship to life.[13]

It was this same adaptivity to changing circumstances that had prompted him to create what he called "practicing membership." This program set forth a daily practice and study of Andrew's teaching for those who wished to deepen their understanding and experience of it without either leaving their lives behind or making a formal commitment to Andrew as a spiritual teacher. It was that level of commitment to which I signed on after having left Peter. Then, about six months before my departure for Montserrat, Andrew initiated the "Student Network." This was a direct response to practicing members, like myself, who found that they wanted to engage with the teaching in a dramatically more committed way, officially take Andrew on as a spiritual teacher, yet not leave their lives "in the world" behind. It was also a response to the growing recognition within his community that perhaps the community model, in and of itself, was incomplete as a vehicle for the growing nature of the teaching. After all, did it truly make sense that everyone deeply interested in Andrew's teaching should live near or with him? If a cultural revolution was indeed the goal, wouldn't it make sense to have committed people live the teaching within the pulsing flesh and blood of that culture and demonstrate with their own lives that something completely different was possible? The consensus was a resounding "yes," and with that the Student Network was created. I joined immediately.

Jason and Ronnit, on the other hand, were "novices." Novices were individuals who had decided that they wished to live together under the umbrella of Andrew's teaching, give their whole lives to him and his teaching, yet not necessarily live in Foxhollow, the location of Andrew's world center in Massachusetts. In such an arrangement there were strict rules and daily practices with an emphasis on shedding the personal life altogether. Finally, there were "formal students" and "committed students," most of whom lived at Foxhollow directly under Andrew's tutelage. Of the nature of their commitment and relationship with Andrew I am not certain, other than to say that it is deep, committed and undoubtedly intense. The important point with respect to all this is that in each case these levels of engagement were conceived as a response to a demand and as such created "platforms of engagement" upon which people could stand without falling back and upon which their confidence could grow in an organic fashion.

The long and the short of it was this: Andrew's teaching, which is about evolution in the most profound sense, was evolving consistently in response to forces, both inner and outer, and was a living expression of the very evolution it called all of us to participate in. In a strange way it appears to be both the path and the expression of the goal simultaneously – constant evolution to higher levels of complexity and integration. It was that fact that had created an opening for me to engage in a way that felt natural and authentic rather than forcing upon me a level of participation that I, in all likelihood, would have found hard to live up to. It was largely because of this that I was sitting here ready to take the next step forward.

As it turned out Gerard – whom I did not know very well – and I had seat assignments fairly close to one another and with a little cajoling we managed to convince the man assigned to sit next to him to trade his aisle seat for mine. That meant we would spend the next eight or so hours making each other's acquaintance more thoroughly, something which I greatly looked forward to.

I have long felt myself drawn to spend time in the company of Andrew's more senior students as they consistently emanated certain qualities I found enviable. First, everyone I'd met over the years who had been involved with Andrew in a serious way was impressively functional. These were not individuals who had opted to live in a spiritual community simply to escape shouldering the burden of life "in the world." On the contrary, many of these individuals had attained uncommon levels of success either before entering the community or while there. Gerard was a perfect example. As mentioned, he earned his living as a "mentalist," and not just any mentalist, mind you, but one of the most accomplished in the world, commanding approximately $10,000 per performance.

This degree of functionality lined up perfectly with an aspect of my former teacher's teaching that I had deeply appreciated and which had made an enormous difference in my own life. That is, he used to rail against what he had appropriately termed "the rent control mentality," by which he meant always finding the easiest, cheapest way to live in order to avoid the pressure of life, under the guise of being "spiritual." On the contrary, like Rudi before him, he felt strongly that the bigger one's inner life was the bigger one's outer life, as a reflection of it, should be. "There's no place to rest," he'd often say. "Whatever level you've attained is simply the jumping-off point for the next level." To this end he'd often advise me to, "take on a little bit more than you can handle. That'll force you to grow and keep expanding your life in all directions." Once, in my early days with him, I jokingly suggested that I wished to hit the Lotto, to which he responded rather pointedly, "Mike, I hope you never hit the Lotto. It'll be the death of you. Learn how to make it." Those teachings have stayed with me, steadfastly helping me in taking bigger and bigger steps with my life, much as he had done with his. It was an ethic of work, ambition and accomplishment that deeply appealed to me and among Andrew's students I saw this same ethic flourish. The recognition that one's spiritual passion need in no way conflict with creative and financial success is, in my view, an important message that needs to be heard more often in our spiritually starved postmodern world and, more importantly, a message that must find expression in the lives of profoundly engaged human beings.

My attraction to Andrew's senior students, however, was not based solely on their high functionality. After all, such individuals may be found in abundance throughout society. There was something more that I found so compelling, something I could only call uncommon dignity and strength of character – qualities which seemed to become visibly more pronounced in direct relation to the length of time they had been involved with the teaching. And while these qualities were equally present in the men and the women, it was mostly to the men that I looked for inspiration, for the simple reason that I am a man and we all tend to look to those of our own gender in search of role models. It has occurred to me on more than one occasion how unusual it is for a 46-year-old man like myself to find a role model in the example of another, often one younger than myself, and think, "Wow, I want to be like that," because I recognized in them some quintessential quality of manhood as yet undeveloped in myself.

I'd recently heard Andrew advise a gathering: *"Watch out for nice guys, especially in spiritual groups. They're the ones out to prove that you have nothing to fear from them. In men, don't look for niceness,"* he'd added, *"look for strength and integrity. A real man should be able to intimidate you with his integrity."* That had stopped me cold. I'd never given this much thought but a little reflection quickly brought to light that I had, in fact, spent the better part of my adult life playing at being a "nice guy." I suppose that's better than being a nasty guy but closer scrutiny revealed it to be little more than a clever ruse useful in convincing both others and myself that "I'm different." Underneath, ego festered freely, having simply hit upon a useful stratagem for being seen as special. It certainly had nothing to do with "intimidating others with one's integrity."

What would it feel like to be intimidated by someone else's integrity? It would feel precisely the way I felt around people like Gerard, who was currently running a last-minute check of his e-mails via a nifty little gadget called a Trêo. It would feel like the best, most authentic part of you was being pulled upon and called to the forefront of the self. It would make you stand up straight and look the man in the eye. And in his gaze you would find a certain transparency and some ineffable quality that might be described as "undivided." It would be a position that that individual would take unselfconsciously because it was simply who he was. And as such his very presence would exert on others something Andrew commonly referred to as "evolutionary tension," a natural pull toward that which is higher and deeper, a silent demand to develop those "quintessential qualities of manhood as yet undeveloped in one's self."

Now, to notice such qualities in someone like Andrew is one thing; after all, he's reputed to be the "enlightened teacher." It's easy to set him upon a pedestal like some alabaster Buddha, an unattainable ideal, and in so doing let oneself off the hook. But when these qualities emerge in individuals who you know started out more or less like yourself, it brings both the promise and the challenge of transformation directly to your own front door. The question, of course, is, will we answer the call? It was a question to which I longed to say "yes."

With the last boarding announcements complete, our tray tables up, seat backs straight and Trêos turned off, we roared off the asphalt and made our way towards Barcelona. As the plane hit cruising altitude, Gerard and I engaged in easy conversation. Initially it revolved around our respective businesses, his as a mentalist, mine as a dog trainer (his definitely the more curious), and how to structure them so that they might generate greater revenue with a lesser time commitment, thus freeing up resources to more deeply engage in "the revolution." I had, over the years, become acutely aware of the good fortune that had enabled me to free myself from the shackles of corporate servitude and become successfully self-employed. Having spent eight years as a corporate jock, thinking that that was the most logical use for my master's degree, I had a painfully clear sense of the mind-numbing routine under which so many labor daily and the often profoundly inhibiting impact of such constraints on one's deepest longings and highest aspirations. That's why I felt so strongly about engaging creatively and effectively with the life process on a business level so that my work could, in some way, become a reflection of my aspirations rather than an inhibition of them. In this regard I found a kindred spirit in Gerard.

Soon, however, our conversation drifted from business to spiritual matters, a shift catalyzed by his passing mention of the fact that he had just emerged from a six-week silent retreat under Andrew's guidance. I had long been fascinated by these lengthy retreats to which Andrew routinely subjected his close students, considering them to be Herculean feats of spiritual endurance (another friend, Craig Hamilton, had once gone through a six-month silent retreat). It occurred to me that now, with ample time on our hands, might be a good opportunity to quiz Gerard about his experience.

"What's your daily routine like on a silent retreat?" I asked curiously.

"Well," he replied casually, "it's about 16 hours a day of meditation and contemplation."

I marveled at this, not only because of the endurance demonstrated by such an undertaking but because of my considerable envy of his ability to steal that much time from the rigors of everyday life to pursue the rigors of the inner life.

"So what was your experience like?"

"Well, it was interesting on a lot of levels," he said, quickly warming to the subject. "First of all, I thought, 'Hey, now that I've got all this time to meditate I'll spend my days just sinking into the Ground of Being.[14] I was expecting a lot of bliss and peace and transcendent consciousness. But it didn't exactly turn out that way."

"That's interesting," I said, somewhat surprised. During my own meditation practice I often found myself distracted by the looming pressure of everything that awaited me the moment meditation was over, the tyranny of my inner check list. Thus I assumed that if one had been entirely relieved of that pressing burden, such distractions would no longer trouble one's mind and thus all obstacles to simply melting into the Ground of one's existence would have been swept aside. "What happened?" I asked.

"Well, my mind just went crazy and wouldn't stop and on top of that I was hounded by sexual thoughts and desire." Once again I was surprised, having assumed that someone associated with this teaching for as long and intensely as Gerard had been would have long transcended such afflictions.

"Did you speak to Andrew about this? How did you handle it?"

"Yeah," he said in a soft but concentrated tone, "I spoke with Andrew and we talked a great deal about the importance of letting everything be as it is."

I had flashbacks to my understanding around this issue that had first emerged during the retreat in Bodhgaya nearly ten years earlier.

"I realized, in a way that I hadn't before, that really letting everything be as it is levels out all experience, from a busy mind full of sexual fantasies to the most sublime spiritual experiences. It all becomes the same. You let it all be as it is and then none of it means anything."

"What are you left with, then?" I asked.

"What do you think?"

The answer flashed through my mind. "You're free to give."

He smiled, dark eyes glinting. "Hey, you got it. That's exactly right."

We settled into silence for a while after that. I considered what he said, realizing that our relentless obsession with the quality of our inner experience so completely consumes us that we literally have very little attention or energy available to give to life. I'd heard this teaching of letting everything be as it is quite often, but there's understanding and then there's understanding. Or perhaps it would be more accurate to say that there are levels of understanding regarding the same teaching that emerge as one's own awareness of and sensitivity to such things deepen. This was equally true for one of the core positions of Andrew's teaching that is most simply articulated in his statement that, "*it doesn't matter what you think and it doesn't matter what you feel, it only matters what you do.*" From this followed his emphasis on being able to bear your experience, no matter what it was, and still do the right thing for the right reasons, especially when it didn't *feel* like the right thing to do. And finally, of course, there was his exhortation to never, ever draw any conclusions about yourself based on any aspect of your inner experience. If you had to draw conclusions about yourself – and, from the point of view of this teaching, you definitely should – it should only be based on what you *do*.

A brief examination of such statements will reveal that when taken together they create a radically different position in relation to our inner experience than the one we're commonly taught. In fact, if we look closely we will find that this position actually has the potential to utterly liberate one from enslavement to and identification with any aspect of their inner experience. In this, the separate self-sense, which is constructed precisely by intense and unquestioned identification with one's mind and emotions, would dissolve and the door to liberation would spontaneously and mysteriously appear on all sides. As I spoke with Gerard, I had already gained some understanding from my own experience of the truth and power of this position (not that I had been able to embody this with any kind of consistency), but this was the first time I had connected it to our capacity to give.

Of course, it made perfect sense. Freed from our fixation on a mind-created and illusory separate self-sense, the energy of Life that animates us all would be free to use our individuated life to care for Itself in its Infinite manifestations. As such it represented not only our own freedom but our capacity to unselfconsciously give in a way that is inconceivable to the ego.

I was struck deeply by this brief and seemingly passing exchange between us as Gerard and I sat there, crammed into our coach seats, streaking through the stratosphere at 600 miles an hour. As we talked I could feel into his depth and in so doing became more aware of my own. I could feel the pull of another's integrity ignite the inspiration to step from my own level of engagement with life to one much greater. As I would soon discover, this conversation set the tone for my entire experience of the upcoming retreat, which I could feel approaching solemnly as we flew into the night, bound for Barcelona and the mountainous monastery of Montserrat awaiting our arrival. As efforts at sleep proved futile, I spent the remaining hours drifting fitfully between awareness of my crumpled, nauseated body and the hazy world of half-dreams where the real and unreal merge in a strange miasma of semi-lucid fantasy.

Sunlight shining in from Gerard's window and the smell of cheap coffee pulled me from that lurid world. Soon, prompted by tin can announcements, we set about filling out customs and immigration forms. Slowly we dropped from the bright blue sky into the cloud cover hovering over Barcelona. Excitement sharpened my consciousness in compensation for lack of sleep. Soon we found ourselves on terra firma once more and after some delays due to harassment by bored and pompous customs officials (who all seem amazingly alike regardless of what country one encounters them in) Gerard and I were hotel bound in a zippy Spanish cab. We had decided to share a room and spend that day and night in Barcelona cleverly disguised as tourists. After a two-hour nap and an hour of meditation we headed out to the Plaça Reial, an old square where the Middle Ages encounter modernity in seamless style, to meet up with Jason, Ronnit and a number of others from the New York Center who'd already been in Barcelona for a week. We sat in a beautiful little sidewalk café off the ancient plaza, enjoyed several courses of exquisite Spanish cuisine and talked excitedly about what had been and what was yet to come.

After lunch and much laughter it was time to explore. We meandered down the cobbled, narrow alleys of an old part of town. The small, flower-lined balconies jutting out from the stone walls of ancient buildings faced each other above us at such intimate proximity that you could, standing on your own balcony, nearly touch a neighbor on their balcony in the facing building. Such architecture harkened back to a time and culture where community was a much more integral part of living than it is today. With the advent of cars and industrialized life, however, the streets of Barcelona became wide and time became short as the fast

pace of modernity consumed the old traditions and ways of living. The beauty
of Barcelona, however, was that wherever you turned, evidence of the old traditions co-existed organically with the new realities. While the old merged with
the new more in some areas than in others, the passage of time and transition
of culture, which had moved Barcelona from its birth in the days of Rome to its
flowering during the Renaissance and finally on to our postmodern present moment, was greatly in evidence on all sides. Old churches and plazas led onto busy
streets choked with cars and busses; ancient buildings with low doors and arched
walkways offered views of gleaming hotels and apartment buildings; and open-air
markets and street vendors in tiny stalls stood near supermarkets, computer stores
and discotheques.

Something else became apparent as we headed down La Rambla, a tree-shaded
boulevard adorned with flower stalls, street performers, assorted kiosks and a general explosion of life, toward the city's port, which had been the focal point of so
much of its turbulent history. Wandering along I slowly became aware of the fact
that, despite the distinct cultural undercurrent that could simply be called the
"Spanishness" of this place, it sported many features that were culturally easy to
identify. Many of the little shops, both in the back streets and along the major
cultural artery of La Rambla, were essentially indistinguishable from their entrepreneurial counterparts back in California. There were New Age bookstores,
home furnishing galleries, tribal arts importers and an assortment of merchants
and vendors, any of whom could have set up shop in the Bay Area and fit in
seamlessly. There was even a headshop with a window display made with such a
psychedelic splash of color that it looked as if a hippie had exploded in it. But it
was more than all that. There was a certain style and attitude among the people
that was also easily recognizable and somehow, despite obvious cultural differences, not "other." The clothing was familiar, the music heard here and there from
loudspeakers in stores and from headsets of scantily clad, pierced teenagers' iPods,
could have been heard anywhere in North America and pretty much anywhere
else in the modern world.

What I was becoming aware of in a way that I never had before was the globalization of culture. And somehow this amounted to more than the mere "cor-
poratization" of modern culture evidenced by the annoying presence of KFC's
and McDonald's – arguably among America's most insidious exports – in even
the most charming locales of old Europe. No, it was an attitude and spirit that
reflected the value system of the secular, postmodern culture, which, for better or
for worse, represents the leading edge of the planet's cultural development. It is
a spirit that is, on the one hand, cheerfully free of the oppressive strictures of the
past and yet at the same time expresses a cynical superficiality that flattens our
view of life into a one-dimensional perspective that is as impervious to wonder
and mystery as chrome and glass are to green and growing things. Endlessly ob-

sessed with slick surfaces, with Tinker Toys, gadgets, entertainment, stimulation and digital distractions of various sorts, it is a culture that, freed from tradition and a higher moral context, has become both obsessed with its clever ability to manipulate experience and simultaneously alienated from the larger mystery of life. Yet at the same time it is educated, liberal, humanistic and creative, but lacking in higher purpose it also lacks a channel into which to pour those precious energies in the service of our world. Of course I belong to that culture and as such am afflicted with both its virtues and its vices. It was the cultivation of the virtues and the addressing of the vices to which Andrew had long set himself, which is why I found myself here considering these things.

Soon our walk along La Rambla led us to the waterfront. This was the city's ancient port, replete with silos, warehouses, cargo ships and cruise ships, all of which still plied the maritime trades that had been the city's lifeblood since its inception several millennia earlier. We wandered along beside the water, a salty breeze tousling our hair, the cries of gulls on the wind, until the path led to an artful promenade beyond which lay the Mare Magnum, a gleaming leisure city of shops, restaurants and theaters that rose like a jewel from its drab surroundings. And just beyond that, a pillar 100 feet high shot from the ground proving, upon closer examination, to be a pedestal for a larger-than-life Christopher Columbus. He struck a bold stance, his eyes questing for the New World beyond the line of the horizon. It was here, some five centuries earlier, that he braved the hazards of the ocean and embarked upon his fateful voyage. That excursion changed the world, dividing it definitively into "old" and "new." One stood for the past and the other for the future; one contained the sum of the known, the other offered uncharted vistas. When Columbus set sail he could not have known that he was triggering the birth of an era so unimaginably different from his own. It was he, in many ways, who set in motion the dramatic sequence of events that has culminated, five long centuries later, in the very cultural globalization of which I had just become aware.

Columbus' voyage had been a watershed in the development of humankind and, fixed on the spot from which he had set out, my scattered perceptions sharpened and resolved into a singularity of understanding. Standing between the sculpture and the ocean, half facing both, I looked over my right shoulder to gaze back in time, first upon Christopher and then beyond him to an ancient fort set on a high hill overlooking the city – once its primary defense against invaders and marauders of every stripe. As I gazed to the left my eyes came to rest on the Mare Magnum, which symbolized in every way our blazing acceleration into the future. With one brief sweep of my eyes I took in the broad sweep of history fully in evidence on all sides: behind me, Columbus pointing from the mists of antiquity to the as yet undiscovered New World; in front of me, the New World fully realized in all the glitter and shine of modernity.

And between the two moved an endless stream of tourists from lands Columbus could only have imagined: Japanese, Chinese, Thai, Vietnamese, Turkish, American, German, French, Australian, Arab, Asian, African, young, old, gay, straight, singles, couples – all combed the city with the same buoyant curiosity that carried me through the tangle of its ancient streets and the graceful curves of its modern boulevards. They spouted an array of languages that might have sent a U.N. interpreter into a spin and sported lifestyles as varied as the cultures and generations from which they came. Yet more striking than the many variations on the human theme was the one that seemed to bind us all together: a globalizing culture that had made available wealth, education and the freedom to travel on an unprecedented scale and with unprecedented speed. Even 50 years ago such a sight would have been inconceivable; aided by the rapid spread of technology, in less than two generations millions upon millions of individuals have been freed from the constraints of the past, from the weight of culture, religion and strictly ethnic ways of seeing. They have benefited from higher education and have embraced a modern worldview. Despite our cultural differences, it was this that made them feel so familiar to me.

Such ruminations on progress and the nature of culture led to still others, these concerned mostly with the nature of the times into which we are heading. I have felt for some time that we lie at the crossroads of two ages, the current age of cultural evolution, which began some six millennia ago being quickly superseded by the age of technological evolution. This presents us with both good news and bad. On the one hand, our rapidly advancing technology promises to deliver us from many of the problems of our imperiled world. On the other, it threatens us in previously inconceivable ways. The ultimate outcome will be determined largely by how we cope with the cultural, philosophical, ethical and spiritual implications of such change. (For a more in-depth discussion of this topic, key to the understanding of this book, please see Appendix 1, *At the Crossroads of Two Ages).*

All of which brings me back to Christopher Columbus pointing from his pedestal to the New World on the waterfront. As I stood there and observed the crowds, I wondered where such individuals, many lacking a higher moral, spiritual and ethical context for their lives, would find the wisdom and vision from which to address the decisions that will inevitably have to be made to deal with a world on fire and a technology accelerating out of control. Of course I too am a product of the postmodern secular world obsessed with individuality and lacking all but the filmiest veneer of moral certitude. And for this reason I hoped to discover and embody a spiritual context that would not only allow me to come to terms with all of this and my place in it, but to find a way to engage creatively with life and help to give rise to a postmodern spirituality capable of addressing the challenges of our time and anchoring us deeply in our own Source. Like Columbus, I also sought a new world and deeply desired to participate in its creation.

As our small troupe left the port to meander back into the heart of Barcelona, I was reassured to be in the company of others who shared in equal measure the interest and passion that had brought me here. That company grew steadily as the day wore on for it seemed that we could scarcely turn a corner or wander into a shop without colliding with yet another familiar face from yet another corner of the globe who, like us, had arrived early and now combed the bustling streets in search of small diversions. By the time darkness had settled over the city a group of perhaps twelve of us had gathered and settled into a stylish vegetarian restaurant. There we talked and laughed until the inevitable pull of jet lag began exerting itself on even the most ardently enthusiastic among us and the allure of soft beds and deep sleep slowly overtook the spirit of adventure. Thus we finally headed for home. There, with my head thrown back on an unfamiliar pillow I fell into a deep sleep.

It was only the dappled play of sunlight dancing on my eyelids that retrieved me from those depths some hours later and, upon waking, I found myself blessedly relieved of both jet lag and the digestive problems that had been a constant companion since the beginning of this trip. After breakfast Gerard and I spent a bit more time visiting tourist attractions and by mid-afternoon we were in a cab headed for Montserrat, some fifty minutes away. Our cab ride took us past the outskirts of Barcelona into a low-lying area dotted with an odd mixture of farmland and industrial plants and, just as it seemed we were bound for rural pasturelands, the saw toothed mountain of Montserrat rose up in the distance like a cluster of broken teeth pushed up from the earth in some primal act of release. That sacred mountain had been a place of Christian devotion for a millennium, its dramatic leap from the valley floor having inspired poets and visionaries through the ages to laud it as a symbol of the inner life and spiritual aspiration. "An immense conflagration of petrified flame," one poet had called it, while another claimed that, "with a saw of gold, the angels hewed the twisting hills." The truth was that the oddly shaped mountain, with its jutting spires of stone pressing each other skyward, was both imposing and austere, and its inaccessibility and commanding view of the surrounding area made it a perfect center for retreat from the world and simultaneous contemplation of both it and its Source. For a thousand years seekers, renunciates, ascetics and monks had made this place a destination on their spiritual journey and it occurred to me that I, in my turn, was now performing a contemporary version of that same pilgrimage.

As we slowly climbed the narrow switchback roads leading to the mountain's peak I was drawn both inward in anticipation of the imminent retreat and outward by the thrill of the view and excitement of the new. To my surprise the road was busy with joggers and bikers struggling up the winding road's merciless grade with bowed heads and stoic determination. Gerard, hanging out the window, supplied them with encouraging cheers and enthusiastic thumbs ups. Finally, as we approached the summit and our destination, my surprise was enhanced by the fact that we were welcomed not by the serene confines of a monastic retreat but by a sea of tourists, vast rows of parking, an abundance of traffic signs and a cadre of crisply dressed security guards asking questions and issuing directions. I suddenly wondered if we had somehow strayed into a parallel dimension in which Montserrat was a spiritual theme park rather than a monastery for reflection and meditation. In truth, it appeared there was little of the monastic life in the air here. What was in the air, and jubilantly so, was sight seeing and entertainment, for this was a full-blown tourist attraction replete with gift shops, cafés, beer and ice cream. It was not until I saw the large sign announcing "Andrew Cohen Retreat" with an arrow pointing down a narrow road to a small group of buildings a bit further on that I was sure we were at the right place.

A few moments later our cab halted in a small plaza ringed by several aging buildings bearing no distinguishing characteristics whatsoever. Judging by the driver's gesturing for cash it seemed that we had arrived. That fact was confirmed the moment we stepped out whereupon we were instantly surrounded by a horde of pleasantly familiar faces. There was Martin from Denmark, a handsome man with auburn hair, dark eyes and gregarious disposition whom I'd made friends with on several previous retreats. We hugged and exchanged warm greetings. Then Gail came along and gave me a warm embrace. She was a formal student of Andrew's, a scrappy brunette and had been a good friend through tough times. For the last year she had been in India running a center for Andrew in Rishikesh and traveling hither and thither across that vast subcontinent to stir interest in his teachings. She was radiant. Then came Deanna, with her bright blue eyes and impish expression. She had also been a student of Peter's who, along with a number of others and myself, had jumped ship and who was now living in London as a "novice." In one's and two's the welcoming committee grew until soon the air was alive with the sounds of many voices exchanging hearty greetings in a colorful array of languages. A lilting syllable of Swedish could be heard colliding with the rough edges of some Hebraic phrase, a baroque curl of French winding itself around a blunt thrust of German, while rolling cadences of Spanish laced themselves throughout and all, of course, were contained within the familiar resonance of English itself, a language which, if I recalled correctly from my childhood,[15] resembled to foreigners speech attempted with a mouth full of marbles. It was great to be here.

After registration I found my room in one of the nearby featureless buildings. I had requested the most basic and least expensive type of room and looked forward to the rugged intimacy that sharing such close quarters and sparse accommodations would likely offer. It would be a nice counterpoint to the "I need my own space" mentality that so often divides those of us with the privilege to be able to afford it. We are so accustomed – addicted even – to having everything to and for ourselves that the togetherness available in communal situations with a shared purpose is an entirely alien experience to most of us. With brief exceptions it was certainly true for me. Five of us had been assigned to a rather austere room in which the shower consisted of a rusty pipe hanging from the ceiling dribbling out a trickle of water so anemic as to better be described as a leak. The room's small central meeting area had three cells running off of it. These were so tiny that they could not properly be referred to as rooms and each sported two small beds equipped with a hard mattress and a wool blanket as scratchy and old as an unshaven hermit. My four roommates consisted of two Germans, one Englishman and another American. My cellmate was a young British man named Anatole who, with his tightly cropped black hair, olive skin and Romanesque nose, looked more like a centurion than a proper English gentleman. He turned out to be an altogether amiable chap with, as I would soon come to see, a fierce degree of spiritual determination. Unpacking took literally no time for there was no unpacking to speak of, nor was there any closet to unpack into. Thus, with a quick shove of our suitcases either under or beside our beds the move in was complete.

All practical details having been tended to, I decided to take a walk around what would, for nearly the next two weeks, be my home. Stepping out into the streets from the cool, stone corridor of my building was as much of a shock on the first day as it would be on the last; I simply could not get used to the interminable swarm of tourists that had overrun this town like a horde of army ants on the skeleton of some long dead delicacy. It was a strange mixture of the sacred and the profane upon which I would repeatedly ruminate during the course of the coming days. At any rate, I wandered from my hostel through an arched gate across the street, up an inclined walk that opened onto a very large plaza. This, in turn, led to a set of impressive doors beyond which sat the basilica, without a doubt the spiritual heart of Montserrat. Far to my right the plaza ended in a short wall upon which rested a series of small arches, each supported by a stone saint and beyond which the wide valley floor spread out far below in vast undulations to distant rises and hills. I headed straight through the next set of doors toward the basilica.

Passing through them led to a central atrium of inlaid marble depicting elaborate insignias and symbols of the Christian faith. On one side stood a Gothic cloister several stories tall and directly ahead, the basilica façade, featuring three massive iron doors above which the twelve apostles stood ensconced in niches overlooking the flow of the faithful. I passed under their stoic gaze into the cool darkness of the church itself. I was immediately touched by the sense of the sacred, no doubt a result of both the countless worshippers that had used this as a place of prayer since its inception in the sixteenth century and the spectacular architecture whose massively vaulted ceilings drew one's eyes and mind up while manipulating an elaborate play of light and shadow across the marble, the gold, the gargoyles, the saints and the many curves and arches whose sole purpose was to sanctify form and glorify the Divine. Venturing further inward I discovered a number of side chapels, each rich with Christian iconography and laden with historical and spiritual significance. Some contained tombs of important historical figures while others served as displays for an assortment of religious art. And above the altar, in a small recessed room on the second floor, sat the church's central feature, "Our Lady of Montserrat," a simply wrought Madonna, her blackened face serene, the Christ child in her lap, flanked by gilded scenes of the nativity on one side and the visitation of Mary on the other. I was stilled into reverence despite my long-standing ambivalence toward Christianity. I walked along the aisles passing worshippers in prayer and reflection until, finding an empty pew, I sat to meditate.

I was quickly drawn inward but equally as quickly I was drawn out again, first by the ring of a cell phone, then a crying baby, then people chatting and laughing, then... The truth was that despite the many faithful who indeed respected the sanctity of this ancient place, many others did not. In fact, an annoyingly large number of people composed themselves with as much quietude and dignity as one might find, say, at the mall. It said much about the current secular culture and it's flat perspective that valued only surfaces and has managed, in near miraculous fashion, to squeeze the sacred even out of the sacred. Even the holiest of places have been reduced to one-dimensional cutout versions of their formers selves, less serving to uplift the human soul than merely to amuse and entertain it. I looked up from my meditation. On the end of my pew sat a man of about thirty, a stroller with a whining infant by his side, drinking a soda and checking emails on his cell phone. His wife snapped flash photos in one of the nearby side chapels. Further along I spotted a column of Japanese marching through with the efficient organization of a factory tour. These were followed by a gaggle of Spanish teenage girls dressed as if headed for spring break at Daytona Beach, the rapidly developing swells and curves of their femininity on easy display for all to see. And so on.

I got up to leave, not as much offended as astounded. At that moment it occurred to me why those in the world who define themselves by tradition, who anchor their self-sense in orthodoxy and who cherish the values of conservatism are revolted by the vulgarity of a culture devoid of higher principles. It was easy to understand the world's violent swing to fundamentalism. And it was equally easy to appreciate the fundamentalist rampage against modernity.[16] In fact, in some strange way I found myself sympathetic to that rage. The growing secular, planetary culture that had resolved into sharp focus for me on Barcelona's waterfront stood, in every way, as an affront to its values. Those, at least in theory, are devoted to a spiritual ideal that cherishes modesty, humility and reverence for the mystery at the source of our existence. Of course these virtues are enshrined (or perhaps entombed) in a tortured, medieval worldview that most of us – the educated elite, both secular and spiritually interested – would find difficult if not impossible to embrace.[17]

Which leaves many of us who are spiritually interested at a crossroads. We cannot go back because the view is too small. Yet there is not much to move forward into. Neither the East-meets-West nor the New Age cocktails of designer spirituality have proven a suitable fit for the needs of our time. Morbid, self-indulgent, or just downright silly, they have promoted the culture of narcissism from whose womb they sprang, but have failed, by and large, to give rise to individuals who can "intimidate you with their integrity." Having replaced the need for submission to the Absolute with the worship of the individual, each a religion of one, society today is more fractured than ever. And much hangs in the balance. My own concern at this point was not simply the matter of my own liberation[18] but a consideration of what we spiritually inclined postmodernists might do to drag the sacred back into the business of living. And not just as an adjunct, a palliative for neurosis and existential angst, but in a way that denies nothing, pulls upon the best parts of our humanity and points the way to an integrated future. Looking around it occurred to me that perhaps Montserrat was an ideal place for the exploration of such questions as the clash of world views was so greatly in evidence all about. Exiting the church, I dared consider what might emerge if the best elements of liberal culture – human rights, environmental care, embrace of the most promising technologies, and so on – were informed by submission to an Absolute Principle without in any way denying our recently liberated humanity or compromising our hard won scientific understanding of the cosmos. That was the culture I wanted to live in and help make manifest. That was why I was with Andrew; and that's why I was in Spain.

I spent the remainder of the afternoon meandering along the many branching paths that wound themselves like vines around the mountain and threaded together a string of abandoned stone dwellings, simple chapels and even a "holy cave," like so many beads on a well-worn rosary. These had all, at one point or another, served as habitations for the various and sundry pilgrims that had walked these trails for the better part of a thousand years. My excursion ended on a small hill upon which stood a simple hermitage, its modest bell tower stretching humbly heavenward from the weathered tile roof, its courtyard decorated with a fountain around which a large mosaic of ornate beasts symbolized the Creation. This was the original monastery of Montserrat, dating back to the tenth century and affording a view that not only spanned the chasm of the ages but also the gulf of air and light that stood between us and the mountains rising from the mist-shrouded valley in the distance. My spirit awed and my mind silenced, it was time now to return to the others.

Later that evening about ninety of us[19] had been gathered together by Chris Parish, a slight, unassuming man in his middle years and one of Andrew's closest students, to announce that we would be in silent retreat for the next eleven days. The silence would commence the following morning. It was not uncommon on retreat for Andrew to select individuals who had made a relatively serious commitment to the teaching to participate in very concentrated practice for the duration of the retreat. Just how concentrated it would be was evident from the schedule posted on a board:

Chanting – 5:15 a.m. to 6:15 a.m.
Meditation – 6:30 a.m. to 7:30 a.m.
Breakfast – 8 a.m. to 9 a.m.
Teaching – 9 a.m. to 11:30 a.m.
Meditation – 12:00 noon to 1 p.m.
Lunch – 1:30 p.m. to 2:30 p.m.
Chanting – 3:30 p.m. to 4:30 p.m.
Teaching – 5 p.m. to 8 p.m.
Dinner – 8:30 p.m. to 9:30 p.m.
Chanting – 9:45 p.m. to 10:30 p.m.

I looked forward to the challenge and rigor of submerging myself in practice in a way I never could at home. This being my third silent retreat I had a sense of what to expect. Obviously we would not be allowed to speak (other than to Andrew during the teaching.) We would also be segregated from the others on retreat, sitting in a separate area of the dining hall. Finally, we would be discouraged from making eye contact with one another. In short, we would be truly on our own with only the teaching to guide us through our experience.

My first silent retreat had come about two and a half years earlier, had tested me in the extreme, and had revealed in a dramatic and surprising way the insidious and ravenous nature of ego as well as the door to freedom from it. The silence, I'd discovered, I could handle. The eating separately – no problem. But not making eye contact presented a surprisingly unyielding straight jacket for the ego. I had not, until that point, realized how much affirmation the ego pulls in for itself simply through meeting the eye of another. "Do you see me?" it desperately wants – no, *needs* – to know. And when the affirmation comes, no matter how slight, the ego swells like a bloated tick, cheerfully returning the favor in an unspoken collusion whose existence only becomes apparent when this avenue of expression is cut off. In fact, this cutting off had the effect on my psyche of poking a stick into an anthill. My initial response to such ego starvation had been raw terror; there was no place to go, no one to turn to, and no way to distract myself from the full fury of the ego's reaction to being marginalized to the point of perfect irrelevance. In that context its ugly face exploded from the dark unconscious into perfect view and, being strapped into silence, I simply had to bear it. This brought on the next surprise, which was that the mere presence of the extremely unpleasant did not in any way prevent the emergence of enlightened consciousness and its expression. This I discovered in the so-called "enlightened communication" groups for which we gathered twice daily and about which I'll say more later. This was a turning point in my understanding of the spiritual life, an understanding that is ever in flux and which I hoped would deepen in the coming days.

After being briefed we were left to our own devices for the remainder of the evening. I returned to the spare confines of my hostel to find my roommates already there, taking full advantage of the last few hours of permissible speech. There was my "cellmate" Anatole from London, Chris, a psychiatrist from Chicago, and Mike and Carl from Germany. Of the latter two, the first was a short, dark haired fellow with ruddy features and a clever smile, while the other was tall, bespectacled and looked intelligent. I was particularly interested in them. Having spent the first ten years of my life in growing up in Germany, I'd wondered much about that culture which, while having left strong traces in me, had not stamped the full measure of its weight into my character. I often wondered how I might have been different had I grown into adulthood there? I looked to them for clues but time being short no startling realization emerged. Nonetheless, being German I felt a strange kinship with these two. Yet while I resonated with their German-ness I felt my own American-ness and the gap between those cultural modes. It struck me at that moment how deeply we are shaped by our surroundings, that inkling throwing into question the sense of rugged individuality to which I, as an American, am particularly prone. I sensed that we are much more shaped by our culture than we like to think and that the sense of being a unique, free thinking individual, independent of his surroundings might be, by and large, a charade. I would get to think on that a good deal more in the days ahead.

The hours swept by nearly unnoticed as we discussed with passionate intensity our interest in the teaching that had brought us here. With silence nearly upon us, it occurred to me how much I would miss this sort of engagement with other men. What made it unusual was not merely the vast context of the teaching itself but the total absence of the macho dimension so common in male gatherings. I considered where men most commonly find brotherhood – business, sports, strippers, and war – and it occurred to me that I was interested in discovering what it means to be a man who is in no way denying his masculinity yet simultaneously free from its darker aspects. What that was I didn't know for I had neither transcended the worst aspects of myself nor brought into fruition the strength and integrity to which Andrew had pointed. Yet it was precisely this aspiration that the five of us shared that evening and within which we discovered, however briefly, the potential inherent in human relationship. It was upon such considerations that our conversation turned until, at nearly one a.m., we finally retired to bed.

NOTES

1. Advaita: literally "non-duality"; a Vedantic doctrine that identifies the individual self (atman) with the ground of reality (brahman). It is associated especially with the Indian philosopher Shankara (788–820).

2. Kundalini: a yogic term indicating the latent female energy believed to lie coiled at the base of the spine. Through the practice of kundalini yoga that energy may be triggered, rising through the chakra (psychic energy centers associated with various aspects of human experience) system to open the chakra in the top of the head, inducing a state of enlightened consciousness.

3. The state of consciousness of the teacher, which is being transmitted directly to the student by mere proximity and attention to the teacher is often also referred to as the transmission of "shakti," the powerful spiritual life force that animates everything, but is particularly pronounced in awakened individuals.

4. Stupa: a Buddhist shrine, temple or pagoda that houses a relic or marks the location of an auspicious event. The Tibetan word is Chorten, which means "the basis of offering." It is a symbol of enlightened mind and the path to its realization.

5. Shakti: from the Sanskrit, meaning power or divine energy, especially in its female principle.

6. Nisargadatta Maharaj: (1897–1981) worked as a cigarette seller in Mumbai (Bombay) but was world renowned for the depth of his enlightenment and admired for his direct and informal teachings, a selection of which are in his most famous book *I Am That*. Nisargadatta is widely considered to be one of the 20th century's most articulate communicators of Advaita Vedanta.

7. Ramana Maharshi: (1879–1950) was born in Tamil Nadu, South India. At sixteen (1896) he had a life-changing experience: while sitting alone in a small room upstairs, a great fear arose in him that he was going to die and he ventured to scrutinize what that might mean. He lay down and turned his attention very keenly inward, realizing that, "Untouched by death here I am still existing and shining. I am indestructible." He soon left home for Arunachala mountain in the town of Tiruvannamalai in Southern India where he spent the rest of his life and became world renowned as the century's greatest master of Advaita Vedanta.

8. Sri Ramakrishna: (1836–1886) Widely considered the greatest Hindu saint of the nineteenth century, he is known for the depth of his enlightenment and habit of exploring all religious paths. One of his most noteworthy devotees was Swami Vivekananda who made his way to America where he helped spark Western interest in Eastern teachings. Ramakrishna was a highly unorthodox and controversial figure in his time and for some time many thought him mad. He was intensely devoted to Kali and was an influential figure in the social and cultural movement known as the Bengal Renaissance.

9. It was only when some of the "other women" found out about each other that the whole charade exploded. For an interesting article on women who sleep with their gurus, see Jessica Roemischer's article, "Women Who Sleep with their Gurus and Why They Love It." In *What is Enlightenment* Magazine, Issue # 26. You can also read the article at http://www.wie.org/j26/women-who-sleep.asp?page=1.

10. A phrase Andrew had coined for the horrific emotional outburst one would be subjected to when the ego of another was laid bare and exposed to the light of day with no possibility of avoidance, denial or escape.

11. It must be said, however, that there have been, throughout history, intrepid thinkers who have, here and there, carried the torch of evolutionary spirituality through their time. While, as is so often the case, they were thoroughly underappreciated by their contemporaries, they did hold

taut a thread of development that is now beginning to bear fruit in a new time and culture. For a fascinating overview of the historical development of evolutionary spirituality see Tom Huston's overview of its best and its brightest at www.andrewcohen.org/teachings/history-evolutionary-spirituality.asp. You can also read his article, *Tracking 300 Years of a Radical Idea,* in issue 35 of *What is Enlightenment?* Magazine.

12. Gerard Senehi, "The Experimentalist." Check him out on the web.

13. To read more about the emergence of Andrew as a teacher see *My Master is Myself* (Lenox, MA: What is Enlightenment Press, 1989), a small journal that Andrew kept during the two week period of his realization and transformation, and *Autobiography of an Awakening* (Lenox, MA: What is Enlightenment Press, 1992), in which he chronicles his awakening, his early experiences as a teacher and the painful rift with his own guru.

14. The Ground of Being is a phrase used to refer to that unnamable mystery in which all being has its roots, that timeless source of time, the root of our very own self that is the target of discovery in all enlightenment teachings.

15. I lived in Germany for the first ten years of my life and did not speak a syllable of English until my arrival in New York, which, of course, forced the issue. And while for a very long time English has been as much a part of me as breathing, I can distinctly recall the days when that was not the case, when to my young immigrant ears it did indeed seem speech attempted with a mouth full of marbles or, perhaps more true to the American stereotype, speech attempted while chewing gum.

16. According to various statistics, approximately sixty percent of the world's population can be considered to be in the fundamentalist camp.

17. Of course, some of the educated elite also revert to fundamentalist views but the amount of denial involved in such a shift of allegiance seems to me to be extreme, a harsh bargain demanding that we set aside large hunks of reason and hard won knowledge in exchange for a brittle sense of existential certainty.

18. Liberation from fear, ignorance (of our true nature) and selfishness; in other words, enlightenment.

19. The retreat totaled about two hundred and forty attendees.

Day 1

An Invitation into Consciousness

The alarm leapt into action at four forty-five in the morning, rattling me out of a fitful half-sleep. During the night my digestive difficulties had returned with mischievous glee and thus my receptivity to rising in the utter absence of daylight was, shall we say, sub-optimal. Nonetheless, rise I did. Stepping over my suitcase and into the main chamber of our room I discovered that one of the other fellows had thoughtfully prepared a small cup of tea for each of us. Since we were now officially in silence I was unable to determine whose generosity of spirit was responsible for this small act of kindness; so I uttered a silent thanks in my heart and released it into the ether. I downed the tea, donned my clothes, shook off the night and headed for the meditation hall.

There I found many of the others already taking their seats. The hall had been neatly arranged with rows of chairs facing a small podium and a series of large windows to our left opening to a brick wall across the narrow alley next to our building. On a small table at the entrance of the room lay a stack of papers with the daily chants printed on them. I grabbed one and found a seat.

I thought back to the first time I heard that Andrew had his students chant various passages from his teachings. It had struck me as rather odd given that I viewed Andrew as the ultimate modern teacher in tune with the times. Chanting, on the other hand, seemed to be a kind of trance inducing ritual from another age that in the sixties had been imported wholesale along with an assortment of other cultural claptrap during the dramatic rise of Western interest in Eastern teachings. Not that I disliked chanting. When I first became interested in Indian spirituality during the early eighties I had spent some time in the Miami Beach Siddha Yoga ashram where chanting was considered a core spiritual practice. Then it was completely new to me and, in fact, I loved it. The ancient chants that we recited were stirring, their beautiful rhythms, cadence and power bearing us up into transcendent consciousness. However, when I met Peter, whose own teacher Rudi had originally brought Swami Muktananda, the late founder of this particular lineage, to the West, he strongly discouraged chanting. In fact, Rudi hated chanting. "I'd rather smoke dope than chant," he was fond of saying.

"At least I'd know what was getting me stoned." Considering that the use of drugs was the one thing absolutely forbidden in Rudi's teaching, this was a rather strong statement. The problem with chanting, both Peter and Rudi believed, was that in creating a transcendent state of consciousness it also created the illusion that one was growing when indeed all that was happening was that one was getting high. "The only thing that'll grow is your ass," Rudi liked to say with respect to such practices. That made sense to me and lined up with my own year's worth of experience with them.

So I was indeed surprised when I discovered that Andrew not only encouraged but also demanded chanting as a spiritual practice from those who'd engaged him as a teacher. However, I found that the purpose of chanting in his teaching was quite different from what I'd seen in the past. Most importantly, it was not conceived in the slightest as an ersatz high. Instead, there were a host of reasons for requiring this practice of his students. I had not fully appreciated what those were until hearing Andrew speak about them on a CD from a teaching in London. First, he had pointed out, that chanting forces the self to renounce the ego because there's something about chanting itself that's as irritating as fingernails on a blackboard if one is identified with ego, but is the easiest thing in the world if one is identified with what he referred to as the Authentic Self.

In a collective context, he'd added, chanting can reveal the presence of ego very quickly because someone identified with ego will always find a way not to be in tune with the rest of the group. They'll either start early or come in late or chant in a way that is nothing short of irritating, all of which represents the plain refusal to be transparent in a group context. On the other hand, when the ego is in a state of submission and someone is really committed, one gets over this hump and the chanting becomes an almost self-generating and thrilling experience of both contemplation and active meditation.

He'd also said that chanting certain aspects of the teaching makes it into a practice in a way that reading them to oneself simply couldn't. One can't really read something a hundred times and have an authentic intellectual relationship with it because the material just becomes too familiar. But chanting actually allows you to engage with the information with a different part of yourself and forces you to connect with it in a way that has an emotional dimension to it. In that dimension there's a certain kind of commitment, inspiration and passion being expressed, no matter what the ego feels like, and that brings surrender and submission into it.

And lastly, because the veiling power of ego is so much stronger than any of us even suspect, on a purely mechanical level the idea is to grind the teaching into the very fabric of the brain matter so that ultimately there could be no circumstance that one could be, *"in this dimension or any other,"* as Andrew had put it, where they'd ever be able to not know this. Therefore, as it turned out, something that for a sophisticated individual can seem like a very primitive form of spiritual practice, in the context of Andrew's teaching, becomes an ultimate challenge to the self and, as such, a very important exercise.

Knowing all that made me much more receptive to chanting and thus, when Chris Parish began the day by speaking briefly regarding the appropriate attitude with respect to this practice I listened with keen attention. He began by pointing out that it's important to audibly verbalize the chant with commitment rather than muttering it under our breath, hoping to go unnoticed. Second, we were to make every effort to stay with the meaning of the words, letting it move into us and inspire contemplation at the deepest level. Rote repetition was clearly not worth much, amounting to little more than spiritual karaoke. He added that doing this properly should result in a state of both profound ease of being and intense alertness, which, he pointed out, is not different from the state of meditation. And finally, once we were autonomously and authentically giving ourselves to the chanting we should find ourselves spontaneously coming into communion with others doing the same. This could potentially result in a sense of union with others such as that experienced in "enlightened communication" groups (again, more on those later).

With that we commenced and slowly the room began to resonate with the day's first chant:

> *The absolute simplicity that can be discovered and experienced directly through the one pointed contemplation of the desire for freedom above everything else is Liberation. That is why intense and profound contemplation of the first tenet, Clarity of Intention, is so important. In fact, that is why the one pointed contemplation of the desire for freedom alone is the most important part of the spiritual life.*

For an hour these words moved through us and filled the space between us. As they represented the foundation of Andrew's teaching their chanting at the outset of the day made perfect sense. If we could anchor ourselves in their meaning it would set the tone for the day.

With chanting complete we were given a fifteen-minute break. I stepped out to watch the day break, the sun casting beams of muted gold across the hazy valleys and a wild storm of church bells hailing a new day. We then meditated for an hour and after a silent breakfast we found ourselves, taut with anticipation, in the teaching hall ready for Andrew.

The room itself was oblong with Andrew's podium stationed on one side facing a long row of large windows overlooking the deep canyon that fell steeply away to the valley floor. Between the podium and the windows sat two hundred and fifty chairs arranged in a semi-circle. The area nearest the podium was carpeted and dotted with meditation cushions for those preferring the floor. On either side of the podium stood a large version of Andrew's two teaching models (see, p. 42-43)

EVOLUTIONARY ENLIGHTENMENT

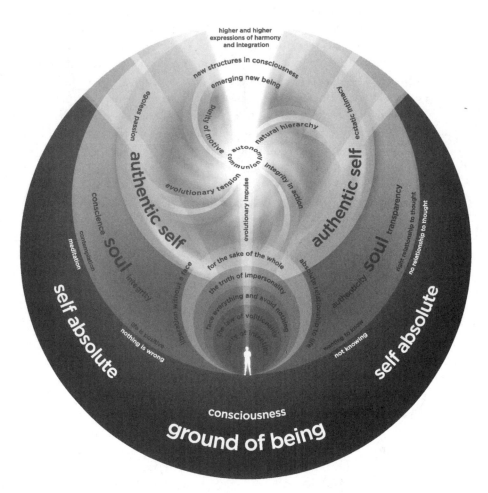

EGO

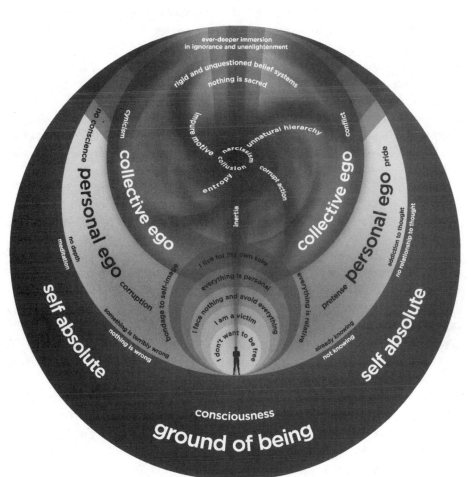

to which he would refer repeatedly in the coming days. Slowly the room filled with people shuffling about in search of a seat and within about fifteen minutes everyone had settled into meditative silence. A few minutes after that Andrew, impeccably dressed as always, slowly walked up and sat on the podium.

After a few moments of silence and then a brief *"good morning,"* he laid out the ground rules for the retreat.

"So, we're going to be meeting here twice a day," he began, *"at nine in the morning and five in the afternoon. Also this room will be open all night for those who might like to meditate and I want to ask everybody to please maintain silence in here at all times.*

"I would also like to ask you not to read anything, including my books, for the duration of these ten days because I'm going to be giving you plenty of things to think about. Along the same lines, please don't speak about anything other than what I'm speaking about in here. Specifically, don't speak about anything personal. Don't ask anyone how they feel, don't ask anyone what their name is, don't speak about the weather, and especially, don't speak about yourself. It's absolutely against the rules to speak about yourself and your history. That's very important! This is not a therapeutic retreat. That's not what I teach and that's not what we're doing here.

"I also don't want you to talk about your opinions including opinions about what I'm teaching. I don't want you to talk about what you already think and what you already believe, because no matter how good the conclusions you've already come to are, they're obviously not good enough, otherwise you wouldn't be here. Therefore I want you to pretend that no one else is interested in your opinions."

Everyone laughed, including Andrew, before he went on.

"This can be very difficult, especially for men, because we're all very proud of what we think we know. But the reason you've come here is because you're interested in my opinions. Therefore, all I want you to do is give your attention to my opinions, which have to do with radical, impersonal, evolutionary Enlightenment. I've been doing this for a very long time. I know what I'm doing and I can guarantee that if you do it my way you're going to get a very big result.

"Now, if you want to speak together that's fine but I want you to speak only about what I'm speaking about in here. There are a lot of big concepts that I use in this teaching. They are morally, philosophically and spiritually challenging so I'll be giving everybody more than enough to think about.

"Finally, I expect everybody to be willing to make effort. We all have habits and the older we get the harder they are to break. So if you want to be a free, liberated person then you have to be willing to make the effort to break deeply ingrained emotional, psychological and even physical habits. So, since you've made the effort to come here I expect you to make effort while you are here.

"When I first started teaching about nineteen years ago I thought it was easy. Unfortunately, I found out the hard way that it's not. So, if you're lazy, weak-minded and self-indulgent you've come to the wrong place! You'll never change. I can guarantee it."

He paused, a sly smile spreading across his face, then added, *"Or, if you want to change, maybe you've come to the right place."*

He finished his opening with that, then asked if anyone had any questions about the guidelines. No one did. Now, I'd heard all this before and understood the reasons for these strict guidelines; however, there was a gravity and an edge to his voice that I had not heard him use at the beginning of retreats. No doubt we would be heading into deeper water soon. My attention was riveted.

"A big theme in my own teaching," Andrew continued, *"has to do with the intention or choice that the individual makes in relationship to life itself. Now, in this teaching we're not depending upon God, Grace or anything else to save us. This teaching is based on the concept of self-liberation. That means that the only way to be saved as an individual is through being willing to make the effort to save oneself. Now, that's quite a big deal and definitely something to think about.*

"Generally, in spiritual teachings, many people have gotten the idea that either some physical or divine non-physical entity or non-entity is somehow going to save them. I can guarantee that that's not going to happen. In my opinion there's no one that can save you other than yourself. A big part of what's wrong with today's spiritual marketplace is that too many of us are seeking to be saved by someone or something else and not enough of us are mature enough to finally be willing to take responsibility for ourselves. So, what I'm teaching will only work according to the degree that the individual is willing to take responsibility for himself or herself. Does that make sense?"

Everyone mumbled half-heartedly in the affirmative as if slightly stunned. This, of course, revealed the depth to which so many of us, myself included, still secretly harbored hopes of being saved. As he said this I had to admit that although I was definitely willing to make effort, still, in the half-hidden depths of my secret self, I did not wish to part with the relief and assurance found in the hope that someone up there is looking out for me.

"You know that there's nobody up there, don't you?" Andrew asked as if reading my mind and pressed further. *"Don't you wish somebody had told you that when you were a kid?"*

Silence.

"I wish someone had told me that," he added in a chipper tone. *"Anyway, there's nobody up there! Can everybody handle that?"*

Another less than convincing affirmative percolated from the group.

He then turned his attention to the two large teaching models set up on either side of him, using his only other didactic tool, a slick little laser pointer, to bring our attention to these representations of what he saw as two fundamentally different modes of human consciousness: the ego[1] and the Authentic Self.

"These models," he began, *"represent what it is that I'm teaching. They're a reference point and over the years I've come to believe that it's very good to have reference points. A couple of months ago a spiritual teacher came to visit me at my center in*

western Massachusetts and we were going for a walk when he said, 'Andrew, isn't it interesting that it's impossible for anyone to see themselves objectively?' In other words, it's not so difficult to see another individual with a reasonable degree of objectivity, but it's almost completely impossible to see ourselves objectively. So, a model or map can be a reference point to help us navigate through life and help us to tell where we are in relationship to our own experience. In other words, it's very difficult, if not impossible, for any of us to tell how well we're doing or where we're at. So models can function like a map. For instance, if you're at sea and want to find out where you are you have to navigate and check certain reference points. This is especially true if you're trying to get somewhere, and in a teaching like this you're definitely trying to get somewhere.

He paused for a moment, and then went on. *"A lot of spiritual teachings these days are not about getting anywhere new. They're about feeling better."*

He paused again, and then qualified this statement. *"By the way, you have to know that when I teach I often speak in very broad strokes and constantly make big, sweeping generalizations. Now, I know that I'm doing this and I'm aware that every individual in the universe does not conform to them and that there are exceptions to everything that I'm saying. However, I do it to make broad, overarching points and establish certain basic truths. Are you all with me?"*

Another wave of affirmatives, this time clearer and more engaged.

"So as I said, in this teaching we're definitely trying to get somewhere. This teaching is about going higher; it's about evolution! I know that everybody here has heard the word evolution before but I wonder how much anyone has really thought about it. Evolution means vertical development! Now, keep in mind that statistically very few people evolve or develop after they become adults. It's a horrible thing. After the mid-twenties it's just kind of a flat line until they die. How's that for a sweeping generalization?"

He burst out in that impish, trademark laugh of his, then added, *"But I'm sure everybody here is an exception,"* which was greeted by laughter from the audience.

"Unfortunately it happens to be true. It's not my fault, but there it is. So there's a difference between approaching a spiritual teaching that is authentically about evolution and development versus a teaching that's going to help you feel better. Most of the stuff out there is usually about feeling better.

"But this teaching is about evolution and development, not about feeling better. There's a big difference. Finding a way to feel better is easy; evolution takes effort and it's hard. So I want you to think about what it means to go from a lower level of development, which means where you are right now, to a higher one." He paused and looked around. *"Is it okay to say that? Sometimes just saying something like that can make people very angry. I can't tell if anybody's angry yet."* He laughed again.

"I'm trying to make some basic points and distinctions here that I hope you'll take seriously. Believe me, I laugh a lot when I teach but the place I'm coming from is deadly serious. To be honest, I often make a lot of jokes in order just to soften everybody up so that when I say some of the stronger things you'll be willing to hear them.

"Now, I've noticed that the concept of evolution or development is very difficult for most of us to think about. You see, on a horizontal scale you can go from, 'I feel bad,' to, 'I feel great,' but there wouldn't necessarily be any vertical development. Sometimes, I've seen a person feel terrible and depressed and then come to a point where they're happy and feel wonderful but no evolution has necessarily occurred. That having been said, it's very difficult to conceive of or conceptualize what evolution and development mean in relationship to our own self.

"Now I want you just to stay with this for a minute because it's very interesting. When we think about the notion of evolution or development it's easy for us to acknowledge that the universe has been in a state of development or evolution for fourteen billion years. Most of us would say, 'Sure, that makes sense.' Along the same lines, we can imagine that a child will grow, evolve and develop over time. Or we can conceive of what it would mean to develop intellectually. What about emotional development? Emotional development means, for example, that if you're an angry and frightened person and go to a therapist for say twenty years – it takes that long most of the time, doesn't it? – maybe you'll find that there'll be some emotional development. You won't be so angry, frightened and paranoid – if you're lucky. That's something we can imagine. And what about physical development? Let's say you're overweight and decide to go on a diet and start exercising. It's easy to imagine that you'd lose weight and develop physically. What about spiritual development, which means going from being a self-centered person to someone who cares more and more about others. You can imagine that, can't you?

"So these are all things we can conceive of. But when I ask you to imagine the evolution of your own consciousness you can't imagine it, can you? Think about it for a minute. Can you imagine your own consciousness evolving? When, in his brief pause, no one said anything Andrew answered his own question. *"We can't do it.*

"From the subjective position it's impossible to conceptualize the evolution of consciousness in relationship to your own self. I can't imagine it. I literally have no idea. You can aspire to evolve to the level of consciousness, but even if your consciousness evolved in real time you cannot imagine what it would look like ten years from now. Only other people can see it. You'll never be able to see it yourself.

"Now, there's another dimension to this. When the evolution of consciousness occurs, what happens in terms of your own subjective experience is that you find that you're less distracted by your fears and personal desires. You're also less distracted by compulsive thoughts and all the emotions that go along with them. They diminish in intensity. But despite the fact that fear, compulsive thinking and desire diminish in intensity, you will still not be able to objectively see the relationship between that and the actual evolution of consciousness itself. Do you know why?"

"Because consciousness is not an object. Does everybody already know that?" Andrew looked around the room, and then repeated himself. *"Does everybody know that consciousness is not an object?"* Then, very quickly, he said, *"say no!"* and

laughed. It struck me as odd that he would assume that we should definitively answer "no." After all, from my own experience I knew that consciousness was not an object. Or so I thought.

When no one responded, he prodded, *"Does everybody know why consciousness is not an object?"*

A middle-aged man with a heavy German accent said, "No."

"Because consciousness is the subject," Andrew replied. *"What does that mean?"* he followed on quickly. *"Well, for example, if you're sitting here giving me your attention, it's the deepest part of yourself that's giving me attention. It's not the part of you that's thinking about what I'm saying. It's just the part of you that's giving me your attention. That's that part of you where consciousness is.*

"Now, when I say consciousness is the subject it also means that everything is external to consciousness itself. In other words, consciousness is primary. Look into your own experience right now. If you do, you'll see that the thoughts you're having are in some way external to the experience of consciousness, or pure subjectivity. Isn't that true? If the experience of consciousness is the centerpoint of all your experience, then you'll notice that thoughts are external, outside, or in some way beyond that centerpoint. It's important to know this and a lot of people don't. Taking this further, you can even see how your emotions are somehow external or slightly beyond this centerpoint of pure subjectivity, this seat or core sense of consciousness. Again, when you experience fear or sexual desire, do you experience them as deeply as you do consciousness itself? Or is the experience of fear or sexual desire somewhere just outside or beyond the experience of consciousness itself?"

As Andrew spoke a strong current of energy entered the room, stilling our minds as we followed his logic inward. The mysterious power of transmission had been ignited.

"You don't have to even close your eyes," he said as people began to do just that. *"You can just pay attention right now. Even if you were overwhelmed by fear or sexual desire you'd still see that it would be somehow external to consciousness itself because consciousness is primary. And if you just feel your physical body you can see that it is like a sheath or a sack around the presence or experience of pure subjectivity. Does that make sense in everybody's experience?"*

A quiet assent rose into the air.

"My fundamental point is that the experience of the subject is primary and that everything else, including the body, the mind, and the emotions is external to the experience of this subjectivity or consciousness itself.

"Now, you can't get any deeper into the self than this pure subject. There's nowhere else to go. That's the last stop. Everything ends with consciousness. In other words, if I drilled a hole in your head and went all the way in to the deepest place I would arrive at this place of pure subjectivity, which is the deepest sense of 'I.' But, the 'I' we're referring to here is not the personal 'I,' or the ego.

"In other words, if we kept penetrating deeper and deeper beyond all the layers of differentiation, what we'd find there is that the experience of consciousness, or the pure subject, is identical for all of us. Right?"

Everyone agreed.

"For example, it feels like something to be a man and it feels like something to be a woman. It also feels like something to be an American and it feels like something to be Danish or Israeli or any other nationality. There's an ethnic dimension to the self. It has a particular flavor to it. If you enter into the collective of a different ethnic group, it feels like you're entering into something very unfamiliar. In the same way, if a woman enters into a group of fifty men or if a man enters into a circle of fifty women, it feels very different. And then if you put all those things together in relationship to your personal life experience, it also feels like something to be you that is in some way unique to you. My personal sense of myself is unique to me and my own particular set of circumstances and this applies to each and every one of us. But if we drill a hole right into your forehead and keep going beyond all these relative differences until we finally get to the end, we will find the pure subjective sense of self, or the experience of consciousness, or simply 'I.' This experience of the subject or consciousness itself is identical for all of us. There's no difference. Whether you're a man or a woman, a Jew or a Christian, an African or an Asian, there's absolutely no difference in what the experience of consciousness, or pure subjectivity, feels like.

"So, once again, what I'm referring to here is the part of your self that is hearing me speak and that is paying attention, that is the very center of your own experience. It's the pure subject. If you forgot that you were a man or a woman, the sense of the subject, of this 'I,' would still be there, wouldn't it? If you forgot whether you are American or Spanish or Israeli or African, this sense or awareness of the pure subject would still be there, wouldn't it? If you forgot about your personal history the subject would still be there. What if the body disappeared? Hmm." He paused to allow for brief reflection. *"Well, think about it for a minute. In deep states of meditation what happens? Body consciousness disappears, right? But the experience of the subject doesn't go anywhere. You're still there! So when I say 'you,' who are you? Who you really are, that deepest and most profound sense of what it means to be you, doesn't go anywhere. Did you know that?"*

Throughout his monologue Andrew's tone had grown in depth and intensity until he threw out these last lines with a kind of impassioned ecstasy, finally adding, *"I wonder,"* with a little laugh.

After a short pause, he went on, *"It's very important to know this. So just for half a minute, can you give attention to that part of your self? If you want to close your eyes you can, but you don't have to. Just give attention to that part of your self that's not male, nor female, nor part of a particular ethnic group; that actually has no relationship to your personal history and yet is the essence of who you are. The point is, you could take everything else away and that would still be there. But if that goes, everything disappears."*

Silence settled over the room as we all briefly attempted to identify that place in ourselves.

"Once again, when I refer to consciousness I'm referring to this experience of pure subjectivity or the 'I' sense. Now, when we talk about the evolution of consciousness, one way of understanding what that means is that the experience of consciousness itself, or that sense of pure subjectivity, of the primordial 'I,' increases, becomes more powerful, more profound, and more intense. So the traditional definition of Eastern Enlightenment is based entirely upon this discovery that consciousness is primary and is what the Self is. Does everybody understand that?"

"Yes's" filled the air like a chorus. *"Good, now the retreat's over,"* Andrew said, clapping his hands as, along with the rest of us, he burst into laughter.

"So this is something I want everybody to give a lot of attention to because it's very, very, very, very, very, important! Most people go through an entire human life and don't know this. Have you noticed that? Even a lot of people who meditate don't know about consciousness although the primary reason to meditate is to put your attention on consciousness.

"So everyone's heard this expression, 'know thyself.' All it means is that the subject, this pure 'I,' is who you are at the deepest level. And so, in the traditional definition of the Eastern Enlightenment, they say that if someone is an enlightened person it's because they have discovered the subject.

"Before they were enlightened they thought they were the ego. Does everybody know what the ego is?"

A few people mumbled that they did.

"It's the personal sense of self. The personal sense of self is the 'you' that was born twenty, thirty, fifty, eighty years ago; the person who's had an infinite number of experiences through historical time. It's the personal line. It's what's referred to when someone calls your name – David, Susan, Andrew, Ruth, Michael, Shirley, or whatever and you say, "yes?"

"But the deepest part of you is the subject. Now if what I'm saying is true – and it is true – it doesn't make sense to live the way that we do. If the deepest part of us is consciousness itself and yet we act or behave as if consciousness is irrelevant, or worse, doesn't even exist, that means what? That we are crazy!

"You see it's consciousness that animates everything including the personal self. That's what I mean when I say that consciousness is primary. If you unplug consciousness, all the lights go out for the personality? That's called death! It's not ego death; it's real death. Ego death is when you die to the fears and desires of the ego and consciousness becomes primary for you. But that doesn't mean that you die; that means you are more alive because then consciousness emerges. It moves from the back to the front.

"In the enlightened state of consciousness the fears and desires of the ego recede into the background if not disappear altogether, yet you're still there. So even when the personal self and all its fears and desires are totally gone, when the memories of your personal stream are completely absent, you can still be completely present.

"These are very basic and important things to understand and it often takes a long time for people to really get it. You can intellectually get it but it won't help you. You have to really get it and when you really understand what consciousness is, it helps you to see how crazy we are because what we give our attention to every day is not consciousness, is it? It's the desires of the personal self, isn't it? And the fears and desires of the personal self are deeply conditioned, which means mechanical, habitual, and unfree. Does that make any sense?"

With that question hanging in the air Andrew paused, leaving us suspended in amazement. The very consciousness from which and of which he spoke could now be felt in the room, its transcendent charge bearing us up with a lightness that coursed through the body and blew the self-sense out in all directions. The morning's fatigue dissolved like a drift of fog under a noonday sun.

"What I do in my teaching," Andrew went on, *"is try and speak about some of these very big yet subtle and challenging concepts in ways that are very simple because one of the things I want to do is help everybody to learn how to think about the human experience – your own human experience—in a new and different way, in the context of Enlightenment itself.*

"So, because it's the beginning of the retreat we have to establish what's primary or fundamental. And what's fundamental for all of us is consciousness itself. Therefore, what I want everybody to do today is to give attention to your own experience of consciousness. So when you walk around outside today and look at the beautiful mountains, don't say to yourself, 'Oh, aren't the mountains beautiful?' Be aware of who's looking at the mountain. Then you're going to become aware of consciousness. Or if you happen to look at your friend, you don't have to say anything to them but you can suddenly be aware of consciousness looking at your friend. Also, consciousness is a feeling, so be aware of what consciousness feels like. This is very easy to do. You don't have to make a lot of effort; just constantly fall back into it.

"Now, if someone knows that consciousness is primary, their whole life is transformed. They're not the same person anymore. They will become a completely different person. So if you're saying to yourself, 'Oh, I already know that,' and your whole life hasn't changed, then it couldn't possibly be true."

That stopped me short because it was precisely what I was thinking. Over the course of the last twenty-five years I have had many experiences of consciousness. But when I asked myself whether or not my life had become completely transformed, by which I understood him to mean enlightened, I could not make such a claim.

"So, as I said earlier, there are different ways of understanding the evolution of consciousness but the first and most primary way to understand it is that the experience of consciousness being primary grows and becomes more intense and profound. Now, don't you think everybody would be very different if they knew who they were at the level of consciousness itself? Unfortunately, however, you could say most of us are stuck

in the front here," Andrew indicated his forehead, *"trapped. Now, is there anybody that's keeping you there at gunpoint? Is anyone forcing you to be lost in your own mind?"*

No one said anything, as if they weren't quite sure about this. *"Well, this is important. Most people feel very victimized by the compulsive thinking of their own mind. And compulsive thinking about whom? About one's own self, of course. Now, once again, is anyone forcing you to do it? You have to be very clear about this. Because if there isn't anybody forcing you then you must be doing it yourself.*

"If you feel like a victim then it's because you consciously or unconsciously believe that someone has a gun to your head, which means that you have no choice. I want everybody to just look objectively and see if anybody is forcing you to think about yourself in such a compulsive way that you live in a state of constant torment? Now, if you see that there's nobody forcing you to do it, then you have to conclude that the only reason you're doing it is because you want to. You see it's all a matter of habit. So, for example, if a junkie is putting heroin in their arm they're doing it because they want to.

"So I want everybody to assume the perspective and position of consciousness itself in relationship to your experience from right now onward. You're on retreat so it should be a very easy thing to do. You have plenty of time to just to give your attention to this, to consciousness. Now, why do I want you to do that? Because what you will notice is that consciousness itself, which is who you are, is already free. So it's not a meaningless exercise. In fact, it's pregnant with potential.

"So just hang back there and pay attention to the subject. Just fall back into it. It doesn't matter where you go in time or in space, you can't get deeper into reality or into life than that. Does that make sense?"

Much nodding on that one though mingled with degrees of stupefaction.

"If we don't know this – and most of us don't know it – then by default we give too much importance to parts of our self that are less primary or more superficial rather than giving the most importance to that which is absolutely primary and fundamental.

"The point is that if you want to know answers to questions like 'what's the right relationship to thinking, to emotions, to the personality, to sexuality,' or more than anything, 'what's the right relationship to life?' then first, you have to find out what's primary and take that position yourself. Then you can go into these questions. But if you don't do that first, how could you even begin to ask questions like that? The answers you're going to get if you go into it superficially are going to be very different than when you go into them very deeply from the perspective of consciousness.

"Now, remember what I said at the outset: that this is a method of self-liberation and that there's nobody up there who's going to save you. Does everybody know that?"

Once again, a chorus of slightly nervous "yeses" met Andrew's question. I had to admit once more that on a deep feeling level I didn't want it to be true. I felt comforted, sensing that some power or force cares about me personally and is thoughtfully arranging the minutiae of the cosmos in my highest interest.

"Are you sure?" Andrew prodded. *"I know a lot of very intellectually sophisticated people that still, when they're alone, think there's somebody up there that's going to save them. But if you want to be a liberated person you have to be willing to let go of a lot of childish ideas including that there's somebody, human or divine, that's going to save you."* After a moment he conceded, *"I know it's a big thing to give up."*

"But for someone who wants to be a liberated person, any hope or anticipation of salvation that exists tomorrow or in the future has to be abandoned. And that's a big thing for people to give up.

"It takes a lot of courage because for a long time human beings have been creating the promise of salvation in the future in order to endure the trials and the tribulations of incarnational or embodied existence and all the suffering inherent in it. And even though these are pre-modern mythical notions, many of us who have grown up in a postmodern context haven't quite given them up yet.

"But there's a direct relationship between the contemplation of consciousness or pure subjectivity and the willingness to let go of all notions of a mythical God or savior and the promise of salvation in the future. They go hand in hand. It's impossible to contemplate consciousness authentically and powerfully in the present moment and still be cherishing hopes of being saved by someone or something in the future. You have to give up the future!"

Andrew paused for a moment, the atmosphere thickening, then asked, *"Can you feel the presence of consciousness in yourself as we're sitting here together?"*

You bet we did! That atmosphere boiled with conscious presence, it's power transcending the mind's ability to distract one from it.

Andrew laughed, *"But that's all the salvation you need. Because, you see, there **really** isn't anybody up there,"* he added emphatically, jesting that, *"I've gone and checked for myself so I can save everyone the trouble."* We all laughed with him but beneath that jocularity was a deep sobriety as we grappled with the depth of superstition in ourselves. I could feel deeply both my own resistance to and embrace of what he was saying and the tension between two radically different modes of understanding.

"Now this is just my opinion, but I'm fairly sure that what's going to happen when you die is very dependent upon what you're doing while you're alive. My sense and my understanding of these things – which is by no means complete – tells me that what we do while we have all our faculties, our health and the power of volition, is what's going to determine how we do after the body drops. There are no guarantees for any of us. How it all turns out is not dependent upon fate or destiny or some kind of higher power or divine intervention. It really has to do with you and the choices you make. And when you really understand that, it changes absolutely everything. When you really grasp that it's completely up to you then you begin to understand what it means to be an authentically mature human being.

"And, by the way, there's a relationship between the fact that it is now completely up to us as individuals and the fact that we happen to be living at the beginning of the 21st century. So what's happened? With the Western Enlightenment², the mythical God fell out of the sky and disappeared for a while. But now, with the discovery of the subject or this primary 'I,' God is re-emerging in our deepest sense of self.

"You see, the primary 'I,' is not just you, it's the 'I' of the whole universe. There is only one 'I' in the universe. Did you know that?"

Silence.

"Well, you do now." His laugh was like an exclamation point. *"I want you to think about this yourself. As you contemplate and become aware of consciousness and this pure subject in yourself, ask yourself, 'is there or could there be another?' There isn't! If you really go into it you'll start to see this and feel it for yourself. And, you see, realizing this is an essential step in the whole process of self-liberation and embracing human maturity because ultimately you have to come home to your Self.*

"Another way to say this is that the only way you can move forward is by returning back to before the beginning. Before the universe was created, before the Big Bang happened, what was there? There was just the subject. There was no world, there was no universe, there was no time, there was no space, there wasn't anything, but there was the subject because you can't destroy the subject. This is really important! It's not just intellectual entertainment. In order to get these things you have to really grapple with them in a fundamental way. And this is what I'm asking you to do."

He paused for a moment, looked around the room and, when most people seemed to have nodded in agreement, he continued.

"In this teaching, there are a few steps to go through. First, we want to move away from a negative relationship to life, which is a life based on the fears and desires of the individual and collective ego.

"Do you know what the collective ego is?" No one responded. *"The fears and desires of the individual ego don't exist in isolation. The things that you're worried about and the things that you want are an expression of the culture from which you've come and the time in which you live. If you were alive two thousand years ago, believe me, you wouldn't be worried about the things you're worried about right now. We're all products of our own time in history. So most of our desires and fears are expressions and manifestations of the culture from which we've come. Therefore the individual ego is related to the cultural or collective ego. This applies to all of us. Nobody exists in isolation."*

Andrew paused for a long moment, then decided to take a few questions. The first came from tall, thin, middle aged man who, judging from his accent, hailed from Australia.

"Dropping aside all ideas of a personal God," he said, "of someone 'up there,' salvation, heaven and all of that, but recognizing that we are true consciousness and not the external ego self, when this body ultimately 'carts it,' as we say…"

"That's an Australian expression?"

"Yeah, and it's a very good one. Carts it, dies, disintegrates, falls away, whatever you want to call it. When that happens, in your thinking, what happens to that true consciousness that the person actually is?"

"Nothing happens. Consciousness doesn't go anywhere. It doesn't travel."

"But does it continue?"

"Notice what happens. You came from Australia, right?"

"Well, so called. I come from planet Earth, but yes, so-called. You asked me but I don't want to buy it because I don't think that way."

"Give me the benefit of the doubt, okay?" Andrew said, cutting through his word game.

"I didn't ask where the consciousness goes to, I asked what happens to it," the man continued.

"I'm trying to help you," Andrew assured him, sensing the adversarial tone in the man's voice. *"So you came from Australia? Just yes or no; did you come from Australia to come on this retreat?"*

"My body did, yes."

"Well, that's my whole point. From the perspective of consciousness there wasn't any movement and there wasn't any travel."

"Quite."

"So that's the point. That's why when you ask, 'what happens to consciousness?' I say, nothing."

"But it continues?"

"Well, when we speak about continuing, then we're speaking about continuing in the context of time. But when we're referring to consciousness, or this pure subject, we're speaking about something that exists beyond time. That's why it's so important. You see, when we speak about liberation or Enlightenment, the traditional definition is that the self-sense is liberated from the belief, conviction, and experience of being trapped in time. So when we discover consciousness, especially if the experience becomes very powerful and profound, there's a simultaneous recognition that who I am is free from time, free from the developmental process, free from the body, free from the whole thing."

"So there's no time other than the creation of man and..."

"Well, I don't want to go that far. But just from the perspective of consciousness itself, there isn't any time. So, you see, consciousness doesn't age and it doesn't develop. We do. But the pure subject is unchanging and unmoving. All right?" He said these last words with finality.

They seemed to have hit their mark for the man issued a satisfied, "Thank you."

Andrew then turned his attention to a forty something German man.

"I am contemplating my consciousness and I go deeper and deeper," he said. "Doing so, I forget the past and the future. I'm here totally present, totally aware and going in deeper. I feel in me like there is a higher presence that is witnessing my contemplating. And with that I am going higher and higher."

"I don't want you to go higher, I just want you to go back inside. Not up. Just back."

"Okay, I can say back, but it is something that is witnessing my contemplating of my consciousness."

"Fine. That's very good. But all I want you to do, just for now, is to be aware of consciousness. That's it, very simple. You can do it with your eyes open right now. Are you aware of consciousness now as we're speaking?"

"Yes."

"That's all I want you to do."

"But behind, or back, or higher there is something I feel that is witnessing my contemplating."

"Okay, well that's it then. That's what I want you to stay with. Okay?"

"Yes."

Next up was a thirty something American woman.

"What about enjoying the mountains outside?" she said airily. "I mean, if I am conscious I look at them and at the same time there's joy and this feeling of wanting to move or something."

"That's absolutely fine," Andrew conceded, *"but just for today I want you to give more attention to who's seeing the mountain than to anything else."*

"Okay."

"The reason I want you to do this is because I want everybody to actually have an experience of the concepts that I'm using. What I'm speaking about is not too difficult to understand intellectually. But I want everybody to experience it so that there'll be a direct relationship between your intellectual understanding and your actual conscious experience."

"I have a feeling of emptiness with the consciousness."

"Good. So all I want you to do is to give your attention to that emptiness. I want you to give more attention to that emptiness than to anything else."

"There's a kind of vagueness…"

"That's because consciousness is not an object. If I say, 'put your attention on this glass,'" he held up his water glass, *"that's an object. But consciousness is not an object. Consciousness is the subject. That's why it's a little more challenging. Everything else that exists is an object from the perspective of consciousness. It's only consciousness that is the subject. Do you understand?"*

"Yes."

"Again, that's why it's a little more tricky to grasp. If I say, 'focus upon a particular thought or a particular feeling or a particular thing outside yourself,' that's easy. But when I say, 'focus on the subject,' then you want the subject to focus upon itself and that's more challenging."

"Yes, I understand and feel it."

"Good," he said, turning away from her and pointing to a dark haired Israeli woman at the back of the room. *"Last one, and then we're going to finish."*

"Andrew," she said, "earlier you talked about the 'evolution' of consciousness and just now, in your response to the Australian gentleman, you mentioned that consciousness is outside time and doesn't move. Were you talking about two kinds of consciousness or are they the same?"

"Well, we're going to be defining evolution in different ways over the course of the retreat, but at this particular moment we're defining the evolution of consciousness as the experience of consciousness becoming more intense.

"Now, for any of us, when the presence or the awareness of consciousness or pure subjectivity grows and becomes more profound, the personality changes instantly. Consciousness makes you drunk. Right?"

"Yes."

"But in a different way than alcohol. It makes you drunk in the enlightening sense. The experience of consciousness is intoxicating. Do you feel it now?"

"Oh yes, definitely."

"The ego, or the frontal self, becomes passive in the presence of consciousness. It becomes soft and malleable. On the other hand, without the presence of consciousness the personality becomes very hard and brittle. Have you noticed that?"

"I have."

"So the experience of consciousness literally pacifies the ego. That's why it is so very important. You can be absolutely sure of something from the perspective of the ego and then, as the experience of consciousness becomes more intense and profound, you realize, 'Oh my god, I was totally crazy.' Happens all the time."

"Yeah, I've noticed that."

"So what I want everybody to do between now and five o'clock is to give attention to the experience of consciousness in your self. So that could mean sitting on a bench and just hanging out but, as you're seeing people walking and cars driving by, your attention should be on consciousness. Then eventually, when you close your eyes, you're going to do that with your own thoughts. It's the same thing. Thoughts are objects in consciousness, aren't they? So that's the idea and it's very important because if you don't want to be a crazy person you have to know how to do this and if you don't know how to do this you're definitely going to be a crazy person. Do you know why? Because then you will inevitably get trapped by the objects, internal or external, that happen to be passing by."

I nodded, being familiar with this exercise but considering that perhaps there are some things you can never know well enough.

"So, we'll meet again at five o'clock and I want to ask everybody to please do what I'm asking you to do. Please do it!" he repeated emphatically. *"Don't go for a walk and think about yourself. Don't go read the newspaper. Don't be lazy. Be active. Pretend it's really important."*

Everyone laughed appreciatively at Andrew's plea and with that the first teaching had come to a close. Andrew unclipped his mike and settled into meditation.

We all followed suit, although to say that I began meditating would be somewhat inaccurate as the delightful expansion of consciousness that meditation is supposed to produce had been a palpable presence in the room for at least an hour. All that was really called for was relaxing into what was already fully happening.

As I settled into myself, the diverse themes of this teaching flitted before my mind's eye. I sat amazed by Andrew's capacity to begin with the most simple points and with them propel us back into the dark interiority of ourselves, then out across the brightly lit contours of our culture, and ultimately into the "I" of the universe itself, before, in the end, returning us full circle to ourselves and handing us the means by which to engage with all he'd just laid out. For me, two points returned with insistence.

What most surprised me was my response to Andrew's statement that there's no one up there. Not that this was exactly news to me. I had had enough direct experience of non-duality to know that. Yet, having not entirely given up the notion of duality, of a "me" in the eternity that I had realized, demanded that I project that "me" into the future and along with that, concern for its well-being. Now, I do understand that if I give up the idea of the "me" that is seen through in the revelation of consciousness then along with it goes the idea of salvation in the future. That "me" caught in the time stream would dissolve into consciousness or pure subjectivity right now and that's where salvation would always lie – here and now. *"That's all the salvation you'll ever need,"* Andrew had said. Now, knowing this and being able to articulate it is one thing, but giving up the future for real and forever is something else altogether. The truth was that my attention and longing were still, at least in large part, snagged on the notion that I was doing the best I can and that a benevolent force was guiding my steps into a blessed future or at least to relief from the difficulties of the present. And attempting to dislodge that deeply embedded notion from the web of my spiritual beliefs seemed suddenly tougher than dislodging a bone from the jaws of a starving dog. It was, after all, a question of ultimate survival, in this case of every sense of who I think I am. The question cannot be shrugged off, as is so often done by those who've had some insight into non-duality, but must be grappled with, with deadly earnestness, for actual transformation to occur.

Which brings me to the second point. Andrew had said that if our lives hadn't been transformed in the most dramatic way then to say that we knew that consciousness was not an object couldn't possibly be true. That had hit me in the gut. I did know that consciousness was not an object – in fact, I found myself insisting on this point – but I had to admit that while that knowledge had indeed altered the trajectory of my life, it had not radically transformed that life itself. The question was, of course, why not? I struggled with the implications, which, simply put, were that I could not know nearly as much as I thought I did. Even so, I ran into fierce resistance to any such considerations and that, in and of itself, was interesting. Truth and self-image were sharply at odds and the turmoil of their collision ran through the quietness of the meditative state.

After about fifteen minutes, Andrew rose and quietly left the room and within a few moments, arms, legs and backs began to creak and stir as people returned from the depths of meditation to their "sacks of consciousness," now rather stiffened from nearly three hours of attentive sitting. My knees and back popped like dry twigs as I slowly gathered my things and headed out of the teaching hall for more meditation back in the practice hall.

Often we cannot fully appreciate something except when it is seen against its opposite. Such was the case as I stepped out onto the streets, along which the tourist throng that had inspired much of the previous day's contemplations, moved. I took a breath, put my attention on the subject and plunged headlong into the fray. I kept my eyes down and attention within before running the gauntlet of sensory assaults. The squeals of children, the shouts of teenagers, the bickering of the elderly, the smell of pungent cheese peddled by sidewalk vendors under the fierce glare of the sun and the acrid stench of cigarettes – all conspired within the jutting cliffs and breathtaking views to send my mind into a spin. But I remembered the subject and in so doing miraculously arrived at the meditation hall with the presence of depth largely intact.

It occurred to me how so much of what we see and take for granted in the glitter and shine of the world pulls us out and away from ourselves in less than half an instant. Without noticing it we overlook the bottomless depth that is doing the looking. And with that the trap is sprung as we are lulled into thinking that that which has coaxed us out can quench the thirst for that which we have, albeit unwittingly, left behind and within.

It was only a turn inward that could hope to recover that depth and turning inward was what we set out to do for the next hour, a task complicated not only by the heat that held us like a clammy hand within the darkness of the hall, but by the shouts of waiters and assorted kitchen staff that echoed sharply off the alley walls from the busy restaurant below. And yet such distractions served a singular function – to remind me that they too were but objects in consciousness and thus drive my attention back into the subject, where all was still despite it all.

Following a short break – enough for a quiet though well-savored lunch and the jotting of a few notes into my journal – we began the first installment of the afternoon chant. It went as follows:

The Most Challenging Spiritual Endeavor

Evolutionary Enlightenment is the most challenging spiritual endeavor because in it there is no promise of escape. Many of us still secretly cherish the hope that one day we will be released from this life process and be able to rest forever beyond the world. Only when we are finally willing to face into the enormity of the

evolutionary context we are living in and its profound transformative implica-
tions for ourselves personally will we begin to develop genuine spiritual maturity.
And that's what the world so desperately needs: mature, enlightened human be-
ings who are willing to wholeheartedly take responsibility for the entire process,
forever — to participate in the creation of the conscious universe, with and as the
very force that created it. That impulse, which is your very own Authentic Self,
can never rest until the light of Consciousness has permeated all matter in the
Universe.

That chant seemed synchronistic as its first few lines addressed the very thing upon which we had begun to touch just hours earlier. Its middle called us to maturity in service to the world and its conclusion held before us a radiant vision that transcended all notions of finitude and limitation.

Nonetheless, I seemed to encounter my own finitude and limitation. Jet lag and sleep deprivation conspired to blur my mind. I struggled in vain to hold on, only the hour's end at long last bringing relief.

I walked back to the teaching hall, braving the throng of tourists once more, and that slap of reality pulled me from my delirium. It was upon that awakening that another followed, a shift or inversion of perception the likes of which I have experienced before but which, on this occasion, became unusually pronounced. Having focused my attention on the subject, the part of myself that perceives, I felt immediately permeated by a vast, unlimited sense of conscious presence. Strangely, it had no location and no boundaries of any sort. Neither did it seem to be defined by beginning or end. And yet it was, in the most undiluted fashion, me, or more accurately, "I." The sense of being "so and so" contained within the larger matrix of reality, was drawn into and subsumed by the sense of being perfectly unlimited and containing everything, including the matrix of reality, within the vastness of myself. And this vastness bubbled with a visceral positivity whose origins lay deep in the mystery of my own Self.

It was in this state of spiritual inversion that I took my seat in the teaching hall. As others shuffled and edged their way to their seats, I noted that the nature of my own current state was more subtle than explosive. This only occurred to me because on prior occasions the opposite had been true. It also led me to wonder why this was the case and from this slight disturbance came an effort to deepen the experience by willing it so. This proved to be useless; however, I concluded that having only been here half a day the results were promising.

We sat for nearly an hour as the current of meditation that trailed in with Andrew drew us into itself. Then, the rustle of Andrew's mike being clipped to his shirt, announced the re-commencement of the teaching.

"So I'd like to hear from you to see if you've done what I've asked you to do and what happened." He said this not in the soft tones of someone drunk on meditation but in the bright, crisp tone of someone ready for action.

"But before we get into that, I want to explain the way I like to do these retreats, which is to take people on a systematic journey through the teaching model. This teaching is a multi-dimensional matrix and what I want to do is give you not only an intellectual understanding of it but to take you through the model experientially. I want to give everyone a way to see themselves objectively, and believe me, that's a big gift! Most people have no idea where they're at. And people who actually do want to evolve need some way to get an objective picture of where they are in relationship to where they think they want to go.

"So I asked everyone to give their attention to the experience of consciousness itself and now I want to know if all of you did that and what happened.

"Remember that I said that the experience of consciousness is primary and prior to everything else and yet most of us do not know that. So I want people to experience this and then discuss it because then we'll actually be talking about something that's real in your experience. I want to establish experientially that consciousness itself has certain qualities or attributes that are of absolute relevance and are incredibly obvious, yet that most of us have no idea about. So I want to know, from your own experience, what the qualities or attributes of consciousness itself are."

He turned his attention to a middle-aged woman to his left who had raised her hand. *"Good, yes. That's the spirit,"* he said, pointing to her.

"Well, I just felt very much at peace and at one with everything." she said in a softly edged accent of uncertain origin.

"Okay, that's good," he said. *"One of the qualities of consciousness is joy, or 'ananda,' or peace."*

"Acceptance."

"Well, acceptance is kind of tricky because once we're into the process of 'accepting' we've already moved slightly beyond consciousness itself. If we talk about acceptance it means we're already involved. But remember consciousness exists prior to and before everything so when we experience consciousness it's not that we feel better because we're accepting something that we weren't accepting before. Rather, it has to do with the nature of consciousness itself.

"Remember when we go back and back and back, consciousness is ONE. When we penetrate through the superficial layers of our identity we finally end up with consciousness, and that's the last stop! You can't get deeper than that. You reach a point of absolute depth. It's the end of the road and it's the same for all of us. My experience of consciousness is identical to yours. Now, I might have examined and explored its nature more than you have but my consciousness itself could not be any different than yours because, as I've said, consciousness itself is one.

"So what's interesting about this exercise is that all I'm asking you to do is give attention to the most primary and foundational dimension of your own experience because anybody who endeavors to know the Self needs to become clear about what the foundation of the Self is. That's what we're trying to do here and I want everybody to know from their own experience because once you know, you know.

"So let's continue."

It was quiet in the room for some time, then just a few tentative hands were raised.

"I want to see more of you raising your hands," Andrew insisted. *"You have to participate. You know what happens if you're passive?"* he asked pointedly, then after a long moment, added, *"You die ignorant!"* He let the weight of this settle in before the final semi-jesting stroke. *"Then you know where you're going to go when you die."* A few giggles leaked into the room but no hearty laughter. With that a few more hands went up and soon Andrew's eyes came to rest on a woman in her forties who looked perplexed.

"The first thing I noticed," she said, "was that whenever I looked, it was always there. At first that was actually irritating."

"Why?" Andrew asked, slightly incredulous.

"Because I couldn't get away from it."

"But why would you want to? If you want to get away from it then you want to die. As I said this morning, consciousness is life. I could see that you might like your awareness of consciousness to go away. Now, why do you think that would be?"

"Habit," she replied swiftly. "With the awareness of consciousness I can't concentrate so much on the personal self."

"Isn't that a relief?"

"After I experienced that for a moment I did say 'yes.'"

"Well, that's a big part of why I put so much emphasis on this. A lot of you are going to find out just what a relief it is."

"There was also a consistency or lack of variation. It's just there."

"So you could say it's unchanging."

"Unchanging, yes."

"Well, that's important. So what we find is that in just about everything else in our experience there's change and variation but there's something about the nature of consciousness that never changes.

"Is there anything else that came up for you about the nature of consciousness?"

"Occasionally when I'd ask myself who is looking, who is feeling, there was a bit of a shock."

"How so?"

"A shock of recognition, like 'oh, this awakeness has always been there.'"

"Good. So when you say shock is it because it's something you didn't know about?"

"I forget it so often and yet it's so familiar."

"Right, good, that's how it works."

With that he turned to an elderly woman, with gray hair pulled back tightly and wrinkles surrounding a tender, wistful smile.

"Hello, yes," he encouraged her.

In a soft tone, as if she had been transported from another realm, she said,

"It was timeless knowledge and it feels exactly like the vibration and sensation of being alive!"

"So what does being alive feel like?"

"Exciting, constant, inquiring."

"That's good but it's one step removed. Consciousness is not inquiring. I want to know what the nature of consciousness is like. You all can look into your experience right now. You don't have to go back anywhere."

Andrew waited for a few moments but the woman seemed stumped. When it was clear that she had nothing else to say he turned to a blue eyed, young man from Sweden.

"Okay, one of the things that stands out in my experience," he began in that characteristic sing-song lilt, "is that it has to no relationship to anything."

"That's very good. It has no relationship to anything because it's primary to everything, right?"

"Yes."

"So that's important! If it has no relationship to anything that means its nature is freedom."

"Yes."

"When you have no relationship to anything, then you're free," Andrew repeated emphatically.

"Yes," the man agreed again.

"So, one important quality of consciousness is freedom." He stated this strongly and his eyes roamed around the faces before him. *"Is everybody paying attention? This is important! All of our problems and difficulties have to do with the network and matrix of relationship and relatedness, right?"*

"Yes."

"Imagine if you discovered that you are absolutely, totally, radically unrelated to everything. All your problems would disappear like that." Andrew snapped his fingers sharply.

"Yes, of course."

"Exactly. So one of the fundamental qualities of the nature of consciousness is that it's not related to anything. It's the foundation of everything but it's not related to anything. Everything relates to it but it's not related to anything else."

"Right."

"So, if consciousness is not related to anything, then how does the experience of it feel?"

"In my experience it's very still and quiet."

"Still and quiet, yes."

"Yes, because it's not moving. It's not going anywhere or coming from anywhere."

"Okay, that's very good. Let's keep going."

He turned to a thirty something, fashionably bespectacled, Israeli man with inquisitive eyes and an intelligent expression. *"Okay, yes,"* Andrew said, indicating him.

"It felt enormous. Big!" He said this almost as if he were gasping for air. "Bigger than big!"

"So that means without boundaries. Is that your point?"

"Yes. Unimaginably big."

"Right. So we cannot imagine 'no boundaries.' That's inconceivable. All we can conceive of is a notion of boundaries. You can even imagine very big boundaries. But it's impossible to imagine no boundaries. If you're using your cognitive faculties all you can imagine is some 'thing.' But some 'thing,' no matter what it is, no matter how big it is, is still going to have boundaries. But if we're speaking about that which has no beginning and no end, which is what 'no boundaries' means, the cognitive faculties literally cannot grasp it. It's important to know that. Consciousness cannot be imagined with thought.

"Often people think of consciousness as a big gray or white cloud that goes on forever, but that's not it. That's still a thing. That's why speaking about consciousness or this pure subjectivity is so challenging. We're trying to understand that which can't be understood with concepts." He paused for a few moments to let this sink in.

"Again," he continued, *"I defy anyone to tell me where in themselves the experience of consciousness begins and where it ends. It's absolutely not locatable."*

"Yes, that was my experience."

"Now, the question is, if you think you already know that, how well do you really know it? You see if you really knew it you'd have to be a free person. If you've come to the recognition that the primary or fundamental dimension of your own self has no beginning and no end, it would have to mean that you're a liberated person. Otherwise, you couldn't possibly know it. Otherwise, it's just an intellectual concept that you've picked up from something that you read. Or maybe at some point you had the direct experience of consciousness or boundaryless-ness but it's no longer real for you. It's no longer alive and it's just become a memory. So if it's become just an old concept and it's dead in the water, it no longer has liberating potential. You see consciousness is ever-present. So when people talk about their past experiences of consciousness it's kind of funny. If consciousness if ever-present then it doesn't go anywhere."

There it was again – the same charge leveled earlier during the day: *"If you say you know this but your life hasn't been dramatically transformed and you're not a free person, then you couldn't possibly know it."* And again, I maintained that I did know it, but, I had to acknowledge that Andrew was closer to the mark than I was, and by a long stretch at that. The fact was that I had had many powerful experiences of consciousness but most of the time I was not living from their realization. That could only mean that I was living in their memory, overlooking the immediacy from which they always arose and which, in fact, is always there. The obvious reason had to be that it is infinitely easier to indulge in powerful memories than to withdraw attention once and for all from the ego's endless preoccupations and commit it, in this moment, to the ever-present presence of depth. Adopting this stance conveniently did not require surrender, yet it allowed me to speak passionately about matters of consciousness from what was, in fact, my own direct experience – albeit in memoriam. And though it was less than what was possible, there was an insidious psychological and emotional payoff. Though relegating me to the ranks of the seeker, it had the advantage of leaving my personal self-sense (read ego) intact. The finder, on the other hand, must take a more courageous stand, retaining no such anchor. Thus, he or she is in a vastly more vulnerable position, which is, I suppose, why Andrew so often referred to the pursuit of enlightenment as *"the search for perfect insecurity."* So I was in an odd position. On the one hand, I was beginning to see that I was cobbling together memories of past experience in an effort to augment what was presently occurring. On the other hand, I could not drop the notion that I already knew what Andrew was pointing to. Thus a kind of tension began to build – Andrew's insistence on one side and mine on the other. These began to circle one another, sizing each other up like fighters in a ring. Uncomfortably split in my loyalties, I returned my attention to the teaching.

"Now, the fundamental sense of boundaries or limitation that most of you experience doesn't come from consciousness. It comes from the fears and desires of the separate self-sense or the ego. It comes from our worldview, from the collective ego, and from the particular culture and place from which we've come. But when we begin to shift our attention and focus on what's primary, which is consciousness itself, the experience of boundaryless-ness has to begin to emerge in your experience. It must. It cannot not happen!

"If it doesn't happen, it's simply because you are not doing what I'm asking you to do. Now, if so far you're not doing what I'm asking you to do, I want you to make the effort to do it. It might be a little difficult but so what?

"You see, consciousness is actually dependent upon all of us to be discovered. It's there all the time but it cannot and will not move on its own. We have to make the effort and through our efforts to discover consciousness, it emerges. But it won't work any other way.

"For human beings, consciousness evolves because of their effort to discover it. It doesn't happen by itself, it won't happen by itself, and it's not going to happen by itself!" He spoke stridently, the repetition driving his point home with the unrelenting insistence of a jackhammer. *"You have to go seeking for it. And when you seek for it, it will emerge. But consciousness is actually dependent upon you. It's not that the potential for consciousness or for its emergence doesn't already exist. It does, but it has to be sought. So if you believe that the ills of the world are due to a lack of consciousness, you should recognize that that is directly related to the fact that we are not going out and seeking it. Do you get my point? It's true, it's true, it's true, it's true, and everything depends on it. So don't be lazy, okay?"*

Andrew's tone was double-edged, combining the heartfelt plea of a parent with their child and the deadly seriousness of a military commander urging his troops into combat. In this he revealed a central aspect of his teaching: the future of our species and of the world as a whole is, at this point, entirely dependent on the willingness of a "significant minority" of individuals to seek and express the very consciousness to which he was pointing.

"Okay, so let's continue," he said, pointing to a young American man with a retreating hairline, which revealed an open, thoughtful face. "So, I guess there are two things that stood out for me," he ventured tentatively. "One was a feeling of being passive as if the active part of myself was not really there."

"Right, exactly."

"It was a kind of indecisiveness, like I didn't know what to do with myself. I was just kind of there."

"Well, if you're not used to giving attention to the subject in yourself, you can suddenly feel like you don't know what to do. That's because we're always busy, busy, busy, doing something or other. So, when you choose to give your attention only to the subject then you are ceasing to do anything except that, which has nothing to do with doing anything other than just being, right?"

"Right."

"So suddenly doing nothing except giving our attention to consciousness can feel a little strange, right?"

"Yes."

"Okay, that's fine. But that being said, what was the nature of your experience of consciousness?"

"Part of it was a feeling of separateness or disconnectedness."

"Disconnected from what?"

"What was going on around me."

"So you were kind of detached."

"Yes."

"So when you give attention to the presence of consciousness you begin to experience some sense of being detached from what's happening outside in the world."

"Right."

"So that's important, isn't it? Normally we feel completely involved and engaged with everything. Yet when we begin to give attention to the experience of consciousness there's a feeling of falling away from the world. When I say the world, I'm talking about all of the objects that arise in consciousness, including thought.

"So there's a world out there," Andrew said, pointing to the jagged canyons beyond the windows. *"But the world out there begins where? In here."* He turned his finger to indicate his head. *"It's your mind, right?"*

"Yes."

"Don't we experience the world through our thoughts?"

"Usually."

"So when you begin to give more and more of your attention to consciousness itself you find yourself falling away from compulsive identification with all the objects that arise in consciousness, beginning with thoughts. Then, when one feels that one is falling away from or out of the world.

"Once again, we experience the world through our identification with thought. The world seems like it's out there but actually our relationship with the world is through thought. So when there's no thought your relationship with what we are calling the world disappears. I want everybody to pay attention to this. Then you'll see for yourself that the world arises simultaneously with thought." He turned back to the young man. *"Do you understand that?*

"Yes," he said slowly.

"So what does this experience of identifying with consciousness and falling away from the world feel like?"

"There's a feeling of restfulness."

"Very good. It feels restful. Someone else said peaceful and boundary-less. That's very interesting." He paused to take a drink of water. *"Good, let's keep going."*

He again looked around the room before his gaze settled upon an older gentleman whose face resembled a composite of Leon Trotsky and Kurt Vonnegut. As it turned out he was a rather distinguished professor of philosophy, which might lead one to think that this dialogue would have been deep and intriguing. Unfortunately, the opposite turned out to be the case. The dialogue that ensued offered an exquisite example of the fossilization of perception that results from living one's life strictly from the neck up. For fifteen minutes Andrew attempted to pry this exceedingly educated and unfailingly polite gentleman away from his addiction to an array of cherished concepts that he'd clearly spent the better part a lifetime cultivating and carefully injecting between himself and reality. Simply put, Andrew attempted to get him to speak from the immediacy of his own experience rather than from his ideas about it. However, after multiple unsuccessful attempts he was forced to concede defeat. It occurred to me that as we get older we all tend to become caricatures of the most troublesome aspects of ourselves and that in many ways this gentleman exemplified what we all do most of the time, namely live from concepts while overlooking the obvious immediacy of our direct experience.

"You are a very sophisticated fellow," Andrew acknowledged at one point. *"But as men our particular thing is that we always like to know. So, that's good because we are curious and we want to figure things out. But then we tend to get very attached to the position of knowing something."*

"Yes. That's why I said it was difficult for me because …" He was, as we all tend to do when put on the spot, making a special case out of himself.

"Very good, sir, but now I want you to continue to explore the experience and nature of consciousness, but from the not-knowing position, okay?"

"To me that's difficult."

"You're not the only one."

"Okay."

"So, " Andrew said, indicating the Ground of Being area on his teaching model (see p. 42-43) *"this not knowing is where you need to hang out. That has to be your fulcrum point for the time being, okay?"*

"Yes, of course," he agreed, reluctantly. Yet despite his reticence and difficulty, it was touching to watch this extremely bright elderly gentleman struggle with his own frustration yet all the while maintaining the utmost respect for Andrew, a man many years his junior.

"You see," Andrew went on, *"otherwise you can't learn anything and without that you can't develop. So again, I want you to continue to explore the nature of your own experience of consciousness from the perspective of not knowing. In fact, there's a word that I add to the 'not knowing,' which really clarifies what it means. That word is 'already.' It's not 'already' knowing. The 'already' changes everything because it's the 'already' knowing that makes it difficult, if not impossible, to learn anything new. So 'already' knowing is the problem. The 'already' part of all of us is what's dead and old and fixed and rigid. Do you get my point?"*

The gentleman nodded his head in agreement though his brows were still knitted in frustration. Of course Andrew, in speaking to him, was addressing all of us.

"So, if you want to be an enlightened person who is a living manifestation and expression of liberated consciousness in time, it's the 'already' part that you have to give up. The 'already' between 'not' and 'knowing' is an island where the ego lives. And it's a horrible place because that's where, from the perspective of Enlightenment, you have the walking dead. They already know. That's the place where the self is defended and protected, rigid, fixed and inflexible. It's living death! So, don't already know. Just explore the experience of subjectivity without drawing any fixed conclusions."

"Very well. I'll do my best," the man finally relented.[3]

As I listened to this dialogue the missing piece of the puzzle regarding my own predicament finally slipped into place. It was the already knowing stance in relation to my own experience that was preventing me from exploring consciousness in a fresh and innocent way. Instead I had taken up residence on that very island of which Andrew spoke, that haven for the living dead that had been meticulously constructed over many long years from all the experiences I'd 'already' had and all the conclusions I'd 'already' drawn about them. It wasn't that the experiences were invalid or the conclusions inaccurate, but simply that they'd formed a sort of barnacle in consciousness from which the fluidity and immediacy of life was effectively banned. That is not to say that I wasn't experiencing many of the qualities of consciousness that Andrew was pointing to – I was – but not with the kind of depth I knew was possible. I'd sensed that something dense, some intangible membrane, some impenetrable skein of half examined ideas, stretched between myself and that depth and now I knew what it was: ego, the lord and master of the kingdom of "already knowing." And that monarch of the psyche was proving resistant to eviction.

In other words, despite recognizing all this, the position proved difficult to relinquish. It was as if that membrane had grown tightly across the field of my vision and lent its own color to every perception. I could not simply "un-remember" my previous experience or "un-know" my previous insights and, given this, I lacked certainty about how to assume the "not already knowing" position. It struck me as odd that on the one hand I knew so much and on the other, so little about what really mattered.

"Remember," Andrew continued, "because consciousness is absolutely foundational to all of our experience, we have to get to know about it. If you don't know consciousness, you don't know yourself. And believe me, without knowing consciousness there is no way out. You are going to be trapped inside your ego right up to the moment that you die. And then what are you going to do?"

No ready answers to that one.

"Earlier we were talking about what happens when you die. What's going to happen to your experience at the level of consciousness when you die if, at that time, you are still fundamentally identified with the fears of desires of the personal ego or the stream of the separate self-sense?" He paused, and then added in a teasing tone, "Well, you know where you're going." Having amused at least himself, he laughed out loud.

His laughter evoked tentative chuckles from the group. After all, who knew? I suspect that most of us, regardless of religious affiliation, believe that whatever it is that happens after we die has something to do with how we lived. I certainly did.

"Well, that's the definition of hell, isn't it?" Andrew added. "You don't have to die to know that. Any reasonably intelligent person already knows that. Look into your experience of what it's like when you're fundamentally and compulsively identified with the fears and desires of the ego. You don't have to die to know that that's hell.

"You know, I've heard some people who have experience with near death experiences say that when you die nothing changes.[4] Now, I can't tell you from my own personal experience whether this is true or not but it definitely makes profound sense to me. Whether it's true or not we'll all find out. But if it's true, that should be a tremendous inspiration to get busy. Because, so the theory goes, you can only evolve with and through this human form along with the mind and the faculty of volition or intention. So, that means if you don't make the effort to liberate yourself now then you're stuck and there's no way out. Wouldn't that be horrible? So the idea is to do the work while you're alive and of sound mind and body, so when your time comes you won't be afraid because you'll know who you are.

"So if it's true that nothing changes when you die, that understanding can help wake people up and bring them to ask themselves 'what am I doing?' That kind of questioning can begin to give a sense of meaning and purpose to our experience of *human incarnation. Meaning and purpose,"* he repeated, *"remember those things? You've all heard these old-fashioned words that come from another era, haven't you?"*

Andrew often pointed out that in today's culture, among those of us with the greatest privilege of wealth, education and freedom, the cultivation of simple virtues such as dignity, self-respect and honor have, by and large, been tossed by the wayside. Such old-fashioned values might make one feel "judged," and that, we are told, is a bad thing.

"So once again," Andrew continued, *"we want to establish what the nature of consciousness is. You know, even having discussions like this is a new thing in terms of the evolution of life. This kind of investigation has only being going on for perhaps three thousand years. Put that in a fourteen billion year process of development and it basically happened this morning. That means that this whole evolutionary or developmental process has begun to inquire into the nature of itself. So when we're entering into this practice of self-inquiry this process that began fourteen billion years ago is asking itself the question: 'Who am I?' In other words, how does the process that initiated itself fourteen billion years ago become aware of itself? Through human beings practicing the art of self-inquiry. No other forms of life can do this. Dogs can't do it. Cats can't do it. The birds and bees can't do it. The trees and the flowers can't do it. Do they have consciousness? Yes, they're alive. Consciousness is life. But they can't seek to know who they are. Consciousness doesn't have the capacity to know itself in lower forms of life. So what we're speaking about here is important beyond you and your own salvation.*

"If you want to put your own spiritual longing in a very big evolutionary, developmental context, this is what's actually happening – life is endeavoring to know itself through the awakening human – through you! Isn't that interesting?" He put this to us with the care of parent explaining something perfectly obvious but quite significant to a youngster still wrapped in its Lilliputian world of childish concerns. *"I think it's very interesting because it literally adds nothing less than a cosmic dimension to the practice of self-inquiry and to our own petty, small, confined, personal, hellish existence. Nothing like a little cosmic perspective to open things up a little bit, right?"* he paused, then prodded, *"Is the context in which we usually live less than cosmic? Most of the time it absolutely is. So this is very, very important."*

I had heard Andrew point this out on any number of occasions but it never ceased to stop me in my tracks, undermining with perfect ruthlessness every belief I've ever had about being some separate, isolated individual groping for meaning and purpose in a universe that has none to offer.

That we are the eyes and ears and heart and mind of the unfolding cosmos awakening to itself has become deeply compelling for me as I have both glimpsed the true nature of my self at the level of consciousness and am aware, at the level of cognition, of the evolutionary process of which I am an expression. And while I still generally live in a self-sense that is largely personal, just a little reflection reveals that we are the sense organs of the mystery beyond the world awakening to itself in its own creation.[5] We are uniquely poised among all the creatures to know both our own Maker as well as the physical context of our emergence – the universe of time and space that is still exploding from its flaming birth in the furnace of the Big Bang. Only we can recognize both the manifest and the unmanifest dimensions of our existence and become the living bridge between them. Building that bridge, as I understood it, was precisely what Andrew was endeavoring to help us do.

"*So one of the things that I am trying to do with this teaching of radical, impersonal, evolutionary Enlightenment,*" he continued, "*is to give people a perspective upon the human experience – their very own human experience – that's nothing less than cosmic. This is not a metaphor! And the way you can begin to see your own experience in a cosmic context without being deluded or megalomaniacal, is through the exploration of consciousness, which will help you to recognize the universal dimension of your own experience.*" He shifted on his cushion and went on.

"*Okay, let's continue with the exploration.*" He turned to a thin, Danish woman a few rows away from him.

"For me it was impersonal," she began.

"*That's very good,*" Andrew said. "*It's not personal, it's not individual, it's not uniquely you alone. It transcends individuality.*"

"*What else can you say about it?*"

"That's all except that I didn't like your question."

"*Which question?*"

"To explore my consciousness."

"*Why?*"

"Because I saw I had no contact with anybody."

"*From the perspective of consciousness?*"

"Yes."

"*Why is that bad?*"

"It's my ego," she offered without hesitation though quietly.

"*That's good. You just saved me about ten minutes of work,*" Andrew joked. Everyone joined in laughter.

"You know," she added, still rather grimly, "during lunch I was looking for eye contact and nobody would look at me. So I asked myself, 'Why am I here? What am I doing here?' Then suddenly I realized," her voice now brightened, "that consciousness is impersonal."

"*That's right.*"

"And it feels good," she added with the thrill of discovery.

"*Because?*" Andrew asked, looking around at all of us indicating that the question was not just for her, before adding, "*I want you all to know why it feels good. It's important to know why.*"

"Because I had no desires and I wasn't judging."

"That's good. So you're saying that consciousness has no desires."

"Yes."

"So this is the essence of the Buddha's teaching. We suffer because we want. When we give up desire or wanting we experience nirvana or heaven. We experience this primordial, unconditional, absolute freedom and that is the whole point of this exercise. That's not an unimportant discovery. So, very good.

"And then you also said you weren't judging. So consciousness has no views or opinions. We do, don't we? We have all kinds of opinions. But in the experience of consciousness there is no opinion or judgment. That's very important!

" So these are things I want you to look into in your own experience because I want you to see what the nature of consciousness is. So far we've said that it has no boundaries, that it's unrelated to anything, that it has no opinions, that it's free from desire, that there is peace and that it's impersonal. Of course, it's not personal on the one hand but on the other hand, it's absolutely personal. Consciousness is the most deeply intimate experience of yourself, isn't it? You can't get more personal or more intimately identified with yourself than consciousness, right?"

Everyone agreed.

" Okay, that's very good!

"Yes," he said, in response to another raised hand.

"I had an experience of lack of fear and self-concern," said an older man near the back.

"Oh, that's good. So in the experience of consciousness there's no fear. That's important, isn't it?"

"Yes."

"So, I want everybody to examine your own experience and see if you can discover the things that I am confirming in other people's experience. I want you to know from your own experience whether it's true that the experience of consciousness is free, fearless, desireless, boundaryless, and free from judgments and opinions. Explore and see for yourself."

"My experience with consciousness," a woman's voice spontaneously added, "is that it's neither warm nor cold, nor good nor sad; it just is. So there aren't any emotional qualities that I could attach to it. It just really is!"

"So there are no emotional qualities?"

"Right."

" No feeling qualities – none at all?" Andrew probed.

"Right."

"I think there are feeling qualities," he ventured. *"For example, some people said peace."*

"Yes," she agreed.

"Isn't there some feeling dimension in your own experience of it?"

"It feels inherently good and positive."

"Well, we don't want to get into whether it's good or not. That's an interpretation of what it means. I want to know just about the nature of the pure experience of consciousness. I think it's neither good nor bad because, as you said, it just is. So, one of the qualities we've identified is that of no boundaries. We also said that it's free, desireless, fearless, and peaceful. These are qualities. So there is a feeling dimension to it. Consciousness is being and being feels like something. It doesn't feel like nothing. It's not absolute voidness. It feels like something, doesn't it?"

"Yes, I guess it does."

"So what does it feel like?"

"It feels vast and still and like I could just stay there forever."

"Okay, very good. 'I feel like I could stay there forever.' What you're saying is true. That's also part of the quality of consciousness. Why is that?"

"There's just no impetus to do anything."

"Okay, good, there's no impetus or desire to do anything, but there's more to it than that. If you say there is no desire to do anything that would imply the absence of certain qualities like desire. But I think when you're aware that 'I could sit here forever' it's usually because you're enjoying yourself, which is a big part of the whole point."

"Yes, I see."

"So if you said, 'I could sit here forever' it means I don't ever want to leave this place. Right?

"Yes."

"Why?"

"Because a lot of the time when I'm moving I'm in the ego and I'm chasing after things and reacting to things and it feels like a tremendous respite from that."

"That's right. You can say that the experience of consciousness is the ultimate vacation. It's better than going to the Bahamas or to Vietnam or Southern Thailand or wherever people go, right?"

"Yes, absolutely."

"It's very important to know that. Everybody needs a vacation, it doesn't matter who you are. Life is hard. Even if you know who you are and you're doing the right things for the right reasons, which is quite a big thing in and of itself, life is still tough. So, everybody needs rest and renewal. The part of yourself that exists in and is engaged with time needs rejuvenation. So, the ultimate vacation is found in the experience of consciousness – guaranteed! You cannot find a better vacation than that. See for yourself. Spend ten days here with me versus ten days on the nicest island in the world and compare how you feel at the end."

A little laughter filtered through the room.

"So the most significant thing you said is that you could stay there forever. Now I want everybody to discover in their own experience why that is. You see, when you experience the nature of consciousness itself – this, 'oh, I could stay here forever,' – then you can

understand why men and women throughout history have run up into little caves and locked themselves up for years on end. Because they wanted to stay there forever."

He paused for a moment to let this observation penetrate. Then he cast about for the next question.

"So, anybody else? Hello."

A middle aged, broad shouldered American man, with a graying mustache, had raised his hand.

"For me, it's a sense of moment to moment observation," he began. "It's also a very expansive feeling and there doesn't seem to be any room for internal dialogue."

"So you said expansive. Anything else?"

"There's a sense of detachment and observation."

"Okay. Once again, the reason the experience of detachment is there is because consciousness exists prior to everything. That means before anything else happened, consciousness is! So when you begin to put your attention on it you instantaneously experience freedom from anything that has happened. That's because what's so compelling about consciousness is that it doesn't exist in time. This is the miraculous nature of it. When you become aware of consciousness, especially when you look deeply into it, you begin to sense that part of yourself that transcends the world. You've heard, 'in the world but not of it?' That's what it means. Transcends means 'exists prior to.'

"Now, part of the nature of the experience of consciousness is detachment. So if someone says, 'be detached,' that's one thing. Then you try to make an effort to let something go. But if you give yourself to the experience of consciousness itself, detachment, or 'freedom from,' will automatically become a part of your experience because consciousness exists prior to the world. It transcends it and that which transcends the world is free from it. So the experience of detachment occurs because you're becoming conscious of that part of yourself that's always free from the process of time and becoming. And because it's free from that process you experience it as detachment. But it's not a detachment that comes from making an effort to let go of. It's one of the natural qualities and attributes of consciousness itself. It's freedom from! It's in the world but not of it!

"Your body is of time and the world process and cannot transcend time. Thought also can't transcend time. Your ordinary human emotions can't transcend time. But consciousness itself, which exists prior to and beyond the time process, is different. And that's why when anyone begins to give attention to the nature of consciousness they experience themselves falling away from and out the world. Yet they're in the world. You look outside and see a world all around you. But suddenly the place you're seeing the world from is prior to and beyond it. You're in the world, but not of it."

"So, why is it so hard to stay there?"

"Well, it just has to do with emotional and psychological habits, because we spend our whole life busy and lost in the process. No one ever said to you when you were a kid," he now affected the tone of a concerned mother, "'You know darling, the *most important thing in life is consciousness and I'd really like you to give your attention to it, because, sweetheart, if you begin to pay attention you'll see that consciousness is the deepest and most fundamental part of your own experience of self. It's who you really are.'"* A few sniggers followed this brief performance. *"No one ever told us this,"* he went on, now in a more serious tone, *"so it's not our fault. But just imagine what it would be like if you were told every day from the age of eight or nine to start to give your attention to consciousness so that it became something that you really knew. And imagine that you began to know it so deeply that it began to influence your perspective and relationship to life absolutely."*

I considered that and immediately thought about my seven-year-old nephew Lucas. Was it truly that easy, I wondered. Would simply driving a child's attention back on itself, and some simple explanation, result in an enlightened human being? Would I have had an easier time with all this if someone had pointed these things out to me when I was young? It would have to be so, I thought, for even a cursory examination of my own predicament revealed how much of it could be attributed simply to the force of habit.

But there is another key piece to this. I recalled a conversation that Andrew had had with a mother some years earlier at a public teaching. She was bemoaning the fact that because of her busy schedule and the endless demands thrust upon her by her child, she was unable to give herself to the cultivation of the perspective he was offering. He responded by asking her, *"Above all, what is it that kids learn from us? Is it what we tell them or is it how we are?"*

"Well, it's how we are," the woman had responded reluctantly.

"Isn't it primarily our fears and neurosis that we bequeath to our kids?" he suggested.

"Yes, I suppose," she'd replied.

"What children need," Andrew responded, *"are enlightened parents. Wouldn't the greatest gift you could give to your child be the knowledge that there's nothing to fear and that life is good, knowledge they would gain simply by being with you?"*

"Yes," she agreed, though somehow she didn't seem happy about it.

I could understand why. Because it's logic was inescapable and, as with everything else Andrew taught, it pointed the finger directly back at her and by extension at all of us. Creating a new world – and this had been Andrew's insistent plea since the day I met him – demanded that each one of us shoulder that burden personally, causing that change to radiate outward from us. Only then might our children become the seeds of a new humanity. But there was no way to lay that expectation on them without putting it on ourselves first. The responsibility of mentoring a child into adulthood could be said to be the greatest reason to pursue the matter of our own transformation rather than a pretext for its avoidance. And though I wasn't a parent, I was an uncle and felt my own responsibility for the next generation as well.

Andrew continued along the same lines. *"So the reason why it's 'so hard' is because we're in the habit of focusing all of our attention on external things. Yet if you begin to give your attention to the nature of consciousness it can become very easy. It's just like learning to work your muscles. And all it is is focusing your attention on that which exists prior to everything else and you're right there. It doesn't take time. It's very easy. You just have to look and it's always there. Now you have ten days for this and it's really easy in a context of being on a retreat. If you're just by yourself living a crazy life where consciousness is not the context, it can be really difficult.*

"You see, if we agree that consciousness is the foundation of all there is, then it would make sense that that discovery should begin to influence what our relationship to life is. If consciousness is foundational but it has no effect on what our actual relationship to life is, then it's really going to be hard. And let's face it, the way most of us live has very little to do with what we're speaking about here. So if the life we live has nothing to do with the knowledge of that which is most fundamental, that's crazy, isn't it?"

"Yes" rose from the crowd like an anthem and with that Andrew turned his attention to an older English woman with thick glasses and hair pulled back into a bun.

"Yes, hello," he said, offering a polite smile.

In an awed tone she said, "I had this incredibly shocking realization that I don't exist and it frightened me."

"How so?"

"Because it conjured up the idea of non-existence which is hard to comprehend."

"That's important. You said, it conjured up the idea of non-existence, which is something that's hard to comprehend. Why do you think that's the case?"

"Well, that's because one is so attached to the personality of the individual life that the idea of letting go of it is frightening. But as I got closer to the experience of consciousness, it became simply awe-inspiring. There was an overwhelming sense of power, of universality. It was all encompassing. I pulled away several times before I could allow myself to be there with this sense of something so immense that I couldn't conceive of it. It was utterly beyond my finite brain to conceive of."

"And yet you were there."

"And yet there I was. And so, as I gradually persevered I found that it wasn't threatening and it wasn't personal and there was nothing to do there. So I allowed myself to be there with it and seemed to merge with it. That's when I had this extraordinarily intense feeling of aliveness. Now, I'm not saying I felt intensely alive. It wasn't like that. I had a feeling of intense 'aliveness.'"

"Right."

"But it was still! Usually if one thinks, 'oh, I feel intensely alive,' it's all agitation and joy and leaping about. It wasn't like that at all. It was utterly serene and like others have said, I could have just stayed there forever. I thought, 'this is life! Hey, I'm experiencing life!' It was unimaginably powerful."

"Okay, good. So this is the one thing that I was hoping we were going to get to before we finished this. It's that there's an absolutely positive and ecstatic dimension to the experience of consciousness at the level of feeling, right?"

"That's right, yes, yes." She was aglow.

"So the experience of ecstasy can be very quiet and very subtle and it can also be powerful and explosive. But whether it's quiet or explosive, if you pay attention you'll notice that ecstasy is one of the qualities of consciousness. That's part of its nature. So that's also something I want you to give attention to. The experience of ecstasy or bliss is interesting because if you pay attention to it and start to have a direct experience of it you'll start to see that, whether the experience is very powerful and intense or very subtle and quiet, it's the same thing.

"Most people are so out of touch with their own experience, so insensitive to themselves, so lacking in the capacity to perceive their own experience, that it's difficult for them to be aware that part of the nature of consciousness is bliss and ecstasy. Most people will only become aware of bliss if the ecstasy meter were around eighty-five out of a hundred. Anything less they wouldn't even feel. But the ecstatic bliss is one with the nature of consciousness. So whether it's one on the meter, which means very subtle and barely perceptible yet present, all the way up to a hundred, where it's overwhelming and literally physically unbearable, it's still this same ecstasy. It doesn't change, it just grows in intensity. So bliss or ecstasy are a significant part of the nature of consciousness along with all the other things that we've mentioned, such as no boundaries, no relationship, freedom from desire, freedom from fear, the fact that everything simply is, beyond concepts, beyond judgments, and that it exists beyond time and beyond the world. These are all of equal importance. When we put all this together we begin to get a real picture of what we're talking about here. We're speaking about the deepest, most intimate sense of what it means to be us."

Andrew paused a long while to let these words hang in the air. Finally he concluded.

"Okay, so that's pretty good. Now, I want everybody to stay with the experience and nature of consciousness between now and when we get together again in the morning."

With that he sank into meditation, pulling us along into its deepening flow.

It is difficult to convey the strange alchemy that permeates the room both during and after a teaching like this. It is one in which words are not mere words but living keys that throw open the doors of perception to the deeper, hidden dimensions in all of us. Such words soon become indistinguishably one with the deeper currents of the universe. Such transmission irrevocably brands both the mind and soul and can sink the roots of authentic transformation deep into the psyche. I hasten to add that this flourish of language is in no way an exercise in literary excess; rather it is a feeble attempt to state an ineffable fact. The truth is that it has been, from the very beginning, this power of transmission, this ability through dialogue to draw others into the same state of consciousness from which he speaks, that has drawn people to Andrew. Even his own teacher flatly stated at the time of Andrew's awakening that, "a teacher like Andrew comes along every six to eight hundred years. What's amazing about Andrew is not only the depth of his Enlightenment but his ability to transmit it to others."[6]

That power of transmission still shimmered both within and without as I headed for my room to grab a shower. This turned out to be so brief and cold as to qualify as asceticism and soon I found myself shouldering my way once more through the swarming crowd as I headed into evening practice. En route I became aware of an austere sense of detachment that, while singular, was in no way separate from life and contained within itself both naked and unshakeable simplicity, as well as unselfconscious dignity. I noticed that even my posture was different – erect and yet at ease – as I opened more deeply to the ever present awakeness that had grown in its dominance of my awareness. I also discovered, to my pleasant surprise, that by putting my attention on that awakeness the sickness, disorientation and fatigue that had dogged me throughout the day faded into the background.

Soon I found myself back to the meditation hall for the last chant of the day.

The Stability of our Transformation

The stability of our transformation depends entirely upon remaining resolutely in the Unknown, never to return again. That means ever abiding in that mysterious place where the mind has no foothold whatsoever. It means always wanting to be nobody more than we want to be somebody. And most importantly, it means surrendering our every breath to the Self Absolute and to the evolutionary impulse that emerges from that Self with a miraculous power to do what can't be done and to say what can't be said for a purpose that cannot be imagined.

While the deep state I was in carried me through the hour's chant, its first two lines swept me into contemplation of the "already knowing" predicament I had stumbled into earlier. How could I come from a place of not already knowing when, in fact, I knew quite a bit, both as a product of direct experience and of intellectual understanding? How could I puncture that membrane that I knew inhibited a deeper level of surrender?

I quickly began seeking mental strategies with which to outwit and outmaneuver the "already" part of myself, that island of ego, which Andrew had referred to as the sanctuary of the living dead. After subjecting myself to exacting mental contortions for some time it became apparent that there are no mental stratagems to trump the endless shapeshifting of the ego. It's not unlike playing chess with yourself. Despite our best efforts at impartiality and objectivity our own selves always defeat us because we already know all the moves in advance. In the same way, as long as we are fundamentally identified with ego we can never outwit or outmaneuver it. It's a maddeningly circular trap from within which there are no solutions, an Escher-like maze of inverted illusions where nothing is as is seems and all tracks lead back on themselves in labyrinthine confusion.

However, it gradually became apparent through the course of the chant that its first two lines held the keys to release. Our transformation is dependent, it told us, *"upon remaining resolutely in the Unknown,"* which meant, *"ever abiding in that mysterious place where the mind has no foothold whatsoever."* If we were we able to rest or abide in the subject, that primordial "I" sense that we'd spent the day exploring, we would indeed be abiding beyond the mind, for the mind is merely an object in that empty no-place that is the root of who we are. Being beyond the mind, of course, would put us beyond the ego's grasp, for its capacity to deceive is deeply rooted there. Strangely, there is nothing there to know; yet everything emerges from that place including knowledge of both the miraculous and the mundane. For years I had heard Andrew speak about action that moved faster than thought and knowledge that appeared from nowhere at the precise moment it was needed. It all came from this "no-place" but access to it carried a considerable price – the need to let go of always already knowing. I'd had brief experiences of such states of spontaneous being, but these episodes were a long way from *"ever abiding"* and *"remaining resolutely"* there. In truth, I found it difficult to imagine what that might mean when defined as the place from which one lived the entirety of one's life. It would require a level of trust, vulnerability, surrender and fearlessness that I could only begin to guess at. Yet that was the target, wasn't it? That was the ultimate antidote to the ego and its carapace of already knowing. I thought about the man's question regarding its being "so hard to stay there." Habit, Andrew had said. It was all a matter of habit. Clearly then, the purpose of spiritual practice was to break this habit and undermine the ego's stranglehold on our soul in favor of developing the new habit of *"abiding in that mysterious place where the mind has no foothold whatsoever."* That insight, thin as it might have been, drove my engagement with the chanting and filled my heart with gratitude for the good fortune of finding myself here.

NOTES

1. Since the word ego has many interpretations it is important to understand that when Andrew refers to it he is not speaking of the self-organizing principle in the psyche that allows us to organize and interpret our experience in an intelligible fashion. Without this part of the self well intact, we would quickly find ourselves institutionalized. What he is referring to can be defined simply as pride and arrogant self-importance, or the insidious need to locate ourselves as standing somehow apart and separate from others and from life at all times, no matter what. In enlightened

consciousness this need to be able to locate oneself as a psychological object disappears or conversely, the disappearance of the compulsive need to see ourselves as being separate is what allows enlightened consciousness to emerge.

2. The Age of Enlightenment refers to the period beginning roughly with the seventeenth century and the burgeoning Age of Reason. As a philosophical and cultural movement, the Enlightenment advocated reason as a means to obtain objective truth about the universe. Emboldened by the revolution in physics begun by Sir Isaac Newton, thinkers of this period reasoned that the same systematic thinking could be focused upon all human activity. The Enlightenment is closely linked with the Scientific Revolution and helped create the intellectual framework for the American and French Revolutions and led to the rise of classical liberalism, democracy and capitalism. In short, it is what gave rise to all of current Western culture.

3. Unfortunately, shortly after this dialogue the gentleman disappeared from the retreat.

4. Listen to an interview with Peter Fenwick at http://www.wie.org/unbound/media. asp?id=75. (This is on WIE Unbound, part of *What is Enlightenment?* magazine's website. It's a subscription service, very cheap, and the first few weeks are free with no obligation. In other words, you can listen to whatever you like at no charge for at least a few weeks.) During part of this interview he plays an audio clip of a hardened air traffic controller who had had a near death experience. Very moving.

5. Along these lines, there has been much interesting speculation lately among those who study evolution, about issues of directionality, convergence and inevitability. Broadly put, directionality suggests that the evolution of the universe is not random, but has direction, moving steadily, if slowly, towards increasing levels of complexity. Convergence means that again and again, among evolutionary lines that are completely unconnected, the same features, both physically and behaviorally, tend to appear. One of the most commonly cited examples in this regard concerns the evolution of the "camera" eye. This type of eye, which is what our eye is, has emerged independently again and again in areas of life that have no connection with each other. Interestingly, consciousness and reflective self-awareness fall into this category as well (it seems that at least some animals – also of unrelated lines such as crows and dolphins – do have levels of reflective self-awareness). This finally leads to the consideration of inevitability. If it is the case that the same mechanisms of development converge again and again to produce an identical outcome, out of near infinite possibilities, was that outcome inevitable? Which, in turn, begs the question of purposefulness? Is there a purposeful drive to the directionality of the evolving universe? Did the universe want to see, hear, feel and ultimately become self-conscious? If everything seems to be driving along similar trajectories (out of endless possibilities), could it be otherwise? Is it possible that the universe really does want to become conscious of itself and that therefore we are its most highly developed instruments toward that end? And if so, what does that mean about who we are? For an interesting discussion of this go to http://www. wie.org/unbound/media.asp?id=148 for a fascinating interview with Simon Conway-Morris. He holds an 'ad hominem' Chair in Evolutionary Palaeobiology at the University of Cambridge.

6. When he first began teaching, this capacity had terrified Andrew because he didn't know if he had a right to take people out that far. However, he said he literally couldn't help it because if people asked him to speak about his experience the "conscious energy that had eaten him alive" would take over and in the face of its power he was utterly helpless to resist.

Day 2

Knowing Nothing – Knowing Everything

Four forty five a.m.; the alarm shrilled. The night had been short but I'd slept deeply and I felt fresh and invigorated. In many ways the previous day had seemed somewhat of an ordeal, largely due to lack of sleep and my annoying colonic catastrophe. However, as I realized this morning, from the ego's perspective discipline and practice always feel like an ordeal. In fact, it occurred to me that when I'm home I frequently bemoan the lack of time for extended practice, yet what does the ego do when that time is suddenly available? Bemoan its very presence. Not today, however; today I felt lucky to be here with the leisure to immerse myself in practice.

The dead stillness of night still held sway over Montserrat as we walked through the pre-dawn darkness across the empty plaza to the meditation hall. There we chanted for an hour. During the fifteen-minute break between chanting and meditation I ventured outside to see the first hints of sunrise paint the eastern sky in pastel hues of pink and gold. Light crept up from behind mist-shrouded mountains while a few solitary birds left their perches in the cliffs below to sweep and dive in the still air of an awakening day. The resonant peal of first one, then two, then a storm of church bells embraced the morning and announced the day. This enduring ritual anchored something of the timeless in the world of time and took me back to the sacred chants of Tibetan monks that had accompanied my morning meditations in Bodhgaya nearly ten years earlier. It was during this time of the day that the sanctity of Montserrat was most deeply felt and each morning of my stay I would stand entranced in the dawning light, letting its luminosity forge a bridge not only between chanting and meditation, but between "my life" and Life itself.

On my walk to breakfast, with drifts of fog winding their way through the hills and valleys below, my awareness remained in the subject. As it did so I became aware of a visceral sensation in my body as if the locus of consciousness within it was not in the head but in the heart. I do not in any way mean this figuratively but literally. As the ease of being in which I was immersed dissolved most mental activity, a spontaneous awareness of beingness in the heart emerged. I cannot ascribe any particular significance to this other than to say that it felt entirely natural and as it should be. It was the commonplace state of frenetic fixation on the contortions of the mind that suddenly seemed extremely unnatural. Why, I wondered, did I choose to spend most of my time there? As Andrew had pointed out the previous day, no one was holding a gun to my head. Habit, of course, was the answer. Habit. Determined to undermine this addiction to the mind I headed into the teaching hall and, after finding a seat, sank back into meditation in preparation for Andrew's arrival.

He arrived shortly and together we meditated for the following hour. Thus, when the teaching commenced the atmosphere was already filled with spiritual power.

"So I wanted to keep going with what we were doing yesterday afternoon," he began, *"which was exploring the nature of consciousness and it's qualities. So I want to hear what you have to say about it and then I'll respond."*

Silence … then more silence. Then a few tentative hands rose here and there. Andrew waited a few moments to see if some burst of collective enthusiasm would lift the weight of inertia and energize the room. None did, so he had to do it for us.

"So once again, what I said yesterday was that you have to participate. You see, I'm very consistent. Yesterday I said that you have to save yourself because no one is going to do it for you. Does everybody remember that?"

A few reluctant "yeses" broke the hesitant silence.

"Oh, I thought you forgot already," Andrew pushed. *"The thing is, a lot of you aren't acting as if you heard me. You see, I've been teaching for a long time now so I do have some sense of the human condition. So if I say something like 'no one is going to save you unless you save yourself' then it would be good if you at least pretended that you heard me. But if you continue to assume a passive position I can tell you, you're not going to make it. You see, what happens on this retreat is a metaphor for real life. The way you behave when you're in here is a reflection of how you relate to your own life. So play for real, play for keeps. A lot of people play with spiritual concepts and ideas in order to feel better temporarily. They don't really want to get to the bottom of things. But someone who takes these things seriously stands out. They're not an ordinary person. And I guarantee that someone like that is going to express a kind of independence that's unusual and live an extraordinary life.*

"So let's continue, but please don't force me to force you to, okay? I really don't like to do it."

That seemed to do the trick and a flurry of hands shot up briskly. Andrew pointed to a middle aged, sandy haired German man with broad shoulders and a respectable command of English.

"When I experience consciousness," he began in a deep tone, "I have a sense of weight, of heaviness, but not as a burden, rather as something massive and somehow grounding or pulling me downwards."

"Right. There's a sense of being pulled right into the center of the universe."

"Yes. It's stabilizing and I feel it as something with a mass, with a lot of weight."

"But you don't mean it in the physical sense, right? In which sense do you mean it?"

"As making me steady and as slowing me down."

"So would that be related to confidence? Is that what you mean?"

"Yes. There's definitely confidence in experiencing that."

"That's very good. So why do you think that is?"

"Well, I think it's because consciousness is where we begin. So it's coming back to where we begin."

"Right. It has to do with knowing who you are. There's a confidence in knowing who you are."

"Yes, it feels at home."

"So I think this weightiness that you're speaking about is the source of a profound sense of self-confidence that has to do with a depth of really knowing something. Knowing something that changes everything."

"Now as you say it, yes."

"Okay, that's very good."

He paused before pointing to a young Dutch man in the back. *"Okay, let's keep going."*

"Consciousness is alive and it's indestructible and …"

"Well, you can't say it's alive because things that are alive also die. But you can say that it's life, right?"

"Right."

"If it's indestructible – and it is – it's not alive. Alive has a beginning. What they traditionally say about consciousness is that it has no birth and no death. It's often referred to as 'the unborn.'"

"Right."

"Okay, what else?"

"I keep going further and further in but there's no end to it."

"Right."

"And it feels like there's some subtle movement in it."

"How so? If it's moving then it's going somewhere, right. So is consciousness going anywhere?"

"No, I don't think so."

"So, we're trying to get somewhere but consciousness isn't going anywhere. But when you discovered that which, as you said, is endless then, because the depth is infinite, the appearance of some kind of movement can be there. But it's not actually the case. Do you understand why that might be?"

"I think so. It feels like when I look there's movement, but there's really not anything moving, I'm just going …"

"It's because the part of you that's observing consciousness feels like it's fixed and every other object that you put your attention on is also fixed – it has a beginning and an end. But suddenly that which appears to be finite, which is the observer, stumbles upon that which is infinite and it's like falling off a cliff. So it's the infinite nature of what we're speaking about that gives the appearance of a sense of movement, but there isn't any actually.

"So what else have you noticed about it?"

"There's a contagious quality to it. The more I look the more I want to see."

"Very good. So the more you see the more you want to see even though you're not seeing any 'thing.' Right?"

"Right."

"So what is it that's so contagious or compelling about something that's not an object? Usually something is compelling because there's some variety in it. For example, if you see a beautiful object, no matter how beautiful it is, after a while it's going to become very familiar."

"Right."

"But now we're talking about something that's not even an object and apparently it's infinitely more compelling. Why do you think that is? This is very important!"

"Well, everything else feels very hollow compared to it."

"No, that doesn't explain it. Do you have a girlfriend?

"Yes."

"Does she appear to be hollow?"

"She wouldn't like it very much if I said that."

Everyone laughed.

"So, this is what I wanted to get to this morning," Andrew said with a certain satisfaction. *"I want to know what it is about consciousness that's so compelling. A lot of people miss this.*

"Do you remember yesterday when we ended we got to the point where one woman was describing her experience of a kind of explosive, ecstatic experience of consciousness and I was saying that in addition to all the other things we mentioned, the nature of consciousness is ecstasy?"

"Yes."

"So what I want you to do now is look beyond just the feeling quality of the ecstasy. I want you to penetrate a little bit more, because there's something else which is a little deeper and which has to do with what you were pointing to when you said it was contagious."

The man appeared to be stumped by this turn of the conversation and with that Andrew turned his attention to a young English woman, pretty and blonde, in the front row.

"It feels like a real paradox," she began. "It feels like coming home where everything is familiar but at the very same time it's always totally new."

"Okay, that's good. But there's something about the newness that's very compelling and I want to know about that."

"Maybe it's related to the sense of discovery."

"That's true. So what is it that we're discovering?"

"Something we didn't know before."

"That's because we weren't looking for it, right?

"Yes."

"Because consciousness is always there so how could we miss it? And yet we do."

"Right."

"Because strangely, we don't seem to know much about it even though it's fundamental and ever present."

"So maybe the thrill of it is in the knowing of it."

"That's very good. That's what I wanted to get to. So what about this knowing?"

"It's not an intellectual knowing."

"Very good. So, what is it about the knowing?"

"It's a deep knowing and sense of connection that is an intimate part of you."

"Right. So I think this knowing something might be one of the most important parts of this. I hope everybody's paying attention. So we said that we're knowing something that is contagious and what I called compelling. So if we put our attention on consciousness and focus just a little bit, suddenly there's this sense of knowing something, which is also connected to the first comment about this weightiness or being rooted. So what is it that is so compelling about 'no thing?' That to me is what's important about this. What is it that we're knowing?"

Andrew turned his attention to an elderly Belgian lady who, despite her slightly quavering voice, spoke with a confident air.

"It's hard for me to say because for me there are no questions there."

"Oh, that's very good. So all questions disappear?"

"Yes, especially the whole question of meaning."

"Why is that?"

"Because I experience meaningfulness."

"Did everyone hear what she said? Meaningfulness! So this knowing is related to…"

"… Meaning."

"So when you say meaning what are you talking about?"

"That there's a purpose to my life. That I'm here for a reason."

"What's your name?"

"Tina."

"Okay, but right now we're just speaking about the nature of consciousness not about Tina's life. We can talk about Tina's life in relationship to consciousness later. But when you said there was meaning that's getting close to it. You were saying when you're aware of consciousness you don't have any questions. So why is it that all questions disappear when you are awake to consciousness?"

Andrew paused and looked about the room as we wrestled with his riddle. Then he took a moment to clarify his methodology.

"*So I want everybody to know that one of the things I emphasize in my teaching has to do with helping people to learn how to inquire and to think. You see, you can have pure or direct experience but that, in and of itself, doesn't mean anything. It's how you interpret the experience you have that's very important. The interpretation of experience is more important even than experience itself. I'll repeat that. It's the interpretation of experience that's more important than experience itself. Should I repeat it again?*"

Everyone laughed and he indeed repeated it again.

"*The interpretation of experience is everything. You need to really think about that, believe me. You see, often we're very sloppy in the way we interpret our experience. So learning how to think about your experience in a way that will liberate is extremely important.*"

Seeming satisfied he moved on to the next question. This one came from an attractive Parisian woman with short, blond hair and sky blue eyes. "What seems to be compelling," she said in a contemplative tone, "is a deep, not knowing something, but knowing everything all at once."

"*That's it. Very good! There's something about the knowing itself where we don't know anything and yet there's this feeling or sense of knowing everything. Isn't that what's so compelling?*"

A collective affirmative rose from the group, as if Andrew had drawn out from us some sudden realization that had been on the verge of emerging but needed an extra push to enter into the light of awareness.

"*That's what's so compelling,*" he said in confirmation of his own question. "*You don't know any 'thing,' because consciousness is not an object and yet there's this sense of knowing everything. When we begin to put our attention on consciousness what begins to reveal itself is a non-relative or absolute dimension or quality. That's why there's the awe and the wonder. It's this sense that whatever it is that one is becoming aware of or in touch with, its nature is everything. It's called fullness.*"

Andrew had touched the heart of something we'd sensed but had been unable to say and then quickly a young American man said in a tone of subdued intensity, "It also feels like a sense of something emerging or a curiosity ..."

"*Right,*" Andrew agreed, "*because from the perspective of consciousness there's only interest in itself, which is the knowing. The knowing of what?*" he asked rhetorically, "*Of some mysterious everything that's not a thing. Fullness. Completeness. So when you meditate on consciousness what's so compelling is this knowing of everything, which is not a thing. It's everything and at the same time it's nothing. Then you can go on forever repeating: everything, nothing; nothing, everything; everything, nothing; always meaning the same thing. As long as you say everything and nothing in the same breath, then you've got it. That's the paradoxical nature of it. If you simply say nothing, it just*" *means void or without attributes. But it's not just empty. It's also full. It's empty of anything, but full of 'everythingness.'*

"So usually when people use the word 'G-O-D,'" Andrew spelled this out with laborious affectation, the "G" word being one he shied away from due to the endless array of "already" known associations that it held for most people, "*it's meant as a metaphor for this everything which is nothing that we're speaking about. Everybody wants to know what 'G-O-D' means. So the real metaphysical or subtle interpretation of that word is this fullness which is empty yet has the quality of everything.*

"*Now, this fullness has an absolute dimension to it. Absolute means overwhelming. That's why IT is so compelling. That's why so many individuals have wanted to go to caves. They wanted to be alone with what they call the Absolute. One could say 'I want to be alone with God.' Same thing. So that's what's so compelling about consciousness.*"

Deliberately and skillfully Andrew had guided us through the half lit nuances of our own experience until suddenly the glorious reality to which he was pointing exploded like a supernova from the beneath the surface of our minds. I was swept up in an expansion of awareness and suspension of time that was shot through with currents of energy and the ecstatic knowledge that this is the Truth. The mysterious flame of transmission burned in every word Andrew said.

"*Now, that's why I said earlier that if you claim, 'Oh I already know this' I would say, 'well if you really know it then your life would have to be dramatically, radically, unalterably, and obviously transformed' because when you are deeply in touch with this knowing of that which is everything, it has to change your life in the most dramatic way. And if it hasn't, then you don't know it or you don't know it nearly as much as you think you do. Fair enough?*"

Fair enough, I thought to myself, fair enough.

"*So then as I've been saying, the real question is how well do we know this? How well do we authentically know that consciousness is primary, that its nature is bliss and fullness, and most importantly that in the nature of consciousness itself lies the knowledge of that which is unqualified or absolute. That knowledge changes everything. And without that knowledge we are lost.*

"*You see, the unenlightened person continually experiences existential doubt in relationship to the two fundamental spiritual questions: who am I and why am I here? And so long as we experience deep existential doubt in relationship to these two questions we are going to be ambivalent about life and about being ourselves. Now this refers to most of us here. Most of us are products of a postmodern, secular culture of materialism. And it's not only us Americans that are guilty of being materialists.*" Then, in an utterly deadpan tone, he added, "*You Europeans are just as bad. In fact, you're better at it than we are because you have better taste.*"

Raucous laughter followed this remark.

"*So the way it works,*" he continued, "*is that at the deepest level – you could say at the level of the soul – we experience this existential doubt which is felt as alienation and a fundamental sense of insecurity. Alienation is this strange and unpleasant feeling of being separated from oneself and simultaneously from life itself. In other words, if you don't know the answer to the questions 'Who am I and why am I here?' in a deep, experiential way that is absolute, you will experience existential doubt in the form of alienation and insecurity.*

"What I'm talking about here is not a psychological problem. I'm talking about existential issues that are deeper than our gross and subtle forms of ego neurosis. So most of us, who are products of a secular culture with materialistic values, suffer deeply at a soul level from this existential doubt, resulting in alienation and insecurity. You see, inherent in being human, at least the more we develop, is a religious or spiritual sense which has to do with the feeling of being connected in the deepest possible way to life itself. It's very simple. And whenever a human being lacks that sense of being connected there is going to be a sense of alienation and insecurity. That's just the way we are.

"Now the problem for many of us is that the answers that many of our religious traditions have given us to the questions of 'who am I and why am I here?' no longer satisfy the more sophisticated, postmodern mind, and that's understandable.

"It's interesting to consider that some human beings are at a lower level of development, say an ethnocentric level.[1] That means that your worldview is dominated by your identity as being part of a particular ethnic group or tribe. Ethnocentric is not very highly developed. In fact, it's very primitive. Yet two thirds of the world's population is at an ethnocentric level of development. Now interestingly, someone at an ethnocentric level of development who believes that what the tradition says is true—if I blow myself up and kill a hundred people I'm going to go to heaven – is free from the existential doubt that many of you suffer from. It's true!" he said in an astonished tone and then wondered aloud, *"Is that a good thing? Well that's another question."*

"The point is that the answers that give the individual, at an ethnocentric level of development, absolute confidence are not the kind of answers that are going to give most of you, who would have to be somewhere around what would be called global-centric or perhaps even a little beyond that—it goes egocentric, ethnocentric, nation-centric, global-centric, and then cosmo-centric – absolute confidence in life. So individuals at a global-centric level of development have begun to see beyond relative, ethnic differences and are starting to have a sense of the 'universal human.' So even the fact that you would be drawn to come on a retreat with me, where we're speaking about religious or spiritual concepts in an evolutionary context, would have to mean that you already have notions about what a 'universal human' would be. And that's probably how you have begun to see yourself and what you are being compelled by. It's just common sense.

"By the way, this is where we're headed. So if we survive," he emphasized this piece, *"you can see that we're headed toward this global-centric notion of a universal human and humanity. Now, two thirds of the planet is at an ethnocentric level of development and perspective. So it's only a small minority that's beginning to see the human experience from the perspective of the universal human, from global-centric*

and beyond. So there is no New Age or Age of Aquarius in the making. If that were going to happen, it would mean that almost four fifths of the world's population would simultaneously have to get to that stage where they were naturally beginning to think about and be attracted to the notion of the universal human. But we're not anywhere near that. I mean, look, at the Global Eight summit. Even my own president, George W. Bush, refused to cooperate with the world in order to do something about global warming. So he's still more concerned with the short-term financial interests of his own country than he is with the survival of the species.

"At any rate, those of us who are products of this secular culture understandably suffer from existential doubt, or alienation and insecurity, consciously or unconsciously, because the answers that the great traditions have given no longer satisfy us. We've outgrown the old but we haven't yet discovered that which is new. Now you have to know that part of human nature is this craving or yearning for a sense of being connected in a way that's absolute. That means at a soul level. So until we experience a sense of absolute connectedness we're going to be seeking and there's going to be, you could say, a 'hole in the soul.' That's why we're starting this retreat at the beginning, with that which is primary or prior to everything else – consciousness itself.

"Remember, for those of us at a global-centric, postmodern level of development, the mythical God has fallen out of the sky and temporarily disappeared. But interestingly, now, as we begin to meditate upon the experience of consciousness, that absolute principle is beginning to appear where? In consciousness itself. Miracle of miracles! It's fascinating, if you look at this in an evolutionary context, to see that the metaphysical God first falls out of the sky and then begins to be recognized as the most fundamental component of the nature of consciousness, which is who we are. That's part of our evolutionary development as a species. Now we're no longer projecting this absolute principle outside of ourselves and that's a sign of big development. We're slowly beginning to wake up to and recognize the fact that the nature of consciousness is the very thing that we were projecting outside of ourselves.

"So once again, the reason that so many of us are so desperately seeking for this absolute principle is because this craving for absolute connectedness is in our human nature. And the only way a human being can experience absolute connectedness in a deep and authentic way is in the spiritual or religious domain. There is no other way, period. That's why so many people like us, who are arriving at this global-centric level of development, are seeking. That's what's happening to you. That's why you're here.

"Now, it's important to experience absolute connectedness because then the existential doubt is gone. Then there's a sense of completeness, fullness and wholeness. And unless a human being is whole, full or complete, they're not going to be able to really be here with any kind of commitment and strength and courage because there's going to be a hole in the soul. That hole has to be filled if we're going to be able to engage with the human experience with a level of commitment, fearlessness and passion that's absolute. That's the whole purpose.

"So this is why I'm having everybody look at the nature of consciousness itself because that's where the universal human who's aspiring towards having a cosmo-centric perspective, is going to find a source of absolute confidence, fullness and wholeness. That's where you're going to find God or that which is unqualified and absolute. And knowing that which is absolute answers every question. Not the relative questions like two plus two equals four, but the existential questions of 'who am I?' and 'why am I here?' It literally erases them and renders you questionless. It removes the existential doubt, the alienation and separation, in a way that is utterly profound.

"But this is work that has to be done. For the postmodern human the exploration of consciousness has to be approached deliberately and with intention. Part of what that means is that as a member of the leading edge of the human species who's consciously aspiring to evolve or become the enlightened universal human, one has to see themselves and their aspiration in an evolutionary context, which means that it's not just about you and your existential doubt. Rather, it has to do with the evolution of the species as yourself. This contextualizes the whole endeavor. Because then what you see is that the longing for completeness, fullness and wholeness in yourself is an expression of the entire species' conscious aspiration to evolve. And as everybody already knows, nothing is more desperately needed today than the evolution of consciousness, right?"

Everyone heartily agreed.

"So what I'm doing now is contextualizing what we've been doing. Context is everything! I guarantee that you will never find the will and strength of intention to do this in the long term if you only want to do it for yourself. It's simply too demanding. If you're interested only for yourself you will find short-term interest. But the only way to sustain the long-term interest is when what's motivating you is much bigger than yourself.

"So the reason that we're looking into the nature of consciousness is, first and foremost, to deal with the existential doubt, which is the hole in the soul of the evolving human who has entered onto the stage of life in this postmodern context where we have come to the end of one age and the beginning of another. You can see that we're between the old and the new right now, right?"

Once again, everyone readily agreed.

"So its important for those people who are beginning to wake up to consciously take responsibility for this transition. Because it is a transition — boy, oh boy, is it ever. You see, up until very recently spiritual seeking was a very personal thing. It was something the individual did for himself. But it's too late for that now. The context now has to be much bigger. There's too much at stake."

Andrew paused and let this thought linger for a few moments before continuing.

"Good, so I want you to stay with the investigation into the experience of consciousness. And, of course, the reason to give attention to consciousness is to fill the hole in your soul because unless that hole is filled your capacity to engage in the life process wholeheartedly, passionately, and unselfconsciously is going to be profoundly inhibited.

And, again, if you believe that you already know about consciousness then the change in yourself must be dramatic and, to be brutally honest, if it isn't you don't know half as much as you think you know. And now, in addition to that, I want you to pay attention to the fact that this is happening in an evolutionary context and consider the significance of that."

With that Andrew concluded and together we submerged once more into the silent depths of meditation. Some twenty minutes later I was making my way along the increasingly familiar walk to the meditation hall, passing the cheese vendors and gift shops on the right and the craggy chasm that fell with such splendor to the valley floor on the left. A sunny breeze stroked my face and the crush of tourists had significantly abated from the previous days. Today was Monday and I could feel its more ordered attitude in the air. I thought about this morning's teaching and back to that day when I'd first heard Andrew talk of the newly emerging evolutionary context of his teaching.

It was less than two weeks after the fall of the towers on September 11th, 2001 when Andrew arrived in Santa Rosa, California to give an evening talk. It had been a long while since I last saw him and I was at the time deep in the throes of attempting to sort out my future with Peter. Though I would not have described it as such at the time, it is clear that while there were a number of philosophical issues at the core of his teaching that I found increasingly troublesome, it was the approach to the spiritual life from the strictly personal vantage point that had begun to assume the feel of a strait jacket. Two key assumptions had in particular begun to irritate me, striking me minimally as philosophically suspect and, at worst, as downright childish. The first involved the view that the earth was a kind of cosmic grade school through whose curriculum we had to pass before graduating to higher planes of education and existence. Considering the vast grandeur of the cosmos, to assume that that near infinitude of manifest existence was created as a kind of campus for the soul struck me increasingly as an impossibly partial view. Conversely, the view that all the effort, sacrifice and determination involved in authentic spiritual transformation should have, as their only end, my graduation from this school struck me as similarly flawed. It magnified my importance, relegating the world to the realm of mere illusion whose sole value lay in serving as a didactic tool for "my journey." The twofold message that evolution in the end concerned only "my development" and that the universe in all its grandeur was conceived merely for that purpose, had indeed come to seem like grade school material, material to be left behind not by graduating to higher planes of consciousness but by embracing a more mature perspective. In short, it seemed time to grow up.

The first stirrings of this discontent had arisen in the aftermath of a powerful spiritual episode some months earlier. At that point I had given the better part of a year to contemplating an aspect of Andrew's teaching that I had neither been able to get out of my head nor digest in its entirety. It seemed lodged in my throat as it were, its presence forcing its contemplation in nearly unabated fashion. Simply put, the teachings on impersonality state that there is really nothing unique or personal about any aspect of our experience and that, in fact, each of us is only an expression of The One Human Experience. Now, in and of itself, that notion was not too difficult to understand. When I experience fear, lust, joy, anger, compassion and the remaining panoply of human feeling and someone else experiences the same, the fact that there is no difference between us seemed obvious. In actuality, it came as a relief to know that neither my suffering nor my joy was mine alone but the shared inheritance of us all. An immediate sense of kinship softened the imagined barriers between the rest of humanity and myself. What I could not comprehend was Andrew's unwavering insistence that when one individual evolves at the level of consciousness the whole race does so as well, and in perfect tandem. Try as I might, I failed to understand this. When an individual evolves an individual evolves. And while they would no doubt exert a profound influence on others and as such on the world as a whole, I simply could not take that extra step that would allow me to see how the evolution of one individual automatically indicated that the whole race had evolved.

With that conundrum continuing to nibble at me, I found myself one night in conversation on this very point with a close friend familiar with the teaching. We spoke at some length without my having moved even an iota closer to a new understanding. Later that night as I lay on my bed and relaxed my mind suddenly, without the faintest warning, a torrent of ecstatic realization crashed over me with the weight and momentum of a psychic tsunami. The seams of my individuated mind were torn apart so quickly that in a fleeting moment the eye of my awareness glimpsed the vast dimensions of the living cosmos. And "I" was now its living center. In that flaming core the obvious burned furiously: the universe and all that it contained is the body of One Living, Conscious Being with whose very life every atom is shot through. In that cosmic body, I, individuated, am but a single cell, though never truly separate from that daunting Unity. From the fire of that insight ensued a cascade of realizations after which one remained glowing like an ember on the black face of a moonless night. In its light burned a new understanding: an organism evolves as an imperative of its cells, those billions of component parts that both inhere in it and upon which is built its existence. If I was just a cell in the body of THAT – which I was – then the degree to which I followed the pull of evolution so, to that same degree, would the organism in which I lived evolve.

This was the first time that I understood that this life was in no way mine and that, if I let go of my grip on the personal view, Life could avail itself of me rather than the other way around. As such, this was the first time that I had caught a glimpse of the fiery core of the teachings on impersonality and as such at the heart of Andrew himself. I understood then that the purpose of this wildly exploding cosmos was in no way to function as a schoolyard for my soul. Rather it was its own purpose – the ever-unfolding handiwork of an Intelligence so vast and sublime as to defy conception or description of any kind. This universe, I saw, was the body of God, infused with God, an ever-evolving expression of God, striving toward some ultimate perfection of Spirit in matter that could be deeply intuited but never truly understood. To the degree that I consciously evolved I was helping this process along literally and in real time. Conversely, to the degree that I was aware of this and chose not to evolve, I would be taking a volitional stand in active opposition to it. I shuddered with the ecstasy of revelation for long, timeless hours that night as this understanding coursed through my veins with desperate urgency. At last, as its intensity lessened, the implications for my spiritual life became increasingly clear. No longer could seeking be seen as merely a personal matter to be pursued at my own whim and for my own ends. Rather, it carried with it the weight of moral obligation as I became aware for the first time of the evolutionary burden of the universe settling upon my not yet fully squared shoulders.

It was within this context that the horror of September 11th bloomed like a stain of blood in my mind. Only then did I truly begin to sense the irreducible intimacy between my own evolution and the decidedly uncertain future of our world. This, in turn, compelled a deepening questioning of the philosophical underpinnings of Peter's entire teaching. Thus, when I saw Andrew speak in Santa Rosa not two weeks after the dramatic demise of the twin towers, the seeds had been sown for an equally dramatic shift in orientation and the end of a relationship that had until that point towered in the center of my life. Hearing Andrew's impassioned call to take on the darkest parts of ourselves in service to and as an expression of the leading edge of a fourteen billion year process of evolution, I found myself immersed once more in the revelatory splendor of some weeks earlier. My heart burst open, releasing a care for the world of which I had been totally unaware and for the first time in my life I began to see what my longing for liberation had to do with that kind of care. A sense of purpose now filtered into me that did not spring from the miserly needs of the personal self, but rather from the Self of the universe and its surging creative imperative. That purpose was not personal in the least yet shot through the personal world with the motives of the impersonal Source of Creation itself. And, as an animating force in one's life, nothing could be greater than that.

I returned to the present and Andrew's exhortation to fill the "hole in our soul" through the direct experience of our own absolute nature so that we might participate in the life process, not only freed of existential doubt but empowered by an unwavering commitment to that process for its own sake. I also understood and appreciated his statement that if we thought we knew this and our life had not been radically, unalterably and irrevocably transformed, then we didn't know it half as much as we thought we did. In this context meditation practice took on new significance. Understanding it more properly I began to see it not merely as a practice to cultivate calmness or "to burn negative psychic tension and develop a strong chakra system," as I had been taught previously, but as a way out of small-mindedness into a big hearted, liberated passion for the transformation of our world. That world, as our mid-day chant reminded us, was in desperate need of "mature, enlightened human beings." Duly inspired, I entered the meditation hall where, for the next hour, I attempted to ignore the echoing shouts of waiters and the thick, humid air, instead delving deeper into the subject, the pure "I," the growing presence of which would illumine the path from the personal to the impersonal.

That hour was followed by a silent lunch and after a further hour of meditation in the teaching hall Andrew was ready to take up the thread once more as we continued with the day's philosophical and spiritual explorations.

"So I wanted to keep going into the qualities of consciousness," he began, *"especially in relationship to the experience of knowing and what it is that one is knowing."*

Many hands now rose simultaneously suggesting that perhaps Andrew's message from earlier that day regarding the need to take responsibility for one's own liberation had gotten through. He turned to a young American man, with a head of brown curls and intense dark eyes.

"So in my vast experience of less than forty-eight hours," he began, "something I've noticed is that consciousness seems to be recognizing itself but the thoughts I'm having aren't necessarily recognizing themselves. They're only a sort of past or future kind of movement."

"Well, thoughts and what we're referring to as consciousness are not the same thing. Thoughts are objects that appear in consciousness. They are not consciousness."

"Well, what's occurring though is that consciousness seems to have an interest in itself. It seems to wants to know itself. Does that make any sense?"

"Well, it definitely seems," Andrew said with an edge of the comic in his tone, *"that this self-infatuation or cosmic narcissism, as it were, is part of the nature of consciousness."*

A vigorous blast of laughter burst through the room. Then, in a tone of "no, but seriously folks," Andrew went on.

"But it's true. If one explores the experience of consciousness without any particular expectations one finds the subject meditating upon its own nature, which, as we discussed this morning, is infinitely compelling. So when consciousness meditates upon itself we come to this non-relative or absolute dimension of experience. And when we cross that line from relative to absolute we feel that something very profound and significant is occurring. No matter who you speak to, when that barrier from relative to absolute is crossed and one begins to become aware of this non-relative dimension of one's own self, it's always powerful because of its absolute nature, which, of course,

is non-other than one's own deepest self. So this afternoon I want everybody to spend a little more time exploring why it's so compelling.

"So, once again, in the nature of consciousness itself there seems to be this experience of knowing something that's not a thing but that changes everything. It's nature is profound and of ultimate value and meaning. That's what I want everybody to focus on. It's the most important thing and it's what people always miss or, if they get it, it's the first thing they forget. And the problem is that the minute you forget this you're seeking all over again. And as long as you're still seeking for absolute conviction there's also still going to be a hole in your soul – this existential doubt, which is experienced as alienation and a sense of being separate from life itself. And that's very problematic.

"Is there anything else about that?"

"Well, yes," the man continued, "Where I'm having difficulty is trying to understand why it is that consciousness wants to know itself. There's a dead end there for me."

"Well, there is no answer to the question of 'why?' That's just what its nature is. That's as far as you can take it. I don't know if there's actually an answer. I mean, I have a pretty good guess but ultimately it doesn't matter.

"What's important about this is to really see that consciousness has its own motive, which is, in this case, to know itself. This knowledge can completely hijack or override the ego's impulses, which is important because usually the directionality of the vehicle – you – is dominated or controlled by the individual and collective ego. But when someone discovers consciousness very deeply, there's a recognition that consciousness has its own motive, the nature of which is also absolute. That's called spiritual transformation. You're on one track and then you discover a kind of depth that blows your circuits. If you discover something that's absolutely true and more real than anything else you've ever experienced, that overrides — at least theoretically — our previously conditioned perspective, which is a personal orientation and worldview, all of which is ultimately relative. The point is that when you discover a non-relative or absolute ground that has its own motive, it overrides in the biggest possible way the sense of being completely lost in the track that one was already on. That's what Enlightenment is all about. It's why I want everybody to really look into consciousness itself because its liberating potential lies in the degree to which we actually recognize its absolute and non-relative nature.

"You see, there's an ultimately rational science to the nature of consciousness," he said, indicating a slight shift in direction. "Isn't that interesting?"

Everyone seemed to agree as evidenced by the rustle of affirmative murmurs throughout the room.

"The great Ken Wilber[2] has come up with concept he calls called 'post-metaphysical spirituality.' Post-metaphysical spirituality means that we want to come up with a way of pursuing the evolution of consciousness without having to assume any metaphysical *givens like, for instance, 'God lives in the sky.' The whole idea behind post-metaphysical spirituality is that you don't have to believe anything. You just explore according to certain principles and find out for yourself.*

"So this is a very rational approach to the exploration of consciousness and Enlightenment, which is also something that's very important for this post-postmodern era at the beginning of the twenty-first century. For more sophisticated people this is really how it's going to have to be, don't you think?"

I certainly thought so. It was a rational spirituality that I'd yearned for since my first experiences of revelation in my early twenties and it was what had first drawn me to the timeless teachings of the East, as well as the growing body of "new physics" books in vogue at the time, including Fritjof Capra's *The Tao of Physics* and Gary Zukav's *The Dancing Wu Li Masters*. Through those books I knew that I wasn't alone in my quest for a new spiritual paradigm, one in which the banishment of reason and embrace of superstition were no longer part of the price of admission.

In all fairness, I did try the old ways along with the new. After all, I had a deep appreciation of history, for this was part of my chosen field of study, and did not assume that all that was old was of necessity dead. Moreover, I'd had an extraordinarily powerful experience of insight and revelation upon my first reading of the Gospel of Matthew. This episode spurred me on briefly with visions of taking up the mantle of the Christian soldier, but even then I felt that that doctrine would have to be reinterpreted in the clear light of both science and mystic revelation.

My brief flirtation with Christianity ultimately turned out to be simply an odd experience. At that time I was spiritually aflame, being plunged almost daily into the crucible of revelation in which the unsuspected realm of the spirit had thrown open its doors to me. It was in this state that I had come to the Gospel of Matthew and discovered in its lines the same voice that spoke so beautifully in the Upanishads and Bhagavad-Gita. However, I could not square this with the angry Father-God also bound within those gold leafed pages, smiting hither and yon with vengeful wrath. Neither could I square the passion, depth and power of Christ himself with the vapid utterances of vain, deluded televangelists in baby blue suits or the stentorian tones of those who insisted that regular church attendance amounted to a down payment on heavenly real estate, into whose possession I would come upon eviction from my current form. Hoping to find Christ-like passion for the mystic life within the dark interior of the Catholic world, I ventured daily to its local seat and plunged for six solid months into its knee numbing rituals. To my surprise, the priests whom I accosted with my passion were less lights shining upon the world as a reflection of their living God and more sackcloth draped guardians of conservatism and a spiritual and cultural status quo. Their long-winded liturgies and services were imbued with none of the passion that must have emboldened the early Christians to face the lions rather than renounce their faith and thus they seemed more an exhortation to a death in life existence rather than its living opposite. Turning my attention to their born again counterparts, I fared no better. In their fire and brimstone company I was the beneficiary of long lectures on "God's lamb" dying for my sins and the inexplicable notion that salvation from certain damnation was to be found in the simple-minded belief in that conjectured sacrifice. I marveled at the contortions of logic that were performed routinely and are best encapsulated by the repeated assertion that the earth's geological fossil record was made up entirely of the "props of Satan" with which the good Lord, in his infinite and inscrutable humor, had chosen to test our faith.

Small wonder that after a six-month dalliance with the emissaries of Christ, I abandoned the endeavor entirely. In order to effectively adhere to the fantastic views of reality that they offered, I would have to set aside the sum of man's knowledge, all of it hard won. It was, after all, science and rational thinking that, fighting tooth and nail with the patriarchs of orthodoxy, had elevated human life in a way religion never had, and that I could not cast aside. Not that I could cast aside the spiritual dimension that had so recently arrived like an unexpected guest. On both counts it turned out I had come to know too much. And yet I knew so little.

That being the case I redoubled my efforts to thread together an integral worldview by refocusing my gaze both to the East and to the latest minute missives from the weird wonderland of quantum mechanics. As I saw it, the Eastern Enlightenment traditions comprised a rational, experiential inquiry into the absolute dimension of reality while the so-called "new physics" was an inquiry of pure science into the fundamental nature of the relative dimension of reality. It was clear that a complete understanding of the life process and our place in it would ultimately have to encompass both these dimensions and everything in between. Thankfully, in both the Eastern and scientific traditions rationality and direct experience were, at least in theory, the guiding principles, which much better suited my postmodern, Western mind.

But both approaches had their shortcomings. First, the scientific approach overlooked the issue of consciousness almost entirely. It relegated sentience to the deadwood category of incidental by-product, a mere "epi-phenomenon" of the very reality that sentience was studying. Second, the Eastern teachings on the absolute dimension of reality, while enlightening us to the fundamental nature of consciousness, say very little about successful strategies for navigating the material world, which is fundamentally viewed as an illusion. At best they instruct us to live an ethical life and, if one's Enlightenment is profound, to share that blessing with others. Neither view alone, nor both together, stood poised to address the complexity of the human predicament.

Attempting to bridge at least some of the gap between these views were the proponents of transpersonal psychology whose presence and popularity grew in great strides during the seventies, eighties and nineties. Calling on the growing body of scientific knowledge regarding the interiority of human experience, they sought to merge it in a "spectrum of consciousness" (a phrase coined by Ken Wilber) with the understanding of its higher potentials as revealed over the millennia by the wisdom of the East. I had been quite enamored of this field during my early explorations as I sought to understand and contextualize the experiences that had so dramatically affected my own life. However, I soon sensed that no amount of therapy, regardless of its kind, could ever lead to Enlightenment. While paying abundant lip service to the absolute dimension of life, it took as its starting point the separate ego and its history, never questioning their fundamental validity and actually, through obsessive examination, strengthening one's identification with them. I could never have articulated this point during those early years, yet somehow I intuited its truth. Somehow, starting with a context of "me" after having had such searing experiences of "That" seemed contrived, painfully limiting, spiritually unsatisfying and fundamentally wrong. It wasn't until years later, hearing Andrew speak about his views on this subject, that I understood why I'd felt the way I'd felt. And today even Ken Wilber, in many ways the godfather of transpersonal psychology, has by and large rejected the sum of its premises, going so far as to refer to therapists as the "pimps for samsara."[3]

While these approaches were infinitely more satisfying than the dogmatism of Christianity, they still did not integrate the timeless truth of non-dual realization with Western scientific understanding, both of the cosmos and the human psyche, and derive from them moral, ethical and practical guidelines for contemporary living in the light of spiritual passion. That's what I was on the hunt for – a teaching that could fuse those elements in a fully satisfying spiritual/theoretical framework and a teacher who would be its living example.

In the course of this pursuit I met psychics and channelers, swamis and lamas, roshis and rimpoches, many of them sweet, some of them powerful, but none able to effectively demonstrate how the mystic life might be lived without any denial of my Western heritage and postmodern sensibilities. It was this nine-year odyssey through the strangely twisting byways of the contemporary spiritual marketplace that ultimately led me to Peter.

In him – and indirectly through his teacher Rudi before him – I had come upon the first credible example of how to embody the timeless truths of Eastern wisdom in an unabashedly Western context. It was the only teaching I'd found that not only embraced the scientific understanding of our world but also encouraged individuals to rise fully to the challenging demands of today's life. In his view, the spiritual and material did not stand in contradiction to one another but were connected symbiotically. He held that if one were indeed having a spiritual life it should be evident in everything they did. This included the worlds of money, business and creative success. Peter abhorred the "rent control mentality," an attitude and strategy of always living in the cheapest, easiest way in order to avoid dirtying one's hands with money and business. His ethic dictated that whatever level one had attained in life could never be seen as an end in itself; instead it constituted a stepping off point that fueled a multilayered process of evolution that was literally without end. Such an ethic appealed to me because it wove into the spiritual life all the threads of my humanity, including those bright strands of ambition and creativity that seem to me among the most thrilling aspects of being alive. None of this was mere philosophy for Peter as he was a living example of his teaching, having worked himself from destitution and flights of suicidal fantasy to extraordinary success in both the spiritual and business worlds. That success he shared in innumerable ways with those who gathered around him. Unfortunately, in the end, I found even his teaching lacking for reasons already mentioned.

In Andrew I saw the realization and fulfillment of the promise inherent in Peter's teaching. I saw a radically realized human being who fully inhabited his Western heritage yet whose enlightened mind set out to reinterpret the timeless truths of liberation fearlessly and without taking a single thing for granted. In so doing, he had developed a teaching that felt to me like the next logical step, not only for my own evolution but also for the evolution of a new spiritual paradigm that sits poised to address the desperate need of our time. That is, it addressed the entirety of current life conditions, empowering the mystic dimension of life to fully inform the postmodern soul robbed of tradition and seeking life-transforming purpose.

"So you can see in the way that I'm teaching," Andrew continued, *"that I'm not asking anybody to believe anything. However, if you do what I am asking you to do you're going to have certain experiences that will show you that what I'm saying is actually true. Then you'll know about consciousness from your own experience and you won't have to take my word for anything. You see, I'm teaching this in a way that is very rational. Don't you think that's very important?"*

Everyone agreed.

"The human race needs to become more rational, don't we?"

More murmured agreement.

"We're not rational enough. Actually, we're completely nuts. That's why we need a rational spirituality.

"But you *have to do it! Remember, there's no mythical God in the sky that's going to save you. Self-salvation is part and parcel of a post-metaphysical approach to spirituality. So don't be lazy. Most people of our ilk are incredibly lazy. We want to have pleasant experiences but we don't want to do any work. We want everything for free."*

Andrew paused for a few moments to let his words settle. He then turned his attention to an Australian man who'd had his hand up for some time.

"Over the last few days," he began, "I've noticed that my thoughts seem to have moved into the background. It's not that they're not there, they just seem, I don't know, far away."

"Very good. The fact that your thoughts are in the background instead of the fore-ground must be a big relief.

"Huge, yeah."

"Well that's important because when thought moves into the background you real-ize, 'Oh my god, I'm not my thoughts.' Before that we falsely assume—usually uncon-sciously – that we are what we think. But when thoughts fall into the background and YOU are in the foreground you realize that thoughts are not inherently who you are. That's a very important discovery.

"The thought stream itself is inherently irrational, chaotic and unpredictable. It's also very conditioned. So unless you take an inquiry like the one we're pursuing right now very seriously, I guarantee that you're going to be lost in your own irrational, crazy mind and then you're going to act out of irrational thoughts and make a mess out of your life. That's how it works.

"So, what we're speaking about here is all part of a coherent way to have a very rational relationship to the human experience, which means your life. Rational means free. It doesn't mean robotic. It means you're in control of yourself. To be free doesn't necessarily mean to feel free. If you want to feel free you just need to have a few drinks. A free person is in control of themselves. They are no longer robots subject to the whims of their conditioned impulses. They may experience those impulses but they are free not to act on them. So everything we're speaking about in here gives everybody the potential to be a radically free human being.

"That's why you have to take it seriously and you have to go into it very deeply yourself. You can sit and listen to me speak about these things and say to yourself, 'Oh that makes sense.' But unless it becomes your own experience it's ultimately going to be pretty useless.

"So therefore I want to continue to investigate the absolute dimension of conscious-ness because it's the discovery of that dimension that changes everything. You see, unless you cross the line from relative to absolute there's no big change, no radical shift in perspective. So I want everybody to continue to explore this experience of knowing, that which is 'everything-slash-nothing' because becoming conscious of THAT is the very thing that changes everything.

"You see, the degree to which someone awakens to and realizes that, is the degree to which they become an enlightened person. So remember what I said this morning: the only way individuals who have grown up within a secular, postmodern context can free themselves from the experience of alienation is through the discovery of the non-relative dimension of consciousness. That's what fills the hole in the soul. You can solve all of your neurotic complexes and quirks and that's not going do anything about the hole in your soul.

"So in order to truly be an expression of an ultimately cosmocentrically-based con-sciousness, the new 'universal human' can have no holes in their soul. That means that they have to be liberated or free from fundamental existential doubt about the nature

of life, being and existence. I don't care how smart you are; I don't care how much you've read or how much you know. Unless you really get this on the experiential level there's going to be a hole in your soul—there's going to be doubt. That's simply the way it works. It's scientific. Now, this can only be done through meditation and contemplation on the non-relative or absolute dimension of consciousness. It's not going happen by itself and it will not happen by itself and it won't happen by itself! You have to do it."

Andrew's emphatic exhortation drew a sober, affirmative response. He paused for a long moment before pointing to a middle-aged German man with close-cropped dark hair and a heavy accent.

"For me, once you get access to this knowing everything is pretty clear. There are no questions anymore."

"That's right, but you have to get really *clear about it. There's a phrase in English, called 'bearing witness.' Have you ever heard that before?"*

"No."

"If you bear witness it means you're someone who's willing to declare to the whole world in the face of all the unbelievers that you've seen this light, that you know it's true."

"Exactly," he said with full conviction.

"You see, once you've seen this absolute dimension it takes courage to stand for it and be an expression of it yourself.

"And today there's another dimension to it. What we're interested in is this post-metaphysical spirituality or a new, rational form of mysticism. That's a new thing and it takes courage to stand behind that also. Have you noticed that a lot of people who are very interested in mysticism are a little crazy and often intellectually weak? It's for this reason that a lot of the New Age movement has profoundly discredited these deeper, metaphysical truths. So in order to give them credit once again we have to have the courage to stand for and be examples of a rational form of mysticism.

"If we can't do that then these timeless truths will not be taken seriously, and for good reason – a lot of crazy people are attracted to metaphysics. But a very rational form of mysticism is a whole new thing. It's a new approach that is desperately needed and that desperately needs us."

"What helps us to sustain the answers we get from this knowing and to assure that ego does not override it with time?" the man asked loudly.

"You have to give it a lot of importance. In fact, you have to give it more importance than you do anything else."

"So it has to be inherent in my value system?"

"It has to be the foundation of your value system," Andrew replied crisply and the man had no more questions.

"Okay good," Andrew said. *"Now, does everybody understand this idea of a rational mysticism?"*

A shuffle of yeses.

"So we have to show everybody that the New Age is for airheads."

With that the room filled with laughter.

"You see," Andrew went on, *"if you authentically embody a rational form of mysticism you'll scare the New Age people away. The word 'rational' frightens sloppy New Age thinking. They equate rational with materialism and they think it stands against God and spirituality. But what they don't see is that they're actually creating more problems for God and spirituality than anyone else because they're making God look like a fool."* A hush fell over the room.

"Can I say that?" he asked with mock caution. It was precisely such strong and straight talk that had given Andrew his controversial reputation. Then he laughed loudly, as he often does when making a serious point.

"Of course, I think they look foolish because frankly they're just silly. For example, this gentleman was saying this morning that he feels this 'weightiness.' That's dignity. Isn't there an inherent sense of dignity, seriousness and self-respect in that weight?" He looked over at the man who had made those remarks, who quietly nodded to Andrew. *"And that's precisely what's missing in a lot of New Age spirituality and also in the East-meets-West spirituality, a great deal of which has become co-opted by New Age thinking. It lacks dignity and seriousness and this is a real problem. That's why it takes courage to stand for and embody a rational mysticism that's founded on clear thinking and is expressed with a dignity and seriousness that it itself makes possible."*

I found myself drifting away as I remembered myself some weeks earlier wandering through downtown Mill Valley – one of the New Age's global nerve centers – idly perusing the various posters and flyers dotting shop windows and bulletin boards. These advertised an assortment of workshops and seminars that reflected what Andrew was talking about. Within a hundred yard radius I was offered the opportunity to have my chakras cleansed, find my soul mate, obtain Buddhist dating tips to facilitate so doing, have my aura read, my past life interpreted, receive therapy for the wounds received therein and in general be the beneficiary of a variety of teachings on accepting, healing, embracing, and nurturing so that I might cultivate the capacity to give myself a very big hug and the courage to acknowledge just how wonderful I really am. It was, as someone once joked, "I Ching, you ching, we all ching" and, incidentally, plenty of "ching-ching" in a lucrative marketplace of spiritual entertainment and customized catering to a culture of near hopeless narcissism. What formed the core of this marketplace was the convergence of several forces including the magic and superstition of New Age thinking, the trivialization of higher truth that constitutes so much of East meets West spirituality and the intense narcissism that is an inherent part of the Age of the Individual. It is an age of "my truth" and "your truth" in which "The Truth" has been reduced to a dusty relic from our religion haunted past. Add to this wealth and a high level of education and one begins to get a sense of the self-congratulatory aplomb within which all of this exits. What is missing is dignity and self-respect. To be sure, in New Age nerve centers like Mill Valley, there is no shortage of nice guys but rarely will one find an individual who can "intimidate you with their integrity," as Andrew defined the authentically spiritual person. In line with this, he'd once observed, *the New Age is everything but the main event.*

Were all of this merely the theater of the absurd that it appears to be on first view, one might simply chuckle and disregard it. Unfortunately, however, the slow seepage of New Age thinking into more serious pursuits shifts its impact from the comic to the tragicomic. And in this tragicomedy, the Bay Area, my home, currently plays a leading role. For this reason, famed integral philosopher Ken Wilber has coined the phrase "the 415 paradigm" (415 referring to the local area code), stating that:

> Much New-Age thinking satisfies the longing for the lost One and Whole, but by actual regression to earlier stages of "oneness" and "wholeness," which are not actually whole in any developed sense, but merely stages of infantile fusion and indissociation, magically and mythically charged. In fact, the more sophisticated New-Age approaches do indeed use a type of recourse to science, but the science is almost always distorted, especially the "new physics" and the "web of life." This pseudo-science hides from evidence and thus is not really science – it is simply a new mythology. Those New-Age worldviews are indeed closed and these movements can survive only in sub-cultural islands. In America one of these sub-cultural islands is found in San Francisco, which is why I call the most prevalent version of the sophisticated New-Age approach the "415 Paradigm." This is why it is so important for integral psychology and all serious post-metaphysical movements to detach themselves wherever possible from such New-Age movements. It is why I myself no longer am a member of the transpersonal movement in America, which has all the earmarks of the New-Age movement.[4]

What has become apparent in my own experience both of myself – for one can never leave oneself out of such equations – and my local culture, is that Wilber is describing a lower level of development masquerading as a higher one while using the cloak of spirituality to obscure this charade.[5]

I remembered Andrew's visit to Mill Valley – which Ken Wilber has coined the epicenter of the "415 paradigm" – some two years earlier. Approximately a hundred and fifty people had gathered at a small church nestled quaintly between the vast heights of ancient redwoods and steep hillsides dotted with multi-million dollar homes. Within a few minutes of the outset of the talk the crowd became restive. Within about half an hour the active heckling commenced. What was it that these "spiritually sophisticated" individuals found so offensive? The presentation of a spirituality that wasn't strictly about them? But what it was that annoyed them doesn't really matter; what was extraordinary was the absence of the basics of human courtesy amongst individuals who considered themselves sensitive, conscious and forward looking. There was no dignity, no self-respect and a complete absence of respect for others. This was the face of a lower level of development masquerading as a higher one under the guise of a convoluted mass of spiritual ideas spread over a nest of brooding egos. The irony was that the majority of "ordinary people" (those not professing interests in higher consciousness and evolution) would have treated Andrew with more respect. That basic quality, however, was entirely absent that night. The point is that the popularization of New Age concepts and their marriage to both narcissism and lower levels of emotional development has robbed individuals of dignity and self-respect, the culture of the liberating power of higher truths, and the higher truths of the credibility needed to affect a desperately needed change in values.

Returning from my reverie I noticed that Andrew was addressing himself to a petite French woman with reddish hair whose hand had been raised for some time.

"Hi, Andrew," she began hesitantly. "I found out that when I watched consciousness, there was no relationship to any material thing."

"That's right. That's the whole idea. Remember, we're going from a negative relationship to life to no relationship to life. A negative relationship to life is the life of the individual and collective ego. But we're going back to before the beginning. There, from the perspective of consciousness, there's no relationship to anything, right?"

"Yes. That's my experience."

"That's freedom, isn't it?"

"Yes. It really was very interesting because sometimes I didn't even know if I am a man or woman."

"That's right, because in consciousness there's no gender. There's no he; there's no she. There is only THAT."

"The other thing that I found very interesting is that there was no need for any further proof of anything."

"Well you have the proof of your own experience, right?"

"Right."

"You get the proof in your own experience and if you look deeply enough you'll always get the proof there. When you pay attention to consciousness, this non-relative or absolute dimension itself becomes the source of one's confidence in being."

"Why is that important?" he asked rhetorically. *"Well, where is it that we usually look for our source of confidence in life? It's not in consciousness,"* he laughed. *"Where is it that we look for confidence?"*

"Ego," someone called out.

"You could say that, but what's certain is that we don't look for our confidence in life in the nature of consciousness.

"But what would human life be like if the knowledge of the absolute dimension of consciousness itself became the source of your confidence in life? My – wouldn't that change everything? Imagine the effect that would have on your relationships?"

Everyone laughed.

"'You didn't tell me you loved me today," he mocked like a wounded lover. *"What happened? Is something wrong?"*

More laughter echoed in the room, this time with self-deprecating undertones as many of us recognized this sentiment in ourselves.

"You see," Andrew continued, *"I'm convinced that for the possibility of a new kind of human relationship to emerge, individual human beings have to find their source of confidence in the absolute or non-relative dimension of consciousness itself. Then, if human beings relate to each other from the knowledge of that dimension, it could change the playing field completely."*

Everyone agreed.

"Easy to talk about – something else to do." Andrew paused, surveying the crowd. *"Nevertheless, you can just begin to imagine how different it would be. Actually, it's too far away to imagine, but you can at least get a sense. Clearly, the potential would be amazing.*

"So, once again, you have to ask yourself: 'where is our attention? Where do we look to find our source of confidence?' Generally, it's not in the nature of consciousness itself. And, once again, why should we look for confidence in the nature of consciousness? Because, as we were saying yesterday, it's primary and fundamental. It's what supports everything. It's what's most trustworthy. Consciousness is very steady. It doesn't have moods, neurotic problems or unfulfilled desires."

Everyone laughed, and then fell into a reflective silence.

Soon Andrew turned his attention to a young Danish woman with long, blonde hair falling over her shoulders.

"I find the 'knowing' compelling and joyful," she said, "but it also gives me a feeling of great responsibility, a sort of a load on my shoulders. It's a kind of responsibility for working with the evolution of human consciousness that's very motivating."

"Well, that sense of responsibility comes from consciousness also, doesn't it?"

"Yes."

"You see, when you meditate deeply on consciousness and begin to experience it directly, it totally undercuts and destroys the ego's narcissistic, pathological fixation upon only its own needs. The famous declaration, 'Not my will, but Thy Will be done,' comes from an individual who is experiencing this kind of depth or the absolute nature of consciousness itself. I think this is very similar to what you are speaking about."

"Yes."

"So that's also why this experience of the non-relative or absolute dimension of consciousness is very important. It frees one from the pathological self-concern of the ego."

"Can this feeling of responsibility come from the ego?" she queried.

"No," Andrew responded simply and definitively.

"Okay."

"Consciousness feels responsible for itself and is actually seeking for itself. It's always happy to find itself, and when it does it's always like the first time." Andrew laughed. *"It's just like my little dog. Every time he sees me he's always happy, just like the first time."*

The image of the wriggling joy of a small dog bouncing with excitement at the return of its master struck a familiar chord in our collective heart, bringing smiles to our faces.

"But it's actually true. When you begin to pay attention to consciousness and then discover it yet again you say, 'Oh my goodness, you're my best friend. It's so good to see you again.' It may have only been five minutes or an hour or a week or ten years, but when you rediscover consciousness it's ever new. It's always like the first time. Nothing else in life is the same the second time. Only the discovery of consciousness is the same every time because it's ever new. Do you understand?"

"Yes."

"It's perpetually, perennially, forever self-seeking. The Self always wants to know itself and always delights in knowing itself. The Self knowing the Self is an endless experience of self-delight."

As Andrew spoke these words we all experienced their truth in the immediacy of our own experience. A spontaneous flow of joy moved through the hall as Andrew took the next question, this one from a middle-aged New Yorker (the accent being unmistakable) with short gray curls and a slightly melancholy expression.

"In its seeking for itself, it seems a little paradoxical because there appears to be a movement or an action but at the same time there's no action at all."

"Exactly. It seems like the self-seeking is happening; it seems like the self-delight is happening but then, from the perspective of consciousness, nothing at all is happening. It is paradoxical, but I think what's more important is just the recognition that for some reason part of the nature of consciousness is self-delight and self-seeking. I think that's more important than the fact that, from one perspective, it's not happening."

"Right," the man replied.

"Some teachers will say, 'nothing's happening and nothing ever happened,' and from a particular perspective they're right. Then it's, 'okay thank you. Now that we've established that, what's next?' You see, the first time you get it it's quite a shock, but then, after you get it, you might need to 'for-get' it because ultimately it's kind of useless information. A lot of people, weak-minded people, get stuck in this trap of 'nothing's happening,' as if it's a really big deal. They're very annoying and boring to be with because they're like robots. They keep repeating, 'nothing's happening.' The thing is, it's just one way of looking at things but it's not the only way.

"The insight that nothing is ultimately happening, which is the absolute perspective of consciousness itself, is helpful when you're in trouble and when bad or tragic things are happening, like when you find out you have cancer, or you lose a limb, or a loved one. At times like that it's helpful to have this background understanding that all these events, while real and painful and even tragic, are still relative. But we don't want to get stuck on that.

"The thing is, people who keep saying 'nothing's happening' become anti-evolutionary forces. Ultimately you have to tell them that their perspective is just one-dimensional. But that's for another discussion." He paused, a soft smile spreading across his face as he turned back to the man. *"Are you having an interesting time?"*

"Yeah."

"Are you giving yourself to what I'm asking people to do?"

"Yes."

"Are you discovering the non-relative or absolute nature of consciousness or the sense of knowing that we're speaking about?"

"Yeah, and I'm discovering that the whole process of knowing doesn't seem to be about knowing nothing. It's the process of knowing itself where there's depth. It also seems that there's no beginning or ending to consciousness."

"Right. So if there's no beginning or ending what does that mean about life and death? That's interesting question, isn't it?"

"It would mean that life and death are relative."

"Right. That's exactly what it would mean. And if that's true wouldn't that be something very important to know about?"

"It's almost as if life and death are no big deal."

"Well, actually, I think it has to be a big deal because we're here. After all, how would consciousness be able to know itself in the world of time, space and causality without these frail and puny human vehicles containing these very highly developed brains? It wouldn't be able to, would it?"

"True, but it seems that death is not a big deal or at least doesn't have the importance that we give it."

"Well, we can say, 'it's not a big deal,' and that's one way of looking at it, which is relatively true. But if we see that birth and death are an inherent part of the creative process then from that perspective it's not about whether or not it's a big deal. You just simply see that it's part of how it all works. And if a lot of birth and death hadn't happened countless billions of times we wouldn't be able to be here having this conversation about the nature of consciousness, would we? So it is a big deal that we're here because we can have this conversation about consciousness. And ultimately, who's talking about consciousness? If the subject is consciousness itself then consciousness is talking about itself. And it must want to talk about itself otherwise why would it be doing it?

"Of course, one could say, 'well, consciousness doesn't need to have this conversation,' but how do you know? Maybe it does. After all, it's the urge towards consciousness that brought all of us together so we could have this conversation about it."

Stirred by this circular logic, everyone laughed aloud along with Andrew at the striking yet odd probability of its being true.

"So I do think that it's a big deal. It's not everything and there are other ways to look at this but I think that, when you really put all the pieces together, being here in this form gives us this miraculous capacity to have this conversation about the non-relative or absolute nature of life and death and being. Not that many people can have conversations like this and throughout history it's always only been a very few individuals who are actually capable of this kind of engagement. Most people are completely unaware of what we're speaking about here.

"So I think consciousness is very interested in this discussion," he added, his tone sharpening to a point. *"It's probably saying, 'look, now I'm talking about myself.' And, as we've been saying, it delights in self-knowing. To the degree that consciousness is aware of itself is the degree to which there's ecstatic self-delight and it's consciousness itself that's urging us towards this kind of conversation. So that's also part of the self-delight. You see how it works?"*

I did and felt swept up in a great spiral of vision by the circle of his logic like a bird flying from an ancient plaza into the radiant eye of the sun. Once more the notion of "my life" dissolved in the infinitude of Life Itself. If consciousness sought itself through me, a movement that I experienced as my most intimate own, who was I then, and where was the frontier between us? All of it dissolved into dust under the subtle weight of insight.

"So if we insist on seeing ourselves in any way, shape or form as being separate from consciousness itself," Andrew went on, *"then we get this kind of strange or distorted perspective that's very dualistic. In a truly non-dual perspective you see that consciousness is all and therefore consciousness must be what's motivating us to have this conversation and delighting in it.*

"Do you think your ego's saying, 'Wow! This is great. I'm having a conversation about consciousness?' Your ego doesn't care. It has all kinds of other desires and interests. But when you realize that it's consciousness itself that's driving the conversation we're having, that really blows your mind."

Returning to his earlier point, he added, *"So even though the 'it's not-a-big-deal-because-nothing-is-happening' perspective is valid, we have to be careful with it because without even realizing it we can verge towards nihilism and we definitely don't want to do that.*

"You know," he added thoughtfully, *"materialists often share the same bed with nihilists. It's not always true. There are materialists who have a very life-positive view. That has to be said. But when materialists start speaking about the nature of consciousness something horrible starts happening. They could be talking about the very*

thing we're talking about now and come to completely different conclusions about what it means. You know what I'm talking about, right?" He looked around, gauging the room for its answer.

I knew what he was talking about: scientism, that darling of the modern mind that holds the universe as a massive sequence of random events bereft of meaning whose vast spaces are inhabited by irremediably separate entities, whose consciousness, in turn, is but an incidental by-product of brain functioning and whose pointless existence will be irrevocably annihilated upon the demise of the physical form. Denying with religious fervor any suggestions of a transcendent principle, it starts from the very conclusion toward which it drives with hell-bent vengeance. Thus it cannot be said to be science in the truest sense – pure and unadulterated curiosity about the nature of reality free from prior conclusions – but more a new mythology seeking structure within the hard structures of science. The upshot is nihilism – the belief that life is pointless, that human values are worthless, and that there exists no objective basis for truth. This dogma has by and large been swallowed hook, line and sinker by the better part of today's sophisticated postmodern elite who have, as a consequence, had their lives eviscerated of meaning and purpose. In their place lies the gaping "hole in the soul," a void screaming to be filled and into which we pour all manner of madness and longing only to find ourselves foiled time and again, for the things of time cannot quench the thirst for that which lies beyond it. The practical consequences of such a hopeless endeavor are widespread and alarming and taken in conjunction with the rampant narcissism of our time are fraying the seams of society in the extreme. So Andrew's brief point about nihilism was no small philosophical matter.

Having made that point he turned his attention to a German woman with rust colored hair and piercing eyes. In a rather dejected tone she said, "I had this unbelievable experience nearly two years ago without paying attention to consciousness. It just happened by itself."

"Yes," Andrew acknowledged, *"that's a spontaneous experience of consciousness."*

"And now I try to give attention to it and…nothing. Why is it so difficult to come to the same point?"

"Well, first of all, you have to forget about what happened in the past. If you have a powerful, spontaneous experience of consciousness – which is not an object – and it becomes a memory, that which was not an object but an actual experience becomes an object in the form of memory. So what you remember is not the thing itself. It's not what actually happened. Therefore what you need to do is forget about it."

"So I totally have to forget about it and start to work hard?"

"Well, I don't know about working hard or not working hard, but you want to do what I'm asking you to do. And you're not going to be able to do what I'm asking you to do unless you can forget about that event because, while it obviously got you here, it has now become an obstacle."

"Okay."

"You see, ultimately we all have to get to the point where no matter what kind of profound, explosive experiences we've had in the past, we let go of them and continue to let go of them until finally we get to the point where we're always letting go. That's the idea: to be free – capital F-R-E-E. To be free means to be free from all experience, including spiritual experience. That means you're always letting go of everything. You're not bringing anything with you. Otherwise a potentially liberating experience becomes like a ball and chain.

"Again, to be free doesn't mean having a particular experience. Having experiences of depth and intensity is important because they give confidence in a higher and deeper dimension of reality. But an experience is not freedom. Freedom is when you're free from experience. No particular experience is freedom and when you're free from experience, that's when you're FREE. So what you need to do now is have the courage to let go of the experience."

"Okay."

"The point is that you're not going to be able to do what I'm asking you to do if you hold whatever experience you want to re-create in your mind. As long as you do that you'll be distracted by the memory. The memory is an object in the form of thought. But the experience of consciousness cannot be captured by thought. So when you realize that then you release the attachment to thought and memory. You just drop it and that's the door to freedom. So I want you to pay attention to consciousness, to the subject, without wanting anything in particular to happen."

"Okay."

This dialogue came to me like a hand reaching down a dark well. I realized I had been doing precisely the same thing that had been hamstringing this woman. Not only had I assumed the 'already knowing' position, I'd been fortifying that position with a wall of memory. I had been trying, through a combination of opening and summoning the long dead past, to force an experience into being. Having heard Andrew pin down this hopeless conundrum I was determined to drop the misguided endeavor.

"I wanted to ask," an elderly Israeli woman asked, "if for a secular person, a non-believer, consciousness is a substitute for religion?"

Andrew considered this for a moment, and then said, *"Well, I would say yes, except that I don't like the word 'substitute.'"*

"So what other word you would use?"

"I don't know," he laughed, *"but the answer is yes."* Then, after mulling it over, he clarified his position. *"What I said is that for individuals who are at a global-centric level of development and are awakening to this 'universal human,' the discovery of consciousness replaces the role that traditional religion played for individuals at lower levels of development."*

"So a religious person believes that if something terrible should happen to them God will be there to take care of them. So for a secular person like myself, in a similar way, I will have consciousness to fall into if something terrible should happen?"

"If you're lucky," Andrew laughed before quickly continuing in a more serious tone. *"So the answer to your question is 'yes,' but that would be the perspective of a very realized person."*

The woman went on. "But if an earthquake happens, I'm like a leaf in the wind."

"But is your consciousness a leaf in the wind?"

She said nothing.

"Remember, what we're saying here is that consciousness itself transcends time. When you pay attention to the experience of consciousness and you become aware of this knowing that I've been speaking about and you realize that there's an absolute dimension to the knowing, there's the recognition of that which is immortal, eternal, timeless and transcendent. So earthquakes don't affect consciousness."

"But they affect me."

"Sure they will. They'll affect part of you. They'll affect your body. They'll affect your mind. They'll affect your personal circumstances, without a doubt."

"So what's my knowing in that case?"

"Well, it has to do with what we were just speaking about. It's that you see that what's happening in the world is a part of the picture but it's not the whole picture."

"The good part?" she said, trying to make a joke.

"Well, whether or not it's a good part of the picture I think depends upon how enlightened you are and how positive your relationship to life is. Whether it's good or bad has to do with your fundamental motives, with what's driving you. For a lot of people it's not so good. Most people are victimized, angry, and frustrated. That's not so good. Again, it has to do with how enlightened their intention and motivation are in relationship to life.

"Remember, I said that the two fundamental spiritual questions are, 'Who am I?' and 'Why am I here?' Do we know who we are and why we're here? Is our life an expression of the deepest answers to those questions? If your life becomes an expression of the deepest answers to those questions then the answer would be that it's good.

"But the lives we lead are not necessarily good. Often they're awful. Many of us here – and we're some of the luckiest people that have ever, ever been born because of wealth and education and privilege – are very unhappy, morbid, self-centered people. That's not good! A person who's angry and victimized wastes the precious opportunity to make their life an expression of the discovery of consciousness. They become consumers, and not just of things, but also of experience itself. They just end up consuming and not giving anything back. That's not good.

"So it depends on how we look at it. But if we're going look at it in the way I was just describing – which is not a popular way to look at it, let me tell you, especially for spiritual teachers who are supposed to see everything in a golden aura of divine light – I think we'll find that for a lot of people it's not a pretty picture. Right?"

"Right," the woman agreed with a laugh. "It's a great loss of energy and life."

"Right. It's a loss of energy but from the perspective of consciousness the potential for something very positive occurring is lost."

"Yes, I see that," she said and then thanked Andrew for his reply.

Andrew surveyed the room. *"So we're almost finished,"* he said, and then, with something like amazement added, *"wow, it's only the second day. I can't even imagine what's going to happen in the next eight days?"*

He had a point. Only two days in and within such a seemingly inconsequential span of time we found ourselves exploring under the full sail of direct experience the deepest nature of that which lies beyond it. In fact, most of us were happily adrift in that undying current and had the retreat ended at that very moment, no doubt everyone would have gone home quite pleased.

After a pause Andrew wound things down. *"Okay, once again, what I want everybody to focus on has to do with giving attention to the nature of consciousness, cultivating a little bit of concentration and recognizing when we become aware of the non-relative or absolute dimension of consciousness itself. I want people to locate that in their own experience because, when you do, you find the ultimate source of freedom and confidence. And that really is everything. When we have access to that and are sure about it, our lives will be transformed. And I feel that meditation absent of that kind of knowledge and understanding is ultimately useless or just some kind of therapy. Okay, everybody?"*

"Okay," came as one voice from the group.

"So then I think we'll leave it at that for the moment," Andrew concluded and with that the session ended and we eased into meditation.

Not long afterwards, walking slowly but purposefully through the late afternoon sunlight, I redoubled my efforts to use every object arising in consciousness to turn awareness back on itself and into the subject as our captain had commanded. That inversion of my attention triggered a shift in perspective that revealed the essential nature of things. However, wandering in that placid light, I found, to my great consternation that as quickly as I was swept into the immovable foundation of Being I was, with equal speed, swept out of it by the relentless tide of thought. Turn upon turn I realized the depth of my addiction, not only to the tantalizing flutter of its movements but even more to the uncanny illusion of "somebodyness" that fixation on this movement spawns. I also noticed that behind the shimmering veneer of thought lie echoes of an unspoken fear – the fear of non-being, the terror of "nobodyness."

Thought not seen through, I realized in a flash, is the heroin of the soul and "I" not seen through is the strung out junkie. I wanted desperately to pull the needle from my arm and understood why Andrew had imposed upon us such a rigorous schedule of practice; we were in spiritual rehab. Habits of self-destruction have to be broken through self-control and the willful imposition of new, life-positive habits. It occurred to me then that if somebodyness were simply a habit then perhaps nobodyness could be cultivated as a kind of counter habit were enough intention devoted to that endeavor. I thought of Gerard secluded in six silent weeks of retreat, immersed in meditation and contemplation for fully eighteen hours a day. No breaks, no days off, no TV. Extreme circumstances call for extreme measures and from the perspective of consciousness it was evident that I, in thralldom to thought, indeed found myself buffeted, in existential terms, by the most extreme of circumstances.

Which brought me back once more to Andrew's insistence that if one truly knows one's deepest nature as being consciousness itself, then one's life would have to be radically transformed. Having already determined that my life, at least when measured against Andrew's exacting standards, had not been radically transformed, I began once more to brood on this point. It ultimately came down to this: it was the "already knowing" position and its augmentation through the gathering of little memories that stood in the way of authentic realization now. Much had gone into the making of this impediment, for I was a spiritually educated fellow. I had heard all the teachers, read all the books, had lots of experience and yet I was not free. Seeing through my ego simply did not seem sufficient to dislodge my self-sense from its bonds or free my soul from serving its whims and fancies. It occurred to me that perhaps all the accumulated knowledge had weighed upon my soul and contributed in no small part to the walls that now encased it. Perhaps what at first had been an ally had, through some inverted alchemy, become not merely a further source of bondage but a near impenetrable barrier against authentic transformation.

The phrase "Zen Mind, Beginner's Mind," echoed dimly from some dust pile of that accumulation. It must be this to which it pointed, I thought; to the ridding oneself of the burden of accumulated knowledge, an undertaking that while theoretically simple proved to be, in actual fact, a formidable challenge. How do we unlearn what we already know? We cannot, of course, and the question misses the entire point. We don't have to unlearn anything; we simply cannot use it as a starting point. What then should be the starting point? Consciousness itself, of course. Ultimately, simply following Andrew's instructions and bringing our attention ever back to the subject should easily solve the entire quandary. We are not that simple, however, and this brings up another point. Andrew had pointed out that most people of our ilk – the fortunate, wealthy, educated elite – are incredibly lazy and possibly even weak-minded, feeling entitled to everything, including spiritual experience and liberation, without the slightest exertion of effort. No doubt this accounts, at least in part, for the plethora of "there's no one to be and nothing to do" spiritual teachings currently bidding for the allegiance of the modern soul. I had only to look into my own experience. I had been following Andrew's instructions for the last two days and while not yet wearying of such exertions I could easily foresee that time when I would, much as I had in the past. The truth is that for most of us, if things don't work out quite well quite quickly, we usually drop whatever the endeavor is (unless, of course, it involves the possibility of large amounts of money or even a small amount of sex) with as much ease as we might an unsatisfactory cell phone service. After all, we, the world's lucky ones, have endless options spread before us, so "hey dude, why be so intense? Just relax, man, it's all good." And while I generally do not adhere to this succinctly stated ethic of much of the "alternative" spiritual world, I had to ask myself: how often did I forgo deep spiritual practice in favor of some more immediately gratifying activity? More often than I cared to admit.

The rationale behind the rigorous practice into which Andrew had plunged us rose in sharp relief against my own feeble spiritual condition. I began to see how much more sustained intensity I had to give. I understood that on the one hand all I had to do to attain perfect liberation was drop everything without hesitation right now, on the other hand the density of past conditioning ensured that the knee jerk reconstruction of myself in the resulting vastness was not far behind. Habit. It all came down to habit. And the miracle of intensive spiritual practice, properly understood, lay in its power to undo the momentum of untold aeons in the span of a single human life. This was the miracle of the spiritual life. This was why Andrew so often spoke of the difference between being serious and being deadly serious. This was the gap that I had yet to bridge.

My next opportunity to bridge that gap came with my arrival in the meditation hall where, with redoubled zeal, I plunged into practice once more. An hour later, at nearly ten, I watched with wonder as the sun withdrew reluctantly behind the western mountains. Its afterglow tinged the sky with feathered tufts of orange and yellow and blue that trailed behind it like luminous banners before receding ahead of the darkness of encroaching night. At ten forty-five, when the last chant ended, I ended the day with a short walk through the brisk evening air. I heard the curiously hollow piping of a thousand tiny frogs hidden in the darkness and it was to the sounds from their diminutive throats that I at long last fell into a deep sleep.

NOTES

1. For an excellent overview of levels of individual and cultural development see Jessica Roemischer's article on Spiral Dynamics in Issue #22 of What is Enlightenment? magazine entitled: The Never Ending Upward Quest available online at http://www.wie.org/j22/beck.asp. Also see Ken Wilber's A Brief History of Everything, (Boston: Shambhala Publications, 2000) and A Theory of Everything, (Boston: Shambhala Publications, 2001).

2. I have referred to Ken Wilber on a previous page and will do so in pages to come. Ken Wilber, often referred to as the "Einstein of consciousness," is the world's leading "integral" philosopher.

His philosophy integrates body, mind, soul, and Spirit with self, culture, and nature. Integral philosophy is rapidly becoming a powerful presence in fields as diverse as politics and spirituality, psychology and business, medicine, and art. Wilber has written sixteen books exploring different facets of human development and cultural evolution. His first book, The Spectrum of Consciousness (1977), written when he was only 23, became a seminal text in the emerging field of transpersonal psychology. His recent book, Boomeritis (2002), is a novelized critique of our postmodern culture and a call to move to a higher, more integral relationship to life. His most recent work, Integral Spirituality (2006), brings to bear the totality of his insights on the fields of religion and spirituality, including the emerging trends in post-metaphysical spirituality. He is a close intellectual associate and friend of Andrew's and the two have had an ongoing series of dialogues entitled Guru and the Pandit, on the pages of What is Enlightenment? magazine.

3. Samsara is a Sanskrit word loosely translated as the world of illusion.

4. This quote has been slightly edited. It's full version can be found at http://wilber.shambhala.com/html/misc/habermas/index.cfm/

5. More crudely put, the pre/trans fallacy simply indicates a lower level of development masquerading as a higher one. A common example involves Vietnam era protestors, a small number of whom were authentically motivated by a higher view of global peace and togetherness while the significantly larger number were motivated by the lesser developed motive of egoistic rage against authority. See Wilber's A Brief History of Everything and also his Integral Spirituality (Boston: Shambhala Publications, 2006) for a much more comprehensive and well-articulated description of this phenomenon.

Day 3

Digging Deeper

This morning I awoke to the hard wall of inertia. It had been a short night and sleep had been elusive. Through a sheer act of will I opened my eyes and stared into the darkness, its density pressing upon me and willing me back into the world of dreams. I realized that any lengthy consideration of this would send me back to sleep, so I threw off the covers, took a deep breath and hoisted myself out of bed. I stumbled into the central area of our small room to retrieve one of the five hot cups of tea that had been prepared by Mike from Germany, who seemed to have undertaken this chore as a kind of religious ritual.

Having struggled into my clothes, I padded down the cold stone stairs into the still plaza now slowly filling with others quietly making their way through the darkness to the meditation hall. This morning's chant hit me like an Odyssean ordeal; its rhythmic cadences caught hold of my consciousness, but rather than drawing me into the power of its words, those rhythms called to me like sirens from the isle of sleep. Only my head dropping suddenly alerted me to this seduction and with that my body and mind lurched upright once more. This swaying between two worlds formed the defining rhythm of the morning's chant. During meditation I fared little better. The coffee I'd bought from a nearby vending machine during the fifteen minute break did less to keep me awake than did the shouts of the maitre'd and the clanging of dishes from the kitchen below. That hour passed in a flow as slow and viscous as oozing amber. I felt like a fly destined to be trapped for eternity in its thickening, maddening midst. At long last, the hour came to its merciful, if procrastinated, close.

A few minutes later, heading for breakfast, I took in deep breaths of cool mountain air in hopes of clearing the fog from between my ears. It seemed to work. At least it seemed to have cleared the way for two strong cups of Spanish coffee to finish the job. Finally I felt awake. And not a moment too soon; the next teaching was about to begin. As had become my custom, I took a seat in the front row of chairs, quietly waiting for the room to fill and Andrew to arrive. I dared not close my eyes lest I should yet again drop into that chasm of sleep that had threatened to engulf me since the early morning. However, once Andrew took his seat upon the dais, all such concerns were dispelled as he led us once more into the still realm of meditation.

It was only when Andrew said, *"Good morning,"* about an hour later and announced, *"Okay, I'm ready to begin,"* that my eyes opened again. Andrew then continued along the same lines that he'd drawn on the previous day.

"Yesterday, we were talking about the absolute dimension of reality that we begin to directly perceive when we put our attention on the nature of consciousness" he said. *"Today I want as many of you as possible to respond to that."*

And with that we were underway.

He turned his attention to four teenagers who sat on the floor directly in front of him. I had been watching them myself the last couple of days with a mixture of curiosity and wonder. What would it be like, I thought, to be sixteen years old and be exposed to these teachings, taking in who knows what? How would it affect a young person's view going forward into the tempest of late adolescence and early adulthood? I could not help but wonder how my own development might have been altered had I heard these teachings at such a pivotal time. But with a little reflection I realized how hopelessly immature I had been at that age. Considering the two teenage boys of the foursome seated before Andrew, it struck me that they must have evolved to a level far above that; after all, they were here. That being said, they struck me less as a youthful Plato and Aristotle than as Tom Sawyer and Huck Finn – tall, gangly and handsome in the making, a gleam of mischief in their eyes, the cocky spring of youth in their step. They guffawed at silly things and I wondered how much of this penetrated their adolescent minds. I shuddered at the thought of ever having to live through that age again. Yet somehow, despite my own confused teenage years spent within the philosophically sanitized confines of a secular household, I'd developed sufficiently to be receptive to higher matters. No doubt then that these kids, with the benefit of such an extraordinary head start, could grow to embrace such matters with much greater depth and maturity at a much younger age than I had.

The two girls presented rather a different picture. I had often heard that girls mature faster than boys and it seemed that these girls were closer by a long shot to womanhood than the boys were to manhood. They were poised and elegant and, of the two, the lightly freckled blonde with her impish smile seemed the most astute, expressing a degree of depth not often found in people twice her age as she addressed Andrew.

"Okay," she began, "so yesterday you told me that if I wasn't finding the Ground of Being in consciousness then I needed to work harder."

"That's right," Andrew agreed.

"So after I left yesterday I definitely worked harder. I meditated a lot more and I actually did find this state of consciousness that you were talking about. And it was very interesting because once I found it, it was like it was always there and I just never saw it."

"Well, you have seen it, you just forgot about it," Andrew corrected her, referring perhaps to previous experiences she'd had under his guidance.

"This is true," she acknowledged and continued, "If I could describe the nature of it, I would say that it was a kind of intense ecstasy that was also calm. And I saw that in light of consciousness everything else in my life that I've been stressing over was sort of obsolete."

"Why is it obsolete?"

"Well, because it just seems like once you discover something as big and as powerful as consciousness nothing else really matters, or at least it doesn't deserve the attention I've been giving it."

"That's good. What else?"

"Well, a lot of the things people were saying I finally realized for myself. I just felt this enormous feeling that was always there and once I put my attention on it, it grew. Discovering this primary part of myself was very powerful. Once I located it, it was so obvious."

"Don't you think it's important that this therefore becomes the foundation or the fulcrum point of our lives?"

"Definitely! It seems like once you realize this then everything in life becomes manageable."

"Because?"

"Because from this perspective these things are secondary and therefore …"

"Everything is secondary."

"Yes, exactly."

"Why?"

"Because everything is relative."

"That's good. Was there anything else?"

"There was this inherent perfection."

"Inherent perfection – that's very good. Do you think there's anything else in life that's perfect?"

"Nope."

"That's very good. You didn't hesitate. You can tell how well somebody knows something in seeing how they hesitate before they answer. That's very good."

With that he turned his attention to the other teenage girl, a pretty brunette with a dark complexion who seemed somewhat shy and reserved.

"Okay. What about you, Emily? How's it going?"

"Well, I've been struggling with trying to experience consciousness but I haven't gotten very far. I tried all last night but I feel kind of trapped in my thoughts."

"You feel trapped in your thoughts? Is anybody keeping you trapped there?"

"No."

"So if there isn't anybody that's keeping you trapped or putting a gun to your head, then where does the notion of being trapped come from?"

"Myself."

"So if nobody's forcing you to be trapped, then how do you draw the conclusion that you are trapped? You do so because you find that your thoughts are very hard to get away from, right?"

"Yes."

"But what would happen if despite the fact that your thoughts are difficult to get away from you just didn't draw the conclusion that you were trapped."

"I'm not sure."

"What it would mean is that despite the fact that your experience wouldn't be the way you wanted it to be, which is quiet and peaceful, you wouldn't conclude that you were trapped. You see, the difference between being free and not being free, or being enlightened or not being enlightened doesn't necessarily have anything to do with the quality or the content of your experience. It could and it often does, but it doesn't necessarily have to. Being free or enlightened has to do with the conclusions that you're drawing about the experience that you're having. Do you understand what I'm saying?"

"I think so."

"So, a lot of people, if they have a little bit of difficulty meditating or giving attention to the nature of consciousness, give up and say 'I can't do it.' They draw the conclusion that they're trapped inside their minds, that there's nothing they can do about it and that that's the end of the story.

"On the other hand, someone who's really interested stays with it and they don't move. Now, not moving is not necessarily a physical posture, even though it could be. The physical posture of being still is a metaphor or a symbolic representation of a certain kind of stoicism or immovable position in relationship to the ultimate truth. So, for example, several people have said that the absolute nature of consciousness is always present. Right?"

"Right."

"So, once somebody knows that very deeply they can consciously take a position in that and say that this is what the truth is. They can put their stake in the ground, shall we say, and never move from that no matter what their experience is. Do you understand that?"

"I think so."

"So a lot of people will bear witness to the absolute nature of reality when they're in an ecstatic or blissful state but when they're not, they're not willing to bear witness or to stand for it. Right?"

"Right."

"So being free or enlightened doesn't necessarily have anything to do with the quality or the content of your experience; it has to do with the relationship that we have to our experience at all times.

"So if you're trying to give your attention to the nature of consciousness and you are doing it wholeheartedly, then you've already won. It doesn't matter what your experience is. Do you understand what I'm saying?"

"Yes."

"A lot of people don't know that. You see the only reason I can sit up here in front of everybody and teach this way is because this is how I practice. You don't need a quiet mind or a peaceful state of consciousness to be a free or liberated human being or to stand in the Truth. Of course, we'd all prefer that, but that's not necessarily how it's going to be, especially not if you're actually living in the world and trying to change things. If you're doing that it's going to be very difficult to maintain some kind of peaceful state because you're pushing up against enormous inertia and resistance and your life becomes like a battlefield.

"So what's more important is to know what the truth is and always be true to that. If knowing what the truth is is always dependent upon being able to experience some kind of peaceful state of mind, then we might as well give up now.

"This requires a much bigger hearted approach. The way many of us operate is if we're emotionally in touch with something, then it's real. But if we're not then it's not real. The problem with all that is that our emotional experience is not only not the deepest part of our experience, it's also the least trustworthy. Right?"

"Yes, that's right."

"So on these retreats I try to systematically help people look at their experience in a particular way that will reveal certain truths. And so, while I am encouraging people to pay attention to the emotional dimension of their experience – because it is an indicator of some of these bigger points – what I'm far more interested in is helping people to simply see what's true. What's really important is that which transcends the significance of the emotional dimension or whatever our experience happens to be at any given moment. Therefore, drawing the conclusion 'I am trapped' is about the worst thing you could possibly do.

"That's what most people do and the only reason most people are trapped is because they draw the conclusion that they're trapped. The thing is, you're not necessarily trapped at all. The way it works is when you look very deeply into your experience and you keep looking, especially if you're very steady and if there's a lot of passion and commitment, you will sooner or later see through the illusion. The veil is going to drop and you're going to see what's true. It might only last for a second, or it might be a lot longer, but sooner or later the illusion is going to fall away. What has to happen then is that we have to be willing to be true to what it is that we see, whether it's apparent to us in every moment or not. Does that make sense?"

"Yes."

"The point is that the nature of our internal subjective experience is not important. Let's say your mind is very, very busy. Does the fact that your mind is very busy deny the fact that there's an absolute or non-relative dimension to reality itself?"

"No."

"Well, there you go. So the only thing that's important is what's ultimately true, not how you happen to feel in relationship to your own chaotic mind in any given moment. Right?"

"Yes."

"Knowing that, to whatever degree, creates a position of objectivity and a kind of cool-headedness. So now, when you look into this question of whether you're actually trapped or not, I want you to see that it doesn't really matter what your mind is doing.

"Now, let's say, you do what I'm asking you to do and suddenly you find that you're experiencing depth, peace, joy, and maybe even ecstasy. All that's going to happen is that that's going to confirm what you already know. So the question is, how many times does anyone of us have to see what the Truth with a capital T is in order to be convinced?"

"Once?"

"Well, I wish it were that simple but apparently it's not. Yet ultimately that's the question: 'How many times is it going to take us to be convinced?' Because until we get to that point in our own development where we can prove we're convinced by the way we live and by the kind of choices that we make, we're going to be waffling around. We're going to be unpredictable and untrustworthy individuals because our relationship to our experience is going to be emotionally based. It will be relative and we're going to be changing our position all the time because there's not going to be any kind of profound rootedness or stability. Do you see the point?"

"Yes."

"So that's why, at the beginning of the retreat, we're looking into absolute nature of consciousness itself – because that is the starting point for everything else. Sound like a good idea?"

"Yes."

"Very good."

As I listened to Andrew I remembered a conversation I'd had with him three years earlier. At that time I was turning the last pages of the last chapter of my life with Peter and on retreat I had asked Andrew a similar question with respect to the fact that the actuality of my inner experience diverged greatly from the endlessly inspired ecstasy that I wished it would be, considering how much of my life had been devoted to spiritual practice.

"Haven't you had enough grace in your life?" Andrew had asked simply and directly. Not being sure what "enough" meant had left me unable to give an intelligent response. The sum of my understanding at that point told me that one should strengthen one's chakra system in order to incinerate negative psychic tension and facilitate the flow of spiritual energy, thus activating the power of kundalini. That primal, fierce energy, the reasoning continued, would then slowly burn away the ego and throughout this process the continued accretion of spiritual experience as well as the development of a psychic mechanism to support a powerful flow of

shakti would ultimately give so much weight and momentum to the process of transformation that what was revealed in the spiritual experience would at length become one's permanent state. Along with this would come a natural diminishing of the ego to little more than a speck of dust, an insubstantial mote drifting in unbroken beams of light, effortlessly contained and easily blown away. It took thirteen years and finally Peter's own example to prove that this simply wasn't the case. I discovered, with dismay, that one could be a spectacular vehicle for spiritual energy – transmitting oceans of shakti and raising kundalini like flaming geysers of oil – yet still remain in the grip of ego, slavishly acting from its basest impulses. Yet this question of how much grace would be sufficient to transform a human life – my life – I had never considered, for in the context of that teaching it simply could not have arisen.

Seeing my vacuous state Andrew asked – no, almost demanded, *"Do you know what the Truth is?"* That question struck me like a ray of light in an interrogation room. I felt squarely on the spot and knew that my answer would have to be informed by the whisper of conscience and thus bear the weight of consequence. "Yes," I said after the briefest hesitation, a ring of self-consciousness tightening about me like a noose. The answer was as audacious as the question. No one before had ever asked me that, for in actuality few would have been in a position to do so. But Andrew, having so profoundly realized the Truth himself, stood in just such a position. My "yes" forced me to eliminate the comfort of an ambiguous response. In such ambiguity one could forever pursue spiritual experience as an end while remaining endlessly ambivalent about the absolute obligation inherent in what one had realized. I realized that that was the position I had been taking for years. Therefore, that "yes" forced me to take a stand and imposed upon me a moral context that I intuitively felt take the measure and cut of a straight jacket for the ego. Thus the sensation of a noose.

"Then when are you going to stop seeking and get on with the process of purification?" Andrew had asked. That question should have ended with an exclamation point because that was precisely how it felt – an exclamation stamped squarely into my forehead. I had no answer. As I said, I had falsely assumed that the process of opening to spiritual energy and the awakening of the fire of kundalini *were* the process of purification. But at that moment, and in the face of Peter's living example, I realized that this was simply not the case. The impact of that realization was at once humiliating and liberating; humiliating because in some deep place in my heart I felt I should have known better; liberating because it freed me to re-evaluate everything and breathe new life into the possibility of transformation and liberation.

"Okay, let's keep going," Andrew said, returning me to the present moment.

A young American man spoke next. "So I'm very excited about the confidence that I've experienced."

"The confidence is based on what?"

"Being able to go to considerable depth by staying with the instructions that you've given us."

"You mean you're able to put your attention on the experience of consciousness?"

"Yes, right."

"Well, going to considerable depth is the whole point of coming on a retreat, isn't it?"

"Yes, absolutely."

"So, what have you found then?"

"What I've found is similar to what other people have been describing. It seems that the bigger my unfocused awareness becomes on the outside, the more depth or focus I'm able to put on the inside. For instance, if I look at the mountain and keep my attention on consciousness, I get this huge expansiveness, this vast unfocused awareness that's not moving."

"What about the absolute, non-relative nature that we've been speaking about? I want to know about that. Do I seem to be grinding this in a little bit? This is the one thing everybody misses and that they think they get."

"The qualities, is that what you're asking about?"

"Yes, but I just want to know about your sense of it. You know, religious or spiritual conviction has to do with the absolute nature of life and death and reality. Isn't that right?"

"Yes."

"Well, I want to know what's most important to you about this."

"Most important for me is that it seems to be the most real thing that I've ever experienced and that gives me enormous confidence. I now know that whether I'm in the presence of it or not doesn't matter because the fact is that it's real and it's unmoving and it's always there. It has enormous depth and purity and clarity and it's exciting because finally there's a reference point rather than being blown about in the wind."

"Okay, that's very good," Andrew said before turning his attention to an older, gray-haired Danish woman.

"I've been experiencing this absolute quality as a challenge to my seriousness," she said gravely.

"It should be," Andrew replied without a moment's hesitation.

"I keep asking myself 'What have I been doing? What have I been doing? I've known this for a long time and what have I been doing?' That's what it does to me. It's like a big slap in the face."

"Well, that's good. Do you mean conscience?"

"I suppose. I mean, if it's so easy to be in this absolute place why am I not manifesting from there all the time? Why am I just mucking about?"

"That's what a lot of people are doing in their lives, aren't they?"

"Yes, I think so."

"Right. So then if we want to start extrapolating in terms of what this absolute dimension means, we could say that what we need for our own human experience at the beginning of the 21st century is an absolute context. And the discovery of the absolute dimension of reality is supposed to create that kind of context for human life."

"So I have to ask myself, 'Why aren't I taking the trouble to live from this place?"

"Well, what's the answer?"

"Laziness. Nothing other than that."

"Well, either you don't really know the absolute or non-relative dimension of reality or you do. But if you really do, how could you deny it?"

"Well, that's what I'm looking at."

"So you just said it was laziness and I'm just wondering, could we really be lazy about something like that? Maybe we just don't know it. But then, how much do we have to know it?"

"Well, that's what I'm asking myself. How much do I have to know it to know it?"

"And what's the answer?"

"That I'm not serious enough."

"Okay, that's good. So what does it mean to be serious then?"

"To honor what I know and not make believe I don't know it."

"So would you say there are infinitely more people who know about this absolute dimension of experience than there are who honor it? Let's say if there are a thousand people who've tasted it and know about it; out of a thousand, how many do you think actually honor it?"

"I'd say there's probably one in a thousand."

"I think you're right. And that's still a high number. And why is that?"

"At this moment it just feels crazy not to honor it."

"Because?"

"Because it's making believe insanity is real. And it actually takes a lot of effort to constantly do that."

"Well, I agree with you. How old are you?"

"Fifty-four."

"So do you think that physical age has anything to do with the urge to become deadly serious about life?"

"Good point. Yes, I do."

"I don't think it does. I don't think age or even life threatening diseases necessarily make people get serious about life except in cases of rare individuals. Don't you find that people are just as crazy and foolish when they get to be fifty, sixty, and seventy as they were when they're eighteen, twenty and thirty? I think the answer is yes, but they just don't have as many excuses for being that crazy as they did when they were younger."

"Yes, that's right. The excuses run out."

"Well, they should if we lived in a sane, rational world. But that's not how we live. Another reason for this is because we all have so many options. 'I could do this or I could do that or I could also do the other thing.' Perhaps, if we didn't have so many options, we'd be better off."

"Yes, because there would be more focus."

"Because options create the illusion ... "

"... of verticalness."

"Right."

"But you're really going horizontal."

"Exactly right."

"You're just doing different colors."

"Does everybody understand what she meant by vertical versus horizontal?" he asked, turning to the rest of us.

Many people indicated that this distinction was rather lost on them.

"Well, vertical represents actual change or transformation right now. Horizontal means you're just going on doing different varieties of the same old thing forever. Most people don't really change, do they?"

"No, even when it's really boring not to change," she said.

"It's very boring not to change," Andrew acknowledged. *"I personally don't get it. I don't understand the resistance. I'll never get it. It's so foreign to how I feel and to the way life seems to me. I can see it and explain it, both philosophically and psycho-dynamically, but for me personally I simply can't get it at all. I can't relate to it with any part of myself.*

"When I was younger I really wanted liberation and I didn't have any doubt about it. The only difference between me and the other people that I knew at the time who said they wanted this was that I wanted it more than they did. I didn't have anything else going for me besides the fact that I really meant it and wanted to go all the way to the other side. I knew that I didn't want to live a so-called 'ordinary' life. I didn't know what an extraordinary or radically transformed life would look like but I had no doubt whatsoever that I did not want to live an ordinary life.

"And also, when I was getting to be twenty-seven, twenty-eight, thirty, I started to see how so many other people were selling out already and it scared me to death. It scared me to such a degree that I emotionally experienced terror when I thought about it."

"It is terrifying."

"It should be. For people who are interested in evolution in real time it should be. So what you're saying is true – that the discovery of the absolute dimension of reality should compel us to embrace a non-relative or extraordinary relationship to life."

"Because nothing else makes sense. That's why it's compelling."

"When you truly know the absolute or non-relative dimension of reality, then noth-ing else makes sense. That's absolutely right. Our experience of THAT is supposed to be a catalyst for radical transformation. It's not an end in itself."

"Right now I'm feeling it burning like a fire."

"Good. All right," he said, winding down the conversation.

He paused and scanned the room where many hands were raised. He called on a young Danish man with finely chiseled features and soft, blond hair.

"Hi," he began hesitantly. "Going from the relative to the subject or the absolute, I have to admit, sometimes scares the hell out of me."

"That's okay. Isn't it good to be scared sometimes?"

"Yes," he answered in a decidedly unconvinced tone and then went on, "this absolute dimension is really compelling and I want to go there, but there's this fear..."

"Well, that's good. Again, don't you think it's good to experience fear once in a while?"

"Yes, but ..." he stammered.

"Don't you think people who never let themselves experience fear aren't alive?"

"Yes."

"So the point is, you have bliss and ecstasy on one side and fear on the other because it's so big and because what you're seeing threatens the relative or ego perspective. It scares it to death. It threatens our desire for comfort, security, and predictability. It's supposed to scare us to death. It's supposed to blow up the very safe non-risk taking relationship to life that most of us live with."

"But is there a way to kind of not fight it?"

"Not fight what?"

"Well, if I'm at that place, it's like I'm really on the edge."

"Edge of what?"

"Total letting go."

"In a good way?"

"Yes, but the ego fights it. I really don't get it. When I start to think about what I'm doing ... wow, it's mind-blowing."

"But isn't that what you came here for? Didn't you want your mind to be blown? Didn't you want it to be too much? Didn't you want to get scared?"

The young man was wide-eyed with fright. "I guess I didn't ... I just wish that I could surrender."

"What do you mean you wish you could surrender?"

"That I didn't get scared."

"But it's good to get scared. That's what I've been saying – it's a very good thing! Most of us are so dull that it's very difficult scare us. With my own students I have to constantly keep thinking up new ways to frighten them."

Everyone laughed at that one, except, I noticed, many of Andrew's senior students as well as Andrew himself.

"It's not funny for me," he said in a deadly serious tone. *"It's because people get so dull that I have to think of new ways to wake them up. After a while I just give up because I don't want to have to do that anymore."*

I had on previous occasions heard Andrew lament how much he dislikes his role as a teacher insofar as it demands that he hold others *to their own stated intentions* when they are caught in the snares of ego and are willing to fight him with a vengeance. It was in the throes of such encounters that Andrew had lost many of his closest students – shot down like soldiers in the struggle for the human soul. I was reminded of Peter's statement, "I don't want to have relationships like that with people anymore," when I had asked him to push me harder upon my return from Bodhgaya nearly a decade earlier. And therein lay the major difference between the two: whereas Peter compromised with others precisely as he compromised with himself, Andrew confronts compromise and hesitation in those submitting to his guidance with the ruthless efficiency of one who cares only for the highest result – authentic evolutionary transformation and the liberation of the soul. Yet at the same time, as he is occasionally forced to remind us, he too is a human being and he has had to pay an outlandish price because of it.

"The thing is, the way that we live is so dull, safe and predictable," Andrew went on. *"So, to start with, if you're afraid of the absolute dimension that means you're actually alive. Most of us aren't afraid enough. Being afraid is a sign that you've touched the real thing. It's a little like the Old Testament perspective in which you're supposed to fear God. Does that make sense to you?"*

"Yes, it does, but I still wish I wasn't scared."

Laughter danced through the room though it was noticeably absent from the young man's face.

"You have to stop wishing that you weren't, because if you weren't then maybe you'd feel better, but so what? The thing is, everybody wants to feel better but feeling better doesn't help. I mean, if you're experiencing physical pain that's a different thing. But when we're talking about feeling badly in relation to this existential hole in one's soul it's not good to feel better. The only relief from having a hole in your soul is having that hole filled with this absolute or non-relative Truth. Anything other than that will just put us to sleep. Do you get my point?"

The young man nodded feebly.

"Comfort, pleasure, beautiful things, drugs, alcohol, sex – they'll all end up just putting us to sleep. And the other thing to consider is that we don't have an infinite amount of time to do this. So the fear is actually good. If you feel better it won't help and from an evolutionary point of view, which we haven't talked much about yet, it could actually hold you back. But if you keep wanting to go further and pushing the edge then fear is always going to be there, especially if you're pushing into that which is new.

"If you play it safe, then you can avoid fear, but then you'll be sleepwalking. So anybody who wants to live at the leading edge has to be willing to bear a certain amount of fear. Because if you're pushing the edge and everyone else is very far behind you it means you're going to be pretty much alone. And who's to say you're not crazy? You

could either be crazy, deranged and self-deluded, or you could be saner than anyone else. So there's a lot to be afraid of. But at least it's not dull and predictable."

The laughter that washed through the room left Andrew unmoved.

"You guys can laugh all you want but the truth is that most people I know choose to live a life that is predictable, safe and secure and nothing radical and new can happen in an environment like that. I'm sorry. It's not because I say so, that's just the way it works. It's scientific. Has everybody heard about inertia? It's the inertia within us that has no interest in that which is new. What I'm speaking about is serious. I'm not speaking in metaphors here."

Andrew paused for a few moments before continuing. *"Okay, I want to hear more about people's experience of the absolute dimension of their experience."*

As Andrew spoke of the cadaverous quality of the "ordinary life," a tide of spiritual urgency washed over me with a renewed sense of sacred obligation. I thrust up my hand and Andrew promptly called on me.

"Okay, Mike."

"You've been asking us to look at the absolute dimension of our own experience," I said, feeling, as I always did when speaking to Andrew, that any eloquence I might have had abruptly left me, "and my experience is that it's not only the deepest nature of my own self but also the source of it."

"Yes."

"And, at the same time it's also the source of everything. So when you just used the word 'God' I thought that it was the perfect word. In terms of my own experience all these qualities we've been talking about are present, but I also experience a demand to embody a lot of those qualities in myself. So my sense of the absolute nature of it also includes a sense of sacred obligation."

"Well, that's why traditionally when people see this thing that we're speaking about they often fall to their knees. Right?"

"Right."

"Okay, that's very good," he said with an air of satisfaction. *"Now we're back on track."* He then turned his attention to the man behind me, a gray headed American man whose eyes, lit with the fire of realization, belied his sad face, which was as soft and layered as melting wax.

"Andrew," he began in a sober tone, "what I can see is this: there's a certain freshness and consistency whenever I focus on consciousness. There's a sameness that has always been there and is still there whenever I focus on it."

"That's right."

"And yet when I first heard you speaking of the absolute it frightened the personal part of me."

"Well, it's as I just said, it is frightening and it's good to be afraid. It's good to have fear of the absolute. At least I'm saying it's good. You heard it from me. A lot of people won't back me up on this but I don't care. It's very good and healthy to have fear of the

absolute. If you don't something is wrong with you. You are morally undeveloped or corrupt. Most of us are morally undeveloped or corrupt anyway."

These words shot out with penetrating impact and precision and cutting through layers of elegant pretense they struck at the core of an unsavory actuality. It was just this sort of ruthless stripping away of the carefully constructed artifice of the persona that had given Andrew his controversial reputation and blown a storm of animosity in his direction from the otherwise soothing winds of the prevailing alternative spiritual culture. To the separate sense of self, the realization of the Absolute represents the ultimate threat, its glory and majesty crushing the felt sense of personal significance. If deeply felt, such revelation forces one to one's knees in submission, a posture disliked by post-modern spiritual sensibilities and the accompanying worship of the individual. In that view such submission is considered antiquated and repressive. In its place it is either explicitly or implicitly held that that Principle should bow before us, making itself ever available to soothe our pain, heal our wounds and meet our needs which, upon but the briefest examination, will be seen to exist in a queue stretching endlessly to an invisible horizon. Yet there is something inherently perverse, even sacrilegious, about this and it was precisely that to which Andrew was pointing.[1]

"*So,*" he continued. "*Don't you feel alive if you feel fear of the absolute?*"

"Yes, no question about that."

"*Good.*"

"I guess the real question is how long do I have to see this purity and sameness and freshness, this no relationship to …"

"*Anything.*"

"Yes, including to my personal story …"

"*Right.*"

"How often do I have to see this before I can just really admit to myself that it is absolute?"

"*Exactly. That's what bearing witness is. And what would be the hesitation to admitting that?*"

"It's not what I'm used to. It's like a full-hearted commitment to what I know is sacred and yet it frightens me. That's all I can say."

"*That's very good. And why does it frighten you?*"

"Because it would mean that I have to stand up. But on a personal level I'm used to being passive or hiding."

"*Right.*"

"So to make that declaration, not to anybody else but just to myself, is like coming out of the woodwork."

"*Yes, exactly. That's very good. 'Coming out of the woodwork.' I like that. As we said, consciousness is seeking for itself.*"

The man seemed to have nothing further to say and Andrew moved on to a middle aged, brown-haired Israeli woman whom I had met at previous retreats.

"Okay, Ruthie."

"I want to speak about my experience of the absolute. First of all it comes and goes. It doesn't stay. But when it comes it feels like it's a direct encounter without any mediations."

"Right."

"And the way I encounter it is not with my usual senses, the intellect or the emotions; not with anything I know about. It's something that is inside me but beyond me at the same time. And there's a feeling that's a kind of knowledge that exists before everything, a part of which is in me. So there's something inside that responds to this experience as if some part of the absolute is also inside me. So it's like the same meeting the same. Does that make any sense?"

"Yes, that's very good. Earlier we were talking about this absolute or non-relative dimension transcending this world. Yesterday I was saying 'in the world but not of the world.' This absolute dimension is in the world but also transcends the world. It's not limited by it in any way. Is that what you were saying?"

"Yes. So the way I encounter it is with something in me that is also absolute."

"That's right. Because we were saying that when you give your attention to the subject you become aware of consciousness observing itself. And, as that begins to happen, your attention begins to fall away from all the objects that arise in consciousness. And then consciousness itself becomes the object of its own attention. And the degree to which that happens is the degree to which you experience this awareness that transcends anything that's relative."

"But because it's very subtle it doesn't stay with me. I can see it and then it goes away."

"Okay, so then you had the direct experience and now what we're speaking about has to do with the emotionally based conviction that comes from being very clear and sure about that."

"I have the conviction."

"So remember that when I first met you you were very cynical about these things. And you liked being cynical. You felt it gave you power. Now you're a lot more convinced about it yourself and infinitely less cynical than you were."

"Yes."

"So, the degree to which we become convinced about this absolute or non-relative dimension and our cynicism diminishes, is the degree to which we actually transform in the deepest way as a human being."

"Yes, I see that."

"So as the existential doubt or alienation from oneself and from life is reduced or goes away altogether this hole in the soul begins to be filled. So what I'm saying is that the transformation we're speaking about has to do with the destruction of cynicism,

which is actually existential doubt. That's what changes a human being at a soul level."

"You're right, but yet this hole in the soul is what brought me to you."

"Yes, I know. Of course that's true also. But the point is that you could say that someone who truly has conviction about this dimension is a completely different kind of person simply because of the fact that the existential doubt is gone. That's what changes everything."

"Yes, I can really bear witness to this."

"Right. I know. That's good. So being willing to bear witness becomes the fulcrum point or the foundation for a kind of absolute shift in a way that nothing else, and I mean nothing else, can.

"Now, that doesn't mean that from the point of this shift there isn't still development and growth, but it means that the ground from which the growth and development is occurring is a completely different ground. And that's the whole point. That's why I'm spending so much time on this — because it's the soil in which everything else is planted."

"It's seeing the world from the perspective of the One."

"Exactly right, that's very good. Everything is seen from the perspective of the One or the absolute wholeness."

"Thank you."

"Okay," Andrew said enthusiastically, the energy in the room now definitely quickening and deepening. He then pointed to an older German man with a spade shaped goatee. *"Hello,"* he said.

"To me it's omnipresent," the man spoke urgently. "It's everywhere, not limited to anything, beyond duality and beyond me."

"You have a direct sense of this?"

"Yes."

"Does that give you conviction?"

"Yes." The urgency in his voice grew.

"As we've been saying, radical transformation is dependent upon the conviction in the absolute or non-relative dimension of reality. It can't be based on anything personal or relative."

"No, it's like beyond the self."

"Yes, exactly."

"It feels like the self is just this little, funny thing in a way."

"On a good day," Andrew laughed. *"Right. That's very good."*

"That's it."

"So you have that conviction?"

"Yes."

"Conviction means it's something that you're sure about."

"Yes, I am sure about it."

"That's the point. You see the conviction has to be there. For instance, the early Christians were killed for their conviction because they also realized this absolute dimension. They were willing to die rather than renounce it. That's conviction."

"I'm willing to take that risk," the man responded passionately. It was clear that he was ecstatic and speaking to Andrew from the depths of the ocean of Being. "I'm experiencing consciousness both as being detached and very passive, as well as being really, really happy and wanting to scream instead of just keeping it inside. My heart is beating wildly and my whole body is full of energy moving up and down. I don't know why my body is reacting like this but I can't help it."

"That's good," Andrew said calmly adding, *"and it doesn't matter."* He never played much to dramatic expressions of ecstasy, I suppose for fear that such histrionics could quickly spin out of control and also because he did not view ecstatic explosions as the main event of the spiritual life. Thus he did not wish to draw excessive attention to their displays. After seeing that the man was okay he quickly moved on to the next person, a tall American woman with sandy hair and the erudite look of a scholar.

"I realize," she began in a studied tone, "that my normal sense of self is defined by what's going on around me, by where I am, by what I'm getting from other people, and by my sense of who I am. In other words, it's always changing. On the other hand, this absolute subject doesn't move no matter where I am. It's always the same and yet it has the all qualities that others have spoken about, like, for instance, this weightyness. The thing is that it's not looking for anything from outside itself. It's never grasping."

"It's not seeking affirmation."

"That's right."

"But it's self-seeking and when it finds itself that's it's own self-affirmation."

"Yes."

"And so when consciousness finds itself what does it want to do? Just endlessly delight in itself – forever, right?"

"Yes, definitely. And I don't want to move away from it."

"Forever, endlessly preoccupied in self-delight."

"Right."

"Whereas we're very concerned with all kinds of other things that never give us the same joy or conviction."

"Yes, that's right. And, it's all so dependent on what's going on around me without ever having a central core to it. The small sense of self, my ego, is very shaky."

"Ego is very shaky?" Andrew responded in a dubious tone. *"Actually, I think it's very strong. It's a very strong enemy and its power to resist higher potentials is enormous. Generally speaking, who's winning the battle in the world?"*

The answer to that question seemed evident to everyone.

"It's a strong and worthy foe. It's not shaky and weak. It's very tough. It's like Darth Vader – tough, strong, and very powerful."

"Yeah, I guess that's right," the woman responded in a tone of "on second thought ..." and lapsed into reflection.

Andrew searched the room for the teaching's last question. He turned his attention to one corner of the room where all those in need of translation were huddled. As it turned out, this section was entirely French, prompting a quip from Andrew.

"So yes, the lady in the back there, in the French ghetto."

A cascade of laughter erupted from every corner of the room including the enclave of French Anglophobes.[2]

"So I wanted to speak about fear," the French woman began (via translation). "I had an experience in meditation where I felt all the cells in my body going faster and faster and ripples of energy surging through me. I suddenly got very scared and then the experience stopped. Afterwards, however, I realized that I was immortal and then the fear wasn't a problem anymore."

"That's great, because this absolute or non-relative dimension of the self that we were pointing to is immortal, right?"

"Yes, but we forget that."

"That's right. That's why we come on retreats like this – to remember."

"Yesterday you asked about how we experience the knowing. Can I talk about that?"

"Yes."

"Relative knowledge is conditioned by our culture and by our education. But the knowledge that transcends our culture and our intellect is non-conditioned. Therefore I can trust it."

"That's right."

"The same knowledge is accessible to everyone and is independent from the observer."

"From the ego, yes. That's very good. Okay? Is that it?"

"Yes. Thank you."

Andrew remained silent for a few moments. It had been a long session and it seemed to have come to a natural close. Then he finished, upbeat and enthusiastic.

"So I want to say that you're all doing very well. After all, we're sitting here for three hours each time we meet, when people usually have trouble sitting still for more than a few minutes. Now I want you to continue looking into everything that we've been speaking about until it becomes absolutely clear. Does everybody understand why?"

We all responded affirmatively.

To drive the point home, Andrew added, *"Because, as I was explaining earlier, this absolute shift only occurs on a foundation of conviction about the absolute or non-relative dimension of life. So if this is not clear you need to make more effort. Therefore, between now and five I want everyone to continue to practice locating the absolute dimension of reality itself. Then, after I'm satisfied that most people, from their own experience, have a clear sense of what I'm speaking about, we will talk about what taking an absolute position in relationship to life is all about."*

With that Andrew ended and we descended once more into the realm of meditation. Only as I rose to leave some minutes later did I realize how exhausted I was.

Despite that exhaustion, I reflected in astonishment that with the passage of just two and a half days it appeared that many of those present were experiencing directly the deepest nature of their own self – something many spend years pursuing. Moreover, that sacred dimension into which Andrew had shepherded us was so palpably present that if anyone wished to explore its nature more deeply all that was required was that they pay attention to the actuality of their own experience right there and then. That dimension had emerged as a living reality among and between us, extinguishing perfectly the need to intellectualize it or seek it in the web of memory. It was simply there – self-evident, ever-present and awesome in its depth. Slowly, as the long, liquid moments drifted by, I emerged from those depths and rose to leave.

The ten-minute walk to the meditation hall was growing more familiar. As I passed through the tourist throng, I kept my eyes cast slightly downward and ahead, studiously avoiding eye contact with others. I recalled how such visual liaisons ranked high in ego's repertoire of strategies in its quest for affirmation. Wishing to delve further into the absolute dimension of reality, I stayed within myself. Yet doing so I became aware of a new sensation, one triggered by the scents and sinuous lines of the many beautiful women who wandered along the streets. Their eyes were easy to avoid; everything else wasn't. Lust, that insistent interloper along the line of my higher desires, had come calling; it wanted me to come out and play. That I did not wish to come out and play carried little weight; it never did. The stroke of the sun's warm rays playing on my skin combined with the numbing fatigue that had returned in full measure worked together to enhance my susceptibility to the charms of this uninvited guest. I looked ahead in my mind's eye and knew precisely what would happen were I to succumb to these feelings. My attention, presently spanning the vastness of Being, would collapse from that expanse into one very narrow and intense sliver of my experience.

This was the crux of one of the most persistent spiritual conundrums to have dogged the human pursuit of higher consciousness. It appears that in many important ways sexuality and spirituality are two realms sharply at odds with one another. Of course, in my most sober moments I realize that this contradiction cannot be fundamental. After all, that primal desire is none other than the insistent engine of life and the throbbing roar of creation, without which spiritual aspiration would not even exist. Clearly both sexual desire and spiritual longing are manifestations of the creative pulse of the cosmos, a symbiosis of the biological and the noetic that form an integrated whole. Yet to date no permanent peaceful co-existence or authentically harmonious integration of their power seems to have emerged.

Repression, we have found painfully, is not the answer; it stunts the flower of desire and drives its roots lustfully burrowing inward to invade the realms of the psyche, poisoning the mind and the aspirations of the soul. Its inverse twin, indulgence, fares no better. The committed pursuit of this strategy is akin to feeding a hungry demon that grows to consume its erstwhile master, sucking away his vital life and leaving behind only a husk, for lust is a hunger that grows in degrees proportionate to its fulfillment. Balance, that theoretical mediation provided by the "sacrament" of marriage, is by and large a fiction, which can best be evidenced by an epidemic of adultery and the flourishing of an erotic economy, offering in its array of goods and services a dish to suit the darkest tastes and predilections.[3]

All this flashed before me in an instant as I walked along those suddenly sultry lanes in the steaming air of Montserrat. I then considered my own relationship to the deep aquifers of lust that pooled beneath the surface of myself. What became immediately apparent was that giving them attention instantly produced an intense narrowing of focus and a ravenous seeking for self. As such they stood in direct contradiction to the expansive selflessness of higher consciousness. And while part of this is purely biological it is simultaneously and intimately connected to the many different motives of ego, both to pleasure and to power. I, like most men, have never been fully a master of this part of myself, having long felt victimized by its, often unwelcome, intrusion into the course of my affairs. I have found it to be an enormous distraction from those things that I truly care about and have been fundamentally confused about its proper role in human life. I am not alone in this. In fact, that no one seems to have sorted all this out in satisfactory fashion is self-evident and definitely hasn't helped. Even Peter, powerful and profoundly awake as he was, gave evidence of his delusion by suggesting to his female students that sex with him would "get them to God faster."

So how was I, an ordinary guy, to deal with all this volatility? On the spot, I decided to do two things: first, to keep my attention on the subject, as Andrew had directed, resisting the temptation to follow fantasies to their ultimately unfulfilling conclusions, and second, to simply bear it. Both strategies were relatively new to me. My normal response to the array of sexual fantasies spun out by the aroused and agitated mind was to indulge in them and ultimately seek relief. This would inevitably and conveniently avoid the need for the second of the two strategies, namely bearing it.

The importance of bearing one's own experience, no matter what it was, without being enslaved by the compulsion to act on it, was a hallmark of Andrew's teaching and, at least as I understood it, a major indicator of just how free one actually was. This places considerable pressure on the individual, pressure that I'd previously been unwilling to shoulder for any significant stretch of time, particularly in this arena. I decided that it was time to issue myself a challenge. Therefore, I resisted the temptation to ogle the girls and made my way with steady strides directly toward meditation. Perhaps, I thought, once I sat and in the absence of such abundant snares for the senses, my libido would desist in its persistence and leave me the hell alone.

Would that it were so. The fact was that no sooner did I close my eyes than a positive torrent of erotic imagery rose in seductive swirls from the cauldron of my mind. It coiled lasciviously in the field of my inner vision. Bear it, I told myself. Let everything be as it is; do not indulge; do not struggle against – simply bear it. This was precisely what I did. What I then found was that often, though not always, simply in renouncing the urge to indulge the theatrics of my mind, its color would soon lose its intensity until it withered to transparency, revealing once more the colorless vastness of Being. However, when I strayed from my intention not only would I get swept up once more in that salacious rush, but the simple act of attention fueled my smoldering desire. For the next hour I navigated between these two extremes.

Steering through that pitching sea was not a vain pursuit, however, for I gained fresh insight and understanding. First, it came to me that we are both angels and demons, a curious concoction of higher and lower, driven by divergent desires to the dense realms of matter and the lofty aeries of the soul. Now, this ragged shred of recognition, I admit, is hardly new. However, it also struck me why this might be so. As human beings we are the ongoing and presumably as yet unfinished product of a process of biological evolution that is billions of years old. In the course of that unfolding the emergence of spiritual aspiration is so recent as to barely warrant notice. Yet there it is, a few thousand years old, consciousness recognizing itself as spirit and aspiring not just to free itself from matter but to fulfill itself in it. And to fulfill that aspiration it must shake off the heavy weight of our ancient origins, our gross materiality and a core biology bequeathed to us from life's infancy. Our center of gravity inarguably lies in that lower nature imprinted within the deep structures of our brain like echoes from our ancient past. It is within those grooves, time worn and deep, that our animal nature lurks and our wild lusts are fired by the burning carnality of life. And it is from those grooves that we must rise, without repression or indulgence, to reach for a higher possibility. We must bear it, as with all of our experience, until we stand in possession of sufficient objectivity to make those choices most closely aligned with our highest aspirations. We must bear it, as Andrew has said, until we come to that point where we can do the right thing for the right reasons even when it doesn't feel like the right thing to do. Of course, I knew all this already but once again, there is knowing it and there is knowing it. Bearing it, I realized, was the only evolutionary response to this predicament; bearing it so that we might bear up spirit and give birth to the next step in human evolution.

I rose from meditation an hour later, spending the rest of the afternoon predictably and uneventfully: lunch, a brief, cold shower and a thirty minute power nap during which I plummeted to the bottom of the deepest sleep. That short dive into nothingness provided a quite unexpected and welcome reinvigoration and by five o'clock I was seated once more in the teaching hall, now alert and ready for further exploration. As the room filled with people, strong gusts of afternoon wind blew up from the canyon behind us, sweeping out the last dregs of heat and carrying in, on angry little squalls, the peal of church bells in the distance. Their unabated vigor combined with our anticipation to stretch the atmosphere about us tighter than a drumskin.

Andrew led us into meditation before taking up the thread again. Then he began by asking people to continue sharing their felt experience of the absolute dimension of the self. A middle aged and attractive French brunette, whom I'd seen at previous retreats, was the first to respond.

"Sometimes this feeling of consciousness is just like a little music in the back of my experience and sometimes it's a deeper immersion, but I never encountered the frightening and terrible aspect that some people have been referring to."

"I don't believe you," Andrew shot back immediately, *"because I've known you for over ten years and I know that you're scared to death of absolute nature of life."*

"Yes, that's true,"

"Okay, so you have encountered it?"

"Yes, but I've never met it directly. I've been scared to death of that."

"So you've been running away from it, you mean?"

"Yes, definitely."

"So you do know about it."

"Yes, I suppose so."

"Okay. So then the question is, 'have we recognized the absolute nature of reality that becomes apparent to us as we begin to contemplate the nature of consciousness?'" He looked at her meaningfully.

"Yes, that's right," she said.

"Then, if we have indeed recognized it we want to admit, 'yes I have.' Does that seem reasonable?"

"Yes."

"Because this is what we have to establish first. Then we want to find out if that recognition has anything to do with the life we live or if it's just some kind of experience we had up on the mountain after which we go back and live as if we didn't know about it."

"Yes, of course. That makes sense."

"So your answer is 'yes you do know about it.'" This was both a question and a statement.

"Yes."

"And you've known about it for a long time, haven't you?"

"Yes and I think that it does give me a fundamental trust in life."

"That's good, but the question is how much. You see, the way it works is this: the absolute dimension can give one a fundamental trust in life but that's not all there is to it. We also have our humanity and there's going to be a play between those two dimensions of our experience. So once we've recognized that the deepest truth is non-relative and that that dimension of the self is attracted to its own non-relative nature, then the awakened or spiritual life would be the authentic and sincere attempt to bridge the gap between the relative and non-relative dimensions of the self. And the degree to which we actually do that is the degree to which we are going to live an extraordinary life. That's the whole point of all this. Do you understand?"

"Yes, I do. Thank you."

With that Andrew turned his attention to young, slender American man with dark hair, dark eyes and an intense expression on his face.

"Hi," he began. "The experience I've been having with the absolute dimension of consciousness is that I feel like butter melting on a frying pan. I feel like I'm becoming one with everything and I'm not here anymore, although something is here."

"Well, the phrase 'I'm not here' means that the ego is gone but 'you' haven't gone anywhere. You see, we usually think that we are the ego or the separate 'I' sense, but when that sense dissolves you find out that you haven't gone anywhere. In fact, you find that you've been there all the time; it's just that you thought you were the ego but suddenly, in an expanded state of consciousness, you realize that you actually never were."

"Yes, that's right. I think what's so important for me is to realize that this is really real and not just my imagination."

"Well, what happens is that everybody who has this kind of experience to whatever degree or intensity will always say that the experience of this non-relative or absolute dimension is always more real than anything else they've ever experienced. So maybe everybody who has this experience is completely crazy, but nonetheless, everybody who has this experience uniformly says the same thing.

"Unfortunately they usually don't live as if they know it. So the whole point, at least in this teaching, is to get around to living up to the very thing that we're experiencing here. That's what gives the experience weight and meaning. In an evolutionary or developmental context that becomes the meter. So the self is endlessly seeking itself and when it discovers itself the stakes go up because you realize that who you really are is not relative but absolute.

"Yet at the same time you also see that there's a body, there's a mind and there's a personality that's part of a world process that, in turn, is in a fourteen billion year

process of evolutionary development and becoming. So then, as the process recognizes its own absolute nature, it finds itself, in its best and freest moments, compelled toward the Self, or its own absolute nature, right?"

"That's right."

"So that puts an enormous amount of creative, evolutionary tension – which is always only positive – on the developmental part of the self, specifically our own humanity, to reach toward its own non-relative or absolute nature. Do you understand?"

"Yes, definitely."

"Good. So the question is: to what degree are we willing to do that? In other words, is bearing witness to Spirit going to be just through some kind of declaration in a moment of passionate recognition or are we actually endeavoring to manifest this ultimately non-relative Truth as our very own self in our very own life?"

He nodded in quiet agreement.

"So when someone does that they make the inner, subjective revelation manifest in the world as themselves. That, at least the way I define it, is what living a spiritual life is all about. In fact, unless we're actually endeavoring to do that sincerely we're not really living a spiritual life at all, we're just playing games."

"That's what I'd like to avoid – playing games."

"Well, you've come to the right place." Andrew said.

Dave, a short, fiftyish American from North Carolina with glasses and a mustache spoke next. I'd seen him on previous retreats and knew that he'd been involved in a fairly serious way with Andrew for some time.

"This is about the knowing aspect of consciousness," he began.

"Okay."

"I've been looking for the doorway into it since you mentioned it and hadn't found it until this afternoon. When it appeared to me I kind of inquired and pushed into it and then suddenly it's almost as if a trap door just opened up. There was just this emptiness and I realized this was an experience of not knowing anything but at the same time that knowing was self-validating."

"That's what happens every time. It's always, always, endlessly self-validating again and again and again. It's always the same and it's ever new and it's always the same and ever new and it can be very subtle or it can be very intense, but it's always the same and it's ever new, right?" Andrew often liked to repeat important points for emphasis.

"Right."

"That's why we need to have these experiences. We need to have them until we say 'yes.'"

"Right."

"So don't be casual about that."

"No, I'm not. What I've noticed is that the longer I stay with that consciousness, the more I see and feel my values changing. I can actually feel the hierarchical nature of it."

"*Right. And remember that the point we want to establish is the absolute nature of reality itself because when we establish that we also realize that this is the 'omega point'* or the prime attractor of the Self to the self.*"

"Right."

"*Of course, the ego or the separate self sense is in complete denial of this 'omega point' or absolute attractor. It literally pretends that it doesn't exist.*"

"Right."

Andrew switched to a slightly mocking tone, playing the part of the cynical ego. "*'Say what? Absolute what? Oh, I wouldn't know anything about that. I don't believe in God. I've outgrown that mythical idea. I'm free.' You get the point?*"

"Definitely."

"*So when this omega point or prime attractor enters into the picture, at least theoretically it's supposed to begin to change everything. Yet ego and our secular, materialistic culture totally deny any kind of absolute principle. They're afraid of absolutes. They look at fascism and communism and say, 'Hey, we don't want to go down that road again.' So there are many good reasons to fear and deny absolutes. But right now what we're trying to do here together is move beyond secular materialism and come up with a new metaphysical, post post-modern version of an absolute principle so we can 'get religion' all over again, but in a new way.*"

"I can see why any real transformation would have to be informed by that."

"*Okay. That's very good.*"

Andrew now turned his attention to a broadly built Irish man.

"*Okay, Finn,*" he said.

"You've been asking us to look into the qualities of consciousness," he began, "and the main one that I've discovered is this fullness."

"*Okay.*"

"I've been sitting with that for two days and it's overwhelming. I just can't contain it."

"*That's great,*" Andrew said, pausing for a moment before going on. "*Fullness means everything – plus. It's like the glass is overflowing.*"

"Yes. But at the same time it's with emptiness. It's emptiness and fullness together."

"*Exactly right.*"

"And you asked yesterday, 'what do we know when we connect with the knowing?'"

"*That's right.*"

"So at first I looked for some thing that I could describe intellectually, but it's not a thing."

"*Right. But what you're knowing is that everything is already complete and full right now and in that knowing there's bliss and joy and freedom. It's that that fills the hole in the soul and erases this existential doubt.*"

"It points to wholeness and healing."

"That's the whole point."

"And then there's a demand to uphold and maintain that truth."

"That's right. That's what we're trying to establish here – the absolute nature of consciousness – and I want as many people as possible and as are willing to, if that is their experience, to claim it." He paused pensively for a moment and then added, *"If they have the guts to do it."*

A thoughtful silence came over the group and Andrew took the next question, this one from a thin, Israeli brunette with fine features and a look of intensity.

In a quiet and reflective tone she said, "It's a very interesting journey you're taking me on and it's stirring up a lot of things for me."

"Well, that's good," Andrew said.

"I feel like I'm a part of everything and everything is a part of me and I also feel that everything is part of the Absolute which itself is love without limits."

"Love without limits?"

"Yes."

"That's a lotta love right there," he jested.

"Yup."

"I think I need a little of that."

Everyone laughed and the woman added, "I bet you have it already."

"Only on a good day," he shot back.

"Well, that's where I am right now," the woman concluded, "and I'm looking forward to seeing where it's going to take me."

"Usually it takes you farther than you want to go," Andrew said in a cautionary tone, *"Usually it takes people too far."*

"Oh, really?" she said, a little surprised.

"Yeah," Andrew said wistfully. *"That's okay though, if that's where you want to go. Remember, I said earlier that when I was younger I knew I wanted to go 'all the way.' So wherever all the way is, it's a metaphor for beyond what you can imagine or think you can handle or bear. It's not a final destination. It just means over the line of what you can control or feel comfortable with."*

Silence reclaimed the room until a young, handsome Dutchman asked the next question.

"I had an experience yesterday of my mind quieting down and my consciousness becoming more intense," he began quietly, "and today I find myself trying to go back to that place but I find myself very much struggling, although I'm willing ..."

"You don't want to go back. You never want to go back," Andrew interjected. He then summarized and reiterated his discussion of why any effort to recreate an experience from the past is doomed to failure, actually hijacking the liberating potential of an experience and turning it to the service of bondage. He then prompted the young man onward.

"I often find myself nervous and frustrated. Is there anything you can say about that?"

"That's too bad," Andrew retorted with mock sympathy.

"That's okay, don't worry about it," the young man replied courteously as if to let Andrew off the hook, which elicited a wave of chuckles from the room. "I also wanted to ask you about …"

"How old are you?" Andrew interrupted.

"Twenty-eight."

"Okay, so you still have time not to end up like a lot of the old timers here." More laughter, though this time less spirited as many of the older folks felt the truthful bite of those words. *"But you're going to have to change your approach otherwise you're going to end up just like them."*

"Yeah, I know," he said, "I do realize that I have to change."

"Good, we all do. We all have to work very hard to free ourselves of our morbid conditioning. Do you understand that?"

"As with a lot of the things that you say, I feel like I understand intellectually but not experientially and therefore it doesn't really manifest in my experience of life."

"Well, like I said, you've got to start somewhere. In other words, if what I'm saying makes sense to you then that should give you confidence. One thing that's very satisfying about this teaching is that it's logically consistent. So for someone who appreciates intellectual consistency this teaching is very satisfying because there aren't any holes in the thinking. You don't have to take any leaps of faith because I don't say things that don't make sense. That should give you confidence."

"Sure."

"Now, you're twenty-eight years old and you seem to be a handsome young man …"

"Thank you," he said politely, spurring another bout of laughter.

"… and you obviously could afford to come here. So that makes you a very lucky person, relatively speaking, right?"

"Yeah."

"Do you feel lucky?"

"At times, when I'm not feeling like a victim, I do feel very lucky."

"Right, but I got the sense that you don't really feel very lucky."

"No, most of the time I don't."

"But that's what the problem is because objectively you are."

"Yes, I see that."

"So in order to become a rational human being we have to make an effort, even if it's only intellectually, to begin to force ourselves, if need be, to deal with the objective facts of our own circumstances. So, for example, if objectively we are quite lucky then we have to force ourselves to act like it even if we don't want to. Don't you think that's a good idea?"

"Yeah."

"I'm sure a lot of therapists wouldn't agree with me but I don't really care. See, how I save myself from going crazy when I have a hard time, which is quite often, is that I look at the facts. I force myself to be objective even if emotionally I don't feel objective or even feel like I want to be objective. That's what saves me."

"Isn't that just relative?'

"Well, who cares? We all have to work with what we've got, right? So, if what we have is the ability to think clearly – because, trust me, a lot of people aren't capable of thinking clearly – then you have to use that capacity to save yourself. That means if you feel one way – frustrated, victimized or whatever – but you have the intellectual capacity to see that this is completely crazy and inappropriate, then you have to save yourself from your own weakness and emotional self-indulgence. If you are objectively lucky you have to act like it. We all do.

"So if you're feeling all those things, then you simply disregard them. This is the shortcut to sanity. But only the most mature human beings can do that. Most people can intellectually recognize what I'm saying but they don't have the willpower or conviction to do it. Of course, if we could all do that, boy, the world would change very quickly."

After a quick drink of water Andrew said, *"So I'm going to get back to this theme later,"* then he paused for a few moments.

"All right," Andrew said in a tone indicating that he was bringing the day's teachings to a close, *"so I want everyone to continue with this until tomorrow morning. Once again, as I've been saying, there's a connection between how profound one's recognition of the absolute dimension of consciousness and reality has been and our potential for transformation. So there's no end to how important this is.*

"Of course, ultimately we want to get to the point where the absolute ground would become the context for human engagement. That's what the new post-modern religious context would ultimately have to be based on, rather than a set of beliefs or myths. It would be based on a direct, non-conceptual, experiential recognition that the individuals who made up the collective would bear witness to. Then, based on this recognition, they would create a new context for human engagement together. So becoming very clear about the non-relative or absolute ground of reality itself is the very foundation for this kind of radical transformation which is why I'm spending so much time on it."

And with that the teaching concluded.

After Andrew's departure the evening routine began - first dinner, then an hour of chanting and finally bed. Moving to the rhythm of that routine, I was once more beset by what had been gathering like bad weather throughout the day, fatigue and insistent sexual tension. This triggered wistful thoughts of Rose and a ludicrous longing to return home. Odd, I thought, how – as the old saying goes – the grass is always greener on the other side. I had been passionately anticipating the arrival of this retreat for months and now, after the passage of a mere three days and with complete disregard for the growing depth and intimacy of our gathering, I was, in the worst and most childish part of myself, aching for a rapid change of venue. Of course, I recognized this as nothing more than the ego's filing of a formal complaint against the squeeze it was experiencing in this highly charged atmosphere. In that spiritual compression its cavalier attitude towards matters of absolute significance simply could not be entertained and it was beginning to moan a sentimental siren song about the long lost wonders of home. How perfectly absurd. I remembered Andrew's exhortation to consider our circumstances objectively and in so doing see through the sham and disregard the whole affair. It was this reflection that drifted as the last definable object through my waning awareness before consciousness dissolved into sleep.

NOTES

1. Interestingly, in his new book, *Integral Spirituality*, Ken Wilber speaks about the three faces of God – God as self, God as other and God as process – pointing out that in the prevailing post-modern spiritual culture, the first and third faces of God are abundantly present while the second is entirely absent. To be more specific, God as self refers to the traditional enlightenment realization, "I am That." God as process refers to the entire process of creation being either God himself or one with God. God as other, however, is that God before whose glory we have to bow down in submission, uttering the eternal proclamation of surrender, "Thy will be done, not mine." And, as Andrew has pointed out, it is only the second face of God that threatens the ego with extinction, which, of course, accounts for its absence in the current spiritual landscape.

2. As it turned out, the translator was a friend of mine and she told me after the retreat that just about everyone in the "French ghetto" spoke passable English but, seemingly as a matter of French cultural pride, refused to do so. Thus this incident provides further proof that cultural stereotypes are often not as far from the mark as political correctness would have us believe.

3. Of course there are Tantric practices that have come to us from the East and that have been eagerly adopted by the East-Meets-West spiritual culture. They promise to bridge this gap by using sexuality as a pathway to the divine. Now, while at their origins or in their purest forms these may indeed have been legitimate vehicles for transformation, I am thoroughly unconvinced of their efficacy in the matter of authentic spiritual liberation when in the hands of individuals seeking to have the best of both worlds strictly for their own ends. I need only look to Peter for the real time results of such practices: confusion and bondage. Moreover, as Andrew has pointed out with respect to such practices, they are suspect from the beginning because from the beginning they posit that two are required to realize the One, a fundamentally dualistic and thus questionable proposition.

4. Omega point is a phrase coined by the French Jesuit Pierre Teilhard de Chardin (1881-1955) to describe the ultimate level of complexity consciousness, considered by him the aim towards which consciousness evolves. Rather than divinity being found "in the heavens" he held that evolution was a process converging toward a "final unity", identical with the end of time and with

God himself. According to Teilhard, the planet is in a process of transformation, metamorphosing from the biosphere into the noosphere. In its original conception, the noosphere is the third phase of Earth's development, preceded by the geosphere (inanimate matter) and the biosphere (biological life). In this thinking, just as the emergence of life dramatically altered the geosphere, the emergence of human cognition fundamentally transforms the biosphere. The word as used by Teilhard also refers to transhuman consciousness emerging from the interactions of human minds as part of a cosmic movement toward the Omega Point.

Day 4

An Absolute Perspective
on Life, Death and Beyond

This morning I rose with a sense of destiny. Not in any grand sense, mind you, only that it contained something of the inevitable, a bit of the preordained and a large measure of the unavoidable. It seemed I had been fated to find myself at odds with the fickle world of sleep. While that realm had eluded me the previous night for reasons of its own, this night I had been forcibly driven from it by the loud assault of my roommate's snoring. Anatole had good reason for his involuntary savagery of sleep; it seemed that seventeen hours daily of concentrated spiritual practice were not enough to cool his ardor for transcendence and thus he felt compelled to add to this regimen supplemental meditation after most others had retreated to sleep. It was not until two or three in the morning that he fell like a stone into a coma and it was from those impenetrable depths that his snoring began like a sawmill in full swing. I, on the other hand, lay awake throughout the night, cut by the ragged edges of sound. Neither earplugs nor the soothing strains of music from my iPod were able to blunt the assault. My irritation was not assuaged by my respect for his endurance, its stark fact taunting me and making me wonder whether I might not be the spiritual equivalent of a ninety-eight pound weakling. Thus I brooded until the alarm mercifully delivered me from the delirium of night and slammed the door on any further hope of sleep.

Addled, I stumbled through the morning ritual: a quick splash of water on my face, the well-intentioned cup of tea and a slow, determined walk to meditation through the darkness. Chanting, sunrise and breakfast completed the routine.

Surprisingly, the day unfolded vastly better than such a night might have led one to expect. This was due in perfect totality to the morning's teaching. Upon its conclusion I was thunderstruck, able only to hold the following thought: no matter the quantity and variety of spiritual experience one has had, no matter how long one's involvement with these or any other teachings, there is simply nothing, and I mean nothing, that can prepare one for a retreat with Andrew Cohen. To put it differently, while so far the power of the retreat had pushed aside layer upon layer of pretense and artifice, I still had the sense of being the undisputed captain of my own experience. That is, I still stood upon a scaffolding of self, constructed of the timbers of accumulated knowledge and fastened, one upon the other, with the resilient twine of memory. And though the transmission had begun to penetrate the empty spaces of that structure, the structure itself still held. This morning, however, that structure was obliterated as I was relieved of the captaincy of self and swept off my feet into the hurricane of the Absolute. And despite the enormity of that event, I never saw it coming.

It would be difficult to overstate the impact of this teaching. It left me so utterly emptied of any personal reference point that I was unable to write in my journal for two days and had, with whatever cognitive function was left to me, determined to abandon the endeavor altogether. All I knew was that in the face of the immensity into which I had been plunged there was simply nothing to say. Words seemed an absurd, even vulgar smear of concepts on the unstained face of the Obvious. Only slowly over subsequent days that sense recede like a reluctant tide; only then was I able to continue with this narrative.

The morning itself had started much as the others – with Andrew doggedly pursuing the line of inquiry that he had set before us on the preceding days. The first question of the day came from a thin Danish woman in her fifties who wished, in most enthusiastic tones, to relate her experience of the Absolute to questions of ecology and practical issues of living. Andrew, apparently sensing she had wandered further afield than his directive had demanded, responded by returning her to the core of the inquiry, insisting that we all stay riveted there.

"So far in the retreat we've just been speaking about this absolute dimension and haven't really entered into the arena of time yet," he pointed out. *"We're just putting our attention on consciousness and seeing what its nature is."*

"Well, that quality of radical unity or oneness just lifted up for me in a powerful way."

"I understand that and many people have been describing this fundamental recognition that the nature of consciousness is the very unity you're speaking about. But still, we're just talking about consciousness itself. We're not talking about people yet and we haven't talked much about the world. The point is that I've asked people to look into the nature of the experience of consciousness itself and as we begin to put our attention there we become aware of the intimations of the timeless dimension. And this is not simply an idea. If anybody really puts their attention on consciousness and begins to explore its nature directly, they're going to begin to have an intuitive sense of that dimension of the self that is primordial that exists before time.

"And because it's primordial it feels so profound. Some people who awaken to this timeless dimension simply refer to it as 'eternity consciousness.'

"But we have to be very careful when we want to apply the experience or intimations of the absolute or timeless dimension of consciousness to the manifest dimension of time in which the world exists, in which there's you and me, because that adds an infinite amount of complexity that we have to deal with. We can't just mash together

the eternal, primordial, timeless dimension of consciousness and the manifest dimension of time without being very careful. Otherwise we're going to probably make some fundamental errors – and a lot of people do that. So we have to go into it very slowly and carefully. That's why I just wanted to establish the basic foundation by going back to before the beginning, before time began.

"'Before time began' always exists right now. When people speak about 'the eternal present' or 'the eternal now' they're talking about the eternal moment beyond time. That eternal moment is always an absolute fact of existence because that's what's supporting everything always, no matter what's happening. Do you understand?"

"Yes, I do."

"Okay. But the thing is, you can't really apply it because there's no relationship between the primordial eternal moment beyond time and the world of time, space and becoming. This is very important to understand."

"Right."

"So the question is, 'what do we do with it then?' He said this rather pointedly.

"Am I supposed to answer that?" the woman asked, as more laughter ensued.

"Well, you could try."

"I think I'm beginning to see that this is the bedrock, the foundation ..."

"That's the point! The foundation of everything. It's very important to become clear about that. It's the foundation of the answer to the question, 'who am I?' Right?"

"Right."

"But it's not a complete answer because if you're only THAT then the world doesn't exist. Some people who have had a profound realization of this unmanifest or timeless dimension of primordial consciousness say 'that's who I am and nothing else is real.' They actually deny the reality of the existence of the world and the universe. They say it's not real, it's just an illusion.' Have you heard that kind of thing before?"

" Yeah," she said.

That "yeah" echoed within myself. And no doubt that echo rang equally within others, for who among us who'd trodden "the path" for some time had not encountered such teachings? I myself had experienced them at several points. First, in my studies of the sacred teachings of the East; second, in my studies with Peter whose teaching, despite its largely life positive position, still held the manifest world to be, in its ultimate essence, a dream; and third, in my own direct experience of the Absolute. From that perspective, where consciousness itself has drowned all notions of independent selfhood and where the unqualified unity of life pulses with such radiance, the world does seem like an insignificant vapor stirring on the glassy surface of Being. As such, its dismissal is rationalized with ease and not without reason.

Yet despite its seeming veracity this view had never fully won me over and I, though having held it, had never done so with a full grip of total commitment. Something had seemed incomplete about it, partial in some essential way that I was able to sense with a vague interior instinct but unable to articulate with clear lines of reason. While not being at odds with the conclusion that that dimension of reality is the most fundamental aspect of existence, to extend that conclusion to suggest that the world is unreal and without significance always rang hollow to me. It seemed a denial of the obvious: that the Creative Principle had, through considerable toil, birthed the manifest dimension of reality and that our bodies, complex and built for action as they are, are here to do something – something of significance. In other words, there is purpose and meaning in manifest existence far beyond the mere transcendence of the process. Otherwise why bother? If life was simply a dream whose ultimate purpose lay in the awakening to one's own Source, enabling a final return to "before the beginning," (that primordial no-place from which all emerged), why bother with the whole event to start with? Such an exercise seems little more than cosmic self-flagellation and stands in denial of the wholeness and perfect positivity that lies at the center of it all. Holding such a view leads to odd and even dangerous conclusions regarding the nature of life and our role in it.[1] At the very least, the dismissal of the world as an insubstantial vapor is a simple 'out' for the weak of mind, an evasive strategy to avoid the inherent complexity of life and its demand that we engage it; at worst it is a straight and slippery road to the moral netherworld of nihilism.

"And when they say the world doesn't exist," Andrew continued, "the people around them all smile and laugh like it's a big inside joke that nobody else knows – the joke being that 'the world isn't real.' Now, obviously they must be a little crazy, don't you think?"

"Oh yeah. That's why I've been drawn to your teaching, because …"

"My teaching is for people who want to be sane but who also want to go all the way beyond the outer limits. It demands a much more rigorous engagement with reality than outdated conclusions that simply don't make sense anymore."

When it became apparent that the young woman had understood and had nothing further to ask, Andrew moved on, this time to a short, heavy set American man near the back of the room.

He said, "I've been looking very intently into what you've been asking us to do and yesterday during the meditation in the afternoon I had a powerful experience which made this absolute position a thousand times clearer and infinitely more real than anything I've ever experienced before."

"What kind of experience was that?"

"Basically I just found myself disappearing. First, I found my bodily and sensory experiences dissolving and drifting further and further away but somehow I was still there. Then these experiences of bliss and joy started to overcome me and going through my body and it just went on and on. This experience was very, very deep and ultimately I had to acknowledge this absolute position."

"Which is what?"

"That THAT is who I am always and I have to acknowledge that foundation. That has to be the position I'm always coming from even when I'm not aware of the presence of that foundation. I mean," his voice trembled and he choked up, "that experience that I had yesterday – well, my daily experience is very, very different than that." He paused and took a deep breath to steady himself. "Yet I knew that I was seeing something real and that from now on I had to always acknowledge, live by, and manifest THAT."

"Okay good. So what does that position mean?"

"It means a lot of things."

"Such as?"

"Well, one of the things that seemed most pronounced was a sense of letting go and having no fear of life because I realized that whatever is happening in the world is still not me. I mean, I'm participating in the world but the foundation of who I am isn't. So being at peace and at ease while at the same time participating two hundred percent in life without fear for myself."

"That's right. You see, to put it in plain English, what this experience of conscious-ness basically tells us is that everything is always okay, no matter what happens or how it seems. That's the non-metaphysical interpretation. From the perspective of the part of you and the part of me that has never been born, everything is always already okay. From the part of you and the part of me that has never been born, that's never entered into the process, there's no relationship – there's only ONE. Right? I AM THAT, there's only THAT and nothing else is real."

"Yeah."

"So the question is: do we get the message? Because if that's true then that should give us a tremendous amount of confidence in the Self, right?"

"Yes, yes. That's right. It also seemed like the whole time I had to keep letting go of everything and that everything was still okay."

"Well, from the perspective of consciousness itself you don't have to let go of anything because nothing exists yet that you need to let go of. If, on the other hand, one is view-ing consciousness from the perspective of the ego then there's this sense of having to let go so one can become one with consciousness."

"Right, right."

"But from the perspective of consciousness itself you don't have to let go of anything because you're not bound to anything and you're already free. Get the idea?"

"Yup."

"You see, depending on which way you look at it the whole picture changes. Once again, the fundamental message of the experience of consciousness is that everything's okay – always has been, always will be. Right?"

"Yes."

"So from the perspective of consciousness there's the recognition of absolute, non-rela-tive fullness. Fullness means everything is overflowing, beyond complete and inherently

perfect. Most people who've been speaking have been saying that that's the nature of this timeless, primordial consciousness."

"Yes, that's right."

"So the question is: do we know that? In terms of the evolution and development of the individual, does the individual know that from the deepest part of themselves, which is the Self Absolute, everything's already okay? And if we think we do know it, how deeply do we know it?"

"Yes. Right."

"So the purpose of this exercise all boils down to what we're speaking about now. Do we know that from the perspective of consciousness everything's already okay? Hmm?"

"It's a big question because …"

Andrew laughed heartily. *"Yes, it's a big question! It's a serious question. It's one that we should waste no time in dealing with and that's what I'm asking everybody. Do you know that from the deepest part of yourself everything is always already okay?"*

"Yes. I mean, it felt like a dying experience."

"Well, that's what it's like! Dying to what?"

"Dying to myself. It was like I was blasted away."

"Dying to the self means what, though?"

"To the ego."

"Which is convinced that what?"

"That something's wrong."

"There you go."

Once again the air was filled with laughter, as if all of this was so self-evident as to barely warrant mention. Andrew, however, wasn't laughing.

"Take this seriously," he admonished everyone. *"Unless you have freed yourself from this fundamental conviction that something's terribly, terribly wrong, don't laugh. You see, it's easy to be smug. But don't be smug unless you've actually dealt with this and can prove by your own example that that position has been destroyed in you at least to the point that that's the example that you're giving to the world. Otherwise don't laugh yet. It's too easy.*

"The thing is, we're not playing games here. You see, if you do it my way you can take care of the whole problem. But the way I'm presenting all this is the hardest way to deal with it and engage every aspect of yourself. So you have to be deadly serious about it. To be honest, most people, I have found, don't have the kind of spiritual strength to do this. So it's funny, but it's not funny, okay?"

"Yes," said the man who had initiated this dialogue; the room was quiet.

Turning back to him, Andrew asked, *"so, what does the ego feel like?"*

"Anxiety."

"Exactly. It's that nagging voice that endlessly insists, 'there's something wrong; I have a problem. There's something wrong; I have a problem. Oh, hi. How are you? There's something wrong; I have a problem. Do you want to be my friend? There's

something wrong; I have a problem.' That's always what's in the background before anything else. And the thing is that most of us can't give that up.

"So that's the ego's position, but when we discover the absolute nature of consciousness then there's the shocking recognition: 'oh, that's not who I am. I'm consciousness itself. I've never been born, I'm never going to die and I never had any problems.' That's the exhilarating thrill in the recognition of the absolute dimension of consciousness itself. It's freedom from the ego's position that, 'I have a problem and something's wrong,' That's why there's so much joy and pleasure in the experience of consciousness. It's a profound relief from the ego's heavy baggage."

"Yes, yes. It was extremely joyous." The man was radiating that joy.

"It always is. But that's what the nature of consciousness is. Consciousness is unbounded. It doesn't have any relationships. It's not involved. So meditation on the absolute nature of consciousness is a withdrawal from our identification with time, with the body, with the personality, and with the mind. And when we withdraw from all that we withdraw from identification with the whole process that's the ego's dominant locus of identification. So as we disengage from the whole process and we begin to identify more with consciousness itself, the burden of that identification falls away. Hmm?"

"Yes, yes."

"And as the burden of that identification falls away then there's lightness of being, which is what Enlightenment is. So what we're doing now is the practice of withdrawal from the ego, which is the false subject, and the result is the emergence of enlightened consciousness."

"Right."

"So when we identify with the subject, which is consciousness itself, we experience freedom for two reasons. First, all of the fears and desires of the ego that we're endlessly troubled with disappear and second, we also fall out of time – which is often experienced as a heavy weight – and that's the ultimate relief."

"Oh, yes," the man agreed.

"So meditation on the absolute nature of consciousness is the ultimate withdrawal from the whole process. When we withdraw from the process we stop identifying with any objects in consciousness and then we begin to become cognizant of the nature of consciousness itself. Consciousness is free. Consciousness is full. Consciousness is eternal."

"Right. It seemed like that recognition was very important even if it was only for a few seconds or minutes."

"Oh yes, it's very important because if you want to know who you are and why you're here then you have to go back to before the beginning and start with consciousness itself because, as we've been saying, consciousness is primary."

"Yes. That's right."

"So the individual, who doesn't know beyond any doubt that consciousness is primary, is convinced that they have a problem and that there's something wrong. And

then they're not convinced that consciousness is primary even if they may have tasted it or glimpsed that fact on occasion.

"But being convinced beyond any doubt radically transforms the personality's relationship to the human experience. It means there would have to be lightness of being in the personality rather than the heaviness that's usually just underneath the surface. And the lightness of being in such a person is not superficial. It's deep and it can't be faked."

"Yes, I understand."

"So that's the whole point of the exercise."

"Yes, I see that now."

"Good. Thank you." With that Andrew was ready to move on to the next person. After looking around, he singled out an older English woman who asked what seemed at first a rather odd question: *"I've misused this space at different times in my life and I want to know if we are going to talk about that later?"*

"Are we going to talk about how you've misused 'this space?'" Andrew asked, adding rather tongue in cheek, *"Do we have to?"*

"I mean, how one can misuse this withdrawal."

"Okay, yes. What about that?"

"Well, I think it's dangerous that when something in the manifest world is too much for me, perhaps because I don't have the skills or the maturity to deal with it, that I can come here, to consciousness, to hide out."

"Well, it could be like that but it doesn't have to be."

"That's not what I want to do with my life."

"Good for you," Andrew said seriously. *"There's a lot of misunderstanding about this. So, as I said earlier, a lot of people don't really understand the experiences that they're having, which is why understanding is even more important in many ways than the experiences themselves.*

"So what you're saying is that escape is not liberation and that's absolutely right. But the test of whether it's a game or not has to do with how profoundly we've been liberated at a deep existential level from the ego's conviction that something's terribly wrong. That's the acid test. And the degree to which that conviction has been burned away will be the degree to which the personality is going to be changed in a way that's not superficial."

"So then one's attention is on transformation not just on experience?"

"That's exactly right. So if someone says, 'I've experienced that there's no time, that the world's an illusion and that I was never born,' then you might ask them, 'so have you given up your neurosis yet?'"

"Yes, I get it."

"Neuroses are always a manifestation of what I call unnatural behavior – responses that somehow don't make sense in the big picture. You see, in a natural state the fundamental existential tension based on the conviction that there's something wrong, is gone.

"Natural means at ease, awake and alert. So if you're not deeply relaxed and deeply at ease within yourself you're not going to be able to be that attentive because a lot of your attention is going to be distracted by your own fear, your own pain and your own anxiety. So if we're distracted by preoccupation with personal pain or fear or anxiety then we're not going to be authentically at ease and we're not going to be able to see clearly. Of course it can get worse than that. The more virulent and nasty expressions of ego are more about competitiveness, ambition, and always needing to see yourself as being better than other people. Right?"

"Right, yes."

"That's the really unwholesome manifestation of ego that nobody talks about. When people talk about the problems that have to do with ego in a spiritual context they usually talk about 'woundedness.'" He laughed that last word out with an edge of sarcasm. *"It's all the position of the victim: the pain, anxiety, insecurity, unworthiness. That's fine and most people can identify with some variation of those. But what they don't talk about are the uglier expressions of ego, which are what create the real problems in the world. You see, the ego is power driven and always wants to be superior.*

"But if someone is convinced that everything's already okay, then these unwholesome ego attributes of ambition and competitiveness and this compulsive need to be superior diminish dramatically or disappear altogether. The whole infatuation with self-image dissolves and there's just the natural state of being profoundly at ease and intensely alert.

"But the narcissist is not at ease and alert. He is infatuated with his own separate image. Narcissists don't have authentic relationships with other human beings because, for a narcissist, other people are just objects with which to adorn themselves.

"So the ego is ugly and very, very problematic for all these reasons. And all of these tendencies exist in most of us in one way or another. So the ego is not just a victim, it's also…"

"A perpetrator."

"Right. It's a Hitler and a Mussolini all wrapped up in one. But what I'm saying is that, if we're deeply convinced about the ultimate nature of consciousness itself, all of these tendencies are going to burn away. Whether they burn away absolutely and completely is another issue, but they have to burn away enough so that the personality becomes transformed in nothing less than a dramatic and radical way. Does that make sense?"

"Yes, very much so."

"And it can get very complicated. You can also have an individual with very strong narcissistic tendencies, with a very deeply compulsive need to see the self as being separate and superior, who has a very profound experience of the absolute dimension of consciousness. What does that dimension tell us? There's only One. I AM THAT. So the narcissist interprets that as "I am the only one" who's better than everyone else.

"So the direct recognition and experience of the non-relative or absolute dimension of consciousness itself can be used by the ego or our narcissistic tendencies for its own

interests also. So the experience of consciousness is extraordinary and wonderful and nothing could ever be more uplifting. But the devil's in the details and life is complex. So we have to be very careful with all this."

"Yes, that's right."

"So therefore I interpret or translate emptiness – pure subjectivity or consciousness in which there are no things – in relationship to transformation as 'transparency.' In other words, if someone has had a deep experience of emptiness at the level of consciousness that means that the personality should then become an expression of transparency. Transparency means there's nothing hidden. It means what you see is what you get. There are no dark shadows."

"So there's no neurosis?"

"Basically, yes. It would mean that. Or if there were it would be benign. So transparency means 'what you see, is what you get.' It's the end of schizophrenia or any kind of fundamental duality in the self. Do you understand?"

"Yes."

"Most of us are quite schizophrenic. As I've been saying for years, often when you get to know people well, you find out that they're little crazy or sometimes even very crazy. Often they're not how they appear, right?"

"Yes."

"So if someone's transparent, then fundamentally there are no hidden dark corners or shadows. Now, that's a tall order."

"By transparent do you also mean congruent?"

"Well, yes. The transparency I'm talking about would have to mean that there would be a fundamental integrity in the self. If there isn't a fundamental integrity in the self then you have these weird, off-balance dimensions of the self that are out of alignment in ways that are dangerous and create all kinds of big problems in real life.

"Now, you should know that the lack of integrity in the self creates more and more problems depending upon how much you actually want to evolve, develop, or become whole in real life. People who have no authentic interest in actually changing or evolving more or less fit in with everyone else unless they're really extreme. That's because most people are crazy and because of that we kind of tolerate and even expect each other to be relatively crazy, don't we?"

"Yes, we do."

"So I think the idea is not to be crazy just like everybody else. I think the whole aspiration should be to become an unusually sane individual in an insane world and that's not an easy thing to do. Hmm?"

"No, it's not."

"So once again, I believe that the potential of the experience of the absolute nature of consciousness is to make all these things possible. The experience of the ecstasy, the joy, the lightness of being and the deep and profound peace and sense of well-being and

'everything is okay-ness' can become the source and fountain of transformation." He looked at the woman directly.

"Definitely."

"That's where you get your soul strength. After all, we're all human beings and as such we're also frail and vulnerable. So someone who's living the spiritual life authentically finds his or her source of strength at this fountain of infinite, unqualified, absolute, 'everything is already okay-ness.' That's very important because life is challenging, especially the more you want to create something totally new and do something that's actually very important.

"And you can always tell whether someone's actually relying on the absolute dimension of consciousness as their source and fundamental reference point or not. When people hesitate, if they're wishy-washy, fearful and half-baked, always bargaining and negotiating, they couldn't be coming from this absolute non-relative position, could they?"

"No, they couldn't."

"So at the beginning of one's path this becoming aware of the absolute dimension of consciousness is an ecstatic discovery. But then, as one gets more serious about it, it's supposed to become the ultimate reference point. And then, of course, the question is: is it or isn't it? If it isn't, then we're not going to change. It's very simple. Then we just had a wonderful experience and it's a big 'so what?' That's how it works." Andrew paused to take a drink, and then asked the questioner, *"Don't you think that this is a very rational way to approach this?"*

"Well, yes," she replied thoughtfully. "It's kind of like it has to inform everything. I can't just back into it as an experience."

"That's very good, I like that."

"Because if I do then I'm misusing it."

"Well, a lot of people do exactly what you're saying, especially these days."

"Yes, that directional thing needs to happen."

"Right. The directional thing we call 'verticality,' it's opposite, of course, being 'horizontal.' Horizontal is backing into it in the way that you're talking about it. It means there's no evolutionary or vertical transformation. The vertical way of looking at is what I'm talking about."

"Yes. And if you're vertical with it then you're not hiding."

"That's right."

"Then it's more militaristic or something."

"Militaristic?" Andrew laughed.

"Yes. Because it creates a definitiveness that the other way doesn't."

"Precisely right."

"And it means standing for something,"

"That's good, yes. You're standing for something. That's the whole point, isn't it?"

"Yes, I see that now."

"So, as I was saying yesterday, if we're going to come up with a post, postmodern rational form of mystical spirituality its foundation would have to be this unqualified non-dual Oneness or the absolute, non-relative dimension of consciousness. And the degree to which it becomes the ultimate reference point for the self, one begins to consciously aspire and feel compelled to manifest that non-relative or absolute oneness in the relative world of duality and multiplicity in all its complexity. Then one becomes a conscious agent of that non-dual realization in the manifest realm and then, instead of living for oneself, to have and to get and to become, one becomes an agent of consciousness itself.

"So, to take it one step further, the degree to which we've realized the non-dual, absolute nature of consciousness can be determined by the degree to which we're actually aspiring to make it manifest in the world of time, where it's not so apparent. Therefore, the expression of Enlightenment becomes the compulsion to make manifest this singularity that one realizes at the level of consciousness.

"So to whatever degree a person is spiritually realized or enlightened is the degree to which they feel they have no choice anymore. Does everybody understand that?"

A chorus of yeses swept through the room.

"It's true. If you meet enlightened people, people that have really seen or experienced this non-dual or absolute dimension, then you'll find that there's a compulsiveness, a drivenness, within them to bring this recognition of singularity into the world of time and space and make it manifest.

"So then the question is, 'are you an egomaniac? Are you still living only to have, to get and to become for yourself? Are you a pathological narcissist who only cares about him or herself? Or are you an enlightened person who's realized this non-dual singularity at the level of consciousness and now feels compelled to make this singularity manifest in the world of time and space,' right?"

"Right," many responded in a burst of inspiration. Andrew was impassioned by what flowed from him with volcanic and spontaneous intensity. I'd seen him like this previously, helplessly swept away by the flood of the Absolute. He seemed driven by an ecstatic surge from the well of that non-dual Ground of which he so passionately spoke and from which the mystery of transmission flowed. We had fallen into one field of experience, a matrix that, revealing itself, simultaneously absorbed us in its splendor.

"Remember everybody, the mythical God fell out of the sky, disappeared for a while and is now reappearing in consciousness as this non-dual Singularity."

It certainly was, right there, right then, closer than my own breath, erupting from the depth of my Self with wild abandon.

"It's only very recently," said Andrew, *"that human beings have developed the capacity to even recognize that that which was seen as an external object is now the very nature of consciousness itself. This non-dual singularity is what the nature of God is. God is One. I AM THAT. So as that non-dual singularity reveals itself*

in consciousness, God becomes manifest in and through that realization in the one who's realizing it.

"And then the realizer becomes a manifest agent of the unmanifest, non-dual Unity in the world of time. You see, only a manifest agent made of flesh and blood with a brain can do that. God as pure Spirit is completely helpless – that means, has no arms, no legs, no brain and no voice. It's not that God or this Absolute Singularity ever ceases to exist. Obviously it doesn't and couldn't. It's just that He, She, or It can't do anything in the world of time and space without arms and legs and a brain. That's the whole point.

"So once again, now we're saying that this absolute, non-dual Unity, which for so long we projected outside the self, has fallen out of the sky as an object and is reappearing as the subject or consciousness itself.

"And in the way that I teach this I say the formless God, which is this fullness, this everythingness, this completeness, changes shape when He, She or It takes form. That movement is from the empty formlessness beyond time and beyond space to form. In the empty, primordial state God has no form and also no desire. Isn't that what everybody's experiencing and isn't that a big relief for the self?

"From the perspective of consciousness there's no desire for anything. All the formless God wants is to BE with Himself, Herself, Itself for eternity, right? Isn't that the nature of it?"

Another chorus of yeses answered as the vastness of Being thrummed like an engine in the room.

"Satchitananda – Being, Consciousness, Bliss—meditating eternally on itSelf! Earlier several people said, 'I could sit here forever.' Well, that's the nature of the unmanifest, formless one Self beyond all pairs of opposites. That's what the nature of the absolute level of consciousness is – always has been, always will be. 'I could sit here forever.'

"But then, when the one Self goes from wanting nothing, wanting only to Be, and decides to take form in creation, God takes the leap from formlessness to form and then the picture changes. Then, suddenly, there's this unthinkably tremendous, enormous and utterly vast desire to become. So if you look at the whole universe, including your own self, what you see is the expression and manifestation of that desire. Now, that's quite a big desire. You have to have an unimaginably explosive desire to do all that. I don't actually think that the human mind is even capable of imagining the enormity of it. We can only just venture to guess how big that desire is.

"But we know it's big because, for example, when you experience sexual desire its nature is overwhelming, right?"

No doubt about that, I thought as murmurs of affirmation answered the question.

"If you want to know how God or the Evolutionary Impulse's desire to create form is experienced at the gross physical level, just look at the experience of sexual desire in *the human body. That's the most powerful experience of desire human beings are capable of having at the physical level. Just think, at those moments when sexual desire is experienced in its greatest intensity, how much you want to fulfill that desire. That's how God feels all the time about creating the universe. And there's no relief. God never experiences relief!*

"So when God goes from formlessness to form it's almost an agonizingly painful state where the desire to create or to become is ever unfulfilled. It's like a constant state of torment. That's why without the unmanifest, formless, absolute nature of consciousness itself, which is always full and complete and ever desireless, as a place of rest, God wouldn't be able to bear His, Her, or Its own passion to create the universe.

"So then, when the awakening human begins to experience that evolutionary or creative impulse not only as sexual desire but at the level of consciousness, it's the same movement. But now it's experienced at the level of consciousness not at the gross physical level. And the way human beings experience the desire to create or become the universe at the level of consciousness is what I was speaking about a few minutes ago – this passionate compulsion to make manifest this non-dual, absolute Unity in the manifest realm. And that urgent, passionate desire is intense. It's as intense as sexual desire when felt at the moments of greatest intensity except that it's at the level of consciousness and that there's no relief; there's no end to it. There's no relief because, as you can see, we're barely getting started here. The project to create the universe in God's own image has barely begun."

What was clear in this ardent and instructive exposition was not simply what it revealed but that Andrew was speaking directly from the living heart of his own experience. It was his passion, his compulsion and desire to create the universe of which he spoke with such conviction. His will had become indistinct from the will of that mystery which lay unseen behind it all. "Thy will, not mine," that timeless declaration of surrender, had eroded every foothold for his personal will and left in its place a frictionless passage for the power of THAT to express its unrelenting desire in the world. It was THAT that was speaking, its force freed in matter and charging through him to call to Itself in us. And we responded. Our hearts heard that call and from those hidden depths that same desire welled up, Self flowing to Self, until the room was awash in only THAT and we were but little crafts upon that sea.

"So when you get into this," Andrew continued, *"you begin to see that how God feels about this entire undertaking is comprised of two completely different views. On one hand, from the perspective of the unmanifest consciousness that has never entered into the process, everything's always already okay. Nothing's happened. And in that God can rest for eternity peacefully and blissfully. But, for the part of God that has entered into the fray and decided to create the universe, this sense of urgent intensity behind it is emotionally, psychologically, spiritually, philosophically and physically overwhelming. That's the Big Bang experienced at the level of consciousness itself.*

"So we can imagine this kind of intensity as a physical experience, but imagine how it feels at the level of consciousness! There would have to be an extremely intense sense of creative urgency. Now, that kind of urgency is a little much for the ego to handle. So, just as the experience of the absolute nature of consciousness sweeps the ego off its feet, so does the recognition of this, what I call 'evolutionary or creative impulse' at the level of consciousness. Its urgency completely sweeps the ego off its feet and overwhelms it. In that urgency the fears and desires of the puny little ego, with all of its narcissistic needs, is rendered radically, totally, and completely irrelevant and the ego, well, it doesn't like that."

Andrew burst out laughing.

"Because then what begins to replace it is the 'Universe Project,' which is the creation of the conscious universe, in which the unmanifest, absolute dimension of consciousness that we've been discovering together here permeates every bit of the relative, time-bound world. Now, once again, in light of that project, the ego's unfulfilled desires, endless needs and narcissistic tendencies are rendered radically – and I emphasize radically – irrelevant.

"So just in the same way that the ego doesn't like to surrender to Unmanifest Emptiness, it likes even less to surrender to the radical urgency of the evolutionary impulse which says, 'my desire to create the universe is the only desire that's important and your desires are irrelevant. Get the point?"

"Yes" rang through the room, the ecstasy now tempered by steely sobriety.

"Okay. So in this teaching the impulse that emerges and drives God to become manifest is what I call the 'Authentic Self.' The Authentic Self could also be called true conscience. It's not the personal conscience; it's the cosmic or universal conscience. It's when you actually begin to experience this sense of evolutionary urgency burning in your own mind, burning in your consciousness, burning in your own veins. It's when you become aware at the level of consciousness that there's something unthinkably big that's absolutely important that must be done NOW. And in light of the recognition of that urgency you see directly that your ego's self concern is completely and frighteningly irrelevant.

"This evolutionary impulse, this Authentic Self, is a serious thing. It's an impersonal function of consciousness itself and it has a powerful, ferocious passion and creative intensity. At the level of consciousness we experience this as a burning concern for that which is absolutely important, which, in this case, is the evolution of consciousness itself.

"So now that we've described what I call the Authentic Self or this shape of God when God goes from the unmanifest to the manifest as the creative impulse, we can speak about what it all has to do with the human situation that we as individuals are in. So remember that in order to live the spiritual life in an evolutionary context in earnest, this non-relative or absolute dimension of consciousness has to be the ultimate reference point. That's because the passion and urgency of the Authentic Self has to be

in balance and you can only really act fearlessly and passionately in the world when you know – and this is paradoxical – that everything's always already okay. In order to have a real integral whole, the passion and ferocious urgency of the Authentic Self has to be balanced through the conscious realization of and abidance in the non-relative or absolute dimension of consciousness itself.

"And everybody, this has to be worked on. This is not just freely given and then that's the end of the story. The potential for all this definitely exists but it has to be cultivated, and cultivated, and cultivated and worked on and developed and created. That's why there's spiritual practice. Spiritual practice means there's a conscious engagement with the evolutionary process for the sake of evolution itself. Because, as another spiritual teacher whom I just met mentioned in one of his books, 'we're all born imperfect.' As if we didn't know that," Andrew laughed, *"but anyway that's one way to put it that everybody's going to understand.*

"But the postmodern, pathological narcissist – which means us – has a problem with the notion that 'I wasn't born perfect.' However, the self must be perfected and that can only happen through conscious engagement with the process of perfecting the self. No one can do that for you; the individual can only do that for him or herself. I hope that's very clear because it's true and it always will be true. And that's the important part of this to let in. We each have to understand that 'I'm imperfect and I want to endeavor to perfect myself because I'm a vehicle for consciousness.' Do you understand?"

Andrew did not wait for an answer but continued, asking rhetorically, *"If you look at postmodern culture you'd think we're a vehicle for what?"* He paused to emphasize his point. *"Pleasure and consumption.*

"But if we're interested in real transformation then the vehicle is what needs to be perfected, and that's the hard part.[2] But if you're not willing to make the effort to perfect yourself, you won't change no matter what you experience. You see, spiritual experience, more often than not, is when we experience our potential for transformation. But it's not a free ride and we have to do the work.

"Now, the problem with this is that the more any of us sees the more we are obligated to change. Before you see what's possible you can plead ignorance. You can say, 'I didn't know. That's very interesting but I had no idea.' So then, when you die, they say, 'that's okay, they get a free pass. They didn't know any better. Forgive them, they know not what they do.' But then they see you and they say, 'oh no, stop that one.'"

At this the spiritual density that had congealed in the room was torn with a paroxysm of laughter.

"And then they say, 'that one, they knew and they didn't do anything about it.' With a devilish gleam in his eye, Andrew added, *"so you know where you're going then, don't you?'* Yet, even through the rolling waves of hilarity it was strikingly evident that Andrew was, at best, only half joking. He followed on more seriously, *"I actually believe that, but I don't think the hell we go to is the kind of place we're used*

to thinking about. You see there's a post, postmodern version of hell also.

"*Remember, I was saying earlier that what some individuals who claim to have had near death experiences – I mean, ultimately how valid this is is anybody's guess – say is, 'well, nothing changes.'*

"*So what would it be like to leave the body knowing what was possible and not having done anything about it? Then you're going to be stuck in some kind of bardo[3] knowing what a complete fool you really are because in that in-between state you'll be able to see how near at hand was your own potential for liberation and the evolution of higher consciousness. These things will become more apparent, imminent and obvious when you're not stuck in the gross realm of your ordinary life, not unlike when you're in a retreat situation like this where your consciousness is expanded. So without the body these things are going to be as obvious to you as they are now, if not more so. And then, knowing that you didn't do anything about it, you're going to be stuck. And then if what they say about reincarnation is true, you have to go through all the hell of being born and growing up all over again, and you also have to reap the consequences of what you haven't done this time around, because there are karmic consequences for our choices. As I said, while I can't ultimately say with certainty whether this is true or not, I can tell you that it's my deepest conviction.*

"*The reason that I have no doubt that the law of karma is true is because I've observed people operating over five, ten, fifteen, even twenty years and I've seen how the choices we make, or don't make, have karmic consequences in this life. Therefore, I don't have to believe in any kind of pre-modern version of reincarnation to know that this stuff is true. I can see the karmic consequences of our own choices in this life. So if that's how it operates in this life then the same laws must operate when we look at these things in a bigger context.*"

Andrew paused for a drink of water and then, with a rather roguish air, he went on. "*So just imagine what it would be like to know and then to be stuck. Do you think you'll be able to turn on the television or go to movies or drink alcohol or take drugs or escape into promiscuous sex without a body? You won't be able to escape! Wouldn't that be horrible?*" His eyes twinkled mischievously.

Once again there was loud laughter. Yet I was immune to it, failing to find even the slightest hint of hilarity in what Andrew had said. On the contrary, what he said struck deep into the raw sense of vulnerability, that undefended and endlessly open sense of being, into which I had been swept as a consequence of hearing his words. I had been opened up and established in that realm that transcends both life and death. From that lofty aerie the naked truth of what Andrew had said lay bare in unadorned austerity; it left my soul trembling and stilled all surface thought, though deep currents of contemplation flowed with concentrated deliberation below. I recalled the early days of discovery and the post-virginal spiritual bliss of my early twenties when the doors of perception had been unwittingly flung open and had flooded my life with the mysteries beyond. First among those mysteries came the irreducibility of inherent immortality. Incinerating every notion of death and birth as the bookends of life, it flung open endless vistas both ahead and behind. Since those days I've learned that death, now seen anew, is not a dark angel of oblivion or brooding harbinger of decay, but a source of blessed perspective and a reminder of the real. And that shapeless specter holds a mirror of precognition in front of me by which I am able to look ahead to that time when I will look back upon my life, stripped bare of pretense, and weigh its actuality against the undeniability of what I had known. It was this, more keenly sensed now than in many years, that was brought to me with unflinching clarity and precluded the casual laughter that still sang lightly in the room.

"But to me the worst part of it," Andrew continued, *"would have to be taking form again, forgetting it all, and having to suffer through the agony of unconsciousness again, not knowing. And then, as you evolve again and all this begins to come back to you, there'd be the memory and the pain of the self-doubt. Because if there's an important step that you need to take and you know it, and you don't, you begin to doubt your capacity to do it. On the other hand, when there's an important step to take and you do take that risk, you develop confidence. And each time you do that your confidence in yourself grows. But each time there's a big step to take and you don't take it, your confidence in your own capacity to do it diminishes. So then your confidence will diminish at the same time that your knowledge that it's a step that you need to take doesn't go away – unless, of course, you begin to deny it, which is often what happens. Then people just start denying that any step has to be taken and start digging themselves deeper and deeper into a completely deluded, lost place.*

"Of course, becoming lost due to your own avoidance and denial also creates pain at a soul level. At a soul level, that part of you that is always awake, there are going to be karmic consequences for all these choices. So you can deceive yourself through avoidance and denial, but the karmic consequences and the pain don't go away. And then, whenever you become more conscious, the pain is going to be there from what you yourself have refused to do.

"At any rate, this is how I believe it works. And I'm drawing these conclusions from what I've actually seen with my own eyes in this life in my role as a teacher and extrapolating that into a larger picture. You can take it or leave it but I'm sure a lot of it is true even if perhaps every single detail isn't. This just simply makes sense. Now, the reason I'm saying all this is not because I'm trying to scare anybody. It's because I'm trying to inspire you to be serious about this. Okay?"

Okay," everyone responded in unison. Sober reflection as well as the unrelenting and devastating surge of spiritual ecstasy had overwhelmed the hilarity of a short time earlier. The heavy curtain of materiality had from the beginning of the teaching been swept aside, the film of appearances torn apart with the power and ecstasy of a psycho-spiritual orgasm, as all sensed boundaries of self were blasted away by the radiant splendor of that dimension beyond time. The previous days' epiphanies had been little more than spiritual foreplay when measured against what now pulsed in the room. As for myself, I was so lost in the endless dimensions of the Self that I could barely find my mind. I had become mute both inwardly and outwardly. Any semblance of a grip on myself, any sense of separate selfhood, had been, at least for the moment, incinerated like a shred of paper dropped onto the surface of the sun. All "already knowing" and its resultant concepts, including that most precious "self-concept," had been swept away like toothpicks in a tornado. Slack-jawed I looked about, seeing all things yet seeing through them, everything and everyone transparent to the still yet pulsing infinitude beyond. It was from that motionless, timeless, deathless apogee of being that the bright light of conscience shone upon the finitude of "my life." In that unfiltered radiance all that I had seen and known stood as the standard against which my life was to be measured both now and beyond and in it withered the listless sense that somehow it didn't matter. "What we do here echoes in Eternity,"[4] resounded with the tenor of a distant drum in my near motionless mind. It was to that drumbeat that I moved both inwardly and outwardly; inwardly into realms of wordless contemplation and outwardly away from the teaching hall into the welcome certainty of the afternoon routine.

Outside the world was suffused in liquid gold. The rocky chasms of Montserrat, the plaza, the basilica, the stone saints and all that lay about me was, despite its seeming solidity, as transparent as everything else. All that had troubled me the preceding days had fled like the shadows of night driven before the birth of the day. My mind was at near standstill. Only inchoate fragments of ideas, wordless textures and intimations, swam before me stripped of verbiage. It was then, my mind crushed under the heel of revelation, that I decided to abandon writing my journal. It seemed a pointless exercise, a self-indulgent, even vulgar, triviality that could no more capture the magnitude of the truth than pornography could capture the essence of love. It took well over two days to reconsider this conclusion and for my mind to regain sufficient mobility to take up writing once again.

It had only been three and a half days in Andrew's company when the weight of his transmission had obliterated all fixed notions of self, peeled away the veil of "samsara," and shown me once again what many people often spend years and endless hours of committed spiritual practice attempting to attain. It was this power of transmission to which Andrew's teacher had referred when he'd said that, "a teacher like Andrew comes along every six to eight hundred years. It's not only the depth of his enlightenment that's extraordinary, but his power to transmit it to others." I was now bearing witness to that extraordinary power. And yet, for Andrew, explosive experiences of enlightenment such as the one into which I had been plunged, represented no final point of realization but merely the authentic beginning of the path. It was the transmission of, to use a Buddhist term, "right view" without which he felt all spiritual pursuits were likely to be misguided and ill-conceived.

It was then, in the consideration of spiritual practice, when it became clear to me that the rigorous practice into which we had been thrust formed a second front in Andrew's assault on the well-defended ego. The first was the fire of transmission, which beat back the ego, that pretender to the throne of self, under its ruthless offensive while the second, the practice, effectively cut off its lines of supply, all those avenues by which it sought affirmation and expression. Thus for days now the ego had been deprived of the very marrow of its existence. The result had been like having my head held mercilessly beneath the waters of the Self. There, washed clean of ego's stain, I stood poised to view all of life, including my own play in it, from the vantage point of the Absolute. There the power of conscience flared, laying its light upon all of my motives, choices and actions, setting them in stark relief against the backdrop of the possible.

The point I contemplated next concerned the relationship between the radically unrelated nature of consciousness itself and the radically related world of our time bound lives. The bridge between these two, I came to realize, had been crafted in the crucible of evolution and was being carried in the hearts of human beings whose existence straddled both dimensions. It was only through them, through us, through me, and the moral capacity of our humanity that the realization of the Absolute could be translated into the world of time. And thus the fundamental question raised in all of this was, "what does having a realization of the Absolute and taking a position in it – claiming it, as Andrew had challenged us – have to do with the position that we are taking in relationship to life?" It was due to the importance of the answer to this question that Andrew placed such unrelenting emphasis on understanding and interpretation when considering the significance of spiritual experience. *"The conclusions that we draw about our experience are more important than the experiences themselves,"* he had said with the redundant intensity of nail gun throughout all the years that I had known him.

My mind, once it had resumed its proper function, turned to such considerations and in so doing stumbled upon a colorful series of instructive memories. The first involved a conversation over dinner with a "nice guy" from Marin who, after I had erred by suggesting that enlightenment indeed carried with it an ethical imperative, angrily insisted (how quickly his hitherto airy tones had been blown aside on that cross current of philosophical vexation) that, "Enlightenment is only the discovery that there's no one to get enlightened. That's it!" His fist pounded on the table as he made this unequivocal pronouncement with shocking vehemence. He, being an adherent of the "neo-advaita" school of thought, held as the central premise of his life that the only reality whatsoever was the Self Absolute, extending that to suggest that any ideas of a personal self that needed to change in any way or adhere to a set of moral principles were simply a barometer of one's ignorance of that ultimate truth. "There's no one to be and nothing to do," was the singular commandment of this school, which from this point of departure concluded that, "whatever you want to do is what God wants you do because there simply is not – never was, never will be – a separate doer with the slightest trace of free will." Any belief in such a doer along with any ideas of right and wrong are considered to be the very worst expression of the ignorance of unenlightenment.

With but scant reflection it is easy to see that the moral vacuum created by this position creates the perfect playground for the ego and its whims, now conveniently liberated from ethical strictures of any kind.[5] The inherent nihilism and absence of sanity in such a view should be equally evident. Apparently, however, it isn't. At least not in the mind of one supposedly enlightened teacher of this school who, upon being questioned about the events of September 11th, blithely proclaimed that if we judged the events of that sinister day as evil, we would be fully expressing our ignorance, having overlooked the happy fact that the billions of microbes that feasted on the carnage that day had received an abundant blessing indeed – a veritable banquet courtesy of al-Qaeda. So who are we to judge? This is a true story![6]

Another view, slightly less insane though equally unexamined, I have already mentioned. It is the schoolyard conception of the cosmos in which the inconceivable expanse of the manifest universe has been provided for the tutelage of the soul on its evolutionary journey *back* to before the beginning, of which I will say more in a moment.

In light of such questionable conclusions, Andrew's insistence that we carefully examine our interpretations of what we experience beyond time seems more than justified. With respect to of neo-advaita, its claims of non-duality fail to stand up to even the most cursory philosophical scrutiny. By affirming one aspect of reality to be ultimately real and casting off the other as perfectly unreal, the single event of which it is all a part has been neatly divided in two. As such there is nothing non-dual about it and its own conclusions stand in denial of its own claims.

The schoolyard scenario, holding that the ultimate purpose of the evolutionary thrust of life is to free us from that which it created, suffers from its own gaps of logic. Alongside the grand dissonance of scale so casually proposed in this view (the entire inconceivably vast universe was created for *my* journey – the first gospel truth of the metaphysics of narcissism) there lies an equally questionable notion. It argues that after taking fourteen billion years of biological development for the evolutionary process to produce self-conscious creatures that could both know their own Maker at the level of consciousness and appreciate, through the power of their intellect, the evolutionary process that led to their own making, the first conclusion they should draw would be to escape from the entire process. And to do what? To return to that which always already existed and from which it all began. As I said earlier, such a view simply defies all logic – physical or metaphysical. If going back to before the beginning was meant to be the endpoint of this explosion of creation, why start in the first place? Thus, even when such teachings employ the term evolution, it is a verbal misappropriation. Evolution involves creation driving forward in ever growing spirals of complexity and integration to no imaginable end point whatsoever. It is not evolving to go *back* to a place of final rest or final anything for that matter. Thus the schoolyard conception of the cosmos is not only fundamentally anti-evolutionary, it is also fundamentally, if subtly, anti-life.

So what then was an appropriate conclusion one might draw regarding the relationship between the unmanifest and the manifest based on the direct experience of the Absolute? What did taking a position in the Absolute have to do with our position in relationship to life? With respect to this, Andrew's lines of reasoning had more fully resonated with my own experience than all the other philosophical musings to which I had been previously exposed. It told me that the inconceivable positivity and inherent perfection burning at the Source, desperately longed for expression in this world. It started, rather than ended, by returning to "before the beginning." That had, after all, been the very nature of our endeavor since the outset of the retreat. But the confidence found in the heart of that Ground should, in his view, serve as a base camp from which to venture forth with the strength and courage to act boldly in life, though not for the sake of our personal evolution as its own end.

To what end then? That we are the first and only creatures – at least in this corner of the cosmos – who, through reflective self-awareness have the capacity to know our own Source and grasp the enormity of the evolutionary process of which we are a product, puts us in a unique position: to be the vehicle through which the Mystery from which all this springs, becomes aware of Itself in Its own creation and as Its own creation. And not only becomes aware of it, but, due to the miracle of surrender, is able to use us as a vehicle for navigation in this world. To even conceive of such a possibility should thrust us into a well of awe so deep that we should, in theory, never quite recover. In that well our myopic world of petty drives should drown forever in an awakening to and recognition of ourselves as nothing less than the sense organs of the cosmos and of That which lies behind it. We are, at least on the plane of potential, God becoming aware of Him, Her, Itself in Its own creation. As such we stand poised to have our lives co-opted for Its creative purposes, giving to our emergence nothing less than cosmic significance. In short, the realization of the Absolute is neither intended to dispossess us of our care for the manifest dimension nor inspire an escape. Rather it should strengthen our ability to participate in it for its own sake thus ennobling our humanity and enabling THAT to act in this world as us. The question is, can we bear it? Or more to the point, can I bear it? Or perhaps even more to the point, will I?

This, of course, lands us squarely back at the crossroads of the moral dimension, caught in the unwavering light of conscience, for there is a fly in the ointment that Andrew had not yet fully begun to address until this morning. *"Ego is the only obstacle"* I have heard him proclaim relentlessly over all the years I've known him. It's influence, he felt, is so corrosive to our capacity to express the "everything's already okayness" in the world that it stunts in the most profound way the flowering of our full humanity and deprives our struggling world of the best of who we are. That being so, the fly in the ointment reveals itself, upon closer scrutiny, to be more like a plague of locusts blackening the sky and reducing a budding crop to a barren waste. Thus I have come to understand that the measure of our spirit cannot be ascertained by the sum of our insight and experience but, as Andrew had suggested, by the degree to which the handiwork of ego – our carefully tended assortment of neuroses and secret drives to power – is denied expression in the world. It was to this that the experience of the Absolute should inspire and empower us. This sentiment, flying in the face of our victim culture, obsessed with therapeutic cures for the wounded self and happy to pathologize the mere aspiration to perfection,[7] has always been what has most attracted me to Andrew's teaching. I sensed that it was here that I might find the dignity in human life, a dignity that grows to full expression only when I am willing to bear witness to and, most importantly, stand up for all I have seen in the unmanifest amongst the vicissitudes of the manifest. As such, this teaching offered no balm with which to anesthetize oneself against life's harsh realities but rather a tonic with which to invigorate the spirit and strengthen the vehicle. Then it might play its proper role in this world. God as pure spirit, he had pointed out, is helpless in this world without access to arms, legs, a brain and, I presume, a spiritual heart capable of knowing what to do with them.

And it is the authentic recognition of this that throws open the doors to spiritual conscience. That guest, having now stepped across the threshold into my heretofore unwitting interiority, stood silently poised, its very presence pressing the question: now that you've seen this, what are you going to do? Are you going to become a vehicle for THAT which you yourself have seen? Or are you going to continue to live for yourself only, relegating THAT to the shadow realm of memory and its creaking treasury of hoarded experience? It was this crash of conscience into my life, this ripping the doors of ignorance off their rusty hinges, that made Andrew's teaching both utterly compelling and perfectly terrifying. And he had so far played his part to perfection, a spiritual Pied Piper leading us into a trap of conscience. He had led us to this trap with our full willingness and had, with this morning's teaching, taken most of us well beyond just claims of ignorance. At least for myself, were I to retain a sliver of integrity, I could not pretend not to know. I had taken the red pill and turned aside the blue.[8] I had gone down the rabbit hole. There was no going back. Not really, at any rate. From this point forward any attempts to retreat from the front, becoming a deserter of conscience as it were, would be bound to have painful karmic repercussions. *"It's better never to start than to start and not finish,"* Andrew was fond of saying for this very reason. And to help stave off such an apostasy of conscience, Andrew had evoked that realm beyond life in which we judge ourselves against the balance of what we knew. In short, having set the context for our lives in the biggest way imaginable he had then, in an inversion of perspective, returned our attention to our lives within that context. All of which reminded me of one of Andrew's most sobering admonitions, burned into me on some previous retreat: *"There is such a thing as the soul and there is such a thing as heaven. And there is such a thing as going in the other direction. So live this teaching as if your life depended on it, because it does."*

All of this echoed wordlessly within as I shouldered my way through the crowds and past the ancient buildings, swept up in the Absolute, free from boundaries, from the weight of the mind, from the pull of desire and the stream of time. Yet somehow I remained aware of my life and its purpose both in that endless radiance and in this more finite world. And for the first time since my arrival the rhythms of the afternoon chant bypassed my labyrinthine mind, striking directly upon the secret membranes of my inner hearing, its full timbre resonating deeply within.

The Most Challenging Spiritual Endeavor

Evolutionary Enlightenment is the most challenging spiritual endeavor because in it there is no promise of escape. Many of us still secretly cherish the hope that one day we will be released from this life process and be able to rest forever beyond the world. Only when we are finally willing to face into the enormity of the evolutionary context we are living in, and its profound transformative implications for ourselves personally, will we begin to develop genuine spiritual maturity. And that's what the world so desperately needs: mature, enlightened human beings who are willing to wholeheartedly take responsibility for the entire process, forever – to participate in the creation of the conscious universe, with and as the very force that created it. That impulse, which is your very own Authentic Self, can never rest until the light of consciousness has permeated all matter in the Universe.

Several hours later, returning to the teaching hall, I couldn't help but wonder whether, having immersed us in the timeless Ground of our deepest Self for nearly four days, Andrew would now strike out in the direction of that Ground's implications, as he had begun to do with such spectacular results in the morning. We would soon see.

The afternoon session was launched into action by a young Australian man, perhaps in his twenties, with an angular face and closely set blue eyes. "Would you mind just saying a little bit about conscience?" he began. "I was confused earlier about what you meant when you said conscience."

"Well, when I talk about conscience it's a deeper, higher sense of purpose and mean-ing," Andrew replied. *"You see, the two fundamental spiritual questions are 'Who am I?' and 'Why am I here?' Right?"*

"Right."

"So, the answer to the first question in relationship to this teaching is, 'I'm that primordial consciousness beyond time and creation.' Which leaves the second question, "Why am I here?" to which this teaching says, 'To create the conscious universe.' Are you with me?"

"Yes," he replied.

"Okay, so what I mean by conscience has to do with awakening to this cosmic, impersonal context for one's own presence in the world. You see, the ego has its own agenda, which relates to one's personal history that is also deeply tied into one's cultural background and to the time and place that one has emerged in the life process."

"Right."

"And, of course, the Authentic Self has a very big purpose, which is always only to create the universe, period. So the conscience that I'm speaking about is when a human being awakens to this cosmic sense of purpose."

"Okay, I see," the man said thoughtfully.

"And that's not a small thing. Traditionally the religious sentiment has always been this discovery of a big cosmic context and an ultimate and absolute sense of purpose. So when I'm speaking about awakening to the Authentic Self that would be the post, postmodern version of that kind of religious sentiment. So, for example, the phrase, "Not my will, but thy will be done," would be an example of that. 'My will' would represent the fears and desires of the personal line. 'Thy will' would be translated as awakening to this Evolutionary or Creative Impulse and Its purpose. Now, Its purpose and agenda are usually very different from the purposes and agenda of the individual ego. So, once again, when I talk about conscience, it generally concerns the awakening to this larger impersonal cosmic sense of purpose."

"So if you're acting from the Authentic Self, or connected to that, would you experience conscience? Would there be any need for it? Because you're coming from a ..."

"But that's what it is! Because purpose creates context. In other words, the postmod-ern self has a very highly developed ego and all of us suffer from almost pathological degrees of narcissism, which means an irrational degree of self-importance, self-infatu-ation and self-concern. So what I'm speaking about as being conscience is the awaken-ing to a higher sense of purpose and meaning, one that usually pulls the rug out from underneath the narcissistic ego's agenda. You see?"

"Yeah."

"And I think that's good although most people don't like it. Once again, the problem for the postmodern self revolves around this pathological self-obsession. Now, it's not our fault. But we're all products of the time we've entered into the process of historical

development, so most of us do suffer from extreme degrees of narcissism. And as a group we tend to be more trapped in compulsive self-concern than any people have ever been, at least en masse. I mean there have always been very self-centered people. But simply never so many who've been given so much and been so lucky and have, at the same time, been so unable to make the highest use and value out of what they've been given.

"And a big problem we have is that in secular culture what's lacking is a sense of purpose and meaning and value. A lot of people really don't know why they're here and that causes there to be a very big 'hole in the soul,' as we were saying earlier. Now, this is the case even though many people wouldn't admit it or even know that that was a problem. Yet without a clear sense of absolute meaning and purpose human beings flounder and for most of us that's what the problem is."

"Right."

"And many people today are very suspicious about any sense of absolute purpose for very good reasons, including religious fundamentalism, what happened in the Second World War with fascism and communism and so on. But just because there have been many pathological forms of absolutism and extremism and just because such mistakes will continue to be made, doesn't mean that what I'm saying isn't true.

"Now, before we discover this Authentic Self and this sense of meaning and purpose the main thing that drives us are our lower instincts – the survival instinct, the seeking for comfort and pleasure and power. And, of course, most people that I run into these days basically do what they want to do. Now, there have never been so many people living on the earth at any time that have been able to do exactly what they wanted to do. And most of us aren't doing that well with it. Most of us have far more freedom than we can actually handle, right?"

"Yes, that's right," the man agreed.

"And why is that? Because there's no sense of purpose!"

"Yup."

"And when you start to talk to a pathological narcissist about purpose they begin backpedaling because they start to hear, 'There's something more important than you.' Andrew burst into childlike laughter. *"And a narcissist will have trouble with that. They'll say, 'Excuse me, can you repeat that?'* Andrew held his hand up to his ear as again he laughed uproariously.

"So I think awakening to the Authentic Self is the strongest medicine the postmodern self could possibly take. It's the ultimate antidote to our problem. Therefore the things we've been discovering regarding the absolute, unqualified, non-relative dimension of consciousness itself are not ends in themselves. They're a means to an end.

"But what a lot of people who are teaching enlightenment these days – if they're for real – will be able to share with you is a similar kind of experience to the one you've been having up until now. But that's about it. And for most people that's more than enough. I mean, we could easily spend ten days on the absolute or non-relative

dimension of consciousness and we'd all leave very happy. But it's not enough because the worst thing for a narcissist is to know only that dimension without a context because it will simply deepen their narcissism.[9]

"You see, I think that the luckiest people in the world – people of our ilk – need to get over ourselves so we can do something, right? That means participate. So, the point is that the discovery of consciousness itself is the ultimate relief from all your personal troubles, all of your pain, all of your hurts, all of your wounds. We've all been hurt, wounded, traumatized, beaten up, had our teeth knocked out, stabbed in the back, had all our money stolen, and on and on.

"Yet for someone who's serious and mature, the absolute dimension of consciousness is the ultimate source of relief and liberation. If you're not serious and mature, which means that you haven't gotten to that point in your own development where you're really willing to take responsibility for yourself, then you need to go see a therapist. Of course, I realize that I'm setting the bar very high here. That being said, if you are very mature, consciousness will set you free. Of course, if you're not, it won't," he laughed, then, tongue in cheek, apologized. *"Sorry."*

"So the endlessly liberating experience of consciousness is the ultimate source of freedom from fear and doubt, but that's a means to an end. And the end is to awaken to the Authentic Self so that we can become liberated and participate very powerfully in the life process. You see, we're here to participate. We're not here just to hang out in states of consciousness that give us glimpses of the Self beyond the world. I mean, that's part of what we're here to experience, but I don't think that's why we have this body. You don't need a body to experience the Absolute. That dimension of self is always already there before we were born. Yet we have arms and legs and a brain that were built for action. That could only mean that we're here to do something. Do you see my point?"

I had first seen that point, collided with it in fact, some years earlier when Andrew had pointed out what, once I had heard it, seemed ridiculously obvious. Of course this body was built for action. One quick look at our hands and its nimble fingers should give a very big clue that we are here to do something, to grasp things, and not merely with our hands but with that powerful mind with which the unfolding evolution of biology seems to have chosen to favor us. The fact that I had failed to understand something so obvious and why I had been nothing short of thunderstruck when Andrew had pointed it out was simple: because I'd been so wrapped up in the pursuit of all experience, spiritual and mundane, as a means to liberation from and transcendence of the world, that engagement with it for its own sake had literally never occurred to me. Having had the obvious pointed out, however, stirred the beginnings of a significant shift in orientation with respect to my own spiritual pursuits and, most importantly, my raison d'être.

"You see, these days a lot of people are very interested in meditation and consciousness. They read books about Enlightenment, do spiritual practices, follow teachers and

so on. But in the end they really just want to escape. They don't want to evolve and they don't want to participate in anything. The whole spiritual pursuit is just another avenue for their narcissism. If you go to a lot of the big New Age centers around the world that's what you'll find. So a lot of people who are attracted to these kinds of subjects aren't necessarily people who are very mature or who really care about anything other than themselves. They're often just looking for a more interesting way to entertain themselves and escape." He gave a slightly ironic laugh.

"I can't tell you how many seekers I've met over the years that, when it suddenly got real and when they found out it wasn't about them having a great experience but that it was actually them changing so they could be useful, boy, their whole expression changed and they lost interest in a minute. They even became offended, often in the extreme. Suddenly it wasn't fun anymore and they didn't want to play. See what I mean?"

"Yes."

"So I think that this post-metaphysical or rational spirituality should be for very serious, mature people, not simply a game for a narcissist to play as a form of entertainment or escapism. It should compel a profound and deep seriousness about being a human being who's alive right now. That does not mean morbidity. It means being deadly serious to the degree that when someone meets such an individual they should feel that there's weight and depth and power and intention. So the awakening of conscience means all these things. Do you understand?"

"Well, yes. It's just that, in my simple way, I imagine conscience as the little voice in the back of my head telling me that I'm doing something wrong."

"Well, this is a much more sophisticated version of that," Andrew retorted with a laugh. Then, without missing a beat, he continued, *"Do you think it's bad to have a little voice in your head telling you you're doing something wrong? Or do you think that now and then it's good to have a little voice say, 'hey, maybe that's not a good idea? Maybe you really don't want to do that.'"* A small wave of laughter rippled through the room *"Is that inherently wrong? Or would you prefer to hear, 'Do whatever you want, it doesn't matter?'"*

"I guess I prefer to have a sense of direction which doesn't require that little voice telling me what to do. It's like a carrot and a stick and the conscience is the stick. I think I'd rather have the carrot."

"But remember, I'm talking about a very evolved, mature and sophisticated version of conscience here. And also remember what those who've had near-death experiences tell us: that so-called voice of conscience doesn't necessarily come from anyone else. It's coming from your Authentic Self which is the best part of you."

"Do you think that's something you have to tune in to?"

"I suppose that if you're in really bad shape you'd have to," he jested. *"The point is that if narcissism or pathological self-concern is a deeply ingrained habit, which it's likely to be if that's been one's fundamental orientation for fifteen, thirty, sixty or more*

years, then you might have to make some effort. Some people find it almost impossible not to think about themselves compulsively all the time. You could tell them two hundred times, 'don't you see how self-centered you are?' and they'll go, 'oh my god, I can't believe it.' Then maybe you say, 'okay, fine,' but ten years later you find yourself having the same conversation. You see? These are strong habits that we have to come to terms with."

"Yeah, I get that."

"And to complicate things even more, the whole notion of change or evolution being the context of a human life is a quite new and a very different orientation to life than what we're used to. So what we're calling the Authentic Self perpetually thrives upon change. The Authentic Self is only interested in change and the ego, or the narcissistic, separate self-sense, hates change. So there's a big conflict there. Do you understand my point?"

"Yeah."

"It's for this reason that I've found this a very difficult concept to share with people. I mean, intellectually it's not hard to understand. But I've noticed that most people, on the level of their actual life, really find this whole idea of perpetual change and development at the deepest level quite hard to get. But when they do, it becomes a part of them. Once you get it at a soul level, you'll never forget it. Lower to higher – that's what the Authentic Self wants. It's an upward thrust, a kind of driver that's an ecstatic compulsion towards higher development and potential. It's a perpetual sense of being driven.

"And by the way, it's exactly the opposite experience of this absolute unmanifest dimension where there's no interest in change whatsoever and all we want to do is BE. 'I could stay like this forever.' That's the Ground of Being. So from this unmanifest perspective, which is before the beginning, how the Self feels and is experienced is that it's not interested in change and it only wants to Be – for eternity. The Self just wants to dwell upon Itself and delight in Itself for eternity. There's no aspiration to be anyone or do anything. It's the ultimate relief and it's ever new. Has that been your experience?"

"Yes, it has."

"But the Authentic Self is the evolutionary impulse and where do you think that came from?" The question was clearly rhetorical. *"Well, it had to come from that very same Ground – the Ground of Being. Where else could it have come from?"*

"Nowhere."

"So that's God in the formless state. But then there was this decision or impulse to take form. That's when God said, 'I want to become Myself in form.' You get it?"

"I do."

"So that's an enormous, Herculean task. Right?"

"Yeah."

"So the minute that impulse was acted upon something else altogether started happening, which was the creation of the universe. That's when time began. That's the theory,

at any rate. So ultimately how this Big Bang theory is going to play out we don't really know. But you don't even have to be that sure about it. All you have to know is that the experience of consciousness in the Ground of Being versus the Authentic Self is radically different. They are two fundamentally different dimensions of consciousness that are both absolute. And this morning I was describing what the difference is. We spoke a lot about the Ground of Being as well as the nature of this Evolutionary Impulse or Authentic Self. 'How does God feel?' we asked, and I said that there is a profoundly intense surge of creative urgency that's experienced. That's what conscience is. It's that big sense of purpose and it has all the awe and grandeur of the cosmos at rest in the Ground of Being when it's in its active dimension, but it's of a different sort. Do you understand?"

"Yes, I do. Thank you very much."

With that Andrew seemed to have summed up his point. After scanning his audience for a few moments his attention returned to the blonde teenage girl who had spoken with him earlier. Her hand was half raised.

"Did you have a question?" he asked her.

"Yes," she said. "From the evolutionary standpoint why was ego created?"

"To make trouble for me," Andrew retorted, exploding in a spontaneous burst of laughter.

The room laughed uproariously with him and it was some moments before he was able to continue.

"So there are different connotations to the word ego but in terms of evolution and development, it's the growing capacity for the individual human being to be able to see themselves as being separate from their environment.

"For example, human beings at lower levels of development had a very difficult time, or perhaps were even incapable, of seeing themselves as being separate from their tribe. So at a tribal level of development the individual sees himself or herself as part of a collective and they literally can't imagine themselves as being separate from that. Their whole identity is related to their particular group. They literally don't have the capacity to see themselves as being a separate individual standing apart from the group. And historically this is largely how it's been.

"So as consciousness has evolved through time and history what has begun to emerge is this capacity for individuation or the capacity for the self to see itself as standing apart from its environment or the context from which it's emerging. So, in a sense, consciousness is disembedding itself slowly and gradually from the context in which it emerged, which is a good thing because in doing so its capacity for objectification develops. That means it can begin to become aware of the context from which it emerged with a growing capacity to see itself as being an observer that, in increasing degrees, sees itself as being other than the context itself.

"Now we can never do that completely. It's impossible for the perspective of the self to be completely unconditioned because part of what conditions the way we see our experience and what gives us perspective are concepts. And all concepts, which are the

way we interpret the experience we have, are somehow culturally embedded in many different ways, all of which is very complex.

"A lot of history and development have gone into the development of our conceptual capacity. So the only way consciousness can completely disembed itself is when it dwells upon Itself. Non-conceptual meditation is the only way we can have an experience of consciousness that's completely and radically disassociated from any context. And that, as we've been speaking about, is the source of ultimate and radical liberation from being embedded or trapped in anything.

"But the use and value of that disappears the minute we enter back into the physical and human world space because then we re-enter into time and we have to engage. And whenever we engage we have to use the equipment that we have, which means we begin to work with concepts – concepts that we use to create different perspectives. Those perspectives are our individual and collective worldviews, and that's how we see.

"So the ego is how consciousness has evolved through time to develop this capacity for individuation, this capacity to be a separate individual. So now the individual has the profound capacity to see its own experience to a large degree as being separate from or no longer absolutely embedded in its own context. And this capacity for individuation and an individual's ability to see his or her own experience as being separate from its own context is a very good thing. Do you understand why?"

"I think so."

"Because individuals and collectives at lower levels of development cannot see beyond their own context. That's their only reality. They literally don't have the capacity to see beyond it. Is that clear?"

"Yeah."

"So the development of this capacity for individuation is a good thing. And it's only very recently in human history that there have been so many individuals that have had this very sophisticated, highly developed capacity for individuation. But because of the particular time in history that this is happening there is no bigger context to moderate this very highly developed capacity for individuation. In other words, historically there was always a mythical god or absolute principle above us that we were subservient to. But we're living in a time in history where, because of the Western Enlightenment, we've freed ourselves from the domination of the patriarchal religions and their worldviews. And, of course, this is what really freed the human intellect and creative potential.

"But because there hasn't been any modifying influence on this highly developed ego to create context for it, for people like you and me who enter into the world space at this particular time, we are the center of the universe. My parents said to me, "Sweetheart, what do you want to do with your life?"

As with so much else, what Andrew was driving at was obvious once it was pointed out. In this case he liked to point out that we are the first generation in all of human history to have been, en masse, presented with this question. He also liked people to consider the effect that repeatedly hearing this question during our formative years would have on our worldview and sense of place. A bit of consideration reveals that it would cause us to feel precisely the way we do: that life is our playground within which to work out our destiny and desires. It's all here for us.

"*Everything was all about me,*" Andrew continued. "*I was the center of the universe and life was all only about me and whatever I wanted to do. We were secular Jews so we didn't believe in God. We didn't believe in anything higher than the personal self. And in the world that I grew up in, which is this upper middle-class life in New York City, the message I was given by my family and all the schools I attended was that I was the center of the universe and everything revolved around me and what I wanted. And it's the same message that all my friends got.*

"*You see, previously there was the emperor, the king, or even the family and respect for elders. But now, not only are there no kings or emperors anymore – thank God – but even the hierarchical family structures are crumbling to the point that they hardly exist anymore. Of course, a lot of the old hierarchies were power-driven 'dominator hierarchies' and they're outmoded now. But what we find is that for the luckiest, wealthiest and most privileged educated classes there's no hierarchy anymore. There's nothing higher than the individual. There are no structures for the self to orient itself in relationship to. The world has become flat! The individual has become the center of the cosmos and that's the problem.*

"*So, as I was saying earlier, historically each culture had its own myths which created context, hierarchy, meaning and purpose. But we've outgrown all the myths from the pre-modern era. We've gotten too sophisticated. Now, that's not a bad thing because we're evolving, but we're at this very delicate transition point where we've outgrown the old but haven't yet created that which is new.*

"*So for those of us highly evolved, individuated beings coming into the world at this interim point, our particular problem is that we have this very highly developed capacity for individuation but there's nothing modifying this highly developed ego. And because there's nothing higher than the individual self we've become infatuated with ourselves to a degree that's extreme.*

"*So when we come upon this Authentic Self, which is the experiential discovery of a universal sense of meaning and purpose, suddenly the ego finds a cosmic context for its own presence here and that's good if we want to evolve. But the ego, having been the center of its own world and its own universe, finds that a very hard message to take.*" Andrew's voice took on a mocking tone. "'*So you mean I'm not the center of the universe? You mean how I feel and what my needs are isn't more important than anything else?*' And then your Authentic Self says, '*No, not at all.*' It says something quite hard for the postmodern ego to take. It says, '*Your value,*' – and this is a very delicate thing I'm trying to say – '*may be dependent upon how much you realize Me. You see the degree of your narcissism, which means your self-concern and your unwillingness to give it up and transcend it, makes you an unfit vehicle. You're not going to be able to carry Me and be a vehicle for this cosmic sense of purpose.' And that's the problem with the narcissistic ego – it profoundly inhibits our capacity to awaken to the Authentic Self and to be able to respond to it. Does that make sense?"*

"Yeah," the young girl responded.

"So in this way we understand why ego, this highly-developed capacity for individuation, is such a miraculous, extraordinary wonder of evolution itself. It's through this capacity for individuation that consciousness has begun to disembed itself. I mean, it's been happening all along, though very slowly. But now there's a profound capacity for consciousness to disembed itself from its environment and to think with greater objectivity about these things than was ever possible before. So that's the positive side of it.

"But the negative side of it is that we've all, as a result of these and other factors, gotten stuck on ourselves. And we are! We really, really are, a lot more than we think. But of course, that's not the end of the story because at the same time the spiritual or evolutionary impulse is very much alive and at work, which is, of course, what draws people to retreats like this. Because many people know that there's more and feel that they're stuck."

"So the ego had a part in this sort of evolutionary thing," the girl stammered in perfectly teenage fashion, "but at this point, its part in history is sort of over? Or, well, I mean, …" After a thoughtful pause she finally blurted it out. "Well, do you think there's a future for ego?"

Riotous laughter swept through the room.

"Well, in the positive sense or the negative sense?" Andrew asked.

"Hmm," she said unsurely.

"Well, let me say that the positive definition of ego is this capacity for individuation which makes it possible to truly become an autonomous individual. So this capacity for authentic autonomy is always good. Right?"

"Yeah, right."

"Autonomy has a lot to do with liberation and authentic freedom. An autonomous individual is one who's capable of thinking very deeply about the nature, meaning and the purpose of life as well as honestly and authentically about one's own self. The majority of people who have very big, highly developed egos don't do that because it's too hard and demanding.

"There are very few individuals willing to make the effort and pay the price to become truly autonomous individuals. Most people are just too lazy and don't care enough. There are so many of us with so much extraordinary potential, but even in the traditional definition of ignorance or unenlightenment, most people are lost and asleep.

"Someone asked the Buddha, 'Are you a god?' to which he said, 'No, I'm awake.' Awake means you're not asleep. What does it mean to be asleep? To be asleep has been

defined in many different ways but one way we could speak about it is as being lost. That means being lost in the individual and collective mindsets, worldviews and values that come to us from our own culture and the particular place that we come from in it.

"So, from the perspective of evolutionary enlightenment, being asleep would mean lost in the materialism and narcissism of postmodern secular culture. And we are all a lot more infected with the narcissism and materialism from postmodern culture than many of us actually believe. That's a very big problem because the ego, the narcissistic separate self-sense, is identified in a deep and fundamental way with the values that come from culture. And let me assure you, this is big stuff to get over.

"The pathological narcissist sees the culture that secular materialism creates as its playground, especially if they have a little bit of wealth. And you don't have to have a lot of wealth to really be able to indulge your narcissistic tendencies these days. It's very easy. There have never been so many options available to human beings throughout history. So, for example, not only are there fifty kinds of toothpaste, but just about anything you want materially or anything you could want to do can be done in more ways than you could even begin to imagine because other people are busy thinking of different ways to be able to make some money out of your unfulfilled desires and endless needs.

"So it's funny but it's also shockingly true and it represents a big part of the world. There are a lot of us, even if perhaps two thirds of the world is still busy just trying to survive day to day. They don't have the luxury of being able to be lost in quite this way." Andrew laughed. *"But believe me, I'm sure they want to. They want what we've got. You see the picture?"*

"Yes, definitely," she said and in a tone indicating that the seriousness of what Andrew was describing was not lost on her.

"Okay. So to answer the question, the ego is both good and bad. On the one hand, it's the best thing that's ever happened to us in terms of the capacity it gives us for self-liberation. On the other hand, it's the biggest problem we have and we need to get over it in the worst kind of way.

"But interestingly, the Authentic Self can only be recognized and realized in our very highly-developed ego, which means only with a very sophisticated and highly developed capacity for individuation. Only such an individual would have the capacity to awaken to and realize what I'm calling the Authentic Self, which is when the Energy and Intelligence that created the universe awakens to itself or becomes aware of itself at the level of consciousness. You start speaking like this to people that are still stuck in pre-modern worldviews and they'll just hear it as blasphemy and come to hang you. Hmm?"

"Yeah."

"So it's good news and bad news."

"Okay, thank you."

"But the whole idea within the context of evolutionary enlightenment is for the individual to have the courage to awaken to the big picture and to the radical implications of that big picture, which is that in order for the evolutionary process at the level of consciousness to move forward it needs individuals who are willing to take responsibility for it. It can't and it won't happen by itself at this point because matter and consciousness are one and consciousness realizes itself through matter. If we weren't here, how would the Energy and Intelligence that created the universe have the capacity to know itself?"

"It couldn't."

"Right. It wouldn't be able to know itself in the manifest realm, in the universe, in time. The Energy and Intelligence that created the universe has no other way to know itself except through us. It can't know itself through my little dog. It can't know itself through this table. It can't know itself through the trees on the mountain, right?"

"Right."

"The trees on the mountain don't have the capacity for consciousness that we do. They have some capacity for consciousness because they're alive. So does my little dog. He's very alive but he doesn't have the capacity for consciousness that you do, hmm? So you couldn't put the evolutionary burden of the universe on his little shoulders because he just doesn't have the machinery."

I smiled at the image of a little Yorkie with the expanding universe resting upon his minute shoulders.

"But we do and because we do it's obvious to me, rightly or wrongly, that we're the ones to do it. We have that capacity for consciousness to become aware of itself through us in the universe of time and space. And if that capacity is not used then what are we going to do? We'll be lost and in all likelihood this experiment in consciousness will not continue, at least not in this corner of the universe. So that's the way I see it.

"This is what I call radical, impersonal, evolutionary enlightenment. Radical, because it's extreme. Impersonal because the Authentic Self, which is a function in consciousness that is one and the same for anyone who awakens to it, completely destroys the ego's sense of self-importance. Evolutionary because what the Authentic Self wants to do is to create the future. Enlightenment because it answers the question, 'Who am I?' with the age-old discovery, 'I am Consciousness.'

"The Authentic Self is the expression and manifestation of the First Cause realizing itself or becoming aware of itself at the level of consciousness. The First Cause is the Big Bang, which was the choice to create and become the universe. The Authentic Self is the part of you and the part of me that consciously realizes that same impulse. It's non-cognitive; it's not an intellectual recognition. It's much deeper. It's a soul-level realization. It's that ecstatic compulsion to participate in the creation of the universe, not because you want to or because it'd be a nice idea, but, in a highly realized individual, because you have no choice anymore. It's 'not my will, but thy will be done.'

"The Authentic Self is a choiceless engagement with life, which means it's beyond ego and beyond narcissism. It's the ultimate destruction of this pathological and

rampant narcissism – and it's a very big deal. A lot of people have a great deal of trouble because narcissism is a tough thing to get over. It's easy to laugh about it and it's good to laugh about it, but the truth is it's not an easy thing to get over because it's such a big part of our conditioning. You get the idea?"

"Yes, I do."

"So the ego is a gift of evolution and this capacity for individuation is a very good thing but unfortunately too many of us have gotten stuck on a good thing. We've gotten trapped in the wrong way on the best thing that we have, right?"

"Yeah," she chuckled.

"So it's a situation that needs to be corrected, hmm? So, for example, if adults like me can't correct it in myself, who are you going to learn from? Because you all need examples of people who've gotten over this thing and are motivated by something deeper than their own narcissism. Right?"

"Yes," she acknowledged.

After a short pause, Andrew, with dramatic flair, wiped his forearm across his brow. *"Whew, that was a long one,"* he said with a grin. Once more, laughter filled the room.

"Okay, we're going to leave it at that for tonight. So once again, if you want to talk about this it's totally fine, but I repeat, you mustn't speak personally! If more of you start talking, which might happen, it's totally fine but you have to promise me that you're not going to speak personally, okay?"

Everyone seemed in agreement.

"The reason I'm saying that is because what I'm calling the Authentic Self can and will emerge if you resist the personal domain. The personal line is the vehicle through which the ego travels. That's its line of communication. So if you cut off its line of communication the ego has no way to come out. So the reason I insist that people don't speak about anything personal is so that what I'm calling the Authentic Self will actually emerge and then people will actually know what I'm talking about.

"You see, the way these retreats are designed is to ensure that as many people as possible have an experience of transcending the ego which means going from a negative relationship to life, which I call 'minus one,' to back to before the beginning, which is Zero, where we experience the absolute, or non-relative dimension of consciousness. So we go from a negative relationship to life to no relationship to life whatsoever and then, ideally, emerge as the Authentic Self which I call 'plus one,' and which is a thoroughly, ecstatically, only positive relationship to life. So hopefully as many of you as possible will have an experience for several days of going between plus-one, which is the Authentic Self, to Zero, which is the Ground of Being and back, while bypassing ego altogether.

"The Authentic Self, by the way, is not self-conscious, not frightened and not competitive. Those of you who have some experience of the Authentic Self know what I'm talking about and those of you who don't will find out that it's quite amazing. You'll

see that the Authentic Self is already fully formed and ready to go. That's what's so miraculous about it. The Authentic Self is inherently whole from the very beginning.

"You see, the experience I want people to have is of this Authentic Self and of the Ground of Being and I want as many of you as possible to see what it's like to spend three, five, eight days just going from the Ground of Being, or Zero, to plus-one, or the Authentic Self. I want you to see what it's like to be you when you go back and forth from the Ground of Being to the Authentic Self and, for at least for a few days, to transcend ego in a very different kind of way than people may have experienced it before.

"So when you experience the Authentic Self, which is already enlightened, then you understand what the Enlightened Self is like when it's engaged with life. The absolute dimension of the Self at the level of consciousness, which many of you have experienced, is consciousness that's completely and radically disengaged from the creative process. But the big question is, 'how does the enlightened Self actually engage with the life process?'

"The traditional response, before this Authentic Self has been discovered, has been compassionate service. That's why so often you see powerfully and authentically enlightened saints serving people who are really in dire straits and helping in so many important ways.

"But the Authentic Self's response is different because it wants to create that which hasn't happened yet and therefore it's slightly different. It's a new potential that's emerging in consciousness and we'll talk more about it tomorrow."

With that Andrew wound up the teaching and, after a short meditation, we dispersed once more. Outside, despite the evening hour, the sun was still bright. My mind, which had been largely incapacitated earlier during the day, was by small degrees beginning to work again. I mulled over the afternoon's teaching and all that had transpired today. Since sunrise we had, after three full days of immersion, emerged from the Ground of Being like divers bringing up pearls. We had then considered the significance of what we had found in those depths in relationship to our human life, both in this world and beyond. From those existential grounds we strode onward – a vanguard of spiritual explorers – into the cultural context within which all of this is playing itself out, paying particular attention to the pivotal nature of the time in which we currently live. Thus, since the outset of the retreat we had traveled from the relative to the Absolute – a three day pilgrimage to the source of the Self – and had, during the previous twelve hours, begun to reverse that course, returning to the relative, bearing the knowledge and living experience of the Absolute. We had gone from fragmentation to wholeness and now, from the perspective of wholeness, had begun to examine that fragmentation.

Aware of this shift I began to consider the afternoon's teaching. The first thing that struck me was the first questioner's difficulty with the concept of conscience. It caused me to reflect on what I understood to be the unspoken ethos of the modern alternative spiritual culture: "I would like to be blessed with as many experiences of spiritual ecstasy as possible and I would like to live a life of effortless and perfect action. However, I do not wish to be told what to do by any agent, exterior or interior, or be made to exert any effort or bear any amount of discomfort in the pursuit of such a goal. After all, why should I? I'm a nice guy or a good girl with honorable intentions and noble aspirations. That should be enough. I exist and that, in itself, makes me important and good."

The unacknowledged subtext of this declaration of the "sensitive self," however, is that those of us who have been brought up with the benefits of wealth, privilege and education and have then had added the blessings of spiritual experience, have somehow become incredibly weak, lazy and self-indulgent. We want everything for nothing as if we somehow deserved it simply because we exist. In short, it is as if, in the wake of such a profusion of good fortune, we have had our spiritual spines surgically removed. Consequently, we are interested in spiritual teachings so long as they deliver the bliss without demands. This explains the immense popularity of the neo-Advaita "no effort" teachings both in the United States and in Europe. "Be as you are, there's nothing to do," they blithely advise us. "You're already perfect. Just stop trying to change or improve anything and allow this liberating truth to wash over you. Don't you know that it's all good?"

Wow! Even as I write I can feel a soothing breeze enfold me in its balmy currents as I smile lazily. Yet my reverie is soon disturbed by that grating voice of conscience, saying: "Is it really true?" Are we really perfect as we are or is there room, on the level of the personality, for just a smidgen of improvement? What if it were true that our value as human beings is related in direct proportion to our fitness as a vehicle for the Authentic Self to emerge into this troubled and divided world? What if being a "nice guy" with a baggage train of good intentions simply wasn't good enough?

Such considerations are like the slap in the face of the "sensitive self," that child of postmodernity which, despite being filled with existential angst, wishes only to have tribute paid to the better of its qualities while glossing over the silently corroding state of its own soul. Sated on a steady diet of its own pretense of "goodness" it explodes in fits of "narcissistic rage" when confronted with inarguable evidence suggesting something other, something darker, even sinister. There are those occasions when the "sensitive self" will confess its imperfections. But it will do so only under great duress and to the degree that it may claim said imperfections to have been branded into it as a helpless victim of circumstance. The modern therapeutic culture has, of course, done nothing to dissuade this notion, flourishing in the soil of such a cultural milieu like a rose in a well-tilled garden. And it is in that selfsame soil that we find strewn about such precious philosophical gems as "don't judge the actor, judge the action," begging the question of where exactly one draws the line? Of course it is in this garden of the "sensitive self" that spiritual conscience, if not having been banished in entirety, has been marginalized to the point of near irrelevance. This explained the young man's question. He did not wish to be "should upon."

But closer scrutiny of this well-tended tract of postmodernity reveals a waft of something unpleasant, an insidious odor perhaps not at first apparent amongst the fragrant floral scents, but drawing increasingly into focus with only the slightest flexing of the cords of moral fiber. Should we linger on such a concentration of conscience we might soon find that odor growing. The fact is that there is something strange about individuals who have been given more wealth and opportunity than any prior generation claiming victimhood in relationship to life and feeling put upon by the demand to elevate the soul because, heaven forbid, in some key interior departments they might be found to be deficient.

Now, you might wonder, and rightfully so, why I should feel entitled to speak so boldly about this depredation of the soul, ranting on as if from the height of moral superiority. The answer is simple: we tend to resent in others precisely that which we secretly most despise in ourselves. The truth is that I cannot exclude myself, even slightly, from this picture for I have also operated from behind the cloak of this moral bankruptcy for the better part of my adult life and I am now endeavoring to dig myself out.

My own embeddedness in this position came fully to light one evening during a rather stormy interaction with Steve Brett, one of Andrew's senior students, whose exterior gave no hint of the spiritual power that lay beneath that unassuming surface. He was, at the time, taking me rather severely to task for a litany of unpleasant expressions of my own unacknowledged unconsciousness.

"The only difference between you and me," he'd said at one point, his eyes flashing and piercing mine, "is that I know I'm a dangerous character and you don't. I know that unless I take responsibility for myself I'll be an out of control egomaniac who is going to leave a trail of destruction in the world. You don't know that yet. You still think you're a nice guy."

"Well, I know that I have a lot of ego," I had objected feebly, "but ..."

"Not enough, you don't," Steve cut me off sharply. He held my gaze briefly and then, in a softer tone, added, "you don't understand. We all want to think we're nice guys, especially us spiritual seekers, but you have to see that it's a sham. The old fashioned Christian proposition is much more apropos. They tell us that we have to come to our knees before God and declare that we're a sinner. That's more like it really. In many ways, that's the beginning of the spiritual life."

I was speechless. The foundations of my worldview were cracking and shifting as the stinging truth of Steve's cutting observations bit deeply into me. The resultant psychic lacerations laid me open and allowed new knowledge to seep in behind the walls of my defenses. Ruefully I realized that I was one of those "nice guys" to which Andrew had referred and against whom he liked to warn others. I, the earnest seeker, it turned out was little more than a pretender, an assemblage of self-serving suppositions that inflated the ego like a swollen bladder.

My mind went back to a quote of Rumi's that had long ago lodged itself in some recessed chamber of my spiritual heart: "the door to Eternity is precisely the shape I make when I am headless on my knees." Headless on my knees, I recognized in that instant to be the diametric opposite of the "nice guy" posture, the latter being little more than a convenient self-deception, a graven image as laden with hubris and presumption as a petty despot is with medals and hollow decorations. I further grasped that should I fail to bring all this onboard I could never authentically "get on with the process of purification," as Andrew had exhorted me, for the simple reason that my starting point would be a groundless fantasy constructed entirely of a deluded collection of assumptions. Conversely, were I to muster the humility to admit to being an "out of control egomaniac" as Steve had suggested, then, as I'd be starting with the facts as they actually were, I might in fact be able to get somewhere. *"Most seekers want to go from where they're not to where they haven't been,"* I once heard Andrew say and I suspect that it was precisely this to which he was pointing.

Humility,[10] I had come to understand, was the key. Nothing new in that yet it was ever new. I had long considered the mystery of that alchemical elixir of which I knew so little. In moments of insight and fleeting transparency I had understood that humility engenders an openness in which could be found the keys to the gateway of authentic transformation. I saw through that gateway the night of Steve's assault on my ego. That encounter with humility, as with all those prior and subsequent, was, in a word, humiliating. That, I suppose, is the nature of the process and the price of admission. No way around it. The ego will always feel humiliated when forced to own up to its own insanity. Interestingly, I had often heard Andrew say that from an enlightenment perspective we are all basically insane, an understanding that has proven as helpful as an arm to a drowning man in coming to terms with all this. Why? Because I realized that the ego is not so much "my problem" as it is "the problem." That little shard of knowledge not only takes a bit of the sting out of a stinging realization, it simultaneously prevents us from taking up a position of specialness in our own madness, another favored ploy of the shapeshifting ego.

So, if we are indeed all crazy – and even a cursory examination of the evidence seems to support this view – one might wonder what we are to do with this information. *"Don't make a problem out of it,"* had been Andrew's advice to one young man some months earlier on this very point. *"Simply assume it's true and don't make a problem out of it."* When I first heard this I felt strangely free; simply put, I could unburden myself of the pretense that it wasn't so. I no longer needed to gush with pained surprise when I encountered further evidence of that very fact. I could simply see its actuality and drop the heavy cargo of pretense like sand bags from a hot air balloon.

What has further helped me in dealing with the unrelenting fact of ego was Andrew's discussion of its singular role in the developmental process. This afternoon he had given as concise and illuminating an explanation of this role as I had ever heard and contextualizing my own experience in this way has and continues to aid me immeasurably on two distinct fronts.

First, it radically depersonalizes the whole business by making it abundantly clear, as I mentioned a moment ago, that this is not particularly "my problem" but simply "the problem," an evolutionary conundrum afflicting the entire race. Along these lines, understanding that the emergence of individuation was an essential prerequisite for winning our autonomy from every structure within which we've been embedded leading, in turn, to the liberation of human independence and creativity, excises much of the guilt from the admission that perhaps we are far more embedded in ego than we'd like to admit. This knowledge injects a much-needed dose of objectivity into an extremely volatile province of the human psyche, for somehow rationally understanding all of this makes it emotionally less objectionable.

Second, such objective understanding can pave the way to an infinitely greater awareness of the obvious, but rarely sensed, fact that we are part of an unimaginably vast process of development. Most of us, myself included, have grown up believing, at least on the feeling level, that we have somehow magically emerged from a vacuum, like a genie from a bottle, and stand alone in the bubble world commonly referred to as "my life." I can easily recall my own early years and the felt sense – though I knew this to be false – that I belonged to perhaps only the third generation of human existence. There were my grandparents, my parents, and then, well, me. Beyond that all seemed vague, unreal and insignificant. At the level of feeling I had no sense of the "deep time" dimension of human emergence and the fact that I was but the tiniest part of the growing tip of the evolutionary spear. I only began to awaken to that dimension when, as a college freshman, I was fascinated with the study of history, thanks to one gifted professor. I will always remember one afternoon when an odd realization dawned on me: somewhere, deep in the mists of time, I have a great, great, great, great, great … grandfather who was a fur-covered, club-wielding cave man not far removed in lifestyle from the basest animals, yet bearing within him a potential of which he was utterly unaware. A hundred thousand years ago my shaggy ancestor, to whom I am connected by a straight line of blood, was by and large endowed with the same DNA of which I am the benefactor. Were we to meet today, however, there would exist a gulf between us that would for all intents and purposes be unbreachable. This, of course, is due to the development and evolution of culture, a phenomenon that has had effects vastly beyond what purely biological evolution has had.

It was this dramatic development that has allowed us to evolve from simple bands of hunter-gatherers to a slowly emerging global community. Along that tumultuous arc, dotted with generation upon generation of ancestors, each evolving by slow degrees from those who came before, we have developed science, the arts, politics, philosophy and the pursuit of meaning. And I, along with us all, am among the most recent milestones upon that road. Along that avenue we have conquered the better part of the natural world and eliminated with ruthless efficiency every threat to our survival save one: ourselves. Thus have we arrived at that critical juncture beyond which physical evolution as a means to our continued survival has been rendered as obsolete as a longsword and a suit of armor. We have mastered our domain – to a fault. This, of course, lands us squarely on the threshold to the realm of moral evolution. That realm, while having undoubtedly evolved alongside that of culture, has done so at a pace significantly out of step with the spectacular ascent of our other capacities. That fact has brought us to a formidable impasse. To anyone paying even the least attention it should be obvious that we are currently in dire need of a solid dose of moral evolution – and fast. Without it the survival and ongoing development of our species is seriously in question – likely to either come to a jarring halt or a collapse into a second dark age. In short, the development of ego, which in many ways has been the greatest aid to the flourishing of our species, has now become the very thing that threatens us either with extinction or dramatic diminution. Thus its transcendence is no longer a mere matter of release from samsara and personal salvation but of physical survival at the species level. That being the case, at least a few individuals – a significant minority in Andrew's lexicon – have to venture into that terrain and through their own effort and example hold open its gates so that in due course others may enter as well and with less exertion than those who came before.

Grasping the nature of my own emergence as part of a developmental stream has been indispensable in helping me to come to terms with and understand my own ego, which, as Steve Brett so clearly helped me to see that night, currently dominates my psychic makeup. More significant than just easing the humiliating sting of this admission, however, was the deepening recognition that I am a process more than I am simply a fixed point in time and space. That understanding has reconfigured the way I see myself and my role in life not unlike a Rubik's cube that has finally had its sides aligned.

There are a number of ways to think about this. The first concerns the realm of pure biology in which, as is now-well known, every few years all the cells and molecules of my body are replaced, meaning that the stuff of which I am composed today is not the stuff of which I was composed say, seven years ago. My very flesh and blood is endlessly reconstituted in a perpetual freeing and releasing of molecules, though somehow among all this flux and change I still remain "me." Plotting the course of said molecules I also find that those that form my body today, or which have cycled through it in the past, have been around since the fiery birth of the universe, only now deigning to lend their capacity to create form to the emergence and temporary sustenance of "me" and soon moving on to do the same for another. All the while the body, its components always being renewed, is aging, another process that belongs to the larger cycle of things and of which we become annoyingly aware as it wears on. In short, our entire physical existence is one mysterious process of movement and change. The only constant being the sense of being itself, its origins outside of and beyond the stream of time.

Along the same lines, when I scrutinize the interior dimensions of self and examine the thoughts, forms and structures that compose the many realms of my psyche, I find there layers of development nesting in narrowing perspective like the rings of an ancient tree stretching back across millennia. Of these, the current state of my ego is merely the latest expression though it is afforded ready access to all the layers upon which it is built. That is, the basest instincts of lust, aggression, dominance and survival that I share in abundance with the most primitive of creatures are readily available to me through a mere hair's breadth shift of attention. At the same time, I have access to the moral codes of culture and civilization that have accrued with the emergence of higher human consciousness and co-exist alongside these drives, exerting a mitigating influence on their raw animal nature. Layered upon all that are the values and principles of my own culture, ethnic background and time in history and upon this lie superimposed the various experiences of my own life, my desires, my dreams and so forth, making "me" the result of multiple, very complex streams of development whose surge forward is ever evolving even as I write these lines. Lastly, and perhaps most grand of all, this must be seen in the context of cosmic evolution, that explosion in motion rushing forward with unrelenting intensity, evolving along its burning trajectory from lower levels of complexity and integration to higher ones and of which I am but the latest product. The inescapable conclusion is that I am that explosion in motion.

And recognizing that changes everything. With just a little contemplation of these facts I find the "fixed point" sense of self-dissolving and awareness expanding infinitely in all directions as my personal story and its claim to ultimate validity relinquish their determined grip on my psyche. In their stead I find myself to be part of a vast, gloriously impersonal process of evolution, yet quickly that insight gives way to the even greater realization that in some miraculous way I am, in fact, that very process itself. But even that soon dissolves in the yet deeper revelation that I am simultaneously that very process *becoming aware of itself.* And while the ultimate impersonality of it all shatters all ideas of specialness like a stack of china hitting the cement, what I find bubbling up from the womb of creation is an uncontainable positivity about being alive.

And as I consider the human predicament several things become immediately apparent. First, it stands to reason that since we have developed over the aeons into what we are now, that we are neither a fixed point nor a finished product. Rather, we are a work in progress, a bridge to some higher potential of which we are as yet unaware in precisely the same way that my great, great, great, great, great … caveman of a grandfather would have been unable to foresee the outrageous development of his distant progeny, namely myself.

Second, and this is the more significant point, we currently find ourselves at a critical crossroads with respect to our future development. That is, while the process of evolution has to date been as self-directed and automatic as digestion,[11] the future development of our species and the growing capacity of That which lies behind it to become aware of itself, and most importantly to act through us, now rests squarely upon our shoulders. The process is no longer automatic. It fully depends upon us.

Sound outrageous? Think about it for a minute. First, with respect to physical evolution, we have cracked the genetic code and, with that encryption key in hand, we are steadily unlocking its potentials. Additionally, we are developing robotics, information technology and nano-technology, all of which are converging and add up to one thing: we are the first and only species, at least in this corner of the galaxy, in a position to direct its own further physical evolution along any trajectory it likes. The process is *entirely* in our hands. Whether we agree with it or not, whether we like it or not, this is simply a fact. Are we going to take advantage of this newly emerging capacity? You bet! Our curiosity and reckless sense of adventure have never yet allowed us to develop a technology and not use it. Upon what trajectory we steer that inevitability is therefore of the utmost importance and is, in turn, entirely dependent upon our moral and spiritual evolution.

Those, in their own turn, also lie entirely in our hands. That is, being the first generation ever to be in a position to be aware of the process of cosmic evolution - and of the Self beyond ego and time - puts us in a position to harness both our critical faculties and spiritual longing to step beyond the belief based religious structures of the past and create a new spiritual paradigm that takes into account the totality of human knowledge and empowers us as conscious agents of the Unmanifest in the world of manifestation. However, the evolution of consciousness beyond ego is a step that we can either choose to take or not. There is nothing automatic about it and no one and no thing can compel us to do this. And the hitch, of course, is the fact that the ego, having as its core agenda only the survival of itself, does not care one whit about any of this. In fact, though it can feign interest with Oscar winning style, when push comes to shove, as it inevitably will, it is actively and violently disinterested. Yet it is clear that if we are to survive, the next step in human evolution must involve the transcendence of the ego, for the miraculous psychic mechanism that has brought us this far now threatens to destroy us just as we sit at the brink of an astounding possibility.

All of which brings me back to the question of conscience that the young man had raised with Andrew during the teaching. The context itself, Andrew had said, awakens spiritual conscience. This rings perfectly true to my own experience. In fact, it awakens it in a way that nothing else could. And once this context has been authentically seen and acknowledged it can't be forgotten. At least I can't seem to shake it. Its realization has irrevocably reframed my own understanding of the spiritual quest, shredding entirely the notion of enlightenment as a means to some form of permanent personal happiness. In short, I can no longer see my own potential for enlightenment and transformation as being in the slightest way separate from this larger picture, which has not so much been imposed upon me as it has revealed to me a sense of moral obligation in a way that years of lectures from pious priests and well-meaning do gooders never could.

This begs the next question: having understood the need to transcend ego for the highest reasons, what are the tools and mechanisms that might enable me to be victorious in so outrageous an endeavor? In short, how do I do it? How do I turn insight into transformation? I was sure that it would be this matter to which Andrew would turn his attention next.

NOTES

1. This is best evidenced in the "neo-advaita" teachings popular today. Neo-advaita refers to a variety of insipid contemporary interpretations of traditional advaita or non-dual teachings that originated in ancient India. These interpretations have largely pulled the teeth of tradition from what was once a potent teaching. For more on this see Jessica Roemischer's stunning satire *Who's Transforming Anyway? Stacey Heartspring Encounters the Postmodern Craze of Neo-Advaita* in issue #34 of *What is Enlightenment?* magazine or read it online at http://www.wie.org/j34/stacey.asp. Also, take a look at Tom Huston's review of the book *The Translucent Revolution* (Novato, Ca.: New World Library, 2005) entitled *Getting Clear about Enlightenment* in issue #31 of *What is Enlightenment?* magazine or read it online at http://www.wie.org/j31/translucent.asp.

2. In Andrew's lexicon perfection can be described as taking unconditional responsibility for ourselves in the name of liberation here and now.

3. Bardo is a Tibetan word that refers to a variety of intermediate states between death and rebirth. Such bardos can be heavenly, hellish and everything in between, their quality determined by the quality of the life one has lived.

4. These lines were spoken by Maximus in the film *Gladiator* and reflect a sentiment to which I have long subscribed but which I have rarely heard more succinctly and passionately stated.

5. This, once again, is what Andrew has often referred to as "negative freedom," which stands in direct opposition to, "the bondage of liberation," in which one is ethically tied to doing the right things for the right reasons.

6. This outrageous statement came from Wayne Liquorman and can be found in the previously referenced article by Jessica Roemischer (*Who's Transform-*

ing Anyway: Stacey Heartspring Encounters the Postmodern Craze of Neo-Advaita in is-sue #34 of *What is Enlightenment?* magazine. It can also be read online at http://www.wie .org/j34/stacey.asp?page=2), who was actually present when he made this statement.

7. Once again defined as the willingness to take full responsibility for every aspect of ourselves in the name of liberation right now.

8. If this reference is unclear, the reader should see the movie *The Matrix*, which will clarify its meaning.

9. I can attest to this affliction as for many years, though on the one hand humbled by my experiences of the Absolute, I had concluded that having had such experiences made me special, privy to some arcane knowledge of which others remained unaware. Thus I perceived myself as more deeply in touch with life and truth than others and, with all the subtlety of pretense netted out, essentially better than them because of it.

10. Humility, Andrew has often pointed out, does not equate with being meek. True humil-ity, in fact, is the fount of true power though not in the egotistical sense. And in our relationships with each other in the context of this teaching, Andrew has added, we should endeavor to create a "hierarchy of humility."

11. An important process shot through with and driven by intelligence and purpose though utterly lacking in consciousness.

Day 5

Meditation is a
Metaphor for Enlightenment

I am not a morning person at the best of times; this much the reader might have guessed from my earlier tales of nocturnal distress. On a retreat such as this sleep is an undeniably precious commodity, but it was one that I was once more denied when, at two-thirty in the morning, my roommate's snoring came crashing through my dreams and continued until I rose in a somnambulistic stupor at four forty-five a.m. During the intervening hours, which passed like the slow, tortured moments of a chemotherapy drip, I lay awake brooding as the bliss and exaltation of the previous day bled away into the night.

How fickle the inner weather, I thought, and how quickly the thrill of just a few hours ago melted away in the face of a stirring breeze of irritation. And how quickly that breeze grew to a storm of despair. One moment in ecstasy, the next in desperation – where was the freedom in that? At that particular moment, nowhere to be found. With stooping shoulders and feet of lead I stumbled across the courtyard to the instant coffee machine – surprisingly good and intensely caffeinated here in Europe where they still do coffee right. As its dark tonic seeped into my veins I considered Andrew's teachings on an absolute relationship to feeling. They astutely point out that our moment-to-moment perspective on life and the conclusions we draw about it are sculpted almost in entirety by the ever-fluctuating waves of our emotional states. If I am soaring among the horizonless vistas of transcendent bliss, as I was not long ago, then all seems possible, including my own outrageous transformation. If, on the other hand, I am being challenged by outrageous irritation, as I was at that moment, such notions are as curtly dismissed as an unwelcome visitor from a foreign land.

An absolute relationship to feeling, Andrew stated unequivocally, was one in which our interest in liberation was always stronger in our relationship to life than our endlessly changing emotional states. What I was most connected with emotionally, standing there in the dark, was my desire for a soft bed, my wife's comforting presence and a heavy silence within which to get some sleep. Yet though I craved relief and entertained fantastic notions of escape, I knew that I would not be going anywhere; that I'd simply wade through my sleep deprived delirium like a zombie, knowing that things would somehow change. They always do. Often, in circumstances like this, the only thing I have going for me is a tenacious stubbornness born of some fundamental understanding that this is more important than anything else and that, at the end of the day, this is where my true heart lies. Perhaps this was what Andrew was pointing to.

Shuffling through the darkness across the cobbled stones I recalled a statement Andrew had made some years earlier and which seemed particularly pertinent now. *"One state can't remember the other,"* he had said, meaning that when someone is basking in the liberating bliss of consciousness beyond ego, they can't remember or relate *whatsoever* to the fears and desires of the ego. Conversely, when someone is traveling the well-worn road of ego they cannot relate *in the least* to the thrill and significance of the enlightened consciousness that they have experienced for themselves. These are two aspects of the self between which there are no lines of communication, which is what so often makes the spiritual journey terribly confusing and causes endless vacillations in one's loyalties to these two rival realms.

As I vacillated between my own divided loyalties, one thing was becoming increasingly clear: ego was not just a realm, it was a beast and it had, over the days, grown weary of its confinement. Now on the prowl and scanning its surroundings suspiciously, it was readying for a fight. I recalled Andrew's comment that ego is a worthy foe indeed, a potent adversary never to be taken lightly. I knew this to be true from previous experience and also knew that its true influence upon our lives is seen only to the degree that we challenge it for real. Rarely faced with such a challenge it is content, mostly, to remain cunningly hidden, running our lives from the shadows while feasting on the life of our soul. Only when incited will it fight for its domain. And it is only when challenged absolutely that its full fury can be known. As only a few dare challenge its insidious reign, its true form is rarely seen or known. *"If a little fear should raise its head most people run for the hills,"* Andrew had once said in this regard, adding that, *"most of us do not bow to the God of Love but to the god of fear."* Most of us, at the slightest flex of ego's power, shudder and quickly negotiate a truce that produces a spurious peace while placing beyond hope authentic victory and the liberation of the soul. And since for this reason the ego is rarely forced to rear up in full power, most people believe that, beyond being a slight glitch in the personality, it barely exists. Which brings to mind the old but apt saying that the greatest trick the devil ever pulled was convincing man that he didn't exist. [1] But I knew better. I knew what would happen if I pushed myself a little harder or placed myself in a context where the possibility for ego to express itself was severely curtailed. What would happen is exactly what was happening now; a grumbling discontent that, finding fuel in sleep deprived irritation was beginning to stir. Anger, the first captain in ego's army of deceit, had risen and its lieutenants, cynicism and despair, were slowly rising in its wake.

All of which brought into sharp relief the need for navigational tools to weather the storms unleashed by the onslaught of such powerful forces. I reminded myself once more of the teachings on an absolute relationship to feeling as well as our instructions for meditation. These simply enjoined us to have no relationship to thought or feeling all the while bearing whatever the winds of inner experience blew in our direction. With those instructions I readied myself for a storm and, much to my surprise, braved it fairly well during the following hours of chanting and meditation. However, I hoped that in the coming teaching Andrew might shed further light on what was quickly becoming a pressing issue.

The teaching commenced with the first question coming from a German woman with a heavy accent.

"I have problems to get contact to my consciousness," she began. "I had contact on the first and the third day with a feeling of emptiness and a touch of wholeness but during the last two days there is much talking in my head and I can't seem to stop it."

"Do you remember when I was speaking to this young woman yesterday?" Andrew asked, pointing to a lady sitting on the floor near him.

"Yes, but I don't know how to destroy this conclusion that I can't contact my consciousness. I tried to go into this and to withdraw my mind, but it is difficult. Sometimes it comes for a little moment, but then it goes away."

"But what I was saying to her was that whether you're in prison or not has to do with the conclusion you draw about what's happening. It doesn't necessarily have anything to do with what's objectively happening. Do you understand?"

"Yes, I think so."

"So you said that for the first couple of days you were having a very nice experience."

"A touch of that; not a deep experience, just a touch of it."

"Okay, but better than it is now, right?"

"Yes."

"And now you find that your mind is more agitated?"

"Yes."

"Right. So what I'm saying is that if you make a problem out of the fact that your mind is agitated then you become agitated. Do you understand?"

"Yes."

"So if you insist that your mind has to be quiet in order for you to be happy or at peace then you're going to have a problem."

"Yes, indeed. So I have."

"Okay, so now what I'm going to explain to you are my teachings about meditation, which I haven't spoken about at all although we've been doing quite a lot of it."

"Okay."

"So, there are two ways to look at it. On the one hand, meditation is a practice that's done through intention, but on the other, it's also something that can happen spontaneously."

"Yes. I had this experience for a while on the second day."

"Very good. So what I'm trying to say is that there's a difference. You can decide to sit still and pay attention to consciousness and practice meditating. Then, at other times, you can actually just spontaneously become aware of the fact that meditation is happening and you're not trying to do it. So I'm making a distinction between making an effort that takes willpower and intention, which is called practice, while the other is a spontaneous experience that doesn't take any effort. Are you with me?"

"Yes, yes."

"Okay, so when we make a decision that we're going to practice meditating, what's more important than the quality and the content of your experience is the position that you're taking in relationship to it. But when you have a spontaneous experience what's important is the fact that you're having a particular experience. Do you understand the difference?"

"Sort of."

"What I'm saying is that what's important when you practice is not the experience that you have, but your relationship to your experience. What's important is the posture of meditation. Do you understand?"

"I think so."

"So the meditation posture is an inner position. It's not a physical posture. It's the posture of freedom."

"Okay."

"So when you have a spontaneous experience, you spontaneously experience freedom at the level of consciousness, right?"

"Yes."

"But when you practice you have to assume the posture of freedom. Freedom is a position that you take in relationship to your experience that has nothing to do with the experience that you're having. Freedom is not the presence or absence of a particular feeling. To be free doesn't mean to feel good. Does that make sense to you?"

"Yes."

"That's an important distinction! So, once again, freedom is not an experience, but a position that we take in relationship to experience. So meditation is a metaphor for the posture of freedom. It's when you inwardly assume, through intention, the posture of freedom. So what's important is the posture that you're assuming and not the quality or the content of your experience. The question is, are you free or not? To be free means that no matter what your experience is, you're free from it."

"Everything is okay."

*"Well, maybe everything won't be okay, but **you'll** be okay. That's the idea. This is a very important thing to understand. Most people don't understand it and, if they do*

understand it, they usually forget it. So this is very important information! However, in order to put into practice what I'm explaining one has to be very serious and mature about this, otherwise we simply won't do it.

"You see, a lot of us are not very mature and also we're very self-indulgent. We put too much importance on the quality and the content of our experience and less on the posture we're assuming in relationship to our experience. So, once again, the important thing to understand is that ultimate freedom has nothing to do with what you're experiencing, which for most of us is a big surprise because often we relate freedom with peace, joy, ecstasy, bliss, and happiness. Are you with me?"

"Yes."

"So it's easy to feel free. Anybody can have the feeling of being free, right?"

"I suppose."

"If you have sex, take drugs, drink alcohol or jump out of a plane with a parachute, you can have the experience of feeling free. But that doesn't mean you are free. So there's a very big difference between the many varieties that the feeling experience of freedom can come in, and actually being a free person. That's the important thing to get very, very clear about, okay?"

"Okay."

"So if we understand that then, when we talk about meditation, as I was saying before, we can talk about it in two ways. First, we can talk about it as a spontaneous experience of higher consciousness that doesn't take effort. Second, we can talk about it as practice, which involves effort, willpower and intention.

"So when we practice meditation or, as I would say, when we practice the posture of freedom, then what we put our attention on is not the quality or the content of our experience, but the posture we're assuming in relationship to the experience that we're having. So looking at it that way, it doesn't really matter if your mind is now more agitated than it was two days ago. What's important is that it doesn't make any difference to you. If it doesn't make any difference to you, then you will be free. Of course you would prefer your mind to be still but if it doesn't happen that way it's not going to affect you in any fundamental way. So you want to shift your attention from the quality and the content of your experience to the position you're taking in relationship to your experience."

"Yes, okay."

"And the reason it's important is that the implications for assuming the posture of freedom have big implications for our relationship to life. In other words, one way to look at it is that to be free means that we're aware of what's happening, which, in turn, means we're not lost in experience. It means that in life we're not lost in our experience, but we're standing in an objective position, bearing witness to the process. So if enlightenment is to mean anything, one of the things it has to mean is that, to a significant degree, we're not lost in the process. As I was explaining yesterday, our consciousness is not embedded in the process but we're standing free from it as the observer. Do you see what I'm saying?"

"Yes."

"So, assuming the posture of freedom is a very important thing to know how to do if you actually want to be a free person. It's not about just sitting still with your eyes closed. It has to do with being a free person in life! Therefore, we want to learn how to be more interested in being free from experience than in needing to have a particular experience in order to feel free. Do you get the point?"

"Yes, okay. I think that's the point I lost the last two days. Thank you."

"Right. But most people lose this point all the time. They hear it and they say thank you and then forget it."

"I hope I don't."

"But the reason we do it is because we all have the habit of relating to our experience through our emotions and anybody who does that is not going to be a free person. So in order to become a mature human being we have to learn how to have a very different relationship to life, one that's not dominated by our emotional experience. It doesn't mean that our emotional experience is irrelevant but it means it has to become secondary, rather than primary. Do you understand?"

"Yes."

"So it's very important and what I'm explaining to you is something that you need to make an effort to practice. And then, when you really understand it, it'll change your whole life because, as I was explaining, ultimately freedom is not an experience; it's a position. Relatively, it's true, but it's also true ultimately. You're free 'from,' you're not free 'because.'"

"That's a new point for me."

"It's a new point for most people."

"Okay."

"But if you understand it, you won't need psychotherapy."

"How do you mean?"

"Well, because it means that you can handle your own emotions. People who can't bear their own emotions lose their objectivity and they need help. But if you really understand this you become your own therapist. Save a lot of money, hmm?"

"Yes, okay," she laughed.

"Is that absolutely clear?"

"Yes, thank you."

Andrew finished, paused and looked around the room for his next question. His gaze settled on another German woman whose features bore the hard lines of frustration. Having been called on, she proceeded to relate her meditation experience and then, apparently not having fully understood Andrew's point, asked essentially the same question as had the woman before her and wondered if Andrew might speak about it in a slightly different way. He agreed.

"Okay. So you have to understand what the state of meditation is. The state of meditation happens when two experiences come together as one. Specifically, you

experience the state of meditation when you're deeply relaxed and profoundly alert. These are ordinarily two contradictory states. For example, when you're very relaxed – very, very, very relaxed – usually what happens is that you fall into an unconscious state. If someone says 'relax … relax … relax,'" he said this in an amusingly soothing tone, *"you usually fall asleep. You'll become unconscious.*

"On the other hand, if someone says 'pay attention,'" Andrew threw out this phrase in a sharp, jarring voice while clapping his hands for dramatic effect, *"then we experience a certain amount of tension or make a tremendous amount of effort. Usually when we're trying to pay attention there's a certain kind of tension within us. Yet the state of meditation is when you're deeply relaxed and simultaneously unusually awake and alert. When these come together as one state that's the meditative state. Does that make sense so far?"*

"Yes, but I don't see how that helps to get in touch with my consciousness."

"Okay, let's look at how to do this technically. First you have to make sure that you're physically very still."

"Yes. That I understand."

"Your back has to be very straight and you want to be very, very still. Then, as you're still, you want to really let yourself be very relaxed and deeply at ease without any tension. At the same time you want to make the effort to pay attention. So you want to relax and pay attention, relax and pay attention, relax and pay attention. To what? To consciousness itself, as we've been saying."

"But when I think about consciousness itself then I'm using my head."

"Yes, but, as I've been explaining it, you're giving attention to something that is not an object. You're giving attention to the subject."

"Yes, I understand."

"That's not thinking! You can't think about something that's not an object or a concept. You can only think about something that is either an object or a concept in consciousness. Consciousness is not an object; consciousness is the subject so you can't really think about it. Therefore the degree to which you give your attention to the subject of consciousness itself is the degree to which you can't really think about it. Thoughts may be going on in the background, but they're going to be irrelevant to what's actually happening because the degree to which you give your attention to the subject, or to consciousness itself, is the degree to which you are putting your attention on something which is not an object. Now, it's challenging because it's a completely different way of focusing our attention. We're always focusing our attention on some thing. And yet here we're focusing our attention on 'no thing.'"

"Yes."

"So the way this works is that some thing, which is the ego self, puts its attention on no thing, on zero. And as it meditates upon and contemplates zero the ego disappears. That's kind of the idea. The ego, which is an object or a thought, can only see itself or its own reflection when it looks at another object. But when the ego gives attention to

zero or emptiness or nothingness, it can't see itself, and if you keep going, the ego falls away and what you find is the subject meditating upon itself. At any rate, technically that's how it works.

"Then, when the ego as the observer dissolves, the experience will be one of transparency. You won't feel that you are standing in any place observing any thing. You won't know where you begin and where you end, where the back is or where the front is. That will all disappear."

"Okay. Thank you," she said, but Andrew went on.

"Now, in relationship to what we've been speaking about, you have to be willing to really put some time into it."

"And I absolutely will."

"Good. Because, you see, you want to go so deeply into this that you get to the point where you really don't care if the whole world disappears and never comes back. Now, that also means your own personal life and the world in which that personal life is occurring. So you want to go so deeply into it that you begin to feel, in a very powerful way that just spontaneously begins to surge up, that you don't really care if the whole world blows up. You want to get to a point where the emotional conviction is overwhelming. Unless you get to that point in your own contemplation of consciousness where you really don't care if the whole world disappears, blows up and never returns, you haven't gone deep enough yet.

"On the other hand, I guarantee that if you do go deeply enough, the ecstasy and the joy of zero, which means having nothing, knowing nothing, and being no one, is spontaneously going to rise up from within you. This deepest absolute dimension of your own self begins to well up and you suddenly find that there is this ecstatic compulsion to be completely free from anything and everything that's ever happened."

"Okay. And that can take a long time."

"It can take a long time or a short time. It doesn't matter how long it takes; it just matters that you get there."

"True."

"Okay, good," Andrew said, concluding this dialogue.

He then looked around the room once more, and then turned to a thin, dark haired German man.

"You explained that it's very important to take no position toward thoughts or feelings during meditation," he said. "Does this apply also to pleasant feelings or experiences of bliss?"

"Definitely, of course."

"Because it's so easy to indulge in them and enjoy them very much."

"Well, you can enjoy them as long as you're not attached to them."

"So even then you try to be some sort of observer or witness of this?"

"No, you don't do anything. So what I was saying is that the freedom has to do with freedom 'from,' so ideally the way it would work is that while you were meditating no

one should be able to have any idea that you were experiencing bliss or you were experiencing intense agitation. Ideally, no one should be able to tell the difference, unless, of course, you told them. What do you think about that?"

"Makes sense."

"So you extrapolate that into a human life. Everybody says 'hello, how are you?' How are you doing? It's a way we treat each other with kindness and respect. But basically you don't really want to know how someone else is, do you?"

"Sometimes."

"Really? When is it that you're interested?"

"When you have some emotional connection with someone."

"When you have an emotional connection. You mean, like with your girlfriend?"

"For example."

"So you say 'how are you feeling sweetheart?' She says 'terrible.' Of course then you ask her 'what's wrong?' but I mean, do you really care how she feels? Isn't it basically that you don't want her to suffer because then she won't bother you?"

A few "oooohs" and hushed murmurs of shock slid tremulously through the room, wending their way between a few stifled laughs. Andrew had just struck another blow, albeit slight, at a sacred cow of postmodernity: the seemingly inviolate and inanely pretentious world of personal romance. And in so doing, he simultaneously faced each of us squarely with our own unspoken pretense. I had no trouble recognizing the sentiment to which he alluded though I was loathe to admit it to myself, largely because the next logical conclusion would have to be that I was an utterly insensitive jerk, which may, in fact, be the case. But in hearing Andrew speak and by the knowing though sheepish response from the crowd, I realized that what he'd described is how at least many of us feel. It was simply one of the many human reactions that we harbor yet simultaneously deny.

Andrew continued. *"So you're hoping when you ask the question that what she's going to say is, 'I feel fine,' right?"*

"Yeah," the man admitted.

"Okay, so basically nobody really cares how you feel. That's my whole point: we don't really care.

"Of course, if somebody is very sick or in a terrible amount of physical pain then you'd want to know because you don't want other people to suffer, all the more so if you care about them. But excluding a dramatic circumstance like that, you're not really interested. At least I'm not and I'm sure most people around us aren't really interested in how other people feel. What a terrible thing to say, hmm?"

"Well, I think I see your point."

"So if we're going to create a new world, which is actually what I want to do, that world would be made up of individuals who could handle their own mind and handle their own emotions so you wouldn't really need to ask them how they were because you knew they were fine, except if something was really wrong.

"You see, the point is you don't want to burden somebody with your emotional ups and downs because you care for them and they have problems of their own. And if they care about you they don't want to burden you either because you have problems of your own, right?"

"Yes."

"Does that sound cold?" Andrew asked rhetorically, quickly answering his own question. *"No, it's not cold at all. That's a new definition of compassion.*

"Remember, I'm talking about radical sanity. I'm talking about an idealistic possibility. I'm not talking about the world we're living in, that's for sure. So what I'm talking about would only become possible if the individuals who made up this new world were capable of handling their own mind and their own emotions. They could bear it. As I always say, if the individual cannot bear his or her own thoughts and emotions someone else is going to have to."

"Yes, that's right."

"Does everybody understand that? If you can't handle your own mind and your own emotions other people inevitably have to suffer the consequences. We don't live in a bubble. So the degree to which the individual refuses to handle their own mind and their own emotions because of a lack of maturity is the degree to which other people inevitably have to suffer as a result. So therefore, if you really care about other people, you will take responsibility for and bear your own experience so they won't have to suffer the consequences. That's true maturity and compassion.

"But most people don't care about other people. You remember when I was speaking about narcissism yesterday? Narcissists don't have real relationships with other human beings because a narcissist is the center of their own universe. For a narcissist other people are just objects that they use to adorn their own image of themselves. They use them like jewelry or like clothes and when it's old or if it's not working they throw it out. A lot of us do that. We don't have real relationships. It's something worth thinking about. What is a real relationship all about anyway?"

"That's a good question."

"So the meditation instruction I gave is very important because it can be the step or the doorway to creating a new world. So it's not just for the individual. If I realize that freedom is a posture I take in relationship to all of my experience rather than any particular experience and I practice that then, in my own way, I'm beginning to help change the world that I'm living in.

"That should mean that I'm no longer going to burden the world with my own emotional and psychological self-indulgence. Because, especially in the arena of human relationships, it's serious, isn't it? That's what creates hell on earth, right? In human relationships, when people don't take responsibility for their own mind and own emotions, it's like emotional and psychological warfare and terrorism. So you can have psychological and emotional suicide bombers, hmm? They sit in front of you and they blow themselves up emotionally and psychologically. Believe me, it creates a lot of damage to

everybody who's nearby, right? That's what's so powerful about being a suicide bomber. So pathological narcissists are often like suicide bombers, you see?

"*So my point is, if you care about human relationships you make damn sure you're very careful about your relationship to your own mind and emotions. Because you realize your relationship to your own mind and emotions is directly connected to your relationship with other human beings because we're all connected to each other on many different levels.*

"*So the beginning of the transformation of human relationship has to do with assuming the posture of freedom within oneself because the only way we can change it is by changing ourselves. You hope other people will do it but all you can do is hope. So then the posture of freedom that we're speaking about is not just something that you would practice as a meditation discipline but it has to do with your fundamental relationship to life and it's actually quite a big thing. Get the idea?*"

"Yes, definitely. It makes total sense."

"*So, in the way that I teach, I always try go from the inner to the outer and see how everything's related to everything else; to see the truly integrated, non-dual, holistic dimension to an authentic philosophy of liberation. Do you understand?*"

"I do."

"*You see, I want to help everybody to think in a different way. So up until very recently what was called mind dharma or mind teachings have all been really about the subjective experience of the individual. But now we want to look into how the individual's subjective relationship to his or her own inner experience relates directly to the world in real time.*

"*This is a new way of looking at enlightenment. It's very important to understand that. This teaching does both of these things simultaneously. If you really pay attention, as I add more and more to this you'll start to see how it's one integrated whole where there's no difference between the individual and the collective. It's not just the individual by him or herself in relationship to his or her own mind. It's the individual, ultimately, in relationship to the cosmos.*

"*You have to think deeply about these things. If you do you're going to see how big it is and when you start to see how big it is you'll begin to recognize that there's an ethical and moral dimension to the evolution or awakening of consciousness. The moral dimension enters into the picture because you realize you are not alone.*

"*However, in our postmodern, secular culture there is literally no moral context for the life that we're living. The highest moral context concerns the rights of the individual. It's freedom of the individual for the individual. Of course, we want to protect those rights. But at this point we've given so much attention to the rights of the individual that we've almost forgotten that the individual is not the most important thing.*

"*We've gone as far as we can with individuation and we've freed the individual from the worst forms of social oppression, which is, of course, good. But now we have to go back to relating the individual to the whole including other individuals. We have to have a larger context.*

"So once again, there's an inherently moral dimension to the evolution of consciousness and that's really the most important thing. Therefore the individual's relationship to his or her mind has a moral dimension to it that transcends the individual's own inner subjective experience. That's a rather interesting way to think about it, isn't it?"

"Definitely."

"Your relationship to your own mind is your relationship to everyone else in both gross and subtle ways. So for instance, let's say you meet somebody and through getting to know them you find that they're always taking responsibility for their own mind and emotions to the point where you can implicitly trust that they're always taking responsibility for themselves. That means you can relax and not be in fear of what they might do. That would give you a tremendous sense of confidence and trust in them. In turn, that would also give you confidence in humanity and its potential and that has a very big effect.

"But then if there's someone you're not really sure of then you're always going to be a little bit afraid and you're not going to be able to relax and to trust. Do you see how it works?"

"Yes, very much so."

"That's why I can say something as outrageous as, 'there's a moral dimension to the individual's relationship to his or her mind and emotions.' It's because it's true! Are you ready for that? Most people say, 'whoa, that's a little too much.'

"But you see, if the world's going to change through the evolution of consciousness this is going to be why it's going to happen. It's not because the savior, whether it's Christ or Buddha or whatever version you like, is going to come and speak on television in a hundred and fifty different languages simultaneously, resulting in the enlightenment of humanity.

"Now, you have to see that even being able to think this way means that we're all really pushing a new edge because it's only individuals who are reaching the level of 'the universal human' who would be able to understand this. Connecting the relationship to the mind and emotions of one individual to consciousness as a whole is quite a step to take. That's because eventually we want to get to what I've been gently directing everybody to, which is that consciousness is the whole point, not the individual. So when the fact of consciousness becomes the central locus for everyone it's going to change everything. I mean, I know we're not there yet, but you can see that that's where we're headed. Does that make sense?"

"Oh, yes. I'd never seen it like that before but it definitely makes sense. Thank you."

He's done it again, I thought. Started with the seed of a small question, in this case someone's particular relationship to the mind and emotions, and grown from that tiny seed a philosophical inquiry as vast as a mighty oak, flinging us out to the biggest perspective and compelling us to consider the most far reaching yet undeniable conclusions about human nature and the play of life. Once more my vision had been broadened beyond its ordinary vistas, as was always the case when my attention was pried away from obsession with myself and pushed in a contemplative direction. And, of course, this addressed the entirety of the predicament into which I had awoken this morning. Freedom is not found in any particular experience but in our relationship to all of our experience, including the fatigue-driven irritation that had welcomed me earlier in the day. In its face could I still live and act as if the highest philosophical principles were driving my life, as if my care for the whole exceeded my care for myself? If so, then that was freedom indeed and if not, well, then it wasn't. It was very simple, but unendingly profound.

After adjusting his position on his cushion Andrew turned his attention to the four teenagers seated on the floor directly in front of him.

"You know," he began, addressing the teens, *"you guys were very restless this morning. Do you guys feel restless?"*

They nodded sheepishly.

"So I just want to explain that it's very important to sit still when you meditate even if your mind is going crazy. You see, your body is the one thing that you can have automatic control over. So even if your mind is going crazy at least your body can be still. But if your mind is going crazy and you can't even control your body there'll be no hope of having even marginal control over yourself in general. And the implications are very big in terms of how one's actually going to behave. Do you understand what I'm saying everybody?" He looked at us all meaningfully. *"So it doesn't matter if your mind is restless or not. You* have *to be still. So it's a really simple exercise but it's important. You see, we should all be able to be still only because we decided to do so. It's not very esoteric but it's important, okay?"*

"Okay" we all said in chorus with the teenagers. With that he went on to the next question.

Once more a German man took the opportunity to speak. "When you want to go into the state of meditation, when you start should you go through the body, you know, focus attention on the feet, relax, then move up and so on?"

"Well, there's nothing wrong with that but the way I approach it is a little bit different. You see I teach this in the hardest and most direct way. In other words, the hardest form of meditation is called 'without seed' or 'without form.' It means without an object. It's much easier to meditate with a meditation object but here we're just jumping right into zero from the very beginning. I mean, there's nothing wrong with a more technical approach to meditation and going through certain steps. But just for the time being, while you're here with me, just leave all that and stay with the main thing, which is just to be still and give your attention to the nature of consciousness without being troubled by whether it's easy or whether it's difficult. Okay?"

"Okay."

"You see if you're lucky you'll discover that the part of you that's already free, that's already enlightened, is not the part of you that's having the experiences. How's that?"

"That makes sense."

"That's good that it makes sense," Andrew laughed. *"I don't understand it myself."*

We all joined in that laughter, myself included, because frankly I didn't really get it either. However, there was an undeniably knife-like quality to this statement, its edge cutting through yet further layers of what I thought I already knew to that empty land of curiosity where nothing was fixed and everything was possible. The cutting shock of this remark sharpened my focus in some kind of sympathetic resonance and alerted my attention to the fact that Andrew was pointing to something of extreme significance that I had, as yet, not fully discovered for myself.

"But this is the difference between enlightenment and a very technical approach to spiritual practice," he went on. *"So, once again, the part of you that's free or that's enlightened is not the same part of you that has spiritual experiences. The thing is, we want to have these experiences of joy, bliss, lightness of being, depth, ecstasy, and freedom because they give us confidence. That's what makes them so important. But in the end it's not really about the experiences. It's about developing so much confidence that you can really assume the posture of freedom that I was speaking about and then just see what happens. Again, it's not about having experiences; it's about something else.*

"So while you're here I just want you to be very still and pay attention. Give your attention to consciousness and allow everything to open, to get very big and see what happens. Sometimes it'll be easy. Sometimes it'll be difficult. Try for it to make no difference to you because you want to be completely even and steady no matter what's happening. That's the idea. You see, in the long term the steadiness is going to give you a lot more strength, confidence, conviction, and freedom than mere experience.

"So steadiness is the position of not being involved. That means from a certain point of view you could say it's a position beyond all opposites. It means you're not involved in heaven and you're not involved in hell. You're taking a position beyond all opposites and all extremes from the highest heavenly bliss to the worst hell of darkness, fear and confusion. Now, obviously your preference would be heaven rather than hell. That's only reasonable. But even in that, you still want to prefer the steadiness. You'll see that the result that will come from the steadiness will be something you don't expect and which is not an experience."

With that Andrew took a breath and a drink of water before, after a short pause, responding to a few more questions. However, these were mostly frivolous and confused, either forcing Andrew to repeat things he'd already spent ample time discussing, or engage in fruitless dialogues, each of which ended with something along the lines of "why don't you think about your question a little more and then we'll come back to it later." None of it mattered much to me, however, for I felt far, far away, having been swept up by his point about the already enlightened part of us not being the part of us that has spiritual experiences. It was there that my attention was riveted in spontaneous contemplation, the world around me dimming and receding. I felt like a hound on the trail of a scent, its nature as yet unclear, the fact of its significance, however, certain. Slowly, as I pursued that trail, driving ever further into the deep woods of self and brushing aside the creepers of accumulated knowledge a new understanding steadily coalesced.

The first thing that struck me and laid open once more the domain of awe and wonder was that everything Andrew had spoken about related perfectly to the question of freedom amidst the changing nature of experience that I'd faced with such grim stoicism in the morning. That fact alone was an astounding reminder of the organic and synchronous nature of these retreats, where one's outer circumstance, inner experience and flow of the teaching dovetailed into one seamless stream of experience that cannot be meaningfully teased apart. A circumstance and experiential quandary had arisen in perfect synchrony with a teaching that addressed it, a trinity of events rising from one source that was ever seeking itself in the world of manifestation. This, of course, meant that the teaching, rather than being received merely on the level of the intellect, could be taken in as living nourishment, providing an organic remedy to a quite real existential problem that had arisen in conjunction with it. In other words, the whole thing was mysteriously alive and utterly non-dual in a way that is as difficult to describe as it is to overlook.

This morning's teachings regarding the posture of meditation being synonymous with the posture of freedom (along with Andrew's insistence that it is not the experiences that we have but the conclusions we draw about them that determine whether we are free or not) triggered a series of memories that slowly converged into deepening understanding. The first such memory stemmed from a retreat I'd attended two years earlier at Andrew's world center in Foxhollow, Massachusetts. There, with the hard grip of winter rendering the landscape into smooth, frozen lines, he had advised us in the warm confines of the meditation hall to *never* draw any conclusions about ourselves based on the quality or content of our inner experience. I had let this sink in and, driven inward both by the teaching and the short, huddled walk through the cruel blasts of arctic wind that sliced through the trees, I began to see how I mechanically and continuously create my separate sense of self by doing exactly that. As the fierce cold strangely slowed my perception of time, I observed how on a literally nanosecond basis I unconsciously draw endless conclusions about myself based on how I happen to feel and what thoughts happen at that moment to be flitting before my mind's eye. I understood in an instant how the accretion of countless such conclusions create the ongoing psychological structure and felt sense of "me," a steady drip of identity into the bottomless lake of Self. It was oddly striking to realize that I literally create "myself" merely through a habitual and unexamined mental act.

Taking this contemplation further, I had considered who I would be if I simply ceased doing that, a consideration to which the answer came in a blinding flash. Such cessation would dissolve my self-image like a sugar cube in tea, leaving in its wake only this vastness of being in which I could not ascribe my self-sense to being a particular somebody yet simultaneously finding myself deeply rooted and profoundly confident in Being itself. I saw, if only for a short time, that I would not have to know who I was in the ordinary sense in order to have absolute confidence in life and my capacity to do the right thing at the right time. I had heard Andrew speak about this mysterious aspect of his own experience endlessly over the years, yet this was the first time that I had seen directly how the unconscious drawing of conclusions about myself, based on the content of my experience, actively prevented the emergence of this inherent state of freedom.

It was then, walking through cutting blasts of icy air while considering these points, that I was hit by something else that seemed to have crept in among the hard gusting winds. Suddenly I seemed to have been cast out of myself and, without the slightest warning, found myself at an entirely new vantage point. My seat of awareness was somehow above and behind myself now, utterly detached and free and from that vantage point I stood holding a sort of dual citizenship. On the one hand my sense of vision and of being in the world came through my eyes, ears and so on as it always had, yet the very seat of my self-sense was up and above, serenely detached, vast, empty and unwaveringly though effortlessly alert. I was both in the world and beyond it, both born and unborn. The small sense of self, so far away now, seemed encased in layers of life like a Russian nesting doll, the outermost layer being that vastness of Self to which there was no outside, which only expanded infinitely in all directions and to which all was interior. I remained like this for a very long time.

That night, as I settled into sleep, I felt myself descending slowly like a pearl dropped into a lake and sinking in lazy turns toward the muddy bottom. When I arrived there all went black. I was asleep. And yet I was as awake as before. The awakeness behind all things had not wavered and I was aware that I was asleep. Again, as I dreamt I was aware that I was dreaming but not in the engaged sense of a lucid dreamer. I was not participating in the dream. I stood as effortlessly detached from that as I had from the waking life. I was simply intensely aware that I was dreaming. It went like that through the night, from deep sleep to dream and back without that awareness so much as flickering. Much later I felt myself rising like a small bubble from the bottom, swelling and scintillating until I reached the surface and life exploded in vivid light and color all about me. I had awoken and yet the awareness remained unbroken and utterly unaffected. In fact, it remained with me for the better part of three days. During that time I was simultaneously aware of the misery of my emotional and physical experience (this was the retreat at which I had suffered so greatly due to the demand for silence and the pressure on my ego) as well as of my ultimate freedom from it.

Reflecting on those icy days in the warm balm of Montserrat it occurred to me that this unmoving, untouchable, ever-present awareness must have been what Andrew had been referring to when he'd said that the already enlightened part of us is not the part that has spiritual experiences. That awareness is simply always there through every changing state, through every moment of life and even through the dark regions of death itself. It remains ever unstained by all experience, hellish or divine. Being ever beyond all, nothing touched it and ultimately THAT is who I always am. That much I knew. However, my conscious awareness of the presence of THAT faded after three short days and the perspective that inhered in THAT seemed to be slipping away like the deep currents of a dream receding and dissipating in the light of day. Yet it was precisely this perspective that Andrew had said this teaching would allow us to assume through intention. And it was meditation that provided the training ground for the assumption of the liberated posture in relation to the vagaries and turbulence of our inner world.

When you are having a spontaneous episode of higher consciousness, Andrew had said, it is the episode itself that is important. However, in the absence of such episodes, it was the posture we assumed in relationship to our experience that was of greatest significance. Making my way to meditation, I considered this again and again, recalling a retreat I had attended three years earlier in Les Courmettes, France during which this distinction was first brought to my attention. There Andrew had gone so far as to say that if two individuals were meditating and one spent an hour absorbed in spiritual intoxication while the other was besieged by the beasts of his unruly mind, if neither moved and neither drew any conclusions about what any of it meant, there would in essence be no difference between them. Both would be free. If, however, the individual who had been intoxicated with the bliss of the Absolute drew some conclusion about what that meant about him or her as an individual, while the other, who had struggled to stay steady amongst the wild streams of the mind, drew no conclusions whatsoever, it would be the latter who would have demonstrated freedom rather than the former. Thus, drawing no conclusions about oneself based on the quality or content of one's inner experience was one of the hallmarks of the liberated state as well as one of the doorways to that state. That is not to say that we wouldn't prefer pleasant experiences to unpleasant ones, it simply means that we would renounce the temptation to draw conclusions about what either type of experience meant about ourselves. This understanding had both radically altered my view of the purpose of meditation and come as a tremendous relief as I began to relinquish evaluating myself in this manner.

That, however, is not the end of the story. Drawing no conclusions about ourselves based on the content or quality of our inner experience was one thing, and a profoundly liberating one at that. But in no way did it mean that we should not draw conclusions about ourselves. On the contrary, Andrew has always been a big advocate of drawing conclusions about ourselves – based on what we did! It is action that is the arbiter of our destiny, not the insane contortions of our churning mind. There is something in this that is as simple and profound as it is obvious and sane. The depth of our spirit and character of our soul is measured only by our actions in the field of time, for in those are revealed our deepest intimations and conclusions about life itself. This standard by which to take the measure of a man (or woman) is elegant and simple and, most importantly, reflects the unflinching truth of actuality. Against that standard the quality of our moment-to-moment inner experience is rendered perfectly irrelevant and approached from the proper perspective is absolutely no obstacle to the living of an extraordinary life. But it can only be truly irrelevant when we have cultivated sufficient objectivity to stand apart from it, empowered to choose to act on those thoughts that are most in line with our highest realization of the truth. And it is such empowerment that meditation, practiced with proper understanding, should enable. And thus enabled a human life is ennobled and filled with dignity. After all, where is the dignity and freedom in slavish dependence on higher states to ensure our sanity in this world? Exactly nowhere. And what good are we to God (if one prefers theological language) if we are willing to stand for Him or Her only when we feel the intoxicating presence of THAT? None whatsoever. Freedom in Andrew's teaching means freedom "from" experience, not "because" of it. And freedom to do what? The right thing! It is this posture of freedom, cultivated through intention and the discipline of meditation that builds the bridge between our episodes of realization and the actuality of our lives in the world. It was here that we could see what non-duality might look like in action and it was also here that the moral dimension entered into the picture.

All of which brought me squarely back to my own predicament. The fatigue of cumulative sleepless nights had proven fertile ground for the ego's stirrings. Exhausted, irritable and filled with self-pity, what was I to do? I knew precisely what would demonstrate a liberated position. First, I would have to refuse to draw any conclusions about myself based on the fact that I presently felt as raw as steak tartar. Second, I would simply have to bear my own discomfort without inflicting it on others. That would mean no lashing out, no small complaints and definitely no "sharing." It meant I would just have to handle it. Simple as that. What it didn't mean was repression. It meant being as conscious as possible of the entirety of my predicament and choosing not to act from it. Third, by keeping my attention on consciousness I should be able to express the best part of myself in such a way that others would have no idea that my inner world was one of turmoil and difficulty. To spare the world from our own miserable ego, Andrew had often said, would be the ultimate expression of our care and compassion for it. It certainly made sense. But then again, we are not sensible creatures.

It was not the first of these points that so irked me: drawing no conclusions about myself based on all of this felt like setting down a sack of stones. It was the latter two that flung themselves against my fledgling conscience. The demand to bear the unpleasantness of my own experience while refusing to express it was the point with which I struggled most as I headed from the teaching hall through the beer drinking, barely dressed crowd filling the walkways of Montserrat. "Bearing it" amounted to an absolute marginalization of my "sensitive self," that easily aggrieved sense of specialness that is quite put off at the idea of having to bear its own suffering in order to spare others the morbid weight of that burden. But that wasn't the worst of it, I grudgingly realized. The worst of it was – and this is a further illustration of ego's ghastly nature – that I resented not getting to tell anyone about bearing my suffering alone so that others wouldn't have to. There would be no laurels for my "heroic endeavor," no spiritual brownie points for so bold a stand in relation to my own experience; for if it was truly heroic it would seem to others as if my difficulties had never existed, which was, of course, the entire point. In the economics of ego this was nothing short of a raw deal – a distinctly unfavorable trade balance involving a big emotional outlay with no payoff whatsoever. At that moment I wasn't sure which was worse: this morally bankrupt position, or my recognition of it. I slowed my pace so that I might delay my arrival at the meditation hall and have time to consider this pivotal point: if there *really* is nothing in it for me in the ordinary sense, am I still authentically interested? I felt that unless I faced this wretched position and my relationship to it head on I would not, as yet, have really looked into the implications of what I was currently involved with.

Once more the moral dimension insisted itself upon my awareness. It became immediately clear that since we don't exist in isolation, as Andrew had pointedly noted, the decision I made with respect to this point would inevitably have consequences far beyond myself. This is not a matter of metaphysical speculation – it is simply obvious. As a result I found myself firmly impaled upon the horns of a dilemma. Simply knowing this meant that I could no longer plead ignorance in relationship to it, that fact adding a high karmic charge to whatever direction I chose to pursue. From that vantage point, deciding that it's too much for me is tantamount to announcing, "screw the world, you bear my pain. I need relief." It was nothing short of a conscious rape of life. As such the karmic consequences of this choice would be much greater for myself than for an individual oblivious to such subtleties. It's better never to start, than to start and not finish, Andrew had said. Anyway, too late for that now.

This, however, is only half the picture. Freeing the world from my ego was not an end in and of itself, though in and of itself it was a worthy goal. Rather, it was what caging the ego in this manner could release into the world through me that mattered most. Imprisoning the ego, hell's diplomat to the psyche, tears open a portal into this world through which the Authentic Self, the God impulse, can emerge and act, having had until that point no arms or legs with which to do so. My arms and legs I could, through conscious choice, lend to that cause and it was this that was the radical promise of this teaching.

This surprising possibility had first revealed itself to me several years earlier during the same winter retreat mentioned above. It was during this retreat that I had been struck by devastating panic attacks as a result of the confinement of my ego. It is important to understand that these were not merely annoying bouts of anxiety and a little sleeplessness, but full-blown episodes of perfect terror that were so consuming that I was convinced they would require hospitalization and an array of medication to fend off. I longed with hallucinatory desperation to simply leave the retreat, to put everything behind me and escape into any form of relief. But alongside this desperate desire lay the knowledge that if I did so I would not be able to face Andrew, my peers or myself with so much as a shred of dignity in future. And for some reason that meant something to me. Which is why, against all odds, I determined to stick it out, come hell or high water.

Both came. Yet despite their unrelenting onslaught I was astounded to find that in our twice daily "enlightened communication" groups[2] my experience of panic, terror and suffocating resistance miraculously did not impede *in the least* the surging forth of the Authentic Self through me. This I had not expected; I had expected, based on the savaged state of my psyche, that nothing of a higher nature could possibly permeate those dense thickets of melancholia and despair and that my access to those dimensions would remain barred until such time as my inner state would once more be transformed into a good mood. As it turned out, however, it seemed that my inner condition was perfectly suited to the emergence of spiritual consciousness so long as I availed myself of Andrew's advice: have no relationship to my inner experience, draw no conclusions about myself based on it, bear it without expressing it, put my attention on consciousness, and be more interested in what was happening between us than what was happening within myself. Thus, despite myself, and because of our collective willingness, something extraordinary emerged between us. We all bore our own experience, whatever it happened to be, and looked toward consciousness together. Sought for, it emerged spectacularly, a dazzling brilliance whose light shone from us and upon us in a glorious and miraculous explosion of the One through the many (a miraculous emergence about which I will have much more to say later). That experience had left only one question unanswered: would I, in the long run, bear and take full responsibility for the worst part of myself in service of a higher possibility even in the absence of any promise of a payoff on the level of the personal? For the truth was that while I had managed, through careful guidance and abundant grace, to peer above the clouds of ignorance into a world of fantastic possibility, my moral, spiritual, and ethical center of gravity lay firmly fixed within the realm of ego. Yet that fantastic possibility required my unfettered participation in order to come into fruition. It wanted me but could not force me. It needed me but offered in exchange nothing in the coin of ego's realm: no specialness, no adulation, and nothing to hold on to in the ordinary sense.

That afternoon in Montserrat, moving as in a dream from meditation to chanting and then to lunch, I forced myself to face this question squarely. If, at the end of the day, it was not about ever-deeper experiences, subtler insights, greater peace and my ability to craft from these a more appealing identity, was I still genuinely interested? And thus I hung suspended between that faceless no place beyond experience and my deeply cherished "sensitive self" beset by crippling fatigue, a tempest of irritation and the all too familiar and insistent stabs of trepidation. Yet despite the inner ferment I determined to take my lessons to heart: have no relationship to any of it and draw no conclusions about what it meant about me. I simply bore my own experience knowing, as I headed into the afternoon teaching, that my actions over time would reveal the allegiance of my heart.

The afternoon teaching set off on an entirely different track than the direction of the morning's teaching. The first question, which established the tenor for the remainder of the afternoon, came from a young, sandy haired Englishman.

Quietly he asked, "I would like to know what the relationship is between soul and Authentic Self?"

In an equally pensive tone Andrew responded, *"Well I've been thinking about that myself lately and I think that when I'm referring to the Authentic Self it's not really the soul because when we talk about the soul there's still a connection to our personal and collective karma. So the soul does refer to a deeper, more authentic, spiritually felt sense of self that's not superficial and that's not the ego, but..."*

"But is it individual?" the young man interjected.

"Well, I think in the soul the individual and collective kind of intermingle," Andrew answered without missing a beat. *"But when I talk about the Authentic Self it's not really what's traditionally referred to as the soul. The Authentic Self is a function in consciousness that exists at a higher level than what is traditionally called the soul and only begins to reveal itself at a very high level of development.*

"So, if we think of the evolution of consciousness in psychological, developmental terms it would start with ego-centric then move to ethno-centric, nation-centric and then world-centric. So egocentric which, in the way I'm using it now is not the same as narcissism, would be the consciousness of the small baby that sees the whole world and everyone and everything in it as an extension of itself. Everything is me. But the self it sees is not the Self in the enlightened sense; it's the ego in the unenlightened sense.

"Ethno-centric, then, would be the identity of the individual having extended and seeing itself as being part of a particular ethnic group or tribe. Then would come nation-centric, where one sees oneself as a member of a particular nation. Then there's world-centric. That's a very sophisticated level of development. That's when the

individual sees him or herself as a citizen of the planet Earth before one sees oneself as a member of a particular tribe or ethnic group or nation.

"For example, I'm Jewish. So more than my Jewish identity – which is not very strong – more than my identity of myself as being an American, I would see myself as a citizen of the whole planet. And I have a feeling that most of the people here are very similar in that way. We all have an ethnic identity and also a national identity but I have a sense that people attracted to a teaching like this are beginning to see themselves more as citizens of one world and members of the human species. So that would be a world or global-centric level of development. In terms of the evolution of consciousness that's a very highly developed level. But there's one level beyond that which is cosmos-centric. There we see ourselves as a citizen of the evolving universe.

"So then you actually see yourself from the perspective of this teaching, which is from the perspective of consciousness itself. The perspective of consciousness is when the individuals begin to see their incarnation in this world in relationship to the evolution of consciousness. That's the cosmo-centric perspective or level of development. It's deeper, higher and more all encompassing than world-centric.

"During one of my conversations with Ken Wilber regarding the Authentic Self, which is my favorite subject and the most important aspect of my teaching, he said that the Authentic Self is the leading edge of the evolution of consciousness right now. He also said the Authentic Self awakens to itself or recognizes itself in consciousness for the first time somewhere between a global-centric and cosmo-centric level of development. So at world-centric and below the Authentic Self has not yet appeared on the screen of human consciousness.

"So, coming back to your question, what I'm referring to as the Authentic Self is not the soul. The Authentic Self is the evolutionary impulse or creative impulse becoming aware of itself at the level of consciousness, which is experienced as this tremendous sense of urgency in relationship to the evolution of consciousness and the evolution of the species. It's the ecstatically realized urge and compulsion to evolve at the level of consciousness itself.

"Just like at the gross physical level we feel the evolutionary impulse as the ecstatic compulsion to procreate, the Authentic Self is experienced as the ecstatic compulsion to evolve at the level of consciousness itself. 'I must, we must' evolve at the level of consciousness. It's not, 'I would like to or that would be a good idea,' but it's 'I must' and this doesn't come from the ego or the mind; it comes from consciousness itself and it's very powerful.

"The soul is a less personal, more profound, deeper and more spiritual dimension of the self than the ego. But what I'm calling the Authentic Self is a function of consciousness and there is absolutely nothing personal about it. The Authentic Self has no karma. There is not a trace of history in it. When we speak about the soul there's a sense of history there in the form of individual and collective karma and there's a deeper felt sense of connection with life.

"But the Authentic Self is completely, radically impersonal. It's free of karma. It's a searing, powerful function of consciousness that is experienced as an ecstatic compulsion to create the future. It's the leading edge of the evolution of consciousness that's just beginning to emerge. That means we have to reach for it. But if you do reach for it it will appear within your own awareness. Are you with me?"

"Oh yes, very much so," the man answered enthusiastically, obviously having caught a glimpse of that very compulsion as Andrew was speaking about it.

Andrew next turned his attention to a young Swedish woman who wanted to know, "Can somebody be truly enlightened without the Authentic Self manifesting in the way you are describing?"

"Oh yes, absolutely," he replied briskly. *"An individual whose worldview has not yet reached global-centric could be enlightened in the traditional, pre-modern sense but their enlightenment would be based upon the profound awakening to the Ground of Being and their emphasis would be on the transcendence of the world not the evolution of consciousness. Their attention would not be on the creation of the future but on the transcendence of the creative process altogether."*

"So, that would really be the difference?"

"Yes, fundamentally. But what's important to know is that the Authentic Self is not the ego at all. It's a completely different part of us. That's why it's so important not only to talk about it but to experience it. The Authentic Self is a completely different line of development. The ego and the Authentic Self are parallel lines that never meet anywhere. The Authentic Self is completely, totally, radically unrelated to the personal line. Do you understand?"

"Yeah, I do."

"But what's so miraculous about the Authentic Self is that it's already enlightened. That's what its nature is.

"Just like when an individual experiences the Ground of Being – this primordial non-relative Ground or 'no place' that exists in a dimension that transcends and exists before time or creation right now – the experience of consciousness comes to the front and the ego – the sense of individuality and all of its karma – fade into the background. So, who the individual is then is an open question. You see, as the experience of consciousness moves to the front, the individual temporarily becomes a different person. The ordinary attributes and tendencies of the personality will seem very distant because the vehicle is now absorbed in a liberated state of consciousness. Do you understand what I'm saying?"

"Oh yeah, definitely."

"Okay. So, with the Authentic Self, which is a different expression of consciousness, the same thing happens. So, whereas the Ground of Being is the state of freedom before time began, the Authentic Self is the passionately felt urge to become. From formlessness, which is the experience of the Ground of Being, to form. 'I want to become the universe.' So what is experienced at the level of consciousness is this ecstatic sense of

urgency and creative passion that is radically impersonal. It's not the ego! That passion and the compulsion that drives it is a function of consciousness itself and when it's experienced something happens to you and what's coming through you is not an individual and it's not ego and it doesn't have any history.

"But at the same time the motive of the Authentic Self is completely different than that of the Ground of Being. The Ground of Being is radically 'free from' while the Authentic Self is the creative impulse. So when the Authentic Self comes to the front the personality and all its attributes also move to the back and the individual changes. I've seen this happen to people many times. Their eyes widen and they suddenly become animated by a kind of power and conviction that is not ordinarily present. And it can happen just like this." Andrew snapped his fingers. *"It's not something that's developed. It's something that just overtakes the personality, usually temporarily. So just as one can be swept away by the consciousness of the Ground of Being, one can similarly be overtaken by the Authentic Self. And then the individual instantly becomes a manifestation of this evolutionary urgency.*

"I remember about four years ago," he said, pointing to a young brunette in front of him, *"when we had the summer retreat in France and Melissa here came into my room and was exploding. When I saw her I said 'wow, who's that?' Do you remember that?"* he asked Melissa.

"Yeah, I do," she replied.

"Well, that was an example of it. You see, you were completely overcome by this passion and this clarity and this conviction and it was quite awe inspiring." He paused, and then added in a teasing tone, *"Then what happened?"*

No response.

"At any rate, I'm just trying to give you a sense of how impersonal it is. So what we want to understand is that on the one hand there's consciousness and on the other is the individual. So the Authentic Self is a function in and of consciousness and in my particular teaching that's what I emphasize the most. It's a new expression and manifestation of enlightenment. So enlightenment, in whichever form, means transcending and going beyond ego. In the pre-modern version that would mean transcending the ego in order to abide in and be one with the Ground of Being, to rest as that one Self, Brahman consciousness, that's never taken form, that's never entered into the world and that's forever free from the whole process. But in enlightenment in an evolutionary context you transcend ego in order to be a manifestation of the Authentic Self, which is the creative, evolutionary impulse manifest in human form.

"You see, we are It. There's nobody up there! No one is going to save us. That means that we're the ones that have to do it. Remember, the mythical god has fallen out of the sky and is now appearing in consciousness as the Authentic Self. Can you see that the implications here are quite big? But what's so extraordinary about this Authentic Self is that there's no ego in it **right now**. *So you can be temporarily overcome by it and temporarily the ego will fall into the background while the radically impersonal,*

utterly free from history, Authentic Self with all of its passion and creative intensity comes to the front.

"Let me give a gross example of what I mean. Consider for a moment sexual energy, which is the creative impulse felt at the gross physical level. Just in terms of the procreative drive and energy itself — is there anything personal about it? Is there any history in it? No! It's a blind energetic function that's not personal, that has no history and that definitely doesn't have a soul!" He laughed impulsively at the last line and with that seemed to wind down his explanation. *"Do you understand?"*

"I do," she said. "Thanks."

I had on numerous occasions heard Andrew use the example of the sexual impulse, as he had just then, and it had helped me tremendously in understanding the impersonal nature of many of the forces he speaks about. As I had discovered yet again yesterday, that energy is wild, its nature is ecstatic, and its faceless surge is shot through with near irresistible power. It cares not one iota for me as an individual. It does not even see me. It has only one purpose – to create life – and I am a mere vehicle for that purpose. It is radically concerned only with that and radically unconcerned with any of the consequences. It doesn't care whether I am single or married, have taken a vow of celibacy or am a lecher, whether I am young and virile or a grizzled old man too feeble to attract fertile young females. It simply presses onward with relentless determination, always looking for vehicles through which it might release itself into this world. It was, in actual fact, no different from the Authentic Self. It too is wild, faceless, fierce and impersonal and it too wanted all of me for its own ends, ends which, rather than being basely biological were elevated in the extreme and even, dare I say, grandly divine. It also did not care one whit about my personal circumstance, being filled with a passion of its own. It did not – could not – see or recognize my personal life and myriad concerns. It is for this reason that when one is in touch with the Authentic Self one's personal life seems so very far away, an ephemeral film in consciousness as insubstantial and transient as the surface of a soapy bubble. Extraordinarily, both the intensity of the biological urge to procreate and the driving power of the spiritual urge to evolve when experienced directly are radically impersonal and tell us something of the fiercely passionate and impersonal nature of the First Cause itself.

With that the teaching moved on as Andrew turned his attention to a middle aged Dutch woman to his right.

Her question could not have been more relevant. "How do we go from the Ground of Being to the Authentic Self?" she wanted to know.

"You have to follow my instructions," Andrew quipped in accompaniment to hearty laughter.

"Okay," she said, a small smile edging its way across her face.

"Which means," Andrew continued looking at all of us, *"that you guys have to*

start talking now. I heard most of you are very quiet, which is fine, but now you have to start talking."

The dining room had indeed been as quiet as a monastery at midnight during the previous days. This was unusual, for more commonly during these gatherings mealtimes were as raucous as high school cafeterias, the atmosphere awash in the din of noisy conversation as groups of perfect strangers sat together and explored the nature of Andrew's teaching in quite spirited fashion. But it had been different on this retreat. Perhaps that difference stemmed from the dining room having been partitioned into two camps, one for those of us in silence and one for those not, with the silence stealing furtively over that boundary to envelop all in its stillness. Perhaps it stemmed from our collective immersion in the mysterious ground of our existence and staying spontaneously in the stillness that it engendered. Perhaps it stemmed from both. Whatever the case, there had been little conversation. Yet in order for the Authentic Self to emerge it required, as Andrew had pointed out, active engagement with life and other human beings.

"You see," Andrew went on, *"the Authentic Self doesn't manifest itself in the meditation position. It only reveals itself through activity. It's not passive. It's creative and therefore you have to begin to engage with one another for it to emerge. So, remember, what we want to do is go from ego or negative one, which is a negative relationship to life, to zero, which is no relationship whatsoever. Zero is the Ground of Being. It means back to before the beginning. It's what we were all experiencing up until thirty, forty minutes ago. Then, when we emerge from zero we want to emerge as the Authentic Self, or plus one. That's the conscious aspiration of the individual in the teaching of evolutionary enlightenment: to become a manifestation of the Authentic Self."*

"Well, I will do what you say but I think I'm stuck in the zero point," she said.

"That's a nice place to be stuck," Andrew laughed.

"Well, I don't know. I've been waiting for a long time for some action to come and it doesn't really happen."

"Right. That's because zero only wants to be. It doesn't want to become."

"Yeah, that's what I mean. I lack the desire to want to become. I feel that I lack the creative impulse to do anything."

"I understand."

"For a long time now I've just been feeling very transparent and not really doing anything and I'm starting to be a little worried. I wonder if I will ever do anything again. But I want to. That's why I'm on this retreat."

"Okay, good. Maybe you came to the right place then."

She did not respond, appearing to sink back into the stillness of being. Andrew looked around the room briefly and indicated the next questioner, this time an American man who asked, "Does the Authentic Self manifest the same in every person?"

"No, not exactly," Andrew replied. *"But it has the same flavor."*

"So what tempers or affects that manifestation then? Is it the personality?"

"Oh, I think it would probably be a multitude of factors," Andrew replied. *"But, the important point is that there is only one Authentic Self just like there's only one Self Absolute. It has fundamentally one quality, one manifestation and one expression. It can be more intense, profound and powerful or less. But it is basically one thing whose qualities are powerful presence, infinite depth, emptiness and fullness. And the Authentic Self has the same searing clarity and intensity as the Ground of Being. So in the same way that the Ground of Being would manifest itself slightly differently through different individuals for a multitude of reasons the Authentic Self would also. But that's not the important part. The important part is that it is so radically impersonal. So no matter what the individual expression is, the foundation itself will always be the same."*

With seemingly nothing else to say on the subject, Andrew turned his attention to an older, balding American gentleman from Texas whom I'd seen on a number of previous retreats.

"Okay, Charlie," Andrew said.

"Andrew, would you describe the Authentic Self?" Charlie began. "It sounds a lot like the evolutionary impulse. What's the difference?"

"Same thing," Andrew said curtly.

"Okay."

"But you've heard me say that many times already," Andrew said in a slightly challenging tone. *"Maybe it's my New York accent that got you, hmm?"*

Everyone laughed. I knew, however, that at best Andrew was only half jesting. He tended to take exception to people asking questions to which they already knew the answers, viewing it not only as inauthentic but simply as a stratagem of the ego, namely the pretense of rediscovering the same thing repeatedly as if it were new in order to avoid becoming responsible for that realization and allowing it to inform one's life. I expected to see him take Charlie to task for this, as I had seen him do with any number of others, but to my surprise he didn't. I was reminded of Andrew's uncanny awareness of his "karmic line" with everyone who became involved with him. By "karmic line" Andrew meant where he stood in relationship to each of his students and where they stood in relationship to him based on the length of time that they had known each other. This line would naturally develop over time and as time passed Andrew was in the not unreasonable habit of expecting more from people that had known him longer and less from those who hadn't. *"From the minute I meet a person,"* he'd often said, *"a clock starts ticking and as time goes by the individual is going to find out whether or not I'm for real and I'm going to find out whether or not they're for real."* It was a sword that cut both ways. But if over time the student became aware that Andrew never wavered from his liberated stand and Andrew became aware that the student indeed wavered from the stand that they'd taken – their declared interest in liberation – then a certain evolutionary friction ensued that was the essence of the student-teacher relationship. But Andrew, being highly sensitive to such matters knew, based on his karmic line with an individual, precisely when to apply pressure and when not to and I secretly wondered whether or not this had anything to do with his easing up on Charlie.

"Everything good?" Andrew inquired.

"Very good."

"Learning anything new?"

"Always."

"Anything specific?"

"Well, just that I'm having deeper experiences than some of the experiences I've had on past retreats."

"Ahuh," Andrew nodded thoughtfully.

"Just a different and deeper perspective. Everything just seems to be growing because on each retreat you describe the same things in a new and different way."

"Well, that's what gives me confidence that I'm not a robot," Andrew laughed loudly. *"So you've seen me what, five years now, more or less?"*

"Something like that."

"Wouldn't you say that I've been developing over those five years? Can you see how the teaching has been evolving and developing right in front of your eyes?"

"Absolutely. It's ever new."

"So what I'm doing is exactly what I want people to do. After all, I can't ask people to do something if I'm not doing it myself. Right?"

"Right."

"That means that I have to be the example of what I'm teaching. But this is what I want people to do and it's very hard for people to understand. You see, when it comes to evolutionary enlightenment we're talking about a completely different orientation or relationship to life than what most people are used to. It's non-static. We don't aspire to reach some kind of static state or to arrive at a particular point and then we've made it. What we're interested in is perpetual development. That's the goal.

"Now, what's important to understand here is that to perpetually develop is exactly the opposite of what the ego wants to do. The ego likes to be left alone, undisturbed. But if you want to perpetually develop you have to keep going and keep going and keep going." His voice now took on the air of a captain driving his cavalry on in a desperate campaign where all hung in the balance. *"Come on, that's not enough! Keep going! No! Keep going! Come on! Keep going! Don't rest,"* he repeated with unrelenting vigor. Everyone laughed at Andrew's theatrics but there was a deadly seriousness behind that comical façade.

"So you can imagine that the ego would go into a rage," Andrew went on. *"The ego wants to be affirmed. It wants to be told 'you're wonderful, you're fantastic, you've done great, sit down, take it easy, relaaaax.'"*

That last word flowed from Andrew's mouth in the soothing textures of a tropical breeze. Inside you just kind of felt "aaaah."

" *The ego wants control and it thrives on a kind of stasis,"* he went on. *"Now, if you don't think that's true intellectually, emotionally it's definitely true. Emotionally where the ego is at is, 'leave me alone!' So the problem — and it's a very big problem — is that the ego doesn't want to keep moving and keep moving and keep moving. It just really doesn't. So there is a conflict between the Authentic Self's ecstatic compulsion to ceaselessly evolve and the ego's deeply felt desire to just be left alone and insistence that 'I'm okay as I am.'"*

I reflected on my own experience and recalled something I'd heard Andrew mention only a few months earlier. It was, as with so much of what he said, a point that was obvious once mentioned but as unreflected upon as air before that point. Specifically, he'd pointed out that until one reaches their mid-twenties there is an almost constant expectation that we develop as human beings on every level from the physical and emotional to the cognitive and intellectual as well as in every other arena of human development. However, beyond that point the demand for continued *vertical* development is supplanted by the demands of survival and the conformist pressure to glide along the well-worn tracks laid out for us by culture and society. In our younger years there's an innate understanding that how we evolve and develop has important consequences for the life we will lead when we are "grown up." However, having passed that threshold into true adulthood, such expectations for *verticality* flatline and further development thereafter occurs along a horizontal trajectory. That is not to say that development does not occur in one's area of expertise, or other undertakings, but the expectation to develop and evolve with one's full humanity is by and large abandoned. This, of course, explains why, over the years so few people actually change and why neurotic idiosyncrasies so often come over time to define one's life as much or more than whatever skills they may have developed over the course of the very same years.

I became unavoidably aware of this painfully suffocating fact in my mid-twenties. At that time I had been working in my first real job since graduating college.[3] All in all, I loved it. I was at long last earning real money of my own, had the respect of co-workers, a responsible position, a little prestige and so on. Things seemed to be unfolding as, for a young man like myself, they should be. Then one Monday morning, as I woke, swung my feet over the side of my bed and gazed through my large bedroom window to take in the full glory of a tropical morning, a staggering realization hit me: this is it. Here are the next forty years of your life: Monday to Friday, work, earn, move up in the world, entertain yourself, maybe have a couple of kids to inject some meaning into your life and then retire. And die. And what about my spiritual passion? What about that explosion of consciousness that had made itself known to me? What about its scream to be released into the world through me? Where did all that fit in other than as a passing interest or curious philosophical hobby? A surge of panic swept through me as I realized that I was being slowly seduced by the worship of the ordinary commonly hailed as the American Dream. That seduction was beginning to take and I freaked out as the reality of it all came crashing down on me like fifty foot surf driven by the angry winds of a hurricane. "The masses lead lives of quiet desperation," asserted itself into my psyche like a haunted cry from the strangled soul of humanity past, present and yet to come. I realized there and then that something had to change, that my soul was on the line and that my destiny hung in the balance. It was this realization that set me off to California in search of a teacher and in pursuit of authentic spiritual liberation.

This move, however, took two years to actualize and during that time I had ample opportunity to consider my realization. I began to understand, in a way that I could not have even a few years earlier, that as one passes into one's late twenties and approaches that sobering thirty year threshold to full adulthood – which, as author Neal Stephenson has wryly observed, is to early adulthood what Sunday morning is to Saturday night,[4] – the enthusiastic passion for change that can characterize one's younger years evaporates like glistening dew from sun scorched sands. Ongoing upward development at the level of one's humanity is simply no longer in the picture beyond a certain point. Moreover, its pursuit is often viewed with cynicism and suspicion by those who have traversed the path of life before us. Of course, they themselves have most commonly walked the rutted paths laid out by those who came before them. For them all forays off that well-worn track into the dark thickets of the unknown are considered dangerous and thus to be avoided. This, it seems, is our mammalian nature: that is, we are hard wired not for perpetual change and transformation but, beyond a certain point, for the status quo. Sameness represents safety in the law of the jungle. I see this biological imperative at work on a daily basis in my work as a dog trainer. Yet that biological imperative bequeathed to us by countless millennia of evolution ultimately offends our deeper and more adventurous sensibilities though, one might reasonably argue, perhaps not enough.

At any rate, as it stands, at a certain point in most of our lives horizontal development trumps vertical transformation unless we proactively take the reins of our life in our own hands and part company, at least insofar as philosophical orientation and life strategies are concerned, with the larger company of our fellows. Now in my mid-forties, I need merely to peruse my inventory of both friends and relations to see how true this is. By and large who they are today is an extension of who they had been in their early adulthood. Their skills in whatever they had pursued have increased commensurate with the march of the years while what once had been mere personality quirks and minor expressions of neurosis have now become the bold strokes and defining features of the canvas of their lives – and often for the worse. Even my "spiritual" friends who had shared with me the explosive revelations of insight that first set me upon this path had by and large relinquished their passion upon crossing the threshold into full adulthood at the apparently fossilizing age of thirty. Passing through that gateway, they had set the train of their lives firmly upon the rails of conformity to lumber along from stop to stop in largely pre-determined fashion, presumably until the end of the line.

To be fair, in casting such judgments I cannot leave myself out of the picture as if I were some cultural anthropologist standing apart carefully categorizing the behavior of others with scientific rigor while participating in none of them. The truth is I too want, at least in part, to coast like a lazy surfer on one of life's tepid waves, digesting the flow of my temporal existence like a pre-chewed meal while adding just enough spice to make it seem other than that, all the while never truly threatening the seemingly obdurate security of the status quo. In fact, I was, by and large, just like everyone else. With one exception: for some mysterious reason I could not help but keep my attention solidly riveted on the interest that had awoken in me with the explosion of consciousness from the core of my being during my early twenties. Since then I had, for that same mysterious reason, consciously chosen to put myself in the tutelage of others who refused to tolerate such an anemic relationship to life and whose own lives expressed anything but "the worship of the ordinary commonly hailed as the American Dream."

The fact is that despite the dramatic differences between Peter and Andrew as teachers, their teachings shared this one golden thread: perpetual change and vertical development should form the only steady pattern and defining feature of one's life. In this regard, both were living examples of their teachings.

I considered these teachings at some length before circling back to the ethical quandary that I had begun to face earlier during the day. Beyond their not insignificant similarity around this central issue of perpetual change and transformation, the two teachings diverged so dramatically as to be rendered incapable of being considered as existing in the same philosophical universe. In Peter's teaching the payoff was always strictly personal. In fact, he'd even once gone so far as to state with dictatorial conviction that if we truly surrender, we will get everything we ever wanted materially. Interestingly, his life had seemed to be an expression of this point. He'd started out as a suicidal young man bereft of both inner and outer resources until, under Rudi's tyrannical affections, he transformed himself both into a vastly successful businessman, writer and authentic master of kundalini yoga. No small feat, to be sure. Yet, in the end, it was still all for himself and he was not in the least abashed about this. In fact, this ethic of radical spiritual self-interest formed a central core of his teaching. He flatly told us on many occasions that even his function as a teacher served simply to catalyze his own further growth and that whatever we did with his teachings was up to us and ultimately none of his concern. And even the final prize, enlightenment, in the end served only one's own ends: freedom from the world process in order to continue one's personal evolution in other realms of the cosmos, this life a mere chrysalis for the next and that one for its successor and so on in perpetuity.

Andrew's teaching formed a perfectly inverted image of this view. The perpetual change and development to which he was relentlessly calling us was never for "me" in any personal sense. Rather, it was for the evolution of consciousness *for its own sake* – a point that though seeming simple is horizonless in its profundity. As such, there are no accolades for the ego, no promises of fulfillment for its endless checklist of unfulfilled desires, not even enlightenment in the sense of escape or relief from becoming for the personal self-sense. There was only the austerity of total surrender and the relentlessness of ceaseless change for a cause always greater than oneself. It was this that had bitten so sharply into my soul earlier in the day, causing me to search deeply in its murky interior and grapple profoundly with both the angels and demons that resided there. This engagement showed that in my deeper self was a nest of deeply mixed motives and set the gravest challenge before my spiritual conscience: did I really want to be free in this way, standing to gain nothing whatsoever for the one asking the question? In response my spiritual ego immediately leapt to attention asserting its sincerity; but that face of ego was, to use the parlance of cyberspace, a mere avatar[5] or two-dimensional, fraudulent representative of its true face. The visage lurking just behind that mask bears a much more sinister expression and darkly unequivocal response: never! I will pretend as long as I can but if cornered and exposed I will fight with the rabid intensity of Grendel – that ravenous beast in the epic *Beowulf* – for my own survival. This is the final and absolute position of the ego. Standing against this denial of the truth is the passion of the Authentic Self and its ever unequivocally positive response for it wants and can see nothing but freedom and creativity without limit. And between them I stand, the final arbiter in the clash of titanic forces, as my own deepest fears collide headlong and clash fiercely with my greatest passion, a collision of forces whose outcome is uncertain and entirely up to me.

These unnerving ruminations flashed through my mind in an instant and, with their impressions lingering like retinal afterburns, I returned my attention to Andrew.

"And so, from the perspective of the Authentic Self the goal is to keep moving," he said, still emphasizing his previous point. *"Moving forward, not backwards!"*

Hearty laughter surged through the room as I reoriented myself to the ongoing conversation.

"But the thing is," Andrew went on, *"if you're continually moving forward and you don't stop then your own experience is one of being free. In evolutionary enlightenment the experience of freedom is not found in resting beyond the creative process of the world and time, which is the one we've been speaking about for the last four days. In evolutionary enlightenment you're free because you're literally engaged with*

the evolutionary process itself at the very edge. So, your freedom is found by constantly leaning forward.

"Now, this is actually felt and experienced as a spontaneous occurrence within yourself when you really surrender to the Authentic Self. It becomes a choiceless response. It doesn't come from an intellectual 'I should.' It comes from the Authentic Self itself, which spontaneously leans forward and leans forward and leans forward, and if you're in a surrendered condition you don't resist it. It's not coming from a mental should and it doesn't involve making effort. At least not when you become well established in the Authentic Self. But in order to become well established in it you might have to make a lot of effort. There is, after all, the ego and its agenda, which we were just discussing and if you're identifying with the ego then you get into problems because there's a real conflict between these two forces. Get it?"

"Yes," said Charlie, "I understand."

"This is a new science of enlightenment. But you have to remember that the ego hates it! So, just in the same way as in the pre-modern enlightenment, our attachments – anything that's going to inhibit the free functioning and flowering of the Authentic Self – have to be given up, in evolutionary enlightenment it works precisely the same way. You have to come to a place within yourself where you're not resisting. Which means that our job, if we're serious about this, is to make ourselves available. Nobody can do more than that. When you're available and that consciousness enters into you, it will use you. But if you're not available the consciousness will surge forward and you'll resist it and that becomes quite problematic. You see how it works?"

"Yep," Charlie said, a broad smile creasing his face.

"So, that's why the ego has to be given up or transcended to a significant degree. Then this consciousness can become the dominant mover of the vehicle. That simply has to happen. It's scientific. Most people don't want to do it. It's too much for them because the ego is a big problem; it really is.

"But that's where we come in. We have been given the power of choice or free agency. Remember, as we concluded the other day, nobody is holding a gun to our head. So we can choose not to resist what we are calling the Authentic Self. That's the good news. It'll probably be the hardest thing you ever did in your life, but what can I say? That's not my fault. It's just how it is. Again, it's scientific.

"You see, these days everybody's interested in evolution. Evolution is a very attractive, sexy word. People love it – especially people interested in the future. They think that's the cutting edge. But when you talk about what it really means, that they have to be willing to give up something for it, like the ego, then they usually lose interest like that." Andrew snapped his fingers. *"You following everything?"*

"Yes," Charlie said, still beaming. "Thank you."

"Okay!" Andrew responded enthusiastically, seeming to have been swept away by the very Authentic Self of which he had been speaking. And once more his eyes

began to sort through the room in search of the next questioner. *"All right,"* he finally said, pointing to another American man near the back of the room.

The man, who had short, dark hair and was probably in his early thirties, asked, "Does the transformation that takes place involve bringing or imbuing more consciousness into my life?"

"Absolutely!" Andrew said, *"It's more like surging through. A tremendous amount of energy, vitality and sense of purposefulness starts pouring through, sometimes to a degree that people find off putting or even frightening, like, 'whoa, this is a little too much.' You know what I mean?"*

"Yeah. I definitely do," he said, sounding as if he were presently at that very edge himself.

"Can I ask another question?" he said more softly.

"Sure."

"It's about morality. It seems like consciousness is the same as morality and that as I become more conscious there's more of a moral imperative that I become aware of."

"Well, definitely in relationship to the Authentic Self because there's a compulsion to create the future that comes from the deepest part of the self. Now the next evolutionary leap, as I see it, is the leap from the individual to a higher collective, a 'higher we.' As we've already seen, we've reached this very high level of individuation so now the next step is going to be a leap beyond being trapped in this individuated separate self to the Authentic Self, which recognizes the non-difference between the individual and the collective. But at the same time our sense of individuality or autonomy is not lost. In fact, it is enhanced. In other words, you're aware of your own autonomy but you simultaneously recognize this radical non-difference with the others. Then you see that the One is the many, not just the many as the One, which is the older way of understanding it. So, the next step has to do with the evolution of consciousness beyond the individual, when the many literally become one organism beyond ego."

"Okay, yes." The man said haltingly, as if he was only kind of getting it. *"See, if you're attuned to the Authentic Self you really begin to see and feel that new organism, which is not a material thing but a state of consciousness, and its desire to emerge. That's the evolution of consciousness. That's the next evolutionary step for our race."*

"Right."

"But the only people who are aware of the fact that it wants to emerge are those individuals who are awake to the Authentic Self. Other people literally don't see it. You can speak to them about it and intellectually they might understand and say, 'oh that makes sense, that's beautiful!' But they don't feel it so it's not really their own experience. It's only individuals that are awake to some degree to the Authentic Self that feel it emotionally and experience that same sense of urgency and compulsion that this must occur.

"So then their attention, the attention of the Authentic Self, is not on the individual, it's on consciousness and that's the big leap! When our attention shifts from

individuality to consciousness it gets radically impersonal and that's a very big shift. So then when you see another individual you don't see another person as much as you see consciousness. You become more interested in the consciousness of the other than you are in their individuality. Their individuality becomes of secondary importance. It's a big shift to move beyond ego to the Authentic Self. Do you understand?"

"Yes, I do."

"So, when this Authentic Self emerges in and between two or more individuals something quite extraordinary happens. This new organism begins to emerge where the many recognize themselves to be that one Authentic Self together while simultaneously not losing any of their own autonomy. As a matter of fact, their autonomy is profoundly liberated while at the same time the Authentic Self awakens to itself through the collective. That's why it's non-dual or paradoxical. So the organism that I'm speaking about is made up of different autonomous individuals who awaken to this one Authentic Self. Are you with me?"

"Yes, I think so."

"This is literal! This is not a metaphor. I'm talking about a real event. So what happens then is that in the Authentic Self there's an emotionally felt compulsion that this must happen. And also that this must be encouraged and protected. You see, that one organism at the level of consciousness has a motive that the individual who is not awake to the Authentic Self does not recognize because they're only concerned with their own ego-based desires and fears."

"Right."

"But the motive of the awakened Authentic Self is completely different. It literally doesn't recognize the fears and desires of the individual's ego. Now, it doesn't mean that you're not respecting the individual; it's just that you're seeing from a different level of consciousness. And what you're seeing is of a different order and dimension. So what you're seeing when you're identified with the Authentic Self is the potential for what I call this new being and you experience the motive to give birth to it. So for an individual who desires to give birth to this new being in the real world, in real time, between real human beings, a moral dimension comes into it. That's because the individuals who make up this new being have to honor, respect and care about the needs and the requirements of the new being more than the concerns of their own individual egos. Right?"

"Right."

"Now, from the perspective of the awakened Authentic Self that understanding doesn't need to be cultivated because it's immediately obvious. When you're awake to Authentic Self, even if only temporarily and to whatever degree, you instantly see it. It's like turning on a light and everything shifts and then you see.

"So, the moral dimension instantly comes into it when the light goes on because you recognize that for this new being to emerge all the individuals have to respect it and care about it more than they care about themselves in an egoic sense. Do you understand?"

"Yes."

"So now when you have the many aspiring to manifest this one new being between each other at the level of consciousness there's a completely different moral dimension that enters into it that has very little to do with the morals and ethics of a world dominated by narcissists. But it's a moral sensibility that is internally revealed and realized rather than externally imposed. You see it, you feel it and you know it intuitively because now this moral sense emerges from this state of consciousness itself, this leap beyond individuality. That's the evolution of morality."

"Wow, that sounds amazing," the man said, astonished.

"It is," Andrew replied. *"Once again, it's a leap beyond the individual where the many become this one. But it's a new 'one,' or a 'higher we' because the many that make up the one realize a level of autonomy that's almost unheard of. You see, usually if many come together then the autonomy has to be sacrificed in order for communion to emerge, right?"*

"Right."

"But in this new emergence the autonomy not only is not sacrificed, but it's realized in a completely new way because the autonomy doesn't come from ego, it comes from the Authentic Self. I mean that's the ideal. So you see, it's really a new thing. It's an ideal that's unrealized as of yet. But I've seen it emerge in brief bursts so I know I'm not imagining it. Do you get the idea?"

"Yes."

"Whew!" Andrew sighed, wiping his brow with his sleeve as if he'd just been carrying something very heavy. We all laughed and I deeply appreciated the passion and effort he put into his words so that we might begin to understand his vision. The well of his energy apparently not entirely drained, Andrew pointed to a mustachioed Frenchman, an evolutionary scientist whom I'd seen at previous retreats, to take a final question.

"Okay, George, you've had your hand up for a while."

"Andrew, if the cosmos-centric is the future of world-centric how can we know when we come across a cosmos-centric person? Is it through his or her actions?"

"Well, I suppose when the Authentic Self or evolutionary impulse has become stronger than the ego in the individual is when you could say that had happened. When the Authentic Self becomes the dominating force or driver of the personality that's when you become a force of the cosmos itself.

"What that means is that you're an individual with egocentric, ethno-centric, nation-centric and world-centric perspectives, but what's fundamentally coming out of you and through you is a cosmos-centric perspective. And it's not just intellectual. It's coming through very loud and clear and that can't be faked."

"So it happens when I don't just visit the Authentic Self space but set up permanent residence there?"

"It will set up permanent residence in you if you're serious enough to get out of the way."

"Okay."

"You see, the Authentic Self is already looking for you. That's how it works. It, being an evolutionary impulse and a function of consciousness, is looking for portals or holes to get through. And the portal or hole appears in your own willingness to transcend ego for real. And then it will happen automatically. It's like water; it can't be stopped."

He said these last few lines with finality and with that the session came to a close. We soon sank into silence and meditation and before long Andrew left the dais and slipped quietly out of the room.

As I rose to leave the hall it seemed that with this teaching the retreat had reached a sort of bifurcation point. We had spent the better part of four days, plus half of the fifth, immersed in the depths of the Self Absolute all the while exploring its implications for our relationship to our mind and to life. Yet with this afternoon's teaching we emerged from that primordial ground in an impassioned exploration of its creative aspect – what Andrew referred to as the Authentic Self. The divide between the two – between being and becoming – had been forded when Andrew began to encourage everyone to engage with one another through dialogue. This was, as I had learned in rather explosive fashion on previous retreats, a prerequisite to "enlightened communication" and the emergence of a radically new state of consciousness to which Andrew simply referred as the New Being and which he had begun to describe in the latter half of this teaching. In the virgin light of this New Being, a radical and entirely novel possibility for human relationship emerged and with it the promise of the seeds of a new culture. (For an in-depth discussion of the history, development and nature of this emergence, please see Appendix 2, The Birth and Evolution of Inter-subjective Enlightenment.) The emergence of this possibility is the overarching goal of Andrew's teaching and its most thrilling aspect. It was also what most inspired me and served as a continual reminder of the moral context for my own pursuit of spiritual liberation.

This consideration stayed with me throughout the remainder of the day, serving as the thread that strung together its remaining activities – dinner, meditation and the day's closing chant. And even as I closed my eyes for sleep near midnight these themes played on my mind like reflections of light on the surface of a still sea.

NOTES

1. The reader might notice that unlike in a previous chapter where the discussion of ego was framed in rather objective, psychological terms, now I'm referring to it in somewhat more mythological terms. The reason is that the internally felt experience of ego is radically different from the objective understanding of it. When stirred it is literally experienced as a living force, a

beast struggling to maintain its grip on and control over the vehicle, namely the body and most importantly the mind and spirit that drive it. When its resistance arises its presence is visceral on the deepest level of feeling and the most difficult thing to do is to maintain an objective relationship to it. In many important ways what is experienced is the perennial struggle between the forces of light and the forces of darkness with the individual human soul poised between these two powerful, and yes, cosmic streams, its fate determined by the choices that it makes in relation to them. While seeming quaintly traditional to the postmodern mind these forces are undeniably real, having been acknowledged in the spiritual mythology of every great culture and tradition of the past. Once again, their radical denial by large segments of our emerging global, secular culture makes one who has encountered these forces directly consider the truth of the well-known statement that "the greatest trick the devil ever pulled was convincing mankind that he didn't exist."

2. These groups involve a number of people coming together with a commitment to containing their own ego and a focused intention to discover what is possible between them when, as a result, they come together beyond ego. And what is possible is extraordinary – the emergence of a collective field of enlightened consciousness in which all the individuals feel more at ease being themselves than they ever have, while simultaneously not being able to tell precisely where one ends and the other begins. "There is no other" is the lived collective experience in such groups. This paradox of perfect autonomy and radical, non-dual communion among many is not only the promise of this teaching but also the next evolutionary leap the race must make in order to assure its continued survival. It is to the emergence of this inspiring possibility that the whole of Andrew's teaching points.

3. I had graduated with a Master's degree in International Relations with a specialization in Economics and landed a job as an analyst in the marketing department at the Port of Miami where I had the good fortune to work with a wonderful group of people who, because of their kind good-naturedness, had made the transition from college to the professional life easy and pleasant.

4. Neal Stephenson, *Snow Crash*, (New York: Bantam Books, 1992) p. 21.

5. An avatar is a movable icon representing a person in cyberspace or virtual reality graphics.

Day 6

Collision with the Finite

Morning came on more gently today. I had slept deeply and beyond the reach of my roommate's snoring. Consequently the buoyant positivity inherent in the teaching and in life itself bubbled to the surface and the early morning darkness, rather than seeming a burden, seemed a deep well of promise. I rose with vigor and ease, something that had eluded me on the chill mornings of the previous days, gratefully drank my tea and padded down the cold stone stairs into the dimly lit courtyard. There I joined with the others who walked in silence to the meditation hall.

This morning I found that simply by putting my attention on that part of myself that was always already awake, ever present as unmoving beingness in the background of my awareness, I could cut through fatigue and inertia in an instant. In that no-place a wellspring of interest simmered with a subtle yet penetrating energy that always longed to participate in life for the highest possible reasons. As I fixed my attention there it occurred to me that too often, especially when I'm tired or distracted, I view practice as a chore, something to get through rather than as a privilege to be treasured; not everyone has such precious opportunity, I realized. Moreover, with practical demands crowding in on all sides in my ordinary life, feeling put upon by deep practice when freed from such constraints seemed, well, to put it plainly, stupid. And worse – what about the obligation to which I'd already given an acknowledging nod on any number of occasions? Where was that on those days when I got out of the wrong side of bed? I walked on, determined to cultivate more of the warrior spirit and embrace practice as both a sacred obligation and a privilege.

This led me to a related consideration: the more we know the greater is our responsibility. I had happened upon this stream of reflection when I noticed on entering the meditation hall that a number of Andrew's senior students were already there, having apparently straightened and prepared the room for the rest of us. In fact, I had noticed over the previous days that the more senior Andrew's students were the greater their share of practical responsibilities appeared to be. Not only did they participate in the long daily practices with the rest of us but also when, at eleven o'clock at night, I headed off to bed I noted with interest that they seemed to be heading off for further unspecified chores and activities. Yet they were also the first ones in the meditation hall, stayed after to clean and were, I'm sure, under enormous pressure from Andrew to push the edge of their own evolution in ways I could not yet imagine. Nonetheless, they stood tall and set an example for the rest of us, one that I set before myself with reverence as I embarked upon the morning practice. And it was a great practice. The meditation was deep and still, the chanting inspired and enlivening and upon emergence from those two hours I felt radiantly alive and ready for the day.

And what a glorious day it was; the sun shone warmly on the ancient cliffs, as we once more found ourselves gathered in the teaching hall for the continuation of our exploration.

"Andrew, I have a question about choice," came the first inquiry of the day from a young Australian man in a faltering voice.

"Okay," Andrew said.

"I'm not clear in your teaching on the concept of choice as opposed to what I've experienced in my own life. For example, what brought me here to the retreat, well, it didn't seem as if I had a choice and if a choice did appear it would really have been because I'd asserted something personal and said, 'I'm not going to come.' Then I could well imagine I might have been tossed around between yes and no. But I don't really get the choice unless I make it into a personal thing and then go against either the information or motivation that I already have. So, am I missing the point?"

"I don't totally understand the question," Andrew said.

"Well, if something comes up on a personal level and I become aware of an emotion or a thought, then as soon as I become aware of it, it appears I have a choice whether to engage with it or just to let it go. So, choice seems to have happened then. But other times, say, like coming here, it was more as if either there was guidance or just simply a movement in me to come. So I responded to that rather than actually deciding to come."

"Well, you know," Andrew said in a sly tone, *"sometimes serial killers say that they just found themselves doing it. They didn't actually decide to do it. They say, 'the next thing I knew my hands were around her neck and she was dead.'"*

"Do I take from that that you're saying that there is a level of choice there and I'm just not aware of it at that moment?"

"No, I think we just have to make a little more effort to be clear about what we're talking about. Now, I'm just not sure what you're saying, but that's what they say; 'next thing I knew, she was dead. It just kind of happened.'"

"Then I'll just sit with it because as far as I can see, I'm asking my question clearly and if it doesn't come across clearly then I'll just sit with it."

"Well, I try to force people to make the effort to be clear. But anyway, I think you're saying that it seemed like the impulse to come here, which was an evolutionary

impulse, was choiceless, and then therefore the implication would be that any time that there was a spontaneous, choiceless compulsion to act, it must be coming from the evolutionary impulse and anything that actually involved a choice—should I or shouldn't I? Will I or won't I? Do I want to or not? — it would have to be ego. That's what you meant, right?

"Yes."

"Okay. So that's why I gave you that example."

"Of the serial killer?"

"Yeah. So it makes sense why I said that, right?"

"Yes."

"Okay. So that means you're wrong, right?" Andrew laughed.

"Well, yes, it's clear …"

"See, the thing is it's a complicated question and it's an important one so we'll go into it. Now, you seem to be saying, 'if it's choiceless it's the Authentic Self and if there's choice, it's ego.' So we agreed that that's probably not the case. Right?"

"Yes."

"So, therefore, what are you asking me?"

The man stammered unsuccessfully for words.

"You see, everybody," Andrew said, looking around the room. *"I put a big emphasis in my teaching on getting people to really slow down and find out what exactly they think, what they believe, what they know and what they don't know. And it's challenging, a little bit excruciating and maybe even a little humiliating, but the only way we can find out where we're actually at is to slow down and really be challenged. And we all have to learn how to make the effort to articulate our own ideas. So most of us think in very sloppy ways. We're rarely, if ever, challenged to think very clearly.*

"You know, I barely graduated high school. A lot of the students that I work with on my own magazine have infinitely more education than I have ever had or ever am going to have in this life and still they find working with me, in terms of me getting them to express their ideas clearly, infinitely more challenging than university ever was. They also tell me that if you're fairly clever you could, as they say in English, B.S. your way through. If you sounded like you knew what you were talking about most professors would accept it as a sign of intelligence.

"So it works the same way in life. Do we actually know what we're talking about? Is what we're speaking about something that we actually know about or is it just something we've heard about? So at least in the way I see it, part of serious spiritual practice has to do with really learning to make the effort to think clearly. And then, ideally, we want there to be a relationship between how articulate we are and who we actually are as a human being. We don't want there to be a big gap between what we know about the human experience and who we actually are as a human being. You see, someone can know quite a lot about the human experience and even about higher states of consciousness and evolutionary theory and still be a really screwed up human being.

"So, in the way I see it, we want all these things to line up and be of a piece — to be whole. And that takes effort. Most people don't know what they're talking about in these areas. And if they do know what they're talking about, more often than not there's a big gap between what they're talking about and who they are. So, we've got to keep all these things in mind and make the effort to be different ourselves."

With that Andrew turned back to the young man who'd asked the question. *"All right, have you figured out what you wanted to know?"*

"Well, I want to know whether I'm making the choice on all levels of my actions."

"You know, it's difficult to answer in a very simple way. Let's say a little boy was brutally beaten repeatedly and sexually abused when he was young. Now often that might create desires to sexually dominate other people. Someone like that might grow up to be a rapist. So he might just very spontaneously have the feeling of wanting to sexually dominate and brutalize other people. So something like that wouldn't come from a choice, from 'I would like to.' It would be more like, 'I was just called to do it. I just saw her and the next thing I knew it was just happening. I didn't really even make a choice.' You see what I'm saying?"

"Yes, I can see that."

"So, there are many different parts of the self and a lot of different issues that go into what makes us tick as human beings. So, in the way that I teach there's always going to be a specific context within which we talk about the human experience. And depending on the context we're going to answer the question differently. So in my teaching the context is one of trying to develop a model of a liberated or a profoundly free, evolved, mature, sane and rational relationship to the human experience, right?"

"Yes."

"So, therefore, what we want to do is to cover all our bases. Which means we want to come up with a model that we can both work with."

"Yeah, that would certainly be helpful."

"So then we're going to say that no matter what the experience, the context is now one of becoming a liberated human being. Right?"

"Yes."

"So, in that context I'm saying that it's always the individual who makes the choice because, you see, if I'm going to be free and if you're going to be free then we have to be in a position to be able to take responsibility for all of our actions. Right?"

"Right."

"In this way we avoid any possibility of any kind of schizophrenic behavior. Do you know what schizophrenic is?"

"I do."

"So in spiritual circles there's a lot of schizophrenic behavior. For instance, over the last few days many of you were saying, 'I disappeared.' That's a common experience when our attention moves away from the ego. But a lot of people use this kind of

experience of emptiness or voidness as an excuse to not take responsibility for the fact that the body seemed to do something. They'll say, 'I didn't do it. It was the body-mind.' That's what they call it." Andrew laughed at the absurdity of the phrase. *"Have you heard this kind of talk before?"*

"Sure."

"So, if it's your body-mind doing it, it's not you. Now, that's a little confusing for me. But there are teachers that have groups this big in front of them saying this kind of thing and everybody's nodding their heads in agreement, saying 'yeah, right. It makes perfect sense.' That scares me and I'd probably want to leave the room right about then because that means anything could happen and there would be nobody taking responsibility for it because 'nobody was doing anything.' It's just the body-mind; it's not the self.

"Many teachers espouse that way of thinking and some of these people are even therapists. They think it's fantastic stuff because they say that's how you gain freedom from your past. That is, since you didn't do anything it's not your fault. And whatever happens isn't your fault because nobody's doing anything anyway. It's just the body-mind that's doing whatever it feels compelled to do because of its own conditioning. And with that you kind of drop the whole business. Even ideas of evolution and self-perfection are abandoned as being foolish, unenlightened activities because the self doesn't do anything and the body-mind does whatever it wants to do. How does that sound for madness?"

No one said a thing, the ethical implications rolling in faster than they could be digested and responded to.

"I'm not kidding. This kind of stuff is being taught all over the world." Andrew paused, and then added wryly, *"It's very big in Germany. Of course, you can understand why that would be but I'm not going to go into that now."* He punctuated that comment with a small laugh and my ears perked up, as they always do when my own German heritage was briefly and uncomfortably brought into the spotlight. The crowd also sputtered with uneasy laughter, due in no small part to the number of Germans among us. Andrew had a penchant for spotlighting with meticulous precision the cultural conditioning of those who gathered around him, both in relationship to liberation and to the whole of life itself and I wondered whether, being in Europe, he would yet shine that light upon the Germans and the peculiarities of their condition. I would find that in due course he would. For the moment, however, he returned to his central theme. *"That's probably one of the most extreme examples but there are different variations on that theme. Are you with me?"*

"I'm with you."

"Now, that view represents one extreme and in the way I teach I go all the way to the other extreme. I say the individual is completely, totally responsible for their own actions, whatever their actions are. What's your first name?"

"Christopher."

"So Christopher's responsible for everything he does. If Christopher wants to be free then Christopher is responsible for his actions.

"'But it's not Christopher's fault, he couldn't help it.' Andrew mocked. *"So if Christopher couldn't help it,"* he asked rhetorically, *"whose fault is it then? This is important, everybody, because look at all the times you've done things that you said you couldn't help. So if Christopher couldn't help it, whose fault was it?"* he now fairly well demanded.

"Andrew, I feel like it's a trick question and it's not too fair. It's like if I'm ignorant then I'm ignorant."

"Yes, I know. But it's a good question nonetheless and I just want everybody to think about it for a minute. You see, often I'll take an extreme example to make a point and then I'll point out that often, when it suits us, what most of us are doing is not that different.

"So if Christopher couldn't help it, whose fault was it? I mean, it's not a trick question; it's an impossible question. If it's not Christopher's fault then it's nobody's fault because Christopher couldn't help it.

"The point is when you think that way there's no traction. There's nothing to grab onto. It's like trying to dig your hands into a wall of ice. You can't grab hold. So if you think that way about yourself you'll never evolve because you'll be living within a self-created ice wall with nothing to grab onto to pull yourself up with. Right?"

"Yes."

"Does everybody understand? This is not unimportant! It might not be as exciting as the more metaphysical concepts are but it's not any less important.

"So in relationship to the whole idea of choice, what I'm in the habit of saying is that whoever it is that's the accumulation of the different layers of self, is responsible for all those layers. So when referring to the self you can include the Self Absolute, the Authentic Self, the ego or personal self, the collective ego, and any other influences driving you including your biological impulses. You put all that in the bag and you say, 'That!' So whoever it is that's choosing includes all those things and the liberated or evolved self would have to be able to be responsible for all of that, you see?"

"Yeah, I do."

"Now, you see, if you get individuals to take responsibility for all those things, well, I can even feel a sense of relief when I say it because then that individual is endeavoring to widen his or her embrace of every single dimension of the human experience to the largest possible degree. I mean, maybe we ultimately aren't going to be able to take responsibility for every single bit of it, but we're going to aspire to that and definitely do our best. That's the goal. To aspire to take absolutely as much responsibility for every single aspect of ourselves as we can — nothing less than that would be enough. And in terms of ethnocentric, tribal-centric, nation-centric, world-centric, cosmo-centric, the

authentically cosmo-centric individual would be an individual that would be aspiring with everything they've got to do all those things. You see?"

"Yes."

"You can see how there's a tremendous sense of relief if you know someone is aspiring to be that conscious and responsible and in control of themselves, right?"

"Right."

"I mean, most people aren't trying to live anything close to what I just described. There are very few people that would consciously aspire to be that responsible. It's only the rarest of the rare, to be brutally frank about it. The last thing most people try and do is to be totally responsible.

"So that's how it works, Christopher. Most of us will be willing to be responsible if we have to. We'd prefer not to have to. Now, for the ego, if you don't have to be responsible an illusion is created. You have to stay with me here and you'll get the sense of it. From the ego's perspective if you don't have to be responsible there's this kind of illusion of almost infinite space in all directions. It's a kind of fake enlightenment state, the reason being that when all the boundaries are kept so vague it's almost like you don't have a past; it's almost like you don't have any karma. From the ego's perspective, if you don't consciously endeavor to take responsibility, everything gets very vague and you live in this grey zone where the past doesn't quite exist. It's almost like you're a liberated person. Are you with me?"

"Yes."

"But when you say to a person, 'you have to be willing to make the Herculean effort to take responsibility for all of your self, every single bit – and the implications are enormous because there are so many impulses and drives that are motivating you that are not very conscious,' – that's a whole other story.

"And, shock and surprise, those impulses are not very conscious because we don't want them to be! Are you paying attention, everybody? That's the problem. We don't want them to be conscious because they might interfere with the ego's image of itself. Remember, the ego, which doesn't take responsibility, lives in this grey zone where it doesn't have a past. It's almost like its own blemish-free universe. You know, the narcissist always looks in the mirror to admire how wonderful they look. But the mirror is very selective, especially if you're unwilling to take responsibility for all of the layers of yourself and all of your conscious and unconscious impulses. If you don't then you're going to see a very pretty picture. I mean, deeply you know it's not true but everybody's living the same lie so there are very few people that are going to crack the mirror and say, 'Look!' Except maybe someone like me. And believe me, there are not too many people like me around who are going to force you to do that.

"So this is what the situation is. And it's much worse than we think. The level of self-deception and delusion and the unwillingness to face the truth and take responsibility for the many dimensions of the self is enormous. The ego does not want to do it.

"I mean, the hardest part of my own teaching work is actually getting people to face themselves authentically. To be honest, I don't find anything more challenging than that. Giving people experiences of the Ground of Being or the Authentic Self is a billion times easier. The absolutely hardest thing to do is to get the individual to take responsibility for him or herself in an enlightenment context. I'm not going to say it's impossible, but it's just one millimeter shy of impossible. There's just nothing harder than that.

"Now, remember, when an individual has to face themselves in an evolutionary, developmental context it gets very heavy. Because if you're going to authentically develop and evolve in a vertical context from a lower level of development to a higher level of development then you have to really face everything. Nothing is more ultimately challenging for the self. Emotionally, psychologically, spiritually and in every other way, it's the ultimate challenge.

"Now, I don't think anybody would argue theoretically with this. But what I'm saying is that emotionally no one wants to do it. People often would rather do just about anything else including maybe even die. I've found this out the hard way in my role as a teacher. The level of resistance and unwillingness to face the self incites nothing less than pathological responses in people. And I really mean it! People get seriously, seriously crazy when they're asked to face, not anyone else, but themselves. I've seen a lot of people go not a little bit crazy, but quite frighteningly crazy, just because of this one point.

"So one psychological definition of ego is that it's a self-defense mechanism that protects the self from too much information that might not be flattering – to put it mildly." Andrew's laugh was laced with the sharp edge of experience. *"Does that make sense to you?"*

"Yes."

"So in light of everything that I'm saying, you can see what an enormous thing it is when I talk about an individual being willing to really take responsibility for every aspect of themselves including a lot of impulses that aren't very conscious and that people don't want them to be. We don't want them to be conscious," he repeated emphatically. *"We don't want them to be conscious. We don't want them to be. I can't overemphasize that.*

"So I'm saying that to be free the individual has to be willing to take responsibility for every aspect of him or herself. Now, whether it's ultimately possible to take responsibility for every single aspect of ourselves, I don't really know. But I do know that it's definitely possible to authentically be willing to and sincerely endeavor to. And in anybody who's assuming that position the ego has already been brought to its knees. So then there's someone that you can really work with. Otherwise the person is going to be fighting you every step of the way. They'll say, 'I want to be free.' Then I'll say, 'well then you have to face yourself.' Then they'll say, 'No.' Well, what am I supposed to do then? They say, 'I want to be free,' then I'll say, 'no, you don't,' and it goes back and forth. So then it's a standoff. Right?"

"Quite."

"In any case, remember that in this teaching the bar is very high. Everybody has to know that. This teaching ultimately challenges all of us, but that's what it is.

"So, in any case, in order to be a free person we have to be willing to take responsibility for every single aspect of ourselves. And remember, there's an evolutionary context for all this. So that means that the individuated self is aspiring to take responsibility for the evolutionary impulse. You see?"

"I do."

"But in order to be a fit vehicle for doing so that individual has to be able to take responsibility for the multidimensional vortex of energy and consciousness and all its contradictory impulses that they are and then move it forward. And they have to do it in some kind of integral or holistic manner. You get it?"

"I get it."

"So it's very simple on the one hand but incredibly complex on the other. But unless the self, which is whatever principle within you that has the capacity to organize all this information, takes responsibility for all these different streams and drives, it isn't going to happen. You see?"

"Yes, I do."

"So it's really a big deal and it's way more than most people are prepared for. But I think, at least objectively, it should be apparent to anybody who's reasonably intelligent that nothing less than that would be enough if we're talking about the evolutionary, integrated and holistic development of the individual. Right?"

"Right."

"So, my man, the Authentic Self had no doubt that it wanted to come here and you said, 'I'm going to go.' The Authentic Self didn't have a decision to make, correct?"

"That seems clear."

"That's right. And Christopher said that's exactly what he wanted to do. So you see, now we've got all bases covered. Right?"

"Right."

"And as long as we keep it that way then we can always know what we're talking about and there's always an individual we can actually engage with, right?"

"Right."

"Then Christopher is going to be this locus or fulcrum of consciousness that we can deal with. And Christopher is going to be this evolutionary force of focused intensity that's going to be moving forward in time. And whatever Christopher is – all those different lines of energy moving out in all directions from that center; the person who just said yes – is going to be responsible for all those different lines. See?"

"Yes."

"So then, whatever Christopher is will become some kind of integrated whole as it moves forward on its evolutionary trajectory. You see what I'm saying?"

"I do."

"And there's nothing more profound that could happen for any one of us than that. Now, this is just an extrapolation of what I was explaining about the development of ego over time, which is this capacity for individuation that we're now expanding to really take on everything that we are from the gross realm to the subtle realm and beyond. And so, in this way, the evolutionary impulse really takes more and more responsibility for its own manifest form in time, which has never happened before in this way. Get my point?"

"I do."

"And by the way, in my teaching this is the second tenet, the Law of Volitionality. Volition is doership. Is that clear?"

"That's clear. That was terrific, thank you." The tone of hesitancy with which the young man had initiated this dialogue had vanished completely.

"Okay, but remember, if we're going to create a new world together then I have to know that when I speak to Christopher, whoever is answering me is going to be taking responsibility for every single aspect of what Christopher is; seen and unseen, known and unknown, gross, subtle and everything in between. Right?"

"Yes."

"That's the definition of a new being, isn't it?"

"Yeah, that's quite thrilling."

"Yeah, and you can see, in terms of the evolution of consciousness, how profound the implications are in that."

"Yes."

"They couldn't be bigger because then the evolution of consciousness is not just some vague, exciting or sexy metaphysical idea but it's also brutally and so profoundly meaningful in terms of the evolution of the species. You see what I'm saying?"

"Oh yes. Definitely."

"So then you can see that what I've been referring to as the universal human, who emerges somewhere between world-centric and cosmo-centric levels of development, would have to be someone who was endeavoring to operate at this very profound level of engagement with the life process and the human experience – much, much deeper than most people even dream of. Right?"

"Right."

"And you could also see that the 'personal' dimension of the human experience and the radically impersonal, cosmic, evolutionary dimension all merge and become non-different until one can't really separate one from the other."

"Yes, that's right."

"Okay, good," Andrew concluded.

He then turned his attention to one of my roommates, Carl, a tall German fellow with an intelligent, angular face and neatly cropped dark hair.

"So, in light of what you've just been saying, it seems that personal enlightenment is very dangerous in the evolutionary context because in some ways it allows you not to take responsibility for all these things."

"You mean in terms of the definition of enlightenment I gave earlier?"

"Yes, that's right."

"I'm going to answer your question but I want to tell a funny story about this first. It's a recent story about a very famous enlightenment teacher, an Indian man who's very popular in Germany. In his teaching there is no doer in the same sense we were speaking about a minute ago. Now, he's an elderly fellow – in his eighties I think - and recently a scandal emerged because he'd been sleeping with many of the luscious young ladies that had been coming to see him. One after the other it came out and then many of them got upset. They don't usually mind if they're the only one but when they find out there was another they get outraged and call it abuse."[1] Andrew threw this in as a quick aside. *"But be that as it may, the funny thing was how he responded. He said, 'I didn't do anything, but it won't happen again.' This is a true story."*

At this the place erupted in laughter at the sheer philosophical absurdity and outrageous hypocrisy of this statement. On the one hand this octogenarian Casanova of consciousness was unabashedly and conveniently taking the position that since there is no doer he didn't actually *do* anything – don't you get it? On the other hand, his somewhat sheepish and belatedly gentlemanly conscience gave unfailing assurances that such transgressions would henceforth cease and desist, suggesting the existence of the very power of choice and doership denied by the first half of his apologetic non-sequitur. Now that's some impressively fuzzy logic, the kind that gives the ego infinite room for maneuvering while simultaneously allowing it to smugly don the cloak of spiritual wisdom.

Interestingly, Ramesh Balsekar, the purveyor of this ecstatic nihilism,[2] is also the guru of one Wayne Liquorman – a karmically curious name for a recovering alcoholic – the popular Advaita[3] teacher who boldly pronounced that the events of 9/11 could not be judged as evil and murderous, since such a conclusion obviously overlooked the consequent banquet upon which New York's multitudinous microbes got to feed for months and failed, all in all, to see the big picture. Don't you get it?

As the riotous laughter in the room faded I enjoyed a secret chuckle and small reminiscence of my own. I had met Ramesh Balsekar on my last trip to India with Peter and my wife Rose, something I had long wanted to do as he was one of the closest disciples of the near legendary Indian Advaita master, Sri Nisargadatta Maharaj, who'd lived his life as a cigarette salesman on the gritty streets of Bombay. Before heading out to Tiruvannamalai to visit the ashram of Ramana Maharshi and prior to our pilgrimage to the Ramakrishna temple at Dakshineswar in Calcutta, we set out to find Ramesh's penthouse apartment in what was, by Indian standards, a rather swank section of Bombay. Ramesh could afford such digs, being the retired President of the Bank of India, a tenure during which he'd also served as translator for his esteemed guru. Nisargadatta Maharaj had indeed needed a translator in his day for he had become quite the destination for Western seekers after the publication of a book of dialogues entitled simply *I Am That* in which his searing transmission of non-dual realization literally burned off the pages. It had seared my mind, to be sure, and I reasoned that Ramesh, having spent years by his teacher's side as a conduit for the transmission of that timeless wisdom, would have become a similarly burning vehicle for it.

When I first met him in his spacious, top floor apartment he seemed, and indeed was, the model of a gracious, elderly gentleman. His smiling eyes flickered with what then I took to be a glimmer of the infinite, yet now I have to wonder whether that flicker, lit by some flame of peace within, was not one of ego enjoying the pseudo liberation from personal responsibility to which Andrew had alluded rather than that of the awakened soul that has been liberated from ego in entirety.

Whatever the case, he was kind and charming and had an infectious charisma. That was fine as far as it went. However, watching him teach some thirty minutes later to a ragtag band of Western seekers I was disappointed; while he certainly radiated a grandfatherly sweetness and did give a transmission of sorts, there was an absence of the kind of fire that had undoubtedly burned in the heart of his guru. His words, spun out in the lyrical sing-song of Indian English, were laced with assurances that everything was perfect as it was; that one should do whatever one wanted to do because that's what God wanted one to do otherwise one wouldn't want to do it because, after all, there is no doer anyway – don't you get it? Ha, ha, ha! I was, frankly, shocked and disappointed, failing altogether to understand how this man's teaching lacked that edge of cutting insight that sheared away the personal and threw open the door to spiritual freedom, qualities that had so characterized the message of his own quick tempered and impassioned guru. I did not, however, fail to grasp that such a teaching, fuzzy edges and all, was seductively dangerous. This frightening lack of a moral center and its sedating influence on the aspiration to change, amounted to spiritual embezzlement, bleeding away the precious assets of the soul while offering the illusion of sedate enrichment – a kind of psychic Enron, if you will. In short, such a teaching deadened the soul to higher purpose and robbed the spirit of meaning, finding its full realization in the conclusion, so eloquently pronounced by Ramesh's most esteemed disciple, that 9/11 was by all accounts a merry event for the blessed microbes of Manhattan.

Pulling myself back from these perplexing reflections and turning again to the teachings at hand, I heard Carl continue, "So in this context, I understood you to say that personal enlightenment can be tricky because it can allow us to avoid facing ourselves."

"*Well,*" Andrew responded, "*it can if it's misunderstood or used in nefarious ways and if the goal is only to be free from the life process rather than to evolve the life process.*"

"Right. So the reason I'm asking is because yesterday you spoke about the emerging new Being, which I've seen in fits and starts, and this clearly seems to be infinitely more challenging than personal liberation."

"Well, you have to understand that in a vertical context – going from a lower level of development to a higher level of development – engaging with the creative process means you're pushing against inertia. And just think how much inertia there is in the universe. From the perspective of consciousness, inertia would be understood as matter that has not become conscious. So you can think of it all the way from a human being who's not enlightened to a wooden table or a rock. That's a lot of inertia. So yes, it's quite challenging."

"Okay, thank you," said Carl, his point having been adequately addressed and with that Andrew moved on. He next looked at a friend of mine, Chris, a mild-mannered, bespectacled psychiatrist from Chicago.

"Okay, Chris," Andrew prompted.

"In my experience," Chris began in an even tone, "there seems to be a surrender dimension to the emergence of the Authentic Self, a volitional 'leaning in' type of thing, and those two seem to … I guess my question is how to reconcile those two because they seem contradictory."

"Reconciling them was what I was doing when I answered Christopher's question. He began by more or less saying, 'well, I didn't choose to come here. It was just surrender. I didn't have any choice.' But in the way that I approach this, I like to emphasize the volitional dimension rather than the surrender dimension, even though surrender, of course, if you're speaking about enlightenment, is the beginning, the middle and the end of the path. But I'd rather interpret it as the individual taking unconditional responsibility for the choice to evolve. It's cleaner, there's an evolutionary context to it and it makes more sense for a Western mind.

"The whole idea of submission is not really familiar to the Western psyche. We don't like to submit, do we? No, we don't." he laughed the answer to his own question. *"If you tell people they're wonderful, they're fantastic, they're the greatest, they're beautiful, they're compassionate, they're generous, they're kind, and they're enlightened, then they don't have problems with submission. But when you tell them all the ways that they really do need to change then suddenly they don't like the whole idea of submission anymore. It loses its romantic shimmer."* He gave another ironic laugh. *"Therefore, it just makes more sense to speak about this in light of taking responsibility for the evolutionary impulse."*

"Well, sometimes I can see that when I think I'm leaning in it's really more of an egoic kind of efforting."

"Who cares who's making the effort as long as it happens? It doesn't matter how you get there. 'God, I ran all the way to the top of the hill and I got there!' he mocked. *"Do you really care who was making the effort? The important thing is that you get there, hmm?"*

"Yeah, right," Chris agreed thoughtfully.

"So somebody could say, 'you know, I was running and something literally came over me and suddenly it wasn't me running. My legs were moving by themselves and

I was in this flow state.' So, of course, that would be the best scenario, however, that's not always going to be the way it's going to work. The most important thing is that you actually get there not whether it was your ego or whether it was your Authentic Self or whatever it was. Hmm?"

"Yeah, I see."

"Because the most important thing is to develop confidence in ourselves and in the fact that we can do it, one way or the other. Right?"

"Right."

"You see, if you don't have confidence in yourself you can't even enter into the territory that we're talking about here. 'Well, I don't know if I can do it,' he went on, returning to his mocking tone. *'Can we sit down and talk about it? I don't know what's the matter with me, blah, blah, blah.' So if that's what's happening, forget it – you should be doing something else. Right?"* Andrew laughed.

Chris smiled slightly and nodded. "Right."

Andrew moved on.

"Okay. You've had your hand up for a while," he said, pointing to a middle-aged Israeli woman.

"If you have a powerful spiritual experience and after that experience you work hard in order to align your life with that, is there a point of no return when you don't always have to fight against your ego?"

"That's a very good question and I have a very good answer because I've thought a lot about this and I think I've figured it out. So everybody should pay attention because this is very important. It really helps to explain a lot of things.

"Let's just say arbitrarily that the sum total of whatever a human being is one hundred percent. Then let's say we have an individual who out of a hundred percent is five percent awake to the evolutionary impulse or the longing for liberation or the Authentic Self. So then ninety-five percent of the vehicle is being driven, dominated or controlled by the fears and desires of the individual and collective ego. But nonetheless, five percent of that individual is awake to the Authentic Self. That means that that individual, to a small but not insignificant degree, is conscious or aware of the urge to evolve at the level of consciousness. So you could meet somebody like that, let's say, in a bookstore and have a fantastic conversation about evolution and enlightenment. You might spend five, six hours speaking with them and not even be aware of time passing because you've really met them on a soul level. And because you were talking about important things the Authentic Self was meeting itself in the other and because of that, with them you found this deep, impersonal connection. And then, when you finally went home, you might say to yourself, 'wow, that was really fantastic. I really met somebody there.'

"Then let's say next week you go back to the same bookstore and you meet someone else, but this talk is even deeper because this person has more spiritual fire and more light coming out of them because they're twenty percent awake to the evolutionary

impulse. You'll be shocked at how powerful and intense is their fire for evolution and enlightenment and you'll think, 'I thought it was good last week. This is four times better.' In fact, it might be so strong that you have to go lie down at home just to kind of recover from it."

Everyone laughed, for Andrew had assumed a rather theatrical air at this point.

"And then, let's say you go back the following week and meet somebody who's twice as awake, passionate and inspired as the individual you met the week before because this individual is forty percent awake to the evolutionary impulse or Authentic Self. It might be so powerful that you'd stop talking and go into a deep meditative state together and the vibration might be so strong other people will feel it and would come and sit at the table with you.

"And on it goes. Now, even for an individual who's forty percent awake to what we're calling the evolutionary impulse or the Authentic Self, it's still ultimately the fears and desires of the individual and collective ego that are driving the car or controlling the vehicle. Do you understand?"

"Yes."

"That means that despite everything the individual is not going to change very much. In other words, an individual can have very powerful experiences of insight and higher states of consciousness, a profound level of understanding and inspiration, but they still won't fundamentally be transformed. In fact, they won't transform in a deep, profound and lasting way until they're awake to the Authentic Self not less than fifty-one percent because until that point the dominating influence over the vehicle is still going to be the individual and collective ego.

"But when the Authentic Self or evolutionary impulse becomes not less than fifty-one percent of the controlling influence then the car changes directions. Then what's in control is the Authentic Self. That doesn't mean that the fears and desires of individual and collective ego have disappeared. They're still present, but now, despite the fact that they're active, they're the weaker part of the self and they're no longer in control the way they were before.

"That helps one to understand why so many people can have deep spiritual experiences, understanding, even passion and inspiration yet still not change. So it's only after we reach that fifty one percent mark that there's a real change. That's when the power of the individual and collective ego over the vehicle suddenly becomes weaker. And then what you could call the truly spiritual motivation becomes who and what the person is then. When you meet such a person you can really see that they're different because something has touched them so deeply that they're fundamentally on a different track. They're not just inspired. They really have become a different kind of person. And if it's real, it's going to stick. Now, this way of understanding it explains a lot."

It certainly did. Ever since I'd left Peter, the question of what to make of it all had gnawed at me with relentless persistence. How could a person, so charged with spiritual power, simultaneously conduct himself with the shocking lack of integrity that he had demonstrated repeatedly in key areas of his life? I had long assumed that if a person were enlightened they would spontaneously demonstrate something approximating ethical perfection or minimally hold a high moral standard to which others would naturally aspire. As a corollary, I had taken it equally for granted that if someone demonstrated a moral standard beneath the waterline of the ordinary then clearly they couldn't be authentically enlightened. In retrospect I have little doubt that I was wrong on both counts, which raises a number of questions, one of which is how, if pushed, one might judge such a person.

This was a key issue for me, having spent thirteen years of my life with an individual who demonstrated with startling simultaneity both these seemingly divergent possibilities. In weighing all this I had to acknowledge that Peter had, over that span of time, bestowed upon me more than I could possibly repay within the abysmally inadequate stretch of one incarnation. He had taken the little discipline I had, helped me forge it into something of substance while giving it direction and purpose. He not only embodied with his own life a bridge between the mystic depths of spiritual realization and the heights of professional excellence, he had also taught me to build that bridge myself. And more than that, he provided the bricks and mortar with which to do it. That is, in a many pragmatic ways he supplied the spiritual as well as material wherewithal that helped me to free myself from the suffocating clutches of corporate life and build for myself the life of an entrepreneur. Around him I witnessed firsthand the power of a categorical commitment to the spiritual life and the miracles such dedication manifests with mind transcending perfection. I was there when he healed others of cancer, transformed psychological and emotional cripples into fully functioning human beings, saved children from sale into brothels and converted personal disasters into unexpected opportunities and foundations for further growth. And all the while he deepened with relentless determination his own grounding in the Absolute. In short, he engaged life more deeply and with greater passion than anyone else I'd ever met. And in so doing he did more to help others and demonstrate a radically different way of life than the next hundred people put together. And yet ...

And yet his wife came to him through an adulterous affair, being married to another of his students who, upon discovering this treachery, promptly and understandably left the teaching. Thereafter he continued to carry on affairs with a veritable queue of female students, all, of course, in the name of Tantra.[4] Having sex with him, he assured them flatly, would get them to God faster. To be fair, he truly, if rather conveniently, believed this, asserting (I discovered this from one of the women later) that the powerful kundalini shakti released during his heated liaisons was like a furnace fueling the ride to the center of the cosmos.[5] When his wife accused him of having affairs he publicly accused her of being a liar and, through the power of others' trust in him, turned his entire student body against her. These offenses, as well as others that I will refrain from recounting, were the most egregious against the most basic standards of ethical conduct.

There were, however, other inconsistencies that became increasingly pronounced with the passage of the years. For instance, as I have already mentioned, in my final years with him Peter became increasingly obsessed with fame, a stark contradiction to his exhortations to become no one and know nothing. Moreover, he had, from the day I'd met him, a striking inability to remember pertinent details of the lives of all but his closest students. I foolishly used to attribute this glaring failure of recall to his powerful presence in and awareness of the moment. It was only after meeting Andrew, whose uncanny ability to remember the most insignificant details from the furthest vistas of his past was nothing short of astounding, that I began to question my understanding. It took considerable time for me to realize and come to terms with what the true picture actually was. As I understand it now, it was this: Andrew, it seemed, being utterly undistracted by any image of himself – for that image had, in the fire of his awakening,[6] been incinerated like a photo in a three alarm inferno – was free to be attentive to the most minute details of his interactions with others. Peter, on the other hand, was so deeply wound into the drama of his own life, that there was little room remaining in his awareness for true attentiveness to others.

As I recalled this string of episodes I drifted off on a series of branching reflections regarding the student-teacher relationship, its nature in the postmodern world and the relationship between enlightenment and ethical behavior. (These are important to the context of this book and are detailed in Appendix 3, Reflections on the Student-Teacher Relationship and the Postmodern World). It was some time before I brought my thoughts back to the present moment in order to rejoin Andrew, *"So then the goal would be that after we'd reached fifty-one percent we would want to increase it to sixty percent, seventy percent and more. But just to get an individual to the fifty-one percent point is an enormous thing. Not too many people get there. Yet the way I see it is that until the individual reaches fifty-one percent they're probably not going to change that much even though they'll be capable of seeing and understanding just about everything. So I believe that we have to work as if our life depends on it to get to fifty-one percent. After that something happens, which is that you literally feel like you're being pulled. That's when we experience this sense of choicelessness, of being compelled, which I refer to as an ecstatic compulsion. We feel pulled or taken, almost as if by a force of gravity.*

"So in the pre-modern definition of enlightenment they said when there's surrender God takes over. But in a postmodern or evolutionary context the impulse or drive of evolution itself is experienced literally like a force of nature that you feel running through your body. You feel it on an energetic level and psychologically it becomes more and more who you actually are and what's driving, even compelling, you. It no longer

takes effort because it's its own driving force that can and will get stronger the more we give ourselves to it."

"So when you arrive at that point there is no longer a choice?"

"Right. When you get beyond fifty-one percent you experience the choiceless dimension. Before that it's something that you can experience psychologically or at moments when you feel very passionate, but it won't ever lead to anything. It'll just be an experience; it won't actually become a function of the self. But after fifty-one percent you experience that choicelessness. It doesn't mean that the fears and desires of the ego are not present or that they won't be problematic; but it means that the Authentic Self has become the dominating presence in the self."

"So up to that point we have to trust and surrender?"

"Well, the trust and surrender have to come from the beginning. After all, who is going to be willing to make so much effort to transcend the ego, a part of themselves that they're still very identified with and attached to? Hmm? Surrender means blind faith and blind trust. Do you understand that?"

"Yes, I think so."

"It means 'I can't see it, but I'll trust and I will just say yes.' That's the implication. Again, the surrender and trust have to be there from the beginning because if you're identified with the fears and desires of the individual and collective ego but you know that you have to override them then the experience will be one of having to override something that feels right and true and authentic. In other words, even if intellectually you recognize that it's not, emotionally you are almost completely identified with it. So the blind faith and trust would be the willingness to override that which feels most authentic and true. Now, that's an ultimate challenge for anybody, right?"

"Right."

"So the surrender has to be there from the beginning. But, whereas in the beginning stage it's going to take a lot of effort, later on it won't because you'll be driven by the part of you that knows more and sees more. So even if there's still an attraction to the ego it won't be as hard to let go of it because now you're on the other side. Do you see the point?"

"I do."

"Now the problem with us is that because of the narcissism we don't like to make effort, we don't like to struggle and we we're not willing to suffer and that's the problem.

"So you see, if you understand this then it helps to understand a lot about how human beings evolve or don't evolve and why and why not."

"Is it ultimately because they don't want to?"

"Exactly," Andrew laughed. *"So in the way I teach the individual is always responsible. It makes things very straightforward. Without the individual being the one who's going to take responsibility for the whole process, you can't move forward. So in a context of evolutionary enlightenment the individual has to be willing to take responsibility for his or her own process of development. Therefore, whether someone evolves*

or not is completely dependent upon them. That's why the foundation of the teaching of evolutionary enlightenment in terms of practice is called 'clarity of intention.'

"People always ask me, 'Andrew, I really like everything you're saying. It's fantastic. How do I do it?' Then I tell them that you have to want it. Then they might say, 'but I do want it. If I didn't want it, I wouldn't be here.' Then I add that they have to want it more than anything else. Now, wanting it more than anything else is not a feeling, it's an action. A feeling is an experience; an action is a whole other thing. So the first tenet of the teaching, 'clarity of intention,' means I want to be free more than anything else so consciousness can evolve through me. It's very simple. But it's the 'more than anything else' that's the challenging part of it. Does everybody understand that?"

A quiet affirmative murmur moved through the room.

"Unless you want to evolve and be free that much you're never going to find the wherewithal to take the kind of responsibility for yourself that I was speaking about earlier. 'How do I do it?' You have to want it more-than-anything-else! And if you don't want it more than anything else nothing's ultimately going to help that much. You can meditate from now until Doomsday and you're not going to change that much. Meditation, while it's an important thing, is not going to make this happen. What does it is you!

"Now the good news about clarity of intention is that it can be cultivated. The truth is I've never met an individual that really wanted to be free more than anything else. They said they did but they didn't mean it. Most people think they want to be free but sooner or later they find that they don't really want to be free. Why? Because it's too hard! And why is it too hard? For all the reasons that I was explaining earlier on. It's such an enormous task.

"So how it becomes possible to want to be free more than anything else is through the conscious cultivation of that very aspiration. And there's a moral and ethical dimension to that cultivation. You see I've never met anybody that for themselves personally would want to accept that much responsibility. I mean most people want to experience higher states of consciousness and moments of inspired passion. But very few want to make the enormous effort to change because it's simply too hard. So, you're not going to do this for yourself because frankly, you don't care that much about yourself. Let's be brutally honest, all most people want to do is feel good. I'll admit it. It doesn't bother me. For myself, all I want to do is feel good and not suffer. That's just how we are.

"But when there's a larger context and a larger purpose that involves everyone else and maybe even, if you're audacious enough to believe it, the evolution of consciousness and our species itself, then you suddenly discover a very big reason you have to do it. It's not for yourself but it's for the sake of the evolution of consciousness itself and you really mean it. 'Not my will, but thy will be done.' That's the surrender we were talking about. That's when the moral dimension enters into the reason why you want to be free more than anything else. The 'more than anything else' is now for a larger purpose. Take my word for it, we are not morally evolved enough to want to do this just for

our self, but the larger purpose can create the moral context and give us the strength to cultivate that aspiration.

"You see, almost everybody, when I ask them, 'do you want to be free?' says, 'of course I want to be free.' Then I'll add, 'more than anything else?' and they'll say, 'well, I never thought about it.' So I say, 'think about it.'" And then people get scared because they're afraid if they honestly look at themselves they're going to find out that while they would like to be free there are other things that they would like more. In fact, when it's just between them and themselves they prefer a whole host of things: mountain climbing; being with their girlfriend; saving the Earth – that's a noble one; driving fast cars or whatever it is.

But anything less than a radically surrendered and committed engagement with the evolution of consciousness in the way we've been speaking about it is not enough. Is everybody with me?"

The atmosphere in the room had sobered considerably. Quietly nodding heads met Andrew's question and he continued.

"If you dare yourself to think about it in this way the ego or the separate self-sense begins to feel enormous pressure."

Andrew glanced over at the headphone clad French enclave. *"Is she doing a good job of translation?"* he asked, indicating an attractive blonde serving that function. Then, semi-jesting, he added, *"Do you feel fear?"*

Everyone burst into laughter though, based on prior experience, I intimated the seriousness behind that quip. Recently Andrew had boldly declared that if you were on retreat with him and did not experience both ecstasy and terror then you simply weren't following instructions. As the last five days had seen a preponderance of ecstasy, that could only mean one thing.

"If she's doing a good translation," he reiterated, *"then you'd feel fear now."* As more laughter echoed through the room I wondered how long this jocularity would last when faced with appraising our prioritization of spiritual freedom over all our other desires.

"So, does everybody follow the idea?" Andrew asked, his tone growing serious now. *"Often people get very inspired and they ask, 'how do I do this? What should I do? Should I meditate four hours a day?' Then I tell them, 'you can if you want to but unless you want to be free more than anything else the meditation's not going to do much for you.' You see, the meditation is an experience but what about the individual who's having the experience? It all comes back to the question that Christopher asked me about the individual taking responsibility for being the one who's doing it? In this case, that would mean taking responsibility for the desire to evolve.*

"So once again, the foundation of the teaching is 'clarity of intention;' it's wanting be free more than anything else so that consciousness can evolve through me. And it's the 'more than anything else' that's the tricky part of it. I want this to be what everybody thinks about between now and when we come back at five today," Andrew

announced. *"Now, I'm sure you're going to find that you didn't want to be free as much as you thought you did. Everybody has a big shock when they were feeling so good and experiencing different kinds of ecstasy and then suddenly they stumble upon the ego, that part of themselves that definitely doesn't want it. It pops their ecstasy bubble. They say, 'oh, the retreat was going so well that I forgot I had an ego. And now you're ruining the party.'"*

Once again laughter filled the room, but Andrew wasn't laughing. *"I'm just saving you some time here. I'm preparing you for what you're going to find. But once you reckon with this then the clarity of intention can be cultivated. It's very important to know that.*

"So again, what we find is that there's a part of you that wants it, which is the Authentic Self, and there's a part of you that doesn't want it. That's why I have two models here." Andrew moved the red dot of his laser pointer to move back and forth between the two large teaching models on either side of him. *"Otherwise I'd only have one. So right here,'* he said, pointing to the first rung of the concentric circles on the ego model, *"it says, 'I don't want to be free.' So if you look inside yourself you're going to find a definite "no, I don't want to be free or evolve more than anything else. Yet at the same time, the very reason you're looking is because you've already found this person,"* he indicated the figure in the Authentic Self model with his laser pointer, *"which is the person who already wants to be free. Otherwise, you wouldn't be here. What brings people to retreats like this is the Authentic Self or the evolutionary impulse. So you've already been saying yes to some degree to that part of yourself, otherwise you wouldn't be here. Is that clear?"*

Lots of sober, attentive yeses this time.

"So one of the many gifts you can get from a retreat like this is that you can easily discover that there's a part of you that wants it and there's a part of you that doesn't. Now that's the beginning of the end of a deluded state. It's a big gift. It doesn't necessarily always feel good but when you know that there's a part of you that wants this and a part of you that doesn't and you're clear about that, and then you'll be in a position to deal with it. But if you falsely assume, as many people do, that you only want this (freedom) *and that this part of you* (ego) *doesn't exist you're not going to be able to make any progress because you're going to be living a lie. Do you understand?"*

It was very quiet now, only the chorus of church bells sounding in the distance.

"So I want you to look into this question of wanting to be free and explore it. And just in case you have any doubt about it, 'more than anything else' is there for a reason. That's the part that's going to create an enormous amount of existential and evolutionary tension. That's why I added it. It pushes you right to the edge. But don't let it intimidate you. Just face it. Have the courage to face and experience it and that's all. You don't have to do anything about it. Can you handle that? Is everybody strong enough philosophically, emotionally, psychologically, and spiritually to handle that? Hmm?"

A small murmur of muted affirmatives greeted that challenge as most of the collective wind and all of the jocularity had been knocked out of our gathering.

"Okay, so between now and five I want everybody to look into the first tenet of the teaching which is 'Clarity of Intention.'"

Seemingly satisfied that everyone concurred, Andrew brought the teaching to a close. I sat quietly for some time after he departed. So he's finally come to it, I thought: The Five Tenets; the teeth of his teaching; the incisors of enlightenment; the scaffolding of liberation. (For a more in-depth and important discussion of the Five Tenets, please see Appendix 4, The Five Fundamental Tenets of Evolutionary Enlightenment). For days now we'd been immersed in the liberating revelation of Being. Now it would be time to consider the implications of that revelation for our lives and the way we lived them. And the place to start was Clarity of Intention and the contemplation of the question of what we most wanted from life. I had traveled down that road on prior expeditions of the soul and I felt a sudden surge of fear. The tenets were indeed the teeth of Andrew's teaching and it was the first one that bit deepest and hardest. It opened a gash in the psyche that if cut well and deep would allow the others entry and empower their transforming work. But the first cut had to be made.

As I walked from the teaching to the meditation hall that morning my ego, which had been squirming for some time, began hyperventilating, frantically looking for ways to avoid facing the first tenet squarely. Sexual desire reared its head with a vengeance and a storm of agitation swept through the swiftly constricting channels of my mind.

"Oh no," I thought, "I can't go through this again." I had struggled with the first tenet in the past, facing the simple question of whether I wanted to be free more than anything else. I had discovered division and despair. Recalling this, depression descended on me.

"Yes you can, you big baby," I chided myself. "Focus on the mission; stay the course."

"Why?" I demanded. "There's nothing in it for you, remember?" I shot a hungry glance at a curvy blonde conversing seductively in French with her equally seductive friends.

"You're a warrior, a fighter," I insisted, ungluing my eyes from the girls. "You understand the context; you know why you're here."

"Bah! Look at her. Damn, she's cute. I could see wanting *that* more than anything else." And I could too.

"Snap out of it, you weakling."

"Why should I?"

"Because."

Back and forth it went in schizophrenic throes like Gollum's madness on Mt. Doom.

"I can't."

"You can."

"Yes."

"No."

"Why should I?"

"You know why."

"Give up."

"Keep going."

"What's the point? You'll never do it. You're too weak – even now!"

"Don't listen to him. You can do it."

"Never. Neeeveeer!" Somewhere inside a fist slammed down concussively.

Feeling the limits of my sanity, I grasped a lifeline from the teaching – no relationship to thought. Shaking my head, I gave my attention to consciousness. Immediately – space; relief. And, while fear and agitation still clung like smoke at the edges of my mind, I could now breathe. I made my way across the sun drenched plaza, passing before the basilica oddly curious how everyone could seem so breezily carefree when, against the walls of my own mind, the forces of ego were massing. Ultimately I disregarded these concerns and settled in for meditation. I let everything be as it is and, desperately, sought *"that mysterious place where the mind has no foothold whatsoever."* I passed through that no-place periodically, finding some relief, but without a doubt the flavor and texture of the retreat were about to change.

During lunch the squeeze on the ego tightened in earnest, that increase predictably tied to ego's decision to become more assertive. In other words, under normal circumstances, with few constraints on ego's actions, it has almost infinite latitude within which to maneuver without bumping into boundaries and is therefore able to remain invisible to its host, freely operating beneath the radar and seeming as if it weren't there. However, with my regained determination to restrict its boundaries dramatically and, threatened by the specter of confrontation with the first tenet, my ego's response - a volatile mixture of fear and rage – was coming to a slow boil.

By the time I returned to the meditation hall for the afternoon session of chanting, all the same sights and sounds that I had previously seen in the radiant light of consciousness I now saw against the brittle textures of irritability and an agitated mind. Many factors conspired to push me to the edge: the stifling humidity that seemed to press the very air from the room; the sweat that covered every pore of my body; the clatter rising from the kitchen below to chew at my fraying nerves; the sexual desire uncoiling itself to invade every cell in my body; the spiritual and physical fatigue that seemed to drain the will to resist from those very same cells; and the one unifying theme that pulled together this symphony of madness – fear of confronting the first tenet in earnest.

It was against this backdrop that Chris Parrish entered the room just as we had begun the chant, in order to point out, in his typically understated yet spiritually potent way, our spectacular lack of success in this aspect of the practice. First, he wryly observed, no sound appeared to be issuing from the entirety of the back of the room despite the convincing movement of lips. Moreover, the collective quality of the chant was rote and soulless, primarily attributed to a failure to stay with the meaning of the words and driven by a tendency to become waylaid by the abstractions of the drifting mind. Finally, with these factors converging, the atmosphere between us entirely lacked the quality of communion that was the larger target of this exercise. As he had on the first day, though now in much more punctuated fashion, Chris explained the importance of each of these elements and urged us to snap out of our spiritual stupor for the purpose of a greater good. If properly pursued, with each individual autonomously meditating on the meaning of the chant while simultaneously endeavoring to harmonize with others doing the same, the result could be the same stirring autonomy and communion to which we had all borne witness during 'enlightened communication' groups. It was this to which Chris implored us.

Chris's challenge, while adding one more strain to my discontent, simultaneously helped me to marshal my resources and redouble my efforts to do the right thing for the right reasons while ignoring the clamor of my ego. At least for the moment. During that hour of chanting I forced myself to follow Chris' instructions and I felt the power of spiritual determination reinvigorate my soul. Thus, due to Chris' intervention, the hour passed quickly. At its end I felt slightly uplifted though that did not last long. Following the concentrated atmosphere of the practice, I was back to dealing with the implicating enormity of the first tenet.

I trudged back to the teaching hall in a stupor. As I settled into my seat it quickly became apparent to me, with some morbid satisfaction, that I was not alone in my reaction. In fact, the silence that now pervaded the room was filled with an entirely different quality than it had on previous days. The stillness of the Absolute, it seemed, had been replaced by the shock of the Absolute. No one moved. The winds that had ripped up the canyon and into our room every afternoon now seemed darker and more ominous against the deadly hush in our midst. The distant ringing of bells borne in on those angry gusts now rang of reckoning, not of release. A riveting sobriety had settled upon us as Andrew entered the room.

The meditation that followed did little to soften the edges of the collective apprehension and when Andrew finally decided to take the first question, the young American man he called on wasted no time in coming to the point.

"I have two lines of inquiry regarding wanting to be free more than anything else," he said hesitantly. "The first thing that I came across in myself is that it would feel nice to be able to say yes but it would not be honest. I mean, it would have to show up in action. So the question I have is does the declaration that I want to be free more than anything else have any value in and of itself?"

"Well, that's a good question," Andrew replied. *"What do you think the answer is?"*

"My sense right now is that only action counts."

"Therefore..."

"Therefore, the answer would be 'no' unless you say that the declaration is also an action."

"Unless you're willing to back it up. If you're willing to back it up then the declaration has absolute, life-transforming value. But if the answer is 'no' then it can have actually the opposite effect.

"So I really want to go into this because the foundation of this whole teaching is really based on this one particular question and it's more important than most people realize. So the main importance of the first tenet lies in the fact that it points toward a non-relative position. Wanting to be free more than anything else is a position a human being chooses in relationship to life that's not relative. So capital F-R-E-E is not relative. You're not 'free-er.' Either you're free or not. The non-relative implications of the word 'free' make this an interesting and very compelling statement.

"Similarly, we were talking about meditation in many different ways over the last few days and I said one of the ways to understand it is that that which is relative begins to contemplate that which is Absolute. Then, the more it actually does so, the more the reflection of that which is Absolute begins to destroy or overwhelm that which is relative. So that's in relationship to the experience of consciousness itself. But now we're talking about in relationship to life. So the statement 'I want to be free more than anything else' sets up that same kind of equation with respect to the individual who is locatable and has freedom of choice. How is the choice or the free agency of the individual going to be used in relationship to that which is non-relative? This is an **ultimately** *challenging question for any individual because when it's taken seriously it compels the individual to engage with a non-relative relationship with the life process.*

"So in contemplating the question one glimpses what the authentically non-relative – which means enlightened – relationship to life should be. And it ultimately challenges the relative notions of who we are, which is, of course, ego. That's why it's such a compelling matter and such a big deal.

"And, of course, when you look into the question, 'do I want to be free more than anything else?' it opens a whole other field of inquiry, which is, 'what would that really mean?' Now, that's an open question. Nobody has figured that out completely yet. But one can't really even enter into the inquiry authentically unless this first question has been answered unequivocally. Does that make sense?"

"Yes, and that actually brings me to the other question I have which is that whether I want to or not, I have to."

"Well, that's another issue. As I mentioned earlier, there is a higher moral or ethical dimension that enters into the picture at a certain point. That's the 'I have to' part."

"But the 'have to' cannot replace saying yes to the want to?"

"I don't think so. How it starts is that first it's a free choice, at least in theory. It's choice that is freely made by the autonomous individual. But after the choice is freely made, over time it becomes a moral obligation. That in itself is evolution, isn't it?"

"Yes."

"But this is why it's without any doubt whatsoever the foundation of the authentic spiritual life and the evolution of consciousness. Wanting to be free 'more than anything else' completely undercuts the ego's position every time. It's the 'more than anything else' that destroys it. That's why it's so powerful. That's why it's the 'position of enlightenment.' Do you understand?"

"Yes."

"That's good. So what did you come up with in relation to the issue of wanting to be free more than anything else?"

"I came up with yes."

"Okay. Very good." Seemingly satisfied, Andrew turned his attention to the next person, an older American woman with a Southern accent.

"During lunch a group of us were talking about this question. So I have some questions about the fact that this desire to be free more than anything else can be cultivated."

"Yes, that's right. What about that?"

"I just wondered if we could talk more about that."

"Well, you see from the perspective of the Authentic self, which is the evolutionary impulse and the part of yourself that brought you here, there's no ambivalence whatsoever about this question. But when anybody begins to look into this question deeply what's going to come to light is both the Authentic Self's doubtless, choiceless position and the ego's profound ambivalence. So, how the desire to be free is cultivated is through choosing to give more of our attention to the Authentic Self's choiceless compulsion to evolve and to delight in its already free state while removing one's attention from the compulsive fears and desires of the individual and collective ego. But you have to be very serious and mature to do that. Most people, to be honest, don't have the maturity because it's a very austere form of contemplation. But that's how it's cultivated."

"When we were talking it was more in terms of the practical things in life. In other words, how do you put yourself in a position where that desire can be cultivated, strengthened."

"That's fine, but I don't want to go into that yet. I just want to go into the questions themselves, not into the practical answers, because that takes the heat off. We just want to go into the dharma of this itself and to get very clear about that first."

"So is the question then about the relationship between the autonomy of the self and the choicelessness of the authentic self?"

"Well, the idea is to line them up. The idea is for the autonomy of the individual to become one with the ecstatic compulsion of the Authentic Self. Does that make sense?"

"Yeah, it does."

"So that's why this question of choice or free agency that we were speaking about earlier today is really such an enormous part of all this. As it should be when evolution becomes aware of itself. If there's no choice there's no autonomy, right?"

"Right."

"And also, if we're talking about an evolutionary, developmental context, that means that the individual is constantly going to be negotiating a field of change. So whenever any individual is doing that there's going to be tremendous unpredictability. In other words, if you're aspiring to create that which is new, that creates a very delicate and inherently complex field of operation, right?"

"Right."

"So if you're living in a very traditional context where what you're supposed to do and how you're supposed to live has already been laid out, then basically all you have to do is follow the rules, right?"

"Yeah."

"Of course, even in real life there are always going to be a lot of complicated choices to be made, but in an evolutionary, developmental context, when you actually endeavor to create something new, it's going to be even that much more complicated. It's inherently very complex."

"And I guess maybe that's the excitement of it."

"Definitely."

"The Unknown, that is."

"Well, from the perspective of the self that has been liberated into the Authentic Self, creating that which is new is the joy of being alive. That's the ecstatic thrill of living an authentically creative life. But so much of the self has to be let go of in order to live in that state of joy that for most people there's too much instability. Most people find it quite emotionally unbearable. Do you know what I mean?"

"Yeah."

"Because where is our attention ordinarily? Is our attention really on creating that which is new perpetually, relentlessly, and endlessly? Or is it something that you're interested in once in a while, but essentially you want a life of predictability, security, comfort, and safety. Do you see what I'm saying?"

"Yeah."

"But if the attention shifts and then what you really are interested in is in perpetually creating that which is new, then the thrill is endless and your sense of security comes from doing that. In fact, if you've gone that far, not doing that is something you find literally physically unbearable and emotionally, psychologically, spiritually, and philosophically suffocating. But you have to go pretty far to start feeling that way.

The Authentic Self thrives when everything's moving. Then you know that everything is right and everything is good and everything is as it should be. But when things are not moving everything is wrong. It's very simple. The Authentic Self thrives on that thrust forward and upward so if everything's moving up then everything's right in the universe and you can sleep well at night. Does that make sense?"

"Yes it does."

"But it's a very different way to live, to think and to feel than we ordinarily do because it's the perpetual creation of that which is new that is driving you. Do you get the point?"

"Yeah."

"So you can see that it is the first tenet of the teaching, the 'I want to be free more than anything else,' that lays the foundation for the authentically creative life. It frees you up to be able to create that which is perpetually new. On the other hand, if you don't want to be free more than anything else you're not going to be in a position to be able to create that which is new because you'll be attached and tied down. So, 'I want to be free more than anything else' is the foundation for being an agent of the evolutionary impulse. It's the only foundation and nothing else will be enough. I, the chooser, want to be free. You won't be able to be an agent of the evolutionary impulse for more than brief moments unless you want to be free more than anything else. It's scientific. If you look at it closely enough you'll see that's simply how it works. Do you get the idea?"

"Yes, I do."

"Very good. So what did you come to?"

"In terms of...?"

"The question."

"Of how to cultivate it?"

"No, of whether you want to be free more than anything else or not."

"I know that I want to want to be free more than anything else."

"You want to want to?"

"Yeah. I think if I'm honest with myself I can say that I probably don't have a full understanding of the implications of wanting to be free more than anything else."

"Well, it's very simple. The implications are always going to be more than your ego can bear."

"Right. That's what I mean."

"Well, that's the whole point of the exercise. It's a non-relative position. It's very simple. It's designed to show you the part of yourself that doesn't want it so you can get a clear picture of exactly what you're talking about. So the answer is that you saw and felt the part of you that did want it – the Authentic Self – and you saw and felt the part of you that didn't, right?"

"Yes, that's right."

"And you feel ambivalent but at least you're clear about the duality there, right?"
"Yeah."
"Okay, that's good. It's not pleasant, but it's helpful, isn't it?"
"It is because I know that in a context like this it's very easy to just make that declaration but when the going gets tough, if I can still act from a place of freedom and still have that conviction, that's the proof of my conviction."
"Right and if you can't do that when the going gets tough then you're not doing it at all. It's easy to be free when it's easy."
"Exactly."
"Anybody can do that."
"Right."
"But it's hard when it's hard. So unless you can pull it off when it's most difficult, then in relationship to the question of wanting to be free more than anything else, it means you do not want it. Hmm?"
"Right. The other thing that came up in the conversation was about the fact that you said that this can be developed and strengthened."
"Cultivated."
"Right. Cultivated. So I can say, 'I want to be free more than anything else' now and sometime down the road realize, 'I want it even more now than I did back then.' Does that make any sense?"
"Well, I suppose if one evolved one would begin to experience more delight and experience a greater thrill in the non-relative dimension as one became a lot clearer about it and had simultaneously given up a lot of emotional and psychological attachments that would hinder one's ability to even experience that thrill and that joy. That would definitely be the case as the self matured. Maturing means that you start seeing what's real, what's not real, what's true and what's not true.
"But from an immature position, in your deepest or highest moments you can probably see that certain things aren't really good for you, right?"
"Yeah."
"They're unwholesome but because one is still seeing from an immature perspective and level of development one isn't willing to let go of it even though one can see intellectually, and maybe even more than that, that it's not wholesome. That's because of attachment. But as one matures one gets to a point where one is no longer attracted to that which is unwholesome. That's a sign of mental health, which is a very rare thing. So the degree of emotional attachment to that which is unwholesome is going to make it correspondingly difficult to experience the ecstatic thrill of wanting to be free more than anything else because there would simply be too much baggage. But as one matures the ecstatic thrill of wanting to be free more than anything else becomes the source and foundation of freedom itself.
"So as we've been saying, the ultimate reference point of the liberated life is the knowledge, recognition and awareness of the already full perfection of the non-relative

*or absolute nature of reality that's in the unmanifest realm at the level of conscious-
ness. And how that translates into the manifest realm is the conscious, soul level choice
to want to be capital F-R-E-E more than anything else. That's the manifestation and
expression of the recognition of fullness in the manifest realm. They're two sides of the
same thing. Does that connection make sense to you?"*

"Yeah."

*"Good. So everybody has to know that I know full well that the first tenet of the
teaching is ultimately challenging. But that's the beauty of it. So it's good to practice
this form of contemplation because if we want to evolve and develop we need to have
a very strong foundation.*

*"The other thing about wanting to be free more than anything else is that it's to-
tally dependent upon you. That's how you find autonomy because then you don't have
to depend upon anyone else. You don't even have to depend upon God. It's completely
freeing. Otherwise you have to wait around for some unmanifest non-entity to save
you. Also, if you want to be free more than anything else then your freedom is also not
dependent upon having particular experiences. You may be inspired by certain experiences but you're not dependent upon them. Of course, the choice to be free would logically be inspired by the experience of higher states, but the freedom itself is no longer
dependent upon having any particular experience.*

*"So if you want to be capital F-R-E-E more than anything else then it's all in
your hands and the whole door to radical autonomy is opened. See how that changes
everything?"*

"Yes."

*"Good, so you should stay with this because if someone is very, very clear about this,
the rest is, relatively speaking, pretty easy, even if it may be very difficult. But if you're
not clear about this you just enter into endless trouble."*

Andrew next turned his attention to Steffen, a German formal student, sitting
behind me in the section reserved for formal students. He was thirty something,
slightly built with dark hair, refined features and elegant glasses. Behind those
glasses, he was pale and wide-eyed. Tight lipped, he asked, "In your answer to this
gentleman you mentioned that the contemplation of the first tenet is very austere.
I was just wondering if you could say more about that because in my own experience, I'm finding more that it takes a very rational and cool-headed approach to
look into these matters."

"Well, you're German so that shouldn't be hard. Germans are very rational…"

"Yes, but I'm seeing that…"

"Even to the point of being completely irrational."

"Yes, exactly. What I'm finding is that the ego responds with all kinds of irrational responses and it's very emotional. Looking into this, I find, has to be very
committed and rational. I was just struck when you mentioned the austerity of
it."

"Well, yeah, but as you already know and as I was saying today, the goal is to become a rational human being, right?"

"Right."

Andrew seemed to have nothing further to say on this point and looked for a long moment into the silence that had filled the room.

When no hands were raised, *"So you guys don't want to talk about this any more? Everybody seems to be stunned into submission. You see, that's the power of the first tenet.*

"This is also what's very unique about the way that I teach. For example, we could speak about the non-relative or absolute nature of reality from the perspective of consciousness itself and that's inherently thrilling, exciting, liberating and intoxicating. But it's not challenging. But when we start seeing that in relationship to choice or free agency, we often recoil. So in the way this stuff is taught, if you just expose people to the non-relative dimension of consciousness you open up a whole field of experience that may not ordinarily be available to them. Now, most people are more than happy with that. They say 'thank you very much, that was wonderful. I'll be eternally grateful,' and everybody will go home quite happy. But then, when you start equating the non-relative or absolute dimension of reality with volition or free agency or choice, wow, that changes the whole picture. That's when it gets real. Get the point?"

A few heads nodded quietly.

"So in relationship to enlightenment in an evolutionary, developmental context, it cannot and won't happen without the wholehearted engagement of choice on the part of the individual. That's just the way it is. Consciousness does not evolve without our conscious participation in the process and our conscious participation in the process comes from the contemplation of wanting to be free more than anything else. See how it works?"

A few more half-hearted yeses and then Andrew turned to the next person, an older Australian man. "Andrew," he began, "I'm inclined to say that I used to think that I had to convince the ego to want to be free more than anything else. Now, from this contemplation, I'm getting the sense that there's no amount of convincing that I could do to make the ego want to be free more than anything else."

"No," Andrew responded emphatically. *"Because the ego doesn't want to be free more than anything else. And, in fact,"* he added forcefully, *"it's never, ever going to want to be free. There, I just saved you a lot of trouble."*

A small wave of lighthearted laughter rippled through the room.

"So you could see when Steffen asked that question that he hasn't figured that out yet. The ego, or the part of him that's panicking, doesn't want this and is never going to. The ego is not the part of you or Steffen or me or anybody that wants to be free. So the ego's never going to help. That's the beauty of this contemplation. That's what makes it all so clear.

"So when this gentleman was asking me how to cultivate clarity of intention I was very specific in my answer. The way you cultivate it is by removing your attention from the fears and desires of the ego. Because if you give the ego an absolute threat and then you begin to pay attention to what the ego's afraid of, and you give more and more of your attention to what the ego's worst fears are, the only thing that's going to happen is you're going to start to work yourself up into a panic."

"Right."

"It's inevitable. If you start giving more and more attention to your worst fears coming true then you start feeling more and more frightened, agitated, frustrated, confused, and desperate, right?"

"Yes, that's right."

"And inevitably when you bring up these big questions it's like turning up the heat, right?"

"Right."

"Okay, so once again, the way to cultivate the desire to be free is very simple. You remove your attention more and more from the fears and desires of the ego and put it more on the aspiration for liberation of the Authentic Self. So you're taking your attention away from the part of you that is never going to want it and put it on the part of you that never wanted anything else. You see?"

"Yes."

"And then what happens is the part of you that never wanted anything else gets stronger and stronger."

"Right."

"And the more you identify with that part of yourself the more you begin to experience that strength yourself."

"Right."

"And then that which seemed to be such a big problem earlier, you now realize isn't a problem at all, not because the problem disappeared but because you're no longer so emotionally identified with what the ego is so invested in and that changes everything. You see?"

"Yes, I do."

"But you have to be very careful with this because the emotions are very strong. See, the emotions, as I'm sure everybody already knows, make people blind. It's not concepts in and of themselves but it's the emotions related to them that blind us so we have to be careful — very careful."

"Right."

"But if you know that the ego doesn't want us to be free, then you understand it from the beginning and it's no surprise. Okay?"

"Yeah, okay."

"So if you feel frustrated it's because you're wondering why your ego is not excited about this. That's called wrong contemplation. Forcing the ego to contemplate freedom

is like torturing yourself. There's no way that could have a beneficial outcome. You'll just drive yourself crazy. So it's easy to understand on the one hand, but it's actually quite complex unless you're very clear what the difference between the ego and the Authentic Self is. So you have to be humble and careful about this because a lot of us don't know the difference. Most people don't know themselves very well. Most of us have a very crude approach to our own experience."

"True."

"So during a retreat is a very good time to pay attention to these distinctions because we can all slow down. We want to learn to make the distinction between the Authentic Self, which is the part of you that already has no doubt about it and is not ambivalent in the least, and the ego. Remember, the Authentic Self is the energy and intelligence that created the universe. It's the evolutionary impulse recognizing itself and becoming aware of itself at the level of consciousness. It has no concern whatsoever for the fears and desires of the ego. You see?"

"Yes."

"So then, if you're very identified with the ego, as obviously Steffen is, then what you have to do is practice the meditative position, which is no relationship with thought. You have to just blindly stop identifying with thought until you start to calm down, realize that the world's not falling apart, and begin to feel some detachment from the intense emotions. And then, as you calm down and calm down and calm down, a space opens up. Then, and not before then, from the perspective of that space, you can begin to put your attention on the Authentic Self. You got that? Do you get how it works?"

"Yes, thank you very much."

Andrew continued, repeating his points, as he often does, in order to drive their importance home. *"So the ego has to be let go of in order to be able to do this, even if only temporarily. Forcing the ego to want freedom will never work."*

"I understand."

"You see, the ego has a lot of conviction about its position. It's very self-righteous. It's very passionate about the inherent reality of its perspective. Does that make sense?"

"Yeah, definitely."

"The ego is sure that its position is valid and if it's not completely valid, well, it's at least partially valid. But it's very sure about it. So self-righteous means if you feel unjustly or unfairly represented then you feel very upset about it."

"Yes."

"So the ego is very sure that at least part of its position is right. The reason I'm making a point of this is because we're talking about the absolute or non-relative dimensions of all this. So the ego might not feel that it's completely right, but it feels if I'm partially right and you don't recognize that – 'you' meaning your own Authentic Self – then it's been unfairly represented. But – because in an enlightenment context you have to engage with the non-relative or absolute dimension to all this – the Authentic Self says that the ego's position is completely wrong. See, that's the challenge. The ego

doesn't mind being a little bit wrong as long as it can also be partially right because if it's partially right then it doesn't have to let go absolutely. Then it can kind of have the best of both worlds."

I thought of Peter briefly and a little shiver shot through me. "Everything Andrew is saying is true," he'd conceded, "but it's so absolute that it doesn't leave any room for one's humanity."

"But in a non-relative or absolute context it could never work that way. So you can begin to see how scientific this is. And in order for a new being to emerge there needs to be a complete reconfiguration of our orientation. Do you understand?"

"Yes, thanks."

"Does everybody understand what I'm saying?" he said to us with tremendous emphasis and an upsurge of passion. *"There's a science to this. That's what's so amazing! And in order to really delight in it and to appreciate it one has to slow down and really let go a little bit. But if you do then you'll see how completely amazing it is."*

He paused briefly, indicating that for the moment he had made his point and was ready for the next question. *"Yes, did you have a question?"* he said to a young, thin American woman with short, red hair near the front who had had her hand up for some time.

"Andrew, I'm wondering what the relationship is between the fifty-one percent that you spoke about and wanting to be free more than anything else. I mean, can I feel this conviction if I'm at like ten percent?"

"Well, at any point you can locate what we're calling the Authentic Self, which is the part of you that's the evolutionary impulse. So you can make the choice to put your attention on that and dwell upon that, which will, over time, change the equation. You see?"

"Yeah."

"Remember, we need to contemplate the nature of the Authentic Self, which is not ambivalent about this at all, until we reach this fifty-one percent point. We have to do whatever we have to do in order to get to that point because once we reach fifty-one percent we become autonomous in this. We become independent agents of the Authentic Self.

"But the thing about the ego is that you have to take it seriously. This is not a game. This is very, very serious stuff we're talking about here. It's not for immature human beings. When we talk about absolute and non-relative we are playing around with very powerful concepts. So the fact that a part of you really doesn't want to have anything to do with this profound level of engagement with life is something you have to take seriously because if you know that, then you'll be able to take responsibility for that part of yourself. But if you don't know it and don't take it very seriously you can end up getting yourself into big trouble. It's like swimming in water that's too deep.

"Now, you may say," Andrew switched to a casual and dismissive tone, *'that's no problem; I know what this is about. I've done it many times.'* Then I'd say *'no, you*

haven't.' Then you might insist, 'I can handle it,' and I'd say, 'no, you can't.' You see? It's arrogance and it's a lack of humility that causes people not to take this seriously enough. So I'm saying that it's very deep water but that it's real, and I'm also saying that it's not a problem if you understand that and if you're a mature adult who's taking responsibility for that choice. Then you know it and you can handle it. See what I'm saying?"

"Yeah, I do. I've been finding this distinction between the ego and the Authentic Self incredibly helpful. I've never really seen it this clearly before."

"Very good. So for the time being I want everybody to really start dealing with these issues. If you can do this, I guarantee it will literally change your whole life.

"You see, most people don't think they have an ego or, if they're willing to admit they have one, they're sure it's not going to be a problem. So when we start really looking into the absolute or the non-relative dimension of the self in relationship to life, in relationship to action and responsibility, then the ego is a big issue – believe me. It's bigger than you think because we're not very conscious about who we are and about the forces that drive us. So there's a lot more to this than it may initially appear. But if you can really meditate on the absolute dimension of what we're speaking about you'll be able to handle it. But you really have to take it on.

"So, for example, the other day I said that the only difference between me and a lot of people that I met when I was on the path was that I had no doubt that I wanted to go all the way. Now, nobody knows what 'all the way' means. You can't have a clear sense of what it means, but you can know that you want that, whatever it means, so that prepares you. Okay?"

"Yes, okay. Thank you very much."

Andrew next turned his attention to Tom, a young, thin sandy haired fellow who was an editor for *What Is Enlightenment* magazine and a very serious student of his.

"A few minutes ago," Tom began, "you said that we can think that the ego is partially right. Intellectually I thought I understood what it meant to learn to live from zero to plus one and disregard the ego entirely. But because of thinking that some part of the ego is valid it's like I've been justifying holding on to part of it. I've always had a visceral resistance to the notion of discounting the ego entirely and absolutely living in the Authentic Self. But just a couple of days ago, while contemplating the absolute nature of consciousness and the Self Absolute I actually started to identify with that as the self. Then I saw the ego, thoughts and everything else associated with it as actually just objects in consciousness. That's when I experienced the actual possibility of completely choosing to move from the Self Absolute into the Authentic Self without identifying with ego at all."

"Right. You also have to understand, even if only theoretically, that unless you're at least willing to completely let go of the ego in its entirety you're never going to be able to be in a position to see it objectively, which is what the goal is because the liberated, autonomous, integrated self would have to be an individual who had a rarified, unusual

capacity for objectivity in relationship to ego. Now, that capacity won't even be begin to emerge until you're willing to just drop the whole thing. So unless the willingness to do that is unequivocal one is never going to be able to truly see it objectively,

"Then the question is, well, what does it mean to be free in an evolutionary context? Now, that's an open question because those answers don't necessarily exist. That's something that needs to be defined and redefined and redefined through ongoing, creative engagement with the whole question. But unless the place we're coming from is the willingness to let go of everything we're not going to be in a position to authentically engage in that kind of inquiry. We will be pretending we are, but actually we'll have a hidden agenda. 'I'm not going to let go of this, but I'm going to pretend I really want to create a new world as long as I can take this little bit of the past with me.' But one is not going to authentically be in a position to know whether that would be a problem or not from the perspective of enlightenment unless the willingness to let go of everything was there from the beginning. So the willingness to do that is what literally puts you in a position where there's a real potential for a new kind of liberated objectivity and that's the whole point. You see?"

"Right. And from that perspective I see the value and importance of meditation too. It's only the willingness to do that that actually makes meditation start having an effect."

"Right. That's the transformative effect because it's the already free, already liberated position that the meditative experience, when it's real, reveals. But again, everybody gets worried about the whole letting go issue. It's a means to an end. The letting go of ego is not just to let go. It's a means to discover or to release a kind of potential in all of us that won't emerge unless we're really willing to do that. When we're willing to let go then all new kinds of creative powers emerge that couldn't possibly otherwise.

"Even just being able to see, let alone act, once you're willing to let go of everything you may find that there are all kinds of things that actually don't need to be let go of because they're not a problem. But you'll find that out after the fact, not before. So you have to be willing to let go of everything and then, from that willingness, will you be in a position to see what actually needs to be let go of, what's problematic and what isn't. But if you're not willing to let go of everything first you won't even get to the point where you'll be in a position to see with a liberated objectivity what it is that actually does need to be let go of because you're still going to be clinging onto whatever you're convinced is important.

"When you really understand it you can see where this is actually scientific. It's not negotiable. It's a step that needs to be taken in order to reach a higher level of development that, in turn, is going to reveal a higher level of autonomy. You get it?"

"Right, yeah."

"Then you can see that it's not a personal thing. So you can see why Steffen asked his question. You could feel that he's really grappling with some terror and that there's an attachment in relationship to this. But you have to know not to do that. You have

to really have the courage to just be very, as he said, cool-headed and objective about it. And now, when you're on a retreat, you really want to give yourself the opportunity to be super cool-headed about it and really see and experiment with it to find out what's possible. So if you can just stay with me in this and go through these steps you will experience the kind of radical objectivity I'm speaking about and you'll know that I'm not making it up.

"This radical objectivity is experienced as this incredibly positive, wholesome expression of evolutionary potential in which there's the sense is that everything's possible. You suddenly realize, oh my God, it really is possible to create a completely different world. Emotionally you experience it as this kind of burning thrill. And in that state everything the ego was worried about you consciously experience as being completely, totally, absolutely, and radically irrelevant, you see?"

"Yes, definitely."

"Whereas from the ego's perspective it's all very relevant. But you have to be willing to let go this much in order to see it for yourself. If this is approached merely with a 'what's good for me' kind of approach you're not going to get it. Because this is not about what's good for the individual. Remember, we're putting attention on consciousness itself, not the individual. That's what changes everything. That's why it's so radical. See my point?"

"Yeah."

"So you have to be willing to let go deeply enough and long enough to experience that. You can't go farther than that. You want to experiment with that and then see how things look. You'll see for yourself that all these things I'm saying make sense. But it's not because I say so. What I'm expressing is not a personal opinion. If you go through these steps yourself, you'll see what I'm saying and why I'm saying it. You'll see where it's coming from. This has nothing to do with opinion. I have no personal vested interest in this. This is just something I've realized, I've understood, I've seen, and that I'm endeavoring to share with people. It's a difficult thing to share with people because it's a perspective that is so completely challenging that at a soul level people get very frightened."

He paused for a moment, a small smile lighting his face as he looked directly at Tom. Then he added, *"But you don't seem that scared to me so that's good.*

"Okay, we're almost at the end. I'll take one more. But I want everybody to keep looking into this question tonight and we're going to continue with it tomorrow because if we get firmly established in this, the rest of it is easy, okay?"

The familiar murmur of assent moved through the room and then he took the final question from an older French man.

"Andrew, when you were speaking about the potential that lies in that dimension where nothing exists and that emerges as the Authentic Self..."

"The unmanifest potential?"

"Yes, the unmanifest potential that's ..."

"Does everybody know what unmanifest potential is? So unmanifest potential is what there was before the universe was born. They say there was just a vacuum before the Big Bang. But it can't be true that nothing existed because the unmanifest potential for everything that exists now had to exist in that emptiness or that void. Now, in an evolutionary context in the way that we're speaking about it, we have to cultivate the willingness to be the stepping stone or the vessel or the portal through which that unmanifest potential will become manifest. The potential is already there, but not the actuality. So it's the willingness to want to be free more than anything else creates the readiness in us to be such a portal. Does that make sense?"

The man, his voice quivering with the thrill of what he seemed to be awakening to in himself at that moment, continued, "When you become aware of that in your own experience, you can choose to engage with that unmanifest potential in yourself and that emerges as the Authentic Self, the ecstatic compulsion to evolve, and it's so ecstatic. It's like the cells of your body become vibrant with life and with a compulsion to come into being and into life."

"Exactly. Becoming such a vessel is the definition of enlightenment in evolutionary context."

"And that gives you a lot of confidence and courage to face your human condition. There's just a lot of confidence and trust in the fact that there is no problem."

"Right. What he's talking about is that when you experience this then you gain enormous trust in your Maker. Your Maker is the energy and intelligence that created the universe. So when you let go enough to be able to experience that kind of energy and intelligence running through your own mind and body then you gain enormous confidence in the Creative Principle itself. Then you see that life and the creative process is not a random event that's just happening with you as a helpless victim that just emerged and now has to suffer the consequences of having become conscious. That's how some materialists or nihilists would have us feel. Then you gain an enormous amount of confidence in the process itself. And from the perspective of evolutionary enlightenment, unless you get to that point you haven't really begun. See? Okay, so we'll finish with that."

And we did. But a few moments after slipping into meditation Andrew suddenly stirred, reattached his microphone to his lapel and added a few final thoughts.

"You see, what I really want, and what's going to happen more over the next few days, is for everyone to experience both this ecstatic thrill of engaging at the level of the Authentic Self, which feels like it could go on forever, and then the joy of diving into the ocean of Being which doesn't want to have anything to do with all that. And I want everyone to delight in seeing the absolute paradox between the ecstasy of the thrill of the Authentic Self of and for the evolutionary process and the part of you that is delighted to have nothing to do with it. To experience both with such intensity is an extraordinary thing. So as you have experiences like that I want you to be aware of

and pay attention to what's happening. They're both a part of you that you experience as a form of ecstasy, but they're different kinds of ecstasy. One is the ecstasy of engagement and one is the ecstasy of disengagement. So when it happens I want you to be cognizant of what's happening. A lot of people experience all kinds of things but they don't know what's happening. So a big part of awakening has to be in the attention to what's happening as it's happening so you know what's happening. It's not a small thing. Hmm?"

He looked around briefly and concluded, *"Okay, then we'll meet again in the morning."*

I sat there stunned, neither swept into the thrill of the Authentic Self nor the still joy of the ocean of Being, but rather pinned between my desire to let go of my life totally and the fear of losing everything. It seemed as if, from the vast, impersonal waters of the Self Absolute, Andrew had swept me up and slammed me face first into the small and the finite world of my own relationship to life. Slamming into that wall like a crash test dummy raised a monumental challenge to the entirety of the way I lived my life.

With that challenge the simmering crisis that had been smoldering with restrained intensity in the recesses of my inner world for nearly two years was now inexorably driving to a final confrontation. This crisis had been initiated about two years earlier at a short retreat with Andrew at his world center in Foxhollow, Massachusetts. There I had been overwhelmed by a passion to give my entire life to this teaching and an equally visceral revulsion against the bourgeois lifestyle, particularly the Northern California variety, which formed the background matrix of my life. The widely accepted virtue of committing the near entirety of my life energy to generating sufficient resources to enable me to own a home (basically four walls to keep the world out while providing sanctuary for our "personal lives" with the attendant modest median price of $700,000) and visit Tahoe on the weekends for various and sundry forms of outdoor entertainment, grated on my newly emerging moral sensibilities. It seemed little more than "the worship of the ordinary, commonly hailed as the American Dream," version 2.0, upgraded, enhanced and with higher resolution. There was so much to do in the world and so few people doing it that to wile away the hours and, though barely noticing it, the days, months and years of my life inhaling world resources while producing little beyond the expectorations of an overfed ego seemed beyond criminal. Additionally I was chafing against the fact that my engagement with Andrew's teachings via our local group failed for a variety of reasons to meet the intensity of my interest in those very teachings. My conclusion, difficult as it had been to arrive at and embrace, was to cast that life off like a pilgrim from old Europe and strike out for Massachusetts in search of a new life and a new world. Mentally I had prepared a plan to clear up my financial responsibilities, leave Rose in possession of my business, set aside some money for myself and depart for a life in the community. Emotionally and on every other level, these were extraordinarily painful conclusions, but I could see no other way to answer the rising call of my conscience.

Then, within a few months of this decision, Andrew initiated a new program simply called the "Student Network," which offered a level of engagement with the teaching much more in line with my own passion and thus dampened to some degree the burning urge to leave "my life" behind. Slowly a new vision emerged from the blurry edges of my view, one forged from the convergence of two influences. First, the teaching itself called for the creation of a new culture based on the radically different values revealed in the collective emergence of the Authentic Self. And while no one could say with any certainty what that new culture might look like, experiments needed to be undertaken in order to find out. In that context it began to become increasingly clear to me that the model for the emergence of this new culture could not simply be found in moving to Andrew's community. Cultural revolution could only happen by engagement with the culture, not withdrawal from it. Duh! In fact, I believe the creation of the Student Network was a response to that very recognition. What then, would living the teachings really look like for one engaged with the so-called mundane world? After all, wasn't what made the world mundane the way one lived in it rather than that lackluster veneer being some essential feature of reality itself? Wasn't it that that needed to be redefined, perhaps even more than the outer circumstances of my life? It was slowly beginning to seem that way to me.

Second, the entire thrust of Peter's teachings – and the one that had most inspired me – had been in this very direction. That is, he held that the breadth and depth of one's spiritual life should be directly reflected in the creativity and success of one's life on every level. "I hope you never hit the Lotto, it'll be the death of you," he'd said to me, adding that I should, "Learn how to make it." He despised the "rent control mentality" and "the bigger your inner life, the bigger your outer life" had carried the weight of divine revelation in his teaching. It was how he lived every day of his life and bearing witness to this had inspired me as much as the combined force of all the kundalini eruptions that I experienced in his presence. With the emergence of the Student Network the abiding inspiration that I had drawn from his teaching in this regard was now subsumed in the larger and infinitely more profound teaching of Evolutionary Enlightenment. In this I felt I had found a way and a reason to bridge the demands of the inner and outer worlds.

But had I really? Sitting there in meditation in Montserrat, in mute terror, I had to ask myself if I had really dealt with the knotty issues of my own relationship to life or had I been doing little more than dubious psychic housecleaning, neatly sweeping things beneath the proverbial rug? Based on the slivers of trepidation that now stabbed into me like voodoo pins into a doll, it seemed rather evident that there must have been much that I had not yet faced. Had I done so I should have found no conflict between the first tenet and myself, and that was clearly not the case.

Throughout the rest of the day I was like a man on the rack, torn in opposite directions. The rug beneath which much had been swept was now being peeled back inch by anguished inch. It quickly became evident that woven into my desire to leave my "ordinary" life behind were the threads of other, less virtuous desires. Chief among these were layers of escapist fantasies revolving around no longer wishing to struggle with the practical demands of that life and imagining that within the welcoming arms of the community I might be freed from worldly woes and be able instead to work in undistracted fashion on projects aligned with a revolution in human consciousness.

Conversely, woven into the desire to remain and make my life an experiment and potential demonstration of a new kind of spiritual endeavor, was simply the fear of renouncing all that that life represented. And what it represented was my relative identity. There was my job, professional reputation, money and in particular all the little daily options to do just what I want, how I want, when I want. Nothing special, just lots of little things, all of which converge to construct the habitat of ego: the freedom to flirt, to wow clients with my expertise; to be "somebody" in countless situations; the endless daily trivia of self-inflation, the surrender of which is the price of transformation. But greater than all these was my connection to Rose. Due to some dissonance in our relationship, the apparently inevitable by-product of twenty years of marriage, I had arrogantly assumed that I could shoulder the emotional burden of leaving with the ease of a weightlifter dusting a shelf. However, what I discovered was that I had been wrong, dead wrong, in fact. The very thought suddenly became unbearable, its visceral sensation being one of having an internal organ violently torn from my body. It felt like emotional suicide.

Under the weight of these considerations I at length concluded, "I can't do this." I conceded the humiliating truth that I amounted to little more than a spiritual weakling, a hypocrite and a coward. How easy it is to hold forth in impassioned tones of walking the hero's journey, of cultivating strength and integrity, of transforming the world. But when it comes to paying the price for that depth of character it appeared I lacked the coin to ante up. Apparently I was in the wrong game. Crushed, I concluded that I simply haven't got what it takes and with that descended into hell.

On the way down I recalled, as if from some half-forgotten dream, the teachings that had just transpired. From them I clutched at two strands. The first was Andrew's admonition not to attempt to convince the ego that this was a good thing, an endeavor tantamount to self-flagellation and destined for predictably disastrous consequences. The second involved a technical fix: no relationship to thought. If, in the throes of panic, he had advised, one could not see beyond the dust storms of the mind one simply had to renounce relationship to thought and then, when the weather had cleared, re-examine one's predicament through the liberated eyes of the Authentic Self. In my dismay I had neglected these lifelines but now I grasped them frantically. The resultant psychic rope burns brought into relief the requisite maturity for assuming this position, which involved the willingness to renounce the very emotional indulgence that had led me to my impasse. And at last, after what seemed an aeon of time, I did just that. With that and the passage of a little further time, the power of the Self ascended once more, displacing the boundaries of self. "Do I want to be a vehicle for this?" I then asked, my mind cleansed of darkness. "Do I want to bring this into the world?" Of course I did and with that the view was clear again.

At that point I recalled Andrew saying that, having assumed the position of the Authentic Self, we should allow ourselves to fully face into the first tenet from that perspective. *"Just go for it,"* he'd encouraged us. *"You're on retreat and you don't have to do anything about it. Just face this question squarely and see what happens."* He had added that unless someone was at least **willing** to drop everything they would never be in a position to actually see what needed dropping and what didn't. In that spirit I went for it and in so doing discovered, to my amazement, that simply considering the willingness to let go of everything **right now** brought an exhilarating rush of liberation. I could feel a weight fall from me as the permission to give myself wholly to the pursuit of liberation proved to be a kind of liberation in itself. It instantly freed me from the world, if only momentarily, and reminded me of Andrew's long standing insistence that simply wanting to be free more than anything else was, in many ways, not that different from actually being free. In fact, he often added that from the outside looking in one would have no way of distinguishing between one who authentically wanted to be free more than anything else and one who indeed was. The path and the goal were one, after all.

Having unearthed the willingness and capacity to consider the first tenet from the perspective of the Authentic Self I once more thought of the practical dimensions of my life and dared myself to ponder just letting it all go. For some time I was able to maintain the thrill, willingness and objectivity of that view and cultivated a steely sobriety with respect to all the practical dimensions. "I can do this," I told myself. "I'll do whatever I need to. Nothing is more important than this." I felt it and I meant it. Soon, however, through the pull of dark compulsion, I found myself once more in dialogue with ego. Waves of imagined scenarios assaulted my determination. My heart writhed as I desperately tried to lay hold of the liberating perspective once more. With grim determination I renounced relationship to thought and from that handhold drew myself up to assume the higher view once more. But it failed to hold and like Sisyphus, I pushed the boulder up the mountain. But each time, on reaching the summit, it slipped from my hands to descend once more into the valley of my devastated self. That torment turned seconds into minutes, minutes into hours, and hours into stretches of time so vast that entire universes could have been born and consumed many times in their terrible duration. Sleep proved no relief. It savaged me with twisted dreams and visions. Angels called me to the light and demons pulled me toward darkness; tormented, I hovered in that half-hell throughout the endless night.

NOTES

1. I would direct the reader once more to Jessica Roemischer's article *Women Who Sleep with their Gurus and Why They Love It* in *What is Enlightenment* Magazine, Issue # 26. You can also read the article at http://www.wie.org/j26/women-who-sleep.asp?page=1.

2. For an interview with Ramesh Balsekar regarding his teaching see Chris Parish's article, *Close Encounters of the Advaita Kind: The Euphoric Nihilism of Ramesh Balsekar* in *What is Enlightenment?* magazine, issue # 14 or you can find it online at http://www.wie.org/j14/balsekar.asp?page=1.

3. For more on neo-Advaita see Jessica Roemischer's previously referenced article *Who's Transforming Anyway? Stacey Heartspring Encounters the Postmodern Craze of Neo-Advaita* in issue #34 of *What is Enlightenment?* magazine or read it online at http://www.wie.org/j34/stacey.asp.

4. Tantra is an esoteric tradition with roots in both Hinduism and Buddhism. It is known for elaborate use of mantra, the importance of female deities and particularly in Hinduism, the ritual use of sexual intercourse. In the West, early European scholars of Asia originally reviled Tantra as an immoral force that had corrupted classical Hinduism. On the other hand many today have embraced it as a celebration of sexuality, feminism and the body. Clearly, in the latter context, the marriage of sexuality with spirituality creates dubious ethical conveniences of all sorts. As mentioned above, Andrew's main philosophical critique of Tantra is that it presumes that the coming together of two is required to realize the One.

5. As crazy as that sounds, anyone exposed even once to the power of that energy would know precisely why, within a certain context, this might not seem unreasonable.

6. "Andrew is dead," he had announced in a missive to his mother immediately upon his awakening, adding later and in a different context that the one who wanted to celebrate the attainment of what he had so striven for was no longer there to celebrate.

Day 7

Liberating the Choosing Faculty

I rose in the morning a broken man. The night's ordeal had driven me to the deplorable conclusion that the bigger part of me lacked not only the spiritual fortitude but also even the slightest interest in anything beyond a selfish life. Sure, in some ways I was interested but only to the point that the "earnest seeker" in me could swell drinking from the lake of Self without diving in and drowning. Pushed beyond that point I faltered, panicked in fact, resisting with surprising vehemence the exalted aspiration to drop a life of pretense for the sake of a higher calling. I should have known that this is what I'd find based on Andrew's endless exhortations on this very point. Had he not said, *"you'll find that you're divided"* on countless occasions? Yet prior to this dreadful night I'd never fully faced that stark and unbecoming truth about myself.

Yet to my even greater horror I found myself unable to give in to this position, unable to enjoy even the dubious comfort of a coward's relief. I could not unsee what I had seen, replacing my eyes with those of another. Consequently, and with great anguish, I committed to do whatever was required, heedless of the pain. I would shut my eyes in a tortured grimace, plunging forward to give myself to Andrew's absolute demand. Yet even in that I sensed no victory, decidedly uncertain of what kind of vessel I would make, for in light of this decision my spirit was broken.

Thus burdened I dragged myself through morning practice with all the zest of a man bound for the gallows before, some dreary hours later, arriving in the teaching hall.

The atmosphere in the room was an odd mixture of solemnity and agitation and the first few questions, seeking to skirt the central issue, were entirely off point. One question concerned enlightened masters controlling the forces of nature, while another involved beneficent aliens bestowing enlightenment upon a struggling humanity (at which Andrew noted that they're not doing a very good job). In many ways this frivolity was not surprising. It was obvious to me, based on my own experience, that this was a semi-conscious ploy on the part of panicked egos to avoid dealing squarely with the implications of candidly considering one's intention. Andrew, seeking to minimize the waste of time, brought us quickly back to point.

"So I want a lot more people to respond to this issue of clarity of intention so that we can move on. As I said yesterday, it's definitely the foundation of everything. Therefore I need everybody to really dig into it, okay? It's the most important thing, it's the hardest thing and most people don't want to deal with it for a lot of different reasons. But I have to do my job and if I'm going to do my job with any kind of integrity then I have to force the issue, right?"

A few timid murmurs broke through the silence.

"Is it fun to force people?" Andrew went on rhetorically. *"No, but what am I going to do? I have to get to the point where I feel like you guys have really sunk your teeth into this."*

At length an American woman mustered the nerve to speak. "So I'm looking into my experience of wanting to be free more than anything else and my question is, what's the relationship between objectivity and clarity of intention? Specifically, yesterday you were talking about emotions and the fact that it's very easy to become blinded by them and that that makes everything a little more challenging. Well, I'm definitely finding that that's true in my experience. In other words, emotionally I'm finding all this a lot more challenging than my experience during the first few days. The first couple of days, during the contemplation of consciousness, it was very easy to have my thoughts go right to the background of my awareness. But over the last couple of days my emotions are extremely highly charged."

"That always happens when I bring up this issue of clarity of intention. People go aaarghh." Andrew leaned back, grabbing his own neck in a strangling motion for dramatic effect.

"Right. So my question is how to approach that. Is clarity of intention the same thing as objectivity?"

"What do you mean?"

"I mean does one have to precede the other? For example, if I'm feeling a particularly charged emotion and I want to take an objective stance with that, it seems like clarity of intention would have to be there before I would be able to take an objective stance."

"That's the idea, because it's an enlightenment context so we're trying to define a reference point that's not an experience."

"So that's what I'm trying to establish. I want to be very clear that that's the stance."

"Right. Clarity of intention is a reference point. It's not an experience and it's not a feeling. It's an absolute position. And it's a completely different orientation to life. The only thing I can compare it to — and it's a terrible comparison — is the commitment some men and women make if they are part of the Special Forces. They make a

commitment to go into a situation that they know is absolutely life threatening. They know that they are not only risking their own life but also that they might have to take life and they are as clear about that as they could possibly be. In other words, they have really looked into it and faced it to such a degree that they've actually changed as human beings – hopefully for the better; hopefully they haven't become monsters" Andrew laughed briefly. *"In other words, they've focused so much on a kind of absolute risk that that ultimate risk becomes a fundamental reference point for their relationships with each other and their relationship to life. Now, once again, it's not really a satisfying metaphor, but I have to come up with something that will give people a sense of how profound a shift this is.*

"For example, if you have a relationship with another person and that relationship is based upon what I was just speaking about it's going to bring out certain qualities which ordinarily wouldn't be called upon and which changes everything – for the better. It makes things absolutely real in a way that compels a much deeper engagement with life. And it also requires a certain kind of steadiness and presence of mind in the face of an absolute context.

"Now, most of us don't think very deeply about life or our own experience. In fact, we don't think very deeply about much. And that's why we're not prepared to engage with the life experience we're having deeply and with intensity. So looking into the clarity of intention is supposed to cultivate a readiness for the challenge of the evolution of consciousness in real time. If you grapple with it it will prepare you for the challenge but if you don't grapple with it authentically you won't be prepared. When push comes to shove you'll find yourself empty handed. It's very simple. So the whole idea behind spiritual practice is that when you're of sound mind and body you're supposed to use all your strength to make the effort to perfect yourself, to evolve, to become a different person.

"But that's not the way we live. The idea of actually using our health and soundness of mind to develop is just an alien concept for us. I mean, there are two ways to look at it. One is doing this so we can actually consciously participate in the evolutionary process. But you could look at it in a much more personal way and say that when you're in trouble and you're being challenged you'll have the strength of mind and clarity of purpose not to fall apart and lose your way. But one way or the other, it boils down to the same thing. Does that make sense?"

"Yes, definitely."

"So I've been speaking about clarity of intention for about nineteen years now and nothing has happened in all those years of teaching to make me doubt this. In fact, all the experience I have up until this very moment only strengthens my conviction about this aspect of the teaching.

"Now, at the beginning of this it's usually all about the individual: 'do I want to be free more than anything else?' But as you get more deeply into it, it becomes less and less about you and more and more about the evolution of consciousness. You see the fifth

tenet says 'for the sake of the whole.' That means your motive evolves from liberation being for your own sake to being for the evolution of consciousness itself. It's not for you anymore; it's for a larger purpose.

"Now, I feel that the post-modern self can only find a source of dignity and self-respect in the discovery of a larger purpose because the extreme narcissism of our time has stripped us of our dignity and authentic self-respect. Self-infatuation is not self-respect! If you respect yourself you authentically respect other people. That means you have real relationships with real people, not objects that you use to adorn your own image. And the only way that the compulsive and pathological narcissism of the post-modern self can be transcended is through the discovery of a larger purpose, not merely through the experience of emptiness or transcendence. It's just not enough."

Andrew paused before turning his attention to a German man who proceeded to ask a long and convoluted question painstakingly detailing his confusion at being tossed between the ego and Authentic Self.

"You're surprised?" Andrew asked in a manner indicating his own total lack of surprise. *"What happens,"* he explained, *"is that when you start looking you find that there's the Authentic Self and the ego but you also see that it couldn't be that simple because there has to be a third party, you, who chooses between them. You said you were looking at the ego and then at the Authentic Self and then you were making a choice for the Authentic Self, not the ego, right?"*

"Right."

"Now, what happens is when you begin to remove your attention from the ego and put more of it on the Authentic Self the ego becomes like a Latin lover, which means it gets very jealous. So if you start putting more of your attention on the Authentic Self the ego feels threatened – and I mean it! It feels danger. It's afraid that maybe it's going to lose your loyalty. So when that happens the ego experiences agitation, often in the extreme. It fears it's going to lose control of you. Therefore you shouldn't be surprised. Sometimes when people begin to have deeper experience of the Ground of Being or of the Authentic Self the ego will get very stirred up. But that doesn't mean that anything is wrong at all. In fact, it might mean that something is very right because you've gotten in touch with something that's real."

That pushed me over the edge. The pressure of the last twenty-four hours was at full boil and bubbling over. My hand shot up impulsively. Andrew turned to me immediately.

"Okay, Michael, yes," he prompted, but then turned suddenly back to the group. *"Does everybody get this?"* he asked insistently, *"because you're all very reticent here."* It was true. A dense silence had settled over the room, its weight bearing down on us all. *"Is it because you're so clear about this?"* he asked, an edge of sarcasm in his tone. *"If it is I'll take your word for it but I try not to take people's word for anything anymore. I've gotten into a lot of trouble taking people's word for things."*

Clearly I was not the only one struck dumb with fear. When no one said anything Andrew turned his attention back to me.

In a sickly tone I said, "Well, I have to say that the contemplation of clarity of intention has just opened up a huge can of worms."

"That's the whole idea. It awakens your kundalini can of worms," he quipped, a joking reference to my prior practice and the fascination with the experience it had engendered.

"I've been contemplating deeply what it would mean to really drop my whole life the way it is …"

"You don't have to drop your whole life," Andrew cut me off abruptly. *"The can of worms it opens up is that if there's anything about your life and the way you're living it that's not basically wholesome then it kind of starts bothering you. You see, ordinarily there are all kinds of things in our relationship to life and in the way that we live that are unwholesome and that we accept, or worse, that we even like. But when we start contemplating wanting to be free more than anything else the things that are unwholesome – that are not really right or straight or clean – start disturbing you. That's the can of worms. So if you want to be free then that's a good thing. But if you don't want to be free then it's like your worst nightmare. Do you get my point?"*

"Well, I guess that's exactly it," I said. "And even over the last few days, as we've been going into the teachings, I've been realizing that as much as I've been involved with this teaching already, there is still a big gap between my understanding of it and really digging in a lot deeper. So this sort of brings it all to a head."

"Isn't that good though?" Andrew asked emphatically. *"Is that bad or is that good?"*

"It's good," I agreed. "It's definitely good."

And at that exact moment I realized just how truly good it was, how clarifying, how empowering to transformation. Simultaneously the weight of my torment fell away from me. I realized in an instant that I'd been torturing myself needlessly, for my life, while not free from egoic shadows, was not overrun by them either. With that the whole dilemma dissolved. I did not have to choose between one thing and the other; I merely had to cleanse what was.

As the tight knot in my soul untied itself I marveled at Andrew's capacity to get to the center of an issue with the precision of a spiritual surgical strike. And in that marveling a flash of insight emerged through the clearing haze of my mind as I realized, as I never had before, who and what was sitting before me. I understood, in a way that is difficult to convey, that speaking to me through Andrew was my very own Self, untainted by any trace of the personal. Ordinarily, the precise nature of Andrew's response to my distress could only have come upon much sharing of the twisted contours of my inner world. Yet within thirty seconds, and in the blessed absence of such sharing, he had delivered, like a passcode, the precise combination of words required to retrieve my spirit from the tomb. I knew in that moment, with as strong a conviction as I have ever known anything, that my own deepest Self had addressed me through Andrew's mouth. And in that instant I also understood why Andrew had titled his first book, a short journal he kept during the dramatic process of his own awakening, "My Master is Myself." This had been no mere sentimentality, simply a statement of outrageous fact. *"Andrew is dead,"* he had written to his mother two decades earlier after every trace of the personal was burned out of him by the conscious energy that, by his own account, had "eaten him alive." What was sitting before me now was a void, a doorway to that absolute dimension of Self that is the Self of us all, adorned with the mind, body and nervous system of Andrew Cohen but freed from every trace of their constraints. I now understood more deeply what he had often said of his own experience, namely that his responses to life occurred faster than thought and thus came spontaneously from that mysterious place that always exists prior to the mind. Andrew had surrendered Andrew and this extraordinary emptiness, along with the fullness of its liberating wisdom, had been the result.

Now, I realize that to state such understanding with respect to another flies in the face of our post-modern culture in which no one can be said to be morally superior, higher, or better than another in any way. But there it is. It is what I knew in the deepest reaches of myself, that flash of understanding parting my mind from its ignorance and revealing things in the light of the simple truth. My master is myself, I kept wordlessly repeating, mystified, as I snapped my attention back to Andrew's voice.

"You see, that's the thing about the Special Forces," he said, tying our conversation to an earlier point, *"when they're out there, that's it. They don't whine…I don't think,"* he added mischievously, eliciting a peal of laughter from the otherwise heavy crowd. *"They're prepared and they're ready to go. That's it. Isn't that cool? Well, I think that's really cool. Maybe it's some kind of male fantasy – I don't really know."*

More short bursts of laughter gave the temporary relief of buoyant levity.

"But once again," he said, returning his attention to me, *"it's because there's commitment and commitment always involves risk. You get the idea? If you want to do something important then you're going to have to be committed and commitment always involves risk. It's not rocket science. Hmm?"*

"Yeah," I agreed.

"And the other thing is that everybody is worried about change. The Buddha told us that everything is changing all the time but – and I've been saying this for years – we all live as if it's not true. We all live as if nothing's ever going to change. We try with everything we've got to create a sense of permanence. But it's not true is it? So what would happen if you were more interested in change than you were in the illusion of stability? Then you would be living more in alignment with the dharma or with the way things actually are. If everything's changing all the time then if you were at one with that truth then you'd be more at one with life itself, wouldn't you? You see it's not

complicated. But the ego's position is that it wants control and stability. So you can see the problem. There's nothing new about what I'm saying but that doesn't mean it's not important."

He paused, looked around the room, which had once again fallen into silence, then said, "*I can't tell how everybody feels about it.*" He gave an exasperated laugh. "*Maybe I struck a chord of some kind,*" he said, to which someone responded simply, "yes."

He looked back at me, his dark eyes fixing me in the timeless for an instant and asked, "*Have we covered it?*"

I nodded yes.

"*Good, man,*" he said with a warrior's camaraderie. Then he added, "*It's California, Mike – that's the thing,*" alluding to the almost impenetrable culture of conservatism and the spiritual status quo that has made the California consciousness scene one of the least receptive places in the world for teachings like these. It was, after all, home to the "415 paradigm" (that insidious blend of sophisticated new age thinking and pathological narcissism) as Ken Wilber had so insightfully put it.

After another round of laughter Andrew said brightly, "*This is good. We have to get clear about these things. Okay, so let's keep going.*" With that he turned his attention to a middle-aged American woman with short gray hair who'd had her hand up for some time.

"Hi," she began rather stiffly. "When I look into my experience to locate the part of me that doesn't want to be free I can identify situations where in the past I could have made more wholesome choices and then based on that I say 'yeah, there was a situation and a time where I didn't want to be free...'"

"*Actually,*" Andrew said, "*if you want to be free you...*"

"There's more..." she curtly interjected. "I'm just looking at this right now, in this very moment, and then I recognize that that's a thought, that's a memory..."

"*What's a thought?*" Andrew asked.

"Looking at that situation. It's a memory; it's a thought so in this moment I can choose to have no relationship to that thought..."

"*What? To bad choices you made in the past?*"

"Just looking at that situation and recognizing it; not getting stuck there but just recognizing 'there was a situation;' I've located that part so I just say 'there it is, that's a thought.' I can choose to have no relationship to that and I can make that decision based on this felt sense that there's no problem there."

The woman continued, but in such a way that what she was trying to say remained unintelligible to anyone including Andrew. On several occasions he attempted to interject but when he did she raised her voice and refused to let him speak. It seemed to me that she was more interested in her question than in any answer it might prompt.

Finally Andrew managed to get a few words in edgewise. *"You're talking about something that happened in the past, right?"*

"I'm just relating how I work through this to get over there," she replied, pointing to the Heaven teaching model.

"Forget about what happened in the past. You don't have to worry about that for the clarity of intention issue. You don't have to deal with your past blunders."

"Well, I'm just starting at the beginning for clarity because the instruction was to look into our experience to locate that place within me that doesn't want to be free."

"But you don't have to look to the past to find that."

"I just look and recall a situation where, based on the choice that I made, I see that I could have made a more wholesome choice..." She continued to repeat the same point she had been trying to make for the past few minutes.

"Yes, but respectfully what I'm saying is that you don't have to look to the past. Just look right now, forget about the past. In order to look into the question of whether you want to be free more than anything else right now or not, and to experience the part of yourself that doesn't you don't have to bring..." I marveled at his patience as he tried to pry open any corner of her mind in order to shed some light on her confusion.

But again, she resisted, now sounding quite annoyed. "Okay, I guess what I'm saying is for the clarity of how I've worked through it is ... for the clarity of the process of working through it..."

"Right, but what I'm saying is that you've added a step that is unnecessary."

"Okay, but what I'm saying is that if I'm in a neutral position if I don't get stuck there in that moment I just say 'this is just a thought. I have no relationship to it...'"

A feeling of exasperation filled the room.

Once more Andrew tried to rescue the situation. *"Okay, but again, respectfully..."*

Now she lost it. "Can I finish?" she snapped aggressively.

"What I'm saying is," Andrew said politely , *"that the way that you're doing it is not the way I asked you to do it. You're describing a way not to let certain things bother you and that's not the issue which is why I keep interrupting you."*

She appeared not to hear him. Andrew attempted several further interventions, all equally fruitless. I marveled at his patience and willingness to wait for the right moment to help her gain a new perspective as well as serve a teaching function for the rest of us. I marveled equally at the obstinacy of ego and made a mental note to be on guard for such behavior in myself.

At length she ran her course, proudly declaring, "Okay, I'm ready to listen now."

Incredulous laughter erupted through the room.

"Oh, you are?" Andrew said ironically. Then thoughtfully he added, *"You're tough, though. That could also be good in the right situation."*

Then he took up his point once more. *"Okay, first of all, something important I wanted to re-emphasize is that on the one hand there's ego and on the other there's the Authentic Self. But there has to be more to it than that because there's obviously a third party also, which is you. You see, you are aware of or can be in touch with the part of yourself that has no doubt about the evolution of consciousness and wanting to be free more than anything else. However, you are also aware of the fears and desires of the ego, which doesn't want to have anything to do with wanting to be free more than anything else. And it's the part of you that's aware of both of these other parts that's making the choices.*

"So that's why the role of choice, of free agency, or volitionality, is so all-important. You see there's not just the ego and the Authentic self. There's 'you,' whoever you are, bearing witness to and experiencing both. So when you – whoever you are – give attention to the fears and desires of the ego and identify with them, the I, or the self that you are, becomes the fears and desires of the ego.

"In the same way if you give your attention to the Authentic Self and this pure passion to create the future, you begin to experience that exhilaration and that passion and that's what you become. So it's for this reason that the role of choice or volition plays such a big part in this teaching.

"So sometimes someone will say, 'the ego's driving me crazy." But if you start to look more closely you'll find that it's not quite that simple. Again, this teaching is based upon the conviction and ultimately the agreement that we all always have freedom of choice. Therefore we say, 'You are not the ego. You are not the Authentic Self. You're that free agency that's choosing to identify with the fears and desires of the ego and thus becoming a manifestation of the ego in real time. Or you are choosing to identify with the Authentic Self or the desire for freedom above anything else and therefore becoming a manifestation of that.'

"So as one begins to study the science of the human psyche and how we work, the discovery and recognition of the fact that there's a choosing faculty changes absolutely everything. So what I have found – and I've seen this at least a billion times – is that when we are identifying with the fears and desires of the ego we will find ourselves denying that there's any choice involved. I guarantee it. Now, nobody taught me these things. This is something I've discovered since I became a teacher. Everything you're hearing me speak about here is something that I've actually learned and am continuing to learn in the field.

"So the ego will, without any conscience, deny any freedom of choice when it suits it. Now, the minute that the self denies the role of choice we can't have this discussion. It comes to an end just like this." Andrew snapped his fingers. *"The lines of communication close and the evolutionary context dissolves immediately.*

"So a very big part of what makes this teaching work has to do with bringing light to this choosing faculty in the self. Because as long as I am awake to and aware of the choosing faculty in my self and I'm never in denial of it, and as long as you are awake

to and aware of the choosing faculty in your self and are never in denial of it, the possibility of creating a new world or a new being together is right there. But the minute either of us or both of us are in denial of this choosing faculty we're locked into the old world of hell and unconsciousness forever. I can't really overemphasize how important this is. It's the bringing light or awareness to the choosing faculty in the self that's completely foundational for this teaching to work.

"So a big part of this exercise of wanting to be free more than anything else is enlightening or bringing light to the choosing faculty in the self and then trying to get the individual to claim it. That's what I'm trying to get all of you to do. I want you to realize that this choosing faculty exists, that it has always existed, and then to claim it for the right reasons. It's a very big step for any human being to take and nothing could be more evolutionary than that.

"Also, the only way to become a truly trustworthy human being is by doing this. If you're not willing to do this you're always going to be a shady character. You know what I mean?"

A low rumble of affirmatives came from the group.

"So there's the ego, there's the Authentic Self and there's the part of you that's aware of both options. Of course, this kind of recognition forces the individual into a confrontation with their own self. That's the whole idea. And we want to confront ourselves in a non-relative or absolute way while we're of sound mind and sound body. In other words, we should inquire into the nature and the meaning of existence while we're in such a condition that we actually can do something about it for real. Get the idea?" Andrew laughed.[1]

"And you have to see that even in relationship to what's happened on the retreat so far, it's not that difficult for human beings to have experiences of higher states of consciousness. Yet the experience of higher states doesn't necessarily force any kind of deep or compelling inquiry nor does it necessarily lead to wisdom. It's important to understand this. So the whole practice of inquiry is about getting human beings to think deeply about their own experience. What I'm trying to do is to get people to begin to make the effort to think deeply and I'm also trying to create a context in which to do it because, as I often say, context is everything. You get the idea?"

Lots of yeses and then a short pause as Andrew took a drink of water before scanning the room for the next question. Soon he turned his attention to an Englishman a few rows ahead of me.

"Is clarity of intention something that will continually have to be struggled with during the course of one's evolution?"

"Ideally, no, but unfortunately it might have to be."

"So at the fifty-one percent stage that you talked about yesterday that question would not be there so much anymore?"

"Yes, that's exactly right. But the reason that you don't want to keep asking the question is that ideally once you answer it, that's where you take your stand in relationship

to life. That's where you put your stake in the ground. Because if you really look into the question in the most absolute way you're capable of and say, 'yes,' then you're creating a completely new context for your life. It's like putting a seed into the ground. It means that you're taking a very conditioned, unfree, human being and they're choosing to have an unconditioned, free relationship to life. That's a very big step to take, isn't it?"

"Yep."

"So the whole idea is that the choice to want to be free, or to be more interested in the evolution of consciousness than anything else, changes the whole context of human existence. And what you need to do when you put that little seed in the earth is protect it. Because remember, you want to get to the fifty-one percent point because beyond that point it doesn't need protection anymore. Then the evolutionary aspiration has become independently self-generating, self-actualizing and autonomous. But until that point that little seed needs to be protected so that it can sprout and grow to be a very strong tree; so strong, in fact, that nothing could pull it down. You see the evolutionary, transformative process is not a game. Therefore, whatever one has to do to protect it one would do and one would continue to do until it gets strong enough, until it reaches this fifty-one percent point, and then it's not a question anymore.

"Now, let's say you say 'yes' and put that little seed in the ground and it sprouts and starts to grow and turns into a little plant. But then you rip it out for a few days, a few weeks, a few months, a few years until eventually you say, 'Oh my god, what did I do? That was the most important—oh, the poor thing.' So then you put it back in and water it. Now, it might take a long time but eventually it'll get going again but it's going to be weak. After all, it's taken quite a beating. But then, just as it starts to get strong again, maybe you pull it out again. You see what's happening? And then you say, 'Oh no, what have I done?' Then you put it back in and then pour a little water on it."

Everyone but Andrew laughed.

"Well, no," he said seriously. *"It's a metaphor but this is what people do with themselves all the time. The thing is, what you're playing with is literally your own soul. You see, self-confidence plays a big role in all this. It's not confidence in the ego or confidence in the Authentic Self. It's confidence that you, whoever you are, can do it. In the end it boils down to that.*

"So you keep pulling it out, putting it back in, pulling it out, putting it back in, and you end up seriously damaging yourself. And if you keep identifying with the fears and desires of the ego they will always rip it up. So, the idea is that you say 'I want to be free more than anything else,' which means that you put the seed in the ground and you won't pull it out. So that's the 'more than anything else' part, which is non-relative. The idea is that you not only won't pull it out but that you also keep nurturing it. You can't just leave it alone. A little seedling like that needs to be nurtured. If you walk away and leave it alone it's going to die. You see, this works according to certain laws that need to be respected.

"So ideally you make that decision once and ideally nobody would say 'yes' casually. Now, I teach in such a way that it would be very difficult for a person to do that. I never tell people, 'It's easy, it's not a problem. Don't worry about it.'" He laughed. *"I don't do that. In fact, I try to make it as difficult as I can. Why? Because I'm trying to wake people up!*

"But what should give you confidence in what I'm saying is that if you pay attention you'll start to see that there's a science to all this. I'm describing natural laws here. I'm not just pulling something out of thin air. And that's what puts the ego in an interesting position. Remember a narcissist is the center of their own universe so they create their own rules. It says, 'What's good for me is good for me.' And in the postmodern world we respect everybody's rights, don't we? Of course that's a good thing. But along with that we notice that especially in spiritual and psychological circles, truth has been relativized. And I'm trying to point people to truths that aren't relative; that are natural laws. But when truth becomes relativized and everybody is respected we say, 'Andrew has his truth. Thank you, Andrew, for sharing.' He said this with mock gentility and with the familiar air of spiritual pretense so common today. He then pointed to a young, dark haired man sitting on the floor in front of him. *"And we say, 'Nick has his truth.' And then we listen and say, 'Thank you for sharing, Nick.' What's your name?"* he asked, turning his attention to the woman sitting nearest to him.

"Anya," she said.

Andrew continued in the same tone. *"And Anya's going to share her truth and we're going to thank her for sharing. And we're going to listen to everybody else share their truth and then everybody will feel good because they've all been heard and we're going to honor and respect each individual equally. Now for a group of narcissists that's very good because everybody will feel respected and honored. The thing is, narcissists don't only want respect, but they want to feel honored, appreciated and recognized, etcetera. However, this teaching is designed to completely destroy that approach. Now, some people find it quite challenging that I don't believe in honoring everybody's truth. But frankly I think it's the worst possible thing we could do if we actually want to evolve. Just so you know, that world of relativized truth is my definition of hell.*

"So ideally, when a person looks into this in the most serious way and then makes a decision that they want to be free more than anything else, hopefully they won't mess around with it. You see, what we want is to become strong. We want to cultivate spiritual strength or strength of character. That means you really mean it and nothing is going to change that.

"Now, the reason why clarity of intention is so complicated is because when this gets real we find that the ego is not served in any way by the desire to be free more than anything else because the aspiration to be free does not honor or respect the ego! In fact, it says, 'Oh! You want to be free more than anything else? Now I can really get you!'" He laughed loudly into the stark silence in the room.

"That's the really challenging part of it," he added. *"Up until the point where one says 'I want to be free more than anything else,' you honor the ego. But the minute you cross that line and say, "No, I want to be free more than anything else," you stop honoring the narcissistic separate self-sense. So that creates all kinds of problems for people. But then it's their choice. That's what they said they wanted to do. You see why it's a big deal? I literally don't think I can overemphasize how big a step this is.*

"So we have higher-state experiences. For example, we spent the first four days just dwelling upon the bliss and ecstasy of what it's like to go beyond ego at the level of consciousness, right?"

"Right," everyone agreed, seeming to remember those days fondly.

"And to go beyond ego at the level of consciousness feels just about better than anything one could ever feel, right?"

Once again, everyone agreed.

"But now we're talking about what it means to go beyond ego, not just as a higher state, but as a real flesh-and-blood human being in real time. That's much more challenging. So the higher state of consciousness is like the bait. That's the seduction. It's also more than that because it convinces people that there's really something to this. Of course, then they want to know, 'Well how do you make it real?' That means, now that you've gone beyond ego in terms of experiencing a higher state, how do you go beyond ego as a human being with all of your humanity intact? It's an integral or integrated whole in which one works in concert with the other.

"You see, my confidence comes from the fact that I know what I'm saying makes a lot of sense. The problem is that we are irrational creatures. But when you take that step and say, 'I want to be free more than anything else, I want to be one with the Authentic Self,' with that step you are saying, 'I want to become a rational human being and I no longer want to be a conditioned robot.' You see, most of us are quite crazy. So when you say, 'I want to be free more than anything else,' that's the beginning of the conscious aspiration to become a truly rational, sane human being who's in control of themselves. And that's a very big step to take. In that step we illuminate the choosing faculty and that's when the possibility of actually becoming a truly sane human being emerges.

"So in a context where we agree that the degree to which we identify with the ego is the degree to which we are crazy, unpredictable and unreliable, we recognize that as long as ego's in the picture we never know what we're going to do. On the other hand, in the Authentic Self there's transparency, which means we always know what we're going to do because we can see. There's nothing opaque that's keeping us from seeing. Transparency is crystal clarity. But when ego is in the way it's hard to see because things get very muddy. The ego can never tell you the complete truth because it always has to have this protective shield. So that's not transparency. The choosing faculty, or the self, if it's identified with the ego is going to be inherently corrupt and it'll have the freedom to do whatever it wants behind its shield. So what we're calling ego here veils the choosing

faculty. That's what creates this lack of transparency in the self. See? So, 'I want to be free more than anything else' means you want to become transparent.

"You get the idea?" he asked emphatically. "*It's not a small thing we're talking about here. Nothing, as far as I know, could be more of a challenge except, I think, whatever we're going to have to go through when we have to let go of the body at the time of death.*

"*Now, I know that a lot of people think it's not possible to become transparent in the way I'm speaking about. Many experts say, 'It's not possible to know yourself that well.' And they also say, 'There's always going to be a shadow, a dark corner that we can't see.' A shadow means there's an unconscious motivation that you're not aware of. So I think it actually is possible, but I'm pretty alone in this. So you should probably not believe me when I say this.*" He laughed at this and we all laughed with him yet what came through Andrew's jesting tone was a deadly seriousness that called each of us to reckon with this in the depth of our own being.

Seemingly satisfied with having made his point, Andrew moved on to the next question from a rather soft-spoken man in the back of the room with an accent from an indeterminate corner of Europe.

"The way I understand freedom of choice," he began, "is that whatever the circumstance is and our action in response to it, we can choose to be detached from both it and its consequences."

"*That's not what I mean,*" Andrew replied.

"So I guess I didn't really understand," the man confessed.

"*I'm talking about becoming responsible for all the choices that we make, not about being detached. Detachment is not the goal here. You see, a lot of people are very in-terested in being detached because their life is such a mess and they have so much bad karma that they can't even bear to face it. So what they're interested in is learning about detachment so they don't have to face into it and suffer. You get the idea?*"

The man said nothing for some moments, apparently unprepared for Andrew's shocking penchant for telling it like it is.

"*Hello?*" Andrew laughed when the man still hadn't said anything some mo-ments later. "*The thing is, you want to get your 'detachment' from the fact that you're facing everything and dealing with it fully, the result of which would also be a sense of deeper integrity.*

"*The thing is, being detached in relationship to what we're speaking about here is not the issue. Detached is a relationship to life from the position of the non-relative or absolute dimension of reality itself. Here detachment from the creative process is the source of ecstasy itself. But from that position you're not engaged; that's why you're de-tached. But the minute you cross the threshold from formlessness to form and come out of this Ground to enter into the manifest realm – that's God going from His formless state and entering into form – you're entering into a world of enormous complexity. So the idea is to take responsibility for your part of that complexity. Then theoretically how it would work is that first you'd get some control of yourself and then, once you've gotten good control of yourself, you'd want to try to extend that outwards and take on even more. You get the idea?"*

"Yes... Well, at least I'm going to think about it."

"Good. So, once again, I know it's a little complicated but detachment is the fundamental position of enlightenment, which is this experience of this unmanifest Ground where everything's already inherently full and perfect. Now, when you know that it's supposed to fill the hole in your soul. And when that hole is filled through the experiential recognition of fullness, that's called ego death. Ego death means you're dying to the conviction that something's terribly, terribly wrong.

"And after you die to this egoic conviction you re-enter into the stream of time with the knowledge of fullness, knowing who you are in the ultimate sense. You see, to put it in very simple terms, before this awakening you thought you were just Andrew, David, Susan, or whoever you thought you were when you had a problem. Then, when you realized that that's never who you were, you died to that part of yourself and then returned realizing who you really are: the Energy and Intelligence that initiated the creative process becoming aware of itself in the form of Andrew, David and Susan. That's ego death and spiritual rebirth. Now, the Energy and Intelligence that initiated the creative process and has realized itself in the form of Andrew, David, Susan, or whoever, has an enormous project on his or her hands.

"Now, Andrew, David and Susan in their unenlightened state will never be able to handle the enormous project to create the universe because they're very busy with other problems." Andrew laughed ecstatically. *"You see the ego has a whole agenda that's very emotionally, psychologically and practically time-consuming. Therefore, it has no time on its calendar for the evolution of consciousness or for the creation of the universe. It's just that simple. So practically, emotionally and in just about every other way, we're distracted and very busy. But the idea is to die to that part of yourself so that your vehicle, your human life, becomes available for the God Project, for the creation of the conscious universe. Suddenly one finds, 'Oh! I'm available. My calendar was booked, but now I realize that I've changed the agenda.' That's how it works, at least in theory. Do you see how it all makes sense?"*

Everyone nodded "yes" as fresh waves of spiritual intoxication cleared the room of the accumulated psychic flotsam of facing the first tenet. .

"So I want you to look into this issue of wanting to be free more than anything else. Also, I spoke a lot about the fundamental role of enlightening the choosing faculty or free agency in the transformative process. Once again, if you really get this it'll change your life.

"So remember, there are higher states of consciousness and the enlightenment, or the bringing light to, the choosing faculty. The choosing faculty is neither the ego nor the authentic self, but it's you! Whatever you choose is what you become. When you really, really let that in very, very deeply, it changes absolutely everything and your destiny

and potential in relation to your own evolutionary predicament fall completely into your own hands – right now! Now, it can be quite overwhelming but nothing could be more thrilling because the miracle of the enlightenment dimension lies in the fact that everything could change at any moment. And really knowing that it really is in your own hands is the most important thing. It doesn't matter what the past has been! It doesn't matter what the past has been!" He repeated this line emphatically at least ten times, then asked, *"Have I said it enough?"* and then repeated it a few more. *"I don't know how many of you believe me but it doesn't matter what the past has been!*

"At any rate, this is why the location, recognition and revelation of the choosing faculty within all of us is so foundational and profoundly important. Because the reason the ego is so difficult to deal with is because it's so laden with emotional conviction. The ego says, 'Yeah, yeah, yeah. Okay. Okay, but I know. He could sit up there all day long and say whatever he wants, but I know...' and then fill in whatever it is. Why? 'Because I feel it.' So the ego is heavy with emotional conviction. But the Authentic Self doesn't recognize it, period. From the perspective of that part of you that wants to be free, the emotional conviction of the ego is pure, as they say in American English, B.S. I don't know how I can make it clearer than that. But it's convincing and so absolutely seductive that only a very sharp, rare individual can resist it and ultimately see through it.

"So in a challenging moment the only way through the overwhelmingly seductive emotional conviction of the ego is by unearthing or bringing awareness to the choosing faculty. People always want to know, 'How do I do this?' This is the answer. You can meditate from now until doomsday. If you don't illuminate, awaken, and take responsibility for the choosing faculty in yourself you're never going to get anywhere. So then the battle is between the awakening to the choosing faculty versus the heavy and absolutely seductive nature of the emotional conviction of the ego. The thing is, when people are emotionally convinced about the ego's position it's almost impossible to change their mind, even if intellectually they agree with you. That's when you start to see how schizophrenic we actually are.

"Now, as I said on the first day, only we can save ourselves. There's no one up there who's going to save us. That's why this is a path of self-liberation. It's very sophisticated stuff but it works if you're really behind it. So you can experience higher states of consciousness and awaken to your already-liberated self as the inherently full Ground of Being. But the way the fullness of the unmanifest Ground translates into an enlightened self, as I teach it, is entirely dependent on bringing enlightenment to the choosing faculty. It'll be the hardest thing you've ever done in your life. I can guarantee it. You shouldn't even doubt it for a second. And why shouldn't it be? If we're really speaking about enlightenment and the evolution of consciousness and it's real then it would have to be ultimately challenging.

"Now, the way you bring light to the choosing faculty is from the strength of conviction that is found through the cultivation of the desire to be free. That's how you begin

to dig yourself out from layers and layers and layers of ignorance and conditioned ways of thinking and feeling. It's heavy, it's thick and it's deep. So someone can laugh and say, 'Ha, ha, ha. It's all an illusion,' and that's fine. But it's just not enough. So yes, from the perspective of the Ground of Being, or the formless Self that's never taken form and that's always who we all ultimately are, none of this matters. And because of that you want to spend as much time in the conscious experience of the formless dimension of the self as possible so that the emotional conviction in its reality gets stronger and stronger and stronger. But you want to use that emotional conviction to dig yourself out from underneath the emotional conviction of the ego.

"Now, as I understand it, this is a very clear expression of a post-postmodern rational, evolutionary spirituality. It puts the entire burden on the individual. Now isn't the liberation and empowerment of the individual what the post-modern world is supposed to be all about? So the demand of evolutionary enlightenment is very legitimate for the post-modern spiritually interested human who wants to be at the cutting edge of development. Are you all with me?"

"Yes," we all answered with both eagerness and solemnity.

"Okay, then we'll finish with that."

Once more silence consumed us. Only the play of bells in the distance and the warm breeze blowing in from the sunlit canyons stirred the atmosphere between us. Before sinking into that no-place revealed by letting things be as they are I marveled briefly at Andrew's amazing ability to steer us into the deepest existential waters, forcing us to confront the biggest questions, incisively responding to our reactions and still, at the very end, leaving us with the most positive possible view. And all the while he never shrank from the ultimately challenging implications of the inquiry upon which we had embarked. Leading us to the edge of ourselves while ruthlessly pushing forward, he'd left us both leaning over the abyss and gazing into unimagined heights, putting in our hands the power to choose between them.

Thus, while the anguish that had burned in me the foregoing day and night had been cleanly swept aside by my interaction with Andrew, it left in its wake much to consider. He had deftly pointed out that it was not my whole life that I needed to let go of, only its unwholesome aspects. That was a relief but it left a wide array of issues yet to sort through. I also realized that what I'd been doing had been shifting my attention and identification back and forth between, as Andrew had put it, the emotionally charged conviction of the ego and the liberated passion of the Authentic Self.

Wandering thoughtfully in the warm sunlight bathing the plazas and walkways of Montserrat I wondered what it would mean to take an absolute stand in the conviction of the Authentic Self. What would it mean, I wondered, to put my stake in the ground there once and for all without ever again entertaining the possibility of stepping back from that absolute commitment. What would

292 • 11 Days at the Edge

it mean if I could forever view the ego's endless heartfelt protestations from the perspective of the Authentic Self, which does not recognize their validity? Of course, with that very thought came a rush of terror that ripped my attention away from this consideration and riveted it once more to the fears of the ego. It was then that the pivotal role of the power of choice became more apparent to me than it had on previous occasions. Somehow, having been through what I'd been through, I managed to keep my wits about me just enough to know what was happening. A shift of attention had occurred and with that shift the entire field of my experience changed in an instant from exhilaration to trepidation. Seeing this, I promptly withdrew my attention from the ego's concerns and fixed it once more upon the Authentic Self's innate desire to move ever forward for the highest reasons. Instantly the thrill of endless possibility ripped through my nervous system, that shift having happened entirely through the galvanizing power of choice, changing the entire playing field instantly. And in that moment my awareness of the choosing faculty was infinitely amplified, as was my recognition of its potential to place the matter of my own liberation directly into my hands. This was something I had previously failed to fully appreciate.

I toyed with this capacity for the remainder of the afternoon, becoming more familiar with the subtleties of its mechanics. By the time the next teaching approached I had succeeded in removing my attention significantly from both the ego and Authentic Self, steadily remaining alert to that part of myself which had the capacity of choice. That capacity seemed to lie so close to the self that I could not locate it as an object, a fact that was in and of itself a source of fascination.

When the session resumed at five it once again took Andrew some time to shepherd us back to the point. At length he succeeded, engaging with an older Scandinavian woman.

"I just wanted to say," she began, "that I want to be a free and liberated person so that must be a yes to the question of clarity of intention."

"So did you find the part in yourself that wants it and the part that doesn't and the fact that there's this choosing faculty?" Andrew asked.

"Yes, I found that and I don't see any doubt in myself right now. I'm just looking forward to seeing what the next challenge will be because frankly, I don't see any doubt right now."

"Well, I guarantee you will. It's all a matter of time." Andrew laughed.

"I'm not scared," she said with a kind of carefree joy. "I'm just looking forward to that. Also, I was very happy too that you brought the 'you' back into the picture. You know, when you were talking about the Authentic Self and the ego I was wondering what happened to the 'you.' Now, with the emphasis on choice I see that the 'you' is back in the picture."

"That's right."

"Can I bring something up that you talked about yesterday; about the soul not being the Authentic Self?"

"That the soul and the Authentic Self are different?"

"Yes."

"Is that important to you?"

"Yes."

"Why might it be important?"

"I think it is because of the discussions about the impersonal and the personal. I wondered where the soul might fit in in all of that. So yesterday when you told us that the soul is personal I thought, well, now it's in the right place again."

"What's in the right place? I said the soul is both individual and collective and that it wasn't just personal. But there is a very personal dimension to it, unlike the Authentic Self, in which there's nothing personal at all. But why is this important to you?"

"Because the soul has always been part of my belief system and view of life."

"Okay, that's good. You see, what I'm trying to teach here is a very new thing. I'm trying to help people gain access to and an understanding of a radically different orientation to life and the human experience that isn't personal at all. Now, what we're calling the soul doesn't play a big part in the practice of this particular perspective. But assuming the perspective that I'm trying to teach here doesn't mean that the soul disappears. It just means that you are not giving it very much of your attention. The same thing goes for the entire personal relationship to life. So if someone can begin to really grasp what I'm trying to teach, which is a very impersonal, very different perspective that could be misinterpreted as being very austere, they'll see that the personal dimension, including the soul, doesn't disappear but, because you are leaving it alone in a way you never have before, it begins to straighten itself out."

"I understand that."

"But most people don't. Most people, because they don't have enough trust, are not willing to let go of the personal dimension, including whatever their idea of the soul is, profoundly enough, in order to see what's actually going to happen. But the so-called personal dimension all the way down to the soul level, which is the deepest you can go to in the personal stream, will straighten itself out by itself if you are willing to leave it alone. Do you understand?"

"Yes."

"But if we are not willing to let go of it as a fundamental point of identification then this self-righting won't be able to occur. That's the issue. That's why I was asking why this is important to you. Do you see what I'm saying?"

"Yes."

"Because if you're still holding on to it, it means that there's a fundamental locus of identification and a false presumption that it really is important. And if that's the case then this self-righting action won't be able to happen. Now remember, there's a context in which this is being said, and the context is enlightenment. Enlightenment is

a metaphor for freedom from the personal dimension. If it's going to be about enlightenment it always has meant and it is always going to mean that there has to be some fundamental letting go of the personal dimension all the way down to the soul level.

"Now, to be quite honest with you, a lot of people and a lot of spiritual teachings are very involved with soul development or soul cultivation, some in ways that are quite serious and authentic and many others that are silly and full of new age superstition and misinformation. But, the thing is, you have to be very careful. Now, if you are really going to go into what enlightenment is all about, you just can't take all that stuff with you and most people simply don't understand that. I encourage you all to look into this for yourselves. If you really want to realize a radically impersonal perspective, which is what enlightenment has always pointed to, whether it's the pre-modern or the post-postmodern version, sooner or later you have to drop the whole thing.[2]

"But if you're willing to let go of the personal dimension, it's going to right itself, especially in a teaching like this because there is a very strong moral and ethical dimension to it. All right?"

"Yes. Thank you."

"Okay, let's keep going," Andrew said and, after some prompting of the reluctant crowd, he turned his attention to a thin British man.

"This morning," he said soberly, "you spoke very strongly about the fact that it's not about the past. I think this relates to what you were just speaking to as well."

"Definitely," Andrew agreed.

"So, when I looked into the part of me that is able to choose it felt like it came u against the consequences of my past."

"Of course that's what's going to happen."

"So, is that part of the whole dropping the personal thing?"

"Well, in relationship to the wanting to be free more than anything else, it means that you were grappling with the question in an authentic and sincere way and that you were experiencing the fear of letting go. But that's not bad. A question like this should bring up fear. I mean, it doesn't have to in every single case. Once in a while there is going to be someone who's already answered the question and it's not an issue for them anymore. But that's very rare. Generally, grappling with this question for real should bring up terror, fear of the future, fear of change and so on because it's confronting the personal part of yourself, the ego, absolutely. That's the whole point of asking the question. Also the idea is to get a very clear picture of where you're at and not to be deluded. Self-deception is very easy so this question can cut through the self-deception and just allow one to see where one stands. And, of course, that's not the end of the story. Then you decide what you want to do from there. But at least you're trying to establish where you are right now so then know what you're actually working with. Make sense?"

"Yeah, it sure does."

With that the man seemed to have nothing further to say and as Andrew moved on in search of the next question I felt somewhat vindicated by his response. At least, I felt, I had truly grappled with this question and was beginning to get a sense of where I was and how I could move forward.

"For me the answer to the question of clarity of intention is yes," said an older English woman whom Andrew had called on. "Inwardly I have been asking for an authentic liberation teaching for quite a long time and it feels like finally I have found one. At the same time I am getting a clearer idea of what that really means. It really feels like you're putting a face to it. And now I realize that I am just at the very beginning of understanding the ramifications of what that means. And I trust the process because I trust that the evolution of consciousness that is bringing me to this place contains all of the things in your teaching model about wholeness and goodness and strength. I mean I believe that it's innately good."

"But you don't have to believe it. I mean, hasn't the fact that that's the case already revealed itself to you in your own experience?"

"Yes, it has."

"Okay, so you don't have to trust that that's the case, do you? You already know that, right?"

"Right, yes, that's true."

"Well, that's important."

"Yes."

"Because, believe me, a lot of people are going to deny that that's the case. They'll either not believe it or through their actions they will say it's not true. You see, the reason this gets very delicate is that once something has been revealed to you and you know it to be absolutely true, then you have to prove that it's true both to yourself and to everyone else."

"Yes."

"So remember, we are going from formlessness to form. And also, this is all in the context of creating something new that hasn't happened before. Now if that's true, it has to go from being merely an intuitive, revelatory flash into the actual, tangible manifestation of that in real time. And that's up to you and to me, right?"

"Yes, and because of that I know that I have to learn about and see much more of the subtleties of the ego that I have not been aware of until now."

"But we all do, and that discovery is endless. It's not possible to get to a point where there's nothing more to know. It doesn't work that way. It never could. In an evolutionary context you are always developing. So you're either seeing more about that which you've already seen or else you are actually seeing things that you never have. But in either case, there's no end to it.

"However, it is possible to get to know enough of what we're speaking about here to make sure that the kind of radical transformation that we're exploring actually does happen. There is no doubt about that! You see, the thing about what I'm teaching

here is that I know that it's entirely possible that anybody who wants to can do this. But it will require everything somebody's got. And it will be the ultimate challenge for anybody. But there is no leap of faith that has to be taken. I'm not asking anybody to go somewhere that's not attainable or that's so far out there that it's beyond the scope of being conceivably possible."

"That's one of the great things about this; it's practical. I mean, it feels like you're giving me practical tools for doing the things that I've always wanted to do with my life."

"Well yes, you see, because when you take the metaphysics away then it really gets very brutally real. It's not up to the will of some kind of higher power or grace or karma or anything else. It's up to you, which is as it should be now. This is post-metaphysical spirituality. It's post-post modern, rational, evolutionary spirituality. That doesn't make it any less dramatic, any less sensational, any less profound, any less miraculous or anything like that. By no means! It just takes the superstition out of it."

Andrew paused for a moment, then concluded with, *"Okay, that was good,"* before seeking out the next question from an Australian woman in the very back of the room.

"Yesterday you used the word transparency," she began thoughtfully, "and that was very inspirational for me and helped clarify my intention."

"Why was that?" Andrew asked.

"Because it just grabs hold of me something fierce. To be in that place of transparency is always where I've wanted to be and if I sense that I'm with someone that has no 'shady character' in them I'm just transfixed."

"Well, the best part of oneself always would be. But to not be a shady character one has to give up quite a bit and change quite a lot. And, of course, the hardest this is to be the example yourself. Right?"

"Right. But I find that very exciting. I mean it might be terrifying at the same time but it's just so clear and something I can really focus my intention on."

"Yeah," Andrew agreed emphatically. *"I think the concept of transparency is very inspiring. At least it is in our best moments."* He laughed a little, then continued in a more sober, measured tone, *"But you have to know, as I was saying, that most people say that what I'm advocating in terms of transparency is simply not possible. I just want you to have that in your head so you'll be ready for it when people tell you that."*

The woman nodded silently but had nothing further to say.

"Andrew," a man called out. "To create something new and to be free sounds very thrilling to me but I cannot grasp any of the practical consequences of that for my life so it's hard to know what I'm choosing for."

"You don't have to worry about that in terms of the first tenet," he replied, adding, *"but you've already been through this exercise with me, haven't you?"* Andrew wasn't fond of people pretending to rediscover the same points over and over again,

viewing it as an egoic strategy to avoid actually taking responsibility for one's knowledge and moving forward with it.

"No, not this deep," he responded. "And I sense that the part of me that's afraid has a lot of questions."

Andrew laughed. *"The part of you that's afraid has a lot of questions? I'm sure they're good questions too: 'and what about this? And what about that?' That's the good, Dutch lawyer in you, right?"* Andrew said, teasing him a little.

Everyone laughed.

"So once again, all I'm asking is that you become clear about the part that does and the part that doesn't and that there's a choosing faculty that's not necessarily either. And in terms of the future, we won't necessarily have a clear picture of it. That's what's so exciting about it."

"So earlier you said that when one connects with the Authentic Self one can experience a very deep sense of purpose for one's life. So is it true that if you really want to be free that there will be some moments that you will have a practical picture about what you will do with that freedom in your life?"

"Yes, definitely, that will happen. Are you worried about that?"

"I'm very curious about that."

"Are you worried about it?"

"Yes, that too."

"If you're that worried about it you'll never have the guts to find out! In order to find out there has to be risk, risk, risk! Risk is where new things happen. Ask any creative person whether they're a scientist, or a musician, or an artist. They'll all tell you that their truly new ideas and sense of extraordinary possibilities emerged when they really let go of everything. That's when something new came up and that's how it works."

"So this freedom, if you choose for it, makes use of personal qualities and talents?"

"In your case, you mean?" Andrew teased again, eliciting more laughter from the group. *"What do you think?"*

"I think if I really choose for it, it will probably try to make use of me and my particular talents and abilities as a vehicle."

"Wouldn't that be a good day?"

"A very good day."

"Isn't that all you need to know about the future?"

"Yes, it is," he responded, his doubt quelled for the moment. Moving right along, Andrew took the next question.

An older Danish woman asked, "Looking into the question 'do I want to be free more than anything else?' I have to answer yes. If I wasn't sure about that I would not have been on this retreat. Of course, I also see the ego and the resistance in that, but that's just what it is."

"And can you see the part of you that's neither?" Andrew wanted to know.

"Yes, and I try to look into the part that is making the choice."

"And?"

"And I was looking into it and asking myself, 'what is this part?' I found it hard to see that separate from what I call my true self. So I had this idea that this must be the soul. But I cannot find the soul in me. I've looked for it and I've had different spiritual experiences in my life but I've never met the soul. So I cannot…"

"That's an interesting point she is making," Andrew said thoughtfully.

"I cannot get the idea of the soul. I mean, frankly I don't know what it is."

"I don't really either. I sometimes I think I do but it's more an idea about what it is than actually something I feel."

"I've been thinking about it because you said, 'There·is a hole in the soul.' And I thought, "What soul?" So where is the hole?"

Uproarious laughter burst through the room and I wondered how Andrew would handle this one. Simultaneously I marveled at his capacity to be disarmingly honest when it came to matters of his own understanding or, in this case, lack thereof.

"But you know what I meant when I talked about the existential doubt, right?"

"Yeah, yeah. I definitely know what you mean."

"So you could say 'a hole in the self.'"

"Yes."

"But with respect to the soul, you could say that it's the sense of a deeper connectedness with life and with people than the one of the ego. It might not be a sense of an absolute connection in the way that we've been speaking about it. It would be somewhere between the ego's connection and this absolute connection."

"So it would not be separate from the Authentic Self?"

"No, the opposite. It has nothing to do with the Authentic Self."

"It's completely separate from either one?"

"Yes, yes."

"But what's the difference between that and the Ground of Being then, which is also connected?"

"The thing is, neither the Ground of Being nor the Authentic Self have a trace of the personal in them. As we were saying during the first few days, in the Ground of Being there's no connection to anything. It's perfectly unrelated to anything."

"So the soul is a deeper sense of the personal?"

"Yes, it's a deeper dimension of the personal part of who we are. So, off the top of my head I'll just come up with whatever example comes into my mind. Let's say you have the first love of your life. Often with their first love people experience a very deep connection that they feel is on the level of the soul. They feel that what they experience with them is more meaningful than what they experience in many of their other relationships. Of course, you can have that deeper kind of connection to other people also,

not just a lover. With some individuals you may feel that your connection is deeper and even that there is a spiritual dimension to it. But it's still personal.

"But what I'm referring to here as the Ground of Being doesn't have a personal dimension to it at all. And equally, when we speak about Authentic Self there's not a personal dimension to it either."

"Okay, I get it."

"Good. And also, in relationship to the soul, that's a part of ourselves where we feel a connection with a sense of meaning and a moral dimension to life, one that is infinitely deeper than the ego's unfulfilled desires, fears, hurts, wounds, and so on. But it's not the moral dimension that I've been speaking about in here. It's more of a sense of meaning that's related to the fact that we are all connected to each other. That's why, when we refer to what is called the soul, there's a weightiness and a very strong emotional dimension to it. But it's not at all what I'm talking about with respect to the Authentic Self."

"So this part of me that's making the choices always knows where it's going? I mean it has its own direction?"

"Well, no. I'm not equating the chooser with the soul. All I'm doing is trying to answer the question about what the soul is."

"But wouldn't the chooser have it's own direction and always know where it was going?"

"Well, not necessarily. I'm saying that the choosing faculty is a function within all of us. And I'm saying that in relationship to the desire to be free in the way that we are describing it we have to locate that choosing faculty. The choosing faculty is more of a function than it is the self. I mean, it is the self, but that same faculty can choose to rape and kill and murder or it can choose to become a living manifestation of the Authentic Self. So whatever the choosing faculty chooses is what the self becomes."

"So what's important is not the choice but who and what is behind that choice?"

"No! What's important is what you choose. That's the whole point."

"Yes, but what you choose must come from somewhere deep inside the self."

"Well, that could be true, but that's not the issue here. What I'm saying is that with respect to what we've been discussing there's the ego, the Authentic Self, the Ground of Being, and we could even add soul. And what I'm saying is that what you — the totality of all these elements — choose is who you become and is what you are. So the whole idea is that you can choose heaven, hell and everything in between and that is precisely who you'll become.

"So in the way that this teaching approaches it, in order for it to be possible to be free the choosing faculty has to be located, because when we locate the choosing faculty everything can change radically at any moment simply through the power of our choice.

"And, as I was explaining earlier, this faculty has the power not only to completely override the emotional conviction of the ego but also the emotional connection to the

soul. For example, there's another way to understand what soul might be. If you're very identified with the ethnic aspect of your personality there could be a lot of karma and history related to that part of who you are. There are all kinds of intense emotions and moral convictions related to that that are very real and that could be really hard to see or to transcend. That also has to do with the soul. But this choosing faculty would make that possible too.

"You see a liberated person is more a manifestation of liberated consciousness than of anything else. They're everything else also. There's an ego, a soul, an ethnic dimension, and every other aspect of culture and time and history. But a truly enlightened or liberated self is going to be an expression and a manifestation of liberated consciousness more than they are an expression of anything else. Their consciousness itself is, in a fundamental and significant way, going to transcend and be free from all these things and that's the whole point.

"You can see very dramatic changes in people depending on what they choose and I've seen this happen many times. I've seen what the personality expresses when they are choosing to identify with the darkest part of themselves and when they choose to identify with the Authentic Self. You can see the same person literally become a different human being. This is something that I find endlessly fascinating. It's the same person, the same body, same eyes, same voice, and same memory. But what you see is a completely different human being. I'm not talking about a little bit different. I'm talking about a dramatic, dramatic shift. You see a person literally change right before your very eyes and in an instant, just like that." Andrew snapped his fingers sharply. *"And it's only because there is a shift in the choice of the locus of identification. And the shift is nothing less than spectacular. So once again, locating the choosing faculty is foundational for a teaching and a perspective like this."*

As Andrew paused to gather himself before scanning the crowd for the next question I drifted off in contemplation. While his point regarding the choosing faculty was growing ever clearer in my mind, what was captivating my attention was his discussion of the soul, a concept that had played little role in my own spiritual pursuits. I perfectly understood the woman's sentiment when she'd said, "I've looked for the soul and haven't found it anywhere."

As a kid I'd foolishly and in perfectly kidlike fashion attempted to locate the soul as some "me" object within the field of my awareness. After several predictably futile attempts, and having no one to turn to with such questions, I abandoned the entire endeavor. Years later, my worldview radically reconfigured by those salvos from the Absolute, the soul remained as traceless as ever. What I had perceived was the undying unity pervading life like red saturating a rose, that unbroken wholeness rendering all separation blissfully invisible to my view. Therefore, the soul remained a nebulous concept as my passion was swept on a tide into the pursuit of the Absolute. Yet simmering in some remote part of me was the niggling sense that in failing to consider that middle ground between the individuated self and the Self Absolute, I failed to consider something of significance. On the brief occasions when I did give this some thought I sensed the soul as a kind of a repository for karma, a reservoir of tendencies that moved from lifetime to lifetime on some evolutionary journey. But that was as far as it went. Therefore, hearing Andrew begin to give considerable energy to inquiring into its nature held its own subtle thrill for, at least in my view, it added one more essential piece to an already peerless teaching. It also demonstrated yet again Andrew's capacity to always change and ceaselessly inquire into life's mysteries with openness and wonder. In other words, I knew this teaching would continue forever to push the edge and thus never stagnate in the rut of fixed positions.

Delighting in that realization, I turned my attention back to the ongoing dialogue just as Andrew turned to the next question, which came from an older Swedish woman.

"So the Authentic Self is already whole and perfectly formed?" she wondered.

"Well, it's already whole," Andrew said, agreeing with the first half of her question before adding, *"but the Authentic Self develops in time. So yes, from the very beginning there is no division, no hurt, fear, pain, hesitation, paranoia, suspicion, unwholesome ambition or anything else in the Authentic Self. The Authentic Self is already completely, totally, radically free and perfectly whole. But it develops in time. I mean, look at the universe!"*

"So that's the impulse that got us here, right?"

"Yes."

"Where I was going with this is that the ego has no interest in learning this stuff, right?"

"Not for real."

"So, the part of us that is learning this and is informing the choosing faculty, is that the Self? I guess that's where I got a little confused. If the part of us that's taking this in is not the ego…"

"The ego can take it all in too," Andrew interrupted. *"The ego is very good at pretending."*

"But that's clearly not going to get us very far."

"Not when push comes to shove. When push comes to shove the ego pulls off the mask. But it will keep on the mask until the last moment. Only when there's no other possibility to 'fake it 'til you make it,' does the mask comes off and you see what you're really dealing with. And believe me, it's not pretty when you see it."

"But the part of us that's taking all this in clearly informs the choosing faculty, right?"

"Yes, sure."

"So I guess I'm not clear about what part of us is taking this in."

"Well, you could say the Authentic Self, which is this raw material, is taking it in."

"That answers my question."

Andrew paused reflectively for a moment. *"To be honest,"* he suddenly said, *"as I'm thinking about it, I don't really think I know the answer to that question."* He, along with everyone else burst into laughter. *"The only way I could authentically answer,"* he went on, *"is simply to say 'whoever you are.' Or, more specifically, 'whoever or whatever it is that's going through this process.'"*

"Okay, whatever works, right?"

"Well, no, it's not whatever works, because how this does work in real time is that one finds that when one identifies with the Authentic Self one has easy access to the kind of information that we're sharing here, especially if one has been exposed to it. However, when people identify with ego they seem to experience some kind of strange amnesia. Then, even if they've had access to it and recognized it they tend to forget because the ego was never interested in this kind of information. The ego doesn't want to know anything about it. So whatever the self is, even if it has absorbed all this information, when it identifies with the ego it won't have access to it. It doesn't mean that the information isn't in there. It is. But it only comes to the surface when the self is identifying with the Authentic Self. So it's very complicated but that's how it works.

"That's why when you asked, 'which part of me is absorbing this?' I said the Authentic Self. But whether that's really true or not I can't really be sure. But I've seen people who have a very profound understanding of this, even for months at a time, seemingly lose all access to it only because they're giving all their attention to how the ego felt. It doesn't mean it's not in there, because I've seen similar people shift and turn on a dime and suddenly," he snapped his fingers, *"it's all there. It's literally like turning on a light. And if you see this it can be frightening because you start realizing how complex we are as human beings and also how crazy we are.*

"So this all has to do with the choosing faculty. That's what turns on the light and turns it off. I have a lot of experience with this and I've seen it happen over and over and over again so I have no doubt that it's absolutely the case. It has nothing to do with karma. It has nothing to do with grace or destiny or anything else. All those things maybe get you to the point where you can actually experience and understand these things but the rest of it is up to you. Is that clear?"

"Yes, it is," the woman said solemnly.

Andrew took another drink, a deep breath and the next question, this one from a Dutch man, who had apparently been involved with Andrew's teaching for some time.

"I have a very strong sense of myself," he began, "and what I notice is that when I'm confronted with something I don't recognize about myself, I contemplate and withdraw."

"What are you referring to?"

"For instance, if I'm expressing doubt or holding back in communication or not expressing the Absolute and someone points out to me that that is happening

I often don't recognize the feedback, withdraw and am unable to respond as I would like to."

"Well, then you have to strengthen your clarity of intention because if it's important enough to you you can't afford to withdraw. Right?"

"Right. But I'm still attached to the sense of self that I experience."

"You're also Dutch so that could be problematic, as you know." A few chuckles surfaced but quickly subsided, as it was apparent that there was something serious passing between Andrew and this student of his. *"What do you think?"*

"Definitely," he agreed.

"Well, you know what I have to say about that.[3] But if what I have to say about that is true, you have to make up your mind about a lot things I've said about the Dutch mentality. And if you come to the conclusion that what I've said is true then, in terms of your own self, you would have to be willing to take responsibility for the implications of being a Dutch man at this particular time and how those forces affect you in relationship to wanting to be free.

"You see, as I said earlier, the ego is individual and collective. So part of who and what we are as a conditioned human being involves a cultural identity – for better and for worse. So coming from any particular culture is going to have both its positive and negative attributes.

"All cultures are different. For instance, you can tell that we're in Spain, not in Germany. There's a different feeling in one place and the other. So when you really look into the human condition you have to get into that part of the picture too. Being American or English or French is all part of it and each has a different feeling. You see, we can't see ourselves outside of the cultural context from which we come because, while not being the whole picture, it's a big part of who we are. So we all have certain tendencies that are based upon our cultural background and therefore we have to take that into consideration as well. The fact is that we're all much more influenced by the culture we come from than we like to believe. And unless you deal with a lot of the things I've had to say about that particular cultural background, it's just not going to work. Make sense?"

"Yes, makes sense," the man responded. Andrew seemed satisfied and moved on to the next question.

A German man wanted to know, "Should we first look at the evolution of consciousness or at letting everything go?"

"First we look at the evolution of consciousness," Andrew replied, *"which then becomes the context from which we look at all these other questions. In this teaching the big context is always the evolution of consciousness, not the liberation of the individual. But since we're all individuals we have to talk about that also, which is what we're doing right now. That's why what we're doing now is a little tougher. This is where it gets brutally real. But it's good and important to do that, don't you think?"*

"Yes, thank you."

"Does anybody else want to say anything?" Andrew asked in that characteristic way that indicated the teaching was approaching its conclusion. *"Did you?"* he asked, pointing to an elderly woman sitting near him in the front.

"I can say without any doubt that I want to be free more than anything else but I'm also aware of the habit to choose feelings and emotions over what I know is good and true and I know that that's evil."

"So what's the good news?" Andrew wanted to know.

"I struggle with it."

"That's the good news?" Andrew asked incredulously.

"No. I guess I'm also aware that I have to free myself and that I have a choice."

"Okay, that's good," he said, turning to everyone to add, *"So what I really want is for everybody to become very, very clear about this choosing faculty because it's a difficult thing to discover and it's a very easy thing to forget. The implications of discovering that there is a choosing faculty are very profound in terms of our capacity to actually change and become different people. It's only the discovery of this choosing faculty within the self that makes it possible to take responsibility for ourselves, which is the whole point of the second tenet of the teaching – the law of volitionality. Only with the discovery of the choosing faculty is it reasonable to expect that one would be responsible for oneself in the very dramatic ways that we've been speaking about.*

"And the other very important point we made today has to do with the discussion of what the soul is and the fact that if we are going to become liberated or enlightened to whatever degree then we also have to liberate ourselves from what we are calling the soul to a significant degree. Of course that doesn't mean it's going to go away. How could it? But our fundamental sense of ourselves has to be liberated from that also because consciousness doesn't have any past.

"You see the degree to which you identify with having a past is the degree to which consciousness itself is going to be weighed down, or at least that's what your experience will be. Of course, consciousness itself could never be trapped because it's always free, but an illusion is going be created that will be real enough for there to be a real suffering individual who feels and acts un-free and creates a mess for themselves and other people. So that's real life.

"So for there to be enlightenment or for lightness of being to become who you are there has to be an enormous shift of attention toward consciousness itself and away from the ego, soul, and all these other things. Remember, it's the evolution of consciousness. So, practically speaking we are literally trying to disembed consciousness from the compulsive identification with individual and collective ego and soul.

"Now, I guarantee you that the experience of consciousness that has been freed from this compulsive identification with the past, no matter what it is, is so exhilarating and so thrilling and so self-affirming that when you experience it, no matter to what degree, you are not going to have any doubt about the fact that there is nothing else that you

could ever possibly want. That's just the nature of what happens. Therefore, you have to be willing to let go of that which is creating the illusion of un-freedom or being trapped in an individual and collective past.

"Don't get me wrong. The past is not bad. In fact, the past is good because, as I was explaining the other day, the past is how we've evolved and developed. So it's important and good but to be emotionally embedded in and identified with it is the biggest problem there is if we actually want to evolve. It's an enormous problem and in fact it's the only problem. Do you see how it works?"

We all indicated our agreement.

"Okay, so we'll continue tomorrow but please, between now and the next time we meet, stay with this line of inquiry." With that Andrew concluded the teaching and we sank once more into meditation.

I was physically, emotionally, and spiritually spent but mercifully set free from the throes of the existential crisis that had threatened my sanity for the previous day and a half.

I began to realize how much more serious I needed to be if I intended to make any real progress in my evolution as a human being. It also became clear to me that a significant slice of the motivation driving my desire to move into Andrew's community had to do with wanting to put myself in an environment where I would not be able to indulge myself in the self-involved ways to which I had grown accustomed. That afternoon I came to see that that represented a serious abdication of responsibility on my part, a denial of the very choosing faculty that we had spent the foregoing hours unearthing. This position, I also realized, had nothing to do with the kind of autonomy that was the backbone of the character and integrity that I was seeking to make my own. I realized that, as long as I don't fully step into my own autonomy in this teaching, I will forever be relegated to the status of follower with respect to Andrew rather than partner, which is what he has called us all to be. The long and the short of it was this: as long as I am fundamentally relying on another or some outside circumstance to ensure my own evolutionary change in real time I will never be a truly reliable and trustworthy human being. That, I now saw, was simply a fact. Therefore, if I wished to win my own dignity, never mind enlightenment, then I had to pursue the purification ensured by living the tenets of this teaching as if my life depended on it for perhaps, as Andrew was fond of pointing out, it actually did.

As I wandered across the plaza spread beneath Montserrat's basilica, this layer of contemplation soon gave way to the next. The directive had been to relinquish the unwholesome aspects of my life. The subtext, of course, read, "for a higher purpose." Heeding this directive, I wondered what it would be like to no longer live for the ego at all. The subtext of this, in turn, was "there's nothing in it for you," a notion to which I had experienced a visceral recoil just two days earlier. That recoil now came around for another visit. Simultaneously I realized that I was yet again examining the entire proposition from the ego's perspective, or as Andrew liked to say, from the bottom up. Turning that position on its head I considered what I might do with my life if I lined it up with the passion of the Authentic Self. Immediately I sensed that that passion would sweep me away. In its throes little or no thought would be given to the ego's mantra: "what about me?" Concern and urgency with respect to furthering the evolutionary agenda would become paramount and in their wake would follow a rush of excitement and a burst of creative energy that would show the ego's concerns for what they are: tin pot tyrants of the psyche committed to a life of trite, petty and selfish insignificance.

I recalled Andrew describing in sumptuous detail a Caribbean vacation replete with sunbathing, Mai-tais, and cheap novels, then asking rhetorically, *"How does that feel from the perspective of the Authentic Self?"* After waiting for a few moments he emphatically answered his own question, *"Like a total waste of time!"* It was a sentiment I fully appreciated, for at those moments that I've been most aligned with the Authentic Self I have found myself overcome by a simultaneous rush of urgency and creativity in which the very idea of spending one's life energy on idle entertainment seemed pathetically small-minded and painfully absurd. That urgency was entirely devoid of any sense of "should," of any browbeating of the conscience with heavy obligation. It was simply the nature of the Authentic Self ever on the move. It did not have to be cultivated. I could simply climb aboard for the ride.

If I chose to. Where I put my attention is what I became. Put it on ego and its whole world emerged in a jarring instant. Put it on sexual desire and with shocking immediacy every axon, dendrite and neuron of my nervous system snapped to attention. Put it on the Authentic Self and burn in a current of wild passion for the unrealized potential of the next moment in a forward explosion without end. It was all up to me.

Later that night, as I lay on my cot, these contradictory streams rushed through me, each an impersonal force of its own, each compelling in its own right, each vying for my attention. And what was I? A choice point, nothing more *and yet nothing less*. And whatever the soul was, it was my actions as a choice point that would determine its destiny, one as yet unwritten.

NOTES

1. In connection to this, I recalled once hearing Andrew respond to woman who had described her hospice experience with the dying in their last moments. In a very beautiful way she had talked of the surrender and openness that comes over people as they prepare to leave this world. Andrew had agreed with her that such experiences are quite beautiful indeed, but had added that it's very easy to surrender then because on your deathbed there's no pressure to live the revelation of the

infinite. That got my attention because, as with so much else of what he said, it made perfect sense. And it brought everything squarely back to my choices now in relation to the infinite. In short, it was vintage Andrew.

2. Interestingly, as Andrew's teaching is constantly evolving due to his own relentless investigation of such questions, he has recently taken more interest in the soul and its cultivation, stating that the first three tenets of his teaching, clarity of intention, the law of volitionality, and face everything and avoid nothing, do just that (see http://www.andrewcohen.org/teachings/path.asp for an overview of the five tenets of the teaching). For an in-depth investigation of the soul and its role in spiritual development see *What Is Enlightenment?* magazine, issue #32, entitled *Death, Rebirth, and Everything in Between: A Scientific and Philosophical Journey.*

3. Andrew's take on the Dutch cultural condition is that, being perhaps the most liberal and permissive culture on the planet today, it also embodies one of the most pathological manifestations of the "green meme" or "Boomeritis" (see previous reference) on the planet. As such, it is also most impervious to Andrew's teaching. Interestingly, California comes in a close second in this area, to the degree, in fact, that Andrew has referred to parts of it as "enemy territory." However, it appears that in recent years the cultural landscape in both areas is shifting slightly as a few individuals are beginning to awaken to the suffocating limitations of a narcissistically infused value system and are longing for a higher view.

Day 8

Face Everything and Avoid Nothing

After four and a half hours of churning sleep, I woke to the cool morning darkness realizing that, with only three days to go, all the streams of self were fully in the mix now: the power of the Authentic Self, the quiet liberation of the Ground of Being, and the ego along with its endless strategies to avoid its own undoing. And I, steering the ship of choice, was plying the choppy waters between them.

This morning currents of ego snaked through my mind, tempting me with thoughts of home and pleasure and freedom from this "bondage of liberation." In fact, home had never seemed so good, least of all when I was there. In actuality, however, I didn't *really* want to leave. On the contrary, I could have stayed another month. Yet the ego, weary of its confinement, was chafing in its bonds. To make matters worse, in addition to fantasies of an Elysian home life, powerful surges of sexual desire continued to pulse remorselessly through every cell of my being. Things were growing desperate. Not only were aged women beginning to look good but if I dared close my eyes, either for rest or meditation, I was overwhelmed by sexual fantasies.

Fortunately, the ego's ploy was as transparent as a car salesman's grin and though its effect was not inconsequential, I was able to lay hold of the twin life-lines of clarity of intention and no relationship to thought, generating sufficient objectivity to keep my nose just above the waterline of madness. I spent my morning, both during chanting and meditation, alternately caught in the currents of desire and liberation and often on the stormy channel between them. Compulsion, revulsion, grasping and surrender all continued as I made my way to the teaching hall. The next hour of tempestuous meditation was relieved only when Andrew resumed the teaching.

"*So, I want to continue where we left off yesterday, speaking about the first tenet of the teaching*" he began. "*Okay,*" he said, pointing to a young American man to his left.

"So, it seemed like the big question last night was about who was the chooser and what the nature of that part of us that chooses is."

"We didn't quite go into that," Andrew replied. *"I just wanted to make everybody clear about the fact that the choosing faculty existed. What it's nature was hasn't been part of the inquiry at all."*

"Well, I guess it's been a part of mine."

"Forget it. It doesn't matter. It's irrelevant. The only thing that's important to know if you want to be free is that it exists. What it is doesn't make any difference. All you have to know is whatever it is is you."

"Right. Okay. That's who we are."

"Then the whole idea is to make ourselves conscious of the fact that this choosing faculty exists and when you realize it is when the door to liberation and radical transformation appears right before your eyes. Do you get the point?"

"Yes."

"Did you forget about that part?"

"No. I guess I was trying to put into context the choice to be free more than anything else because I see that that choice is the portal through which the Absolute comes into the world and creation. And I was seeing the magnitude of the moment-to-moment choice for freedom and life and evolution as opposed to choosing the ego and keeping that consciousness in its embedded state. So I was just trying to put that into in the context of…"

"But you want to remember that in this kind of inquiry we don't want to get too abstract. For the inquiry to be fruitful and powerful it always has to be in direct alignment with your own aspiration for freedom in the present moment. Otherwise it just gets abstract, theoretical and irrelevant."

"Hmm, right," the man assented.

"There's no risk in just exercising your cognitive faculties. Anybody can do that. The idea is to use the inquiry as a way to liberate your own self. Okay?"

"Yes, okay."

"Good. Okay. So…" Andrew was about to go on to the next question when the young man raised another question.

"There was something more in terms of the practical implications of clarity of intention. I found, or we found in a group context through inquiry, that there is really no neutral ground."

"What do you mean?" Andrew asked.

"Well, anytime that you choose to become, you either are choosing freedom or not choosing freedom."

"That's very good."

"So there's no way to remain neutral once you make that choice."

"Not once you become conscious of who you are and what the process is."

"Right."

"But before you become conscious it might as well be neutral ground because you're not driving the car. You're just along for the ride."

"But if you…"

"But you want to say that from the minute you begin to wake up and become aware of who you are and what's actually occurring then you have to choose. But up until that point we've all had about fourteen billion years of a free ride."

I laughed briefly with everyone else while also appreciating Andrew's point.

"So there not being any neutral ground depends upon the degree to which you actually become aware of the fact that you're part of a developmental process that is becoming aware of itself and that you have free agency. In accordance with your degree of recognition of free agency comes the growing realization that there is, as you put it, no neutral ground. But not before that. It's entirely dependent upon your awakening."

"I can see that now."

"Okay. Good. But just to put it very bluntly, most human beings haven't gotten to that point."

"Right."

"So even to begin to appreciate or recognize intellectually that that would be the case is quite a sophisticated perspective."

"Right. And so, from that perspective, the only neutral ground is the Ground of Being."

"Yes, that's very true. But when you begin to awaken to the delicacy, the subtlety and the profound implications of your own capacity for consciousness in this developmental context it's supposed to shock you out of your infatuation with the fears and desires of the ego. In the shock of this awakening you realize, 'Hey, wait a minute. The fears and desires of my ego are such an infinitesimal part of such an enormous picture and the most important part of that picture has to do with consciousness becoming aware of itself through me.'

"You can see that this is something that's just beginning to happen. And now it's beginning to happen through you. And then you begin to see how big the implications are. And again, that's supposed to shock you out of your compulsive identification with the ego. And if it doesn't, then something's wrong with you. I mean that! I don't know what more anybody would need to know, assuming they weren't totally crazy.

"And that's what's different about looking at enlightenment in an evolutionary context. It's the discovery of the purposefulness of your own incarnation. Suddenly your own incarnation becomes infinitely more purposeful than the ego's agenda could ever be.

"It's really just a matter of seeing things as they are. Again, that's supposed to shock you out of being entrenched in an unenlightened perspective in which you're not really very available. Does it always work that way? No. And I honestly don't know why not. I don't know what more anybody would need to know to give them strength, courage, conviction and all the inspiration they should ever need."

The bittersweet exasperation in Andrew's voice was heartrending. Suddenly I saw him in another light. Not merely the enlightened teacher, he appeared to be someone both blessed and cursed by the dual edge of a vision that at once overwhelmed the bounds of personal selfhood and silenced every doubt and pang strangling the human heart. There he sat, pouring the depth and realization of his own extraordinary life out before us, begging us to take in that vision so that our own lives might pulse with the depth of purpose that had consumed him. Inwardly I bowed my head in gratitude.

"So just remember," he went on, *"when you're doing the inquiry, it has to relate directly to your own potential for liberation in the present moment. We don't want to get lost in theoretical abstractions. It's easy to do because the ideas in themselves can be compelling. But you want to put yourself right in the center of the picture. You practice inquiry to liberate yourself, not to entertain your intellect. You want to feel that the power of the inquiry is doing something to you on a cellular level, just like when I'm sitting here speaking. It should be the same kind of explosive intensity and you should feel that you're being shaken to your core by what it is that you're recognizing. If it's anything less than that it's ultimately probably not going to be very useful. Okay? How's that for raising the bar?"*

"I guess I can see now that there was definitely a part of my ego that was attached to the question I was asking. I mean I did feel authentic and..."

"You see, the thing is, when you started talking there was a way that you were removed from what you were saying in a way that revealed what you were doing with your inquiry. I could hear it the minute you opened your mouth."

"Yes. I can see that now," the man said humbly.

A short silence filled the room as Andrew scanned for the next question.

He turned his attention to a Dutch woman who asked a long and convoluted question that amounted to two things: first, that she already understood everything that Andrew had said and was indeed spontaneously living it; and second, she couldn't understand the big deal with respect to the choosing faculty that Andrew had gone to such lengths to clarify.

"I think I know and how can you tell that I don't know?" she demanded before adding, with respect to the choosing faculty, "What's all the fuss about?"

"Well," he responded with an easy air, *"I think the fuss is that most people don't know it and a great deal of the time, even if they did recognize it in their best moment, they would probably deny it. So it is a big deal and I've been saying why it's a big deal over and over again. Once again, when you locate this choosing faculty the potential for your own radical transformation opens up right in front of you and is not dependent on anyone else including a higher power. So that's a big deal, I think."*

"It is a big deal," she now responded as if this was perfectly obvious and couldn't understand why Andrew was pointing it out, "but..."

"But you said, 'what's the big deal?'"

"What if it happened some time ago?" she followed up, sidestepping Andrew and presumably referring to her own elevated position.

"Does that mean it's not a big deal right now?"

"No, it is a big deal."

"But you said, what's the big deal?"

"Yeah, but I don't know why…" she faltered slightly.

"You see, I could speak about the first tenet of this teaching forever although it's not an issue I personally struggle with. But whenever I talk about it it's a big deal and it's always fresh and new because of what IT is. Certain things are just so important that when you're really in touch with how important they are you get very excited when you speak about them."

"Yeah, and that's what all your life and all my life is about then."

"Ideally."

"And how do you tell it's not? I mean, it sounds as if nobody really understands it."

"Is this an abstract question?" Andrew asked, finally cutting through to the heart of the matter.

"I don't know," she said. "Maybe."

"Well then don't worry about it. Just be concerned with yourself and with the things we're speaking about here. Nothing else matters right now. Okay?"

"Okay."

"Certain things that are absolutely true and of absolute importance are always going to be exciting, fresh and new. You can never become so familiar with them that they don't interest you anymore or don't set your heart on fire, especially if you really know them. You'll just never be able to get over them. That's how you can tell if someone really knows. That might be part of the answer to your question."

With that he brought this interaction to a close and pointed to Mark, a middle-aged American man and student in the New York center, who sat in the first row of chairs directly in front of him. *"Okay, Mark."*

"Hi, Andrew. I don't have a question, but I did want to see if I was thinking clearly."

"Okay."

"With regard to clarity of intention, when I said 'yes' to wanting to be free more than anything else, although it wasn't apparent to me at the time, it seems that at the moment that I said 'yes' it set up a new context."

"That's the idea."

"So it was transformative in that."

"That's right."

"And then, from that first 'yes,' it's a matter of me being responsible for that 'yes' rather than continually choosing for it over and over again."

"Exactly."

"So it's almost like you get one time to say 'yes.'

"Ideally that's exactly how it works. One shot. You don't want to keep renegotiating the position"

"Then in a way that new context transforms what ethical behavior is because…"

"Because now the ethical behavior would have to be true to…"

"To that! To the clarity of intention. To wanting to be free more than anything else."

"Well. That's how I see it."

"That's what I thought."

"So the implications of what you're saying are quite profound. You're saying that there are moral implications for coming to the point where you make the decision that you want to be free more than anything else. But what if you don't feel that way tomorrow morning? What are you going to do then, hmm?"

"No, I have to give up any rights I have to…"

"To be an emotionally self-indulgent, self-centered person? Is that what you mean?"

"Yeah, that pretty much nailed it."

"Well, what kind of freedom would we have left if we couldn't be emotionally self-indulgent anymore? Hmm?" Andrew teased. *"It doesn't sound like very much fun to me. It sounds like it would be boring. Wouldn't it?"*

"Well, that's…" the man began, but Andrew went on.

" So we're defining freedom now, right? To the ego, being told that you're no longer allowed to be emotionally self-indulgent feels like being put it in prison. It feels like you're a Nazi commandant. To the ego freedom means, 'I can do whatever I want whenever I want to do it and I can operate according to how I feel.' Of course, then I would say, 'If you want to be free more than anything else, that's actually not the way it works. It's quite the opposite because once you say that it changes all the rules.'

"So then you have to appreciate why it's a choice and that's why we're talking about it. That decision to be true to the fact that there's a moral obligation when you acknowledge a higher context is a choice. It's not an experience. It's not a small distinction."

"So I see then that in this context suffering becomes unethical."

"Well, I wouldn't go that far," Andrew laughed incredulously. *"You've left me behind on that one. I say outrageous things all the time but I would never say suffering is unethical. That's a dangerous way to talk and you could be rightfully accused of being a lunatic. That's taking it too far. This has to be reasonably attainable. So suffering is part of life and there's no way any one of us is not going to suffer emotionally, psychologically, spiritually or physically. It's part of the life process and there's no way around it. But that's not the issue.*

"However, what you could say is that the experience of emotional, psychological or even physical suffering would not be an excuse not to live according to these higher principles that emerge in the evolutionary enlightenment context. That would be a different way of putting it. Doesn't that sound more reasonable?"

"Yes."

"Suffering is unethical," Andrew burst out in a fit of laughter. *"Wow! I'd have to say 'thank you very much and see you later' on that one.*

"Okay. So who else had their hand up? It was you?" he asked, pointing to an elderly German woman. *"Okay, yes."*

"Yesterday you said a sentence that struck me deeply," she began. "It was, 'the past is good.'"

"I said that it wasn't bad."

"Oh, yes. The past is not bad. So I am German and I thought it's impossible for me to accept this sentence. My past as a German does not feel good. So in order to accept this sentence I had to let go of something very deep and then I felt a very deep sorrow. There was compassion for what has happened and in that a very deep pain. And then I felt a great love, a love that was greater than the evil that happened."

All my attention went to this woman who, with her grey hair and kindly expression had to be about my mother's age. She, like my mother, had probably been a child during the Second World War and thus had witnessed the horror first hand. I immediately felt a thin sense of kinship with her for I too was at least marginally German, having spent the first ten years of my life growing up in Germany. Interestingly, throughout that time I knew little or nothing of the Second World War. I did know there had been a war because I had seen the gutted hulks of the many ruined buildings left standing in German cities to serve as a reminder to future generations. But I knew nothing of Nazis, the Holocaust, Hitler and the fascist legacy of my own people. It was not until I arrived in the States that I learned of the Second World War in all its gruesome brutality. This is understandable; what parent would tell that story to a child not even ten years old? Since those days, however, I'd thought a great deal about the legacy of my people and seeing the anguish in that aging woman's eyes brought those reflections back to me.

"When I said the past is good," Andrew's voice cut through my reflections, *"what I was speaking about was, as Ken Wilber would say, to transcend but include it. Because without the past we wouldn't be able to be where we are now. So even this dawning insight that 'I am the Creative Principle beginning to become aware of itself' has taken a long time to even begin to emerge as a potential in consciousness.*

"Now, it doesn't mean that everything that's happened in the past is good or everything that even we personally have done in the past is good. It doesn't mean that everything that's in our own past karma, individual or collective, is good. Not by any stretch of the imagination! But we have to understand that we're all standing upon the shoulders of our forefathers."

"Yes, that's true," she agreed.

"It's important to understand that some things in our individual and collective karma are evil. So if one was German, and if the horrors of what the German people

collectively did hasn't been faced on an individual basis, even if one physically had nothing to do with it – because if one is German then, at a soul level, that's going to be part of who one is – it's going to continue."

"Yes, that's right," she acknowledged.

"Because the way we free ourselves from the past is by facing everything without conditions which is what most people do not want to do. And this is also how we free ourselves from our personal history. You see, often, on a personal level, there are many things that we have done that have caused a lot of harm and created a lot of suffering.

"So unless we are willing to face our past, distant or recent, without conditions – and most people don't have the emotional strength and courage for this – we'll never be free from it. We have to face it all, and not only once, but always, you see?"

"Yes, I understand."

"So this is the third tenet of the teaching: facing everything and avoiding nothing. Ultimately, enlightenment means the self beyond ego. So it's only the ego that has a self-image that it wants to protect. For example, one might see oneself in this case as being a good German. They might say to themselves, 'I would never do anything like that.'"

"Yes."

"Because a lot of Germans are in denial, right?"

"Yes, that's right."

"Okay. So the image that the self has does not accurately represent the truth. The ego is an image that we have of ourselves that is false. And this is true in relationship to our collective past as well as our personal history. We all like to see ourselves in a very positive light.

"Now, if we are identifying less and less with the fears and desires of the individual and collective ego and more and more with the longing for liberation, there's going to be less and less fear, hesitation and resistance to facing absolutely everything about the self because the place that we're looking from won't be the ego. Therefore, we'll be able to bear whatever it is that we need to because we really do want to be free. We really, really do.

"We want to liberate our own capacity to experience consciousness and because we want to be free we'll find the strength and the moral courage to face what needs to be faced. And it's only through facing everything and avoiding nothing that we can free ourselves from the past. There's simply no other way that it can possibly happen.

"If you want to be free from the past in the present moment you have to be willing to face everything and avoid nothing right now and not just once but in every single moment. That's the liberated position in relationship to time and in relationship to individual and collective karma. And who and what we are is a mixture of those things.

"So initially there has to be a willingness to face everything and ultimately we want to get to the point where that's something that's happening naturally. Spontaneously *facing everything and avoiding nothing would be the goal you would aspire to reach and ultimately you'd want to get to the point where we couldn't do otherwise.*

"The liberated self couldn't do otherwise because in it the motive to avoid seeing anything other than it actually is would have been destroyed. So the ego, in the context of the third tenet of the teaching, is the motive to avoid. So as long as there's a motive to avoid there's going to be a divided self or, to use psychological terms, there's going to be a big shadow.

"I could say with an enormous degree of confidence that this is probably the most challenging part of the teaching for everyone. Most people have the biggest difficulty facing themselves unconditionally."

"I understand exactly what you are saying," she said, this time with conviction in her tone. "I feel that I'm quite courageous to go for my choice but I feel that I have one edge that I come up against again and again that I cannot overcome."

"Which is what?"

"To experience these states of consciousness really deeply. That means that I have to give myself up or to let go of myself completely. I feel like fighting for something that I want and I don't get it."

"What are you fighting for?"

"For complete freedom."

"So I'm not sure what you're saying now. What about it?"

"I feel that I can't go to these higher states of consciousness."

"Why not?"

"I don't know. I think there must be something in the way."

"Like what?"

"Maybe fear. I don't know."

"Oh, fear. The fear is the fear of emptiness, or the fear of zero. Zero means being nobody."

"Yes, probably that's it."

"Yes, that's the problem many people have. And women have more of a fear of zero or emptiness than men do, even though men also are frightened of it. It's called no sense of self that you can locate and no picture of yourself that you can identify."[1]

"Yes."

"It's like disappearing into emptiness. You can't find yourself anywhere. You can't locate yourself. There's only consciousness. There's no object there. A lot of people feel, 'If I can't find myself I don't want to go there.'"

"Right. Shall I stay with it then?"

"Well, it's just something to consider, don't you think?"

"I don't know if I can reach it by considering it."

"Why? Do you think it's too mental?"

"Yes, that's right."

"Why is that?"

"Maybe also because I am a woman."

"So women aren't good thinkers?"

"We are good thinkers but we must base it on true experience. That's my inner path, I feel."

"But do you think there's such a thing as a unique inner path? Isn't it the same for all of us in the end?"

"The principles are the same and the path is different."

"Okay, right. But what if we stop thinking about the fact that the path's different for everybody? Maybe that's a relative issue that's not absolutely important. Maybe what's more important is the simple truth of what we're speaking about that applies to all of us equally in every moment. Then that removes all these 'different paths for different people' ideas in a minute. Then you just have what's true and your relationship to it.

"'No,'" he said, now switching to the mildly mocking tone he loved to employ when laying bare questionable contemporary spiritual ideas. *"'I have my own way to go about it. And so does she. And so does he. We want to honor your path and she wants to honor hers and I need you to honor mine.'"*

"Well, I guess you go straight away to these states. And I don't know what my consciousness is doing. I mean it's obviously very different from yours."

Andrew laughed. *"So what's the good news? Are you happy?"*

"The good news is that…"

"Are you happy?"

"…your teaching fits…"

"Are you happy?"

"…in exactly in what I am needing and that is…"

"Are you happy?"

"Am I happy?" she suddenly asked herself reflectively. "I feel fulfilled."

"Well that usually means that one is happy."

"Yes," she laughed.

"'I'm feeling fulfilled,' is a pretty good definition of happiness, isn't it?"

"Yes."

"You see the reason there's a little struggle going on right now is because I'm really nailing everybody to the wall here. So I want you to appreciate what I'm doing. It's a little bit harder than just speaking about the absolute or non-relative nature of consciousness itself because we can all float up there forever. But this is the most help you can ever receive because I'm forcing you to take yourself on in the biggest possible context and it's very challenging to do that.

"So, I would encourage you to try and drop this whole idea of different people having different paths. You see it's only true relatively. It's a relative point that loses its significance when you begin to look at the absolute nature of what it is that we're speaking about. Then there's just the Truth, which you either recognize and acknowledge or

not. And if you do then there's the question of whether you're dealing with it right now or not. That's all there is to it. Then the different paths idea goes.

"Because even the whole notion of a path is a relative concept that involves time and an individual who has to go on a journey to get somewhere. So relatively speaking that's obviously true. But since this is an enlightenment context, in the non-dual dimension of all this, that's not true. There's just this larger perspective or Absolute Reality as it is and the degree to which we are we willing to deal with it and be true to it now.

"So facing everything and avoiding nothing unconditionally removes all obstacles. Now, nobody on God's earth can get you to face everything and avoid nothing. It's something we have to choose to do on our own.

"So, for example, yesterday we were speaking about transparency. What makes it possible to manifest transparency is when the individual faces everything and avoids nothing about themselves. Now, some people would say that it's not technically possible for any human being to do that. But I can tell you that it's possible to face everything and avoid nothing enough to achieve the goal that I'm speaking about and to make all the difference in the world. Do you understand?"

"Yes, thank you."

"So, just to get back to your original question. If the German people are going to really change, then individual Germans have to face this event. It has to be faced because it wasn't an individual that did that. It was, for the most part, all of the German people who collaborated. They weren't brainwashed. You can't be brainwashed unless you're willing to be brainwashed. You have to be willing to believe whatever it is. It's just like people who are in crazy cults. They have to want to believe things that don't make sense. When someone offers any one of us overly simplistic solutions to life's inherent complexity we have to want the burden of complexity to be removed from our shoulders in order to accept it. The thing is, life is inherently emotionally and psychologically complex and challenging.

"So, the worst part of each and every one of us doesn't want to deal with the complexity. And in order to not to have to face the complexity we'll often be willing to sell our soul, our higher conscience and our own deeper human instincts in order not to have to think for ourselves or bear the burden of complexity."

"That's right."

"And the Germans aren't the only ones. I mean, look what's happening in many places in the world today. There are many forms of the same kind of ethnic cleansing taking place.

"And you have to be able to see that even in all of us these lower tendencies exist. The capacity for unimaginable evil exists within us all. Part of it just has to do with certain lower level instincts and impulses that are involved with survival and domination. And when we have a highly sophisticated mind that is all hooked up with this biological mechanism that hasn't outgrown a lot of instincts of survival, domination

and control it creates a very complex and confusing picture. The fact is, given the right conditions there's no telling what we would be capable of doing. That's just true. It's actually been scientifically proven. So to what degree do we individually face our own capacity for evil, hmm? None of us ever knows what we're going to do in a very challenging situation. The only way to find out is by being tested and certain things we hope we're never going to have to find out. But nevertheless, part of facing everything and avoiding nothing also involves facing this part of ourselves. Do you get my point?"

"Yes."

"So, there's a lot that we need to be able to take responsibility for if we want to be a free, independent human being. And it has to with being able to handle knowing that we're capable of the most unspeakable evil as a real potential.

"Anyway, so what we've been speaking about this morning is the third tenet of the teaching."

"The word 'tenet.' You didn't explain it yet," the woman pointed out.

"Well, it just means those five circles." Andrew, using his laser pointer, indicated the large teaching model behind him on his left side. *"We call them tenets. They clearly explain how to do this. In other words, if, at the level of consciousness, you directly experience what it is that I'm speaking about all the time, the five tenets explain what the state of consciousness that you are experiencing is based on.*

"So when you're spontaneously experiencing a state of absolute freedom with no resistance and no fear whatsoever then you're going to want to be free more than anything else. You won't need to struggle with it. You won't be ambivalent about it at all. Do you understand?"

"Yes."

"You won't have any doubt whatsoever, not even in your little toenail. And because you have transcended the fears and desires of the individual and collective ego in a very fundamental way, the motive to avoid has also been significantly transcended. You see such an individual actually feels an emotional desire to be responsible for themselves. Can you imagine that? That's moral development. So the tenets say that if you're a free or liberated person, this would be what your relationship to life was naturally and spontaneously.

"And then it also says that if this is not your spontaneous condition but you want to be a liberated person, this is how you do it." He pointed at the model once more. *"So if that's not the case now, then you'd look into this first tenet, 'wanting to be free more than anything else,' which we've been doing, and then the second one, which is 'the law of volitionality,' which is about taking responsibility for yourself. Then, of course, there's the third one, 'facing everything and avoiding nothing.'*

"And ultimately you find they're really not separate. They describe one position. It's an enlightened position in relationship to the human experience. It's not divided into five separate pieces like it is here on the model but it's actually just one position. If you

want to be free then you're going to want to be responsible and you're going to want to face everything. Why? Because you want to be free. What could be simpler than that?"

"I understand now. It's very clear, thank you."

"So now we're talking about the third tenet. The thing about facing everything and avoiding nothing is that it's the way we burn up accumulated karma."

Andrew paused for a moment to look around the room at everyone. Then he asked, *"Does everybody know what bad karma is?"*

Some people answered in the affirmative and others in the negative so Andrew offered a brief discussion of his understanding of karma.

"Bad karma is experienced as an irrational conditioned response that's unwholesome and negative. That's the loosest way I could describe it. It's why we behave in crazy ways. So one way to look at this – and it's definitely not the only way – is that it's all the unconscious motives that we experience, in a very subtle but also very powerful way, that resist transparency, that resist this extraordinary call to evolve, that says, 'No!' to all of that. And while first you feel it emotionally as a visceral No!' eventually you just feel nothing. Ultimately, when you hang onto the 'No!' long enough, you don't even feel that any more; you just feel nothing. You feel dull. It's like when you stick a needle in somebody and they don't feel anything. Their nerves go dead.

"So you have physical nerves but you also have psychic nerves. They're the nerves that are connected to your soul and if you keep resisting they go dead and you can't even feel them any more. Then you don't even feel your own resistance. That's the worst possible state to be in. Now that's some bad karma," he laughed.

"But what that comes from first of all is your individual and collective past. So, for example, let's say someone was born in Germany. So, there's the fact that this evil had been perpetrated and that's a very hard thing to face. You don't have to have been part of it. Even to face the magnitude of it is ultimately challenging on a human level. You can imagine how much more difficult it would be to face if you knew that your own people, maybe even your own family, had been involved. Then that starts to touch you and implicate you whether you were involved or not. It would be very hard emotionally and psychologically to deal with that because we're dealing with a magnitude of evil that is impossible to grasp. Right?"

"Right," the woman replied very quietly.

"So then there would be fear and you'd be withdrawing and then maybe turning away. So how that would show up in conditioned behavior would be through avoidance and denial and that would affect your personality. Wouldn't it?"

"Yes. Yes it would." Her voice had grown quieter still.

"There'd be a lack of awareness. You'd start to feel overcome by all kinds of feelings that you couldn't control and didn't understand. And also certain things might make you angry that shouldn't and you wouldn't be able to control the anger. There would be all these kinds of things. Right?"

"Yes."

"So I'm just using this as an example of conditioned behavior. Now, once again, conditioned behavior can be a result of what has happened to us. For example if you were just born in Germany at a particular time then you're going to have to suffer the consequences one way or another simply because that's where you showed up. Right?"

"Yes."

"So then it could also be what happened to you when you were younger. And there's also the possibility that you brought things with you. So if we look at evolution in a context of the possibility of reincarnation, which might be a part of it, then maybe we don't come here with a clean slate. Maybe there are a lot of conditioned responses we're bringing in with us.

"So there's all of that and then, at a certain point when we're very young, we start responding. And as we begin participating we're going to start creating karma ourselves for a lot of good reasons. So, there's a lot of all that in all of us and how it manifests is in blind, unconscious, deeply conditioned behavior.

"So one way to define bad karma is that it would mean the existence of these negative impulses that were very emotionally charged and that we either felt strongly, or were in denial of and didn't even feel at all, but that still existed. These, of course, incapacitate our own potential for a real spiritual vitality. So that's my definition of bad karma and there's a lot of it. Do you understand?"

"Yes, I do," she said. Small tears showed in the corners of her eyes as the weight of it all saddled her soul, yet simultaneously a slight smile curved the corner of her mouth as the possibility of freedom from it all also appeared before her.

Listening to this exchange time seemed to slow as the sum of my own half-digested ruminations upon my German heritage welled up from deep within myself (these are discussed in Appendix 5, On Being German – Reflections on Facing Everything and Avoiding Nothing). I considered all of it in light of the third tenet, though I had never done so as deeply as at the moment I heard Andrew's exchange with this sweet German lady. It convinced me that there was more for me to face and I was reminded of an excerpt from the third tenet, the reading of which formed part of my weekly practice:

> "What does it really mean to face everything and avoid nothing? It means we have to ceaselessly inquire into the true nature of what it is that is motivating us to make the choices that we make. Do we have the humility to face into the aggressive and frighteningly selfish nature of many our own actions? Do we have that kind of courage? Because if we refuse to face the darkest parts of ourselves, we will never be able to transcend them. Only if we truly want to be free more than anything else will we find the integrity of interest that will enable us to face everything and avoid nothing, no matter how difficult or challenging it may be.
>
> "But facing everything means facing everything, not only our darkest impulses. Facing everything means daring to face wholeheartedly into the infinite depth our

own Self, a depth that reveals a mystery so awe-inspiring that it simply cannot be imagined. But more often than not, we're unwilling…to face the profoundly liberating implications of our own potential because we're simply not prepared to accept that which our mind cannot comprehend. Always living in denial of our darkness and ever fearful of the overwhelming brightness of our own unexplored heights, the inevitable result can only be mediocrity."[2]

It was this last line that always struck me most deeply and which burned most brightly in my reflections. It occurred to me that this was precisely what we'd been doing since retreat's outset – facing into the "infinite depth of our own Self" and its liberating potential as well as the darkness that inhabits us all so that we might transcend the selfish mediocrity that defines so many of our lives and embrace our birthright as co-creators of the conscious universe. It is this vision that has consistently inspired me and given me the wherewithal to keep pushing against myself, to face into my own inertia and unexamined motivations of which, I was certain, there was more than a little yet to be faced.

"And what keeps all this bad karma alive," someone said from the audience as I turned my attention from my own thoughts back to the teaching, "is that we're not willing to face it or look at it, right?"

"What keeps it alive," Andrew responded, *"is not being aware of it. When you're not aware of it you blindly act out of it. But what makes it more problematic is when you are aware of it and then you deny it."*

"I can understand that."

"That changes everything because, up until that point, you know you're ignorant. It doesn't mean you're innocent! It means you're ignorant. There's a big difference," he laughed. *"But in an evolutionary context, if you actually become aware of it and then choose to resist it, it makes everything much worse.*

"You see opening yourself up in this was is not a game. It's like opening up a Pandora's box and it takes a lot of courage. That's why the first tenet is so fundamental. Because if you, whoever you are, want to be free more than anything else, you'll be able to take it. If you don't want to be free it'll be too much for you emotionally and psychologically and you'll resist and deny it. Then you'll be in worse shape than you were before you even knew because, as much as you deny it, part of you can never forget. So then you end up in a really bad place. Now, many of you have probably heard the line that, with respect to the authentic spiritual path, it's better never to start than to start and not finish. The reason why is that you start playing around with things that you shouldn't play around with unless you intend to really follow through because if you stop you're going to be much worse off than you were before you ever started. So again, the wanting to be free more than anything else makes all things possible. This is something I've been saying since I began teaching and it's as true today as it was then.

"*So this third tenet is an expression and manifestation of the liberated state or relationship to life and it's also the hardest and most challenging one to practice for obvious reasons. But if you want to be free more than anything else you're not going to resist. Why? Because what you want is freedom! So whatever it is, you'll be able to handle it.*"

"So there are really no excuses whatsoever for not handling whatever comes up?"

"*Well, as I said, if you're serious then you do and if you're not you won't. It's a personal choice. But the hardest part of the path of evolutionary enlightenment is this particular aspect of it. It has to do with attachment to the self-image. If you're really invested in seeing yourself in a particular way you're just not going to be able to do it. You see, the image has to go, the image has to go, the image has to go…*" Andrew repeated this five or six more times for emphasis.

"*So ultimately you have to go from knowing who you are to not having any idea. That's the leap she was speaking about.*" He pointed back to the elderly German woman. "*It's going from knowing to not knowing. Now, for most people it's terrifying not to have any idea who they are but if you really want to be free you have to be willing to hold that position of not having any idea for more than a second.*

"*And in the same way with inquiry, as I was speaking to this man about earlier,*" he pointed to the young man with whom he'd started this morning's teaching. "*You have to be coming from this not knowing who you are and then go into it, not sitting off to the side in a safe, comfortable place. If you sit on the side in a comfortable position it's just ideas. But if you step out of that fixed sense of self it becomes a dynamic, creative, explosive process. Get the idea?*"

"Yes, I do. Thank you."

Andrew moved on, his dark eyes shot through with light as they scanned the room. Soon they fell upon on the delicate features of a thirty-something Swedish woman.

"As I considered wanting to be free more than anything else," she said, "I realized that I had always thought of the Authentic Self as personal. That's why I thought that the soul was my access to higher consciousness. And, now I realize that the Authentic Self is impersonal." She laughed out the last line with a sense of recognizing something so obvious that it seemed nearly absurd.

"*It's not personal,*" Andrew agreed.

"No. I can see that. And that's probably why I didn't really know what to think about my soul as we were talking about it yesterday."

"*So it's a big step when you realize that it isn't personal. So the enlightened mind is not a personal place, is it? Hmm?*"

"No, it's not."

"*It doesn't have a masculine face or a feminine face, does it?*"

"No. Not at all!"

"Now, the soul has been very popular for millennia," Andrew laughed along with everyone else. *"But you can imagine that as we evolve, how we see it is going to change. But in order for it to change we have a lot of work to do. You see, as I've been saying over the last few days, you can experience instantaneous radical liberation from the individual and collective soul and all the karma inherent in it right now. But it's not enough. You have to face all that karma to really be free of it because, although the Authentic Self doesn't have any karma... we do!*

"But you can begin to see what could be possible if we really did this. Imagine the kind of beings we could become over a long period of time if we finally freed ourselves from all this heavy baggage. It would actually be quite extraordinary. So, in terms of a long-term trajectory, you could see what could be possible in the distant future if people like us do our part now. See what I'm saying? So then you want to see that the part that you could potentially be playing in this larger developmental context is quite enormous."

Once again, Andrew managed to explode the limiting ways I thought about the significance of my own potential for transformation. Once again, he had the bigger view. And contemplating it challenged my mind's plasticity, stretching it in dimensions and directions I'd not imagined possible. What might we be like in five thousand years if this new being emerged? How would radical autonomy and perfect communion transform the face of humanity? What could we accomplish? At length my imagination failed me, except that I knew it would be good

Andrew looked around the room, and then turned to a thirty-something Dutch woman with short blond hair and piercing blue eyes.

She said, "The other day when I was meditating I went from the zero point to the creative impulse and experienced a beautiful vision. But I quickly lost my bearings because it scared the hell out of me..."

"Wow, that's cool," Andrew said, genuinely impressed. *"That means you really stepped outside yourself in that instant."*

"Yeah and I've been in a process since because I can see that my ego has a different agenda than my Authentic Self."

"Definitely."

"Where I get lost is the gap between where I am today and where I'm going to be if I'm going to do this. On the one hand I feel like it's not a choice but rather something I have to do. On the other, I feel like I will end up there eventually anyway."

"Well, the ego probably gets kind of scared there, right."

"Yes, and I'm trying to redefine the wanting to be free more than anything else in this light."

"It's all in your hands."

"Right," she said quietly.

"There are no guarantees in life," Andrew said in a direct tone. *"Did you know that?"*

"Yes, of course. I know that," she responded, humbled and conciliatory in the face of the obvious.

Andrew turned his gaze to the teenagers sitting on the floor directly in front of him. *"Did you guys know that?"* he queried.

They smiled agreeably and nodded in such a way that it was impossible to tell whether or not what he'd said had actually landed.

"Did you know that God doesn't give you a slip when you come into the world that says, 'I guarantee you're going to have a good life.'" His impish smile was greeted with a few chuckles and additional nodding from the kids.

"Nobody told me that," he added emphatically. *"I always had some crazy idea that you were entitled to have a good life. I think that if you come from a good enough background that's one of the things you falsely assume. Well, it's not true."*

I considered what he said and at that instant realized that not only had that long been true for myself, but in many ways it continues to be. In tandem with this realization I recalled a recent teaching during which Andrew had pointed out that our generation was the first ever in the hundred thousand year span of human history in which people were routinely asked, "Honey, what would you like to do when you grow up?" I'd never actually thought about this and hearing it was an awakening to the fact that we enjoy unprecedented and, until very recently, literally unimaginable freedoms with the casual ease of a teenager popping gum. I had also never thought about the next consideration Andrew had suggested, namely the impact of this question on the developing psyche of a child. The effect would be akin to an I.V. drip injecting a steady dose of "Life is your oyster, darling. It's here for you to do with what you want" into the matrix of the child's developing mind. Now, while all this was indeed the product of hard won civic and economic freedoms and nothing we would want to relinquish, simply considering the impact of these freedoms on one's mind is an interesting exercise. In so doing one finds yet another of the many causes underlying the pathological narcissism afflicting our time. The message kids need to hear these days, Andrew liked to point out, was not, "It's your life, do whatever your little heart desires," but rather, "life needs you. As the beneficiary of so much good fortune, what will you bring to it?" Hearing this always caused me to slow down and re-evaluate the network of assumptions that formed the backdrop of my own life and, as of late, make adjustments in attitude accordingly.

"I think that if you're born poor and miserable," he went on, *"you know that that's not true. Of course, that's not necessarily good either. But in light of the fact that we're not guaranteed a good life, good health, happiness, longevity or anything else, the choice to be free more than anything else becomes all the more urgent.*

"Again, if you consciously or unconsciously assume that somehow it will all work itself out in my life you have to let in that that's not necessarily the case at all. In fact, it usually doesn't work out that well in the end, does it?" He paused for effect, and

then rhetorically asked once more, *"Does it usually work out fabulously?"* before answering his own question, *"No."*

After another pause and with a little smile he added the punch line. *"But it can if you want it to."* Turning his attention back to the woman who'd originally asked the question, he said, *"Does that make sense?"*

"Yes," she replied.

"But that's a big deal because it involves you taking control of the car. You wake up and jump out of the back seat where you've been sleeping and go 'Oh my god, what's happening?' as you leap into the front seat where you take control of the vehicle – literally!

"And then life can be quite extraordinary and fabulous, though not necessarily easy. It's still going to be ultimately challenging but because you've found out who you are and why you're here, and because of the discovery of an absolute commitment you're completely engaged with the whole process and that's what changes everything. It really does. Are you with me?"

"Yes, I am. So what I really need is more surrender, right?"

"Well, that's the whole point, because there's just no way we can know about the future. So since that's just the bottom line what we need to become clear about is 'Who am I and why am I here?' It's when you discover the answer to these questions that you can know what the most appropriate relationship to the life experience would be and then assume that position. That's when the show really begins. That's when a new life begins. Everything leading up to that doesn't really count. Of course, it counts to the ego because it says, 'Well, that's my life and that's everything.' But when you awaken to the Authentic Self it's the start of a completely different life. It literally feels discontinuous. Of course many things are going to continue as they did before but on a fundamental or soul level you're going to be living a completely different life for completely different reasons. It's literally like living one life and then living another. You see?"

"Yes, I do. Thank you."

Andrew looked at his watch, which lay stretched on the carpet in front of him. We'd been going at it for about two hours and the atmosphere in the room bristled with a current of meditation that showed no signs of abating. Andrew looked around and called on yet another woman, the men having remained strangely mute during this teaching.

Also German, she said, "Yesterday you talked about the shift between the position of the ego and the position of the Authentic Self and that can happen in a split second."

"Right."

"Well, I experienced that rather strongly. The day before yesterday I inquired deeply into the issue of wanting to be free more than anything else and the answer that came was, 'I'd rather not.' Then yesterday I was in a group where we sought to locate the choosing faculty and what I experienced was that giving that interested part of me more attention suddenly changed the whole picture."

"Right. That's what happens."

"And also being with a group that was inquiring collectively really raised the energy."

"Of course. That's because the Authentic Self in one calls the Authentic Self in others to itself. That's the whole point. If you're together with another individual or individuals who are really manifesting this perspective it can pull you out of your ego just like that." Andrew snapped his fingers. *"And then in an instant you can see how totally insane you were just five seconds before. Am I exaggerating?"*

"No, not at all."

"That's how extreme it is. So it's good that you came out of it but it's bad when you realize how crazy we are. Hmm?"

"Yes."

"The thing is, the state of being crazy in and of itself isn't problematic. It's what we do when we're in that state that's the problem. See?"

"Yes, definitely."

Following that exchange, Andrew went on to the next question. This time he called on a Dutch man who, judging by the familiarity of their initial greeting, he seemed to have known for some time.

"I've been struggling with the question of wanting to be free for a long time now and inside me it feels like some kind of inner court of law. So with respect to this question, I can hear the ego go, 'well…'"

"Sounds like the other side has a good Dutch lawyer," Andrew cut him off good-naturedly, as everyone laughed.

"That's why I wanted to ask you about caging the ego." The man pointed to a smaller model behind Andrew entitled simply "Caging the Ego." "I think you've already spoken about it but if you have some good clues about how to actually do it, it would be very helpful in this inner court of law."

"No," said Andrew. *"You have to take responsibility for that yourself. No one can help you with that."*

"I think I can identify what the ego wants to do…"

Once again, Andrew cut him off. *"You have to go up to the lawyer on the other side and just take a gun and pull the trigger."* An explosion of laughter burst through the room. When it had died down a bit he added, *"Then you walk out of court a free man,"* which called for yet another round of slightly hysterical laughter.

"I didn't think about that one," the man quipped. "Thank you, now I know."

He was ready to let it go at that but Andrew had more to say. *"You know, it's a rational discussion up to a point but beyond a certain point it becomes irrational to keep talking about things to which you already know the answer."*

"That's the conclusion? That the answer…" the man began.

"When you're having a debate about something you've already found the answer to," Andrew cut across him to drive his point home more deeply, *"that's irrational.*

If you don't know and it's something you're in the process of understanding then you need to have a line of inquiry in order to understand it. But once you've completely understood it, there's nothing to talk about, is there?"

"No, there isn't," he said sheepishly.

"The thing is, if you want to keep talking about it it's because you're convinced philosophically and intellectually but not emotionally. That's the problem and that's a very bad place to be. It's a real predicament.

"So what do you do then? Do you give the emotional discomfort weight and importance or not? If you do so then you dig yourself into a hole. And if you keep holding on to the significance of the emotional resistance what's going to happen over time is that you're going to start to reinterpret the conclusion you've already come to and rewrite the whole thing. You're going to start seeing that black is white and white is black, not because it is but because you want it to be. Do you see what I'm saying?"

"Yes, I think so."

"Well, in other words, one can engage in a philosophical, spiritual, even moral line of inquiry which, if it's done ethically, is going to lead to certain conclusions. Now, the conclusions that are reached will be objectively valid based on your own criteria. However, that doesn't mean that emotionally your ego is going to be happy about it. In other words, objectively you might come to certain conclusions that emotionally you don't like. It's basically how a little child feels when they can't get what they want. The little child doesn't care if they've already had three ice creams and you say they can't have a fourth one. If they're really a spoiled brat they might throw a temper tantrum. They don't care.

"In the same way, the little spoiled child inside each of us doesn't care what's rationally appropriate, let alone experience concern about higher philosophical and spiritual principles. So you can engage in the kind of philosophically, spiritually and morally driven inquiry that we've been pursuing here in a way that's intellectually sound and reach certain conclusions, yet simultaneously find that emotionally they will make you feel horrible. That's when you start to see the gap or the division in the self. That's why there are two different models in the teaching." He turned briefly to look over each shoulder and shone the red dot from his laser pointer on the large models on either side of him.

"So when that happens, many people think, 'oh, I haven't thought about it deeply enough.' But it's not true. They have actually already thought about it deeply and they can think it through again a hundred times. But they will still come to the same conclusion and continue to find that emotionally it still feels terrible.

"So then they're in a predicament. They can either go with the conclusions that they've come to simply because they're right although it feels wrong in which case they're going with their higher faculties. Or they can do the opposite and go with how it feels while completely denying all the conclusions that they themselves have come to. In other words, they can go with what feels emotionally justified but is morally and philosophically corrupt.

"Of course, what we want is that the conclusions that we've come to after we've done a rigorous moral, ethical, philosophical inquiry make us feel good."

"But that doesn't happen?"

"Well, it can and will happen but you have to pay a price for that. It can happen if you let go of the ego. But if you don't, the highest and most appropriate conclusions are going to make you feel terrible. That's just how it works.

"But it gets worse because if you deny your higher faculties and the conclusions that you yourself have come to through spiritual and philosophical inquiry and go with your emotional conviction you fall into self-deception. That's when you start lying to yourself and distorting the facts, because what we all desperately want is for our world-view to line up with our emotional conviction. But if you choose the ego then your worldview is going to have to accommodate the ego's preferences, which are going to differ significantly from the conclusions you came to when you weren't acknowledging them and just wanted to know what was true? Are you with me?"

"Yeah," the man said soberly.

"Whew, that was hard," Andrew said, wiping his brow for effect. More laughter swept through the room before he continued. *"What I'm saying is very important with respect to this realignment and recalibration of the self. You see the idea is that through using your best rational, philosophical, moral and spiritual capacities for profound inquiry you recalibrate and restructure your own worldview. And once you've done that based on your own criteria then you have to drag the rest of yourself along. Do you get my point?"*

A collective yes issued from the group.

"This is the unspoken, nitty-gritty truth about transformation and it's absolutely scientific. The problem is that most of us are quite corrupt in the sense that there's an enormous gap between where we're capable of seeing and where and how we live and who and how we are. That's the gap we want to bridge through spiritual cultivation, development and evolution. It's that gap that shows you the absolute contradiction between the ego's position and the mind of enlightenment.

"So the sincere individual has to bear the emotional discomfort. Because the fact is that if you're not willing to bear the emotional discomfort of the enormous contradictions that exist within you someone else is going to have to suffer the consequences.

"So your capacity to be able to cognize this and grapple with the gap between what makes perfect sense and how insane we are emotionally is very important. Remember, in post-modern, secular culture there is no moral, philosophical, spiritual, ethical context for human life. So we're not in the habit of thinking this way about life, about ourselves and about self-cultivation, are we? Therefore, if we're products of a materialistic, narcissistic culture nothing could be more disturbing than thinking a lot about things like this. But it's good to be disturbed for the right reasons," he said with an exclamatory clap of his hands. *"Don't you think?"*

We all agreed, the moral and ethical logic behind these assertions being unassailable. Apparently having nothing more to say on that subject, Andrew went on to summarize the morning's teaching.

"So between now and when we meet at five I want everybody just to consider this. First of all, we talked about the third tenet, facing everything and avoiding nothing. We saw that the individual and collective ego has a big motive to avoid a lot. At the same time we saw that the aspiration to be free more than anything else means becoming one with the evolutionary impulse, which is the Authentic Self, in which there is no motive to avoid anything.

"And the other thing I was speaking about involves entering into an inspired line of philosophical and spiritual inquiry, reaching certain conclusions that make perfect sense to us, and then finding that there's a big gap between what we see makes perfect sense and how we feel emotionally. Then it's understanding that bridging that gap is what spiritual practice is all about and also that it is possible to get to the point where the conclusions that you come to after going through that line of inquiry will make you feel very good.

"And you have to understand that this shift from our fundamental choices in life being emotionally based to being more philosophically and spiritually inspired has to happen. Of course we would all like to always be in touch with the emotional implications of spiritual and philosophical truth, but, hey, it might not happen. Maybe your life's going to be a lot more complicated than that. Maybe you've identified with the fears and desires of the ego for so long that it's something you're going to have to be negotiating with, maybe forever. Maybe not, but that's a possibility.

"Therefore, maybe the only way to do it that's reliable and not dependent upon emotions and feelings has to do with making the effort to become very clear about what 'The Way' is. And that can be cultivated. And also, when you are true to what 'The Way' is, even if you feel very much the opposite, it gives you confidence in yourself. That means that your own clarity and insight and realization is the stronger part of who you are as a human being than the emotions connected to your ego. And then you're not a slave to your lower emotions any more. That's the beginning of a real, liberated self. Do you see how sane that is? There are no metaphysics in that. There's no leap of faith. You don't have to trust something that you can't see. Do you see how important that is for a post-metaphysical, rational, evolutionary spirituality?"

We all answered soberly in the affirmative.

"Calling people to be rational sounds good but to pull it off in real life is an enormous leap that requires an tremendous commitment. Do you all get the idea?"

More affirmatives and with that the teaching concluded.

After Andrew had left the room I took my now familiar walk across the plaza under the balmy weight of a sunny day. The smell of the cheese vendors, the rattle of trolley cars and the glint of golden mugs of beer greeted me on my way to meditation. While I was not nearly as troubled as I had been on previous days, thanks to speaking with Andrew, I was increasingly aware of the machinery of my psyche, of its drives and motivations and the growing intensity of its demands. I had not spoken in eight and a half days, had jailed my steadfast companion, the ego, and was engaged in rigorous spiritual practice for seventeen hours a day. I was also exhausted from cumulative sleep deprivation. My psychic defenses had been ground down and with those defenses beaten back the divided reality of my inner condition confronted me remorselessly.

Stripped bare of pretense, what did I see glaring at me? When I looked unflinchingly, what was it that I most wanted from life? It was all quite simple, actually. I wanted the variegated sexual experiences of a Middle Eastern sheikh, that desire swelling by the hour; the widespread appreciation of my creative genius together with an attendant bumper crop of material bounty; and most importantly, to suffer no service or obligation to anyone or anything. Hey, I wanted to be a rock star. And, after all, who didn't? But there was more. I addition to this profusion of desires and my full appreciation of their perfectly banal nature, I further discovered enormous resistance to letting them go. For years this had been a source of great confusion and I had long attempted to negotiate a truce between those warring sides of myself. And while I had begun to come to a rational understanding of the forces at work, emotionally this did not help at all. And herein lay the challenge – how to stand my ground in the face of the overwhelming temptation not to do so. Doing the right thing even when it didn't feel like the right thing to do; *especially* when it didn't feel like the right thing to do. This was the spiritual battleground on which the mettle of each of us would be tested and on which the character of our souls would be forged. And on this field I swayed between my commitment to stand against the powers of ego and my desire to join their ranks. The clash of these forces ravaged me, tearing into my meditation with lurid fantasies and visions and causing my chanting to stumble like a drunk on a cobbled street. Over the next several hours that battle raged.

When I found myself seated in the teaching hall again, the keening winds from the canyon gusting wildly into the hall, I was raw and exhausted. I just wanted to do what I wanted to do and be relieved of this interminable grinding. As Andrew entered the room, I pulled together the frayed ends of my attention in the hope that his wisdom and transmission would yet again provide a lifeline to sanity.

"I want to continue where we left off earlier in the day," he began. *"We were speaking about the discovery of a moral, ethical, philosophical, and spiritual context that made perfect sense yet that we felt very ambivalent about emotionally. It's that split between our higher rational capacities and the narcissistic self's innate disinterests in moral obligation, a spiritual and philosophical context, a hierarchy of values, universal truths, and so on."*

Andrew paused a few moments with a look that clearly invited questions. None came.

"Have you thought about that a little bit?" he pressed after a moment of silence. *"It's not irrelevant."* The silence, rather than lifting, deepened. *"Does that mean yes, you've been thinking about it?"* he asked again, pushing for a response. *"It's actually very, very important. You see, we can speak about the evolution of consciousness in*

many different ways but one of the most hands-on, realistic and authentic ways to talk about it has to do with this real split in the self."

Silence.

"*Does that mean yes? Is everybody with me on this? I can't tell because hardly anybody's raising their hand.*"

There were some uncomfortable stirrings in the room and I suspect that most others were as stunned as I was in the face of the same forces that had so insisted themselves upon me. Finally a Dutch woman raised her hand.

Andrew indicated in her direction. "*Okay, what did you have to say about it?*"

She took the mike rather hesitantly but finally spoke. "When I was looking into the part of me that didn't want to evolve I saw the shadow side of my ego and for the first time I understood that when I'm in the shadow side of the ego I'm really messing stuff up and I realized that that creates karma. So for the first time I really got in my body what karma really is."

"*Okay, that's very good but I want to speak specifically about this split in the self. You see, this is an evolutionary issue and very few people are this interested in evolution.*" Andrew looked around as silent tension lingered in the room. No one responded so he went on. "*For some reason you guys are making me repeat myself. But I want you to think about this deeply because this really is the whole thing.*" Nothing. "*Is it humiliating? Maybe that's the reason why you're not responding. Personally I find it very exciting.*"

Quietly the Dutch woman said, "It feels like that's what the work is."

"*Yeah, definitely it is. Maybe it's more obvious to you than it is to me.*"

"Our commitment has to make us do it even when we don't want to or we're all caught up in our emotions."

"*Right. But the point I'm trying to make is that when you think about the evolution of consciousness in a spiritual context you think about it in terms of the experience of higher states of consciousness, bliss, and swirling, thrilling insights, right?*"

"Yeah, right."

"*So how those swirling insights and ecstatic revelations become a concrete manifestation of evolutionary transformation in real time has to do with what we're talking about now, which is a little bit more demanding, you see?*"

"Yes, I do."

"*I'm talking about you and me here. That's what makes this very real. It takes all the mystery out of it. You see, the evolution of consciousness is a very romantic and inspiring concept, but this is the brass tacks. It involves first having an ecstatic experience of your pure evolutionary potential at the level of consciousness itself because that's what's going to convince you emotionally that it's something you're interested in. But then you have to ask what the implications of the evolution of consciousness are. What does it actually mean? That's what we've been doing. Now, once that's been established then we're confronted with a gap between where we want to go because it makes perfect sense to the best part of our self and where we're really dug in emotionally.*"

She had nothing to say.

"Okay. I guess it's not a very popular topic so far."

Andrew looked around the room once more where a few hands were finally beginning to rise.

Soon he called on an American man with whom he'd spoken a few days earlier. He asked, "We had this discussion after lunch today where we just focused on the third tenet and were distinguishing between when we were on the edge of something and when we were avoiding something. And in that we had this collective realization that that was something that could change very, very quickly."

"Oh yes," Andrew said brightly, *"that's the beauty of it because remember, we've been talking about free agency, haven't we?"*

"Yes, we have."

"And I was talking about how glorious and important this is as an emergent evolutionary potential. That should be more than enough to make everybody happier than they can even bear. But I know you guys don't really appreciate it because you're not looking at your own emergence in a cosmic – which means fourteen billion year – context. You're just looking at your own little, tiny, minuscule, hardly even measures on the scale, brief flash in the pan existence and thinking it's a big deal. But how could it possibly be a big deal?" Andrew laughed. *"In terms of evolutionary time, one life hardly counts. So what I'm saying is that this emerging recognition of free agency at this developmental level between world-centric and cosmo-centric is a really big deal.*

"Believe me, you take it for granted. But if you really begin to look at your own experience in nothing less than a cosmic context you won't take the notion of free agency for granted. Even in relationship to the emergence of civil rights, the liberation of women, the notion of equality in relationship to freedom of choice, the emergence of the choosing faculty is very new in terms of our evolutionary development. But in spite of that you all take it for granted, right?"

Of course we all did and we mumbled in something like agreement.

"Yet now we're applying the whole notion of freedom of choice at the highest possible level, which is in relationship to the evolution of consciousness."

Andrew paused to get a sense of the atmosphere in the room. *"I still feel that many of you don't really get what a big deal it is because you take it for granted. You shouldn't do that.*

"You have to look beyond your own little life here. Otherwise you're not going to get the energy or the passion or the courage to do this. You really have to make the effort to become aware of the context. This doesn't come naturally and believe me, the context is always bigger than you think. Now, once you become intellectually aware of it you then have to become emotionally connected with the implications of being part of this enormous context. Then you will not take it for granted. You'll feel how precious it is and you'll treasure it. This is the only way consciousness is going to evolve.

"Evolutionary consciousness is not going to descend from the heavens, you see. Consciousness from this point on is only going to evolve through the awakening of this volitional faculty in the individual. If you have sex and your children have sex and your children's children have sex, that's not going to produce the evolution of consciousness. It's going to produce the raw materials. However, the evolution of consciousness now is not like biological evolution because — and this is the whole point — to the degree that consciousness awakens to itself or becomes aware of itself is the degree to which evolution itself falls into the hands of the self that recognizes the process. Once that happens, it's up to you. Do you understand?"

I understood, though no doubt dimly in relation to the depth possible with respect to this weighty philosophical point.

"This is a very hard thing to communicate to people," Andrew went on. *"Remember, there's nobody 'up there' and 'nothing out there.' Therefore, the degree to which we realize this is the degree to which it is up to us and only us. "Us" means whoever it is that's actually realizing this. It's not going to happen by itself. If it were we wouldn't have to waste our time on a retreat like this."*

"Right," the man agreed.

"Well, obviously that's not the case."

"No, clearly not."

"So you have to see that your aspiration to awaken, to evolve and develop spiritually demands your response to it. After all, it takes two to tango. It's just like sex. Sex is a creative act, at least theoretically."

"Right," he hesitated.

"But in the creative dimension two have to come together. There's an engagement. And it's the same with the evolutionary impulse. It will emerge in consciousness, but then the individual has to respond to that awakening. And the intensity of the response itself creates this friction or this fire that drives the development of higher consciousness. That's where the whole notion of free agency or conscious choice enters into the picture and that's why it's really everything. So as I've been saying repeatedly, there's the pure ecstatic, revelatory experience of insight through which you realize your evolutionary potential at the level of consciousness. It's like when you fall in love and get into kind of an ecstatic, drunken state, but only temporarily. Temporarily you see what things could be like if you were really living according to the highest principles. It's not the best example but it's the only one I could come up with." He laughed apologetically. *"But do you understand what I mean?"*

Everyone nodded.

"That's a real experience of ecstatic free-flowing unity with the absence of conflict. And it's a free ride for a while but after a while you realize, 'Oh, it's not that easy. This is going to take some work."

Having been married for over twenty years the truth of that remark was inescapable. In the wake of that truth, the uneasy silence still hung about the room.

Picking up on it Andrew said, *"I can't tell if I am I doing something wrong?"*

"No, no," said the man with whom he'd been speaking. "I think we're just actively avoiding that very fact that we are..."

"I wouldn't even say that," Andrew interjected. *"I'm just not sure. Maybe everybody's already got it and I'm repeating myself pointlessly."*

"No, I don't think so," the man insisted.

"Oh, okay. You see, for me the simplicity and clarity of it as well as its comprehensive nature thrills me to no end. I endlessly delight in the inclusive nature of what it is that I'm trying to share with everybody here." He said this with almost childlike glee.

For a few moments Andrew added nothing more, then slowly turned his attention to an English woman with whom he had spoken previously.

"I'm actually not sure if this applies because I was looking into facing everything and avoiding nothing and I was kind of taking it layer by layer into my individual experience because, as you said, we have to really look into it as ourselves."

"That's right."

"So I got to a point where I really saw my ego and how I think I'm really great, you know?"

"Yeah, we know about that," Andrew said slightly impatiently.

"But it was just such a realization. Like here I am thinking I'm so great when I'm actually not. When I look at my life and the things I've done and not done it just kind of hit me."

"But you see, the point is that narcissism is a kind of strange and false presumption that we're great that's not based on any evidence. But at the same time, I think that from an evolutionary standpoint we should aspire to be great, but our aspirations for greatness needs to be demonstrated. In other words, we need to do great things. Then we actually will be great and there will be evidence of that fact which is something else altogether. But in terms of the narcissism there's this strange presumption, 'I'm great because I exist.'"

"Actually, my thought was more that I'm doing pretty good. So then, when I was really being honest with myself, I said to myself, 'Wow, you think you're doing pretty good but are you actually doing good?' I mean, when I really look, when I really face everything, am I really doing that great?"

"Yeah, right. Well, the question's relative. Doing good compared to what? If you say, compared to the other crazy, deluded narcissists, yeah, you might be doing okay. But if you really look at this in terms of the evolution of consciousness it changes everything."

"Yeah, that's right. And as I looked at it I felt a deep sense of humility in recognizing that I could even think that I'm so great."

"But we all have to assume that we probably are narcissists. Maybe you're not but the likelihood is yes, you are. Now, I'm not blaming anybody for it. It's not our fault. It just that that's our lot in life. If you're born in very lucky circumstances with wealth and opportunity and the message is that life is your playground, you can't help but draw the conclusion that you're great."

"Yeah, so even though the whole thing felt kind of heavy, the discovery of this humility was actually the best part of the experience."

"So, look," Andrew said, pointing over his shoulder to the Authentic Self model behind him, *"humility's there."* His little red laser dot danced on the word.

"Yeah, I saw that."

"And what's on the other side of it?" Andrew asked, pointing to the ego model over his other shoulder.

"Arrogance."

"Yeah, that's it. You see, a lot of people think arrogance is kind of an angry state but it's not. For most people it's simply a barely conscious conviction that they're better and it's hard to get them to even become aware of it. It's a very subtle and also not really subtle conviction that you're better than the other."

"Yeah, so this kind of feeling of being humble puts you right down at the bottom again."

"You don't have to be at the bottom. I think that in relation to what we're speaking about here a more appropriate way to understand it is that you don't presume you're better. In fact, you're not presuming anything in particular."

"Yeah, so that's why it kind of puts you at the Ground of Being because in humility there's no face."

"Exactly right. That's the idea."

"It becomes what you call transparency."

"That's how it works. So as I was saying before, you have to understand that there's going to be a very challenging gap between our capacity to experience our evolutionary potential at the level of consciousness and the way we actually operate in real time as real human beings. It's that gap that needs to be negotiated. Does that make sense?"

A very solemn "yes" issued from the group.

"If you get that and become inspired to respond to it then you're going to be in very good shape. Why? Because it means you're going to want to embrace the transformative implications of the higher state experiences, which will challenge you ultimately for all the reasons that we've been speaking about. It's the emotional willingness to do that, which is the wanting it more than anything else that creates the actual capacity to do it. It's that that will enable us to find some way to be victorious in the face of the emotional embeddedness.

"Now, some experts would tell you that if you're emotionally embedded then you need some kind of psychotherapy that's going to help you let go of a psychologically and emotionally entrenched position. The problem in psychotherapy, however, is that there's no higher moral, ethical, philosophical, and spiritual context, or if there is one, it's very mushy. Do you know what mushy means? Soft, soft, soft! Undeveloped, not sharp, clear, austere, demanding and rigorous.

"The other problem with the psychological orientation is that there's much too much emphasis on the suffering of the individual. Now, I understand that that's part

of the orientation. But everything depends on how we look at being emotionally embedded. So, from a psychological position you're going to see that there are certain psychological and emotional reasons for this embeddedness that the individual is blind to. And because of that they're acting unconsciously and causing other people to suffer. And therefore they need help and compassion, right?"

"Right."

"What happened to evolution, though?"

He let the question hang in the air for a moment.

"You see, you have to watch what happens because the minute your attention becomes focused upon the psychological and emotional suffering of the individual, even if it's ever so slight, you lose the evolutionary context in an instant." He snapped his fingers. *"Did you see how that happened?"*

We all agreed for even as he said it we could feel the evolutionary tension that he had created since the teaching had begun to drain from the room with a rush.

"It's very interesting how that happens. Did you follow that?"

Lots of yeses.

"A lot of people don't know this. This is kind of an unusual way to look at it. So again, the minute you begin to give attention to the suffering of the individual you're going to lose the higher context. You should look at this for yourself and see whether you begin to see it in your own experience. Seeing things from the perspective of the wounded self is called a 'bottom up perspective.' In it the wounded self is in need of healing and is looking up, up, up, up at the possibility of higher evolutionary potential.

"On the other hand, the 'top down' perspective, which is what this teaching is only about, is when you awaken this faculty of consciousness and evolutionary potential to such a degree that the individual directly sees it at the level of consciousness in the form of pure experience, insight, and revelation. Then, from the perspective of the individual's direct, experiential realization and understanding of that potential, you look back down from the top at our emotional and psychological predicament. So the perspective I'm sharing with all of you is called 'top down.' It means that you're looking down at the same issue from a higher perspective.

"The other perspective, for instance, that of transpersonal psychology, is looking from the bottom up and these are two completely different ways seeing exactly the same predicament. But the way you look at whatever the predicament is changes everything. *From the bottom up your perspective is completely different than from the top down. It's not a little bit different; it's absolutely different. So once again, the perspective of this teaching is **only** top down. That's why it's so challenging. The top down perspective doesn't recognize the suffering individual as being important because it's from the perspective of consciousness, or that part of you that's not suffering. When you look at that mess from the Authentic Self's perspective versus from the perspective of a part of you that is suffering and yet still wants to evolve, it looks* very *different.*

"So that's bottom up versus top down and, believe me, there are not very many people in the world who know about this stuff and who are authentically embracing a top down view. Theoretically it's understood by a few people. But very few, if any, are actively embracing the top down perspective. It's very, very new!

"Of course, the reason why it's so challenging is because of what Ken Wilber calls the 'sensitive self,' which is what I'm referring to as the narcissistic separate self-sense. The 'I'm so special and important because I exist' self. In this teaching or from the top down perspective the sensitive self or, to put it simply, the big ego, is completely eradicated. It's destroyed, eviscerated. Why? Because it's not seen. It's completely ignored. Now, the worst thing you can do to a narcissist is to ignore him or her because what the narcissist or the sensitive self thrives on is attention. The worst insult is ignoring it and the top down perspective does not acknowledge in any way the sensitive self and its plight, predicament or, God forbid, even feelings. So it's very radical.

"It's very important to be clear about these things because there are many people that will talk about similar ideas – enlightenment and evolution – but they're going to be talking about them from the bottom up and mean something completely different. It might sound very similar but they're not the same. 'Top down' is a different animal altogether. It's a new thing. You can see why. By its very nature it would require an extraordinary commitment.

"So this teaching model represents a top down perspective." He flashed his laser pointer back across his shoulder onto the Authentic Self model. *"That's why it's so minimalistic. If we were going to look at things from the bottom up we'd need to fill out the picture a little bit more. We'd need to know a lot more about the narcissistic, separate self, its history and its make-up and what makes it tick because in that context it would be really important. After all, the separate, sensitive self or ego is a very complex, multidimensional animal. But the minute you make that flip from bottom up to top down the complexity of the developmental context of the individual becomes irrelevant. That's a pretty dramatic statement. But that's what happens because you're making a leap in identification. So the leap in identification, if it's real, is also going to be a leap in emotional allegiance because then what you're going to be identifying with is the Authentic Self not with the sensitive self and its predicament.*

"Now, the Authentic Self has feelings and emotions also. It wants to create the universe and there are a lot of emotions behind such a dramatic undertaking. But believe me, they're not personal! Do you get the idea, everybody?"

No one said a word, yet now the silence was less an indicator of resistance and more one of astonishment; as Andrew spoke of the "top down" perspective that very perspective swept us up in its glorious view. That was the view of the enlightened mind and its emotion was the creative passion of the very Energy and Intelligence that lay behind the whole of life. It wanted ever more life and ever more of Itself in life. And it wanted it in the most desperate way. So desperate, in fact, that in the rush of that driving passion the significance of 'me and my problems' vanished like a ghost. "The drama of the moment is like a fart in hurricane," Peter used to say and as funny as that might sound, it perfectly captured the essence of scale between the personal and impersonal.

"The enormity of this flip cannot be underestimated," Andrew said at the precise moment that this fact became apparent to us. *"I keep repeating this because I want some of you to get a sense of what I'm talking about here. So the Authentic Self has an emotional dimension too, but it's not personal. A lot of people who have an experience of the Authentic Self see it through the filter of the personal or sensitive self. But that's not it! The top down perspective that I'm teaching is when you see the ego or the sensitive self from the perspective of the Authentic Self and that's radically different, radically different, radically different."* Andrew was impassioned, fire flowing from the darkness of his eyes. *"So the Authentic Self experiences no compassion whatsoever for the suffering of the sensitive self and it's not because I say so and it's not because I'm a Nazi. It's because that's the nature of the Authentic Self. Just try to understand the scientific nature of what I'm talking about. It's not that the Authentic Self lacks compassion. It just literally cannot relate to it as being real because from the perspective of the Authentic Self, the problems of the sensitive self don't exist.*

"Try and imagine a point five thousand years in the future – or maybe fifty thousand years, it might take that long – when what we're calling the Authentic Self had really emerged. Imagine that the sensitive self had died a long time ago and the world was inhabited by these universal humans who are awake to the Authentic Self and for whom this whole personal dimension in the experience of consciousness disappeared so long ago that it wasn't even a reference point. Now, imagine if you met one of these beings and started talking about your personal problems. They would go..." Andrew made a face expressing baffled curiosity. *"It's not that they lack compassion, you see. They just would not be able to relate to it and wouldn't know how to respond. So from the Authentic Self, that's the perspective. It's radically impersonal because we're talking about consciousness and consciousness does not have a face.*

"So the top down view is something you do need to make a little effort to lean into it because it's quite radical, it's quite dramatic, it's quite a new thing and it's definitely real. And to really get it, in a sense your whole world has to turn upside down. And once you get it, it will change your whole worldview and that's the whole idea. But this is something you really need to work on a little bit and that's why you're on retreat."

Andrew paused to let us take in his transmission us more fully. A current of spiritual power pulled us ever deeper and higher. I felt as transparent as I did solid, as empty as rooted in substance and the turmoil that had plagued me not long before was, for the moment, gone. After all, one state can't remember the other. And more than that, as Andrew had noted, it does not even recognize it. There was only the bliss of Being, the sublime awe of insight, and the thrill of possibility.

"Nobody thinks this way," Andrew went on. *"Most enlightenment teachers don't think this way at all. This is why looking into the gap between this higher perspective*

and where we're emotionally embedded is so important. Because how is it that we're going to be able to actualize this top down perspective now? Because we're not five, ten, or fifty thousand years in the future, are we?"

"No," we responded in a soft chorus.

"It's 2005 and the Authentic Self is just now beginning to awakening to itself. So this is the bare emergence of this kind of shift and therefore, in a very profound sense, we have to be the pioneers of this emergent potential. You know, if this whole process continues we're going to reach...I mean, it's something we can't really imagine. But we can try. You can see that eventually we're going to reach someplace way beyond where we are now that's going to be, in some sense, similar to what I was describing. But if we're the ones that need to make that leap now for the sake of the evolution of con-sciousness and of the species, then the question is how are we going to do it?

"Now, the only way that I can see it being done is in the way that we've been speaking about it. That's why I'm really, really emphasizing it. You see, the emotional embeddedness is not going to disappear like this," he said, snapping his fingers. "But your own moral, ethical, philosophical and spiritual perspective can be cultivated through rigorous inquiry. And this different relationship to your own experience can be consciously embraced and assumed for the sake of the evolution of consciousness through the power of choice. Of course, when you're in an ecstatic state of revelation and spontaneous insight it'll be painfully obvious and ridiculously easy. But at other times it will be the most difficult thing you've ever done. But one way or the other, it's not going to make any difference to you because the only thing that's important is that this actually happens. That's top down!"

It sure was and at that moment I knew it in the marrow of my bones and in the unplumbed depths of my soul.

"So, for example when you're emotionally in touch with the thrill of the Authentic Self you find all kinds of emotional, psychological and spiritual strength to deal with your own fear, insecurity, frustration, anxiety, confusion, neurosis, lusts," (it seemed to to me he emphasized the last word), *"and all forms of irrational compulsions. Somehow you find that you can handle all of it, not because they have disappeared but because you are awake to a higher context. That's what changes everything! It's not a compassionate ear that allows you to do that. From the top down perspective it doesn't matter if the sensitive self feels better about itself or not. It's totally irrelevant. Do you see what a big step this is? Do you understand why it's called radical impersonal evo-lutionary enlightenment?"*

An awed chorus of assent rose in the room.

"Because the personal dimension is not important and that's very hard for people to take. It's kind of a new thing. Most of the spirituality that people are getting into today is very personally oriented, even if there is an enlightenment dimension to it. But when it's not personally focused at all what emerges is a context in which we can all meet. It's very different than the world we usually live in. If the context is not personal,

then in a very dramatic and instantaneous way it enlarges to one in which we can come together that is completely different. And it's a different world only because the personal dimension is either absent or completely in the background. That alone is what changes absolutely everything. But it's a dramatic leap. Now, I know that this is more than most people can handle but you can see that if there's a particular personal process that I need to go through I'm not going to be available, right?"

"Right," a few voices agreed.

"I know that's kind of a tall order. I do realize that. But I've got to say it anyway so at least some of you can theoretically understand it. As long as there is some particular personal process that I need to go through for which I need time I'm not going to be available now. I may be available, if I'm lucky, whenever it is that I've gone through this particular process, but it will probably only lead to another process, which will lead to another process, which will lead to another process.

"So on the one hand, it could not get more challenging than dropping this whole orientation, but on the other hand it makes sense when you really begin to understand the nature of enlightenment in which there is no time. The nature of the Authentic Self is that it doesn't have any personal issues and that it's already liberated right now.

"Now, the so-called personal issues don't necessarily disappear from the top down perspective. That would be unrealistic. But they don't have to. What has to happen is you have to get the individual to the point where they realize that it's completely within their means to be able to handle whatever personal issues they need to handle in order to change. So if you are consciously making the effort to embrace the top down perspective you will have all the strength of character to be able to deal with your own neurosis.

"Do you get the idea?" Andrew was passionate and went on without waiting for a response. *"It really makes sense and it's true. But it's only true in real time and real life with real people who make this flip from the bottom up to the top down, which only you can do. I can't do it for you. This is an absolutely individual matter. It's an enormous, heroic leap and it's more dependent on understanding than it is on experience. You need the experience to convince you of its truth, but once you're experientially convinced all more experience is going to do from that time on is just convince you again and again and again of the very same thing. So once you're experientially convinced, that's enough. After that the main event is just bridging that gap. This is the whole thing. Do you get the idea?"*

Did I ever. The shocked silence had deepened with the deepening of revelation, and Andrew's call to heroism sounded like a trumpet at the break of day.

"This, of course, embraces the fourth tenet of the teaching," he went on, *"which is the law of impersonality. The law of impersonality points to the non-personal perspective upon the human experience and this top down perspective is radically non-personal. From the bottom up, it's all personal, including the whole idea of my path and my journey. From the top down it's not. It's the evolution of consciousness and you're either participating in that consciously or you're not. Or maybe you are to a certain*

degree but whatever the case, it's not 'your' journey. It's the evolution of consciousness. Do you see how perspective is everything? Perspective is everything and perspective is more important than experience. Experience without perspective is useless."

He could not seem to stress the point enough and paused to let its power penetrate. After a long moment, he went on.

"I'm telling you, I've worked hard to get you guys into the state you're in now, so you should appreciate that. It basically took me all morning and all afternoon, but now at least I feel a sense of victory and relief because I really felt like I was going a little crazy today."

It was both excruciatingly and ecstatically evident that Andrew had indeed been waging a battle against our inertia throughout the day.

"But now I want you to see what it's taken to get you guys this far. I want you to understand that the perspective that you're seeing at this moment is what I teach and is the very thing that these models represent." He pointed over his shoulders once more.

I was awed, not only by where Andrew had taken us but also by his acute awareness of the atmosphere in the room. I had noticed this sensitivity many times over the years and its power never seemed to wane. He was always one with the very field he created. It was as if he had some inner finger on a psychic pulse and was able to detect the slightest flutter in its rhythm, attuning himself to the subtlety of its shifting beats in order to affect precisely that change in consciousness needed to share his vision.

"Not many people understand this," he went on. *They may understand enlightenment and the concept of evolution, but not this top down perspective. Even if they understand it theoretically, very few people are taking it seriously. But it's for a good reason. It's because authentically embracing a top down perspective is way out on the cutting edge far beyond where most people live or have any intention of going in real time.*

"But I'm hoping that that's going to change because, you see, if I can get a small but significant number of committed people – a small army – to actually embrace a top down view it could trigger some kind of very significant rupture in the status quo. Something could really change. If you can get people to hold it there's a shift that's going to happen. You can feel the shift that's happened in the room. If enough people authentically embrace this view and hold it it's going to hold some outer edge and keep it steady. Do you understand what I'm saying?"

There was a collective and exhilarated assent.

"Okay, good, so I'll leave it at that for now."

Andrew finished and quickly sank into meditation, the weight of his presence pulling us down with him. The energy and ecstasy that had surged through the room during our first few days now returned in its full power. My view on the turbulent highs and lows of my own experience since the beginning of the retreat now came fully through the eyes of the enlightened mind, from the summit of consciousness, veritably from the "top down." And the view from that summit was vast. From it the peaks and valleys of my own experience appeared as they were, that is, not mine in any particular sense but simply the expression of one vast, universal movement of becoming. More than I was having "my experience", I was having the human experience. More than I was an individual, I was an expression of human emergence and that emergence itself was but one expression of the creative surge behind the entire evolving universe. And that very surge, at the deepest root of self, was precisely who and what I was in this and every moment. From that perspective my very human predicament and all those psychological and emotional knots that I had long experienced as "my problem" I now saw as "the problem," an affliction affecting the entire race equally. Therefore, to the degree that I was willing to take on board full responsibility for "my problem" in some small measure I would be taking responsibility for "the problem" as well. Minimally, I would be ridding the world of my ego.

But there was so much more. This exploration was no mere adventure in the pursuit of personal liberation. Its goal was nothing less than a revolution in consciousness and culture. Years earlier Andrew had said to me, "Welcome to the revolution," and the passion behind that statement, the passion to create a "rupture" in the status quo, flamed unabated even now. Even now, despite two decades of the equally unabated cynicism of the wider culture, Andrew remained an "idealist with revolutionary inclinations." Such was the power of his inspiration. Such was the depth of his realization.

In my own heart inspiration danced a delicate dance with the whispering hiss of doubt. In the heated throes of revelation all things seemed possible yet when that ardor cooled, an evolutionary breakthrough in the psychic density of the current culture seemed less likely than an orchid sprouting on the moon. Elated by vision yet tempered by realism was how I often saw myself, that position itself lending subtle credence to the cynical view. Yet Andrew, pushed ever onward by some visionary muse, accepted no such "reasonable objections." "Revolution" was his trademark sign-off and once, when asked what product he offered to the world, he responded without a moment's hesitation, "Total Victory!"

My own "tempered realism" was struck a welcome blow upon discovering that the Renaissance had been sparked by the spirited deliberations of no more than five hundred people, their daring hauling mankind up by its bootstraps and out of the Dark Ages, launching the Western Enlightenment and giving birth to the Modern Age. That recognition tempered my "realism" with a solid dose of vision, allowing me to give myself permission to share in Andrew's view much more fully. It had also caused me to inspect with greater depth the mechanics of cultural change. I quickly discovered that great cultural transformations have always been triggered by the committed action of a handful of the inspired who pushed the culture to a tipping point.[3] Beyond that point, and by rapidly increasing degrees, others could inhabit the new structures of thought so carefully erected by the few. And then others, and others still, until what once ruled the imagination of a few became the view of the many. So why should today be any different? Why should there exist such cynicism with respect to the possibility of radical change? Why indeed, since it has already happened once within the lifetime of many readers of this book? After all, didn't the sixties irreversibly alter the face of our culture? Did they not introduce new structures in thought that most of us take as commonplace today: civil rights, women's rights, environmental sanity, and so much more? And who is to say these were the last? In an evolving universe, how could they be?

Creating new structures in consciousness—that is what this teaching was about and what Andrew had referred to in his closing remarks. There had been much talk about this among Andrew's students in earlier years, which went something like this: currently we operate from an interlocking network of structures in consciousness, a system of emotional, psychological and biological habits that have been bequeathed to us by near countless millennia of biological and cultural development and have culminated in the super-sophisticated postmodern ego. Because these structures have long been in place, because they have been inhabited by millions upon millions of our progenitors across the slowly unfolding ages, they are as deeply felt as an ancestral home, as easy to wear as a favorite garment, as close and familiar as skin. They have become a habit of the race.

However, new habits can be built, new structures laid down. Historically this begins with the pioneers – Galileo, Descartes, Martin Luther, and so on. They lay the foundations and raise the new structure. These are then inhabited by their first intrepid followers and ultimately by the larger mass of humanity, a process that often, though not always, occurs within the lifetime of the originating pioneers. It is along these lines that Andrew has envisioned change from the very beginning. Except in this case the structures exist not merely in the realm of ideas but within the very fabric of consciousness itself. There exists both theoretical and experiential support for such a view. With respect to the theoretical, there is Jung's notion of the collective unconscious, which postulates the existence of various archetypes and patterns that form fields which, though without mass or energy do, however, shape an individual's self-perception and relationship to life. Rupert Sheldrake's theory of morphic resonance and morphogenetic fields falls into this category also, holding that for each species, including the human race, there exists a morphic field which stores the collective knowledge of that species and makes that knowledge more readily available to members of successive generations regardless of location.[4] And of course there are other evolutionary and developmental theories, including the work of Don Beck and the developmental framework known as Spiral Dynamics[5], that lend further support to Andrew's vision of the possibility of fomenting a cultural revolution.

Which brings us to the experiential side. The most significant development here is that the initial emergence of the Authentic Self in collectives of extremely committed individuals took twelve years of super-human effort to bring into being yet now, only a few years later, that same emergence has become increasingly accessible to larger and larger numbers of people, many of whom have had no previous spiritual experience whatsoever (see Appendix 2, The Birth and Evolution of Inter-subjective Enlightenment). And while they are not yet permanently inhabiting this new structure, they have begun to rent space there, a fact that lends itself to a further acceleration of momentum. This emergence and its rapidly evolving nature is, in my view, one of the most significant and encouraging elements of Andrew's undertaking and, taken along with the theoretical frameworks just mentioned, provides the best antidote to the cynical insistence that nothing truly outrageous is actually possible.

A few committed people holding an edge in consciousness for everyone else and for the sake of the evolution of consciousness itself - that is what Andrew has given his life to. Over the twelve years that I've known him, he has never wavered from his relentless pursuit of this outrageous possibility. It was either an insane vision or one of profound sanity. From the aerie of the top down view, my own current vantage point, which it was was clear to me. Andrew's vision opened the door to an evolutionary leap in human development and the creation of a new platform from which to address the frightening dangers by which we currently threaten ourselves with extinction. For better or for worse, I knew that I would throw in my lot on the side of "outrageous possibility."

Thus elevated I left the teaching hall to walk to meditation. As I did so I became acutely aware that to the very degree that my vision had thus expanded, my awareness of the darker drives and forces within myself was elevated also. Lust, panic, resentment, inertia, and their long wagontrain of relations went on their brightly-lit parade. Yet somehow the indistinct though irreducible seat of my awareness had become very far removed from even that, and from its lofty perch I viewed the hollow pageantry of ego.

In the vast space of that easy wakefulness, another pitched battle appeared to be brewing, though at the moment it seemed but a distant swirl of dust. I considered Andrew's words regarding the power of conscious choice. We take it for granted, he had said. It does not often occur to us that such choice is, from an evolutionary standpoint, as recent a development as the latest newsflash from the Web. Nowhere in the natural world does such choice exist. And even with us it is new; not only is it a uniquely human emergence but also a relatively recent one. And its significance is vast, not only with respect to personal liberation but also for the evolution of consciousness itself. If we are indeed the First Cause awakening to itself in Its own creation then, upon awakening to that astounding fact, the whole process crashes directly into our laps. We are free human beings, fully empowered to do as we will, as we *choose*. And, once having awoken to the possibility, we can manifest the Authentic Self through the simple power of choice. And by embracing the "top down" view, especially together, we stand poised to hold a field, a structure in consciousness, at the very edge of the possible. What might arise from that field for the sake of the whole is difficult to say, but given the nature of its blinding positivity we can say with certainty that it would undoubtedly be good.

As I considered the weight of such realizations and their personal implications I was struck by a curious irony. As Andrew had pointed out, the sensitive self views itself as possessed of inherent greatness even against the striking void of any supporting evidence. Moreover, it demands respect for that spurious greatness, being as easily offended as a petty lordling by the absence of esteem from those by whom it is surrounded. This was a sentiment to which I could easily relate. "I am great because I exist and have noble aspirations." Yet when asked to step up and be counted for the highest reasons – for it was nothing less than greatness to which we were being called – the sensitive self runs for cover behind the veil of "who me? What can I do?" or behind the cynical insistence that nothing great is really possible. When called to consider our own potential for authentic greatness we all too often shrink back, retreating to a shadow world where nothing is what it seems and where pretense decides the day. We are a mess indeed, I thought. But we can also straighten ourselves out in most dramatic fashion by choosing to do so and aligning the full power of our humanity forcefully behind that choice.

I was reflecting on all these thoughts as I entered the meditation hall and there I was informed that I had been assigned to a cleaning detail, duties to commence after lunch. I was grateful for this opportunity. After days of alternately sitting, walking, meditating, chanting, and listening to teachings, I craved any physical activity. Soon enough, I found myself moving chairs aside, sliding a broom this way and that to corral the vagrant dust balls that hid in every corner. The change in routine felt great despite the fact that in that thick, hot air I felt as listless and lethargic as a Louisiana swamp. As I swept and moved, I remained established in the "top down" view into which Andrew had inducted us earlier. And from this perspective I continued to be aware of the ongoing clash of forces within myself. Yet I saw them objectively and for what they were, enabling me to study them with a measure of detached, even idle, curiosity usually absent when held in the wiry strength of their grip. And so it went for some time.

Then, suddenly and without the slightest warning a black voice shot forth from some interior darkness, honed with the bloody edge of a guillotine. It proclaimed in a diabolical rage, "He's crazy." This was no idle ripple of the mind, but a furious howl from somewhere deep within myself. If there was a devil and he had a voice then this was surely it. The hairs on the back of my neck bristled and as I listened more closely it came again, a storm of fury from the underworld. "He's crazy," it railed. "Space beings five thousand years from now – bah." That last word was flung out on the psychic equivalent of spit. "A madman! He wants me to give up 'my life' for some insane, utopian vision of the future. The outrage! The nerve. What about me? Right now? What right has he got to play with my life?" This vicious invective spun on, and through the same mind's eye that had recently seen from the summit, I now saw myself tearing at his flesh with the talons of my rage. I was appalled, rocking back on my heels from the sheer impact of this assault. I had no idea that that had been in there. I had no idea that the seemingly familiar terrain of my very own skin harbored such a demon. This was more than simple resistance; it was homicidal indignation and I was simply stunned.

After a while I managed to pull back, to decline the magnetic attraction to that awfully seductive voice and give my attention to the Authentic Self, assuming the view from the top down once more. And everything looked different again. Light glinted through the brooding thunderheads and optimistic brightness illuminated my inner landscape once again. But that voice had stopped me in my tracks, truly scared me, and set me to thinking more deeply about the forces I was meddling with. It was clear that I had unleashed a beast and I saw that were I to entertain it, the upshot could be grave. That voice was the voice of the devil, and metaphorical as that might be, it was also brutally real. It violently opposed all that the teaching stood for, all that Andrew stood for, and all that I wanted to stand for: selflessness, integrity, pure motive and every form of higher aspiration. It wished, in the most fervent way, to destroy them all, for each threatened its survival absolutely. I considered for a moment the ethical gymnastics I would have to perform were I to heed this angry voice and turn my back on all that had been given me. Were I to go down that road, yet preserve my spiritual self-image, that precious crown of ego, I would have, at all costs, to place upon Andrew the mantle of the demon so that I might be relieved of its burden. I shuddered at this twisted bargain under whose auspices light is cast as darkness and darkness cast as light.

Thinking about this it was immediately obvious why some who had been deeply involved with Andrew and had, for one reason or another, parted from the teaching went to such extraordinary lengths to vilify him in as public and relentless a manner as possible. Such tactics were required for the individuals involved to make the case, first to themselves and then to others, that Andrew was a monster; then they could deny the monster in themselves. Thus they have resorted to extreme distortions of truth and vitriolic character assassination, for painting him as an incarnation of evil was the only way to inure themselves against the betrayal of their own souls. Most did not have the humility to say, "it was too much for me," (though some did) for such an admission proved too weighty for their spiritual egos to bear. It all made perfect sense now. And it put me on guard against that possibility within myself. That egoic monster was alive in us all.

That reflection threw me back to the mid-nineties and the early days of my association with Andrew. At that time he had already become quite a controversial figure due to his simple demand for integrity – his demand that what one had realized inform how they lived. This seemingly sane demand created a storm of self-righteous indignation both in individuals upon whom Andrew exerted pressure and in the larger culture as well. Both were a form of "narcissistic rage," an expression of that selfsame monster that had sprung from the shadows at me, demanding its right to exist and consuming even spiritual experience in its bid to stay in power. Of course, Andrew being who he is did not pull punches. When I first met him he was vocally critical of other spiritual teachers for their ethical failures in all the usual areas: sex, finances and the related profusion of abuses of power. But this was not his biggest crime. His biggest crime by far was naming names. That crossed some unspoken line of collusion amongst the millions of members of the "I'm only human" spiritual culture of which, I would come to find soon enough, Peter was a member in exceedingly good standing. For his transgression Andrew was ostracized from the wider spiritual community as, on all fronts, it closed ranks against him. However, he fiercely maintained his simple point: if one had indeed attained a high level of spiritual realization, it was then a moral obligation to live in such a way that the absolute love that they had realized be known in the world through the expression of integrity. Conversely, he posed the grating question: if individuals who are supposed to have or actually have attained a high level of spiritual realization behave in accordance with an ethical standard that is far beneath that of an ordinary person, what then could the significance of enlightenment possibly be? (For an in-depth discussion of Andrew's legendary battles around this point with his own students as well as much of the postmodern spiritual culture please see Appendix 6, The Controversy around Andrew Cohen: Purity, Corruption and Spiritual Authority Figures).

This was a simple point that I have spent many years considering and, of course, it brought everything directly back to me. Was I willing to demonstrate integrity and live in alignment with what I actually have realized? Did I have that kind of courage? Did I aspire to that kind of greatness? I liked to think so, but, as Andrew had said during the teaching, where was the evidence? Ah, there was the rub. Yet bridging the gap between who I was and who I aspired to be was the very reason I was attracted to him in the first place. Which, of course, set up an interesting dynamic. The job of the authentic teacher is to push the student further than he or she would ever go willingly, which all but guarantees intense friction between the absolute demand of the teacher, who, as I had realized earlier, is none other than one's very own Self, and the ego of the student and its vehement insistence on survival. When that confrontation comes, the student has to have perfect trust in the teacher otherwise the voice of doubt and cynicism will win the day. Did that prospect frighten me? You bet. Did I have the stomach for it? I couldn't say since, unlike others, I had not yet been pushed that far.

None of us knows what we will do when a life and death crisis puts everything on the line for real, right now. Right now! All I can do is prepare myself as best as I can. *"Ego death is not a game,"* Andrew has consistently said over the years. Did I know that? Yes, I did! Could I handle it? I wasn't sure. What I was sure of was that in the face of such forces I had to be humble, never arrogantly assuming that "of course I could do it." Such arrogance, it seemed to me, lies at the root of failure, ensuring that the strength of character and spiritual conviction needed to let go for real would be unavailable when the demand to do so came. And then where would I be? Facing the betrayal of my own soul and, in a perverse inversion of reality, heap my own self-hatred for doing so directly upon Andrew as others had done. Would that be the bargain I would have to strike in order to endure living with myself? It was a sobering consideration.

Once more I realized what I was – a choice point between competing forces. And the choices I make will, and always do, manifest that which is of most significance to me. If I wanted freedom, my choices would make manifest more and more of that; if I didn't then they wouldn't. It was brutal, inescapable and perfectly equitable spiritual arithmetic and its stark simplicity both frightened and inspired me. The stakes were high and the game was real but at least I knew I was alive. And from the top down view I knew that I, we, all of us that had *really* heard this teaching were potential flagstones for the future upon which the very force behind creation could step into our deeply troubled world. And at that moment it was clear to me that, whatever else might enter the picture, nothing could ever be more important than that.

NOTES

1. Over the years Andrew, on the basis of extensive experience with his female body of students, has had much to say about the nature of women's conditioning in relationship to liberation. His observations on this sensitive subject are more extensive in nature than can even be hinted at in a footnote. However, by the time this book is published, a new issue of *What is Enlightenment?* magazine (Issue #36) dedicated to this topic should be widely available and will no doubt contain a discussion of this topic. You may also want to examine Elizabeth Debold's series of articles in the magazine entitled "*Where are the Women?*" These can be found in a section of the magazine's website entitled *The New Women's Liberation Movement*, (http://www.wie.org/women/).

2. Andrew Cohen, *Embracing Heaven and Earth*, (Lenox, MA: What is Enlightenment? Press, 2000) p.32.

3. See the book, *The Tipping Point*, by Malcolm Gladwell; (Little, Brown and Company, 2000)

4. See previous reference to Rupert Sheldrake's *A New Science of Life*.

5. See previous references on Spiral Dynamics. Or simply google Don Beck.

Day 9

The Birth of a New Consciousness

When I woke the first bells of morning had not yet rung and the cool breeze that eased through the window carried not just the smell of cold, ancient stones but the singsong chirping of those little frogs that, crooning through the night, made this place their home. A day and a half to go, I thought, as I stretched my weary limbs. Something had changed in me this morning. While the turmoil of the preceding days had not relented, my relationship to it had changed. I had somehow resigned myself to it all and assumed a stoic attitude of endurance. In some ways this was a relief and, no longer needing things to be other than they were, I was able to focus. I was able to resist the temptation to treat the remaining days with a casualness born of the knowledge of their impending end. I left my cell, retrieved my steaming cup of tea, splashed some cold water on my face and headed out for two hours of practice. Later, sitting outside on a bench between chanting and meditation, I watched the sky grow pink with the first hints of sun. It was one of those timeless moments when, in contemplation of nature's serene majesty, all troubles dissolved in an instant of radiant perfection. I breathed in a touch of that radiance and held it within me throughout the meditation.

At breakfast I noticed a change in the weather. While my side of the dining hall was as steeped in silence as it had been on previous days, that stillness no longer seemed to affect the other side of the hall. There all was abuzz with lively conversation, as Andrew's directive to discuss the teachings had been taken up vigorously. For some time I listened, wondering if the dynamic ecstasy of the Authentic Self was at that moment burning through the room. It was difficult to tell, however, and soon I returned to my own ruminations over cereal, coffee and toast. I then headed downstairs to the teaching hall and found a seat, wondering where Andrew might take us today.

A bit over an hour later he started the day, softly saying, *"So we can continue where we finished last night,"* as he pulled us from meditation and clipped on his tiny mike.

"This is more of an observation than a question," the first woman he called on said. "I've heard the expressions top down and bottom up before but I never really understood them until yesterday. And you mentioned the fourth tenet in relation to top down view but it seems to me that the only thing that guarantees the top down view is the fifth tenet. Everything else is personal."

"Well, that's the idea. When you really start to understand what the perspective is that's how it works."

"Yeah," she agreed, "well, I got it."

"Good. It's a big thing to get. And just because you get it once doesn't mean you really get it at all. You can't really get it until you actually begin to live it. Anything prior to that is just spiritual and philosophical entertainment. That's when you experience a thrill, which is not a bad thing or a put-down. But there's no proof that someone really gets it unless they can actually live it."

"I understand that. It re-hangs the world in a profound way."

"Absolutely. It completely re-hangs it. Everything gets turned upside-down. Or," he added with a chuckle, *"right side up. It all depends on what your perspective is. But as I was saying last night, there are people who understand this top down view theoretically, but it's a very rare thing to actually be able to live it. Of course, I personally believe that anybody who's intelligent and developed enough to conceptually grasp it should be able to live it in real time if it's important enough to them and if they want to badly enough."*

"It seems to me that's what the fifth tenet, for the sake of the whole, is all about." *"Yeah, definitely,"* Andrew said with finality, turning his attention to an Australian lady.

"So, as soon as I closed my eyes after your description of the 'top down' view I had a direct and vivid experience of the Authentic Self and…"

"When did that happen?"

"Pretty much immediately after I closed my eyes at the end of your talk last night."

"And what happened then, when you closed your eyes?"

"My first intention was to completely let go of the personality. And then this vivid presence of the Authentic Self appeared in consciousness and the main message, or effect I guess, was that there's only one, which wasn't what I had imagined or expected before."

"So this is subtle but I need to explain it again. I know it's a difficult thing to grasp but the Authentic Self can only be recognized through action. So through calm reflection you can't see it; it's only seen through activity. Remember, first there was nothing and then something came from nothing and it's only through the emergence of something that the Authentic self can be recognized. It's only in and through action, not through calm reflection."

"Okay," she said uncertainly.

"But this is something that takes a little bit of time to get and I know it's a little hard to understand. You see, the Authentic Self is a compulsion to act and it's also

activity itself. But there's nothing passive about it. It's never a witness; it's only an actor."

"Okay." The hesitation in her voice had not diminished.

"It's a difficult thing to get, but you can get it. What you have to do is let go enough to feel this thing acting in you and then you're going to know what it is. Or else you can see when someone else is lit up with it and then you can recognize what it looks like. But it'll never reveal itself in calm reflection. It can't, because, as I said, its nature is activity."

"So I'm wondering what it was that I saw."

"Well, what happened was very good and it was obviously very important."

"But that's not the Authentic Self?"

"By definition it couldn't be."

"Okay," she said, gathering her thoughts. "The impression that I got was this is the self of the world."

"Yeah, that's right," Andrew said brightly and then, after a slight pause, added, *"You see, what happened yesterday is that at a certain point during my talk the room flipped from 'bottom up' to 'top down' so everybody was starting to see the 'top down' perspective. Now, that's a big thing."*

He paused again, and then drove home the point once more.

"Again, this thing about the Authentic Self being only an action is hard to get. But just consider that that's the energy and intelligence that created the universe – the Creative Principle – and because of that it only becomes evident in activity. That's what its nature is."

He let that sink in for a few moments before pointing to Piotr, a Polish student from Chicago whom I'd seen on previous retreats.

"Oh wow," Andrew said in a playful tone, *"he hardly ever speaks so when he does, it's a big moment. I definitely don't want to let that pass."*

"You just said that the Authentic Self can only manifest through activity. Does that include mental and intellectual activity?"

"Yes, definitely. Mental activity is a form of activity. But the Authentic Self can't emerge just through calm reflection. There needs to be engagement. Remember on Star Trek when Captain Kirk said, 'Engage?' Everyone laughed. "It's like that."

"So you're saying that thinking is activity and can be expressed through the thinking Authentic Self, right?"

"Well sure, there can be creative, passionate and inspired thinking, right?"

"Yes."

"I'm just saying that in the meditative state, the Authentic Self doesn't appear. In the meditative state is when you're going into the Ground. Make sense?"

"Yeah, it does."

"Anything else?"

"No."

Andrew paused thoughtfully, as if looking for a different angle from which to make his point. *"For example, you could say that at the gross physical level, sexual energy is always experienced as activity, right?"*

"Yes."

"It's never passive. It's only passive when it dissipates. Even if you just experience its potentiality it's always active. Right?"

"Right."

"So that's what I mean. It's very easy to get when you see that the Ground of Being is this absolutely passive, still, nothing ever happening at all, no place of no activity whatsoever. The Authentic Self is the exact opposite. So this example can help you to really let in what that distinction is all about.

"The Authentic Self is not something that you can just bear witness to, you see. It's you in action. Unless you are in action to some degree you're not going to be able to know what it is as a subjective experience. You can't be a separate witness of it in yourself. You have to act or it has to act in you. Does that make sense?"

"Yeah, it does."

"And in a retreat context like this when you're speaking together, if you strictly avoid the personal domain in a very disciplined way and you avoid getting lost in theoretical abstractions, keeping your self at the very center of the inquiry without it being personal, this thing that we're talking about as the Authentic Self will come to the front.

"Have any of you experienced it?"

Instantly about eighty hands shot into the air. I was shocked because so far no one had mentioned anything of the collective emergence of the Authentic Self.

Andrew's eyes widened. *"Oh. I didn't know that,"* I was as surprised as he seemed to be. *"So, of those of you who did, I'd like some of you to describe what the experience as like."*

He turned his attention to a soft-spoken German man.

"It feels like it's no longer 'I am here and you are there.' It feels like 'we are here.' And I think it's possible, for example, that if there is a problem that we can come together like this and find a solution far away from the perspective of the ego. It's like it goes to the back so something new can come into the group."

"Well, what's the new thing? We're just talking about the conscious experience of the Authentic Self. I want to know what it feels like."

The man pondered a moment but came up with nothing. Andrew moved on to the next person, this time a young Danish woman.

"In our group last evening it was like the experience of the new being emerging..."

"But what did the Authentic Self feel like?" he interjected.

"It felt like a tremendous transparency."

"And?"

"And a feeling of communion although we were still very autonomous."

"Yeah, I get it," he said a bit impatiently, seeing that the lady was using his language but not really answering his question.

"You're talking around it but I want to know what your direct experience was like. What did it FEEL like? Do you know what feeling is? If I do this," he smacked himself sharply on the forehead with his laser pointer, *"I say, 'ow, it hurts."* Everyone laughed, as Andrew seemed to have surprised himself with the impact of his own blow. *"I'm not talking about the relationship between the pointer and my head,"* he said, rubbing his forehead. *"I want to know just what the feeling was."*

"It was a feeling of ecstasy and of intensity…"

"That's more like it."

"In a way, like in the Ground of Being, it's bliss that came alive."

"Okay, that's pretty good. So it was alive and it was ecstatic and there was intensity to it. Not bad."

He went next to a young American man.

"It feels like there's this joy and unknowing feeling that I keep pushing into and that keeps looking at itself and keeps pushing forward and forward."

"Can you say more about it than it just being an unknowing feeling? If you said unknowing feeling it means that there's a purity to it but I'd like to know more about what the thing itself feels like."

"It feels fresh."

"Right. What about the energetic dimension of it?"

"It feels vibrant."

"Right. There you go. That wasn't that hard was it? It was vibrant. It wasn't passive was it?"

"No."

"There's a very active quality to it, right."

"Right."

"You see I'm not making this up and I want you to articulate your experience so that you know what I'm talking about and so that when you look at that model you'll know that it's actually representing something that's real and you'll know exactly what it's referring to. Do you understand?"

"Yes."

This focus on the precise articulation of one's inner experience had been a key feature of Andrew's teaching since I first met him. He set the example in this regard. Such articulation demanded that we needed to be more attentive to what was going on inside our own skins than we were in the habit of being. It also required cultivating the capacity to discriminate about precisely what it was that we either had experienced or were experiencing. After all, as Andrew never tired of saying, it was not merely experience but our understanding of it that determined its impact on our lives.

"Okay, who else?" He asked. *"Yes,"* he said pointing to another English lady.

"To me it's this feeling state of shaking and of every cell in my body just going crazy."

"Right. Once again, there's a certain kind of intensity that's vibrant and alive."

"Yes, and it's very exciting. So I heard what you said yesterday about being aware of the different states of feeling in the three places. In the Ground of Being I'm completely comfortable and it's the only place I'm still."

"Right."

"Outside of that I'm either in total vertigo or in this incredible, thrilling, exciting passion. And I think that's the Authentic Self."

"That's what it is."

"I'm sensing now that I need to not be such a thrill junkie for this incredible high that I'm getting and learn how to use it in a wiser and more practical manner."

"That's very good," Andrew said, *"but I just want to establish what it is for the moment."*

He went to the next person, another English woman.

"At the beginning it felt compelling and I didn't understand why, but once I began to feel that it was very important it became both challenging and exhilarating and I found a huge amount of passion going into what I was doing…"

"What you're saying is beautiful but it's still one step removed."

"Can you tell me what the one step is?"

"Well, you're talking about *something and I want to know the quality of the thing itself. That's all."*

I was suddenly reminded of the first few days of the retreat during which Andrew had gone to such great lengths to force us to articulate our experience of the Ground of Being. Here we were again, now leaning into the experience of the Authentic Self and learning to discriminate between the qualitative differences of these two divergent yet singular modes of consciousness.

He moved on, this time to a middle-aged German woman.

"Well, for me it feels like a very concentrated energy."

"Yes."

"And also I had this experience of wondering how the words I was speaking were coming out of my mouth."

"What does that mean?"

"That means that I could describe my thoughts with words I never thought I would use."

"Right. That's very good. Did you all hear what she said? Andrew was trying to bring our attention to something significant. *"She was saying things that she didn't think she knew."*

"Yes, that's right," she enthusiastically agreed.

Andrew let that comment hang in the air. Then he added, *"that's exactly how I do this. A lot of people think I really know what I'm talking about. I have no idea."*

Everyone laughed but there was something significant and extraordinary in what Andrew was pointing out. *"That's how it works,"* he reiterated. *"Very good. So you see, that's the Authentic Self."*

Andrew had once defined the quest for enlightenment as *"the search for perfect insecurity."* What he had meant was that in that state one surrenders all "already knowing" in a trust so deep that from it the power of the Self can emerge from the deep well of its mystery directly into this world. The result? Actions faster than thought, perfectly unpremeditated and always tailored to the needs of the moment. But to be a vehicle for that miraculous unfolding someone would not only have to have surrendered to that mystery absolutely, fallen into its well, as it were, but would also have to be willing to bear the enormous insecurity of extending themselves fully while literally having no idea of what was next. Only trust and surrender of the profoundest kind would enable such transcendent spontaneity.

I only had two points of connection to such a state within my own experience. The first came from nearly two decades as a serious Judo competitor during which, in my highest moments, I traversed that mysterious realm of performance known simply as "the zone." "The zone," as all accomplished athletes know, is that timeless instant of perfection where everything lines up to produce a flawless physical feat. And that perfection, though utilizing all one's skill and training, simultaneously transcends all such categories. In "the zone" the mind dissolves in unselfconsciousness and a power from beyond it sweeps in, synchronizing a display of physical perfection that no amount of calculation and cognition could account for. The only other times I've found myself thus lost in "the zone," ecstatically swept up on some force of life itself, was during "enlightened communication" groups. There, in the absence of the least premeditation, the most profound things would emerge from my mouth with a life of their own, the realization of what they were pointing to arising simultaneous with their expression. Thus I was as much of a recipient of their wisdom as anyone else.

In "the zone" we are one with life, free from fear, from self-consciousness and every form of knowing. There is no sense of being a doer, only doing and the freedom is absolute. And yet for most of us it lasts only an instant. *"Imagine living your whole life from that place,"* I'd heard Andrew say often and therefore, when he said, *"that's exactly how I do this,"* I knew he wasn't kidding. *"You guys think I really know this stuff but I don't"* he'd insisted previously much as he had just now. *"It's not something I carry around with me in that way. Yet miraculously, the moment I begin to speak about it, it simply appears."*

I have frequently considered this extraordinary state of consciousness and what it might mean to live there. But in all honesty I still find it difficult to grasp. Moments of athletic perfection and spontaneous revelation were one thing. But these were, after all, merely the briefest forays away from the familiar reference point of self, ending always in a return. What would it be like to never return to that reference point, to that place of preparedness and knowing? And though I could not say for sure, I sensed that it would have to be both the greatest thrill and the ultimate terror. It was where our longing for "zero" collided with our fear of no longer being able to locate ourselves as objects in our own minds. Yet that was the price for freedom, for *"liberation without a face,"* as Andrew liked to say. In this context I considered more fully a segment of the chant we had repeated hundreds of times in the last few days: *"The stability of our transformation depends entirely upon remaining resolutely in the unknown, never to return again. That means ever abiding in that mysterious place where the mind has no foothold whatsoever. It means always wanting to be nobody more than we want to be somebody. And most importantly, it means surrendering our every breath to the Self Absolute and the evolutionary impulse that emerges from that Self…"* It was that mysterious place from which Andrew lived constantly and from which this teaching emerged. And it was that mystery that the woman with whom Andrew was speaking was just beginning to discover.

"That's exactly what happens," Andrew reiterated, referring to the spontaneous response that had so surprised her. *"So you described the energetic quality as concentrated?"*

"Yes. I would describe it as very concentrated and I could feel how it changes when people fall a little bit back."

"Back into what?"

"Something like ego or opinions."

"So they fall back into the personal?"

"Yes."

"So when you fall back into the personal the Authentic Self simply disappears, right?"

"Yes. I feel like the energy changed then."

"That's right, the energy definitely changes. But the point here, which just confirms everything I've been saying, is that the personal dimension is a completely different dimension of reality and the self than the ego and there's no, and I mean no, connection between them. This is a very hard point to get but they're parallel lines that never cross anywhere. The ego and the Authentic Self literally have no relationship. And I just don't know how to make that clear except repeating it over and over again. There's never a moment where you're in both. It's only one or the other and they never meet. As you were experiencing in your discussion, when someone fell back into the personal the Authentic Self disappears. Right?"

"But we had one person in our group who was very conscious of this and who brought us all back and you could also feel that on an energetic level."

"Yes, that's right. But my point is that when the personal appears the Authentic Self disappears. That's just the way it works."

"Okay, yes. I understand."

"Okay. So once again, it's got to be one or the other. That's how it works technically; that's how it works scientifically. Not because I say so but simply because that's how it is. That's why the ego has to be transcended in order for one to become a manifestation of the Authentic Self. It will not work any other way. When you begin to see it happening in front of your eyes and it's not theoretical anymore then it's quite fascinating, isn't it? Hmm?"

"Yes. Yes, it is. And now I also remember that when this very concentrated energy appeared I automatically came out of my own personal state."

"Exactly!"

"I was listening to what someone had said and suddenly I felt the personal self just fall to the back."

"Exactly. It's not subtle. It's a very dramatic shift, isn't it?"

"Oh yes, quite."

"Very good," he said softly. *"So, you see, I'm not making this stuff up. I'm talking about something that's real."*

"Yes, very real." Her eyes had the most sober expression.

"And do you understand how and why the Authentic Self only emerges in action and why you can only see it through activity?"

"Yes, I do."

"That's very good. Okay."

Andrew paused for a moment and then, looking to the back of the room, asked, *"All right, did you have your hand up?"* pointing to an Australian woman with curly gray hair.

"It feels like a stream of energy that's definitely moving forward," she said. "I never experience it turning back to something that was. It feels like it's always wanting to know more of everything."

"Wanting to know more of everything. That's good. And what was the energetic quality?"

"The energetic quality is one of insistence and never resting."

"Right," Andrew said, his voice rising a little with excitement. *"If it's never resting, that's very energetic, isn't it?"* He laughed.

We nodded acknowledgment.

"So therefore the Authentic Self couldn't be a person because all people need rest. Right?"

More acknowledgment. Once again, Andrew was slowing us down in order to get us to fully appreciate what he was pointing to.

"Remember I said that the Authentic Self is a function of consciousness; it's not an individual."

"And I experience it as never being satisfied," the woman added.

"That's right. Never being satisfied."

"Because there's always more to do or to explore."

"Well, that's because it's the creative impulse. And I said it's never fulfilled—there's never satiation. It's relentlessly creative."

"Right, right," she agreed enthusiastically.

"So, once again, it's a function of consciousness and when you awaken to it your experience is like plugging into a wall socket."

"Yes, that's exactly it."

"But it's not just an energetic experience. It has a self quality because it's a function of consciousness and a state of consciousness."

"Right."

"And it has direction."

"Oh, yes,"

"These are important things to recognize. It's a state of consciousness that has direction and the direction is vertical."

"Absolutely."

"It's not horizontal, it's driving up. And then, when you awaken to the Authentic Self there's a quality or sense of ... "

"Purpose," she said with conviction.

"Right. So when you experience it, one of its qualities is this inherent sense of profound purpose and meaning."

"Right."

"In fact, on the experiential level this purposefulness almost seems to be the most dominant feature of what its nature is. So the instant you become conscious or aware of the Authentic Self it will be obvious. No one's going to have to say, 'Shh! Listen! This is very important!'" he whispered conspiratorially.

"No," she laughed.

"Because if you're awake to the Authentic Self you'll find that purposefulness is its nature. So if you put all these things together you really begin to get some sense of what it is. So there's this intense, ecstatic, energetic dimension that has direction."

"Right."

"In the Ground of Being there's no directionality, is there?"

"No."

"But in the Authentic Self there's this very intensely vertical surge and sense of purpose that's endless. So, as we discovered in the first few days, when one awakens to the Ground of Being there's this sense that 'I could sit here forever.' Right?"

"Yeah."

"Then, in the Authentic Self, the sense is, I could create..."

"Forever," she finished the sentence.

"Forever," Andrew repeated. *"Remember, I said I wanted to know what God felt like. How would God feel about all this? So a human being cannot conceive of the notion of creating unendingly. But if you were the Creative Impulse itself there wouldn't*

be any sense of time or limitation. So it's this kind of eternal, ceaseless, ecstatic creative surge and, if you pay attention, you find that its nature is liberation itself because the Authentic Self is already free. If you look at the quality of that state of consciousness do you notice that in that state you're already free?"

"Yes, yes," she agreed passionately.

"And, instantaneously there's perfect liberation."

"Yes."

"It's perfect liberation because the Creative Impulse itself is already free. So you know how I've been saying over and over again that the Authentic Self has no neuroses, no self-doubt, no self-consciousness and no personal ambition."

"No thinking about that at all."

"Exactly. There's no thinking about that. And so what I'm saying is that when the individual experiences the Authentic Self what they experience is instantaneously spontaneous liberation because as the Authentic Self you are inherently free because that's the nature of the Authentic Self already. Already!" he repeated for emphasis.

"Yes, right."

"It's the same as when you experience the Ground of Being, its nature being inherent freedom from becoming, freedom from the world, freedom from everything because that's what it already is.

"Now, you can't have absolutely an equal interest in both the manifest dimension and the unmanifest. You're always going to have to have a preference. So most enlightenment teachings, which are liberation teachings because the state of consciousness they point to in the Ground of Being is inherently free, express a preference for the unmanifest.

"But with the Authentic Self it'll be the Creative Principle that will be experienced, which is this endless passion to create the universe. So in this teaching we're biased a little bit more towards the Authentic Self because we're interested in evolution and the creative dimension. After all, this is post-postmodern evolutionary spirituality in which the universal human is taking control of the process.

"Remember, the mythical God fell out of the sky, disappeared, and is now emerging as the true face of consciousness itself. So therefore the post-postmodern human who is endeavoring to become a manifest expression of the 'universal human' is consciously endeavoring to get into the driver's seat as the Authentic Self. Are you with me?"

"Yes."

"So now that the evolutionary process is beginning to become aware of itself, we reinterpret the meaning and significance of enlightenment in a developmental context. That's why we're calling it 'evolutionary enlightenment.' And enlightenment, as I've been saying, always means beyond ego. In evolutionary enlightenment that means beyond ego as the Authentic Self.

"By contrast, in pre-modern enlightenment the goal was the realization of the Ground of Being. To transcend the fears and desires of the individual and collective ego you give

up all your attachment to the world and abide forever in the eternal empty ground of the Unmanifest. But in evolutionary enlightenment you want to transcend the ego so you can be the Authentic Self in which there is the instantaneous, conscious experience of liberation here and now because that's its nature. Do you see how it works?"

"Yes, I do. Thank you."

"Good."

After repositioning himself on his cushion, Andrew called on the next person, this time an Australian man. *"Yes, sir?"*

"I also had this intense sense of vitality," he said, "but the intensity of it very much waxed and waned depending on whether I really engaged in the conversation or whether I'd sort of sat back a little. But whenever I re-engaged the intensity became far stronger."

"From the non-personal dimension, right?" Andrew asked.

"Yes. And although I didn't equate it with freedom at the time, there was a wonderful lightness of being that I experienced, which, as soon as you were talking about freedom, I recognized."

"So can you see the enormous potential in that?"

"Oh, absolutely. Without a doubt."

"Can't you see that from the perspective of the Authentic Self literally anything seems possible?"

"Yes, there's no question about it at all."

"Because in the Authentic Self there's no fear, there's no doubt and there's no self-consciousness. There's only this surge, right?"

"It's true. I mean…"

"This surge into the future starting right now. Always! Right?"

I could sense the fire pumping through Andrew's veins as he spoke.

"Right. And clearly, clearly dependent on my willingness to engage with it because, as I said, when I sat back I could sense the intensity dropping off."

"Yeah, because then you became a witness."

"I did."

"Then you're separating yourself from the thing itself."

"Yes, that's true."

"You see, you want to get to the point where being a witness and being completely engaged are not separate. You want to be able to observe and to participate at exactly the same time so that in the experience of witnessing you're not separate at all. Are you with me?"

"I am."

"That would be a more non-dual event."

"Yes, because I was aware at the time when I was pulling back the intensity would drop off…"

"Right. But what would life be like if we didn't pull back?"

"Revolutionary," he said with excited awe.

"*Oh!*" Andrew said in a long, drawn out way, feigning surprise and pitching the room into laughter once more. "*So if we pull back, that means there's time on and time off, right?*"

"Yes."

"*So does the Creative Principle or the Energy and Intelligence that created the universe have time off or need time off?*"

"No."

It seemed an absurd question when put this way, but then, who thinks like this?

"*Well that's the whole point. So who are you, then?*" He posed the question rhetorically and then answered it in the whining voice of the sensitive self. "*'Well, I don't know if I'm really, you know, up for that. I mean, it's…blah, blah, blah.' So it's only the ego that has doubts and hesitations. It's only the ego that wants time for itself. It's only the ego that needs to go through a process. The Authentic Self doesn't need to go through any process, does it?*"

"No, it doesn't."

"*As you experience it for yourself you'll see that I'm not making this up. It's because that's the nature of the Authentic Self already. It doesn't need to go through any process. It also doesn't need any time. The Authentic Self is never not ready.*"

"That was clear."

"*Exactly, but the thing is that as you experience the Authentic Self you begin to see what you're playing with and then you begin to see how, for example, everything I'm speaking about here fits together and how much sense it makes – and not just theoretically. Everything I'm speaking about is in relationship to real potentials. And it's not far away. That's the whole thing. It's not far away. It's right there and it doesn't take time. Does the Authentic Self need ramping up? Does it need to start slow and then turn it up gradually?*"

Everyone laughed and in that moment the urgency, intensity and passion were indeed right there and everything of which Andrew spoke was as obvious as sunshine.

"No, no. It's either there or it's not."

"*Well, it's always fully functioning. The minute you create the right conditions for its emergence it will emerge without hesitation, already going a hundred miles an hour. Because, once again, the Authentic Self is a function of consciousness itself. See what I'm saying?*"

"Yes."

"*So all we need to do is create the right conditions and it emerges. See?*"

"I do."

"*So once you begin to understand this experientially you'll see why I keep saying that the personal line and the Authentic Self are two completely different lines of development. And as long as one is identified in a very deep way with the personal domain the Authentic Self cannot emerge.*

"So, for example, if you, in relationship to your neurotic issues or narcissistic tendencies are not willing to make the effort to drop them, then the Authentic Self will not emerge. Therefore, the idea is to do whatever you need to do to relinquish your emotional attachment to your narcissistic proclivities.

"A narcissist is emotionally infatuated with himself. All they want to do is see themselves at all times and therefore they manipulate all the objects in their life in order to be able to see their own reflection. It's that habit that has to break. It means that you have to drop the mirror, which would mean that you couldn't see your reflection anymore, and that's a big deal. It means you can't use other people and circumstances for your own narcissistic needs anymore. And nobody can drop the mirror for you. You have to do it. It's the same with the infinite variety of ways that all our neurotic issues around fear, desire and god knows what else, manifest in us. Whatever it is and however it is for you is completely irrelevant. The point is, once you've recognized a much larger impersonal context and way of seeing, if you're not willing to make the effort to drop it you're actually standing in direct opposition to the evolutionary process itself.

"Now, as I've said, anyone who is able to understand what I'm talking about should be entirely capable of dropping it because of the choosing faculty that we've spent two days talking about and which we all agreed exists. It doesn't mean that the neurosis and narcissism go away, but it does mean that you drop your emotional investment in and attachment to them, which is something else altogether and which we can have control over. Do you see how that could work? Hmm?"

"Yes, definitely," he said soberly.

"You see, the problem with narcissism and neurosis is that we're emotionally invested in the worst parts of ourselves. And the thing is, we love it. We don't hate it. That's why we're so sick. We joke about it, but the truth is we're completely in love with it. It's a very morbid and unwholesome predicament. So we can laugh about it, but it's not funny because we do ruin our own lives and the lives of others simply because of our unwillingness to let go of it. We love our suffering because we love all the self-importance. You see, in a lot of our emotional and psychological pain the narcissistic self-sense experiences an incredible degree of self-importance and that's horrible. For far too many of us our sense of self is empowered by our experience of suffering so we really have to find enough interest in evolution to drop that."

As he said this I recalled the first time that I recognized this fact directly. It was shortly after having met Andrew, at which time I was burdened by extreme financial distress and had plummeted into deep depression, spending weeks on end squirming in a world of self-pity. There I was, witness to an interminable parade of "I'm not good enough; look what I've done; I'm thirty five years old and have nothing to show for it," ad nauseum. One morning, after weeks of bearing the heavy burden of self-hatred, in a flash of insight I saw through what I instantly knew to have been a charade all along. That is, I recognized the self-indulgence involved in wrapping the facts of a difficult situation in layer upon layer of acute self-pity. Was my situation painful? It was. Did it seem inescapable? It did. But beyond that I recognized, in a deeply morbid way, that by donning the cloak of "poor me" I got to be special, very special. In the folds of that cloak it was the "me" that was more pronounced than the "poor," and that "me" had taken center stage to act out a dark farce. My suffering made me special and for that satisfaction a part of me was willing to pay the price in pain. In that instant I realized how little the ego, that pretender to friendship, actually cares about me. In fact, it cares not one whit about me, about my welfare, about whether I feel good or bad – it cares only for its own position at the center. Ego cares only about ego and its ability to locate itself at all costs at all times and in any way possible at the very center. And there was nothing like intense emotional distress to act as a focal point for such ruthless cunning.

It was also during this time that I first discovered the power of choice and its capacity to transform my relationship to my inner world in an instant. I realized that while I did not have to deny the emotional pain of my present circumstance whatsoever, I also did not have to chew on it relentlessly, twisting myself into a knot of misery sitting alone in the center of an uncaring cosmos. I noticed that if I simply let things be, most of the heaviness vanished, leaving behind a thread of distress in line with actual circumstance. Proportionate to reality, the discomfort no longer plunged me into depression. In fact, by letting things be and refusing to engage with my own morbidity, the space opened up for the practical facts of my life to shift to such a degree that within a week of this realization my fortunes had fully reversed, and in nothing short of miraculous fashion.

Since then I have often considered the damage we inflict upon ourselves by meditating upon our self-pity and neurosis, upon the "poor me." It is in this fashion that we box ourselves into an imaginary hell. And while imaginary, the consequences are real enough. Yet does the ego care? Not as long as it gets to "wallow in the wallowing," as Peter used to say. Not as long as it gets to be special and not as long as it gets to occupy the central seat in that self-created hell world. Now at forty-six years old, poised at the apex between coming into this life and going out of it, I am able to look down both sides of that divide and continue to observe with both fascination and trepidation the evolution over time of neurotic self-indulgence. What begins as a colorful collection of personality quirks in our twenties grows like a tumor, digging deep into the psyche until, years later, with age stripping away the strength to maintain the façade of "normalcy," it transforms us into caricatures of ourselves, into harsh etchings of the "poor me." As such persons, or with such persons, both authentic relationship and the emergence of the elevated human potentials that we were presently exploring are banished from the realm of possibility.

"*So this is why the ego's got to go,*" Andrew pointed out. "*Then this function of consciousness, which is inherently egoless, can come to the front and do its thing. So, the whole process and practice of purification, which has been a central feature of the spiritual life for millennia, doesn't come from God. You see, enlightenment has to do with the experiential discovery of certain parts of the self at the level of consciousness that are already pure. The Ground of Being doesn't need to be purified because purity is its nature already. In the same way, the evolutionary, creative impulse of the Authentic Self doesn't need to be purified because its nature as this energetic function of consciousness is already pure. But we, as individuals, are a different story altogether. So the whole question of pure or impure motivation in relationship to ego only we can deal with. Consciousness cannot deal with these issues because consciousness itself doesn't have these problems. So you're the only one who can choose to do whatever it is that you need to do to get control of the worst parts of your self. And worst means evil. The definition of good and evil – which we haven't spoken about at all so far – in an evolutionary context is very simple: that which is good is what encourages and inspires this creative impulse and enables it to grow and to move forward; that which is evil is that which actually inhibits it.*"

"Yes, that makes sense," the Australian man said.

"*So there are forces in ourselves that can and will inhibit the emergence of our own creative, evolutionary potential as well as that in others. You better believe it! So another word for spiritual practice would be self-cultivation. The cultivation of the self, at least in the way that I teach it, is all about doing whatever it is that we need to do so that we can be a vehicle for consciousness itself. See how simple it is? When you look at it in a post-metaphysical context it becomes more practical than anything else. But that doesn't make it any less daunting.*" Andrew laughed in a way that suggested that no matter what he said, he couldn't overemphasize this point.

"*And if you understand what I'm saying now then you want to put this together with what I was explaining last night about the 'bottom up' versus 'top down' perspective. When spiritual practice is 'bottom up' your relationship with ego is going to be very different than if it's top-down. From a 'bottom up' perspective you're still going to be personally identified with the ego. You're not going to see it as the enemy because it's still going to be part of you and you would never want see part of your self as an enemy because you're a good person. You're just not perfect.*" He laughed again. "*You see, from the 'bottom up' you're seeing the ego from the perspective of the personal dimension, which is the ego itself. But from the 'top down' you're seeing the personal dimension from the perspective of consciousness itself whether it's the Ground of Being or the Authentic Self and then the context of your spiritual practice is going to be very different. Now, even though you can do spiritual practice from a 'bottom up' perspective and be talking about evolution, about going beyond ego and all those things, it's going to look very different than if it's from the 'top down' because, as I said, it's really from the perspective of consciousness itself.*

Andrew paused for a few moments to allow this new point to settle into our awareness. Then he continued, *"Do you all see how the teaching fits together? If you keep going into it you'll find that it's an integral, evolutionary perspective. And if you really understand it, it changes your relationship to life, to your own experience and to others in a way that's nothing short of dramatic. So this spiritual practice, self-cultivation, path of purification or whatever you want to call it, is an essential component of the teaching that nobody can do for you. Spiritual practice in this context means that you are making the effort to cage your ego.*

"And when you begin to understand this you'll see that effort and spontaneity begin to come together in a kind of perfect balance that begins to reveal itself. Suddenly you'll find that the whole notion of effort doesn't even mean anything to you anymore. In other words, once you see what the goal is in this very big perspective, when it's necessary to make effort, you do and when it's not necessary to make effort, you don't. But you're no longer even drawing a distinction because you just do whatever you have to do in order to achieve the goal. You see what a big perspective that is?" It was a rhetorical question as most of us were at least intuiting this view at that moment.

"So when you understand what the view is then you can actually practice, but if you don't understand it, you can't really practice because you don't know what you're doing. So I hope that some of you can grasp why the view or perspective is really the whole thing and the rest of it is you just bridging the gap. If you don't have the view you can make all the effort you want but you're going to go in circles forever and wonder why you're not getting anywhere. But if you have it and you want to make progress and evolve more than anything else, you will. You have to. Nothing can stop you.

"So the view is when you see what we've been talking about in here in your own heart, in your own soul, and in your own mind. Then the perspective of evolutionary enlightenment is actually living within you. And then as your practice develops, your relationship to your own mind, to your own emotions, to other people, to the world, to life itself, will become an expression of that perspective. So the act of becoming a different person with different values requires practice and when you become a different person with different values in a world of materialism and narcissism that's *revolutionary.*

"When I think about it, it sounds very much like Buddha dharma. When the Buddha would teach he would begin by giving people what he called 'Right View', and then they would begin to practice. So in traditional or original Buddhism they say that you can't practice without the Right View. But in today's spiritual world a lot of people say, 'no, you need to practice in order to get 'right view.' And the traditional response would be, 'you can't do that. You have to get the view first.' So it's the same thing in this teaching. You have to get the view first. If you understand this it will really blow your mind because then you start seeing that it's not about having a particular experience. It has to do with gaining a certain perspective and doing whatever you need to do to maintain it through cultivating yourself."

Andrew paused once more before concluding. *"Okay, I think I've said enough,"* he laughed. *"So I'm very happy about this. Do you all see what's happened in the last twenty-four hours? We've taken an enormous leap from where we were to where are right now."*

We indicated our assent and with that Andrew concluded and we all settled into meditation once more.

Right view. As long as I've known Andrew he has unfailingly maintained that his first job as a teacher is to provide the seeker with "right view," a direct experience of precisely what it was that he was teaching. In this case that would be either an experience of the Ground of Being, the Authentic Self or, in all likelihood, both. His first job as a teacher then was to prove himself to the prospective student. Having done so, it then fell to the prospective student to prove him or herself to him as a teacher. Such was the dynamic of an authentic student-teacher relationship.

It occurred to me that for the previous nine days Andrew had been giving us right view – on steroids. He had provided us with powerful experiences not only of the Ground, our very own source, but also of the Authentic Self, the creative surge behind the evolving universe and the surge of our own lives. He had then helped us to interpret those experiences, in light of all he had learned in two decades as a spiritual teacher. Thus he had been crafting "right view" with meticulous precision from day one, culminating in the "top-down" view from which most of us now saw. It occurred to me that this was what Andrew had been doing from the very first day of his teaching career – directly transmitting the experience of enlightenment through mere association and dialogue. The content and thrust of that dialogue had changed but its essence remained the same – powerful, direct transmission. I had read numerous accounts of how he and those who gathered around him in the early years used to spend weeks immersed in the ecstasy of Self-realization. Once, when I casually mentioned this to Alka, his wife, she looked at me incredulously and asked, "Weeks? We used to spend months like that." Yet even then, for Andrew such immersion in the bliss of the Self merely signified the beginning of the path rather than its culmination. Right view. It all began with right view.

I considered the journey Andrew had taken us on since the beginning of the retreat nine days earlier. He'd brought us from glory to glory and laid out the path in between, rocky gulleys and all. That is, we'd spent the first four or so days diving deeply into the realization of the Ground of existence. We'd then explored the reality of our relationship to life and examined the mechanisms by which we could, if we chose to, straighten ourselves out, aligning ourselves with our realization. And now, as the retreat was nearing its end, Andrew had facilitated the emergence of what such straightening out would empower – the ecstatic eruption of the Authentic Self in the individual and collective along with the recognition of its monumental potential. From glory to glory, and every step of the journey experiential. There was nothing to believe, no articles of faith, nothing to take Andrew's word for. Simply in following his guidance to look into ourselves, "right view" revealed itself. This made everything real, inspiring and personally implicating. Having seen the view from the inside out was post-metaphysical spirituality in its nascence. And, even with all the troubles of the previous days, I reveled in it. I wanted to be part of this revolution more than I wanted anything else. And therefore, though fatigued, I was exhilarated and spent the afternoon in calm reflection.

The next session began with several people sharing the burning thrill of their alternating immersion in the Ground of Being and Authentic Self. There was an intoxicated, slightly out of control quality to these dialogues, as people seemed to have difficulty forming full sentences. They were literally drunk on consciousness. Andrew listened quietly, serving as a calm anchor. One woman said with tremulous intensity that the very ground under her feet seemed to be shaking and that her body felt as if it might explode. In a tone of "but of course" Andrew replied that that's what's supposed to happen and if it didn't one hadn't "gotten it" yet. Talk about right view! Soon things settled a bit and the questions resumed along the lines of inquiry that had begun in the morning. First Andrew engaged with an Israeli woman.

"I want to know," she began in a kind of challenging tone, "according to your teaching is our activity for creating a new world through our Authentic Self the only meaning and significance of life."

"Versus what?" Andrew asked.

"I don't know versus what, but is that the answer to the question, 'Why are we here?'"

"Yes. For the Authentic Self creating the universe is the raison d'etre."

"And are there people that are working and creating but without Authentic Self?"

"Yes. Certainly."

"So they are working the same as us but the only difference is that they are suffering more because of their ego?"

"No. The point is that the Authentic Self is the creative impulse. Many people experience the creative impulse in many different ways, but now we're talking about recognizing the creative impulse at the level of consciousness itself. It means you're actually aware of it. You're aware of it and also you know what it is. You can experience it and respond to it without understanding what it is or knowing what it is in this way."

"So the difference is the knowing."

"That's the whole thing, yeah."

"But they are creating as much as…"

"Well, the creative impulse is all around us, right?"

"Right."

"I was talking with Ken Wilber about this once and he said what would've happened in earlier times when this impulse was felt by people who were interested in the kinds of things that we're speaking about here is that they would have experienced an urge to create which would have expressed itself in various forms of art. That would've been the only outlet. But now we're becoming objectively aware of the creative impulse itself and that changes everything."

"Thank you," she said, seemingly satisfied with this response and having nothing further to add. Andrew moved on, his eyes settling on an American woman with pulled- back blond hair.

"I wanted to say," she began in a tone of sober respect, "that so many tumblers have been falling into place for me during this retreat that I'm just awed by it. I'm really beginning to see how all of this fits together. I've been meditating for seven or eight years and I actually never understood why we meditate until this retreat and I'm just so grateful."

"You used to do Buddhist practice, right?"

"Yeah, that's right. But no one really ever explained this 'top down' approach. I mean we just kind of kept doing it and doing it and eventually the message became, 'well, you'll get to the point where you can have peace and be able to control your mind,' but I just never really got why. But when I was in conversation around the tables and the Authentic Self was really manifesting powerfully, I was experiencing this human joy and bliss and the longing and the joy of the Authentic Self itself because it was able to come into form. So that just gives me such great inspiration for actually doing the work that..."

"But the Authentic Self is never happy about doing anything..." Andrew interjected. *"It's not happy about doing something because it's not self-conscious in that way and it never experiences time. So it can't stand back and feel happy about a job well done or say, 'Aren't I having a great time?' But* **you** *can."*

"Oh. Maybe that was me then," she laughed, little tears of joy glistening in her eyes.

"But it's important to understand that. It's just a function of consciousness. It's nature is many of the things that you described but the Authentic Self doesn't have the capacity to step back and be aware of its own experience in that kind of way. Does that make sense?"

"Yeah."

"The Authentic Self is not happy that something is happening because that ecstatic, passionate intensity is what its nature is already. See the point?"

"I do. Can I ask another question?"

"Certainly."

"What did you mean the other day when you were asking us to really look into the clarity of intention and you were saying, 'Well, just imagine that the

Authentic Self or the creative impulse is waiting for your answer'? Were you joking or is that really serious?"

"*It's serious.*"

"Maybe that's what I was experiencing."

"*Well, the Authentic Self is always seeking for itself and it wants to take over the universe, right?*"

"Yeah."

"*Because you could start to see, as one of you said this morning, that when the personal dimension comes into the picture then the Authentic Self just goes into retreat, right?*"

"Yeah."

"*And it'll only return when the personal is being held in check.*"

"Right."

"*So when I say it's self-seeking it's much like sexual energy or the creative impulse. So you can see that sexual energy has a certain nature and it has a motive, which is creative. In the same way, there's a powerful, inherent motive in the energy of consciousness itself and the experience of it is many of the things that we've been speaking about. However, from the perspective of the empty ground there's no motive whatsoever. There's just Being itself.*

"*But when a human being awakens to the Creative Impulse or the Authentic Self then that human being – who was the one with a hole in their soul – experiences that motive as the discovery of absolute meaning and purpose. But that meaning and purpose is already inherently the nature of the Authentic Self because of its motive, which is to create the universe.*"

"Yes, that makes sense."

"*But what you said is true. A lot of people don't know why they do spiritual practice. They just do it and the why is often very vague.*"

"Yeah. I mean it was such a…"

"*You need to know why you're doing it and it has to be goal-oriented. Hmm?*"

"Yeah. I mean my experience was that I just lost motivation because I really didn't understand why I was doing it. It was something I kind of had to do. However, my experience of both the Ground of Being and the Authentic Self give me the inspiration and desire to deal with my ego where it is. And as you were saying, now that I have the view I can go about bridging the gap between my center of gravity and what I've realized as my own potential. I just never really got that before."

"*Okay, good.*"

I remembered a story I'd heard Andrew tell on several occasions, which concerned a comment one of his Buddhist meditation teachers had made upon hearing of Andrew's awakening. Derisively, he had said, "The problem with Andrew was always that he was only ever interested in enlightenment and that he never just wanted to settle into the practice." That's quite a thing to say by someone teaching enlightenment - and a pertinent comment on today's East-meets-West spiritual culture.

"All right," I heard Andrew say, as the microphone went to a French woman.

"Is how deep one can go in the Ground of Being the same as how far one can express the Authentic Self?" she asked through the translator.

"What do you mean?"

"Well, there's something I don't quite understand. So I see that I've got the ego or the Authentic Self and that the difference between them is black and white, but at the same time it's as if there are different levels of being able to express the Authentic Self, right?"

"Well, no. There's just degrees of intensity of more or less. But what's the question about it?"

"I guess that was the question."

"It's funny," Andrew said, *"but I just want to point out that every question that's been asked almost since we started this afternoon has been in the abstract category. For some reason, and I don't know why, suddenly everybody's like, "Oh, now I got it so now we're going to get abstract."* He laughed, and then added, *"So don't do that."*

"Well, maybe the reason I ask," the woman continued, "is because I want to be able to discriminate more clearly in the discussions whether I'm really coming from the Authentic Self or if that is just some kind of self-deception because it seems as if I'm still self-conscious when I come from the Authentic Self."

"You wouldn't be though because there isn't any self-consciousness in the Authentic Self," he pointed out once more and then, apparently knowing this person, he added, *"but you're very self-conscious anyway, aren't you? Isn't being very self-conscious your natural state."*

"Yeah, definitely," she acknowledged.

"That's the problem," Andrew laughed.

"So that means that when I'm self-conscious I cannot express the Authentic Self. Is that it?"

"Right."

"But that means that I am expressing ego then?"

"Right."

"Oh."

"That's what self-consciousness is. It's the sense that I'm aware of myself as being separate."

"Yeah, I see."

"I'm here. You're there. I'm having this conversation with you. You're having this conversation with me and we have like two-hundred and forty people that are listening to us." Everyone laughed as it appeared that Andrew was endeavoring to make her

squirm even more in self-consciousness simply so she could become aware of its visceral feeling quality.

"Not being self-conscious, on the other hand, means that you're not aware of yourself as being separate. You're not aware of yourself as being separate!" he repeated and then once more, just for emphasis: *"You are not aware of yourself as being separate! I could still have a conversation with you, with you sitting over there and me sitting over here and me being aware that you're sitting there and I'm sitting here. Are you with me?"*

"Yes."

"And I'm aware that there are a lot of people looking and listening. But I can be aware of all those things and simultaneously not be aware at all of any emotionally felt sense of separation. Do you understand?"

"Yes, I think so."

"Once again, you can be aware that you're there and that I'm here and that there's a conversation happening between two people that have different qualities. One's a female. One's a male. One's Dutch. One's American. But you can be aware of all those things without experiencing any emotionally felt sense of separation at all—at all—at all! Absolutely none. Do you understand?

"So the separation we're talking about" he went on, *"has to do with an emotional sense of distance. So you can be aware of difference yet not have any emotional experience of it."*

"What do you mean by emotional experience?"

"Well, self-consciousness is basically an emotional experience. It means I am aware of myself as being separate. Therefore, while I might be having a conversation with you I'm still going to be more aware of myself than of you. I'm going to be self-conscious in a way that distorts my perception because I'd be getting a little bit lost in my personal field of sensory experience."

"Okay."

"Therefore, I'm here and I'm having a feeling relationship to what's happening in my inner field of awareness and then I see you more as an object that's out there somewhere. I'm aware that you exist and I might even be able to hear what you're saying enough to be able to feign actually having a lucid or reasonably intelligent conversation with you. But the majority of my attention is going to be focused upon my own personal experience of myself with you as an object in that field of experience, right?"

"Right, I can relate to that." She wasn't the only one, a fact we acknowledged with a brief burst of laughter.

"But when there's no emotionally felt sense of separation then the other is not objectified. There's literally no wall whatsoever. So there's no emotionally felt difference between speaking to one person or speaking to another or just sitting quietly with my eyes closed. It's all just one field. Do you understand?"

"Yeah."

I had to wonder how many of us really understood this. What Andrew was describing was his own experience. It was something that I'd experienced at moments and could deeply intuit based on that past experience, but it was far from where I lived. I relished such descriptions of enlightened awareness, told from the inside out by someone who actually lived there.

"So for the Authentic Self there is no sense of otherness, especially not in relationship to other people. That's one of the things that's so miraculous about it. You literally experience absolutely no separation, gap, ego defenses or any wall between your self and another whatsoever. Even in dialogue it's not like you're having a conversation with another person, but almost like you're thinking out loud with yourself. Just because something comes out of one mouth over there or another over here, it's still one Authentic Self. It's non-different and when that's experienced in a very profound way it's quite a shock to the system.

"The ego can only have a relationship with other separate individuals," Andrew continued, "and it's all very personal. But the Authentic Self only has a relationship with itself. So it's not a little bit different or slightly different; it's completely and radically different. So did you ever experience that?"

I certainly had had such experiences during various enlightened communication groups, validating Andrew's description in my own experience. However, it appeared that the young Dutch woman, had not. "I don't think so," she responded to Andrew's query. "Not in the way you're describing it. I thought I did, but…"

"It's harder for Dutch people," Andrew said without jest in his voice. "You've heard me say that before, right?"

"Yeah, you say lot's of things about Dutch people," she acknowledged, half grudgingly, half knowingly as the silence was ruptured with laughter.

Andrew wasn't laughing, though. He'd spent much time over the years attempting to pry open a breach in the Dutch mentality as he saw it. It had only been a couple of years since he had headed for Holland with the intention of closing his centers due to a collective lack of response to his message. While there, in a public talk he attacked the entirety of the smugly self-satisfied, ultra-egalitarian, anti-hierarchical, doggedly narcissistic Dutch mind-set (which differed from its California cousin by only the slightest degree) head on. Astonishingly, he received a standing ovation – something that never happens in Holland, for too much approval might raise one too far above others and thus comprise an affront to the pathologically egalitarian sensibilities – for his audience recognized the truth in his words and, to everyone's shock, respected him for his forceful critique. In a stunning acknowledgement of that critique, Andrew's teachings began to flourish in Holland and, in fact, continue to do so as a growing group of individuals are beginning to grapple with their cultural conditioning in a serious way.

"Well, it is harder for Dutch people, to experience freedom from self-consciousness, isn't it?" Andrew asked.

"Yeah, it's true."

"So remember there's individual and collective ego and therefore part of our own ego has to be an expression of the culture from which we've come, right?"

"Yes."

"As we were saying earlier during the retreat, it's all part of the self. So there's our ethnic background, our sense of being part of a particular gender and many other things that influence our sense of ourselves, right?"

"Yes, but I somehow had this idea that it was kind of easy to come from the Authentic Self…"

"Well, the Authentic Self is always at ease."

"I meant making the leap from the ego to the Authentic Self."

"I know, but I'm just trying to make the distinction that the Authentic Self is always at ease. It doesn't experience fear or self-consciousness. So it's always easy for the Authentic Self. It may or may not be easy for you. So if you're a very self-conscious person then it might be quite a leap to let yourself go into the Authentic Self. There might be that much more hesitation, resistance and fear about it, right?"

"Yeah."

"But that's not the problem of the Authentic Self."

"No, I realize that."

"Okay good," Andrew laughed.

"Can I ask you something more now?"

"Sure."

"In the meditation today I really tried to let go into the Ground of Being and fall into it. But as I got more and more of a sense of this Ground I just got self-aware again and again and again."

"You mean you'd go in and come back out of it?"

"Yeah."

"Do you see how it's a psychological habit?"

"Yeah. It was really difficult to make the jump although I really wanted to. It was as if I could jump a little bit and then go back again." She paused thoughtfully for a moment, and then went on, "Well, in the Ground of Being the whole world disappears and yourself also, right?"

"That's on a good day. That's exactly it, yeah," Andrew laughed.

"So what I felt was this holding on to the sense of self."

"But you did feel the disappearing start to happen?"

"Yeah."

"Isn't that thrilling?"

"It was absolutely great, yeah."

"Well, that's the whole idea and the more the better."

"Yeah, definitely. Thanks."

Andrew shifted slightly on his cushion and took the next question from a young American man.

"So, Andrew, first of all I want to appreciate your efforts yesterday to drag us out of our collective stupor. I really felt the shift in the whole group and myself. It was pretty profound and I experienced it as a lightness in myself…"

"Well, the thing is," Andrew interrupted, *"I was speaking quite a lot about the gap between our capacity to intellectually appreciate a higher moral, ethical, philosophical and spiritual potential and where we actually live emotionally and what we're actually up to. I also talked about the moral and ethical implications of bridging that gap. And I kept repeating it and understandably a lot of people were kind of viscerally and involuntarily balking. So there's a word for that, which is right here,"* he pointed to the appropriate place on the ego model, *"and it is called inertia."* Everyone laughed. *"So inertia is just naturally there. It's part of the universe. You understand?"*

"Yeah."

"But so I think what was being felt by everybody was inertia, which was the resistance to bridging the gap between a higher potential that made perfect sense to us and a willingness to meet the implications in real time because the implications are big. I think the individual and collective ego was saying, 'whoa' and I kept repeating it because the more people didn't respond the more I felt that what I was saying made such deep sense that it was making me more excited. That set up a certain amount of tension and there was a gap until I spoke about this top-down perspective. Finally everybody seemed to get it and that seemed to relieve the tension."

"Right."

"Whether it actually relieved the tension or not remains to be seen. It's usually not that simple," he laughed. *"But at least I think suddenly many people understood the difference between bottom-up and top-down. That in itself is enlightening because, as I said, not many people do. But then you see the enormous potential inherent in this completely new perspective. It's very exciting."*

"Yeah. So I felt that shift in myself and I could see the power of the collective in initiating that shift. I can see the amazing potential for a new way of coming together."

"Yes, that's true, but at the same time we all have to be careful of collectives because with a collective or group it's very easy to lose your autonomy and just go with whatever direction any particular group or collective is headed in, right?"

"Yeah, that's right."

"You have to be very careful not to lose your autonomy or objectivity because any collective context is by its nature going to have a certain view. But part of what the teaching is about is striving to reach a higher level of development where we can be in a collective context and our autonomy is not lost at all, but rather is actually developed.

"So, by the way, a collective context starts with two people: husband and wife, boyfriend and girlfriend," he paused for a moment, a sly grin on his face, *"man and dog."* Another burst of laughter filled the room. *"But the point is, whenever there's kind of a shared viewpoint and emotional experience, which is a big part of what the human experience is all about, often our potential for autonomy decreases in a profound way and in the worst case, disappears all together. Right?"*

"So there's a danger, but there's also…"

"But that's how human beings function. We haven't taken that step yet where being alone is not any different than being together. This leap has to be taken and that's what this teaching is all about. It's supposed to actualize this potential for being alone and being together as being exactly the same experience. That's the 'new being' that the teaching refers to and that's a different world. It's something radically new. Now, if you look at the implications of a statement like that, well, they're enormous. And that's why I keep saying that it's the personal sense of self or the personal stream that is the big obstacle to this evolutionary leap.

"Yesterday, when I was describing what it would be like in five thousand or maybe fifty thousand years if this process were to continue, maybe some people got a sense of it. But as we've been saying and as some of you have experienced, when the personal emerges the Authentic Self disappears. That's because the personal self is 'the other.' On the other hand, when the personal self recedes the Authentic Self comes to the front and then being alone and being together are exactly the same thing because the Authentic Self is one. And if we can do that with real people in real time then something very important is actually happening. Does that make sense?"

A murmur of both affirmation and astonishment moved through us as the living possibility of what Andrew was pointing to blossomed in the collective.

"But it's very different and the implications are nothing less than radical in terms of our unrealized human potential. That's why this step beyond individuality really must be the next step for our race. And just to be clear, we don't lose our individuality; we go beyond it. We transcend it. It's not lost. So usually, in a collective context we lose our individuality in a way that isn't good. That's what happened in Nazi Germany. That's an extreme example, but in many subtle ways these kinds of things happen all the time. But if the opposite would begin to happen it would represent a complete re-ordering of things. It would be a vertical step up, an evolutionary leap in the development of our species. So the Authentic Self is already ready to go and it's only the ego or the separate self-sense that would have enormous hesitation about such a step. It should be obvious why," he laughed. *You get the idea?"*

We all agreed once more.

"So for the remainder of our time here, which is another day and a half, you all should really, deeply consider these things. Because, once again, one can have experiences but the experiences have implications. So think about what it would be like if being together was just like being alone.

"And remember, the thing that's very compelling about the Authentic Self is that it's seeking for itself. Human beings are social animals. Whether you personally feel like one or not is another issue," Andrew laughed. *"And also, as you all probably know, human development and the evolution of consciousness take place through human interaction. It's through the stimulation and engagement of human interaction that culture develops and evolves and it's also how the brain develops.*

"So if you really look into the evolution of consciousness in light of the discovery of the Authentic Self then what's actually happening when we're together in our relationships becomes more and more important and meaningful. Then the context of our relationships – of why we're together and what we're actually doing together – begins to become more significant than it ever appeared to be. So what is the context for our relationships? Is it ego? Is it the past? Or is the context for our relationship the ground for something new and creative? So the implications get bigger, more apparent and more tangible. That's when the inner and the outer begin to merge and become indistinct. Often we have our spiritual life including our spiritual practice, which is something we do when we're alone. But what if there wasn't any distinction between being alone and in relationship? What if it was all just one thing?"

I understood what he meant and again marveled at the potential for individual and cultural transformation inherent in enlightened consciousness. It was something I had suspected all those years ago when that consciousness had first intruded so unexpectedly into my life. It was also something that I had longed to participate in and help actualize, both then and throughout the twenty-six years between then and now. And now that possibility rang more true than ever.

"You know it's interesting to note," Andrew added as an afterthought, *"that in some of the most progressive countries like Holland and Scandinavia where the individual has more freedom and rights than anywhere else in the world, the sense of alienation is most extreme."*

This statement was followed by a short, awkward silence in which most of us took in the curious irony of that fact.

"Right?" Andrew insisted and the silence retreated in the wake of soft laughter. *"All right,"* he said, before going on to the next question.

This time the microphone passed to an older English woman, her gray hair neatly pulled into a bun, "I'm getting a sense that the 'top down' and the 'bottom up' are both important for the picture to be whole."

"How so?"

"For integrity of the self."

"So how would that work together then?"

"Well, I think if one can make them work together that there would be an integrity and wholeness."

"Right, that would definitely have to be true but the whole idea here is that once we're able to embrace the top-down perspective, then we totally abandon the bottom-up one."

"Oh, we abandon it?" she said, surprised.

"Yeah," Andrew said jovially.

"Oh." She sounded slightly taken aback, clearly not having expected this response.

"But you can only abandon the bottom-up perspective when you can actually embrace the top-down view," he added.

"Okay," she said, sounding slightly relieved.

"And so the sixty-four thousand dollar question of course is, when is an individual authentically ready to make that flip? When will they be willing to assume the top-down perspective? You see, the top-down view is exclusive. You can't mix a 'bottom up' and a 'top down' view. It has to be one or the other. That's why it is what it is, which is non-relative or absolute."

I had heard Andrew speak before about a conversation he'd had with Ken Wilber during which Ken had asked him this very question. At the time Andrew had had no ready answer. It was only some months later that the answer, seemingly obvious in retrospect, came to him. A person will not be ready to wholeheartedly embrace the 'top down' view, he concluded, until they are ready to embrace wholly the fifth tenet of the teaching, "for the sake of the whole." In other words, when an individual's motivation shifts authentically from wanting liberation only for themselves to wanting it for the sake of the evolution of consciousness itself, then, and only then, will he or she be able to embrace the 'top down' view and jettison its opposite.

"Now in terms of what you're saying," he continued, *"a model could be created where you take the 'bottom up' perspective to that point where this flip could be made from the ego's perspective to the perspective of the Authentic Self. At that moment the bottom-up perspective would be relinquished and the top-down perspective would be embraced. It's important to understand, however, that from the top-down way of looking at it, the bottom-up then becomes not only irrelevant, but destructive."*

"How so?"

"Because these two views are like oil and water. The 'top down' perspective cannot be seen from the 'bottom up' and vice versa. So that's why, practically speaking, when an individual authentically embraces the 'top down' view they can't pick up the 'bottom up' ever again—I mean ideally. Of course, after the flip is made the stakes go up, because in the 'bottom up' perspective you have all kinds of time and room for your own particular process, right?"

"Right."

"But when the flip's made that time's up. It's over. You've gotta do it now." Andrew snapped his fingers. *"And then if the person says, 'but I'm not ready!' you'd say, 'well*

then, what are you doing up here?'" Everyone laughed. *"Now that doesn't deny evolution or the constant need for self-perfection. That never ends. But practically speaking it means that we made that flip to not less than fifty-one percent Authentic Self. It means that our center of gravity and the perspective that we live from and stand for is of the Authentic Self, not the ego."*

"Yeah. I understand."

"That's why when people start talking about their 'issues' and their 'I have this and I have that' you're not going to be able to relate to it because you realize you're actually feeding something that from the perspective of the Authentic Self isn't real. But from the 'bottom up' it's very real. So you're literally stepping out of one world and entering into another. And we have to stay out of the old world because, in terms of the evolution of consciousness, if our resolve is not strong, and if we're still listening to the old voices, the old world can pull us back down. And then we lose the absolute conviction that we had known when we were in touch with the Authentic Self. That conviction is everything and the soul gets profoundly shaken by being pulled back down like that. It doesn't mean it's impossible to pull ourselves back up to the 'top down' perspective but it means we have to work that much harder. Dropping back down shakes your faith in your own capacity to do it and it also strengthens this wounded self-sense, which is the last thing that we want more of. But not doing that requires an act of renunciation. The fact is that once you take that step you have to resist what will at times be an overwhelming temptation to go back to the old way of looking at things."

"Yes, I can understand that."

"Remember, we said the minimum requirement to make the flip is not less than fifty-one percent. So even if the individual was say fifty-six percent Authentic Self that would leave intact forty-four percent of the individual and collective ego and all its attachment and identification, much of which might be so deeply conditioned that it would go beyond even one life. So that's still a lot of temptation. But if you've made that step to fifty-one percent you will have the wherewithal to resist the temptation. Now you can see that if you haven't reached the fifty-one percent point yet, and most people haven't, how much work one would have to do, how much courage, strength of purpose, clarity of vision and faith would have to be cultivated, in order to strengthen oneself until one got to the point when it was fifty-one percent. And that's just the way it really is, you see?"

"I do."

"So this top-down perspective is something to be worked for and consciously cultivated through effort, willpower and big-heartedness. It takes a lot of courage to be able to bear your own insecurity and your own fear and your own doubt as well as that of others and not to give in to it. And you don't have to be at fifty-one percent to be able to do that. You just have to be earnest. See what I'm saying?"

"Yes."

"Okay good. But the thing is, the top-down is a radically different perspective. It's a different feeling state and it's a completely different relationship with the human expe-

rience that people who are still very identified with the 'bottom up' perspective, which is the ego's point of view, are going to find threatening and won't understand. They'll feel you've lost your humanity, you've lost your soul, and you've lost your heart and actually what they don't know is that you've found all those things. But because they're still identified with all of the things that you are bending over backwards to let go of you can't engage on that level anymore. You just can't do it because there's something else that's too important and that's what they won't understand. They'll say, 'what's happened to you?' and you'll say, 'The most important thing that could ever happen.' Then they'll say, 'but I don't feel it. I don't feel connected with you anymore,' and you'll say, 'I'm right here.' 'I know,' they'll say, 'but I don't feel you; something's happened.' But it's because they want to feel that personal thing and all you can say is, 'I'm sorry.' But then they'll feel offended and think it's a lack of love. But it's not a lack of love, of affection or care. It's that you've changed.

"So the ego seeks for itself just like the Authentic Self seeks for itself. So if the ego is seeking for itself and doesn't find itself it feels hurt or offended. But it has nothing to do with any kind of personal hurt or offense, it's just literally that you've shifted into a different perspective and the shift is nothing less than that big. So it's an enormous leap and it can't be underestimated. But one way or the other, the 'top down' and the 'bottom up' cannot sleep in the same bed – the bed being you."

Andrew paused for a few moments, as if considering another point or reaching for some strand of memory. Suddenly he seemed to have hit on it.

"You know, when I started teaching a long time ago I was very open-minded. In those days I was willing to try anything. So with some people who were with me and who obviously had issues that they weren't dealing with, I just experimented and sent them to different kinds of therapists. In every single case their identification with the wounded self increased dramatically within days. The sense that they had a problem and the sense of specialness in relationship to that fact increased by leaps and bounds literally overnight and every single time."

I had heard Andrew proclaim for years that psychotherapy and enlightenment are two streams heading in opposite directions and that the former could never lead to the latter; that, in fact, the former would profoundly inhibit the latter. This earned him no small amount of ire while in California, where therapist's offices line the streets like coffee shops and therapists are busier than plumbers.

"Okay, yes?" He called on a young German woman with thick glasses.

"I heard you say on one of your CDs that it's not enough to have a big heart, that you have to find the right heart. And just now you said, 'you have to have a big heart.' So what heart is it that you're talking about?"

"Well, what do you think I'm talking about? You're an intelligent woman."

"The heart of the Authentic Self."

"Right. So there would be a big-heartedness that would be strong enough not to be seduced, not to fall apart under very strong temptations to get smaller."

"Yeah. So that's what you…"

"In other words, part of growing or evolving involves suffering, hmm?"

"Yes."

"When you embrace that which is new you have to let go of that which is old."

"Right."

"And it won't happen just once because if you're continually growing you're continually having to let go of that which is old and all the emotional investment in it. So it would also take a very big heart to be able to bear the pain involved in that. You understand?"

"Yes. Okay."

I'd given a lot of thought to this aspect of the teaching and it was something to which even Peter had alluded repeatedly. Nonetheless, the entire notion took some getting used to. What I hoped, and I doubt I stand alone in this, was that I would struggle to a point, overcome some major obstacles with heroic spirit, then land on the white sands of a distant shore where I might enjoy the blissful fruits of my endeavor with spiritual leisure and ease. However, I continue to discover that this is simply not the case, growing slowly into the more mature understanding that authentic transformation is ongoing and always carries an emotional price. Spiritual economics 101 – there are no free lunches. And it is our willingness to pay that price that determines how extraordinary will be our transformation and our life in the world. We all must learn to bear our own insanity so we can authentically rise above it and it occurs to me that the visceral friction and discomfort inherent in such a stand is nothing less than the feeling of karma burning in real time. We become furnaces within which the old structures burn to ashes but we must be willing stand in that fire not once, but again and again, becoming as familiar with the tendrils of its flames as we have with the psychic debris that is burning. "To make the strongest steel," Rudi used to say, "you heat it, hammer it, fold it, plunge it into water and repeat," and you want to "strike while the iron is hot and keep striking." Along these lines he often added his motto that "work brings more work." It was a spiritual ethic strikingly in line with what Andrew taught.

"But the big-heartedness means" Andrew went on *"that you're connected with this higher view, or this call of the Self, and that you won't compromise it even if it might be easier for you in relationship to yourself or in relationship to other people. See what I'm saying?"*

"Yeah, definitely."

"Okay, we'll finish with that. So between now and tomorrow morning I want everybody to stay with this, especially with looking into this question of the 'bottom up' versus 'top down' perspectives and this whole notion of what the Self is, in terms of being alone being the same as being with others."

And with that we finished. He'd done it again: swept us into spiritual ecstasy. At that moment "no otherness" held the room in a seamless embrace. Being with others was indeed no different than being with oneself. In that room there was only One of us. Hearing Andrew speak of the experiential non-difference between being alone and being with others – obviously his own experience – brought me yet again to the awed recognition of how empty he actually was and hearing him speak of the requisite big-heartedness to really take this all the way, caused me to more deeply appreciate his own big-heartedness, his love for the truth, his love for the deepest and highest in us all. And that that big-heartedness has remained unsullied in the face of unending assaults speaks much of just how big a heart it really is. How much easier to have compromised just a little. In exchange for spiritual ecstasy and the void of an ethical demand, the world would have loved him, thrown flowers at his feet, and carried him to the pulpit on their willing shoulders. *"I could make this about myself in a second,"* he had said in the past, *"and you wouldn't even know it."* But he didn't. Because of that very transparency, integrity and big-heartedness to which he was calling us all, he simply couldn't do it. And for that the world may come to love him yet. I, for one, will remain forever grateful for, without a living, breathing embodiment of those qualities, I would have succumbed to my own cynicism long ago. As such, of course, Andrew stood both as an affront to the spiritual status quo and as a magnet for those yearning for a higher standard. Thus, from the first moment that consciousness fully availed itself of him nearly two decades earlier, Andrew's life has been defined equally by the forces of attraction and repulsion. I had been fully captured by the force of his attraction. I had seen the vision, acknowledged it and thus crossed a line. And I knew that despite the ups and downs that had beleaguered me in the past - and would no doubt continue to do so in the future - I had to somehow hold that line. I had to lay hold of the lifeline this teaching had handed me so that I might haul myself out of the "bottom up" perspective to stand in its "top down" opposite.

I considered once more the forces inside me, which ranged far and wide and heralded from warring camps. Yet all this was contained within the ecstasy of spiritual vision and an expansion of self that stretched every boundary of whatever I'd thought of as "me." I both wanted this retreat to be over and to go on forever. I felt I was breaking at the seams, yet was simultaneously held together by the power of a seamless mystery. It was that same power that had flowed from Andrew from the very first day.

I was exhausted and exhilarated as I approached the plaza on my way to meditation. Beneath the stone saints perched in their alcoves above the wide gates of the cathedral, I saw others from the silent retreat dotting the plaza, which had largely emptied of the day's crush of tourists. The sun's rays slanted in at that angle indicating its imminent descent. The day's heat had receded, its warm residue rising softly from the stone tiles beneath my feet. That gilded half-light bestowed a transcendent glow on the atmosphere, the coarse film of materiality seeming peeled back to reveal the radiance beneath. Life was lit from within. Stepping into that languid scene as if into a dream, I found myself suddenly borne up by the sweetest strains of sound. Breathless, I stood transfixed and noticed that those about me stood spellbound in equal measure. Cascades of golden notes poured from large windows above those unmoving saints of stone. Behind them, recessed and unseen, a choral group cast a faceless serenade upon us, layer upon layer of liquid sound spilling into the shimmer of the setting sun. The impact was wondrous. My heart opened and the torment of the previous days left me, seeming never to have existed at all. Tears welled in my eyes as those pristine voices, seemingly unblemished by any corporeal stain, gave expression to the sacred realms, the higher states and revelation within which we'd been immersed now for days. I felt lifted up, freed from all earthly bonds, every cell vibrating with the ecstasy of love. I stood there transfixed and melted as those voices cut into my heart like shining blades of light.

Finally I made my way to the side of the plaza overlooking the landscape beyond. Long rows of low jagged mountains jutted from the earth, falling away layer by layer into the misty distance. The sky was vast and clear in the dying sun. Beneath that crystalline canopy the small, scattered clouds assumed a celestial bearing, weaving strands of light into their billowy fabrics to glow incandescent, in golds and pinks and opalescent fire. Little ships of color languishing across the sky, they drew me into trancelike contemplation.

Why was it that nature, in all its remorseless efficiency, should create images that strike the soul as achingly sublime? Where did this sense of beauty come from and what purpose did it serve? It did not serve the animals, the seasons or the courses of the galaxies. It did not serve the stillness of a winter landscape, the sun slipping away beneath a purpling sky, or the rustling of palm fronds in a tropic breeze. Yet each of these was filled with it. "The painter is in the painting," came to me just then and I sensed that beauty is its own purpose and its own fulfillment. We are that by which THAT becomes aware of Itself and Its splendor in Its own creation. The eyes are not merely the windows to the soul, but the windows of the soul and of THAT which lies behind it. We are the sense organs of the cosmos. And also its means of engagement. We are its arms and its legs and it calls us to a union of the One with the many and the many with the One from whose embrace the future can unfurl. That is what I knew in that moment and in that citadel of vision I stood and stood in silent wonder.

NOTES

1. According to traditional Buddhist teachings, right view is the beginning and the end of the path. It means to see and to understand things as they really are. It is not necessarily an intellectual capacity, just as wisdom is not just a matter of intelligence. Right view is attained, sustained, and enhanced through all capacities of mind. It begins with intuitive insight and ends with complete understanding of the true nature of all things. In short, right view could be simply put as getting the big picture.

Day 10

The Transformation of Human Relationship

I had spent the waning hours of the previous day straddling the peaks of epiphany and awoke this morning in one of the valleys between them. However, this fact now held more fascination than confusion as I observed yet again that states of consciousness change faster than the weather and that volatility served as an ongoing reminder that context, not experience, is the doorway to liberation. Interestingly, beneath my struggle with exhaustion and the weariness of routine, I discovered a certain satisfaction connected to doing the right thing for the right reasons. Dignity, that's what it was, self-contained and immune to pretense. This, I realized, was the seed of who and what I could become were I to pledge myself to this standard perpetually.

And thus once more I, along with ninety others, chanted into the silence of the morning, stood in the cool sunrise, and meditated to the clamor of the kitchen stirring to life below. Once more I kept to myself during breakfast though I longed desperately to speak. And once more I found myself seated before Andrew, ready to plunge yet again into the unfolding mystery of consciousness.

"So we can continue from where we left off last night," he began after an hour's meditation and then turned his attention to a young Australian woman who had quickly raised her hand.

"I want to tell you about the big bang that happened in the dining room last night," she said, her voice quivering with enthusiasm. "There's probably seventy versions of this but we'd all be talking about the same thing, which was really the evolution of consciousness and the emerging of a new being." Her voice faltered.

"Okay, go on," Andrew encouraged her.

"Well, I can tell it from my vantage point. After dinner there were about six tables of people left in the dining room and many were starting to leave. But I know that at our table we felt that we still wanted to keep going. We had had this discussion and we were starting to think that maybe we wanted to get together with others and that we should move. There was this sense that we've got to do something. I think somebody said that this 'urge to merge,'" – she laughed a little at that – "was really taking a hold. And so we said, 'Okay, there are a few people over there; we'll go and talk to them and get them to come over.' And when we started doing that we thought, 'hey, let's get in a circle,' and suddenly the whole room came together. Spontaneously everybody at all the different tables just got up and we all formed one big circle. And it was sort of like a like a chain reaction without anybody talking about it. We just all came together very powerfully."

"This was late last night?" Andrew asked.

"Yes. And then—I don't even know how long we stayed there; a few hours at least —we had a very powerful discussion and there was an incredibly strong sense of conviction in everyone."

"So, was everybody listening?"

"Yes. And that really felt like where the power of it was."

"Well, if you can have seventy or so people having one conversation with everybody actually listening, that's quite an accomplishment. In just about any other circumstance that would be impossible, right?"

"Yes."

"Assuming that the conversation was not directed and also that nobody knows each other."

"Right."

"So if people don't know each other and you're not even addressing each other by name and there's a kind natural order occurring, that's quite unusual."

"It was really unusual because it was like everybody was drawn to something. It wasn't about yourself at all. It was very creative and it was about contributing to something new that was not about any one of us in particular. So it wasn't like anybody went into long…"

"Monologues?"

"Right. Everybody kept it moving. And then it was really interesting, because it felt that it was evolving and changing during that time."

"How did it feel?"

"At times it felt really ecstatic and at other times it felt like it slowed down and we were really grappling. At those times it was demanding that we go deeper into something and that we shouldn't just let it go because there was also a sense of, 'Oh, we could just break here.' At one point there was actually a break because a whole lot of people rushed to the toilet. But then we actually did come back together. That was a kind of dangerous point because we could have kind of lost it."

Suddenly a man who had apparently been part of this group said, "but it became more powerful after that."

The woman agreed. "And after that, yes, it was more powerful, because we all recognized that we had to make more effort."

"And did you?"

"Yes. Yes, we did."

"And then what happened?"

"And then we went deeper. That's when we really felt that we were grappling and that it really became clear that we were going into the unknown. That's what was challenging us at that point."

"What was challenging you?"

"What was challenging us was that we wanted to go deeper but we didn't know where we were going with it."

"That's wonderful! So you could see even in a context like this where the Authentic Self emerges in so many individuals that you were all working together and that this whole process couldn't work without you. Because for consciousness to be able to function in a creative direction you have to have a sentient being, right?"

"Yes."

"So you were all there and then there was a willingness to co-operate, engage with and participate in what was spontaneously emerging and beginning to open up. So you could say on one hand it was happening by itself but on the other it wasn't because you were also making it happen."

"Yes."

"So in terms of how evolution at the level of consciousness works, it's not going to happen by itself. There has to be conscious agency and there needs to be a balance between that and the spontaneous emergence. Because you saw that you could have left it, but because something powerful and very thrilling had happened many of you had realized that that wasn't enough. Hmm?"

"Yes."

"So you can see then how much there is to do, because basically we're just getting started, right."

"Right."

"We're just scratching the surface. And so you could see how much there is to do and how far there is to go and how if we don't do it, it's not going to happen — 'we' being people who realize this. So do you see how all these things I've been emphasizing have to come together at one time for this to work."

"Yes."

"That's very good."

"There's another point that I've been contemplating that has to do with being alone and being together being one and the same?"

"Yes."

"For some reason that really struck me deeply. For that to be so I have to really know who I am."

"What do you mean?"

"Well, not only that I am embodied consciousness but that I am complete already."

"You mean the Authentic Self is already whole."

"Yes, that."

"So whoever was engaging in that inquiry wasn't preoccupied with any kind of self-doubt, self-concern, unworthiness, self-hatred, ambition, sense of superiority, or anything else like that, right?"

"Yes, that's right."

"So what happens when all that, which is nothing but ego, is tangibly absent in a collective? A new being emerges and a new world opens up – right now! It's not something that happens in the future." He paused for a moment and then asked pointedly, *"And what does that new being want to do?"*

"It wants to keep creating the future," she responded without a trace of hesitation.

"Right," Andrew agreed. *"It wants to create the future. Not because I say so but because that's what its nature is."*

"Yes."

"And you could see that the minute you refocused the energy to move forward it was automatically present. It didn't need to be cultivated. You just had to redirect your attention and then it was there. That's the nature of the Authentic Self. That's where it always is. And our job, as I've been saying, is just to do whatever we need to do to facilitate that process."

"Yes."

"So the miracle of an experience like this and a teaching like this is that a technically unenlightened person can experience and become that egoless state in the most creative way – just like that." He snapped his fingers.

"Yes and it takes letting go of everything," she said slightly dramatically.

"Well, yes. But I mean, you've only been here a few days. All most of you did was just show up. I think that's something that needs to be recognized. Because from the point of view of the ego or the separate self-sense it seems that this is something that's very far away and involves some arduous endeavor that's going to take a long time and require a level of austerity that seems almost inconceivable. And yet, you can see how it's literally near at hand, if only one is willing. And once again, you can see how this potential that was manifesting itself is just the beginning."

"Yes. Yes."

"And once this authentic creative process at the level of consciousness starts, you would find that if you were to meet the next time you'll start right from where you left off. It'll pick up and keep going. Now what would happen if everyone that was there was actually committed to seeing it through, no matter what it took?"

"Well, we talked about that."

"Oh, you did?"

"Yes. "

"And what happened when you did that?"

"Well, there was a really powerful conviction in the group that you could feel and an extraordinary sense of the importance of the commitment to this. We talked about it feeling like being in the army."

"Because at first it's an ecstatic experience and then it becomes a conscious obligation."

"Yes, right."

"Now you can see how the ego's perspective literally lives on another planet from where you were last night?"

"Oh, yes."

"The fears and desires of the separate self-sense could not care less about what was happening last night?"

"Yes. It's very different."

"Right. And that's why, as I've been saying, they're two completely different aspects of the self that have absolutely nothing to do with each other. Is that clear?"

"Yes."

"That's very good." Andrew was delighted. This emergence was what he had dedicated his life to and to see it bear fruit before his eyes clearly lit up his heart.

At this point a sea of hands swayed in the air, as others wanted to share their experience.

"Okay, Christine," he said to a young woman.

"So there were quite a few of us and the shift really happened when we all recognized that we were being much too casual and started to look for the sacredness in what we were doing. And when we all decided to make more effort we could feel we were going much deeper. And the difference was that then we had an emotional connection with the purpose. And from that point everything changed in the circle. We were all focused, listening each other, and we were just one, really one, all the same. And the care was inherent in us. There was no thought of moral obligation or anything like that. We were just acting, just doing it and all of us felt that we just wanted to keep it going. No matter what, we just didn't want to do anything to stop it."

"Yes. Very good! That's the nature of it," he said, and then looking around through the forest of upraised arms, he called on a middle-aged American man. *"Okay, yes."*

"So, in terms of that casualness, my experience of it was that in the beginning of the group there were quite a few of us expressing awe and wonder with this sense of 'look at what's happening; look at what we're doing' isn't this amazing' and so on. And then we realized that with that kind of thinking we weren't really pushing it to the edge. It was more like collective narcissism." He laughed sheepishly. "And when that became apparent people realized that we had to push deeper into it and not just look at ourselves thinking what a great thing we'd accomplished."

"Right," Andrew agreed.

"And also in terms of the complete other planet that the ego exists on, I had this sense that when we were pushing into the edge there was an energy and a kind of tension that the ego might interpret as anxiety or fear or something like that. But from this place that we were in that was felt more as just an excitement and a thrill and there was an ecstatic urge to push into that tension."

"That's great! Very good."

Andrew went to the next person, an older Swedish woman. *"Yes, hi,"* he said.

"I just want to follow up on his comments. At one point there was this kind of ecstatic experience and then something shifted and what became clear was how much evolutionary tension was in the room and how much was actually demanded of us in order to really participate in what was happening. So there was a need to be willing to actually bear that tension and discomfort in order to go deeper and do what was being demanded of us."

"Oh, you mean, you have to suffer a little bit for evolution to happen?" Andrew jested.

"Yes," the woman laughed.

"I didn't think that was in the contract," Andrew continued in a teasing tone. *"So you're saying you have to bear discomfort in order to evolve?"*

"Yes."

"Oh, I didn't know that," he said, a sly grin stretching across his face. *"So everybody talked about that and felt that was a reasonable expectation?"*

"Yes."

"Well, that's very noble." Andrew was only half-jesting now and few people laughed. *"No, I mean it,"* he said. *"Usually if suffering's involved people lose interest real quick."*

"Yes, that's right," the woman agreed. She paused for a moment, and then shifted the subject slightly. "Some people mentioned that there was some self-consciousness but that despite that there was a need to just participate anyway. And then someone asked, 'Are we really having a top down perspective here?' And it was clear that we were because despite whatever hanging on or clinging we were doing there was an agreement that we actually had to continue despite that."

"So how come you stopped? I mean, why did you go to bed? I'm just curious. Did it come to a natural end or what?"

"It seemed like it had come to a natural end and then someone said, 'this might be a good place to close.'"

"Fantastic! That's very good. So then you have to recognize that there is a part of ourselves, this Authentic Self, that wants this coming together of individuals beyond individuality."

"Yes, that's right," several people agreed immediately.

"Because only an individual can creatively participate with others. If you're a drone or a sheep or a robot you're not going to have anything to contribute. You can't creatively

participate. You can only do what you're told. It's only an authentic individual that can participate in and independently contribute to the creative process, right?"

"Yes, that's right."

"But now you can see that if you set up the right circumstances and create the environment this kind of thing is going to happen. And even more, it seems like it wants to happen or is ready to happen. Hmm?"

"Oh yeah, definitely."

"Okay, that's good."

Andrew paused, then turned his attention to an older French gentleman named George, who was an evolutionary scientist.

"I was at the table that formed the first small circle," he began, "and I observed the relationship between free agency and collective spontaneity. You see, we didn't have a plan for creating a big circle but within a few minutes a second group moved away from its table and formed a larger circle until it became a chain reaction. And it was just so beautiful to see how a new a new order can unfold from many small individuals who didn't have a grand plan in mind. But it felt like the collective Authentic Self was working through us and at the end I…"

"But the plan's already there," Andrew interjected.

"Yes, but without any mind directing it. That's what I observed."

"That's right. It's almost like if you set up the right conditions then it becomes a magnetic compulsion."

"Yes."

"But once that magnetic context is created you can't just sit there. You have to engage with it. That's the beauty of it.

"So you can see that the Authentic Self wanted everybody to come together. It's always seeking for itself. But the minute you come together, you have to start giving something to it. So the creative dimension is you actually giving yourself to it. So you can see, in terms of the evolutionary potential, the compulsion to come together in that way is important, but it's not enough. I mean, that part almost happened by itself. Right?"

"Yes."

"But the next level, which is the creative dimension, involves conscious engagement with the process. And once you consciously engage with this potential, nothing could be more thrilling. Because you know something new and big is happening but you don't know what its limit is. What you do know is that it's absolutely important because you're discovering a completely unknown or radically new and profound dimension of your own self that's almost unheard of, right?"

"Yes and I observed one more thing at the end when we felt that it was time to finish and the tables needed to go back. Then this very same quality of the Authentic Self that many of us had been experiencing in one form of action, the action of inquiry, transformed in rearranging the physical space with a quality of attention that was just a straight continuation of the same presence, the same qualities that we had in the inquiry. And in that moment I felt that this is the kind of consciousness from which we would be able to solve complex problems and go at it in a totally new way. So it's not just the sitting in the circle in which the Authentic Self manifested, but in the movement of physical action as well."

"Well, yes, absolutely, because if you're engaged and coming together beyond ego to, number one, inquire but then also to actually do something, I mean, that's a completely new potential for our species."

"Yes, that's right. That's how it felt."

"Because one is just the thrill of inquiry and consciousness beyond the individual, which is fundamental, especially if we're going to create a new context in consciousness. We have to create a new context in consciousness, don't we?"

"Oh yes, very much."

"For the sake of our future we have to create a new moral, ethical, philosophical and spiritual context beyond this culture of narcissism and materialism in order to help us make sense out of the human experience. And that has to be consciously created because it doesn't exist yet."

"No, it doesn't," George agreed.

"So, the way to do that is obviously going to be through this very focused inquiry. That's one dimension. But another has to do with actually accomplishing tasks, right?"

"Yes."

"Because you see, the biggest problems we have involve the nature of relationships. What's the problem with our world? We don't get along! So that's where we have to start and then we can look into just about anything.

"For instance, what's the nature of friendship? What's the nature of friendship beyond ego? You can have an ego-based friendship, which is very personal and which is usually what it's about, or you can have friendship that's about the evolution of consciousness, which is a completely different context and different order of friendship. What would be the nature of romantic or sexual relationship? Usually it's very personal and completely interlinked in a matrix of unexamined ideas about what it's all supposed to mean that come from culture, past and present.[1] What about family? That's an interesting question, especially now at the beginning of the twenty-first century when the family almost doesn't exist anymore as any kind of functioning unit. So these are a lot of important questions to examine from this new perspective because relationship is the structure of culture, right?"

"Yes."

"If you want to create a new world you have to question everything. And then in this context we also have to examine how it is that we work together to do whatever it is that we do. We all know how hard it is to work together. Creative people in the arts, in business, in science – everywhere – often have difficulty working together. There are

so many ways in which we don't want to come together. There are so many ego-based motives that are multi-dimensional in nature and come from very different parts of ourselves. Yet there's so much that we have to do together.

"So you can see that once this Authentic Self would begin to emerge and gain some real foothold that it would eventually end up restructuring everything we're talking about because the part of the self that would be driving our actions wouldn't be the ego. And that would literally change nothing less than everything. It would have to. Of course, I'm talking about well, well, well into the distant future. But that means that we have to do our bit now.

"So what would that world look like? Well, we don't really know. There aren't any examples. But you know it would look good. And when you have the kind of experience that you had last night you can see that the potential in this is neither imaginary nor theoretical. It's literally imminent. And then you can see that if you were to follow through on the potential that revealed itself that you'd have to sacrifice everything for it because the old way of being and this shockingly new potential simply don't go together."

I was reminded of Jesus saying that you cannot put new wine into old wineskins.

"So it's that very potential that all of you were experiencing last night which is what the upper half of the model is really all about." He used his laser pointer to indicate the top section of the Authentic Self model. *"So you see that at the bottom of the model is Clarity of Intention, which we've spoken quite a lot about. Do you remember clarity of intention?"* he asked as if we might have liked to forget about it. *"Remember the individual who wanted to be free more than anything else? Is that still in your memory?"* He laughed along with everyone else. So much had happened since that aspect of our investigation, yet the difficulty that had been involved in that inquiry still lingered. *"It's still as important now as it was then, no matter how you feel.*

"So it's the individual wanting to be free more than anything else in the bottom half of the model that makes possible the emergence of everything in the top half. You see, the way it works is that the lower half of the model represents the individual and the upper half is collective. So the lower half of the model describes what the individual's relationship to life has to be in order to facilitate the emergence of the Six Principles, which is what you guys were all experiencing last night.

He directed our attention to each of the six principles at the top of the model. *"I imagine there probably wasn't much natural hierarchy, though some must have been there. I imagine how it worked is that some of you who have a bit of experience were doing a little bit of guiding. It must have been."* A few people nodded. *"Yes?"* he asked and they nodded again. *"How could it have not been the case? Without that you wouldn't have pushed forward, right?"* They agreed; it had to have been the case. In every one of these groups that I'd ever participated in it was the skilled facilitation of a handful of individuals that made the difference between an interesting discussion and an explosion in consciousness within which everyone was swept into the "ecstatic intimacy of incarnational non-duality."

"*So,*" Andrew said, returning our attention to the model, "*the next of these six principles is Evolutionary Tension. Evolutionary tension is a creative, positive tension. Usually when we hear the word tension it's considered to be something negative. But this is different. Evolutionary tension is what makes you sit up straight and pay attention when you hear something important, when you care about something, when you experience respect for someone or when you experience awe. Evolutionary tension is a higher context. For example, somebody said, 'at a certain point last night we were becoming casual.' So that's when the evolutionary tension dissipates. But the minute it comes back you feel you're focused and attentive and your respect for self and other is present in your awareness once again, as is your care for the larger context.*

"*So, the spiritual life has to be pregnant with evolutionary tension. With no evolutionary tension there's no spiritual life. Then life is casual and self-indulgent. Evolutionary tension is what creates self-respect, respect for others, a sense of order and a context for right relationship. It's the ground for everything and without it nothing can happen.*

"*The opposite of evolutionary tension is here,*" he pointed to the ego model. "*It's inertia. Are you aware of the difference between inertia and evolutionary tension?*" A few people mumbled affirmatives. "*Inertia is when you don't want to get out of bed. It's when you don't care. That's quite different than the way a lot of you were feeling last night. Last night you all cared and you expected everyone else to care because to be there they had to. If they didn't care it would have been problematic. Hmm?*"

Vigorous nods of agreement followed.

"*Their presence would have been a hole through which all of the creative tension that was building would have drained out. That's when you have inertia. If someone doesn't care you could also call that inertia but when they do care, that's what creates the evolutionary tension.*

"*So autonomy and communion,*" he said, pointing with his laser to the next pair of principles on the model, "*which is what the goal is and what you were experiencing last night, is directly related to clarity of intention. If the individual wants it more than anything else, and at least for the moment everyone did last night, that means when you come together in this context each individual is independently supporting the environment that was making this possible. Everyone was giving of themselves so that this could actually occur. So there's a direct relationship between the individual and his or her relationship to what it was you were doing and it actually being possible.*"

Moving on to the next set of principles, he said, "*So then there's the purity of motive and it sounds like there was a lot of that. Purity of motive is when you really care and when the caring is egoless. It's when you want the thing to happen and you know it's not about you. You care more about that than you do about yourself. So purity of motive is the egoless recognition of that purely felt impulse to create that which is new, in this case the evolution of consciousness. And then integrity of action is the willingness to follow through on that, even under pressure. Even under pressure,"* he repeated. *"Life creates pressure and it's usually when we're under pressure that we'll back down on the follow through. There's often a gap between the awakening of pure motive, which a lot of people experience arising in consciousness, and following through, which is the integrity of action. So purity of motive is a conscious experience and the integrity of action is the follow through on the awakening of pure motivation. Now the proof of the stability of the kind of transformation we're speaking about, the stability in this 'top down' perspective, would be when an individual could sustain this awakened pure motive for the evolution of consciousness and back it up over and over and over again through integrity of action. Integrity of action is something that you can see. It's tangible. It's an action. It's not just an inner experience. So how you can tell what people are made of once you get to know them is by how profound the consistent follow through is in terms of integrity of action. And the consistency is everything.*

"Let's say you meet somebody and they express pure motive through integrity of action in an evolutionary context three times in a row. Now that's a lot for anybody. Then you might actually begin to think, 'Wow! This could be an extraordinary person.' Now, I'm talking about integrity of action in an evolutionary, developmental context, which means it's vertical. And in a vertical context the stakes would always be going up. That's the nature of it. So integrity of action would mean that bit-by-bit the individual would be taking on more and more and more. Now keep in mind, we're speaking about the evolution of consciousness, not doing more dishes.

"So this is a serious thing. For the self-sense at a soul level what could more challenging than that? So, you could say that for many of you last night was a kind of an initiatory event. Some of you have had this experience before, even though it's ever new and always like the first time. But that means you now have even more responsibility than you did last night for the very thing that just happened. How would it be if this happened again this afternoon but you just decided to lay back? You couldn't do that because the experience you've already had would mean that to be true to your actual level and depth of experience you'd have to be right up on the edge, just one small step beyond where you were last night. This is true for everybody.

"So this is very democratic and there's a perfect science to how it works. I'm talking about natural hierarchy, which is the most difficult one of the six principles to explain. Natural hierarchy, which is a law of how the Authentic Self works, demands that in relationship to integrity of action each individual be willing to be absolutely true to their actual level of experience. Not more than that. But nothing less would be enough for the evolutionary process to be taken forward. Remember, evolution doesn't happen by itself. It happens through individuals who are consciously taking responsibility for the process. So if they consciously take responsibility for the process it would mean that we're literally creating a living developmental context. And each time they'd have to

keep taking that one little step forward because they'd learn more and gain more confidence in this new terrain. And the more confidence they gain the more responsibility they have to assume in actually creating it.

"So this is natural hierarchy and evolutionary tension and how they work together." He pointed over his shoulder to the model once more. *"Now this puts an enormous amount of pressure and expectation upon an individual to be true. As ecstatic as that event was last night, since the ego's not dead, it's just taking a coffee break, sooner or later the individual is going to say, 'okay, that's enough already.' Because you're always going to be poking them in the back, saying, 'no, one step more.' And sooner or later it's inevitable that the individual is going to encounter that part of themselves that fiercely resists all of this. Now, because the Authentic Self is relentlessly surging forward that's going to set up a conflict because, in order for this developmental process to continue, each individual has to keep going, in spite of all that.*

"So what I want you to understand is that at least theoretically this is a perfect science. There are certain laws that are not made up by human beings but that are consciously recognized. In the awakening of consciousness itself these laws simultaneously appear and as we evolve we simply recognize this to be the way. And the degree to which they're recognized, if we want this to work perfectly, we as individuals have to conform or surrender to them and act upon them without hesitation. Now, I know that a lot of you like to use the word surrender. Well, here you have to conform or surrender to the science of how this evolutionary process works."

Surrender, it seemed, was key, being every bit as relevant to the new enlightenment as to the old. "A deeper sense of surrender" had been Rudi's last words in this world and *"surrender is the beginning, the middle and the end of the path,"* Andrew had said on any number of occasions. In fact, he'd said that in his own life as a seeker, all he had had was clarity of intention and surrender, which were enough to take anyone all the way. Being so busy with endless action, I often forget about this aspect of the spiritual path. Meditate, chant, attend retreats, participate in discussions, push the edge, work and so on. In that crush of activity, albeit spiritual, the simple act of letting go often escapes me, though that simple act should be present in all activity. Paradoxically it seems that the letting go of ego requires will, intention and action. Striking this balance between the active and the passive was, I believe, at least in part what Andrew was pointing to. In other words, in order to facilitate the emergence of the new being, we had to let go of self-consciousness and self-concern and, through effort – intense effort, even, if needed — move into the unknowable emptiness that lies just beyond them. At the same time, when caught in the emergence of that mystery one had to simply let oneself be swept up by it. One had to simply not resist. It seemed a poised balance between effort and surrender and the edge between them is, at least in part, the edge I believe we have to push.

Andrew continued. *"You see, in a group the minute anyone, but especially the more experienced individuals, would hesitate, resist or just hold back even a little bit, the tension in the collective would drop. And at first it would be imperceptible because there would be so many other things happening. There might be newer people and everybody would say, 'oh, this is totally amazing,' and not notice. But the leading edge would have fallen. And then what are they going to do? You see, the minute anyone drops that edge where's the reference point? It has to be ego. There's nowhere else to go. Once that tension is dropped, which is your own edge, the only place you're going to fall back to is into self-consciousness. So now there's a gap between where you were and where you're supposed to be or where you could have been. That means now you're going to have to work that much harder to bridge that gap.*

"I hope you all see how unbelievably delicate this is. But this is the nature of how this process works. We're talking about the evolution of consciousness beyond the individual, beyond the individual, beyond the individual!" He could not have been more emphatic. *"This is not merely about the evolution of consciousness of the individual. But in order for this to work the individual has to co-operate absolutely. Without absolute co-operation, commitment, surrender and this willingness to keep leaning forward, the process is going to fall back onto itself because, for it to keep moving forward, the edge has to be constantly pushed. If it's not, the process will literally cave back upon itself. Do you understand? It's a science with its own dynamic."*

A murmur of assent rose and the atmosphere was laden with both passion and sober reflection.

"So this is what natural hierarchy and evolutionary tension are all about," he went on. *"Natural hierarchy means that each individual has to be willing to be true to their own level of actual experience. No more than that would be expected but nothing less than that would be enough. It's completely reasonable."*

How often had I heard Andrew say, *"I'm one of the most reasonable people you're ever going to meet"*? It was hard to argue with him. *"What if all of us lived up to what we already knew?"* he'd frequently asked us. *"Well, the world we live in would look completely different."* It was unassailable logic. Yet most of us don't live up to what we already know, except perhaps in our very finest moments. At least I don't. In connection to this, and as I have already mentioned, Andrew has often said that *"the minute I meet someone a clock starts ticking and over time I begin to see what people are made of."* He has also often spoken of an individual's "karmic line" with him, meaning that he is aware of each individual's experience both with him and with the teaching and that there is an expectation of real-time development based on that. For instance, if someone had known Andrew for ten years, what was expected of them both in their relationship to the teaching and to life as a whole, differed greatly from what might be expected from someone who had been involved for six months or a year. Of course, this makes complete sense. Unfortunately, Andrew, in most cases, has to push quite hard in order to get an individual to take responsibility and manifest what they already know. So I understood natural hierarchy to be about what would emerge between people if everyone authentically lived up to what they already knew. In such a scenario the unnatural "dominator hierarchies" of pretense and self-importance would dissolve in the spontaneous emergence of the true and right relationship between individuals. Now that's a new world.

"I'm hoping you're getting a sense," Andrew continued, "of how this is a newly emerging science of the evolution of consciousness beyond the individual. But for it to work beyond a blast like last night you can see what has to happen. In other words, you can see the degree of conscious co-operation, commitment, and engagement on the part of the individual that's required, right?"

This time everyone agreed more vigorously.

Andrew paused, glanced back over his shoulder at the model and went on to the next set of two principles.

"Autonomy and communion." He repeated it several times lest we should overlook the profundity of both of those emerging as one state.

"Ecstatic communion is the blissful experience of no ego boundaries. It's boundaryless, radical intimacy. It's more profound than physical or sexual intimacy because it's not a physical event. In other words, there's not this physical form to work through. It's the direct, ecstatic experience of no ego boundaries at the level of consciousness, which is, as I was saying yesterday, when you literally experience no gap or no boundary with the other whatsoever. This is not metaphorical but an actual, literal experience. But it's not losing touch with the implications of autonomy that's important for actual evolution to occur and that seems to be the most challenging part of this. Because if you get people in the right state and they're in a good mood, something like what happened last night is likely to occur. But then we want to take what happened last night and start working with it in order to create the future. Now that puts an enormous amount of responsibility on the individuals.

"But if the individuals are living the five tenets and come together the six principles have to emerge. The five tenets create the foundation from which the six principles are going to emerge. So the question is, when the six principles emerge, do they emerge as a passing spontaneous eruption, which is a glimpse of our future potential, or is it deeper than that? Is it the beginning of a process that's going to become ongoing? That's much more challenging. You see, what I'm interested in is taking the kind of experience you had last night and refining and developing it. Then it's not a flash any more. Then you're actually engaging with the creative process at a much deeper level that's very conscious and deliberate. And that's infinitely more implicating. Do you all get the idea?"

We indicated that we did.

"So now you understand what the words radical, impersonal, evolutionary enlightenment mean. It's radical because it's so far out on the edge. It's impersonal because *that's the nature of the Authentic Self and of the whole process. The evolutionary part you understand and the enlightenment part we've covered. Now you see that it's called that for a specific reason."*

Andrew was silent for a few moments before he turned his attention to a Swedish man who'd also been a participant in the previous night's events.

"I have been sitting with a question the whole morning and it came up again when you mentioned the risk of it falling back on itself again. I wonder if you could say more about staying on the edge and not letting this process fall back on itself?"

"That not happening," Andrew replied, *"has to do with this whole question of natural hierarchy and for anyone to understand that would require them to have some time and experience with this process. Then what they would begin to get is an insight into not just what's happening in a highly charged situation like that, but what's happening all the time. Because you can extrapolate what's happening in that context into almost every human circumstance. So, for instance, to what degree are we staying at our particular edge autonomously in relationship to our self and in the context of our relationships with each other? Of course, this kind of inquiry can happen in many ways and in multidimensional contexts. So when you really begin to understand this you can see what it would mean to create an authentically evolutionary developmental context for the human experience. And then you can translate that into a new kind of dharma with respect to the question: what does it mean to be awake?*

"So from an evolutionary viewpoint it would mean to be awake to this developmental context in many different situations, some of which are less important and some of which are more important. That's when the moral dimension of this evolutionary context emerges. This emerging moral dimension would have to imply being true to and honoring the developmental context of relationship. If there's a developmental context for relationship it injects a certain amount of evolutionary tension. Remember, that's positive."

"Right," everyone readily agreed.

"And that gets very tricky when you get to know people well. 'Why don't you just accept me as I am?'" he mocked in the pleading, whining tone of the sensitive self. *"That's often what we want. 'If you loved me...' You get the idea? So that's what the ego wants. 'Just accept me as I am.' But in an evolutionary context we want to accept each other as we are now as long as it's different than we were before and it's going to be different in the future."*

Many of us laughed, but was it really funny? I thought of all the ways in which we hold each other down, fetter each other in suffocating bonds, in relationships where nothing is ever to change unless strictly according to custom, a paint by numbers life in which we play a game of "I'll pretend that you are who you think you are so long as you pretend that I am who I think I am." Narcissism and collusion on Andrew's model are opposite to autonomy and communion and this, I think, is why.

"I'm not kidding," Andrew said emphatically. *"I want you to think about it. It's a completely different way of thinking about human relationship.*

"So once again, the credo would be, 'I'll accept you now as long as you're different than you were before and are going to be different in the future than you are right now.' And then you'd expect that from them also. Do you understand how completely radical that is? Hmm?" He didn't wait for the answer. *"So then, if you begin to let that in, you can really see how an evolutionary developmental context would be authentically translated into an interpersonal context. And then, in a relationship that was based on this commitment to the evolution of consciousness, both people would be moving forward together. Not in parallel lines. Not 'in our own ways because we're all individuals.' But if I was moving forward and you were moving forward and we were in a relationship we couldn't help but be feeding and compelling each other through the dynamic of our own individual development. Now that's a completely different kind of relationship. It's inherently creative and that's the whole point. It has nothing to do with how we live, with 'If you love me, you'll accept me as I am.'"* He laughed at the absurdity. *"Think about it,"* he urged us.

He paused briefly before continuing with a related point.

"Did you know that most adults don't develop?" he asked, echoing my reflections of a few days earlier. *"Beyond a certain point it's just a horizontal line."* He looked pointedly at the four teenagers sitting directly in front of him and asked them, *'Do you know that?'* They said nothing. *"They don't know that,"* he said to the rest of us, *"because when you're young you feel all your hormones and your youth and you think you're going to be surging ahead forever. It's just a physical experience that doesn't necessarily mean anything because when you're young everything is new and you think it's all very exciting. But pretty soon you just flat line out."*

The adults had fallen strangely silent.

"I had a talk with these guys," he said, indicating the two teenage boys from the group of four youngsters in front of him, *"and one of them was talking about how when he gets older he wants to have a nice house. I thought to myself, Jesus! when I was sixteen the last thing on my mind was having a house. That's the kind of thing you wouldn't think of until you were much older, right?"*

Everyone agreed, laughing. Like Andrew, at sixteen such a thing was as far from my mind as a group of Christian zealots from a Grateful Dead show. Actually, it was not on my mind at all. Not that my mind was any deeper than a puddle in the street. Yet the concerns that drifted on its murky surface contained nothing of the practical, the predictable and the ultimately suffocating. I realized at that moment that I'd never thought I'd get old enough to say "kids nowadays," disappointed headshake and all. And yet, here I found myself doing just that – for exactly the opposite reasons that my parents and their friends had shaken their heads at us. Time sure has a sense of irony, I thought. But there it was. I recalled a recent interview with an aging Harvard psychology professor bemoaning the banal conservatism of campus youth and expressing his desire for more LSD on campus. I wondered if this young man's vision of his future reflected the much maligned apathy, conservatism and nihilism of today's youth that I'd heard so much about. I sure hoped not. These kids are the future, I thought like my parents before me. And I trembled slightly.

"You don't want to be thinking about things like that at your age," Andrew laughed, along with everyone else. The young man blushed a little. *"So what happens with most adults is that we don't evolve or develop any more beyond a certain point. After that point, usually in your mid-twenties, it's kind of a flatline and then you die. Do you guys get what I'm talking about?"* He addressed the teens directly though their looks showed little comprehension. Of course he was also speaking to us all and I in particular was sobered by his observation.

"Now obviously there are exceptions," he went on. *"But generally speaking that's more or less how it is. So if that's true you have to consider that what I just described to you about an authentically evolutionary engagement with the human experience that was perpetual and unbroken, ultimately creating a new context for relationship, could not be more radical. It literally could not be different than the way life is generally lived and nothing could be more demanding than that. Do you get the idea?"*

Most of us were definitely getting a sense of what he was saying.

Directing himself once more to the young man in front of him, Andrew said, *"The reason I said that about the house is because, as a concept, that house represents something that's very static. So you see, if you blow up the house in your mind now then the whole universe will open up for you. But if you have that as some kind of object in your future it'll strangle your soul to death. And all these older people were laughing because they knew. So if you don't believe me you could trust them because there's thousands of years of experience here."* Riotous laughter shredded the solemnity, dying away only with considerable time.

"Okay, so that's good," Andrew said at length, seemingly satisfied with where we'd gone this morning. *"I'd like everybody to stay with this whole notion of the evolution of consciousness, how it relates to everything and how radical it really is.*

"What I'm describing here is a perfect ideal which would be very hard to pull off in real time even under the best of circumstances. But at least you can understand what the goal is. Whether we reach it or not is another issue. But there's no way you'd ever be able to even begin to reach it if you didn't at least have a conception of it. And it's important that when you're actually experientially in touch with the imminent nature of this potential that you begin to dig in and work with these concepts because that's when you can really do something. If you're just working with concepts but you're not actually in touch at an experiential level with what they mean then it'll just be an interesting idea. But when you're actually in touch with the evolutionary potential or the Authentic Self and then you're working with concepts like this, then it can be very powerful.

"Okay, we'll finish with that."
And we did.

I had been deeply touched when I heard of what had happened in that gathering on the previous night. I have been part of such emergences and have been moved most profoundly both by their sacred nature and what they heralded for the future. Yet it was the question of suffering and our willingness to endure it for the sake of evolution that had most stirred me this morning – perhaps due to my own plight much of the retreat. The sensitive self, my own close companion, feels keenly its entitlement to the good life, to career, a caring spouse, health, leisure and the bounty of good fortune. That self, after all, is a good person, a "nice guy" with good intentions doing his best who therefore does not deserve to suffer. So what about that then? What about suffering? Is it something to be eliminated at all costs and in all arenas? Is it necessarily a sign of something being wrong? Or is there, contrary to post-modern sensibilities, a rightful place for it on the stage of human drama, or even a necessary one? Is the bearing of psychological and emotional discomfort not a necessary pre-requisite for living a life not constrained by the bonds of mediocrity; a life of authentic transformation? These were important questions that challenged current conventions in spiritual thinking.

I sat silently in the teaching hall after most people had left and considered this, turning the question inside out. Where did the question of peace and the end of suffering enter into the spiritual equation? How have they become so inextricably intertwined? The answer is obvious: in the experiential discovery of one's own Self beyond time, that "no place, no time, no thing" that always exists before the beginning right now and in which is found perfect stillness, perfect fullness and the perfect cessation of every troubling ripple to stir the surface of being. That was Home; Heaven; Nirvana; perfect bliss and peace forever. That is its nature and that is what is and always will be endlessly compelling about it. But that is not the realm of manifestation and is therefore only half the picture. The other half is the churning world of form, of becoming, of constant change and movement, of an evolutionary trajectory heading ever to realms of greater complexity. And in that half, consciousness is seeking not simply to liberate itself from matter but to liberate itself in matter and make matter a reflection of itself – an endeavor vastly complicated by our identification with that very matter. Unfortunately, the process of disembedding our consciousness from matter is slightly more arduous than the "be as you are" spiritual crowd – which has embraced the end of suffering as the goal of spiritual life – would be comfortable admitting. In fact, if the ego and the Authentic Self are two layers of self that cannot occupy the same space at the same time then the shift from one to the other might unavoidably involve the shouldering of emotional and psychological burdens and the willingness to suffer.

All life is suffering, the Buddha observed. And while in today's wealthy West that is not as true as it was in the days of Gautama – harsh days when life was "brutish, nasty and short" – it is undeniable that suffering seems to be woven deeply into life's complex fabric. The fact is that all of us suffer but most of us do it stupidly. Peter, quoting his own teacher Rudi, used to say that "you can pay for your life consciously or you can pay for your life unconsciously. Either way you pay." I have always found this statement to be deeply profound. What is it that we suffer for and what are the results? Mostly we suffer for love and for money, for fear and desire, acting on these to create more of the same. And thus the wheel of karma grinds on. But this is not true for us all. What about Gandhi, Martin Luther King, Nelson Mandela and others, the great souls who have lived determined to raise the lot of mankind? They suffered, enormously in fact, but for a great purpose. Their raison d'etre was not the personal experience of unbroken wellbeing, the seeming target of most post-modern spirituality. It was the transformation of the race and the realization of a higher potential. And few would argue that to such ends strife and difficulty engender nobility, dignity and the elevation of the soul.

So what are the ends to which we aspire? In the context of this teaching our aspiration is to the transformation of human relationship. *"What's the problem with the world? We don't get along."* That much is obvious, though I wonder how deeply we truly consider this. It seems that we have simply come to take this for granted, an inescapable part of being human. *"Relationship is the structure of culture,"* Andrew had observed. Thus what happens in relationship has inevitable consequences for culture. And what is relationship?, I ask myself. It starts with me and just one other person. My wife, my friends, family, co-workers and the remaining network of associations within which I live. Of course, new networks need to be created for a new culture to emerge. As a one-sided venture this cannot work. And with each other we aspire to create new structures in consciousness, an emergence between us of an order of magnitude so beyond what human relationship is now as to seem nearly inconceivable. That's what's so exciting. And, because the structures of ego inhibit this emergence we must struggle both individually and together in order to transcend them. Our effort, our passion, our will and our surrender are required, for it will not happen by itself.

And within this emergence, this radical potential for human relationship beyond ego and the pathology of narcissism, lie the seeds to the solutions of the woes that beset our race. This leap beyond the individual is demanded by evolutionary logic. For those at the leading edge, where else is there to go? Further individuation can only breed more narcissism, deepening division, and an insanely splintered self and culture. The inexorable evolutionary drive can only be to go beyond the individual altogether so that our hard won individuation – that precious gift of evolution – is not lost but transcended and liberated in the service of a new humanity.

And that, at least in my view, is a cause worthy of struggle and yes, even suffering. And why should it be otherwise? Why should I not be willing to bear discomfort and insecurity for the sake of the miraculous? Why should I not pay for my life consciously? *"Is the willingness to suffer for the sake of evolution a reasonable expectation?"* Andrew had put to us earlier. Without a doubt, I thought, so let's get real. What is my own emotional discomfort for the sake of a higher calling when measured against the unbearably real physical suffering routinely endured by the majority of the world's population? Nursed at the breast of good fortune, what right did I have to insist that I not suffer? How could I justify employing that good fortune for the mere alleviation of my own discomfort – small by comparison to others – rather than invest it in a purpose that, if fully realized, would stand to benefit the whole in inconceivable ways? I could not. In the culture of narcissism and materialism, Andrew had often said, good old-fashioned virtues like dignity, self-respect, honor and nobility have fallen noticeably out of fashion, replaced with self-acceptance, healing of the inner child and endless displays of victim consciousness. I no longer wished to worship at the altar of such self-indulgence, seeking rather to stand for something that might not only justify my existence, but perhaps even imbue it with those good, old-fashioned values.

The long and the short of it was that evolution, both physical and spiritual, allows for the natural unfolding of things including the emergence of the unexpected and miraculous. Yet such evolution entails struggle, conflict and yes, even suffering; such seems to be the way of things. In the world of becoming, galaxies explode, asteroids rip into planets, volcanoes rupture the land and tornadoes tear through the landscape. Life grows and withers to a rhythm of its own, one that moves ever forward in some grand march of destiny whose glory we can intuit but never fully grasp. So why should my life be different, as if separate from that? How could it be, being one with that? And so I suspected that the thrust and purpose of my own life might be discovered in aligning myself with that which lies behind it, always driving it forward. And that, in turn, would engender a vastness of view and strength of character that ultimately transcends all questions of effort and surrender, of peace versus strife. And it was that to which I most aspired.

That aspiration carried me through the day, through meditation and chanting, through silent walks in sunny, crowded walkways and through the ceaseless churn of my crazy mind.

The afternoon session began in intellectual and spiritual disarray. The first two questions fielded by Andrew were so odd and disjointed that a full twenty minutes passed while Andrew attempted to pry from the questioners precisely what they were asking before he gave up. Then, after a few moments, he turned his attention to the freckled teenage blonde directly in front of him.

"So, I was having a talk with her about two hours ago," Andrew said, *"and she asked me this question to which I said, 'Maybe you should ask it in front of everybody because I'm sure they'd be interested.' So what did you have to say?"* he asked turning to her.

"From what I understood earlier," she said in voice as faltering and self-conscious as it was curious and determined, "consciousness evolves when two or more people who are embodying the five tenets come together."

"Well," Andrew replied, *"it can also evolve through a single individual. You don't need two."*

"Okay. So my question is that if consciousness is everywhere and in everyone and everything, when one person evolves or pushes the edge, does it sort of raise the bar and raise the consciousness of everybody or just that individual or group?"

"That's a very good question, don't you think?" Andrew asked and everyone agreed. *"So what do you think the answer is?"* he asked her.

"I think that it would evolve for everybody because…"

"Automatically?" Andrew interjected.

"Well, that's my question."

"So do you think that if one person evolves everybody's going to get enlightened at the same time because suddenly one did?" His laugh contained a touch of mischief.

"Well…" she stammered.

"You know, some people say that there's going to be the Second Coming. Have you ever heard about that?"

"Yeah, I have."

"So in all the great traditions there's a version of the Second Coming. Judaism, Christianity, Islam, Hinduism, they all have some version of it. Did you know that?"

"Yep."

"It's going to be the great return of The One." Now, with a storytelling air he said, *"And when The Great One comes back – it's usually a man,"* he added, slightly tongue in cheek – *"he's going to bring this new consciousness to everybody all at the same time. That's what they say at any rate."*

"Oh, wow!" she replied in a tone suggesting that she wasn't sure whether her leg was being pulled or whether she was expected to heartily agree.

"Yeah," Andrew said grandly, inciting a burst of hilarity. *"Well, there are billions of people in the world that actually believe this."*

"Oh, I'm sure," she said, sounding a little relieved that Andrew wasn't party to such beliefs.

"So, who knows, it could be true. But in that way of thinking the idea is that the evolved consciousness of this one great being will affect either all the individuals of the particular tribe that he's a part of or all of humanity. So in that way of looking at it you'd say the answer would be yes, right?"

"Yes." She sounded as if she wasn't sure where this was going.

"They say if the messiah comes everybody's consciousness is going to evolve automatically because he has come back to save all of us. The savior returns!" he pronounced dramatically. *"When the savior returns then everybody, for lack of a better way of*

putting it, becomes enlightened, goes beyond ego, realizes this one mind and one heart all at the same instant. It will be the end of war, division and hatred and then the result would be a Golden Age. A lot of the great traditions - and also a good deal of New Age thinking - promise us that there's going to be a Golden Age which means that it's something that happens to everybody. Everybody wakes up to the one mind, one heart, one truth, one consciousness, all at the same time and then it's the end of all our troubles forever. It's like being in heaven."

"But..."

"So that's what many traditions, including a lot of New Age and assorted other spiritual groups, believe. They believe there's going to be a switch, there's going to be one moment where everything's going to flip. It's usually preceded by some really bad, dark period and then everything's going to be better than it's ever been. So, as many people see it, the consciousness of one highly evolved divine individual will affect the consciousness of the whole."

I recalled with amusement attending a gathering in the mid-eighties to bear witness to and help usher in something called the "Harmonic Convergence," during which, according to some ancient Mayan calendar, the energies of the world would align in the way Andrew had just described. I didn't really believe it at the time but the thing is I wanted to.

"Is that what you believe?" she asked Andrew.

Cannonades of laughter burst into the air.

"What do you think?" he asked.

"Well, to tell you the truth, I really don't know because I feel that..."

"You really have no idea?" Andrew asked, slightly astonished.

"I can venture to guess, but as far as knowing for sure, I don't."

"I don't know if that's good or bad," Andrew laughed. *"It's probably not good."*

"But you say that in the traditional sense, that God has fallen out of the sky and is now..."

"No, no, no. I said it depends on who you are."

"Oh, yeah."

"It depends what your belief system is. So if your system of beliefs tells you that God or an Absolute Principle or divine Godhead lives up in the sky and you believe that, then he or she or it hasn't fallen out of the sky. But if you are individuals like most of us here, you fall into the camp in which he, she or it has fallen out of the sky. And that's also the situation you're in, right?"

"Yeah," she agreed.

"But the question you're asking is an important one. So what's the relationship between the evolution of the consciousness of the individual and everyone else?"

"Yeah, maybe that's the question."

"Now, the answers aren't as obvious as you would think because the evolution of consciousness is the journey from the gross to the subtle. Do you understand that?"

"Yes."

"So even to be able to see certain things, to become aware of them, one's conscious-ness, sensitivity, understanding and perspective have to have evolved and developed."

"Yeah."

"So even in order to be able to appreciate what the evolution of consciousness would mean in and of itself would require a very high level of development. I'm sure the ma-jority of human beings living on the planet right now probably would have no idea what the evolution of consciousness really meant."

"Yeah, I think that's true."

"So if the majority of human beings living on the planet wouldn't really have any way to grapple with the concept of the evolution of consciousness, what would that mean about the question that you asked?"

No answer.

"I was once speaking to a Tibetan Buddhist Rimpoche about this. He was a great man and considered to be a living Buddha by his own people. He said that you could be in the presence of a living Buddha but you wouldn't necessarily know it unless you were evolved enough to be able to recognize who he was. So in terms of the evolution of consciousness it's a journey from the gross to the subtle and in order to be able to even begin to glimpse these very high levels of human potential we can't be too far away ourselves, otherwise it would be totally beyond our grasp. We wouldn't be able to understand it intellectually and experientially it's going to be so far away from any reference point that we're simply not going to have any way of understanding it."

"Yeah, I think I get that. So what you're saying is that unless someone has at least some awareness of consciousness, it won't matter to them whether conscious-ness itself evolves or not because they're not really tapped in to it."

"Right, that's the whole point. Then they have no way of knowing."

"But, isn't it true that in your vision of the future, fifty thousand years from now, everyone is awakened to this?"

"But the point is everyone is never going to be at the same place. Think about it for a minute. You're in school, right?"

"Right."

"So some people are at the top of the class, other people at the bottom, a lot of people in the middle, right?"

"Yeah."

"Some people are so smart that they have to go to a special school for smart kids and other people are in such bad shape that they couldn't even handle the easiest level, right?"

"Yeah, that's true."

"Okay. So, in terms of this evolution of consciousness in the way we're speaking about it, that's also true. There's never going to be a moment when everything's just going to equalize because if we're part of a developmental process it always has to start

at the beginning and everybody apparently has to go through all the same stuff and – at least according to evolutionary theory – you can't jump any steps. So, one of those steps is the one that we're speaking about; the one required in order to even be able to appreciate all this."

"Yeah, that makes a lot of sense."

"The point is, as the individual gains the capacity to recognize these things they simultaneously begin to appreciate their significance. So you could say that the degree to which you are able to recognize and appreciate these higher levels is the degree to which the actual living presence of those higher levels will begin to have a magnetic effect on you. At first, as you begin to see it, it'll just be some light that's barely flickering out in the sky. But the clearer it becomes, the more compelling it's going to become. It'll be like a tractor beam that's calling you to it. But for that to happen, you have to at least be able to begin to see it, right?"

"Yes."

"So the answer to your question is both yes and no. So what these higher levels are continues to develop over time. The highest levels ten thousand years ago are not the highest levels now because consciousness has evolved and is still evolving. So in terms of the evolution of consciousness itself, whatever the leading edge is, will always be this omega point that's calling consciousness to itself. So you could say that on some kind of very subtle, almost imperceptible level, it has to have some effect on everyone to some degree just because it exists as the leading edge. But most people are so unconscious and so lost in lower levels of development that it's not anything they would perceive or even be aware of. But for those individuals who are closer to those levels, they'll begin to see them and they'll exert a pull on those just behind them. Do you understand?"

"Yeah, I do."

"It's kind of complicated, isn't it?"

"It is, but it's interesting also."

"Because we have to be careful that we don't reduce consciousness. In other words, if we're going from the gross to the subtle there's a vertical dimension to it. And as I said on the very first day and have been saying every day since, the vertical dimension is very tricky for us to understand. Going from lower to higher, from the gross to the subtle. And the more subtle it is, the harder it is to perceive, right?"

"Yeah."

"So then it requires more development and self-cultivation so we can develop and evolve and begin to be in a position where we can grasp these things."

"That makes a lot of sense."

"Because we can see that left to our own devices we tend to sink down to a lower level of development where a lot of the things we're talking about in here are the last things on our mind."

"Yes."

"But then when we come together like this and begin to focus our attention individually and collectively on these higher potentials, eventually they actually begin to emerge. Hmm?"

"Yeah."

"But in order for that to happen most people have to do something like this. They have to come on a retreat in order to retreat from the ordinary, everyday state of consciousness, stage of development, relationship to life and so on. But when we withdraw, focus and concentrate we can begin to cultivate our own capacity to realize these higher levels and when we do that then the dramatic and miraculous thing is that they do appear. We begin to actually experience potentials that ordinarily are not apparent to us. So can you see how subtle and how delicate it is?"

"Yeah, definitely."

"So the point is, it just depends on which way you look at it. When these higher potentials exist, then the leading edge for everybody has been pushed forward. But then, to be honest, how many people would even be able to recognize what that leading edge was? Not that many."

"Right."

"But the fact that it's there means that for those people who begin to get in that vicinity, they're suddenly going to see it. That's why throughout history there have always been individuals who have been pushing the leading edge. And they're not pushing it for themselves, they're pushing it for everyone else."

"The people who create that edge are pioneers because they're forging territory that hasn't been traversed yet. It's new. But then for the people who follow, that leading edge becomes — and this is something that Ken Wilber has spoken a lot about — tracks that have been laid down and then other people have easier and easier access to it. It's almost like if you're climbing up a mountain and you're the first one, it's going to be a lot harder because there's no path. And then there'll be someone else and someone else and someone else and eventually there'll actually be a clear path. Then, for the other individuals who are going to follow, it'll be clearly laid out.

"So can you see that the evolution of consciousness is a creative process because we're actually creating new potentials?"

"Yeah, I can."

"So this is a new way of understanding how it all works. The old way of thinking about it is that God's already figured everything out and we just have to catch up. In that way of thinking there's nothing new under the sun.

"For instance, they say that if you read the Koran, the Old Testament, the Bhagavad-Gita, the Upanishads or whatever, that everything's already there. But if this is a creative process then God hasn't already figured it all out because God figures it out as we figure it out. You see, that's the most exciting understanding in terms of the evolutionary perspective. What we're calling God, which is the energy and intelligence that initiated the creative process and that's driving it right now, figures it out as we do.

A lot of people can't handle that. They get scared. They'll say, 'Whoa. You mean Big Daddy or Big Mommy isn't up there already and hasn't already figured it out for all of us?' That makes people feel uncomfortable. See, that's why I keep saying, there's nobody up there. But the exciting thing about this evolutionary perspective is that what we're calling God, this Energy and Intelligence that initiated the creative process, figures it out as we do."

"So this is like climbing a mountain that doesn't end."

"Exactly right.

"And there is no end to this. In other traditions and other ways it was like you got to the peak and that was it. You just got to hang out there until you died. And in this way it's just like there's always something new that you're pushing for."

"Well yes, because we're talking about the evolution of our capacity for consciousness or knowing. This is the Energy and Intelligence that initiated the creative process emerging in and through matter. And when you understand that that's literally what's happening and that the Creative Principle figures it out as we do, nothing could be more exciting. It creates a sense of urgency and purpose. And, for people who have the wherewithal to be able to handle it, nothing could be more exciting. Especially now, in the time that we're living in, because, as I've been saying, the old worldviews are obviously outdated and we have to create new ones. They don't already exist. So do you get the idea now with respect to your question?"

"Yeah. It's very interesting."

"So do you understand now why it's a journey from the gross to the subtle?"

"Definitely."

"So in this context what it means to be asleep or unconscious means that one is not aware of this depth of subtlety. So you can see that ultimately the evolution of our own potential as a species is completely dependent upon the awakening to these increasingly subtle perspectives. It means actually being able to see them, feel them, know them and then actualize them more and more and more. You understand?"

"Yes."

"And realizing that, you would see how important it is to be engaged in the process, as we were speaking about earlier today, because that's how development happens. The individuals throughout history who have taken these steps forward are people who were completely engaged with the process. And the problem with too many of us is we're not willing to be. That's the problem with ego and that's our particular issue right now.

"And also when these new potentials emerge, it's always been small groups that have taken these first leaps. You understand?"

"Yes, I do."

"It's never some kind of mass awakening. It doesn't work that way."

"Yeah, I didn't think so."

"You have an individual and then a small group of individuals who are at the head pursuing a new possibility that's way beyond where the status quo is."

"Yeah. But when a group of people pushes the edge, don't they in a sense bring others with them? Like, once the bar is lifted, wouldn't people rise to the occasion?"

"Well, yeah, because you're creating new pathways for others to follow and eventually they will. See?"

"Yeah, I do."

"And can you imagine what it would be like if, for example, this were explained to you as you were growing up? Well, it would totally change your worldview because then by the time you got to be your age it would be something you'd take for granted. It wouldn't be like some weird theory or outlandish spiritual concept. It would be the foundation and ground of your worldview, which would also inform the kind of choices you'd make in relationship to the life that you would endeavor to live."

"So when people become aware of these new levels it would show through in their life and in their actions and stuff, right?"

"Well, ideally."

"Yeah, ideally. So by evolving consciousness the individual in a way – this is going to sound weird–changes the world."

"Exactly. That's why I said the answer is absolutely yes and absolutely no. It depends how you look at it. So from the perspective of consciousness it's yes, and in the most dramatic way. But, I mean, not that many people are going to know about it. But that doesn't mean it's not true or that the extraordinary potential that's there isn't real. It doesn't mean it's any less miraculous. So as you begin to understand that you see how important it is that we all do our bit; that we all make the effort to evolve for the sake of this very potential we're speaking about. If we all play our own part in the process then that would be living a holy life, a life at one with the universe. Then everybody would be playing his or her part in the grand scheme of things? You get the idea?"

"Yes. Yes, I do. So is it a more worthy task to try to get a few select people to raise to a very high level of consciousness or a larger group to raise to, like, five percent?"

"You want to do both."

"You want to do both?" she repeated.

"Yeah, both at the same time."

"So you want to do everything?" she said in a half kidding tone that suggested that this might be a mildly ridiculous and overly ambitious notion.

Everyone laughed.

"Well, you need to do both" Andrew continued good naturedly, *"because the real issues that we as a species have to deal with now have very little to do with the kinds of things we've been speaking about in here."*

"Yeah."

"The biggest problem now is getting people from a tribal-centric perspective – which is where most of the planet's population lives – to global-centric one. That's really where

we need to get quickly so we'll begin to be able to work together to save ourselves from ourselves."

"Yeah."

"So a lot of the rarefied things we're speaking about here are way beyond that."

"Yeah."

"Because if we don't survive there's not much value that the kind of things we've been speaking about here are going to have, right?"

"Yeah. But once you have this perspective, it ideally would affect your life in a way that would enable you to make more wholesome decisions and therefore help save humanity."

"Absolutely. Once you really begin to get this whole notion of being part of the developmental process yourself, then, when you make this shift beyond your ego or your narcissism, there's a sense of care for the process, which is you! Do you have a sense of that?"

"Yeah, I do."

"Because then you want it to work out. You begin to really care about it. And it's not just your particular group or tribe, or even nation. But you want it all to work. And you really feel it. And I think there are a lot of people in the world today who feel that way. There are a lot of us who care and really want this all to work out."

"It seems to me," she said, struggling, "that on this retreat I've been realizing and understanding everything at an intellectual level but when I think about going home in a couple of days, back to my life and school and all that stuff, what a difference all this will really make for me. And what you just said clarified that for me."

"In which sense?"

"In the very practical sense of knowing that if we don't change quickly, we're all going to die."

Everyone laughed, not because what she was saying wasn't true but simply because there was something funny in her unpretentious, youthful bluntness.

"But if we gain this new perspective," she went on, "it will make it so that people will change and therefore all the things that are wrong with the world will have to change also because people will care that much."

"That's the idea. But, you see, for that to happen there needs to be nothing less than a cultural revolution because not enough people care enough yet. It has to be a real uprising that would be international. Hmm?"

"Yeah, that makes a lot of sense."

"So, anyway, you asked a very good question. And as you can see, the answer's kind of complex."

"Yes. But I think it really helped me clarify the importance of all the unconsciousness in real life. And not just as an idea, but in a very real way."

"So there are two dimensions to that. On the one hand, you have to make an effort to evolve your own consciousness. That's number one. And then, in concert, you have to do what you can to evolve the consciousness of the whole. So in our own ways we all have to do both. And how that would look in real life would be different for different people because people have different capacities and talents. But once again, simply put, we all have to do both."

"Yeah, I see that."

"I mean, if you just want to try and wake everyone else up, but you're not making an effort constantly to evolve yourself, it doesn't really work, does it?"

"No, of course not."

"And then if you're only interested in your own development but don't care about everyone else, what kind of person does that make you?"

"A selfish one."

"Right. And also, it means you don't get it."

"Yeah, right."

"But if more and more of us were doing both with commitment, you see, then that's going to generate a tremendous amount of positive evolutionary tension. Do you get the idea?"

"Definitely."

"So then there's a direct relationship between the inner development of the consciousness of the individual and his or her relationship with the world. And there would be a dynamic tension created between those two. And ideally that would be sustained and over time get more powerful. Both the inner development of the individual and his or her engagement with the world process would become more and more dynamic, powerful and profound. And, if you've got many people doing that simultaneously in this very dynamic way, it would have to have a powerful effect. But the inner development of the individual always has to always lead and be what's informing the engagement with the world process. Does that make sense?"

"Yes."

"So when you go back to school, are you going to get lost in your teenage world there?"

"No, I..."

"I would hope not. Because, you see, if you have integrity as a person then one can't have conversations like this and not have it mean something. Get my point?"

"Yes, definitely."

"Otherwise everyone would wonder what kind of person you were, right?" He laughed at his own words.

"That would be a little scary," she agreed.

"I've known a lot of scary people in my time," he laughed again. *"So, in terms of the integrity of our own development, the practice of inquiry, in the way that we've been pursuing it, has to mean something about our own evolution and development*

practically, morally, ethically, philosophically and spiritually. It can't be just a form of intellectual or spiritual entertainment." Andrew paused to look at the broad smile spread across the young girl's face. *"Why are you smiling?"*

"Because I was thinking about what I could do in my school to try to express this stuff."

"What came to your mind?"

"Going over the loudspeaker and reciting all the tenets." This time the whole room laughed uproariously. "And I was thinking that that really wouldn't work, but…"

"But I'm sure there are a lot of other things you could do that people might be more receptive to. I'm sure that a lot of your more sensitive, smarter friends and acquaintances are already interested in a lot of these things."

"I'm sure they are, but not by the same names."

"That's fine. It doesn't matter what you call it.

"But you're old enough to know that as a world and a world culture we're headed for big trouble."

"Yeah."

"I mean when you're sixteen you're old enough to begin to see that it's actually true and that it's not something that somebody's made up. It's not a game or a joke but it's actually real. So if that's true then that knowledge would have to inform your relationship to life, your engagement with life, your curiosity about it and the way you think about the future, right?"

"Yes."

"So if you're interested in the future then you have to ask how deep or profound your perspective is. Because remember, we see everything in context. So how big is it? Of course, the biggest context is going to be cosmos-centric, which is the spiritual perspective. That's the ultimate perspective that any human being could have upon the life experience.

"So even if we're dealing with a global crisis of overpopulation, mass extinction, the destruction of the environment and all the other lovely things that are happening, including the challenges we face as individuals in our personal lives, what's the ultimate context in which all that's being seen? Is it being seen from the perspective of consciousness itself, which is the only place from which we realize a liberated perspective? Because if we are going to get really involved in the life process for the biggest reasons, for it to work, we have to do it from a perspective or place of inherent freedom in ourselves. Does that make sense?"

"Yes, it does."

"Really?" he said somewhat astonished. *"If it's true that's very good. So what I'm saying is, on one hand, there are big problems that desperately need to be responded to but the biggest context is one of consciousness itself and consciousness is always free from any process that it's a part of, right?"*

"Yeah."

"It's a strange paradox, but it's driving the process and it's also free from it at the same time. So the idea here is that we want to both radically and completely engage with the process and at the same time experience our inherent freedom from it. Do you understand that?"

"Yeah."

"So the spiritual dimension of it has to do with seeing any and all circumstances, from your own personal challenges to the biggest challenges we face as a global species from the perspective of consciousness itself. That's not an easy thing to do. That requires the cultivation and capacity for the kind of subtlety that we were speaking about a few minutes ago because the goal here is to be completely involved and committed and at the same time be established in an ongoing realization of inherent freedom from the whole process at exactly the same time."

"Well, I mean, from the cosmic point of view, global issues aren't really that important."

"Well, no, they are important, but the place you're seeing them from is the biggest possible perspective."

"Right, I see."

"You have to know that the most important thing is perspective because it's the context in which you see anything. The minute you open your eyes from a meditative state you interpret what you're seeing through perspectives. You cannot see anything without perspective. It's simply not possible. Perspective is how you organize the information to create a coherent picture. So some perspectives are more developed, more evolved, more sophisticated, and more inclusive than others, right?"

"Yes, definitely."

"So we need to learn ways to cultivate these bigger perspectives. That's what's going to make it possible for us to be able to respond to life from an ever-deeper and higher place."

"Right."

"So the kind of things we're speaking about now is what the practice of religion and spirituality is going to be about in our future. See how it all works and how one informs the other?"

"Yes, I do."

"So once again, you have to be free from the process in order to be able to engage wholeheartedly in it. If you're not free from it, you're going to be too personally invested in something or other, which will inhibit your capacity to be able to see clearly. So you need to free yourself from the process in order to cultivate the capacity for clear seeing, which will in turn enable you to engage in the process in new ways. And on it goes and then you just have to stay with it.

"But the spiritual dimension has to do with letting go of the personal dimension. There's no enlightenment without doing that. If you let go of the personal dimension,

whether it's from the perspective of the Ground of Being or the Authentic Self, you'll experience instantaneous liberation, not in the future but now, because that's the nature of consciousness itself. And the perspective that you realize then is the one through which and from which you want to engage with the life process. One feeds the other and in an evolutionary or developmental context it has to be ongoing, until the very end. Do you understand?"

"Yeah."

"You mean I don't get to retire and go to Florida?" he mocked.

"Will that be the very end?" the young lady quipped.

"If you go to hell, yeah," Andrew shot back and we all laughed.

"Okay, thank you very much," she said and slowly the laughter subsided.

"So did you realize from our discussion that even if you're sixteen, there's no escape?"

"Yes."

"See, when I was your age, I thought that the whole world was going to change because that was the end of the sixties revolution. I was too young to be at the center of it, so I just caught the tail end. But I was old enough to experience the promise that was in the air. The time I lived in was very different than the time you're living in. And I really thought that the whole world was going to change because it really felt like it was. There was a lot of idealism in the air. I mean, it was tangible and a lot of people felt that a new age and a new time were at hand. And part of the reason for that was that there were a lot of mini-revolutions happening in society – individual rights, civil rights, women's rights, protests against the war and so on. And also, because of the psychedelic drugs people were taking…"

The girl giggled dismissively, as if such a thing were simply absurd.

"No, it's not funny," Andrew said in a serious tone. *"You see, by taking some of these psychedelics, people's consciousness would evolve temporarily because of what was happening chemically in the brain and they would actually experience these higher potentials. And because it was so easy – all you had to do was take a pill and you could actually see heaven – many, many people experienced higher and rarefied states and potentials all at the same time. That's why it seemed that a huge transformation in the culture and a new world were literally just right around the corner.*

"But the point is, the evolution of consciousness is a lot harder than just taking a pill. If you take the pill you'll be able to glimpse what's possible, but that doesn't mean it's yours. It's something we actually have to work for. But in those days that's how it felt. Of course, since it's a lot harder than just taking a pill, it didn't happen. But what we're speaking about on this retreat is about doing it authentically."

I flashed back, in a manner of speaking, to the days when the ingestion of psychedelics and the potentials they revealed had loomed large in my own life. (For more on the subject of psychedelics and their relationship to spiritual transformation, please see appendix 7, Ruminations on Psychedelics and Spiritual Transformation).

"Thank you," the young lady said, taking his point about making it happen in real time.

"So is it apparent to you that if, to some degree, this was the context for whatever you were doing in your life, it would change everything?"

"Yes."

"Good. That's what's important. Because without that, what is there? All you have is the material experience. And that's what most people have – the experience of their body and their senses, right?"

"Yeah."

"That's why sex is such a big deal. It's the only access to transcendence or escape that all those people have. Without consciousness, that's all you have. You're trapped in form."

"Interesting."

"Yes, it is interesting, isn't it?"

"Very."

"It's good to just stand back, watch and see how true it is."

"Yeah."

"So many people are trapped and then the luckiest people on the planet, like yourself and a lot of other people, are being hypnotized by this stupid culture of materialism and narcissism. Hypnotized," he repeated emphatically. *"And young people aren't stupid. They grow up, look around and see that there's no sense of meaning and so then they withdraw into a kind of cynicism, nihilism and arrogance, which just results in people not caring, right?"*

"Yeah, definitely."

"That's the result. And then what happens? Then you're as much part of the problem as everyone else. You're not above it or beyond it in any way."

"Right."

"Things aren't good."

"Yeah, I know."

Andrew left it at that, the unspoken conclusion suggesting that it was incumbent upon her to begin to shape her young life into something that was part of the solution rather than part of the problem.

I sat there surprised and inspired by the probing dialogue this sixteen year-old girl had just had with Andrew. I thought back to myself at that age and it took less than a nanosecond to know that, had my life depended on it, there wasn't a snowball's chance in hell that I could have carried on a conversation like that with anyone. Thus I marveled at her courage, her maturity and her capacity for vision, hoping that there were many more like her.

Andrew wasted no time in moving to the next question, motioning to another young woman.

"One of the things you said," she began, "is that if we go 'top-down' then we have to quit processing anything."

"No. We don't have to quit processing anything. We have to give up the attachment to having time to go through a process ourselves."

"Can you say more about the difference between the two?"

"Well, yeah. If you need to go through a process then you're not ready now."

"But what about processing stuff?"

"What do you mean?"

"I took it to mean if we're coming from a 'top-down' perspective we would connect with the evolutionary process and move from there and wouldn't process whatever came up because that would bring us into the ego."

"No, that's not quite it. It's a good question but what I'm speaking about has a very specific meaning and it's easy to misunderstand. You see any way you look at it, life and development are a process. They're one process after another all the way from the gross to the subtle, right?"

"Yeah."

"But what I specifically mean is that the Authentic Self, which is a function of consciousness, is absolutely ready right now. It doesn't need time to prepare itself, to look over its notes, have a last supper, take some vitamins, have some heart-to-heart talks with loved ones, do some more therapy or learn some new exercises, right?"

"Yes," the young lady agreed.

"You see, to that the Authentic Self would say, 'Do whatever you need to do, but I'm going to be as ready when you get back from all those things as I am now.' Are you with me?"

"Yes."

"Good. So the Authentic Self is ready right now. It doesn't need to go through a process.

"Okay, I got that," she said, though traces of uncertainty lingered in her tone.

"Well, that's all it means."

"But does this apply if something goes wrong in life."

"Things always do."

"In other words, you don't process it but simply go back to the Authentic Self. I mean, with respect, for example, to one's interaction with somebody else, would you want to know, well, hey what did you do? What did I do? What do we think about it? What do we feel about it? and so on?"

"Well, if things go wrong you'll often want to understand why they went wrong so that next time you'll do it differently. And also, if the opposite happens, if things go very well, you might also want to know why that happened so you could do that again. So thinking about what went right or wrong and why is not part of what I mean about processing not being a good thing."

"Okay, I see."

"So what I mean by not processing has to do with any and all excuses the indi-vidual self comes up with for not being ready for prime time right now. That's what clarity of intention is all about.

"'Are you ready now?' he suddenly demanded in a boisterous, theatrical tone. *"'Well, I don't know,'"* he replied to himself in mousy fashion. *"'I need more time to think about it.' 'Oh, okay. Sorry,'"* he said with mock sensibility. *"That's what it means. You see what I mean?"*

"Yes, I do."

"Because as the Authentic Self you can be ready right now to engage with the evo-lutionary, developmental process full-bore and with complete commitment. You're not going to be, 'Well, I don't know. Let me stick my toe in and see how it feels. Then we'll talk,' right?"

"Right."

"Because then you need time to check it out. And even after that you're not so sure. Maybe you'll change your mind."

"So that's inertia?" she replied as both a question and a comment.

"That's ego."

"Okay."

"So the Authentic Self is not playing games. It says, 'I know who I am and I know why I'm here.' So once you know that, the ego's need to process simply means, 'I need more time.' We all need time until we know unequivocally and absolutely 'who I am and why I'm here.' When you know that you don't need time anymore. And then when you engage in this developmental process you'll be at a hundred percent. And this pro-cess doesn't need individuals that are half-baked, right?"

"Yes, that's right."

"So that's the whole point. The ego or separate self-sense is always in a process of recovery."

"Yeah, getting it together; studying a little more, and so on," she said.

"Right. And the Authentic Self is not. So you would have to make a choice. And then you would have to be able to take the risk of being a hundred percent ready to go while at the same time still feeling, at least in part, 'Well, I'm not really ready.'"

"Yeah, that's a challenge."

"That's the big challenge," Andrew repeated. *"I mean, exactly what would it mean to be fully ready? Would it mean that you are one hundred percent physically fit, that you're emotionally and psychologically functioning at the highest level and that there's not a trace of a shadow or any stain in you? Would it mean that everything about you is just fantastic and couldn't be better and that you've also done everything you could have ever wanted to do? Would it mean that not only are you at your optimal level of functioning in all the lines of development in every part of the self, but you've also done, tried and experimented with every possibility so there's nothing else that you could possibly want to do? Is that when you're going to be ready?"* Everyone laughed

at these absurd propositions, knowing full well that on even the most propitious journey along the road of life none ever reach such a perfected state. *"Because that's the game the ego's playing and most people actually believe it. Of course, real life could never work that way."*

"True," she conceded.

"Okay, but the ego's perspective, which is warped, would lead you to believe 'Well, I'm not ready yet, I'm not ready yet, I'm not ready yet.' And if you give it all the time it wants it will still always say, 'Yeah, but I'm still not ready.'

"So, if you want to put it in a Christian context you could say that God wants those people who would give their heart."

That sent a silent shock through my heart, made it quiver with a tender ache.

"'Not my will, but thy will be done,' right? So, do you think that cripples aren't allowed? You see the way we think about this is insane. It doesn't mean anything. It's absolutely useless. Do you see how foolish we are?" Andrew grew passionate on this point.

"Yeah, I definitely do."

"Okay. So all this 'processing' is giving undue significance to our..."

"Ego."

"Yeah. And this is a very important point that's very hard for people to get. So, for the ego it seems reasonable because, 'I'm hurt and wounded, traumatized, and victimized. I lost an arm, a leg, a tooth, I have brain damage, I was sexually abused,' and all the rest of it. It all seems very reasonable from the perspective of the sensitive, narcissistic, separate self-sense. But for the Authentic Self it's all always perfectly irrelevant. So who has the courage to throw all that to the wind and proclaim, 'Not my will be done, thy will be done?' That's the traditional declaration of unconditional surrender for a higher purpose – always has been, always will be. It's not when you think you're ready. From that perspective you'll never be ready because you'll never be good enough because there'll always be more that's possible, right?"

"Yes, definitely."

"So what's dramatic is seeing crazy, fractured human beings turn into dramatically transformed individuals. So if you want to put it in theological terms, it's a leap of faith. You see, the ego is not only disinterested in these higher potentials, it has no faith in them."

"True."

"So the unenlightened individual who lacks faith and conviction is going to always be giving more weight to what they think about themselves than what God thinks or what the Authentic Self is. And it's a totally warped perspective that is giving too much weight to the wrong part of us. It doesn't mean those things aren't true, because we all have a lot of developing that we are going to continue to need to do. Just because this flip occurs doesn't mean that this ongoing development doesn't need to occur perpetually and endlessly. But it has to do with where we are putting ourselves and our relationship

to life. So, at a certain point it becomes a matter of faith in something you can't see. Are you with me?"

"Yes."

"So that's what I mean by giving up the processing which specifically refers to this point of giving yourself time. You see, I have no doubt that if one is deeply willing to do this for the biggest reasons—not the motive to be someone or even to be an enlightened person – which means 'I have no choice and I'm absolutely needed because we all are,' that that's enough if we have the courage and commitment to follow through on that and that alone. Beyond that we'll all be given whatever it is we need to take those steps. But it's not on our terms. It'll never be on the ego's terms and that's what the ego can never understand. It doesn't work that way. And as you get into it, it's less and less on the ego's terms, and more and more on the terms of this larger impulse. You get the idea?"

"Yes, I definitely do. Thank you."

"Very good. So we're almost at the end of the retreat but please remember that it's not over until after the session tomorrow morning."

We all agreed and then sank into silence, only the sound of ringing bells on the wind moving in that stillness.

As my eyes closed tears welled up, compelled by a surge of emotions. When Andrew said that God only wants our hearts I felt mine melt. How could I be so foolish, so arrogant, setting ever in the future the only thing that God wants now? How steadfastly I deceive myself and keep my face from His, arguing ever for more time from behind a shield of false humility. I was devastated by my own stupidity and the monumental majesty of the Truth. The sheer grandeur of what had been laid out before us over the past ten days struck me then like some grand fugue, its themes and currents intertwined, streaming forward in one great harmony, the discordant notes of human struggle – my struggle – finding their rightful place among the greater themes and movements of spiritual unfolding. Andrew had robbed me of excuses and left me empty handed, staring mutely into the light of That which always wants me now, as I am, for Itself.

NOTES

1. For a more in-depth discussion of this go to the following web page: http://www.andrew-cohen.org/notes/index.php?/weblog/blog/love_sex_and_spiritual_evolution/

Day 11

The Absolute is Always Too Much

"Today is it," I thought upon waking to the cool air drifting in through the large, half-open windows. The, short, serrated nights, sawn through with snoring, were now behind me and soon exhaustion would be also. But so would the warm cups of tea prepared with such care each morning, the stirring sunrises and morning bells, and most of all, the currents of meditation, introspection and revelation that had carried me through this outrageous journey into the very heart of Life. Little wonder that as I rose I was buffeted by both melancholy and exhilaration.

As I moved through the familiar rhythms of chanting, of meditation and of walking among old buildings and the stones of ancient hills, I was aware that these were the last moments of what now seemed a long standing ritual. Time slowed. Small details resolved themselves into sharper focus as I sought to etch it all into my mind. The intoning of the bronze bells, the growing warmth of the morning sun on my face, the birds taking flight, the smell of coffee and baking bread. All these impressed themselves upon my senses more forcefully this morning; their singular intention – to abide with me so that they might raise themselves on future days and ferry me back in reverie to the moments that passed beneath me now like water. And while I knew that I would soon be swept back into speech and interaction and irrevocably forward into life I would, despite my difficulties, deeply miss this place and all that I had found here.

That same sense of suspension between things hung over our gathering as we assembled in the teaching hall one last time. Even as the stillness settled, there were subtle signs, the small fidgeting of nervous hands, casual glances between people that hadn't been there before and an air of mild unrest that indicated something was about to change, that the future was calling and the present dissolving in the wake of its pull. Yet when Andrew entered the room, neatly dressed and as composed as he had been every day, timeless presence entered with him. The power of *this* moment reasserted itself as we fixed our gaze on that dimension from which the miracle of this teaching had emerged and unfolded itself, petal by petal, in the days that had passed behind us.

We meditated for an hour, sinking once more into that Ground that had now become the shared field of our experience, before rising from those depths to explore one final time the extraordinary potential of enlightenment in the twenty-first century.

Methodically, Andrew clipped on his mike and surveyed the room. *"So this is our last session together,"* he said, *"and if anyone has any questions they'd like to ask before we finish they can do that now."* Soon his gaze settled on the Dutch lawyer with whom he'd spoken some days earlier.

"I was wondering," he began softly, "how this teaching can be implemented in the profit-oriented business of today."

Andrew paused for a long moment to consider the question. Finally he said in a thoughtful tone, *"I don't have enough experience working with people who are doing business to be able to give a clear answer to that question. I've spoken a couple of times at different organizations though it wasn't really very in depth. But at least by now you can see that this teaching is all about how we can come together so there obviously has to be a big connection there."*

"Right," the man agreed, though somewhat dubiously. "But do you think it's possible to mix this teaching with the profit oriented business of today?" he repeated insistently.

"Profit oriented business," Andrew repeated back to him in an exclamatory tone. *"What do you mean by profit oriented?"*

"Well, the businesses that are…"

Sensing his direction, Andrew cut him off. *"If I provide a service for you doesn't it make sense that you should give me something in return and vice versa? Isn't that how it works in life?"*

"At this point, yes," the man admitted reluctantly.

"Well, how are we going to survive if there's not some form of commerce that's mutually benefiting? If, as we've been saying, there's nobody up there, then we have to do it."

"Yes, I guess that's right."

"So when you say profit does that mean having evil intentions?"

A small series of chuckles crept through the crowd.

"I don't know. It depends."

"Well, I'm asking you because when you said profit-oriented I wasn't sure what you meant."

"It can be both, actually."

"I know that's why I'm asking you."

"I guess if it's from an evil intention then it's not possible to mix the two, but if it's not then it is."

"Right," Andrew agreed. *"So if it's an evil intention then all you're interested in is profit and you're willing to destroy other people and the planet simply so you can profit from them, right?"*

"Right."

"Of course, a lot of corporations operate that way. They're only interested in profit and nothing else. Clearly then, those are evil intentions and obviously this teaching wouldn't work with that kind of motivation. But if the motivation were different then I'm sure it would be able to help quite a bit, hmm?"

"Right. I think so too."

"Good," Andrew said matter-of-factly, concluding the dialogue.

This brief exchange triggered a number of strong associations for me, all carrying an intense emotional charge. The first revolved around the strong loathing I felt toward the all too common assumption of "spiritual types" that money is somehow dirty, "the root of all evil," and thus well beneath them. I have never found this to be anything other than a strange form of poverty elitism, an insipid excuse to hide behind a veil of moral superiority one's lack of creativity, courage and the willingness to struggle to make something of oneself. This was an illusion which was thoroughly destroyed in me by my lengthy association with Peter. He, like Rudi before him, would not put up with such nonsense. It was his view that if someone was truly living a spiritual life and becoming a vehicle for the "Higher Creative Energy in the Universe," that fact should have abundant manifestation on the level of their material life. [1] And that level, as with everything else, should continually evolve. As a Westerner with entrepreneurial inclinations, this simply made sense to me and in this regard Peter himself was a powerful example.

In fact, this aspect of his teaching, this rejection of the "rent control mentality," was both empowering and exciting as it set before me a clear example of how to live a profoundly spiritual life within the context of an unabashedly Western existence while compromising neither. I feel it is incumbent upon those of us who live with strong spiritual interests, creativity and a socioeconomic environment that makes financial success possible, to endeavor to become role models for a new possibility, one in which financial success and spiritual depth feed and support one another, rather than standing in active opposition. If some of us can do this on an individual level then perhaps new possibilities might emerge on a larger level as well.

That larger level would range from the world of small business to that of mega-corporations. With respect to the latter, however, I must admit that I had long shared the cynical view about the possibility of corporations serving higher interests, having spent years trapped in a corporate nightmare myself. There I lived like Dilbert, the popular comic strip office drone. Little more than an indentured wage slave, I toiled in what amounted to a corporate Yugoslavia, a balkanized entity where petty leaders vied for position and control to the detriment of the organization as a whole and where personal victories over internal adversaries were as highly prized as corporate profits. It was a machine in which people were simply "resources," having their life drained from them and their souls hung out to dry. What remained were human husks surviving the daily grind, reduced to fantasizing about hitting the lotto and telling their boss to "shove it."

I have often wondered since those days how much latent creativity lies untapped and remains ultimately wasted in these graveyards for the soul. I personally functioned at no more than thirty percent of my capacity during my corporate servitude. That was more than adequate for the job and was the sum of what such a dispiriting environment could obtain from me. I had much more to offer but no reason to do so. And I was not alone. Many bright people worked in my company and do in all such organizations. Yet the collective clearly didn't reflect that fact. The fact is that most who toil in such circumstances, from the perspective of the possible, lead lives of stunted creativity to their own detriment and the detriment of the whole.

All this, of course, describes only the interior dimension, both of the individual and the organization. What of the exterior? There, as we all know, it gets dramatically worse. Few would argue that by and large corporations are the most powerful force on the planet today. And, due to a corrupt value system and narrow-minded obsession with quarterly profits, that force is often destructive. That being the case, I had to concede that the young man's question, though irritating to my entrepreneurial, Type-A, sensibilities, was not without merit.

When I left the corporate world to strike out on my own I set out to prove, in my own very tiny way, that engaging in commerce with other human beings for the purpose of earning a profit didn't have to stand in opposition to the deepest and highest values in life. In this I have succeeded at least in some measure and to my own satisfaction. And along those lines and in light of Andrew's teachings, I have come to believe that while at present corporations are largely less than a benevolent force on the stage of world events, the potential for that to change in dramatic ways definitely exists. In fact, that potential, if realized, could play a significant role in contributing to the salvation of our world.

One of the contributions of the teaching to this development lies in the emergence of the Authentic Self in the context of "enlightened communication." There the individuals merge and become one self in "ecstatic intimacy" without sacrificing their autonomy and with access to a level of intellect and insight that is normally unavailable. Were that acuity to be directed at the very real and practical concerns of commerce with a conscience, the very real and practical upshot could be nothing short of staggering. Andrew's organization, EnlightenNext, is a striking example. With a tiny core team of committed individuals the creative output of that organization is nothing short of staggering. There is an award winning magazine, award winning website, graduate program in conscious evolution, an international speaker series, worldwide evolutionary enlightenment courses, seminars, global centers, retreats, and soon, branches to address both global warming and the endless crises in Africa. All of this from a core of around fifty people, all of whom are intensely engaged in the matter of their own evolutionary development. And all of whom are holding the space of enlightened consciousness as the ground from which all of this activity occurs. This ongoing success is a potential model for others and, at the very least, through the fact of its existence, can help destroy the cynicism about such a possibility.

That some hopeful signs are indeed emerging from the corporate world was recently discussed in an issue of *What is Enlightenment?* magazine entitled "The Business of Saving the World." In its pages we are introduced to some extraordinary people and their work from within the machine to help transform corporations into agents of positive social change. No one denies that there is an extremely long way to go and that such individuals and corporations represent only the tiniest percentage of global commerce today. However, since the rate of change is changing[2] and nothing motivates change like a crisis of survival,[3] there is a chance that such small stirrings of conscience might contribute to the very revolution that could help set things to right. That, at least, is the view and hope that I hold and is part of what continues to inspire me to demonstrate that creativity, financial success and liberated consciousness do not stand in opposition to one another but rather stand to support each other in a way that has never existed before.

All this flashed through my mind during Andrew's brief dialogue with the cynical Dutch lawyer. That concluded, he next turned his attention to a German woman.

"Yesterday you said something about the experience of being on your own and being in a group as the same," she said. "Could you elaborate on that or say more about it?"

Andrew paused thoughtfully for a moment. Then he said, *"I'm not sure I can. What did you have in mind?"*

"What do I have in mind?" she returned somewhat puzzled.

"Well, I mean, I kind of said it, so I'm not sure what more you're interested in."

"Well, I wanted to know more about the implications of that."

"Isn't the implication obvious?"

"Yes," she returned sheepishly.

"I thought so. The implication is that it's vertical? From the many to the One — that's how it goes.

"The higher One though, right?"

"Yes, the higher One."

What Andrew meant by this was that merely coming together for a shared purpose is not enough to guarantee a desirable and beneficial result. After all, as we all know, the Nazis did that to great and devastating effect. I'd heard Andrew refer to this sort of coming together as a "lower we" – a domain into which we definitely do not want to tread – whereas what we were striving for was the coming together as a "higher we," the new, collective emergence of the Authentic Self.

"From the many egos to the one Authentic Self," Andrew clarified. *"That's when the one Authentic Self is aware of itself as being the many but simultaneously as being the One. So the implications are enormous, aren't they?"*

"Yes. Yes, indeed."

"The implications are utterly profound in every way you could possibly consider them when thinking about human life.

"So was there anything else?"

"No, it's just that I'm blown away that it's so enormous and that the implications are so huge."

"Oh, yeah," Andrew agreed with enthusiasm. *"But isn't it thrilling?"*

"Yeah, absolutely," she returned with similar passion.

"Remember, we've been posing the question, 'Who am I and why am I here?' So I asked, 'what do we all have to discover for change and a sense of purpose and meaning?' So when you discover the Authentic Self you discover purpose and meaning in a way that's quite shocking."

"It is indeed."

"And the implications are profound beyond measure. They're so big that we know that no matter how much we could ever respond it would never be enough because what has to happen is so enormous."

"Yes."

"So therefore we would all have more than we could possibly handle or accomplish. And so all we can do is try and do as much as we possibly can."

"Right."

"But from the perspective of the Authentic Self nothing less than that would be enough. Unless we did everything we possibly could, it wouldn't be enough. That means each and every one of us! Because if it wasn't everything, then we're still leaving room for the ego and that's not a transformed, liberated anything."

"Yes," she agreed with breathless enthusiasm. "That's why yesterday when I came out of the session I told myself 'no more vacation ever from consciousness.'"

"Well, that's exactly right. Very good."

Andrew searched briefly for the next questioner. He soon went back to a German man with whom he'd spoken on several prior occasions.

"Hi," he said in a rather stiff tone. "I need clarification if possible. I sense this creative impulse very strongly. It engages all my senses and I can feel it as a totality in my entire body. But then the meditation feels like it's working against the evolutionary tension and the creative forces that are in play."

"No, it doesn't work against it."

"That's why I'm asking for clarification."

"I said meditation is completely the opposite, but it doesn't work against it at all. Remember, everything came from nothing, including you and I, didn't it?"

"Yes."

"Before your mother and father created you, where were you?"

"The Ground of Being?"

"Yeah, that's right. So you existed as an unmanifest potential, right?"

"Right."

"So where does the unmanifest potential abide?"

"In the Ground of Being?"

"Well, yeah, it lives in this void which is pregnant with unmanifest potential. But in its unmanifest state there's nothing there. It's literally less than a thought though it still exists. Everything that exists has always had the potential to exist otherwise it couldn't exist, right?"

"Right."

"So everything that exists comes from the same place including you and me. So if that's where we come from it also has to be ultimately what we're made up of. Doesn't it?"

"Yes."

"So you could say that in a non-relative or absolute sense there isn't any difference between where we've come from – this unmanifest potential abiding in this vacuum – and who and what we are as these embodied, material, beings with consciousness and its capacity for awareness. So in an absolute sense there literally is no difference between the forms we're in now and the forms we were in before we came into existence. That's the really non-relative way of looking at it. So from that perspective there isn't any difference between that state and this state. It's all only one."

"Yes, that's right."

"Now, this is just one way of looking at it but it's truthful from the non-relative perspective.

"But there's another way of looking at the same thing and it's completely opposite. In this unmanifest ground there's no impulse to become – at all! There's only Being, not becoming. So, when you begin to give attention to the non-relative dimension of consciousness itself you begin to experience the nature of that dimension of your own self, and the nature of that dimension of your own self is the nature of that dimension of at all times – before, during and after the creative process. It's a constant. However, in this manifest domain the only constant is that everything's changing all the time, right?"

"Yes."

"So it's literally like going from one dimension to another, one perspective to another, but there's no conflict between them. And more importantly, what happens is that as we meditate upon zero or no-thing-ness in an evolutionary context, we find that our capacity and willingness to transcend and to let go of the fears and desires of the ego increases. Meditating upon zero should weaken those attachments because the more you experience the already full condition of the Unmanifest Ground, the more you are convinced emotionally that fullness is the ultimate truth of all of life and

death. So that should help you to be able to let go of the fears and desires of the ego so that you'll be able to embrace the fire and passion of the Authentic Self to create the universe. See what I'm saying?"

"Yeah, I do. That's what I was wondering because I can see that from the Ground of Being I can really increase my awareness of consciousness in the manifest state of the Authentic Self. But I found that when I came from the state of Authentic Self then I really struggled in the meditation."

"Right, but there's no need to struggle. It can only help. And you also want to understand that this Unmanifest Ground is a very significant part of who and what we all are. So if that's something we don't know about then it means we don't know who we are and where we've come from."

"Right."

"It's always the ground we're standing on and if we don't know that then we're living in ignorance of our own source and that has very real, tangible effects on our sense of who we are. And also, the conscious experience of that Ground, as I was saying earlier, is the ultimate relief and release from manifest existence, even from the passion and intensity of the Authentic Self. We might even want relief and release from that because, after all, we're human beings, aren't we? We can't ever deny our humanity. There's a very real human dimension to all this. There's not only a physical dimension but also an emotional dimension, a psychological dimension, a psychic dimension, and so on.

"So how much of the Authentic Self can any of us bear? That's the question. We can never forget that we're human beings first and foremost. But it's the kind of human beings we are that we've been talking about. So since we are human beings, then for the evolution and cultivation of our own capacity to be more authentically human – which means not conditioned robots – spending long periods of time in this Ground has the potential to liberate the self-sense from a very conditioned relationship to the human experience. Therefore, it can be an enormous help towards giving us a greater and greater capacity to become the Authentic Self. Do you understand?"

"Yes, I do. Thank you."

"So you've got to do it every day. I think that until you can consistently and over a long period of time demonstrate through your own actions that you are aware of what you're doing, you should meditate every single day for as long as you possibly can as if your life depended on it.

"Earlier these kids were saying," indicating the four teenagers in front of him, *"'Oh wow, my mind is driving me crazy. I can't believe it.' So I told them that the only thing that happens when you meditate is that you become aware of what's happening in there all the time that you're just not aware of. And they went, 'Really?' They thought that because of meditation it was getting worse and speeding up. So I told them that that's not the case; that that's just how crazy we are all the time. It's only because you're stopping and beginning to pay attention to how your mind works that you see what's*

happening. Of course when you see that you can't believe how out of control it is.

"Therefore, you can see that if we're not really paying attention, if we're not very aware of what makes us tick and how the self functions at a mechanical level, then the left hand doesn't know what the right hand's doing. In other words, why we're not conscious. Are you with me?"

"Yes, definitely."

"So then the meditative posture – not necessarily the physical posture – is a practice and a symbol for awareness, isn't it?"

"It is."

"So now you're making an effort to pay attention and to be aware. And that effort needs to be made until you can demonstrate that you're no longer acting out of unconscious impulses or motives. And that's quite a tall order. Meditation in and of itself is not going to be enough to get you there. All I can say is it helps. But what's more important than anything else is the first tenet of the teaching, which is wanting to be conscious more than anything else.

"So if you want to be conscious more than anything else then things like paying attention will help a lot, not because you're practicing paying attention but because you want to be conscious. A lot of people meditate and it makes absolutely no difference. They don't change at all. They meditate for years and they don't change one single bit. Now, why do you think that is? Because they're not interested! They don't want to change. But if you want to change then every effort you make in order to do so is going to bear fruit because you want to change. You see?"

The painful simplicity of this struck me once more. In the end everything comes down to what we truly want. All else is secondary.

"Yes," the German man agreed.

"Because you yourself are going to be paying attention to what you're doing, why you're doing it and what the nature of your experience is all the time, not just when you're sitting. Like meditation, this should become a natural state."

"All the time; that's the challenge," he lamented.

"That's when it counts though. So if you want to become conscious you will. If anybody wants to become conscious, what could possibly prevent that?"

"Nothing."

"If you want to increase your capacity for consciousness it literally cannot be stopped. But if you don't want that, then it's not going to happen. You could go through some kind of outward ritual or routine that might feign or evoke the pretense that that was something you were interested in, but if you don't become more conscious it could only mean that you're not interested in becoming more conscious. Do you understand?"

"Yes, definitely."

"So that's why the first tenet is the foundation of absolutely everything. Everything always returns to the free agency of the individual."

"Okay."

Andrew shifted his position, took a sip of water and went to the next question, this one from Imants, the tall, thin older Australian fellow "Hi Andrew," he began.

"Hi."

"Okay, here we go," he said as if having to get up his nerve to dive off the edge of a cliff. "I wanted to report on my experience of the Authentic Self last night and this morning. And I want to bear witness to it because I think it's very important in terms of my own development and in terms of the development of consciousness. So what really struck me about the Authentic Self was its incredible physicality."

"Physicality?" Andrew answered back in puzzlement. *"How so?"*

"Just the sheer energy that was created by the simple perspective of intention and interest. Like when we first sat down in the circle at probably about nine thirty last night, it was just the sheer act of committing oneself in terms of interest and leaning forward into the group that evoked the beginning of the emergence of the Authentic Self and that experience lasted until about four o'clock this morning."

"Wow, you were there all night?"

"Well, no. I moved from there. But the experience didn't leave me and one of the things that I did actually physically experience – and I've had trouble with this issue – was the being alone and being together as being one."

"You're saying you had trouble with it. Does that mean you didn't understand it, you didn't like it, or both?"

"I think I didn't like it and therefore I didn't want to understand it."

"Well, usually one has something to do with the other there," Andrew laughed.

"Yeah, yeah, that's right. My experience was that I moved from the group but the presence of the Authentic Self didn't leave me at all. And in terms of the nature of the Authentic Self, I was looking into my experience to try and describe what that expansion or that evolution of consciousness actually was. And what I saw was that it was basically a field that came from nothing, enveloped me and then moved into the circle. And then, as people were talking, their fields emerged and there was a mixing of these fields.

"When I left the group, which was about quarter to one, as I went up the back stairs I saw Christopher from Australia, a friend of mine, come out as well. When I got to the top of the stairs my ego said to me, 'Keep going, keep going, you don't want to keep this experience going. Don't wait for him.' But I waited for him and then we had this amazing conversation in which we talked about this issue of physicality, of how the field of this Authentic Self was actually in every single molecule in the body. And we were both experiencing this extraordinary lightness of being.

"And for the first time in my life," his voice quivered with emotion now, "as we were just walking in the darkness talking about our experience of the Authentic

Self, I experienced true intimacy with another human being. And this morning, when I was contemplating that, I realized that from the ego self we would have discussed that event in a completely different way. We would have gone back into the past and we would have made personal comments. And I think it was the complete absence of the personal from the physical body that just gave us this incredible lightness of being, clarity and expansion of the mind.

"I mean, the ego mind says, 'The Authentic Self is all fine intellectually, but it doesn't really exist.' But I can tell you that in terms of my own experience," he paused in awe for a moment as sympathetic laughter welled from the group, "the Authentic Self is a living, real, intelligent phenomenon and I have an obligation to be always available for it."

"So you mean I'm not making it up?" Andrew said, tongue firmly in cheek.

"Well, there was some speculation about that prior to the experience," – everyone laughed heartily at that – "but no, you're not making it up at all. Not in terms of my experience, anyway."

"So, you said you never experienced intimacy like that in your whole life, right?"

"Yeah, which is a crazy thing to say, given that…"

"Why? It's not crazy if it's true."

"Well, it's crazy in the sense that I've always regarded myself," he paused for a moment as if to reorganize his thoughts, then went on, "maybe it's that this sensitive self has regarded myself as being a very intimate, caring, and compassionate person."

"Oh, interesting. Caring and compassionate?"

"Yeah."

"Is there any compassion in the Authentic Self as you experienced it?"

"Actually, you often mention that the Authentic Self doesn't really care for us as individuals. Well, given the experience of this physicality and the fact that every single molecule was vibrating with this intense sense of energy, this lightness of being, this cleansing and rejuvenation, I'd have to say that the Authentic Self was expressing a care for my vehicle, so…"

"Well, hold it, though. You're just describing what the nature of the Authentic Self is. But I think you can't really go farther than that. You can say, 'Its nature is energy, lightness of being and so on,' but you can't say, 'It has compassion for,' because it's a function of consciousness. It's not an individual. Only an individual can have empathy for another. But the Authentic Self is a function of consciousness so it's not capable of empathy."

"But the by-product of this physicality just seemed to be very powerful and positive."

"Well, I'm not denying that it's powerful and positive at all. But we were discussing this question about compassion."

"Well, I don't think it is compassionate."

"Right, because that's not part of its nature. But there's a ferocious, radically austere, passionate concern for truth, right?"

"Absolutely, yeah."

"Because the Authentic Self can't bear pretense."

"Yeah, and that's an incredibly liberating relationship to have to one's experience."

"Right. But before we get there, if what I'm saying is true – that that's the nature of the Authentic Self – that's fascinating and something to think about in and of itself. If, when you are experiencing this function of consciousness coming awake and alive within you, one of its qualities is intolerance for pretense, that's quite profound. That means a lot about the nature of the Authentic Self itself. Right?"

"Oh, absolutely."

"It's not a small point."

"As you were speaking, I was recalling what happened during the first group discussion. In it I had the sense that something was speaking through me but I wasn't actually saying the words."

"Right."

"There was no thought. It was spontaneous and it just came and came and came."

"Yes, that's right. That's how it works. But the point I'm making is that if it's true that when one is awake to the nature of the Authentic Self there's an automatic intolerance for pretense then it's quite significant. So what's the opposite of pretense? Authenticity, right?"

"Right, yes."

"You experience the profound intimacy because of the presence of authenticity in the self. And then, if the other is also awake to the Authentic Self then, when that authenticity meets authenticity there is automatically going to be the experience of profound intimacy."

"Yes, very much."

"So many people say when they experience the Authentic Self, 'I've never experienced such profound intimacy in my entire life.'"

"So I wasn't the only one?"

Everyone laughed again.

"Well that's the nature of the experience of the Authentic Self. What everybody says is, "It's a different level of intimacy that's profound beyond any kind of experience of intimacy I've ever had – bar none.' And I'm saying the reason has to do with the presence of authenticity in self and other. That's what changes absolutely everything. Authenticity means ego-less. It means the veil of pretense falls away."

"Yes, that's my experience exactly."

"What's fascinating is that the Authentic Self is intolerant and has no time for pretense. However, often, though not always, when we think of the word compassion it

means that if someone who is full of pretense and self-importance were to come up to you and want to engage you from that level, if you are a compassionate person you'd be expected to spend as much time as they wanted to take listening to whatever it is. Why? Because you're such a compassionate soul.

"So what if you were awake to the Authentic Self and someone who was feeling a lot of self-concern wanted your attention but, because you were awake to the Authentic Self, you just couldn't respond to it? It's not that you wouldn't want to. It's just that there was no way you could even begin to relate to where they were coming from, however real it obviously was for them. Now, there's no doubt that that individual would experience that as lacking compassion.

"So the narcissistic separate self-sense is always looking for attention for itself. It doesn't matter how it gets it. But the Authentic Self is not interested in having attention on itself. It's inherently interested in authenticity and nothing else. That's what's so miraculous about it. And when you experience it, you experience that automatically, just like that." Andrew snapped his fingers sharply. *"It's instantaneous.*

"So it's a completely different self and there is an enormous clash between the ego and the Authentic Self. Remember, I said they're parallel lines that never meet. Never! And not only do they not meet but there will be a conflict between the pure passion for authenticity of the Authentic Self and this compulsive craving for affirmation and attention of the narcissistic separate self-sense. That's why the ego has to be transcended. And that takes practice and work and discipline. It takes commitment and more commitment and more commitment and more commitment and more commitment. Do you understand?" Andrew was emphatic and passionate.

"Yes. Yes, I do."

"And the reason is that if you or I or any one of us have been living in the grips of the narcissistic separate self-sense or ego, for twenty, thirty, fifty or seventy years and we've also been cultivating our narcissism by compulsively and aggressively identifying with the fears and desires of the individual and collective ego, then we're often willing victims and even collaborators." There was a little laughter at this, though it was soft and sober. *"So our hands, so to speak, are not clean.*

"Yet we believe that the worst part of our self is our best friend. So what's important about the kind of dramatic experience that Imants is describing is that it's living proof of your potential to be a liberated self or enlightened self right now. But in order to sustain that potential you have to be willing to pay a price for it and the price is always going to be a lot bigger than you think. Of course, it's not hard to understand why, because if we've been cultivating these narcissistic tendencies for decades they're not going to go on a permanent vacation just because you tasted the bliss and the glory of the Authentic Self. So you need to have these kinds of experiences in order to be convinced and then you have to get to the point where you're so convinced that you're literally doubtless. Of course then your back is against the wall. Once you bear witness and you're doubtless then you have to be willing to do whatever it is that you need to

do and make any effort you need to make in order to be true to what it is that you no longer have any doubt about.

"If someone is not experientially convinced, you can't expect much from them. But if they are it's different because now they know and that's supposed to change everything. So if there's integrity in the self or in the soul, then you'll fight for it. If not, then you can say that you have real spiritual problems. If you're not willing to fight to save your own soul, your own self, in order to liberate the Authentic Self and evolve consciousness, then you have spiritual problems. Wouldn't you say that?"

There was a humbled murmur of agreement. He just had such a way of saying things, of honing in on an important point so that it exploded in your soul like flaming punctuation.

"Interesting way to put it, isn't it? It can't just be called an issue of narcissistic proclivities once you've tasted your own spiritual nature as the Authentic Self or the Ground of Being. Because if you've realized that and experienced it to a point of doubtlessness and yet are unwilling to do whatever you need to do to cultivate those capacities in your self, then that's a spiritual sickness. So where's the compassion in that statement?" he jested with a little laugh. Everyone else was silent.

"You see, whenever we begin to acknowledge the presence of free agency, from whence comes the whole notion of compassion, hmm?" He paused for a moment to let the question linger. No one replied. *"There are a lot of people in this world,"* he went on, *"that need your compassion but it's not the teeming world of narcissists just like you. There are billions of people that need your empathy and compassion, literally, figuratively and practically, but it's not the luckiest people that have ever been born; this army of pathologically self-concerned people who have more opportunities than human beings have ever had and who don't appreciate it. They're not the individuals that need your compassion. You don't help a weak and self-indulgent person by feeling sorry for them or having empathy for them. By doing that you actually empower the worst part of them, which is the belief that they have a problem or that there's something in the way. So there are many gross and subtle ways in which we all empower the worst parts of ourselves and each other and in that we are each other's worst enemies. So if you want the world to change then you have to stop doing that. Now your refusal to play that game might be interpreted as a lack of care on the part of other people but that's their problem. The truth is that it's actually the opposite of what they think because you really do care, but it's about evolution and development.*

"So what we want to do is support the best and the highest in each other and also, dare I say, even expect that from each other. Isn't that what a new world would be like? That's not the world we're living in now," he added pointedly. *"In the world we're living in now, none of this would be regarded very highly, would it?"* It was hard to deny this point.

It was just this kind of talk – this frontal assault on the collective narcissism that defines our culture – that has earned Andrew the enmity of so much of the spiritual world. His pointed derision of the spiritual status quo, of the therapeutic, wounded child, poor me, self-indulgent pursuit of emotional well being for its own sake, was met by violent derision in turn. Many have said, and angrily so, that Andrew is arrogant, aggressive, rude and lacking in compassion, all the while skirting the simple and central issue of whether what he said was actually true. Yet it was precisely the force of this argument that had so exerted its moral compulsion upon me. It was this that I thought of when my ego screamed. It was also what I thought of when I shopped at Whole Foods, surrounded by walls of produce and wine and fish and a cornucopia of harvest bounty while so much of the world starves. It was what I thought of when I popped up my laptop, surfed the web, cruised in my car, went to the movies and enjoyed any of a thousand privileges available to me on a daily basis, all of which are hopelessly beyond reach for five billion of my fellow humans. Not that I felt guilty for such privilege. I had gotten over that. But what was I giving in return? What was I doing for those five billion souls who could only dream of living my life? How could I justly complain of my difficulties when they pale by comparison to real difficulties? How could I claim victimhood, lowering the bar for myself like a wounded soldier, a psychic cripple needing a hand up, never ready for action quite now? And, should I choose to take that stand, did I deserve the compassion of others? Would group hugs, therapy and endless affirmations ever make me ready? God wants only our hearts. And to give that heart to a higher purpose, to one that, if realized, could empower the best of us to care for the whole with a passion unbridled from the reins of the ego and to express that care with the fullness of our lives; that would be an act of true wisdom and compassion.

"*So I was talking with these two young boys yesterday,*" Andrew went on, indicating the two teenagers, "*and I was trying, in a nice way, to give them a different message than their parents do. I was kind of saying, 'Hey, guys. I expect more from you and so does life. And you should expect more from yourselves.' And I could tell that no one had ever talked to them like that before. They both looked at me with this expression that said, 'You mean it matters?'*"

"*See, in the old days young men and women used to have mentors. These are supposed be people that you look up to and that are role models who expect more from you. They get you to expect more from yourself and that restructures the whole self-system.*"

I thought of my first and most influential martial arts teacher, Frank Payne, who in many ways saved my life by performing precisely this function.

"*But in the culture we're living in now these things don't exist anymore. And it's terrible!*"

"*So we want to get to the point where we begin to expect more from each other and are maybe a bit less tolerant. So part of changing consciousness also has to do with our level of expectation, starting always, of course, with ourselves. You can't expect from others what you're not demanding of yourself first.*"

"So in a vertical context the standard for the individual with him or her self and also in an inter-subjective relational context, begins to go up slowly. And that's something we can all learn to cultivate. That's the non-metaphysical, practical dimension of evolutionary, post-metaphysical spirituality. It's called growing up and out of this terrible state that we're in.

"Of course, if you're a very self-indulgent person you're not going to tend to expect much either from yourself or from others. In fact, you're going to be careful not to expect too much from others because – you know what? – they're going to start expecting more from you and you wouldn't want that." Andrew laughed ironically. *"It'll be like, 'Hey, I'll do my thing, you'll do your thing. I'll leave you alone, you leave me alone.' And then you'll call that freedom. Isn't that what freedom is like for the privileged, educated elite in the postmodern world? It's a horrible ghetto we live in. So understanding this is also part and parcel of the cultivation of a new context in consciousness. Do you understand?"*

"Oh, I absolutely do."

Andrew then called upon a thirty-something German woman with closely cropped, copper hair and flashing blue eyes. Her words were edged with spiritual intensity, little flames dancing on each syllable.

"From what you said before I guess I have a spiritual sickness," she said, "because…"

Andrew burst out laughing and assured her that, *"It's okay, there's a hospital upstairs."* With everyone doubled over in laughter, it took some time before she was able to continue.

"What my problem really is is that people seem to run away from me because I am too impatient and come on too strong with this perspective. So I wonder how can I make a difference if everybody's running away."

"Well, you can't force these kinds of things on people who aren't interested. It's not fair to impose this, right?"

"Yeah," she reluctantly agreed, then countered, "but then again, it would not be truthful if I didn't."

"Well, I understand that, but you have to be careful with whom you're going to choose to be truthful."

"I tried with family and friends."

"Bad idea," Andrew said instantly and there was more laughter.

"It didn't work out very well."

"The family's the worst place to start."

"Well, yeah," she said somberly. "But it made me think that if it was possible to somehow present this in a more compassionate way…"

"If you want to suffer…" Andrew let the sentence hang in the air, it's meaning ringing in everything that wasn't said. More laughter. Then he went on, *"The thing is, in this postmodern family context the conditioned, emotional and*

psychological baggage is so thick that it's almost impossible. I mean, there are rare exceptions but it's usually very, very, very tough."

"So I should start somewhere else?"

"I definitely would."

"Okay, thanks." She was happy to let it go at that, but Andrew always wanted to get to the deeper structures behind things.

"But you shouldn't be surprised that it's so difficult in a context like that because that's where everything is more personal than it ever is anywhere else. You see, often the family is where everyone takes everyone else for granted. You already think you know people. 'Well, I know her. She's my sister, she's my daughter, she's my mother,' and so on. And it's very hard to break that which is why, in most cases, you can't even begin to talk about anything like we're talking about in a conscious way."

"But my family's very open and I was thinking if I could do it in a more compassionate way, maybe…"

"Well, obviously they're not as open as you think."

"Well, they didn't respond too well," she admitted.

"Well, I know, that's my point. But that shouldn't surprise you because the Authentic Self is radically free and doesn't respect, recognize or acknowledge the significance of the personal dimension at all."

"Yeah, that's why they think I'm rude or coming on too hard."

"But listen. You have to understand that there's a biological connection with your family. It's in your blood. And there's a connection between this biological connection and our personal identification. They're all tied up together and it's a really tough one to break. For example, my brother and I never had a good relationship when we were younger. In fact, it was terrible. And now I see him maybe once every five years. If I call him, then he'll be happy to see me, but he'll never ever call me. So I saw him about six months ago when I was in New York and we went out together. The thing is, I always have this strange experience when I see him because when I look at him, his physical form, I feel this incredible sense of intimacy and closeness just because of the biological memory. And because of the biological memory and because of how close he feels, emotionally I want to experience intimacy with him. But we have literally nothing in common — at all! So when I see him, I just think, 'well this is a very strange person.' But, of course, I've always seen him that way, which is a whole other issue. But there's such a gap between us!

"So with your family there's always going to be some felt sense of intimacy due to the biological connection, but that doesn't necessarily mean anything. And also, when you discover who you really are at the level of consciousness, it becomes even stranger because you can have the experience of being in the company of someone who the lower or more primitive part of yourself feels this connection with but with whom this higher part of you experiences none whatsoever. In fact, you often can feel much closer with a stranger, someone you met on the bus perhaps and with whom you had a good

conversation about something important, than you do with someone with whom you have this strong biological connection. But you have to understand that there are different parts of yourself that experience these connections for different reasons."

"I guess I never really thought about it like that before."

"So the Authentic Self can only meet itself in a context where only that is seen as being important. So, to be honest, it's only really with another autonomous individual who's reached that point in their own development that they want to be free more than anything else that the Authentic Self in you could meet itself in another in that place of unconditioned freedom and from there really go to new places together. There's no baggage then."

"I understand. So I guess at the point where I'm at, I have to want to be free more than I want friends."

"Well, it depends on what your definition of friends is. Who are your friends? What does it mean to have a friend? And to what part of yourself are you talking about? So usually a friendship is very personally based. It has to do with history, time, and the personal dimension of the self. So when you discover the Authentic Self, there's no time involved and the proof is that you can have this experience of shocking, radical intimacy with a person that you have no history whatsoever with. And yet you can feel closer than close, an unbearable sense of no separation, no gap whatsoever with this person. So what does it mean to have a friend? It's an open question because at this point to have friendship is usually based on something personal.

"Now, I live a very unusual life, so it's not good to compare yourself to me, but my relationships with people—except in a couple of unusual cases—are really only dependent upon this Authentic Self. So that makes my life very complicated and very, very problematic. It's very difficult for me to have relationships with people because what I'm talking about here is what I live. It's not a game for me and it's not something I move in and out of. That's where I live. However, I'm also a human being just like you. But my human relationships have to be dependent upon this. Otherwise I can't do it because then I have to compromise and I have to become somebody I'm not. And I won't do that for anybody." He paused, and then added in a softer tone, *"I can't.*

"So then it gets very hard for me to have personal relationships or even friendships with people because I can only do it to the degree that someone's willing to actually meet me in this place. And then, once they meet me in this place, they have to stay with me, because remember, the Authentic Self is a function of consciousness that's inherently evolutionary. That means we have to keep moving forward together."

Now that's some kind of friendship, I thought.

"So, if Imants was in the Authentic Self and met Christopher and Christopher wanted to sit back and talk about this thing that happened yesterday Imants probably wouldn't want to do that because he'd want to meet now. What happened yesterday is yesterday. Who cares? But the Authentic Self is always at that edge and is always moving forward and it won't go back. So, for example, for a friendship or any human

relationship to be truly creative or evolutionary we have to travel forward in evolutionary time at the level of consciousness together. Then our human connection is going to have that sizzling, searing quality of newness and creativity and to me that's ultimately what human relationship in the highest form should be all about.

"But, I mean, most people are in no condition to actually be able to pull that off in real time. They might say, 'Oh, that sounds great.' But to really do it, each and every one of us have to pay a very big price. This doesn't come free. But that, to me, is what the nature of real spiritual friendship is all about. It's inherently creative and you're moving forward together. And in order to move forward together you each have to be interested in creating the future together and constantly dropping the past. It doesn't mean you forget the past. We shouldn't ever forget anything that happens because everything that happens is important, especially in the real world. But you don't want it to be a form of baggage that's tying you down.

"So the Authentic Self in you is craving that. But you have to understand that the Authentic Self is only seeking for Itself. The Authentic Self doesn't care about your biological history. It's a different part of the self. I can't overemphasize how profound that really is. You can have very frightening moments when you don't know who you are anymore because a lot of the normal things that meant something to you and that you felt emotionally connected to suddenly don't mean anything to you anymore. That can make your felt sense of humanity feel quite uncomfortable. But once you really understand what's happening and what a thrilling thing this is, you have a different relationship to it. Because eventually, if you pursue this, what will happen is that the Authentic Self will be who you are more than you are anything else. I mean, it's never going to be completely who you are, but it's going to be that fifty-one percent, if not more. So that's going to be fundamentally what you've chosen to be and what you've become in real time. Of course, then you're going to pay the price to stay there, which is letting go of everything else. You can't take it all with you and the Authentic Self doesn't wait for anybody.

"Remember, the Authentic Self is a function of consciousness. It's evolution in action at the level of consciousness, which means that it's moving forward. It doesn't run in place and there's a ferocious intensity to it. Remember the Big Bang? It's ferocious. And look at nature – it's ferocious. Tidal waves and volcanic eruptions; animals tearing each other apart; sexuality – this is also a manifestation and expression of nature in action. It's not good or bad. That's just what its nature is.

"So at the level of consciousness, how you experience this is that it's just moving forward. And the degree to which you awaken to the Authentic Self is the degree to which your interest is in moving forward. It's not a personal thing. It has nothing to do with friendship or family or anything like that. So the individual who experiences the ecstatic thrill of the Authentic Self knows who they are and gets their absolute sense of confidence in life and being and purpose and self. But that's not where most people are living. An apt metaphor for how most of us live would be like old people hobbling *along.*" Everyone laughed, but Andrew remained serious. "*Well, look at it. The Authentic Self is going – metaphorically speaking – at the speed of light, waiting for no one. Now, what do old people do? Take small steps very cautiously, always looking at the ground and always talking about the past.*" Convulsions of laughter now filled the air. "*Well, that's what the ego does.*

"*So, once again, the degree to which any of you have the kind of experience that Imants was describing and that some of you were talking about yesterday, you're going to realize that what I'm saying actually is true. It's real and it's powerful. That's why it's evolutionary enlightenment. Enlightenment is the non-relative or absolute dimension of life and being in consciousness. And the non-relative or absolute dimension is simply that, absolute – and it's always way too much. That's what absolute means. So that which is relative is something we can kind of handle and work with. But when it's non-relative or absolute it's inherently too much. It-is-too-much! That's what its nature is and why it's evolutionary 'enlightenment.' Enlightenment is a metaphor for the non-relative or 'too-much' dimension. So, for the enlightened self the relationship to life would be always playing with and pushing that which is too much in a world where that's exactly what nobody wants. Oh sure, people always want things to improve a little bit, but they don't want things to become too much. Everybody can handle a little bit because if you get a little bit it makes a boring, mundane life a little more interesting.*" Andrew's laugh was edged with irony. "*But when it's too much, it literally means too much. And then, in evolutionary enlightenment what that would mean is that you'd be constantly living in the context of it being too much. Now, the Authentic Self can handle it because that's what its nature is but the ego will find that absolutely unbearable – absolutely unbearable! That's why the ego has got to go! Do you get the idea?*"

Everyone agreed loudly.

"*Okay, so we'll finish with that.*"

A long, silent pause was followed in my own mind by the resounding echo of Andrew's statement, "*The Absolute is always too much,*" which struck me as the perfect exclamation point and grand finale to the entire retreat. And then, just like that, it was over.

People rose and slowly began to mill about, stretch, chat and so on. I sat there with the somewhat disorienting realization that I was now free to talk, that the daily routine of practice and meditation had come to an end and that I could, by and large, do as I liked. Having finally come to that point, I wasn't sure how I felt about it. Largely, I couldn't believe it was over. I experienced a strange and simultaneous sense of both the expansion and the collapse of time. On the one hand, it seemed an eternity since we'd started, with time stretched like taffy extending behind me. On the other hand, time seemed to collapse, the beginning of the retreat seeming just seconds ago.

I sat there a while longer paralyzed by the cross currents of contrary forces. Cascades of bittersweet emotion coursed through me: an ecstatic surge of spiritual passion; the desperate longing to sit there forever, permanently fixed outside the stream of time; an equally desperate desire to charge forward into the stream of time, a silver clad soldier in God's army bearing the Gospel of Evolution; the desire for companionship and dialogue; the sentimental sadness associated with endings and more than anything the overwhelming sense of spiritual "shock and awe." I simply could not believe what I had been through and dimly began to sense the impossibility of sharing the depth of what had occurred here with others who had not been in attendance. This fact I found strangely troubling.

Soon, however, such ruminations were dispersed by the growing clamor of the bustling crowd. Hesitantly I rose, still, due to habit, avoiding eye contact yet silently casting about for a familiar face with whom to break the silence. I passed by clusters of people discussing their travel arrangements, exchanging addresses and phone numbers or simply giving each other hugs and catching up. I headed up the stairs to the cafeteria, which I knew would by now be transformed into a lively marketplace of books, videos and information tables regarding the activities of EnlightenNext and the global dissemination of these teachings. At one of those tables I spotted my friend Elizabeth Debold, a senior editor of *What is Enlightenment?* magazine, noted feminist author and driving force behind creating a new movement of women's liberation.[4] She had also been in the silent retreat and stood leaning against the wall near her table. I walked over and stood beside her. We exchanged knowing looks that expressed a singular sentiment: "Oh my God!"

It was in her company that I decided to break my ten and a half day silence. This I did with an ever so articulate "whoa" accompanied by raised eyebrows and an extravagant exhalation. I leaned against the wall next to her. She smiled and slowly, softly we began to engage in conversation. As it unfolded she shared with me her sense that throughout the retreat, and even at this very moment, we had been caught up in the wide, wild upward rush of consciousness, a river unbroken and ever One, a surge in whose great flow we were just eddies swirling along the banks. This metaphor so aptly captured my own experience that once more I was overcome with emotion and nearly struck to the floor by the roar of shakti within. Tears welled in my eyes, their salty chemistry a swirl of awe, humility, exhaustion, trepidation, and uncontainable exhilaration. I bristled with life as did she and we stood for some time, sharing our initial impressions in the wake of a spiritual storm. After a while she was compelled to attend to her duties, excusing herself politely.

I moved on. Now more confident in my capacity for speech, I felt much like a man regaining the use of his legs after having spent weeks in gravity-free space. The first few wobbles hadn't been so bad and soon the bottled up energy of the last ten days demanded expression in interaction. After perusing the materials spread out about the cafeteria, I sat at a table where I was soon joined by a number of men who had also been in the silent retreat. We talked at length and with

444 • 11 Days at the Edge

great animation, finding that much of our experience had been identical. This was especially evident with respect to the intense desire that had tormented me for much of the time. When one man after another related the difficulty they too had experienced running the daily gauntlet of barely clad women that swarmed like butterflies along the walkways of Montserrat, I was astonished. Stupidly, I had thought that I was alone in this struggle. After all, gazing about the peaceful atmosphere of the meditation hall, what I had seen were ninety people beautifully composed, seated upright and alert with a Buddha's poise, seemingly absorbed in the depths of the Self. I, on the other hand, had spent much of that time traversing the sewers of the psyche and thus had felt ill fit to sit with this lot. Of course, I should have known better, everything being as impersonal as it was.

There was something exhilarating about this conversation. It was not simply the camaraderie of men in a spiritual context that was thrilling. It was the capacity, through each other, to explore issues of men's conditioning in a way that we never could in a mixed gender group. No doubt the same was true for women. It was for this very reason that Andrew put so much emphasis on men coming together with men and women coming together with women. He had long felt that only when a significant degree of transparency had been attained in both contexts could men and women come together in anything approaching authentic equality.

My experience with the men was totally liberating. We sat for a long time discussing the thorny issue of sexuality. We concluded, as I had some days earlier, that neither individually nor as a race had we sorted out the proper relationship to this part of ourselves. Whatever it was, however, one of the men pointed out, it would have to be a relationship that was not victimized. Most men feel victimized by their sexuality, he said, and this was certainly my own experience. In this context we discussed the importance of not struggling with the associated thoughts, images and impulses, for by expressing fear of our minds we would actually empower the very impulse from which we were attempting to gain distance. During the retreat I had settled on a strategy of just being easy with the impulses, not fighting them, but definitely not indulging them – an easy thing to do in the often visually active interior of the meditative state – and then gently moving my attention back to the spiritual practice. Staying easy with it, returning with that ease to the practice over and over again and not making a problem out of it; this had made the whole thing just bearable. And that was it, wasn't it? – the willingness to bear all of our experience without making a problem out of it. This was key in Andrew's approach to liberation, a possibility empowered by our choosing faculty and fueled by the fierce intention to be free. Autonomy and choice were the pillars of freedom.

And thus autonomy entered into the field of our conversation. Several of us wondered why Andrew hadn't had us gather for "enlightened communication" as he had on previous retreats. One man, a senior student, replied that over the last few years in Andrew's work with his students much progress had been made in the area of communion – the simultaneous coming together of many in oneness beyond ego. However, as this emergence required intensely committed individuals, the grounding of such individuals in unshakeable autonomy was paramount. As another friend of mine had put it to me, "you have to become so strong in this that even if Andrew and everyone in this teaching disappeared right now you would still stand for it unwaveringly. You see," he added, "Andrew doesn't want followers. Followers are a dime a dozen and when the going gets tough they're nowhere to be found. Andrew wants partners, people who are fully and autonomously established in this and are willing to stand for it side by side with him." And for that, we agreed, diving deep into practice is essential, such spiritual calisthenics loosening the ego's grip on the soul while cultivating the strength, space and clarity to see through it. In short, radical autonomy was key to ecstatic communion.

With respect to this I must return to the issue of chanting which had formed a central feature of our daily practice. As mentioned, on numerous occasions throughout the retreat, Chris Parish had tried in various ways to guide, encourage, instruct, harass and cajole us into a level of engagement with this practice which we had not yet achieved. At times he upbraided us in the manner of an English gentleman for being too disjointed, pointing us steadily in the direction of greater communion. At other times, when we were indeed together he pointed out that we were droning on, repeating by rote the phrases while strikingly divorced from their meaning. At those times he urged us on to greater autonomy, to investing ourselves fully and independently in the meaning and spirit of these phrases. The goal, of course, was for these two aspects of the chanting to merge into one state where autonomy and communion were paradoxically yet undeniably indistinguishable in precisely the same way they were during the best moments of "enlightened communication." This, unfortunately, never happened. There were times when we came close, when a certain resonant hum began to emerge, transcending the merely auditory and embracing another dimension, but these times were not often. There was something toward which we had striven but of which, in the end, we had fallen short.

Interestingly, some months later Rose attended Andrew's winter retreat in Rishikesh, India. During that gathering she was part of a similar group that had been brought together for this same kind of intensive practice. However, rather than struggling with the chanting as we had, it seemed that that group started off from precisely the point at which ours had finished. This was reported by a number of people who had attended both retreats. From there they jetted into the spiritual stratosphere. The sessions, by all accounts, had been nothing short of the blissful blending of autonomy and communion and the emergence of the new consciousness toward which Chris had unsuccessfully tried to steer us. What's extraordinary about this is that it yet again points to the non-local nature of consciousness and the fact that it is indeed possible to lay down grooves in that consciousness for others to follow.[5] This increasingly undeniable fact has been evidenced repeatedly in the development of this teaching over the years, specifically with respect to the practice of enlightened communication, but somehow that never seems to diminish its miraculous nature. It seemed that we had indeed laid some tracks, as far as they went, during our retreat in Montserrat, and when this endeavor was taken up five months later on the other side of the world by a different group of people, they were able to catch the train at precisely the station where we'd stepped off. The implications of this phenomenon for a revolution in consciousness are staggering. They fill me with a constant stream of hope that despite the currently desperate plight of humanity, unimaginable potential lies just on the other side of our willingness to pursue it. And what could be more thrilling than that?

At any rate, at long last our gathering broke up. I spent the remainder of the day connecting with all the friends whom I'd been unable speak to for the last ten days. Unfortunately it was all rather hurried, with many in the throes of imminent departure. The afternoon was a whirl of activity, of hugs and greetings, of compressed, intense philosophical debates, of address exchanges and, of course, passionate assurances that we'd all be in touch again soon. And so the day waxed and finally waned.

The sun's lazy descent behind the mountains was slowly followed by a fingernail moon sharpening against the dimming sky. With it a crisp night wind rose and a twinkle of stars appeared above the dark shapes of the hills and the valleys below. A group of perhaps thirty of us who were staying on embarked on a leisurely walk along the darkened trail that wound its way between the crags of the mountain's side. The trail ended on a dramatic promontory jutting out between the stones that offered a breathtaking vista revealing the true scale of things. The lights of the cathedral and teaching hall were now distant and tiny, set in what seemed like gaping jaws of stone. We stood there, spellbound in that wonder induced by the grandeur of nature and of life and spoke about all that had transpired, what it meant to us and how we might go forward in bringing it to life. The conversation between us was amiable and intimate though many of us did not know each other. We were bound by a common vision and that was enough. Several hours passed before we began to disperse. But many of us, shot through with passion, continued in smaller groups to carry our discussions into the night. My own night closed at two a.m. in the company of three friends standing together in the dimly lit, shadowed courtyard of the old basilica. There we marveled in hushed whispers at the faith, passion and conviction of those early Christians who chose to be thrown to the lions rather than abandon their stand and together, though hoping never to face such choices ourselves, we solemnly sought within for such courage to fuel our own surge forward. And then, at length, time won out and we all retreated to our rooms. At last I gave myself to the darkness of sleep.

The following day had been arranged as a "Student Member" day during which those of us in the so-called "Student Network" gathered to discuss how we would take the impact of this retreat home to our communities. We met repeatedly throughout the day, endeavoring to translate the visionary into the practical. In so doing the unifying phrase and concept that emerged was that of creating a "culture of engagement." This was distinguished from what one might call a "culture of recruitment." That is, during our discussions it occurred to us that there are a whole host of small and large organizations that share with us an integral vision in the service of the transformation of humanity. That being the case, it did not appear integral in the least that we should each pursue our respective goals, separated into tiny enclaves. Rather, it seemed that we should reach out, join forces and create strategic alliances with others of a similar bent, thereby fostering a growing front of individuals and organizations committed to a global change of consciousness as the foundation for every other sort of change. So the day went on like that. We met as a large group, broke up into smaller ones, created to do lists and action items and point persons and so on. It was an exhilarating and inspiring expression of the Authentic Self in action that took us from sunrise to nearly sunset.

In the late afternoon we met as a group with Andrew. It was an open and informal forum during which we could ask him or share with him anything that we liked. Most people asked questions relevant to their situation in their respective communities, some had specific personal questions and others simply thanked him for what he had laid out before us during the retreat. The atmosphere was relaxed and positive though supercharged with evolutionary tension. As I heard others speak with Andrew, my mind ran to a thread of contemplation that had woven itself through my experience since before leaving for the retreat. It had, in fact, begun in the conversation with my friend that Fourth of July night just prior to my departure. I had wondered then how I could, upon my return, share with him what had happened here in a manner that might convey at least a fraction of its magnitude. I had realized then that I could not and that realization struck me again upon the close of the retreat. I also realized that I could not share the nature of such a retreat in any form of simple conversation with anyone – it was just too deep, too broad and too all encompassing to be reduced to any clever netting out. There could be no Cliff Notes for this. How then, I thought, could I share with those who were interested what it was like to be on retreat with Andrew? How could I convey the life transforming message and view that had so profoundly potentiated my own quest for transformation? It was in considering this quandary that the idea for this book slowly began to congeal in my mind until, sitting in that room with Andrew, I felt compelled to speak with him about it.

I decided to do this in private and managed to speak with Andrew just after this meeting. I began by pointing out that while he had published a consider-able number of books, none gave a comprehensive overview of the teaching and neither did they convey a sense of what it was like to be on retreat with him. Moreover, none provided a larger cultural and global context within which to set the teaching as he had done for us during the retreat. I then shared with him the fact that the two books that left the greatest spiritual impression upon me had been Irina Tweedie's *Daughter of Fire*[6] and Nisargadatta Maharaj's *I Am That*.[7] The former was an extraordinary account, in journal form, of one wom-an's transformation at the feet of her Sufi master and the other was comprised of a series of dialogues between one of the twentieth century's most notable Advaita masters and the hundreds of seekers that came to him over the course of the years. Both books possessed an impact vastly beyond the words on the page, imbuing the reader with the living presence and timeless transmission of the masters themselves. As I had kept a retreat journal it occurred to me that in weaving its contents together with the full content of Andrew's talks an interest-ing and possibly similarly inspiring book might result. Knowing that Andrew had not, to date, entrusted his words to anyone other than his closest students I was not sure how he would respond. However, to my very pleasant surprise, he heartily agreed. He clapped me on the shoulder, gave me two thumbs up and simply said, *"Go for it."*

Thus, the next morning, as a group of us awaited our cab in the quiet plaza before our hotel, luggage in hand, tickets and passports at the ready, I felt a mul-tilayered sense of purpose. The foremost thrust of that purpose went straight to the issue of living the teachings in a radically more committed way than I had to date. This would, without a doubt, have tangible results on the level of my "day to day" life, which, as Andrew was fond of pointing out, was actually all there was. Second, I would set out on the writing of this book. This would, I hoped, not only carry the power of Andrew's transmission into the hearts of the caring, those individuals possessed both of spiritual longing and a longing to change the world, but also help destroy the cynicism of so many of us who have abandoned the hope of a life of true meaning and ultimate purpose, a life of integrity and honor com-mitted to the highest in us all.

Finally, I stepped into the cab with Gerard, Ronnit, Jason and the others and slowly we wound our way down the side of the jagged mountain. Once in the valley its stillness slipped as quickly into the past as an autumn leaf on a rushing stream while the world we had suspended and the future it contained rushed in equal measure to receive us. Cell phones rang, Treo's flashed emails, the news crackled on the radio and Barcelona rose in the distance. We joked and laughed in the back, then jostled our luggage through airport queues and checkpoints, shopped duty free and at last settled into our seats for the long flight home.

NOTES

1. Peter was fond of telling an instructive tale from his own life in this regard. Some years after he had begun studying with Rudi, Rudi asked him to move to Texas and open an ashram, which he did. Once he had been there for a time Rudi went to visit him and hold a retreat at the ashram. Toward the end of the weekend Peter and Rudi were driving through the streets of Denton when Rudi pointed out the window and said to him, "You see that mall over there?" indicating a small strip mall off to one side. "Yeah," Peter replied. "I want you to buy it," said Rudi in as commonplace a tone as if he were asking to have the salt passed. Peter looked at him dumbfounded. "But Rudi," he replied, "I don't have any money. How am I supposed to do that?" Rudi just cast him one of his withering looks and said, "Schmuck! Anybody can do it with money. Figure it out." Knowing better than to argue with his guru concerning such requests, Peter went to the mall manager only to discover that the mall was indeed for sale (there had been no sign to that effect out front) for the not insignificant sum of $40,000 at that time (early 70's). In the next two to three months Peter harnessed all his resources and creative energy to start multiple businesses and miraculously come up with the money to buy the mall. He learned to pull himself up by his bootstraps and create something from next to nothing. He proceeded to convert that mall into a further series of successful businesses, which he ultimately sold in order to buy what remained of Rudi's art business after Rudi's passing. This allowed him to return to New York where, through all the years I knew him, he continued to develop his business skills to generate vast sums of money, most of which was used to continue to deepen and make more available his spiritual life and teaching. It is an instructive tale and an inspiring example of how one's creative capacity and spiritual life can be developed in tandem, one being in no way inhibitive of the other.

2. For an interesting discussion of the Law of Accelerating Returns, see Ray Kurzweil's discussion on this topic at http://www.kurzweilai.net/articles/art0134.html?printable=1.

3. This is a point on which most evolutionary thinkers agree: survival threats spawn adaptation. Therefore survival threats, unpleasant as they are, are in many ways key to the evolutionary process. For a more in-depth discussion of this please see previously referenced material by Don Beck and Spiral Dynamics.

4. For more please see http://www.wie.org/women/.

5. See previous references to Rupert Sheldrake's *A New Science of Life*, as well as previously referenced works by Ken Wilber including the *Guru and the Pandit* dialogues featured in *What is Enlightenment?* magazine.

6. Irina Tweedie, *Daughter of Fire: A Diary of a Spiritual Training with a Sufi Master,* (The Golden Sufi Center: New Ed. Edition, 1995).

7. Nisargadatta Maharaj, *I Am That*, (Acorn Press; Reprint Edition, 1990).

Epilogue

Heading Home

About an hour later I gazed out the window to see a blue ocean and bright day spread out in all directions. The thin thread of the Spanish coastline had faded into the distance some time earlier. We had reached cruising altitude, the seat belt sign was off and the first bad movie had been announced. I had been seated next to Gerard and we talked in relaxed fashion about what had transpired and what lay ahead. However, within another hour or so we had exhausted those topics. Now we were bored. As the conversation had gotten around to work Gerard suddenly asked me brightly, "you've never seen my show, have you?"

"No," I answered. "I haven't,"

If you will recall, Gerard[1] is a mentalist, and, as I had discovered during our previous conversations, one of the world's foremost in this odd profession. "You want to do some tricks?" I asked in a prodding tone.

Gerard gave me a mock glare. "I don't do tricks."

"Oh, sorry. What exactly is it that you do, then?" I asked earnestly.

"I'm a psychic entertainer."

"Okay," I said, having no real idea what that meant.

"C'mon. Let's go see the others."

We walked over to the other side of the plane and found Jason, Ronnit, Kevin and Holly, the very group with whom we had first had lunch upon our arrival in Barcelona. We huddled together and made small talk for a few minutes.

Then Gerard asked if anyone had a deck of cards. Holly did and handed them to him. Gerard fanned the deck out in front of me. "Pick a card, memorize it and slide it back into the deck."

I did so thinking, hey I thought you said you didn't do tricks. But I kept my mouth shut.

Gerard shuffled the deck several times, then placed it on the cabin floor. I looked at him curiously. He waved his hand over the deck from about waist level and – I kid you not – the bottom half of the deck slid to the left, the top half slid to the right and my card shimmied itself out until it was resting on the floor in front of the two divided stacks. I gaped at him stupidly while the others, who had apparently seen this act before, laughed wildly.

Gerard then pulled a five Euro note out of his pocket, had me hold it between my thumb and forefinger from one end, and placed his own hands on either side of mine at a distance of about six inches. "Do you believe in telekinesis?" he asked.

"I don't not believe in it."

Suddenly the bill that had been hanging limply from my fingers began to flap in my hand as if I were holding it out a car window going forty-five miles per hour. This time I gaped and gasped. The laughter in our group was now mixed with "whoas."

Gerard, smiling, looked around and asked if anyone had brought any books with them. Kevin and Holly each retrieved a paperback from their bags. Gerard gave me one and held on to the other. "Go stand about ten feet away," he said.

I did. He then began flipping the pages in the book he was holding. "Tell me when to stop."

"Stop," I said after a few seconds.

He looked at the book in his hands and said, "okay, this is page one sixty nine. Open your book to page one sixty nine."

Once more I complied.

"Look at the first line of that page, read it to yourself and hold it in your mind."

I read and held.

Gerard grabbed a pencil and a napkin and began scribbling. After a few moments he handed me the napkin. With the exception of two small words, the sentence he had written on the napkin was the very one from the book sitting in my hands. Now I just stood there mutely. I may have uttered a "whoa." I don't remember.

Gerard's face was split with an ear to ear grin. "Okay, one more," he said. He handed me a shred of paper and a pen. "Think of a person you knew a long time ago that you were very close with and that I would have no way of knowing either through you or any mutual friends. Then write that person's name on the paper."

I settled on a name and wrote it down.

"Okay, now fold the paper up and give it to someone in the group."

I handed it to Ronnit.

"Now, think of what it was that you used to do with this individual and hold those images in your mind."

Once again I complied, resurrecting thirty year-old memories to perform before me like a play.

"I see fighting," Gerard said, pressing three fingers to his forehead above his tightly closed eyes. "I see mats, a gymnasium…is it Rocky?"

At that moment I nearly fell over, my knees buckling as if some prankster had popped them out from behind me.

"Yeah, that's it," I said wild-eyed. "Rocky was my best friend in junior high school and high school. All we did was practice Judo together. We lived, breathed and ate it. How the hell…" I said nothing further for some time, my face flushed with disbelief. Everyone else was laughing.

We went on for some time until at length Gerard wrapped up his performance. As we headed back to our seats together I said to him, "I get it now. Not tricks."

"Right," he smiled.

With that we settled back into our seats and fell silent. I rustled through my carry on in search of a book and soon retrieved a title I had brought along – *The Universe Story* by Brian Swimme – and began reading. On the first page I read a quote that slowed my racing mind and drew me into deep reflection.

> Originating power brought forth a universe. All the energy that would ever exist in the entire course of time erupted as a single quantum – a singular gift – existence. If in the future, stars would blaze and lizards would blink in their light, these actions would be powered by the same numinous energy that flared forth at the dawn of time.
>
> There was no place in the universe that was separate from the originating power of the universe. Each thing of the universe had its very roots in this realm. Even space-time itself was tossing, churning, foaming out of the originating reality, instant by instant. Each of the sextillion particles that foamed into existence had its root in this quantum vacuum, this originating reality.
>
> The birth of the universe was not an event in time. Time begins simultaneously with the birth of existence. The realm or power that brings forth the universe is not itself an event in time, nor a position in space, but is rather the very matrix out of which the conditions arise that enable temporal events to occur in space. Though the originating power gave birth to the universe fifteen billion years ago[2], this realm of power is not simply located there at that point of time, but is rather a condition of every moment of the universe, past, present and to come.[3]

I read the passage several times before turning the book over to peruse its title once more: *The Universe Story.* I thought about this for a while. How unused we are to thinking of our life in an evolutionary context. How unused we are, in fact, to thinking about anything in an evolutionary context. The whole notion is so new that the bulk of the debate about it is still polarized between the absurd insistence of creationists that the Bible is the only science text we'll ever need and the equally absurd insistence of the evangelical materialists out to convince us—with the full fury of religious fervor – that the universe is a pointless sequence of random events devoid of meaning or purpose. Educated and authentically interested debate is nearly nowhere to be found.

With time on my hands I considered the issue in light of all that I'd just been through. First, it occurred to me that people like myself, post-modern individuals unfettered by religious dogma or tradition – lack a story that gives meaning to their lives. Yet the need for such a story is as essential to being human as speech and higher thought. In fact, it is much of what makes us human. We are the only creatures who ask "why?" And we are the only ones lost without an answer. Each age has had its stories and all were appropriate to their time. They encompassed the sum of human knowledge and provided a cosmic thread upon which all could hang the details of their lives, finding in them meaning, purpose and a sense of belonging to a higher order – an apparently innate human hunger. However, for many of us these stories have, in the light of scientific knowledge, been reduced to little more than fairy tales. They have lost their power. Their spell has been broken. We have grown up.

But the story of evolution has not yet been told. Not in full measure at any rate, for its full measure is just beginning to emerge. And the more it emerges, the greater its power to stupefy. It is a grander tale than all the others, more mesmerizing than the myths of old, for it is powered by the light of scientific knowledge and was, as I had discovered, married to the depths of mystic revelation. It is a story that could capture the post-modern mind and hold even it, with all of its sophistication, in thrall to the miraculous.

Perhaps most miraculous is that the evolutionary process happened at all. Fourteen billion years ago something burst from nothing. On this, most agree. What could be more mysterious, more miraculous than that? Something came from literally no thing! No time, no space, not even emptiness per se. Just an inconceivable, dimensionless "no thing" with the intelligence and power to explode out of itself an unfolding cosmos. And that it had directionality and intelligence – a point long denied by the ruling priesthood of "scientism" [4] – becomes increasingly evident upon closer examination, particularly in light of the revelation of Enlightenment in which we experientially discover the living Power at the center of it all.

I considered the twin philosophical pillars of scientism – randomness and purposelessness – in the light of things I had both learned and experienced directly. First I pondered randomness and reminded myself that, as the sole explanatory variable for the world we see around us, it is today viewed as one-dimensional and insufficient by the majority of the scientific community. There are too many thinly sliced variables that had to conjoin just so and insufficient time for pure chance to account for the universe that has given birth to us.

In fact, some particularly assiduous researchers, employing complicated statistical models, concluded long ago that our universe having emerged as it is by chance is approximately as likely as a troupe of monkeys striking a keyboard with primate frenzy until producing a play by Shakespeare, a tornado ripping through a trailer park and assembling a 747, or a cave of dripping stalactites producing over incalculable eons a fully functioning locomotive. And actually, as it turns out, the eons are not incalculable. Further computations by further assiduous scientists determined that the actual span of time required for such unlikely outcomes ranges in the neighborhood of a billion billion years. The problem is that the cosmos has only had roughly on the order of fourteen billion years within which to pull off the unlikely sprouting up of life. In fact, as it turns out the paltry mini-eon of fourteen billion years does not even allow sufficient time for the development by pure chance of a single modest enzyme.[5] Another, equally mind-boggling way to consider it is that the chance of those aforementioned thinly sliced variables aligning to produce a universe containing life is one out of 10^{123}. To appreciate the magnitude of that number, consider that it contains more zeroes than there are protons in the Universe. In fact, in scientific circles any statistical chance that is less than one out of 10^{50} is considered essentially an impossibility. As Robert Godwin puts it in his entertaining and highly compelling work, *One Cosmos Under God*:

> Interestingly, even a cosmic intelligence conceived of in the most crude and childish manner – perhaps as a bigheaded scientists named Yacub sitting behind the cosmic console, actually twiddling knobs – is *more* likely than pure randomness resulting in that one chance in 10^{123}. From a strictly rational standpoint, the existence of God is not more improbable than the existence of blind laws of nature. Indeed, some have made the point that it is logically incoherent to argue over whether or not a higher intelligence exists in the universe. Rather, if such a higher intelligence is even philosophically *possible*, then it is logically *necessary*, as compared with the alternative, that is, the almost impossible odds against randomness resulting in such fantastic order and complexity.[6]

But there is more. The above considers the realm of cosmic evolution. The following humorous quote from Ken Wilber's book *A Brief History of Everything* examines the same problem in the realm of evolutionary biology:

> Take the standard notion that wings simply evolved from forelegs. It takes perhaps a hundred mutations to produce a functional wing from a leg – half a wing will not do. A half-wing is no good as a leg and no good as wing – you can't run and you can't fly. It has no adaptive value whatsoever. In other words, with a half-wing you are dinner. The wing will work only if these hundred mutations *happen all at once,* in one animal – and also these *same* mutations must occur *simultaneously* in another animal of the opposite sex, and then they have to somehow find each other, have dinner, a few drinks, mate, and have offspring with real functioning wings.[7]

Once again, randomness, though indeed explaining much, falls short in key areas repeatedly. In other words, whatever formative impulse is driving the universe forward, it is not *solely* the play of chance.

This raises the question of purposefulness or directionality. Hardcore adherents of scientism proclaim, with the conviction of revival tent preachers, that neither of these play a role in the unfolding cosmos. Yet standing back far enough from the process one finds that despite the fact that evolution meanders more than it progresses, there is definite directionality – that direction being from lower to higher levels of complexity and integration, and, along with that, to ever greater levels of "interiority" or consciousness and sentience. Not only that, but with each new level of complexity the entire process seems to speed up.

Let's step way back and take a quick stroll along the evolutionary landscape. At the zero hour we find the eruption of the Big Bang out of a point of infinitely dense matter referred to simply as the "singularity." Only after nine billion years of cosmic churning and expansion did our sun begin to burn in its place and draw the planets into the orbit of its flaming light. About a billion years later the first rudiments of life poked their heads through matter in the unimpressive forms of single-celled organisms. Not much, one might say, but vastly different from what came before both in terms of complexity and interiority (considering that there was no interiority, the primary feature of all sentience, prior to this.) For more than two billion years these organisms teemed in the primordial soup before collaborating to create the first multi-celled organisms. Then, some six hundred million years later, life burst across the globe in an eruption of forms known as the "Cambrian explosion." About four hundred million years later, the first vertebrates and land plants emerged. Some two hundred million years after that the first four limbed animals began scurrying about. Another two hundred million years passed before the first mammals emerged. A hundred and fifty million more before the first monkeys started swinging from the trees. Thirty million years later the first chimps appeared and sixteen million years later they began to walk upright. From walking upright to cave painting and praying took four million years. Ten thousand years later the first human settlements formed and four thousand years thereafter writing emerged. From the invention of writing to the emergence of the Roman Empire took another four thousand years. From the Roman Empire to the Industrial Revolution: eighteen hundred years – things are definitely picking up now. With the passage of another hundred years we have the emergence of flight. Sixty-six years later we put a man on the moon and twenty years later finds us at the dawn of the "Information Age."[8]

There exist an abundance of ways to be astonished by the drama of this unfolding, not the least of which is the sheer scale of time and the shockingly recent emergence of human beings – little more than an ember kicked out of an exploding inferno. Of course the very point of this illustration is often to highlight the inconceivable depth of time against which our emergence is barely discernible.

Rather than quailing at the insignificance of man, however, I marvel at the contrast between the abyssal yawn of time that passed before the rising of the rudiments of life and the steadily increasing pace of change thereafter. It took somewhere on the order of ten billion years for cosmic evolution to cough up the first cellular organisms and with them the first twitch of consciousness, triggering the age of biological evolution. Thereafter, with each new complexification of organisms came greater consciousness and greater interiority; and with each of these the process was potentiated, the spans of time between each leap and the next dramatically diminishing. Not only that, but with each complexification novel properties emerged that were not characteristic of the component parts. For instance, when molecules first came together to form single celled organisms, those organisms possessed "novel emergent properties" – life and sentience among others – that were not characteristic of molecules. Some have used the term "holon" to describe such aggregation, potentiation and emergence, which appear to be a constant feature of the entire evolutionary process.[9] At any rate, with the rise of more complex forms of consciousness, that potentiation became super-charged. This was most evident with the rise of self-reflective consciousness – consciousness that is aware of itself as both subject and object. I imagine that this traces back to the days when our ancestors first buried their dead in wonderment and sorrow and with such interment planted the seeds of philosophical wondering, of questioning "Who am I" and "Why am I here." And between that time and the invention of writing – that event triggering cultural evolution – humans were, for the very first time, able to experience their own Source in the form of enlightened awareness. This was a dramatically new evolutionary emergence. For the first time the Source was able to know itself in its own creation. And look what has happened since the rise of self-reflective awareness. In that brief instant of cosmic time human culture and knowledge have leaped forward at a breathtaking pace, that pace itself relentlessly accelerating into and forward from this very moment. We have now triggered what Joel Garreau has termed the age of "radical evolution." (See his book, *Radical Evolution*, already mentioned in Chapter 1.)

Why radical? Because so much has changed. For nearly fourteen billion years the process has been driven by some mysterious combination of randomness, natural selection and a teleological – and, I believe, intelligent – drive towards greater complexity and deepening interiority. But now, in our time, on our planet, natural selection and other automatic processes have been trumped by the emergence of human choice as the primary driver of *all further evolution* on the planet. That choice itself, as Andrew had pointed out, is a strikingly recent evolutionary emergence, first rising as a potential with the rise of early man and now being actualized and potentiated through the blistering advance of modern culture and the ongoing liberation of human rights. No people in human history have had the freedom of choice that we in the modernized world daily take for granted. And what is driving that choice? By and large, narcissism. Today we – the luckiest, wealthiest, most privileged people to have ever lived – stripped of the context, meaning and sense of belonging provided by tradition, have collapsed into ourselves. Radically empowered as individuals and painfully alienated from life, our choices will determine the evolutionary destiny *of all life on this planet*. We are, in the words of Mary Evelyn Tucker,[10] at a "Noah's Ark" moment, deciding which life forms will move with us into the future and which ones won't. Additionally, we are now the sole arbiters of the future evolution of our own biology. That is, with the dramatic advances in technology, we are the first and only species ever poised to engineer its own further evolution. And, in the absence of a moral, philosophical and spiritual framework – a new story of meaning for our time – how are we to exercise such power? How are we to exercise choice?

It is the story of the evolving universe itself – which I have outlined, albeit in shamefully cursory fashion, above[11] – that, in my mind, stands poised to provide a new framework – a new moral theology if you will – and return to us a sense of purpose and meaning. That story gives post-modern, highly sophisticated individuals – who tend to view themselves as the end product of the evolutionary process – something beyond themselves to stand in awe before and align themselves with. This is doubly true when seen in the context of enlightenment. In that context the outrageous truth is revealed: we are that Source to which enlightenment awakens us awakening to itself in the very process that it started. And now, only through human choice can that process be moved forward.

Thus we stand at an historic moment when the evolutionary process, having fallen into our hands, is balanced on the edge of a knife, poised between the birth of the new and the looming specter of collapse. It is this recognition that has caused Joel Garreau, Karen Armstrong and many others to argue that we are entering a second "axial age." I recalled Garreau's ruminations once more, "If our narratives of how the world works are not matching the facts, are we seeking a new era of sense, intelligibility, clarity, continuity and unity? If profound restatements of how the world works arose all over the planet the last time we had a transition on the scale of that from biological evolution to cultural evolution, will it happen again as we move from cultural evolution to technological evolution?…This is a spiritual crisis."[12]

Before considering that further, I leaned my head back and gazed out the window at an infinity of sea and sky drifting slowly by, the muted thrum of the engines droning just on the edge of awareness, a colorless ambience of sound conducive to reflection. Drifts and chunks of Andrew's teachings passed before my half closed eyes like leaves stirred up on a gentle gust of wind. One held my attention more than all the others. This was the pivotal question of human choice – my choice. In the midst of the immensity of evolutionary unfolding there I stood, at once perfectly one with the process and perfectly alone in it, with only my capacity for choice to help determine my destiny. With my awakening to the Authentic Self, and the Authentic Self awakening to Itself through me, the future of the process had landed squarely in my lap. And in light of what I had seen, my choice could represent only one of two positions: to participate in the evolutionary process for the highest reasons or to actively stand in opposition to it. I could no longer seek neutrality in the blessed refuge of ignorance. I simply knew too much.

I experienced once more the visceral recoil that had beset me during the retreat. There's nothing in it for me, I remembered, shuddering slightly. There really isn't! In fact, the "me" to whom this so mattered stood to lose everything including itself. But from which perspective was I seeing at that moment? The ego's, of course. Shifting my attention to the perspective of the Authentic Self transformed the landscape immediately. Instantly the thrill of it all overtook me once again. Who am I? I asked myself. If, at the deepest level, I am the Authentic Self, the radically free, perfectly unselfconscious power that initiated the creative process at the beginning of time, then what else was there to do? And who else was there to do it? If ultimately *I am That* awakening to Myself in My creation after toiling for fourteen billion years and "there are no others," who else could possibly do it? If there was only one Self and I was that Self, how could it be any different? In that radically non-dual perspective the ego's view was instantly incinerated. There was only an urgent, ecstatic and relentless push into the future.

So what of me and my humanity poised as a choice point between these two possibilities? For some time I shifted back and forth between them, dwelling upon the nature of choice and spiritual conscience. I could not turn my back on this. That much I knew. But could I really do it? Did I have the strength of character, the conviction, the passion, and the mettle? In short, was I good enough? I remembered what Andrew had said: God only wants our hearts, not our perfection. *"Do you think that cripples aren't allowed?"* he had poignantly asked us. If we give our hearts, he had said, the rest of our humanity would straighten itself out in due course. And that much I could do. I could give my heart and work with everything I've got to not only *"become a living expression of the opposite of everything that's wrong with the world,"* but to help move the evolutionary process forward. Then, through my conscious choice, I could potentially further both the deepening interiority of the cosmos and the evolving creativity of its outer manifestation. That was something worth working for. I recalled once more the words of historian Felipe Fernández-Armesto: "That humans are uniquely rational, intellectual, spiritual, self-aware, creative, conscientious, moral or godlike seems to be a myth - an article of faith to which we cling in defiance of the evidence...[However], if we want to stay human through the changes that we face - we had better not discard that myth, but start trying to live up to it."[13] And that was precisely what I intended to do.

In the light of this sentiment I examined my experience of the previous days. It had been agony and ecstasy, a long series of ups and downs modulating far beyond the frequencies of normalcy. Those modulations reflected the nature of the forces at work; that infinite density of primordial matter and infinite freedom of consciousness tangled in mixed proportions with my soul in between, struggling to right itself and become a force for good in this world. *If you don't experience both ecstasy and terror,"* Andrew had said, *"you're not doing what I'm asking you to do."* I had experienced both, never arriving at some plateau of steadiness with respect to either or anything in between. It was the context that pulled me through. And that, as I understood it now, was evolution itself. It was that that empowered steadiness, not inwardly, but in one's outer expression, in what one stood for in real time with one's very life. It was that that empowered "doing the right thing even when it didn't feel like the right thing to do." It was that that gave rise to the dignity and strength of character that had and continues to inspire me so. And those I could make my own by firstly, wanting to more than anything else, and then by heeding Andrew's simple though taxing advice: letting things be as they are; bearing the vicissitudes of my inner volatility; drawing no conclusions about myself based on any aspect of it; and standing for what I have seen even when I don't see it. It is by taking this position in relation to all of my experience and to life itself that consciousness evolves through choice. It is in that that the Source not only discovers itself in life but can also, in partnership with my evolving humanity, move that process forward. It is in this fashion that Love Absolute can be known in this world in all its fierce intensity, not merely as interior revelation but as living outer fact. Would fear, hesitation and inertia ever disappear completely? Who can say? They might remain my irksome companions to the very end. But the liberating news was that it didn't have to matter. Their potency stemmed by the higher view, I can be free now. Free to no longer inhibit the Authentic Self. Free to provide it a portal into this world. Free to offer these arms and legs, this heart and this soul for the transformed future of our world.

And that future, that looming uncertainty into which we rush with abandon, lies greatly imperiled. We are locked in a race between the currents of destruction and the new tides of life. And on those new tides' fragile crests plays the promise of a "higher we" and the nascence of a new humanity. That is the promise of this teaching. From the dim light of consciousness pooling feebly within the walls of single cells to its increasing radiance in burgeoning complexity; from its first weak glimmers to the miracle of self-reflection, growing complexity and deepening interiority have bloomed into the modern self, each new blossom bestowing the novel and the unexpected. And now onward–onward towards the awakened collective and its emergent novelties: radical autonomy, perfect communion, deep intelligence and seamless unity with THAT behind it all, surging forward irrepressibly with infinite care for the totality of evolutionary unfolding. Love Absolute, moving as one with many hearts and many minds amongst the turbid streams of the world; needing all yet waiting for none, pursuing its own unfathomable destiny – the full realization of consciousness in matter until all of creation is alive with THAT.

This is the story of evolution that has not yet been told, a story whose pages we have barely begun to turn and whose chapters we will help to write. And while what kind of story it will be cannot be said, one thing is certain: it will not be one in which we are the hapless puppets of a distant master, our salvation determined by adherence to the letters in a book and tightly clasped beliefs in antiquated notions. It will be a story in which, freed from both the safety and the fetters of the past, we can march forward in the boots of our own experience, empowered by and wholly one with the Source of life itself. And along that road lie hidden wells of creativity waiting to be tapped, waiting to surprise us with the power of the sacred to transcend all notions of the possible, *"to do what can't be done and to say what can't be said for a purpose that cannot be imagined."*

That was a story in which I wished to play my part, not merely as a chronicler reporting from the front like some journalist of the soul, but as a real player, a broker of destiny from whose very flesh and blood the future would be wrought. Was I willing to pay the price? Time would tell. But at that moment, turning my face to the golden glow of the setting sun, nothing seemed more certain. A pleasant fatigue began to wash over me in that buttery light and I lay back, closing my eyes, and letting my mind drift into abstraction. And just before sinking into the deeper flows of self and melting into sleep an old memory surfaced with a smile. It was Andrew speaking to me on the phone all those years ago upon my return from Bodhgaya. His voice, ringing with the love and the demand of the Absolute, echoed insistently and open-armed, *"Welcome to the revolution."*

NOTES

1. Gerard Senehi, "The Experimentalist" Check him out on the web.
2. Since the writing of this book the latest scientific data indicates 13.7 billion years.
3. Brian Swimme, *The Universe Story,* (New York: Harper Collins Publishers, 1992) p.17.
4. Once again, scientism is a dogmatically reductionist view of the world that holds, both as its starting point and the conclusion toward which it drives, that the universe is fundamentally and only the result of the random interactions of physical objects and that all phenomenon can be reduced to them. It vehemently denies any higher power or intelligence and reduces the full interiority of human experience to chemistry and physics. It is an "ism" because while cloaking itself in the mantle of science it denies the scientific spirit of open-minded inquiry, starting from a conclusion

rather than simply examining facts and letting them take one where they will. It is not a search for Truth but rather a dogmatic pronouncement of it and a correspondingly limited search only for supporting evidence.

5. Ken Wilber, *A Brief History of Everything*, p. 23.

6. Robert Godwin, *One Cosmos Under God: The Unification of Matter, Life, Mind & Spirit*, Paragon House, 2004, pp. 34-35.

7. Ken Wilber, Ibid., p.20.

8. This little timeline was stitched together by perusing Carl Sagan's "Cosmic Calendar," which may be found on the web; also by listening to a talk given by author Joel Garreau at a "Voices from the Edge" event sponsored by EnlightenNext.

9. Holon is a term referring to "any entity that is itself a whole and simultaneously *part* of another whole." (Ken Wilber, *A Brief History of Everything*, p. 23) All of reality is comprised of holons and holons extend infinitely up and down the developmental scale. In other words, break any holon apart and there are supporting structures or holons beneath it. Break down a molecule and you have atoms; break down the atoms and you have subatomic particles; break those down and, to the ongoing consternation of reductionists, you get infinitely smaller ones, ad infinitum. Apparently there is no bottom. In the opposite direction the same appears to be true, there is no ceiling, at least so long as the evolutionary process continues, driving inexorably onward toward ever increasing complexity.

10. Mary Evelyn Tucker is a professor of religion and co-director of the Forum on Religion and Ecology. For more about her see http://www.wie.org/bios/mary-evelyn-tucker.asp.

11. For a much more interesting and comprehensive account of the "Universe Story," see this fantastic overview with Brian Swimme: http://www.global-mindshift.org/memes/swimmeseries/step1-3.asp?bandwidth=high_video.

12. Joel Garreau, *Radical Evolution*, pp. 259-260.

13. Garreau, *Radical Evolution*, pp. 237-238.

Appendix 1

At the Crossroads of Two Ages

As I walked along Barcelona's waterfront I considered Columbus, the intrepid mariner, pointing from his pedestal with conviction to the sea and imagined him 500 years earlier sailing his little wooden ships to a new world and into a new age. Things moved slowly then and change was measured in decades and centuries. I gazed at him again, now pointing beyond the slick display of modernity along the piers to the silver line of the horizon. Time had sped up almost immeasurably and I imagined him now pointing into the uncertainty of our future. It stopped me on the spot, riveted in contemplation of the cusp upon which we now stand. It was the clear recognition that I as an individual and we as a race stand poised once more on a brink between the old world and the new. We are at a crossroads between two ages as different from one another as Columbus' was from our own. While five centuries lay between his age and ours, just a few decades lie between ours and the next, perhaps even less than that. With the rate of change accelerating, the blistering pace of the last decades' technological progress is no indicator whatsoever of its pace in the next. All we know is that it will be faster – a lot faster. And that acceleration is likely to continue so long as we as a species do. Of course, there's the rub; with all our clever ingenuity we have raised ourselves, at least at the leading edge, to undreamed of heights.[1] We have stolen fire from the gods. Yet the question is, will we use it to spread light or incinerate the house? This question is no longer rhetorical or theoretical; it is the urgent reality of our time. We are among the first generations faced with the challenge of either saving the planet – and ourselves, incidentally – or destroying it. Never has the promise and the peril of human emergence been greater. And it was our rapid acceleration into the yawning unknown of our imminent future with its promising technologies and its quite flawed, though no less promising, humans that most struck me as I stood there between Columbus and the sea. I was in search of a new world, one that would bring forth the best of our humanity while constraining its darkness, one that might usher in a better age while holding at bay a dark one.

Much of my thinking in this regard had been influenced by the reading and writing I had done for *What is Enlightenment?* magazine,[2] most of which concerned the relatively near future of technology and its implications for our time, our planet and ourselves. The long and the short of it was that we are entering an age of such technological prowess and sophistication that we are changing the world and ourselves at a pace faster than we can comprehend. The implications of these changes are wide-ranging, leaving no aspect of human life untouched, and while all those who are familiar with the subject matter agree that they are inevitable and imminent, many disagree about their implications.

The trend of development that had seemed most significant to me was that of the rapid approach of our "post-human" future. "Post-human?" What exactly does that mean? It means beyond human; it means that we are the first generation of the first species to be in a position to engineer its own future evolution. We sit poised to be able, within the next few decades, not only to conquer every physical ailment to beset our species and design its continued evolution as we see fit, but even to contemplate the previously unthinkable specter of physical immortality. One of the world's leading and most well respected anti-aging researchers has boldly proclaimed that by the year 2100 the average human life expectancy will be around 5,000 years.[3] Even if that is only ten percent true, the implications are staggering not only on a societal and cultural level but on a moral, ethical and spiritual one, as well. In such a world human life will be as different from our own as ours is from that of Columbus' time. And even that does not quite capture it.

What makes such bold claims plausible is that the rate of change itself is changing. Speak to the experts or better yet, just take a look around, and it soon becomes evident that we are accelerating at ever-greater levels. In fact, we are at the "knee of a curve" of an exponential rate of technological development, which in plain English means that if we graphed out an exponential rate of increase, i.e. two plus two equals four, four plus four equals eight and so on, we would find that for quite some time that graph would remain relatively flat, rising only at a very modest angle. In historical terms what that means is that for millennia human technological progress advanced very, very, very slowly, doubling only in long increments of time – increments that until recently no single generation could even notice. However, at some point the cumulative effect of this doubling would become increasingly dramatic at which point the graph would begin to curve upward significantly, taking on the shape of a bent knee; hence the phrase, "knee of the curve." In accordance with this principle, that historical doubling has slowly increased its pace until, in our present age, we find ourselves at that knee. The so-called law of accelerating returns has become one of the defining features of our time. We are the first generation for whom the last twenty years are no indicator whatsoever of what we can expect in the next twenty for the simple reason that the rate of change itself is accelerating ever faster. Ultimately our graph, and by extrapolation our level of technological change and innovation, would rise in a straight line up as the acceleration approached a rate that for all intents and purposes might be considered infinite. That point is referred to by the experts as a "singularity" or an "event horizon," a phrase borrowed from cosmology and used to refer to a point beyond which it is literally impossible to guess what might happen next because, beyond that line, all known rules and laws simply break down. According to a wide array of well-respected experts, we are rapidly approaching a singularity in our technological development, a threshold that will not only redefine who we are as human beings but create a world we simply cannot envision and whose implications at this point are almost entirely beyond us.[4]

Technologically speaking, a key factor in the rapid approach of our "post-human" future is the rapid development and convergence of four key technologies: genetics, robotics, information, and nano processes. Collectively these technologies are often referred to as the GRIN technologies and between them we will not only revolutionize every human enterprise but we will redefine the very meaning of the word "human" as it becomes increasingly difficult to differentiate between man and his creations. That is, within the next twenty-five to thirty years, about the time required to pay off that new mortgage, not only will human beings be dramatically enhanced or "augmented" through feats of genetic engineering, robotic attachments, implanted computer chips and molecule sized "nanobots" that will control and enhance our bodies in presently inconceivable ways, but machines and artificial intelligences (AIs) will have become so lifelike that it will be difficult to deny that they are, in fact, alive. Whatever definition of consciousness or sentience one favors, it will be impossible by those standards to argue that these AIs are not self-aware. As difficult as such notions are for even the most sophisticated among us, the truth is that even at this very moment there is much serious talk not only about the wide-ranging impact of greater than human intelligence, but how best to handle that intelligence when it becomes self-aware. According to Joel Garreau, author of *Radical Evolution*, by the year 2029 it is likely that machines will be as or more creative than their human progenitors, producing music, visual art and much more quite on their own[5]. They will have read and stored the entire written, accumulated knowledge of mankind and, in addition, ninety-nine percent of the world's processing power will be non-human. Stranger than all of this, however, is the fact that machine rights will be as large a social issue in that very near future as civil rights is in our current time.

Clearly, such radical changes will leave no aspect of our lives and culture untouched. What the impact of such dramatic technological innovation will be is currently the subject of heated debate between warring schools of thought. Some argue that it will usher in a golden age of progress and with it the remediation of all our planetary problems, while others insist with equal fervor that this marks the beginning of the end of the human race. The latter conjure up such heartwarming scenarios as rogue scientists creating "white plagues"[6] that could eradicate all life on the planet within a matter of days.

As mad as all this sounds, none of it should be taken lightly. Many of the world's brightest thinkers, while disagreeing strongly on the implications of these changes, unanimously agree that we are currently entering the "bio-intelligence age." In fact, a conservative D.C. policy institute has recently produced a document for presidential cabinet members outlining these changes in order to help prepare the country for them. Put all this in the context of our present world crisis including global warming, deforestation, extreme poverty, HIV/AIDS, refugees, fundamentalism, terrorism and the fact that we are ushering in the sixth extinction period in the planet's five billion years and it becomes clear that we are entering a pivotal era in human history or, as some people are calling it, an "inflection point." And what we as individuals choose to do will determine everything.

Joel Garreau, noted religious scholar Karen Armstrong, and a growing number of others believe that we are entering a new "axial period"[7] during which humanity's entire worldview will shift dramatically as we leap into a new way of seeing ourselves in the universe. Garreau believes that "the search for spiritual breakthroughs during the first axial age was no less urgent than that of our current technological breakthroughs, both driven by a universal search for meaning and value, which many believe is hard wired in the very human nature we are changing." He also wonders, "if our narratives of how the world works are not matching the facts, are we seeking a new era of sense, intelligibility, clarity, continuity and unity? If profound restatements of how the world works arose all over the planet the last time we had a transition on the scale of that from biological evolution to cultural evolution, will it happen again as we move from cultural evolution to technological evolution?" He poignantly argues that, "this is a spiritual crisis. It's not about science,"[8] and quotes noted historian Felipe Fernández-Armesto, who tells us, "That humans are uniquely rational, intellectual, spiritual, self-aware, creative, conscientious, moral or godlike seems to be a myth – an article of faith to which we cling in defiance of the evidence...[However], if we want to stay human through the changes that we face – we had better not discard that myth, but start trying to live up to it."[9]

As human beings at the cusp of an evolutionary crisis that is as much spiritual as it is physical, we must learn to embody the radically whole view of life revealed in the depths of spiritual experience and express it in a way that embraces the entirety of current life conditions. It has become clear that neither traditional religion, nor the so-called New Age, nor the various and sundry "East meets West" spiritual practices stand poised to adequately meet this challenge. The only thing that makes deep sense is a thorough re-evaluation of the whole picture, taking the totality of the human predicament, both inner and outer, into account and constructing an entirely new approach that leaves nothing out. It was precisely this that I felt was embodied in the teachings of "radical, impersonal, evolutionary Enlightenment," the brain and soulchild of Andrew Cohen. These teachings, as

I understood them, were a direct spiritual response to the dramatic needs of our time. They provided a way to begin to live up to the myth of the "godlike" human, not for our own sakes, but for everyone else's, as well as for the evolutionary process itself. It was in the context of these teachings that I began to see what my own potential for spiritual development had to do with the burgeoning world crisis that is impinging on us from all sides and of which too many of us who are actually in a position to respond remain blissfully and dangerously unaware.

NOTES

1. That is not in any way to deny that the overwhelming majority of humanity still lives in conditions of poverty and degradation. It simply means that, as a percentage of the population and as an absolute number, vastly more people today enjoy a standard of living inconceivably higher than at any other time in history. Hundreds of millions of people are free to travel where they want, learn what they like, marry whom they love and eat with abandon, enjoying a lifestyle not even imagined by royalty of the past.

2. Nothing major, just a handful of book reviews. However, they did require reading the books and these were, in each case, quite compelling, thought provoking and even shocking.

3. As stated in *Fantastic Voyage: Live Long Enough to Live Forever* by Ray Kurzweil & Terry Grossman, M.D. (Rodale Inc., 2004).

4. See Ray Kurzweil's books, *Fantastic Voyage, The Age of Spiritual Machines, The Singularity is Near*. You can also find interviews with Mr. Kurzweil at www.wie.org/unbound. This is a subscription service of *What is Enlightenment?* Magazine in which many of the background interviews for the magazine's articles are available for download. At this writing the fee is $10 per month but they usually offer a free trial period during which to download whatever you like without obligation to actually subscribe. Tha being said, it's an extraordinary resource for hearing today's leading thinkers in dialogue on what is closest to their hearts.

5. See Joel Garreau's *Radical Evolution* for an in-depth discussion of these topics. *Radical Evolution: The Promise and Peril of Enhancing our Minds, our Bodies – and What it Means to be Human,* Doubleday Publishing, 2005.

6. "White plague" is a phrase coined by science fiction writer Frank Herbert in a book of the same title. It refers to a genocidal plague that can be engineered to kill only certain types of individuals, women, in the case of the novel. It can also be used to simply refer to a genocidal plague.

7. The term Axial Period was coined by the philosopher Karl Jaspers and refers to the historical period in which most major philosophical and spiritual traditions arose independently across the globe. In his view, this period, from around 800 to 200 BCE, gave birth to everything that, since then, man has been able to be. While the leaders who inspired these changes were philosophers and spiritual realizers, the change was radical, affecting forever after all aspects of culture, for it transformed consciousness itself. The Axial Period featured three defining characteristics: 1) reference to another dimension that transcends this one; 2) the authority of a universal moral code and 3) a type of higher thought that has authority over the secular world, both informing and changing it. This was a major change from pre-axial thought in which cultural identity was strictly tribal or ethnic,

resting on a common pool of genes. Individuals existed to perpetuate their own survival. They were oriented to the forces of nature, lacked a nameable religion. Religion, science, and morality formed one indivisible whole that defined the foundation of their ethnic cultural tradition. Thereafter, however, ethnic cultures were linked into a common umbrella culture by refocusing human attention on superhuman realities and goals which transcended the boundaries of their tribal cultures.

8. Joel Garreau, *Radical Evolution: The Promise and Peril of Enhancing our Minds, Our Bodies, And What It Means to Human*, (Doubleday, 2005) pp. 259-260.

9. Garreau, *Radical Evolution*, pp. 237-238.

Appendix 2

The Birth and Evolution of
Inter-subjective Enlightenment

My first introduction to "inter-subjective" enlightenment had come, strangely enough, at the very same retreat where the foundations of my sanity were shaken by fits of anxiety and where, perforce, I had learned more than I ever wanted to about bearing my own experience. Twice a day during that retreat our small, stoic coterie, otherwise pressed into silence, was assembled in a circle for a discussion facilitated by several of Andrew's senior students, the format of which has since been labeled simply as "enlightened communication."

In this gathering we were encouraged to initiate our dialogue with anything that had struck us as poignant or significant during the foregoing teaching. From there we were to collectively delve deeply into the subject matter to see what understanding might be unearthed. However, this was not to be simply a free flowing, anything goes kind of discussion. Rather, certain conversational constraints and parameters for participation were given as ground rules. These were designed, much in the way of a chemical experiment, to enhance the possibility of producing a very specific result. They included the avoidance of the personal, speaking directly from the authenticity of one's immediate experience in relation to whatever the point was and steering clear of abstractions and opinions. Along the same lines, we were encouraged to abandon the position of "already knowing" while simultaneously bringing an intense interest unburdened by the past or images of self – an attitude of simply "wanting to know" – to the table. Not that we had to forget everything we knew – an impossible feat, after all. We were simply to renounce it as a platform from which to dive into the swirl of the conversation. Not already knowing but wanting to know – that was the key.

Once in the mix, we were advised to *really* listen to one another and respond directly to whatever point they had made rather than waiting with baited breath, as we are so wont to, for them to finish their point simply so that we might paste ours atop it. Within those guidelines everyone was required to participate, participation being defined as giving one's full attention and absolute priority to what was happening within the group rather than to any aspect of one's internal experience – including one's own self-consciousness and insecurities – with an unqualified willingness to participate from the very edge of one's own experience. Hanging back in a comfortable, safely passive position was not permitted and the group facilitators would be quick to point out if anyone assumed such a posture of fainthearted neutrality. On the other hand, tossing out into the space between us any handy philosophical flotsam simply in order to be seen as participating was equally unacceptable. Both were seen as expressions of ego, the former a fear driven to hide out for pride, the latter its hollow bravado. The authentic response had to emerge spontaneously from the immediacy of one's own experience in direct response to a point another had made from that very same place within themselves. And in so doing, we were to listen from the deepest part of ourselves for the points to respond to, ever seeking with the deep intuition of spiritual longing those that would move the conversation into the realms of the deeper and higher.

Key to this experiment was the presence of skilled facilitators for it was they who, whenever the conversation seemed to sputter and ebb, bouncing along the rocky bottom of possibilities, would point out what had caused this sudden descent into one-dimensional mediocrity – always an unwitting transgression of one of the ground rules – and reorient us to a more upward trending conversational current. Each time such a course correction was made, our collective navigational skills improved until, in relatively short order, we found our way around the riptides of ego and into the center of that elevating current.

And when that happened something exploded between us – a veritable supernova in consciousness – an eruption not merely inner or outer but both in a way that transcended either. Suddenly we crossed some threshold together and an electric charge shot into the stream of conversation. Each of us leaned wide-eyed from the edge of our chair into an emerging field of consciousness. Our collective attention was fixed unflinchingly in the center of the room where an invisible vortex of conscious energy opened and spiraled upwards. Utterly transcendent yet not quiet in the least, we were swept along in its ecstatic flow. In turn, that very power cycled back to inform the ego-free engagement that had given it birth, deepening our dialogue immeasurably and yielding up understanding and insight to the collective vastly beyond what any of us could hope to penetrate alone. An unseen though deeply felt field drew us in as One Enlightened Mind emerged among us, conveying Its intelligence to whoever spoke, shocking the speaker with what spontaneously flowed from his or her mouth, for each knew that their own innate intelligence alone could never have given rise to such understanding. Simultaneously and seamlessly the full magnificence of each person's autonomy and creative individuality were realized in a way previously unimaginable as all barriers of fear and mistrust melted away in the splendor of Being. Faster than thought, unpremeditated in any way, the engagement spiraled upwards toward what struck the soul as an endless horizon.

As I gazed into the eyes of others what I found returning my gaze, to my unending astonishment, were not others at all but rather my very own Self. This is not to be taken in the vein of metaphoric speech. Rather, it was the literal experience of non-dual, boundaryless being realized through engagement with others. The one Self emerged in the many not only as timeless peace but also as radical, creative intensity. Where "I" ended and "they" began was impossible to say yet simultaneously I'd never felt more "myself" than at that very moment. Unafraid, unencumbered by the past, unburdened by any ideas about myself, I was free. Free to participate in life unselfconsciously and with utter abandon, driven by the highest motives, untainted by the stain of ego.[1]

As this driving intensity deepened and broadened in the midst of our gathering, two elements key to its sustenance soon became apparent. First, at the slightest expression of ego the current of energy raising us all fell like a dying bird from a blue sky, the depth of its plunge dictated in direct proportion by the height of ego's ascent. This fact fulfilled a crucial didactic function for we all quickly became conscious of the felt difference between ego and Authentic Self. With that knowledge distilled from the flow of our experience, we could now begin to discriminate and choose between them. And it was with the emergence of this capacity that the moral dimension unveiled itself, not imposed from without like stone tablets from on high but revealed from within like a thousand roses blooming in the heart. The message was one – it's all up to you! Neatly put, in light of this revelation it was now incumbent upon each of us, when we expressed ego – and we all did at one time or another – to immediately corral it and prevent its further expression. And when we collectively caged the ego in this fashion the surge of the Authentic Self was released once more in all its radiant potency.

All of which highlights the second point, namely that while the significance of the Authentic Self's emergence utterly transcended the significance of any individual, it depended upon each of them in equal measure. In other words, despite the innate power of the Authentic Self, its emergence into the world is as delicate as a butterfly and utterly dependent upon human character and all its frailty. It quickly became apparent that any one of us could take this emergence down and bring it crashing through the floor simply by releasing our ego from its hastily fashioned bonds.[2] Which also meant that without a total commitment on everyone's part to contain the enemy within this new Being, powerful as it was, would lay dormant beneath the surface, rendered helpless under the weight of our unwillingness. In short, it needed us in the most desperate way and thus each individual in the room was paradoxically of ultimate significance. It was only through the coming together beyond ego of those who have recognized this that a rift might be opened in consciousness through which the new Being could be born.

And it was without a doubt a new Being. One that far transcended its parts yet, as I have said, fully depended upon them. As atoms form molecules, that in turn give rise to cells, who in turn collaborate in ingenious and mysterious fashion to form organisms, each of these including yet profoundly transcending its component parts to give rise to a life far beyond it, so did the selfhood of many, transcended and subsumed yet simultaneously strengthened and freed, give birth to a new form of consciousness vastly beyond it. It was the birth of the One in the many, not merely the return of the many to the One, the stated and unarguably lofty goal of pre-modern enlightenment in which the individual soul dissolves in the ocean of Being to find its release from material bondage. In this journey awareness of and abidance in the One formed the ground for relatedness between the many. And that ground empowered the many to engage with life and with each other as an expression of the non-dual creative mystery beyond time in a way previously inconceivable.

When Andrew would speak about this extraordinary collective leap in which autonomy and communion fuse as one state, neither impinging one iota on the domain of the other though being perfectly one, he often used the phrase "ecstatic intimacy" to describe its core quality. In it stood revealed a newly emerging human evolutionary potential, one that those of us who could feel it, see it and taste it knew we had best reach for in earnest. *"What's the problem with human beings?"* Andrew liked to ask rhetorically. *"We don't get along."* An obvious though not unimportant point. Clearly, what had revealed itself to the forty or so of us during that particular retreat demonstrated the existence of an entirely new possibility for human relationship. Inherent in it was more than the promise of quelling egoic conflict, though that alone would be a grand attainment indeed. Of equal or greater significance was the emergence of this vastly higher intelligence that had thrust itself through the surface of ourselves and begun to animate the very individuals who given it birth. Intrinsic to this emergence of the one "enlightened mind" through the many was the potential for collectively discovering solutions to the increasing and rapidly converging problems of a world spinning out of control. It was this vastly higher intelligence emerging in many individuals simultaneously and its potential, through a collective, to address the very real problems that we face as a planet that was of the greatest significance. Einstein was reputed to have said something along the lines of "you can't solve a problem from the same level of consciousness that created it." Perhaps this leap from egoic individualism to the ecstatic intimacy of awakened autonomy and communion represented evolution's response to the current human predicament. That, at least, was our sense of it.

There was so much that was extraordinary about this surge of "ecstatic intimacy." Not the least of it was that it did not demand that we be enlightened in the traditional sense, nor that we had spent many years in disciplined meditation – not that such practices would be unhelpful[3] – in order to facilitate its emergence. Rather, it simply asked that we shoulder the burden of our own egos (for if we don't someone else will have to), be moved by an authentic interest and be willing to subject ourselves to a few ego-binding rules of engagement. Not that these were small matters. As I've already related, I suffered terribly during this retreat, an onslaught of phobic demons preying on the fraying edges of my mind. Shouldering this, while staying attuned to my interest, demanded more than I thought it possible to muster. Yet somehow I managed it. No doubt others had their own loads to bear. Yet it was precisely that collective willingness to bear the secret burdens of our own insanity, all the while extending ourselves fully into what was emerging between us, which enabled this rupture in consciousness to occur. Once unleashed it moved outward and upward, driven by a life of its own, asking only that we stay true to that task, remaining open as portals to the unknown and miraculous.

And in all that was miraculous what struck me as most poignant was that we needed each other to travel upon this road successfully. This was no solitary venture for the lone spiritual hero. No one of us, no matter how committed or spiritually gifted, could open this rift in duality and thus give birth to the New Being. Only through collective engagement could the doorway to this new world be swung open to reveal the features of a virgin landscape. And in this the gap between self and other, that trench of division from whose fissures oozed all the troubles of the world, was bridged in a dramatic leap whose promise is as yet almost fully unexplored. It is the promise of a new humanity made whole by the intersubjective[4] revelation of the Absolute and freed to explore its evolutionary potential in the ever-changing world of form.

A collective form of spiritual practice was born to further that venture, a new spiritual science that cut time radically out of the picture, opening the world to enlightened awareness with astonishing efficacy. That is, in the secret chambers of the solitary psyche the ego, so deeply enmeshed in the fabric of selfhood as to be nearly traceless, is free to operate invisibly and indulge in endless self-deception. Yet in the company of others, such guile is quickly brought to light; for while we each take an abiding interest in the welfare of our own egos, we have absolutely none in that of another. This distinctly one-sided arrangement served our situation exceedingly well, for when ego surged from any of us it was seen and cornered in an instant by the larger collective and its imperatives. Then, if its host was at all in the thrall of spiritual conscience, they would quickly retract their daemon, returning it to its cage so that the journey might venture onward unhindered. In other words, through such collective engagement the whole business of individual self-deception was dramatically short-circuited and undermined. Which is, of course, the entire point. As such, the power to effect change, both individually and collectively, was vastly enhanced. This potentially bodes well for transformation on a larger scale within the confines of a rapidly shrinking time horizon – for as a species the last few grains of time for business as usual do indeed seem to be trickling out of the hourglass.

It must be added that this emergent phenomenon did not evolve spontaneously or through the kind of synchronous, effortless spiritual unfolding so highly prized in the rich fantasy world of much of the alternative spiritual culture. Rather it was the direct result of an unrelenting and fiercely committed effort on Andrew's part to force this emergence into being. To hear him tell it, not long after his own awakening and the birth of his career as a teacher, a latent potential came to him in a flash of insight. He had been sitting, observing a number of his students as they gathered together under the intoxicating influence of his transmission, when he noticed the welling up between them of something that far transcended the importance of any of the individuals involved. It was then that he intuited what he then termed impersonal enlightenment or enlightenment beyond the individual. "What is the difference between personal and impersonal enlightenment?" someone had queried all those years ago, to which he'd responded, *"What is the difference between a burning match and a raging forest fire?"* And thus, though he had nothing to show for his intuition in real time in those days, Andrew attempted to share with those around him the vast gulf between these two manifestations of human potential.

By Andrew's own admission, very few initially got it. Nonetheless, true to his vision, he began pushing his students to transcend ego collectively and for a cause that eclipsed their own personal enlightenment in measure beyond measure. To say that he encountered a little resistance would be like characterizing the Second World War as a mere border skirmish. In fact, the resistance he encountered from many of his own students was ferocious as was Andrew's response to the resistance. *"There's blood all over these walls,"* he'd once confessed in somber reference to the embattled history of the walls within which our retreat as well as our advance to the frontiers of consciousness had played itself out. People had bled. Many had left. And Andrew, above all, paid a bloodprice as many he had held as near and dear not only left, but also often turned on him with a vengeance. Yet Andrew stood his ground, suspended over that abyss of dubious certainty shared by both visionaries and madmen. And he kept up the pressure.

Then, early in the new millennium on a retreat near the sun-baked coast of southern France, an explosion occurred between a group of his closest female students that confirmed in real time that perhaps Andrew was not mad after all – a possibility even he had considered more than once. Not only did they catalyze through their engagement the same upward rush of consciousness that had swept us away, but also each of them individually remained firmly rooted in the enlightened state for the better part of three months. After careful interviews of those involved and deep consideration of the event, Andrew realized that what he had intuited so many years earlier had reared its head in earnest and with singular power for the first time in a demonstrable and objective way. It had taken twelve years. It would take several more for that nascent potential to rise once more from the collective field, this time brought out by a group of men who had labored long and hard under the exacting edge of Andrew's guidance. It took twelve years for the Authentic Self to emerge the first time; then two and a half more years for the second emergence; and the third came six or so months later. The next emergence came even more quickly. And each time it happened between different groups of people; and each time the result was stronger. In fact, it seemed that the emergence itself had not only gained momentum but was evolving independent of the vehicles that had given rise to it. That is, in some strange way it appeared that each new emergence of the Authentic Self began precisely where the old one had left off, as if it had a life and momentum of its own. Very quickly thereafter the phenomenon began to spread to other groups of students around the world (none of whom had been involved in the initial events of emergence) and the enabling rules of engagement we were given as a prelude to our gathering began to become evident, nearly writing themselves. It was not long before the Authentic Self regularly emerged on retreats between people who had had no previous exposure to Andrew's teaching. And soon thereafter a handful of Andrew's senior students took this phenomenon public in experiential seminars on "enlightened communication."

What had taken a seeming eternity and a Herculean, sustained campaign among a small group of intensely committed individuals was now exploding with but the slightest provocation between individuals who, in many cases, had little or no experience with spiritual disciplines and matters of a higher nature. For enthusiasts of the theory of morphic resonance[5] here was compelling evidence of its veracity. Something was emerging in the field of human consciousness and each such emergence rendered the subsequent one easier, making available to individuals with little or no experience what had taken twelve years of unrelenting spiritual effort to facilitate the first time. An infectious sense of revolution permeated the body of Andrew's students and I gladly counted myself in their company, however ancillary I might have been to the larger flow of events.

On every retreat since the one mentioned above the Authentic Self swirled with the wild intensity of a forest fire amongst the attendees within hours of the first teaching. In fact, this emergence soon became so commonplace that it was becoming increasingly easy for those of us caught in that swirl to take it for granted – inappropriately so. At one point this caused Steve Brett to admonish a number of us to have enormous reverence and respect for all those who'd come before us, those who had labored to bring this new being into existence and made all this possible for us. They'd paid a much higher price than we'd had to, bestowing upon us, as beneficiaries of their sacrifice, a debt of silent gratitude. And most sobering of all, many of them we no longer counted among our number for, unable to bear the nearly unbearable, they had fallen in the assault on the ego. Yet it was their sacrifice, along with those who had somehow survived the scourging of their egos, which had made the once unthinkable so readily real. For this reason, as well as for the future potential of human consciousness that this sacred emergence heralded, we were strongly cautioned against a casual attitude with respect to what we were participating in. I personally understood this to mean that the silent debt of gratitude that I had incurred through my participation could only be repaid by my own sustained and earnest endeavor to do all within my power to make of myself a fit vehicle for the continued unfolding of this mysterious process.

And it was a process that continued apace. In fact, it was the increasing speed and regularity with which all this had emerged on every retreat since I had formally joined Andrew's teaching three years prior to the retreat in Montserrat that had caused me to note with surprise the silence that had permeated the dining room during that gathering. I had noted with similar surprise that among those of us who had been culled from the larger group for the rigorous schedule of silence and practice there had been no focused gatherings for "enlightened communication," as there had been on every previous retreat. Why this was so would become apparent to me later.

Having witnessed all of this has given me great faith in the capacity of this emergence to effect portentous changes in the nature of human consciousness.[6] Indeed, this phenomenon appears to have gained a life of its own, growing in depth and dimension with each emergence. There is often the sense, as uncanny as it is undeniable, that whatever forms the peak of its emergence in one gathering becomes the foundation for its successor regardless of the individuals involved or the physical and temporal distance between events. Mysteriously, any emergence anywhere in the world fully informs the next. It took twelve years and untold strength of spirit for this new potential to first poke its head into the world and now it flits into its far-flung reaches daily. And in at least one locale – Andrew's community in Massachusetts – the Authentic Self appears to have taken up permanent residence, being sustained by around fifty people whose commitment is holding that portal open for others. And while the numbers are small the pattern is striking and, dare I say, even encouraging despite the daunting array of looming crises whose shadows stretch across our world.

Andrew has often referred to himself as an idealist with revolutionary inclinations. In what is evolving around him it seems he has found a way to vent both these passions into the world. His idealism is reflected in the slow emergence, at his relentless and unyielding behest, of a new culture of engagement between human beings, one freed from the insidious veil of ego. His revolutionary fervor finds its expression in the unimaginably positive power unleashed by such an engagement with even a small number of committed individuals – "a significant minority," as Andrew refers to them.

There is historical precedent for cautious optimism here as all major shifts in human culture have begun with the thinnest sliver of its leading edge leaning into new possibilities. Consider that about a thousand forward thinking individuals, many of whom risked much, ignited the fire of the Renaissance. Yet soon the force of their commitment breached a "tipping point" (see the book of the same name by Malcolm Gladwell), releasing a cavalcade of transformation that catapulted collective development forward at an accelerating and irreversible pace after the many bleak centuries of stagnation known simply as "the Dark Ages."

It may well be that once again we find ourselves at such a tipping point, with humanity perched precariously on the edge of a decidedly uncertain future. Should we follow the old ways, our range of potential destinations is depressingly limited – if you are a pessimist, extinction, and for the optimist, an evolutionary dark age of unspeakable suffering. However, there are a number of promising though nascent signs. All are delicate and none have as yet established a firm foothold in the greater mass of the human psyche. The promise inherent in this teaching is one of them. Fortunately, the end of this tale is not yet told for we are at present writing it. Where it ends will be determined largely by the choices of those who recognize its potential.

NOTES

1. See the Supermind video online at http://www.andrewcohen.org/supermind/.

2. That is to say, those bonds were only hastily fashioned by some of us. Others had spent many years cultivating through intense spiritual practices the kind of "soul strength" for an authentic and more than fleeting caging of the ego. It was due to their capacity to "hold the space" for all of us, as well as providing practical guidance, that this emergence was possible.

3. In fact, they would be extremely helpful which explains why Andrew insists on intensive and sustained spiritual practices by his students. These strengthen the mechanisms by which the Ground of Being might be experienced directly as well as by which the ego might be caged permanently.

4. Simply meaning between subjects as opposed to purely subjective which indicates only one.

5. Morphic resonance is a term coined by Dr. Rupert Sheldrake, which he defines as "the influence of like upon like through or across space or time." It is based on the conjectured existence of "morphogenetic fields," that contain species-specific characteristics both physical and non-physical. For an in-depth discussion of this see Sheldrake's books, especially *The Presence of the Past: Morphic Resonance and the Habits of Nature,* (Crown Publishing, 1st Edition, 1988) and *A New Science of Life,* (Park St. Press, Reprint Ed., 1995).

6. Human consciousness has been evolving for tens of thousands of years. Many of us commonly assume that people ten thousand years ago were just like us with the exception that we know more today, eat better and dress differently. However, a great deal of research has indicated that this simply isn't the case. Notable distinctions are often made between the self-sense of an individual in a strictly oral, pre-modern tradition who has never seen their name on paper and that of one raised in a literate society. For an interesting discussion of this and much else see Thomas de Zengotita's book, *Mediated: How the Media Shapes your World and the Way you Live in It,* (New York: Bloomsbury Publishing, 2005).

Appendix 3

Reflections on the Student-Teacher Relationship and the Postmodern World

O
n the sixth day of the retreat Andrew began speaking about the significance of crossing, what he called "the fifty-one percent" mark. This caused me to reflect deeply on my own relationship with Peter, the nature of the student-teacher relationship in today's culture as well as the connection between enlightenment and ethical behavior. With respect to these subjects, I departed from my narrative at the point where I was describing Peter's inability to remember significant details of the lives of his students and contrasting that with Andrew's extraordinary capacity to remember the most minute details of the lives of people who came to him. Below I continue this narrative and venture more deeply into an exploration of these matters.

Peter could, for instance, on any given retreat, relay repeated tales of his latest business, travel and spiritual adventures without the slightest diminution of enthusiasm, while remaining steadfastly immune to similar details in the lives of those around him. To be fair, he was an inspired storyteller and the telling of teaching tales formed a key part of his transmission. As for those of us around him, we had little trouble listening for the stories were humorous, entertaining and as laced with teachings as Grimm's fairy tales. But the point is this: he loved talking about his own life. He reveled in the spotlight, the power of enlightened consciousness having done little to dim the narcissism that burns within us all. In fact, the opposite appeared oddly to be true. That narcissism seemed to swell, prospering like a shrewd merchant cleverly poised on the rising tide of his transmission. In short, he grew ever more fascinated with his own life, in part no doubt because his life indeed was fascinating, and that fascination, like an insectile plague, consumed ever increasing swaths of the acreage of his awareness. Now, in none of this do I mean to suggest even in the mildest fashion that he did not care deeply for people; he did, and in abundance. The sobering point here is that within the confines of a single nervous system an astounding degree of narcissism was able to co-exist in highly collusive fashion with profoundly awakened awareness. That was the key issue, which in turn begs the question of how to reasonably square these things.

Andrew's formulation of percentages has helped enormously in this regard, allowing me to explore this troublesome issue and arrive at some outposts of understanding. If, let's say, Peter's development had risen to the forty-nine percent mark, the light of awareness that would stream forth from him would, by comparison to average, be nearly blinding, as, in fact, it was. In the presence of such an individual, as Andrew had suggested, one would experience the power of transmission and be drawn spontaneously into a meditative state, as one inarguably did in Peter's presence. In fact, in the face of such an individual, the blaze of their light would obscure the darker terrain of their psyche much as staring into the sun would blot out the surrounding landscape. Yet behind the heavy brilliance of that light, fifty-one percent of that individual would remain tethered to the whims of ego, that ego now paradoxically empowered due to its intimate association with the Self. This phenomenon led Andrew to identify an insidious and treacherous spiritual pathology and coin the phrase "the enlightened ego."

From the perspective of moral development, this, it seemed to me, was a precarious and frightening place to be, a near foolproof prison for the psyche in which the incentive to dislodge oneself from the constraints of ego was scant indeed. That is, with forty-nine percent of the vehicle under the dominion of the Self Absolute the individual's depth of insight and spiritual fluency would be profound indeed, passing as a near peerless level of enlightenment to all but the most spiritually astute. As such the individual's ability to be a force for good in the world would be considerable, as would their power to influence others to a variety of other decidedly less lofty ends. With ready access to higher states of consciousness and the resultant charisma to draw others into the circle of one's light, where exactly is the incentive to change? What else could one want? This, I think, is no small question. It was, I believe, with this predicament in mind that some years ago Andrew had remarked that once the shift in consciousness to enlightened awareness had been made the state of the personality was essentially frozen in place. This chilling potential for the freezing of the soul is the reason Andrew cited for his strong emphasis on the purification of the vehicle prior to the occurrence of that dramatic shift in consciousness. Having looked first hand into the perplexing and strangely morphing face of the enlightened ego, this is an issue of no small import for me and has caused me to take Andrew's teachings on the cultivation of pure motive with the utmost seriousness.

Staying with the equation of percentages, the next question that occurs to me is how one might know when an individual has crossed that fifty-one percent line and thus passed beyond the field of ego's domination. The only answer that has to date presented itself in the wake of that wondering is when an individual is no longer living only for themselves and when this fact is, *on a consistent basis,* dramatically and objectively obvious to those around them. Here again, however, Peter presented a curious amalgamation. Much of what he did benefited those around him in the most dramatic ways, myself included. Yet he never shied away from insisting, often vehemently, that ultimately his sole motivation was his own growth and development. "I'm getting mine (liberation)," he often said, adding that, "what you all do with this teaching is up to you." That sentiment is characteristic of the path of "personal enlightenment," which, at the end of the day, has little to do with others and everything to do with oneself and as such can be potentially hijacked by the worst aspects of our narcissistic tendencies. All of which points once more to purity of motive as the antidote to such egoic predation and thus its cultivation is of ultimate significance. The only fertile soil that I have discovered for such cultivation is found in the evolutionary context – the recognition that my own evolution or lack thereof has consequences far beyond myself – and my care for that. *"Context is everything,"* Andrew was fond of saying for this very reason. In this light it becomes increasingly evident that reaching the fifty one percent mark, and the potential of that to undermine the foundations of the "enlightened ego," is an attainment of the greatest significance, far transcending lofty inspiration and even the ready accessibility to heightened states of consciousness and the power to transmit them to others.

Continuing along this trajectory in my attempts to sort out my relationship with Peter as well as my understanding of the student-teacher relationship in general, I have considered other rings of moderating influence on the expression of enlightened consciousness. For instance, Andrew often discusses three factors that profoundly shape that expression: context, perspective and depth. Contexts are simply layers of moderating influence that exist regardless of our awareness of them. For example, culture is a layer of context that affects us all regardless of whether we acknowledge it or not. Perspective relates to our awareness of and relationship to these contexts. And depth simply concerns the depth of our experience and its proximity to the center of life. So, for instance, an individual could possess tremendous depth but if the context for that depth is merely one's own liberation and the perspective is that of the narcissistic self sense then in that expression of enlightenment one might very well find what I found in Peter – powerful awakening conjoined with a fundamentally self-centered directive.

To further complicate matters, I have also considered Wilber's concept of lines of development, which holds that there are many aspects to our humanity, each a line of development that evolves along its own trajectory, a progression that is by no means equivalent on all fronts. Therefore an individual might have a highly developed line of spiritual development alongside a moderately developed cognitive line and a patently juvenile line of sexual development,[1] weaving of such asymmetry a strange and complex fabric. There has been, on the contemporary spiritual scene, both traditional and alternative, no shortage of examples of such shocking discontinuities over the last few decades. That fact has cast considerable and justifiable doubts in the minds of many upon, not

only the role of spiritual authority figures, but on the significance of enlightened consciousness itself.

The more I consider these things and attempt to decipher what they might
mean about Peter and my relationship with him the more difficult it becomes to
arrive at any ultimate conclusions. In fact, even in discussing what I have so far
I am merely considering the moral and ethical position of the teacher independent of the context within which they exist. Expanding the investigation outward
quickly adds further layers of complexity to an already knotty circumstance. For
instance, extending the inquiry just one ring beyond the teacher himself we arrive
at the psyche of the seeker who lays at the teacher's feet the dubious gift of their
kaleidoscopic motivations. Of course, in an ideal world the teacher would be a
perfect manifestation of the Self Absolute and the seeker would harbor nothing
other than an authentic and ardent longing for liberation itself. That, however, is
not the world we live in. The fact is that most seekers arrive at the teacher's door
in search of many things, not the least of which is a deep desire to be affirmed,
possibly even as special and unique. Now, there is nothing more affirming to
the deepest part of ourselves than the ecstasy of spiritual experience. When that
spiritual experience is triggered as the result of contact with a spiritually powerful
person many levels of the self and many streams of motivation flow together into
one river of experience, the sorting out of which is a tricky endeavor indeed. Add
to this the primeval background radiation of relentless sexual longing and the
resultant brew is a volatile one indeed.

In my own case, while the sexual dynamic was absent from this brew, the
desire for affirmation from a powerful spiritual figure was definitely not. Like
so many of us, I grew up in the asphyxiating grip of insecurity, self-hatred and
unworthiness, which formed the emotional matrix and backdrop for the powerful spiritual experiences that first set me out in search of a teacher. Were I to say
that the hunger for egoic affirmation did not play into this equation I would,
in fact, be glibly skirting the truth. That being said, I must add that Peter did a
rather remarkable job of tearing my need for affirmation away from my authentic spiritual desire, not catering to the former while richly nourishing the latter.
The point is that we have to stretch substantially in order to fully appreciate the
delicate predicament of the teacher. On the one hand, the teacher is relentlessly
driven to share his or her awakening with others because that is the nature of the
Self. On the other hand, they are as likely to be as beset by the assorted weaknesses
of their personalities as the rest of us. Add to that the student's baggage train of
neurosis (and willingness to purchase affirmation and spiritual intoxication at
near any price) and we can begin to appreciate the depth of purity and surrender
demanded from the authentic teacher. Turning an ethical spotlight upon myself
and posing the question of how I might fare in the face of such temptation I could
not, definitively, declare that I would be beyond its reach. And yet that is precisely

the level of integrity that is demanded if the transmission of enlightenment is to remain uncorrupted by the blight of ego. It was also that level of integrity that had so attracted me to Andrew.

Setting these considerations in the larger social context – the post-modern Western world and its anti-hierarchical bias – adds yet another rung of complexity. As Andrew had already pointed out, we live at a time where many of us, for a variety of perfectly good reasons, have rejected the religious structures of the past. Consequently, whatever larger context once existed to help us orient ourselves to life and our role in it has been razed. What has risen from its ruins is the culture of the individual and its dual offspring of narcissism and materialism, and both are fed on the philosophical gruel of moral relativism and an aversion to every form of hierarchy.[2] In short, we are on our own. Add to that the fact that most enlightenment traditions, viewing the world as ultimately unreal, offer little guidance with respect to life in it, including the turbid realms of ethics and the interpersonal, and one finds the student-teacher relationship on shaky ground indeed. The upshot is this: in all but the most powerful cases of awakening that experience is likely to be interpreted through the filmy values of a superficial culture and the light of realization will be accordingly discolored; it is this tainted light that will meet the medley of the seeker's mixed motivations.

Ironically, this perplexing state of affairs has descended upon us at precisely that time when, in a spiritually impoverished Western world, authentic visionaries bearing the message of liberation and a living example of a life beyond ego are desperately needed. There lurks among us an aching and silent desperation for moral certainty, for authentic role models of higher possibilities and yet so many spiritual authority figures have let us down, often in spectacular fashion. Thus today's would-be teacher of enlightenment is emerging at a time when that role has been dramatically diminished and is being redefined within nested layers of complexity and with as yet inconclusive results.[3]

All of which brings me back to considering the question that has played with annoying persistence at the back of my mind since leaving Peter: how do I judge him? And after giving this matter considerable thought I must conclude that I am in no position whatsoever to judge him. Nonetheless three sentiments spring up in concert with this larger conclusion. First is gratitude for a debt that can never be repaid in the currency of ordinary life. Second is colossal disappointment for what might have been. Andrew once pointed out that in failing to vanquish our egos for real we are ripping off the world of our own potential for transformation. There was so much of consequence in Peter's teaching, particularly with respect to bridging the gap between traditional enlightenment and a creative, fully engaged life among the challenging realities of the Western world. All of this now lies compromised on the altar of self-indulgence and is likely to wither like so much chaff, never being carried into the cultural winds of the wider world. Third, and perhaps most importantly, is sobering humility in the face of the forces at work. While it has long been said that the quest for liberation from ego's obscurations is singularly the most challenging endeavor within the sweep of human possibilities, confronting this in the viscera of one's own experience is both humbling and unnerving.

In the face of such forces it is not only the need for a deep well of humility that I have come to recognize but also for the intensely engaged purification of my own humanity. In line with this, and in view of the menacing specter of the 'enlightened ego', lies the importance of driving with sharply honed intention toward that fifty-one percent mark. Beyond that line lies safe haven from the long arm of ego. Beyond that line, Andrew had pointed out, the momentum and motivation of the Authentic Self are in ascendance, dominating the psyche and undermining the foundations of ego's miserly ambitions. Not that they would fail to make themselves known, for no doubt they would; but the compelling nature of both their angst and aspirations would have been thinned to transparency and thus their occluding nature dissolved. In short, their power to rule the destiny of my soul would have been vanquished and that freedom toward which I might still have to push would now exert its own inexorable pull. Beyond the fifty-one percent mark, ego's corrupting spell lies broken and with it the fiction of a personal life. Beyond that a new life is born.

NOTES

1. For much more on this see Wilber's works, *A Brief History of Everything* and *A Theory of Everything*.

2. For a more in-depth discussion of this phenomenon you can visit the "Spiral Dynamics" page at WIE.org: http://www.wie.org/directory/spiral-dynamics.asp. For an excellent general overview see Jessica Roemischer's article, *The Never Ending Upward Quest*, (http://www.wie.org/j22/beck.asp). Also, Ken Wilber's book, *Boomeritis* (Boston: Shambhala Publications, 2002) offers an in-depth, novelized exploration of the post-modern ethical predicament. Finally, for an entertaining video exploration of this subject go to: www.andrewcohen.org/notes/?/weblog/blog/boomeritis/.

3. For an in-depth exploration of the topic of spiritual authority figures see *What is Enlightenment?* magazine, issue #31, entitled *Spirituality vs. Religion: Where do you Stand?* You can also find it at http://www.wie.org/j31/.

Appendix 4

— The Path and the Goal are One —

The Five Fundamental Tenets of Evolutionary Enlightenment

The Five Tenets represent the supporting architecture of Andrew's teaching, the cornerstones of the liberated perspective and relationship to life. Taken together they formed one position, albeit with five faces: Clarity of Intention, The Law of Volitionality, Face Everything and Avoid Nothing, The Truth of Impersonality and For the Sake of the Whole. They were, according to Andrew, both the path and the goal. *"The path and the goal are one,"* he was fond of saying. I had heard this proclamation for years and for years had failed to understand it. A path is a road to a destination, I had long believed. Spiritual practice was the path, enlightenment its goal and in my mind these were absolute distinctions. I had questioned Andrew about this many years ago and though he had spent considerable time attempting to explain this paradoxical statement I had utterly failed to grasp it. It was not until about three years prior to the present retreat, at a similar gathering in Les Courmettes, France that I began to grasp what he meant and intuit its liberating implications.

As Andrew explained during that retreat, the Five Tenets described the spontaneous experience of someone abiding in the enlightened *state*. That is, in that state they naturally wished to be free more than anything else and indeed were; they did not view themselves as victimized by any aspect of their experience and thus their faculty of choice stood inherently unhindered; they faced everything without hesitation because, self-image having dissolved, the motive to avoid or deny anything in order to protect that image had been transcended; they spontaneously saw through the illusion of the personal and, that being the case, effortlessly and unselfconsciously cared for the whole. As such, the Five Tenets described the goal. Simultaneously and paradoxically, they described the way to get there: if one was aspiring to abide in that lofty state he or she would have to want to be free more than they wanted anything else in life; they would have to take total and unconditional responsibility for themselves and forever relinquish the victim position; they would have to face everything and avoid nothing whatsoever when it came to confronting their deepest drives and motivations; they would have to endeavor to see through the illusory film of separate uniqueness that the personal view creates and ultimately they would have to endeavor to deliver the final coup-de-grace to the ego by caring more for the welfare of the whole than for themselves. Thus, the very elements that described the goal also described the means to arrive there.

I remember the moment that the significance of this paradoxical convergence marked a seismic shift in my understanding. It had been a warm and humid day, the height of summer in southern France, with several hundred of us gathered in a tent in the gently sloping hills. It was here that I first heard Andrew describe the distinction between the enlightened *state* and the enlightened *perspective*. That distinction had previously eluded me though its significance is monumental. The enlightened *state*, Andrew had explained, descends upon us not through any act of will but through the mysterious descent of Grace. None knows when, where and how they will be touched by that benediction of the Absolute. When swept up in the sheer rapture of that smile from the Self the significance of the experience lies in the simple fact of the experience itself. And in that experience we see with new eyes. That seeing is a *perspective*, a radically new way of apprehending life, and that new apprehension, that *perspective* can be adopted in the absence of the *state* through an act of choice. That simple choice empowers the possibility of living an entirely different kind of life and that perspective is described by the Five Tenets.

The implications are profound and numerous, first among them being that from now on we need no longer approach God as hungry beggars pleading for an endless flow of Grace in order to steadfastly stand for Him. Rather, in recognition of and submission to what we have seen we can adopt that perspective and thus forge a partnership with the Creative Principle that will enable us to move from where we are to what we have recognized, through Grace, as our own highest potential. Through choice, we can shoulder the burden of our own egos and see through the eyes of enlightenment, thereby aligning ourselves with the First Cause – the mystery behind existence – and its imperatives. And finally, because the enlightened state and the enlightened perspective are ultimately non-separate, by assuming the perspective we increase significantly the chance of more frequent visits of the state, for assuming the perspective removes the obstacles to its emergence which is, after all, nothing more than our "natural state." I found all this, upon apprehending it, to be nothing short of miraculous – a science and psychology of enlightenment that perfectly joined the worlds of longing and surrender, of effort and of Grace. I had finally understood what Andrew meant when he referred to the Five Tenets as both the path and the goal and why he continually exhorted all who came to him to live them "as if their life depended on it."

To drive home the significance of this, Andrew often pointed out that if two individuals stood side by side, one living the Five Tenets flawlessly though not enlightened in the traditional sense and the other spontaneously and perfectly enlightened, looking at them from the outside no one would be able to know the difference because, in fact, little difference would exist between them. Both would be free from ego, though one might have to bear its presence within their awareness. In either case, ego's hold over the personality and its power to express itself would be aborted. Moreover, should the experience of Grace descend upon an individual living the tenets to perfection, it would find within them more fruitful ground for transformation than in God's beggar pleading for Grace. In short, the tenets describe a unified perspective on and relationship to the human experience – one free from ego. They are the means for purifying the vehicle, providing the traction for progress to the fifty-one percent mark and safeguarding against the corrupting influence of ego, whose power so often takes both seekers and finders directly to the mat.

The path and the goal are one. The tenets are the means of purification and simultaneously its result. An earnest engagement with them is singularly the most challenging endeavor one could strive to undertake. Not only had Andrew said this a thousand times, it was also true to my own experience, partial as it was. Striking out upon that road holds the promise of unleashing the unimagined heights of our potential but not without taking us down the shadow road of ourselves.

Appendix 5

On Being German –
Reflections on Facing Everything and Avoiding Nothing

As a youngster I had never developed a well-defined sense of national identity. We had moved to the States when I was ten – prior to the age when such things dig themselves deeply into one's psyche – and although through my formative years I had absorbed much of the essence of Germanness, no strong sense of national identity had yet congealed around it. In fact, such issues had never occurred to me until my arrival in New York. Thereafter, however, they became unavoidable. For the first few years both my linguistic deficit and the jeering taunts of "Nazi" by schoolyard bullies served to give rise for the first time to my sense of otherness. It also made me wonder what a Nazi was. And slowly I began to find out. Thus, at the same time that my awareness of my people's past was growing, so was my identity as an American. The upshot was that I could not fully embrace either identity, which must have put my parents in an awkward position.

On the one hand, avoiding a discussion of Germany's dark past became impossible: references to Nazi Germany and the American liberation of Europe littered the culture like so much ticker tape along a parade route for the troops. On the other hand, my parents, most notably my father, went to great lengths to educate me about my people's honorable past. After all, Germany's history had not been as strictly one-dimensional as portrayed by an American culture obsessed with its own glory, power, and righteousness. In fact, Germany had given rise to many of the world's greatest musicians, artists, philosophers and scientists, a fact now sadly overshadowed by more recent and more sinister events. But one could not deny what had happened either. It was a complicated subject and so we rarely talked about it. But it was, at least for me, always in the background. Thus it was in those early years that I became increasingly aware of the conflicted self-image that I now believe plagues Germans everywhere.

I developed an interesting strategy for dealing with this schizophrenia. First, as the years went by – and along with them the process of cultural assimilation – I began to develop a growing identity as being an American. This was as natural as it was convenient. I now got to be one of the "good guys," which somehow made looking at the facts a little less painful. At the same time, I developed an abiding fascination with what had happened, the result of which was an undergraduate degree in history and intensive study of the subject. I wanted to know how otherwise good people could have sunken to such barbarism. And in particular, I was on the hunt both for mitigating circumstances and for examples of "good Germans" who had resisted the tide of evil. I found both. But the motive behind the search, I must admit, at least in part involved a strategy of avoidance.

I occasionally asked my parents the obvious question: what did our family do during the war? And on occasion I was treated to reassuring stories of my grandfather's virtuous actions during that difficult time. He had, after all, formed part of the French occupation and had been in a position to do as much good as harm. It seems that he had chosen the former with such vigor that after the war the French resistance had stood by his side and prevented his prosecution by the Allies. Such stories removed a palpable weight from my shoulders and I have no reason whatsoever to doubt them. However, the fact that I should need them tells a deeper tale. It tells of a hunger in the psyche to deny its latent darkness. After all, why should I, who was utterly blameless in these events, be concerned with what my grandfather did? His character, either for good or ill, meant nothing about me. Or did it? On some deep level I must have worried that it did. And in this I was not alone.

This fact was brought to my attention in a conversation with Chris Parish. Upon sharing this story with him he surprised me with his reply, "You know, Mike, every German person I've ever met has told me a story like that. In fact, if you talk to enough Germans today you'd find it hard to imagine that anything ever happened at all. After all, everyone you meet had a relative who somehow stood against Hitler and no one seems to have had relatives who did anything wrong. Very odd, that," he added in his comically bone dry and unabashedly English way. That stopped me in my tracks. I'd never spoken much to other Germans about the war largely because I didn't know any. But Chris' response caused me to take a deeper look at the layers of denial and my own need to see myself as fundamentally good. It was then that I first began to consider that perhaps I had long ago shifted my fundamental national identification to one of being American rather than German at least partially out of a convenience of conscience. No doubt it was that same convenience that was responsible for the current popularity in Germany of the "neo-Advaita" teachings that Andrew had mentioned previously. After all, if there is no doer then it must have all been God's will and we can conveniently lay the whole nightmare at His blessed feet.

It was this abdication of responsibility and convenient denial with which Andrew had taken issue and with which Germans, for obvious reasons, have particular issues. Currently my understanding of it is this: the fact that the genocidal madness happened and that the capacity for monumental evil is there in all of us is not necessarily a problem at all. It just is what it is. However, denying that it exists creates enormous distortions in the psyche. I've seen such distortions play out firsthand in people very close to me and the result is nothing short of bizarre. I've also seen it in myself. The fact is that any denial will call into immediate play all the ego's stratagems of self-protection and twist the person's psyche ranging in degree from the merely neurotic to the severely pathological. And while this is true for all of us, it is doubly true for people like myself whose cultural inheritance contains something as unspeakable as the wanton, wholesale murder of the Third Reich.

All of this points to the significance of embracing the third tenet in earnest if we are ever going to truly know ourselves and, with that knowledge in hand, be able to rise above whatever our inheritance is from our past.

Appendix 6

The Controversy around Andrew Cohen:
Purity, Corruption and Spiritual Authority Figures

I recently read an illuminating preface to Andrew's booklet, *In Defense of the Guru Principle*[1] by one Professor James R. Lewis,[2] a specialist in non-traditional religions who has studied religious controversies for the past fifteen years. Based on his experience he had initially concluded that Andrew's suggestion – that he attracted so much hostility due to his insistence on spiritual purity – was off the mark. However, as he states in his short essay, "I was having difficulty putting my finger on exactly what it was…" After some incredibly negative press, Professor Lewis had initially concluded that Andrew and his community were "suffering at the hands of an irresponsible mass media more interested in exploiting sensationalism than in the less than titillating truth."[3] Wanting to sort this out for himself he decided to visit the home of Andrew and his community in Massachusetts to do a little field research.

"I was frankly impressed," he said of his visit, adding that "not only was it clear that Andrew Cohen led a simple, unpretentious lifestyle congruent with his teachings, but I also found Cohen's students uniformly mature, likeable and mentally alert. I had studied many spiritual movements at close range, but in all those years had never encountered a group with which I felt more comfortable."[4]

While at the community he spent much time speaking with students about their experiences with bad press. The biggest problem, it turned out, was less the rancorous articles freely published in a number of magazines and newspapers, but their complete inability to get their own rebuttals printed. Lewis cites one "spiritual" magazine that had written a horribly negative and one-sided article about Andrew without so much as checking the simple facts of the story, whose content they swallowed wholesale from disgruntled former students. Yet when Andrew wrote a measured rebuttal the magazine refused to print it for being "too critical," despite the fact that they had eviscerated Andrew on the very same pages. Even the *L.A. Times* and the *Boston Globe* got in on the act, refusing to print letters to the editor from Andrew's students. Reading of these episodes, I was reminded of an event I'd heard about in the mid-nineties when Andrew was roundly criticizing other spiritual teachers for their ethical shortcomings. At the time someone suggested to a senior editor at a major magazine touting the benefits of yoga and meditation that it might be interesting to do an article on Andrew and his teaching work, to which the editor flatly responded, "We'll do an article on Andrew Cohen when there's a scandal in his community." This from a magazine claiming to be a beacon of spirituality for our post-modern culture. All were waiting for Andrew to fall. In 1994 the late Suzanne Segal, who was becoming recognized as a powerful teacher in her own right due to the publication of her extraordinary story of awakening entitled simply, *Collision with the Infinite*, said to Andrew, "Everybody out there is waiting for you to make a mistake." She herself had been amazed at the controversy swirling around Andrew who, in his own words, had naively assumed, "that the spiritual world at large would welcome with open arms my unwillingness to compromise the truth *for anyone*. How wrong I was."[5]

How wrong he was indeed. Even his mother turned against him. Soon after Andrew's awakening he had sent her a letter boldly declaring, *"Andrew is dead."* He then invited her to come to India to see what had happened. Upon her arrival she immediately recognized the magnitude of her son's transformation and when asked whether she wished him to relate to her as his mother or as his student she declared for the latter. However, when pushed, like any other student, to confront her ego she turned on him vengefully. After an ugly parting she wrote a book portraying Andrew as a dangerously deluded megalomaniac who plied the same spiritual waters as Jim Jones and David Koresh. Shortly before its publication she casually informed him that in its pages he would be cast, "as a dangerously deluded and frighteningly pathological figure whose insatiable thirst for absolute power over pathetic and weak-minded individuals is couched within the pretense of a passionate interest in the spiritual Enlightenment of humanity."[6] Moreover, she added with a conspiratorial wink, that she hoped that he wouldn't be upset that she'd changed significant facts in order to add drama, thus making the book more saleable. Literary license and all that. "Little did I know," Andrew later said of this event, "that even the conversation we were having at the moment would itself become, in her book, so distorted as to have no resemblance whatsoever to what was actually occurring between us."[7] In perfect alignment with this vicious and mean spirited assault, his mother called some time after the book's publication to inquire whether or not Andrew had as yet slept with any of his students.

That the answer to that question and others like it was and continues to be a resounding "NO" has undoubtedly been an irritating source of consternation to Andrew's angry detractors. For all their vitriol and grotesque distortion, the noteworthy truth is that during the twenty years of Andrew's relentless push to spiritual and cultural revolution, there has never been a single scandal to compromise the stand he had taken: to become a living expression of the opposite of everything that's wrong with the world. Yet in taking this stand Andrew ignited powerful forces that converged in incendiary fashion.

Among them was Andrew's own understanding of the significance of enlightenment itself: *"What has always intrigued me is that many people appear to be interested in the experience of love while they so often seem mysteriously able to avoid its implications…many have been drawn to me initially because of the experience of love that they have felt in my presence. And while the majority may be more than satisfied with that, for me it has never been enough. I have never been able to allow those who have come to me to settle merely for the experience of feeling better[8]…It is because the demand to drown and truly lose oneself in that ocean for eternity is not made often enough that so many seekers end up satisfied with being mere voyeurs of their own Self, rather than living expressions of it…The course of my life as a teacher has been defined by my continuous insistence that the experience of love and bliss is meaningless when it is not supported by a life lived with true integrity…Ironically, it is because of this that I have been the object of much controversy…[and] it is precisely this that has simultaneously attracted some and repelled others."* As Andrew says elsewhere, he has never *"been able to divorce the experience of love from its absolute demand."*[10]

That demand collided with the collective inertia of the alternative spiritual culture like an asteroid crashing into earth. Fascinated with itself and content to be "voyeurs," that culture would rise to fight tooth and nail in defense of its position, a position that put nothing on the line and vehemently affirmed the "sensitive self" in its false regency over consciousness. As Professor Lewis observes, "it began to dawn on me (after visiting Andrew's community) that what was going on here was something other than what I had first supposed. While a number of critical pieces had appeared in the mainstream press, it was becoming increasingly evident that the real nexus of the controversy was to be found within the spiritual subculture itself. Although his critical analysis of this subculture has been couched in relatively mild terms, Cohen has breathed life into his critique by establishing a community of students who have responded to the call to awaken. Had he merely been a critical voice, or had members of the Impersonal Enlightenment Fellowship (now EnlightenNext) quietly pursued enlightenment without stepping on anyone else's toes, the response might have been different. In combination, however, the dual thrust of Cohen's challenge fundamentally calls into question the vested interests of the 'spiritual establishment' – that informal network of organizations, publications and teachers who have become comfortable with something less than the goal of ultimate freedom.

"I began to see that the attention of the mainstream media had obscured the basic source of the controversy. Long after the *Los Angeles Times* and *The Boston Globe* will have forgotten about Andrew Cohen, the spiritual establishment will continue to attack him. This 'establishment' might be nothing more than an informal network of people who know people who know yet other people. In whatever way it is organized, however, it is clear that it has closed ranks against Cohen and is actively trying to discredit him. And, contrary to the conclusion I had reached in my initial evaluation, the attack has been provoked by the very reason indicated by Cohen."[11] That reason, of course, was his unyielding demand for integrity with respect to what one has realized. A small thing, it would seem, though apparently not insignificant.

The final, and I suppose root force behind this bad chemistry was that self-same voice that had so shocked me with its vehemence and murderous aggression. "He's crazy," it had said, pretending to seek my rescue from the clutches of a madman. "Run for your life," it had suggested with panicked urgency. "I'm your friend." That traitorous voice lay submerged within the ego's deepest structures and clearly recognized the threat to itself in Andrew. Cornered, forced to face its own exile or destruction, it attempted a powerful sleight of hand, projecting its own darkness upon the other while pretending to wear their light. It has become abundantly clear to me that the violent backlash that Andrew has suffered from much of the spiritual culture is but a collective manifestation of that very same voice. After all, ego is both individual and collective.

NOTES

1. Andrew Cohen, *In Defense of the Guru Principle*, (Lenox, MA: What is Enlightenment Press, 1999).

2. James R. Lewis is Dean of Humanities and Professor of Religious Studies at the World University of America, and Senior Editor at the Center for Academic Publication. He is a world-recognized authority on non-traditional religions, and is the author of *Cults in America*, the authoritative *Encyclopedia of Cults, Sects and New Religions*, and *Doomsday Prophecies*.

3. Cohen, *In Defense of the Guru Principle*, pp. xii-xvii

4. Ibid.

5. Ibid.

6. Ibid.

7. Ibid.

8. Ibid., pp. 3-4

9. Ibid., pp. 4-5

10. Ibid., p.3

11. Ibid., p. xvi

Appendix 7

Ruminations on Psychedelics and Spiritual Transformation

It was in the early eighties, during my first year of college when my roommate, a chemistry major, introduced me to the world of psychedelics. The effects of these chemicals irrevocably changed my life, tearing through my secular worldview like a tornado through a trailer park and throwing open the realm of Enlightenment. Within a few months, the doors of perception ripped from their hinges, my life was awash both in the world's spiritual literature and a sea of psychedelics so vast that we referred to our bulging stash as our "psychedelicatessen." There, on any given day, one might find not only psilocybin and mescaline but also LSD, DMT, DET, 2CB, MDA, MDMA, MDE and an alphabet soup of other chemicals that I can no longer remember. Soon "transcendental medication" had become our spiritual practice and "better living through chemistry" our motto. Life had become interesting indeed.

So interesting, in fact, that we had convinced ourselves that we had hit the spiritual lotto. That is, from much reading I had discovered that, while some ancient cultures employed psychedelic substances in their arsenal of spiritual practice, the majority did not. On the contrary, they advocated strict rules and disciplines to gain entry into the very realms into which we, supplied with the chemical keys to entrance, journeyed daily. Given that I wondered why one would bother with such practices. By all accounts, they were difficult and time consuming, demanding a level of dedication rarely found in human beings. When one could, at the pop of pill or a pull on a pipe, induce such extraordinary states instantaneously, wasn't this an enormous waste of time? Hadn't we found a terrific shortcut? With the arrogance of youth fully on my side, it certainly seemed so. After all, we were living in a modern age, one of speed and instant gratification where journeys that had once taken months and years could now be undertaken in hours or days. So why should the journey to different states of consciousness be any different? Why not use the new modes of transportation, now so readily available? With youth, enthusiasm and new technology, why waste time with what the ancients did?

Despite cheerfully adopting this viewpoint, which conveniently demanded no discipline or fortitude, I began to suspect that the psychedelic merry-go-round couldn't last forever. That suspicion would not become conviction until some years later upon leaving school armed with an advanced degree and a radically re-adjusted worldview. It was only then that I realized that the problem with merry-go-rounds was that they never go anywhere and that despite the jubilant whirl the scenery never changes. Further, I realized that staying on them keeps one trapped at the carnival long after the crowds have gone, dividing one from life, ensnared in myopic reverie. It was also becoming abundantly clear that the drugs, while ecstatic and illuminating, were not facilitating the kind of transformation that would allow me to stay in touch with the extraordinary depth that they routinely revealed. In other words, the love I was experiencing was not necessarily turning me into a more loving person; the unqualified unity I was experiencing was not making me less self-centered and divided; and the ecstasies were not truly making me happier. Reluctantly I began to acknowledge that work needed to be done in order to render the personality more susceptible to sustaining spiritual conscious-ness and, most importantly to manifesting it in the world. While I don't have a sliver of regret for partaking of those mystic molecules, I have not done so in many years nor harbored a craving to do so. It was as Andrew had said: glimpsing heaven was one thing; taking up residence there was something else altogether. That had to be worked for and earned.

About the Author

Mike Wombacher was born in Germany in 1959, and emigrated to the United States with his family when he was ten. In 1983 he graduated from Florida State University with a Master's Degree in International Relations, and then spent eight years working in the corporate world and has started several businesses.

Mike has been deeply involved in the post-modern spiritual scene for over twenty-five years. He met Andrew Cohen some fourteen years ago and watched Andrew's teaching develop from a radical call for personal enlightenment to an equally radical call to enlightenment beyond the individual with global implications. And, after monumental struggles, he has watched him succeed, with his body of students, in giving birth to the first seeds of a new stage of human evolution.

Photograph: Barbara Vaughn

As a writer he has long desired to chronicle the development of this teaching, the personal and cultural resistance to it, and the promise inherent in it based on the real-time experience of a growing group of individuals, himself included. It was this passion that compelled him to write of his experience of attending a long retreat with Andrew Cohen in the summer of 2005 in Montserrat, Spain.

Mike is currently heavily involved in bringing the vision described in this book to life in the world. He teaches courses on Evolutionary Enlightenment around the Bay Area and the West Coast.

FINDHORN PRESS

*Books, Card Sets,
CDs & DVDs
that inspire and uplift*

For a complete catalogue,
please contact:

Findhorn Press Ltd
305a The Park, Findhorn
Forres IV36 3TE
Scotland, UK

Telephone +44-(0)1309-690582
Fax +44-(0)1309-690036
eMail info@findhornpress.com

or consult our catalogue online
(with secure order facility) on
www.findhornpress.com